D1805947

Traction And Transmission, Volume 5...

Anonymous

Nabu Public Domain Reprints:

You are holding a reproduction of an original work published before 1923 that is in the public domain in the United States of America, and possibly other countries. You may freely copy and distribute this work as no entity (individual or corporate) has a copyright on the body of the work. This book may contain prior copyright references, and library stamps (as most of these works were scanned from library copies). These have been scanned and retained as part of the historical artifact.

This book may have occasional imperfections such as missing or blurred pages, poor pictures, errant marks, etc. that were either part of the original artifact, or were introduced by the scanning process. We believe this work is culturally important, and despite the imperfections, have elected to bring it back into print as part of our continuing commitment to the preservation of printed works worldwide. We appreciate your understanding of the imperfections in the preservation process, and hope you enjoy this valuable book.

LIBRARY OF THE
UNIVERSITY OF MICHIGAN

DEPARTMENT
OF
ENGINEERING

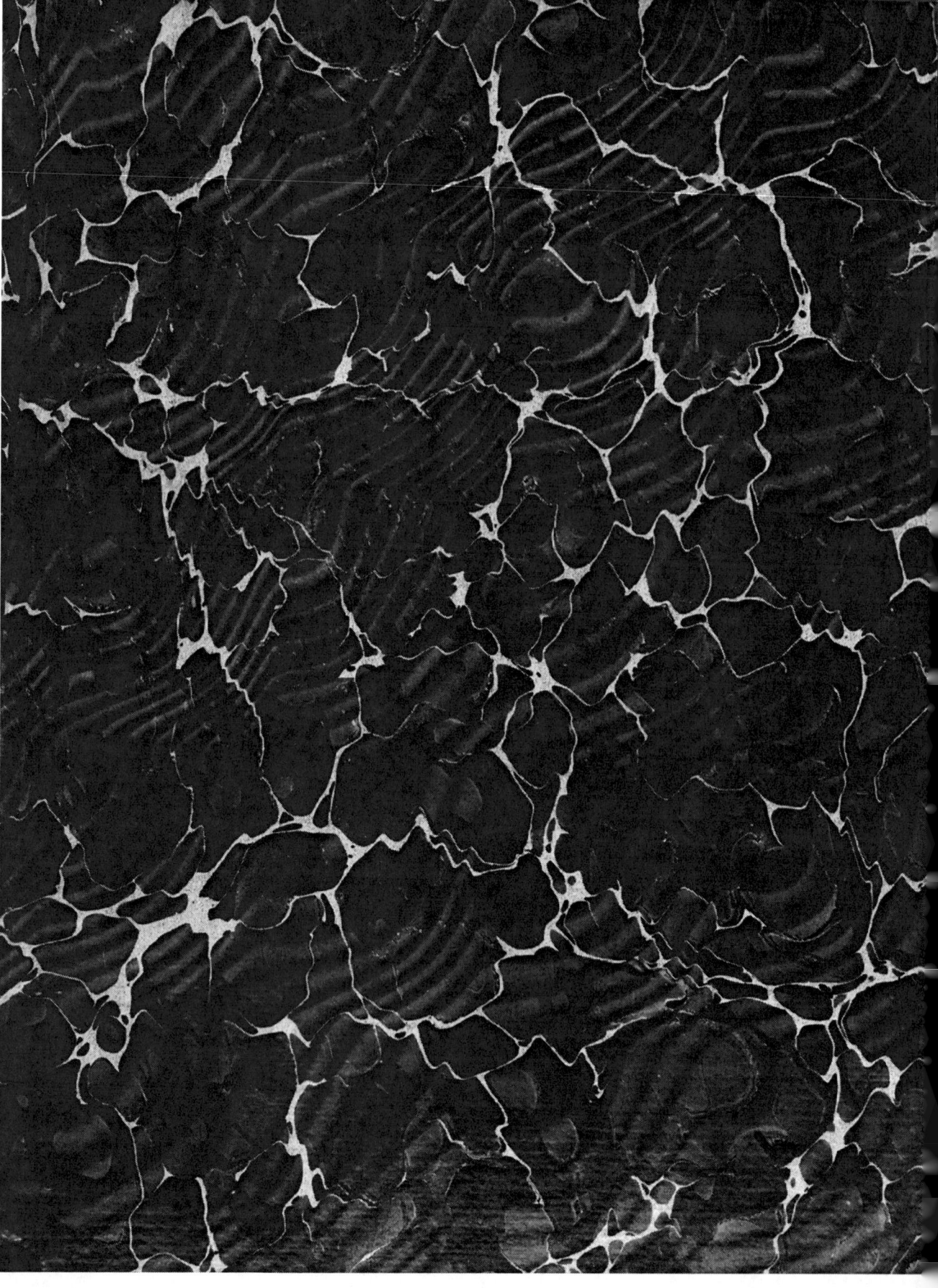

LIBRARY

TA
1
.T76

TRACTION

AND

TRANSMISSION

A MONTHLY SUPPLEMENT

TO

"ENGINEERING"

VOL. V

SEPTEMBER TO DECEMBER, 1902

LONDON
35 & 36, BEDFORD STREET, STRAND, W.C.

—

GENERAL INDEX

ILLUSTRATIONS IN TEXT

INDEX TO PLATES

THE PATHS OF PROGRESS

A MONTHLY REVIEW

ELECTRICITY AND ETHICS

JUDGING from the experience of the Institution of Electrical Engineers with the President of the Board of Trade, and the continuous failure to interest members of Parliament in questions touching electrical development, it seems almost time to despair of any assistance from the politicians. The industry is indeed in a truly difficult position when its only hope of relief from Municipal vexations and restrictions is to appeal to the gentlemen who are under the delusion that those Municipal bodies faithfully reflect public opinion, and that they—the members of Parliament—represent, merely in another place, the same constituents as the aldermen and councillors represent at the town hall. In theory, this is true; in practice it is almost ludicrously false. Except at times of abnormal local excitement, local authorities do not indicate the majority of the rate-payers, and far less do they represent the greater portion of the rateable property. It has been ascertained that on an average only from 30 to 40 per cent. of the rate-payers go to the poll, and little more than half of these return the candidate of their choice; so that the average town councillor is elected by about 20 per cent. of the rate-payers,

many of them taking small interest in his programme, but assiduously nursed and whipped up by his organisers. To say that such a person represents public opinion is arrant nonsense. Yet the president of the Board of Trade plaintively argues that he is helpless, and hints that if they want reforms, electrical engineers and investors must first convert the aldermen and councillors, to whose absolute control electrical business in this country has been handed over by the complacent ignorance of the Legislature.

Strongest proof of the distinctly unrepresentative character of most local authorities is to be found on occasions when a poll of the rate-payers needs to be taken as part of the procedure in the promotion of a Bill for extending the trading powers of the council. Municipalities make desperate efforts to avoid these polls, for the simple reason that the result is almost invariably a heavy adverse majority. A few recent cases, taken at haphazard from districts of various size and character, are those of Birmingham, York, South Shields, Crewe, Romford, and Finchley, the people in every instance prohibiting the further invasion of commercial fields by bodies elected for the maintenance of public order and public health.

In ordinary times, however, the attitude of the majority is one of indolence and indifference. There is no hope of holding their constant attention to broad questions of industrial policy. All that can be done is to form a compact and persevering minority ready to strike as occasion offers. Only note what an influence in politics is exercised by, for example, the Temperance Party or the Nonconformist Conscience—quite out of proportion to their actual voting strength. Why is it that the Education Bill fills columns and columns of the popular newspapers, while the commercial development of electricity is only alluded to in rare and obscure paragraphs? Not because there is any general interest in elementary education in itself, but simply and solely because there is an opening for contentious religious feeling. Could we but divert some of this zeal to the promotion of electrical freedom, the end of the struggle would be in sight; and as it appears useless to keep on preaching cold economic truths to a heedless generation, is it not worth while to direct public attention to the ethical by-products obtainable by means of great electric power and traction schemes?

THE LIMITS OF CONCEPTION

The public mind is necessarily always halting in the rear when scientific development requires its support. To the trained and refined intellect of those who are capable of independent thought there is a wider view, a more distant horizon; and whereas the general mass of the inhabitants of this world appear to regard every short step in advance as a firm foothold on the pinnacle of human endeavour, the minority, endowed with what may be termed the faculty of logical imagination, recognise that they have only mounted another rung of a ladder which is interminable perhaps, but the ascent of which affords a more and more expansive prospect. What, for example, does electricity mean to the mass of mankind? Only yesterday it was an amusing freak of nature, of which the only practical purpose was apparently to give shocks of more or less medical value. The telegraph and telephone were regarded first as playthings, secondly as rather useful but expensive means of communication, thirdly, as almost necessaries of life, and lastly,—private enterprise having at

great risk, and with incessant labour, converted a toy into a great commercial utility—there arises in State and Municipality a demand for public ownership, the sole basis of which, admitted or denied, is the popular belief that we have reached finality in this branch of electrical invention, and that the financial future is all profit and no risk. In just the same way, the transmission of electric current by means of wires for arc and incandescent lighting was taken to be the last word in this department, and now many local "leaders" are astonished and dismayed to find that a more important use of the current is to drive machinery from large power distribution centres, which leave the much glorified Municipal electric light works hopelessly out of the competition. Having to choose between blocking the progress of industrial science and conserving the rate-payers' vested interests, the local authorities unanimously decide in favour of the latter course, just as they will carefully preserve the virgin purity of their own street corner tramway system rather than allow a company to afford them cheap and rapid access to all parts of the county. Year in and year out, such questions are approached by those in power with the same pitiable narrowness of view. They are quite incapable of building up anything for posterity but debts.

Meanwhile the great public remain stolidly indifferent. Unable to look ahead, the masses consider that this struggle is merely to settle the question whether one party or another shall pocket the immediate profit of electrical work. They have no philosophical or humanitarian outlook. That there must be still a multitude of undiscovered uses for electricity which will be more or less rapidly revealed in proportion to the amount of liberty and encouragement granted to the engineer and his capitalist backers—of this they are ignorant, and it is by sheer ignorance that the national policy in respect of these matters is dictated.

THE SIEGE OF GARDEN CITY

In bringing about reforms in this country, an ounce of emotion has always been worth a ton of reason, and many general elections have been won, not by argument, but a good "cry." Electrical science must have sentiment on its side. We must show its connection with the housing problem and the horrors of overcrowding, and explain to the multitude how free development of traction and power schemes will break up the "large wens" which our towns have become. There are a great many worthy people who are so much affected by the disgusting uncleanness of industrial low life and its attendant and really excusable vices of intemperance and immorality, that, in order to obtain some consolation for their wounded souls, they will fly to quack remedies and become converts to all sorts of curious social sects. Consider, for example, the strange mixture of very amiable but almost entirely unpractical people who form the Garden City Association, and who propose to found an industrial Eden on communist principles. Bishops and business men, artists and politicians mingle with leisured Socialists of all denominations in their devotion to this ideal. Each one has his own notion of what the city will be. Sir William Richmond, for example, demands that it shall be modelled on ancient Athens, and that the citizens shall eschew all thoughts of money making. But all the City Gardeners are alike in one point : all have a lofty scorn of details, and none has apparently more than a yawning acquaintance with economic laws. They are animated and united by philanthropic sentiment, and they would rather attempt something, however impracticable, than admit the impossibility of accomplishing anything at all. Such well-meaning people can do a great deal of harm to their fellow-beings, and we have been informed that there is another place besides Garden City which is paved with good intentions. The fact to be recognised, however, is that popular sympathy is a tremendous force, and that it is almost impossible to make any impression on the Legislature without its aid. Logic has, so far, failed as a weapon in the hands of the electrical engineer, and he will almost certainly produce more practical results if he addresses himself direct to the hearts of the people. They are only ignorant of the blessings which his work can give them because nobody has ever made a sustained effort to teach them. The great mass of the public do not even know yet that electric light is cleaner, and safer, and healthier than gas or oil, and when it is offered to them, refuse to consider anything but its relative cost. Much less are they aware that electric power distribution over wide areas, combined with electric light railway systems, would, by greatly multiplying

suitable industrial sites, quickly sweep away the abominable conditions under which so many of the labouring population are living to-day. Even the Garden City enthusiasts make their plans without any reference to electrical progress. The subject has never come within their ken. Members of the profession read admirable and learned papers to one another, but until Mr. Swinburne invaded the Board of Trade and disturbed the serene and conscientious indifference of Mr. Gerald Balfour, no step had ever been taken to draw wide public attention to the national importance of encouraging electrical development.

MUNICIPAL OBSTRUCTION TO NATIONAL GROWTH

The "Housing Question" furnishes the best opportunity to the electrical engineer to enlist popular support, for it can easily be seen that it is he and not the average alderman who is the best friend of the suffering poor. This department of the subject necessitates plain speaking. Both in their personal interest and in their corporate welfare, members of local councils are opposed to plans which may have the effect of reducing the local population by assisting the decentralisation and redistribution of industries. Aldermen and councillors nearly all belong to the trading class, and the relief of overcrowding by the removal of the workers to more open districts would diminish the takings of the shops and public houses, whose abundant prosperity is dependent upon the swarming of the people in their vicinity. To use the pitiless logic of Mr. W. L. Madgen's pamphlet on "Industrial Redistribution," "in the neighbourhood where human beings are herded together one thousand to the acre, and where there is a death rate running up to thirty per thousand, the general dealer and the undertaker cannot take a broad and impartial view of the overcrowding question." Yet it is they who sit in the councils, and are deputed by the Government to deal with this most pressing problem of our time — they whose personal interest is not to disperse the people, but to keep them cooped up.

As private individuals they can do little in this direction; but in their corporate capacity they are entrusted by the Legislature with the power of borrowing millions of money for the purpose of "improving" the town. And the methods they may adopt are briefly these :—

(1) They may erect and maintain at the public expense, block dwellings, tenements, and cottages, which they let at uncommercial rents. Such "Municipal enterprise" is a financial burden to the community, but it is advantageous to the retail traders, especially the publicans, because it keeps the people huddled together near the shops and public-houses.

(2) They may establish Municipal trading undertakings, enabling them to offer "direct employment" to working men at high wages, thus increasing their spending power—a further gain to the tradesmen and the slum landlords.

(3) They may construct internal tramways which stir up the crowd where it is thickest, but do not provide an outlet, and which are, of course, mainly supported by "the pennies of the poor." Where a surplus is shown, the so-called "profit in aid of rates" is, in effect, simply a form of indirect taxation imposed upon the workers for the benefit of the middle and upper classes.

The most curious development is that these few immediately interested parties, by getting themselves elected on the council, have the power of dragging the general body of rate-payers into partnership with them. Municipalisation involves the whole of the rate-payers in the financing of certain trading departments. It follows, therefore, that the burden of any commercial risk due to dispersal of population, instead of being borne merely by the tradesmen who deal with the masses, is thrown upon the general inhabitants in their rate-paying capacity. Most departments of Municipal trading so far entered upon can only be guaranteed against heavy loss by the maintenance of the dense population for whose convenience they were ostensibly designed. If the staple trade of a town declined, and the population fell, say from one hundred thousand to eighty thousand, the Municipal gas and electricity works and tramways, most probably laid down in anticipation of greater, rather than less density, would be seriously reduced in value. The municipalisers have thus succeeded, by the creation of these speculative vested interests, in making the relief of overcrowding a most costly matter to the pockets of the rate-payers. In the present anomalous state of the law, the councillors of such a town can practically veto the over-running of the population into the open country outside their boundaries by blocking comprehensive schemes of electric traction and power distribution, while, on the other hand, they consider it as one of their primary civic duties to lure and retain the working classes in their overcrowded quarters by means of cheap block dwellings, direct employment, and other adventitious attractions.

THE REACTIONARY PROGRESSIVES

Between the Urban District Council of Little Pedlington and the London County Council there is only a difference of degree. It was suddenly discovered recently that the glass trade was being partially diverted from London to the provinces owing to the more favourable conditions there prevalent. Naturally the London County Councillors, who take such a tender interest in the over-crowding question, rejoiced. Did they? Read the debate on the subject in the Council, and you will find therein nothing but cries of alarm, howls of indignation, resolutions to stop the migration of industry at all costs. Yet, if you listen to these people on a public platform, you will hear how much they deplore the horrible over-crowding of London, and how speedily they would institute wonderful reforms if only the wretched Conservative Government would let them. They use the housing problem to work up public feeling and thus gain their political ends, but it is absurd to suppose that the party in power at Spring Gardens has any real desire to see the population of London on the decline, when they are horror-struck to learn that a number of glass manufacturers have moved into the country. The very councillors who conspire with the trades unions to drive business out of the country altogether by inserting meddlesome wages clauses in their contracts are the first to raise the alarm when an industry shows signs of leaving London for the provinces. Their point of view is purely parochial. Like any other local authority, the L.C.C. will resist any schemes for relieving overcrowding by the only possible remedy, namely, the reduction of the population within the area of its rate collection. Any enterprising company which proposes to construct light railways for enabling us to rush out of London into the open country is regarded by the L.C.C. as an enemy, and is kept outside the boundary. In the matter of "tube" railways, the Council has no jurisdiction, and its grief is profound. So much so that, towards the end of the Session, it was announced in the daily press that "a combination of Moderates and Progressives" were planning a grand attack on the new tube schemes, and were petitioning Parliament to postpone its sanction to them "so that the public interests can be more thoroughly safeguarded." At Spring Gardens, "public interest" is not associated with the early provision of cheap and rapid means of transit; the term "public interest" merely signifies the blocking of all such schemes until the County Council itself is empowered to carry them out at the risk of the rate-payers. If, to take another example, the public interest alone in its ordinary sense had been considered, the Council could easily have assisted a company to provide a steamboat service on the Thames; but it preferred to see the enterprise fail, because its ambition extends to a fleet flying the "Jolly Roger" of the

this sermon? Most unfortunately the electrical engineer and investor have a melancholy interest in every fresh development of the Municipal trading policy. The greater the number of directions in which this mischievous practice spreads of employing public trust funds for competing with private trade, the more hopeless is the entanglement in which the electrical industry finds itself. "Forward" is the motto of the electricians and the municipaliser, but forward in diametrically opposite ways. The great need of the country is the provision of facilities for the mobilisation of industry, the smoothing of the paths of progress. And the requisite conditions for the maintenance and increase of national prosperity are obviously the cheapening of production by the adoption of the best scientific methods, and the conservation of the energies of the people by the improvement of their environment. In the form of a genealogical tree the following table purports to show how all these things depend upon free play being granted to the electrical engineer and the capitalist behind him :—

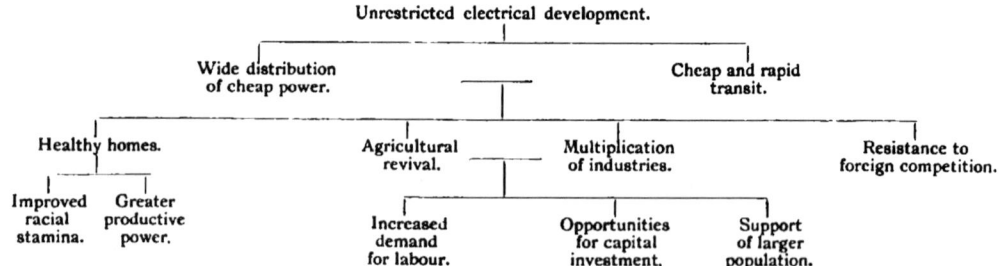

L.C.C. A scheme has been prepared giving estimates of receipts and expenditure which, if embodied in a company prospectus, would be rightly denounced as one of the wildest of "wild cats," and which will unquestionably, if carried out, create a permanent burden on the rate-payers for the benefit of the riverside population, who care very little for penny steamers, after all, to judge from the long experience of those who have catered for them in the past.

A COLLISION OF POLICIES

In what way, it may be asked, do penny Municipal steamboats affect the progress of electrical science, which is the subject of

But the electrical industry has to fight its way to freedom through the dense and stolid mass of Municipal obstruction. The electrician proposes to alter the map of England. The Municipal councillors and officials are in nearly every case personally interested to a greater or less extent in keeping things as they are. Let there be no mistake about it, the electrical engineer's enemy is not merely a few ill-considered legislative enactments; it is a strong and selfish general policy, which attacks any trade that presents an opening, and which only by accident and legislative indulgence has made electricity its chief victim. Present-day Municipal policy in most towns is one of bitter exclusiveness and boundless cupidity. If they had their way, the "Progressives" would rapidly convert London into a communist settlement, and they would be but feebly opposed by the so-called "Moderates," who on most occasions are merely underdone Progressives. For a start they are burning to acquire a monopoly in means of transit. Their ideal is to see the magic letters "L.C.C." on every tram-car, omnibus, tube railway carriage, and steamboat. It is this tendency, as a whole, that the electrical and allied engineering industries have to struggle against, and that, by checking their growth and paralysing their energies, prevents the nation from making steady progress in the directions already indicated. Municipalisation is thus the greatest foe not only of capital, but also of labour, inasmuch as it tends to quench the spirit of commercial adventure and to produce industrial stagnation.

THE APPEAL TO THE PUBLIC

Like "Hamlet," the electrical engineer finds the times "out of joint." Upon him falls the burden of reforming what has gradually become almost the settled policy of the local governing bodies, and he has small chance of success unless he can gain the sympathetic ear of the British public. It is a hard task to do this by controversy with local authorities. It is almost as though an Arkwright were compelled to obtain the permission of the old-fashioned spinners and weavers before being able to make use of textile machinery. A Municipality owning its little electric light works and tramways is in almost exactly the same position in relation to comprehensive modern schemes of power distribution and traction, as the owner of an old hand-loom when confronted with the introduction of revolutionary inventions. The only difference is that the old weavers smashed machinery in defiance of the law, while Municipalities, animated by just the same motives, block the advance of science with the assistance of the law.

Having failed to rouse the interest of the politicians in the industrial future of the country, it is apparently necessary to make a wider and more popular appeal. If one can make no impression upon those who, in theory, represent the people, but, in practice, misrepresent them most wofully, the only resource is to go direct to their masters. The electrical engineer has a case which ought to touch his audience both on the rational and the emotional side. He can claim that he is a most valuable public servant who is practically prevented from fulfilling his duties; that if allowed to go to work he can, in a few years, sweep away the evils of overcrowding, which must be productive of serious deterioration of the national physique, and of daily incalculable misery and vice; that he can industrially fertilise this country so as to render it capable of yielding healthy and remunerative occupation to more than twice the present population; and incidentally it is unfortunately incumbent upon him to show that the reactionary Municipal policy is not merely a negative, but a positive hindrance; that is to say, it does not only prevent him from reforming existing abuses, but it is piling up additional difficulties, and consolidating the forces of obstruction.

RAILWAY ECONOMICS

V.—LONDON LOCOMOTION

By the Hon. Robert P. Porter

I.—Introduction

London, with an area of one-fifth of 1 per cent. of the United Kingdom, contains 15 per cent. of the population. The county of London, at the last census, had a population of 4,586,524; Greater London had a population of 6,581,077. The administrative county of London, comprising portions of the ancient counties of Middlesex, Surrey, and Kent, has an area of 74,828 acres. Greater London, or the Metropolitan police district, includes, of course, the county of London, the county of Middlesex, and parts of the counties of Surrey, Kent, Essex, and Hertfordshire, representing an area of 443,421 acres. In studying the problem of London locomotion, these two distinct areas must be kept in mind, as well as a constantly growing area extending in almost every direction from the Metropolis for a distance, say, of thirty miles from the centre, into districts being rapidly settled by people whose occupation or business is in London. In describing this process of extension, Mr. Robert Donald recently said: "All the towns in Greater London are natural outgrowths of the parent city. London, in its onward march, picks up smaller hamlets and absorbs them. It turns old cities which, if left alone, would have long since sunk into insignificance, into populous towns. London, in fact, from the Bank to the limits of the police area, and far beyond, is one homogeneous body, one vast community of interests, each part of which is dependent on the other." And, he might have added, the continued harmonious growth of these districts must in a large measure depend upon the means provided for rapid transit between them and the city. The two districts in Greater London where population has probably increased most rapidly seem to be the north-east half of Middlesex county, and that part of Essex nearest London —what may be termed the Willesden, Tottenham, and Enfield district of Middlesex, and the West and East Ham and Walthamstow district of Essex. Here are a few instances from each district:—

TABLE I.—GROWTH OF POPULATION IN TWO METROPOLITAN DISTRICTS

Willesden and Tottenham District.			West and East Ham District.		
Registration Sub-district.	Population.		Registration Sub-district.	Population.	
	1881.	1901.		1881.	1901.
Willesden	27,613	114,815	West Ham	128,953	267,308
Hendon	10,484	22,450	East Ham	10,706	95,970
Finchley	17,615	33,692	Wanstead	—	—
Hornsey	37,078	72,056	Leyton	32,430	108,097
Tottenham	46,453	135,702	Chigwell	10,544	17,653
Edmonton	23,463	61,892	Ilford	7,645	41,240
Enfield	18,944	42,738	Barking	9,203	21,547
Total	181,650	484,345		199,481	551,815

It will be seen the population has increased in the Willesden and Tottenham district 175 per cent. in twenty years, and in the west and east district about the same. The totals above given do not represent the entire population of those districts of London, for I have only taken some of the more important places. To these two districts we shall find, as we proceed with our study, both Mr. Yerkes and Mr. Morgan have directed their attention, the western district containing the terminals of two of Mr. Yerkes' railways—the Great Northern and Strand, and the Charing Cross, Euston, and Hampstead — and the eastern district the terminals of two of Mr. Morgan's proposed tube railways—the North-Eastern, and the City North-Eastern and Suburban Railways. What may be termed the Surrey group of towns—the field of the London United Electric Tramway Company's activity — have not shown such remarkable growth, but only a steady increase during the twenty years: Croydon from 78,811 to 133,885; Wimbledon from 15,950 to 41,604; Kingston, Surbiton, and Esher from 47,414 to 78,000; while the growth of Hampton, creased from 24,134 to 46,445, ranking first, while Bromley, Beckenham, Chislehurst, and some others, all show liberal increase. Where there has been such a steady growth in every

Diagram of London and Thirty-mile Circuit

Richmond, and Mortlake has been about from 47,000 to 75,000. In Kent the increase in population has been about the same as in Surrey; Bexley, which has in-

direction it is hardly worth while to dwell on the increase in certain spots, unless to emphasise the claim of some, that in places where the railway facilities are good, quick,

Plate I

Densities of Population in Greater London

U of M

RAILWAY ECONOMICS

No.701

and cheap—there will be found the greatest growth of population. Up to a certain point this has been undoubtedly true of both the districts given in the above Table. The Great Eastern Railway has accomplished wonders in handling the traffic of the growing towns in Essex, while the Great Northern, Midland, and North-Western, have all had a share in improving means of transportation, and in attracting the population to the north-eastern part of Middlesex. But, whatever may have been done in the past, both of these districts need additional facilities at the present time, and both stand a fairly good chance of obtaining what they want.

Mr. Edgar Harper, the able statistical officer of the London County Council, has given in a recent report, some interesting data on the density of population outside the county boundary, and he ascribes it to two main causes.

(a) The existence of old-established towns, such as Croydon, Kingston, Richmond, Uxbridge.

(b) The travelling facilities afforded to workmen and third-class passengers by railway companies.

As I have said, the largest population in 1901, and the greatest increase during twenty years, are found in West Ham, Willesden, Walthamstow, and Woodford, Wanstead, East Ham, and Little Ilford. In all these areas there exist reasonable and cheap facilities for railway travelling to and from business centres. On the other hand, in districts where no facilities for cheap travelling exist, and where the railway journey is relatively long—such as Uxbridge, Edgware, Waltham Abbey, Orpington, and South Mimms—the population has not increased, and the density is less than one person to the acre. This makes me think that electric tramways or light electric railways, may be safely built in any of these districts around London, no matter what the density of the population. Cheap and quick travelling will soon bring the traffic. In the United States the tramway has always been the forerunner of population, and in nine cases out of ten, population has quickly followed. Mr. Harper hits the nail square on the head when he says: " In order to obtain the desired object it is essential that the new railways should run well into those undeveloped areas, and not stop short at the edge of the thickly populated districts, as they now for the most

part do. If the railway companies wait for a population to grow up before providing trains, it is quite likely that the population will never come; but if they found a cheap and convenient service, including an adequate number of working men's trains, past experience goes to show that the development of a new district is greatly facilitated and accelerated by such action. In other words, this is a case where provident supply will practically create demand." In this direction an instructive comparison is given by Mr. Harper, between the north and north-east part of the belt beyond the county boundary, and the remainder of the belt. In the north and north-east he takes the 1901 totals of Hornsey, Tottenham, Walthamstow, and Woodford, Wanstead, and Leyton, East Ham, and Little Ilford, and West Ham districts, with a total area of 26,299 acres, and a population of 789,064 persons, or 30.0 to the acre. Serving this area there are fairly good workmen's trains. The remainder of the belt includes Finchley, Hendon, Willesden, Acton, Brentford, Chiswick, Mortlake, Wimbledon, Mitcham, Croydon, Beckenham, Bromley, Chislehurst, and Bexley; these, collectively, have an area of 108,294 acres, and a population of 674,886 persons, or 6.8 to the acre. In this district, workmen's trains are the exception. Even within the county boundary there are districts having much less dense populations than 30 per acre, viz., Eltham (19), Charlton and Kidbrook (11.5), Putney (15.3), Lewisham (19.1), and Plumstead (22.2). Electric tramways and light railways will in the future deal with these undeveloped districts, and where the tramway spreads, there we shall find the increase in population during the next decade. Statistics demonstrate that the great increase in the building of small houses, to the east and north-east of London, has been facilitated by the policy of certain railway companies in catering to third-class passengers, and especially to working people. In districts served by railway companies which do not provide adequately for the working class, large tracts of land remain undeveloped, or are only sparsely populated. Nearly 20 per cent. of the population of London, or one out of every five persons—men, women, and children—live in overcrowded tenements with more than two occupants per room. The proportion of people so living is greatest in the central and eastern districts of London. In Central London East, the proportion is 38.5 per cent.; in Central London West, 29.76 per cent.; in Central London South, 25.09 per cent.; and in East London, 25.78 per cent. In individual districts the proportions are so large as 38.68 per cent. in Shoreditch; 34.23 in Bethnal Green; 38.08 per cent. in Holborn; 38.78 per cent. in Clerkenwell; 39.33 per cent. in St. George's in the East; 43.5 per cent. in Whitechapel; and 44.24 per cent. in St. Luke's. In the last named nearly half the population live in overcrowded tenements. It is, therefore, impossible to discuss the locomotion service in London without some knowledge of the density of population and of the housing of the working classes. No true solution of the problem is possible that does not provide better facilities for this class of inhabitants as well as for the thousands that are annually displaced by improvements of all kinds which involve the destruction of many dwelling houses.

II.—A General Review

Those who have been called upon to deal with what has not inaptly been called "the tangle of London locomotion" are confronted with a condition which cannot be changed, and which is entirely unlike the similar problem in any other city of the world. What could be done in London, if one only had a clean, white sheet of paper, and unlimited capital, combined with modern electrical engineering skill, may be an interesting subject for speculation, but it will not aid in the practical solution of the problem of how to circulate the living stream of human beings through the congested and inadequate arteries of the Metropolis. A study of the map of London reveals the enormous spaces occupied by the station sheds, warehouses, depôts, yards, junctions, and tracks of the railways which now hold all available entrances into the city, and no inconsiderable space within the boundaries of the county. If these vast complications of lines, with their embankments, bridges, arches, and viaducts, could all be swept away, we hear some say, and a comprehensive plan with modern appliances inaugurated, the vast crowds of people could be carried daily to and from their work, and an immense area released for building and other purposes. The same results might be accomplished if

it were practicable for these great systems of railways to discharge the bulk of their passengers on an outer circle, and bring them up to the well-reorganised centres of traffic by means of harmoniously arranged and electrically equipped, subway, tubular, and surface trains. These are good topics for essays, but the competition for the London traffic is far too keen and too ably directed on all sides to admit of any treatment that does not take into consideration vested interests, which really means existing conditions. And then, while the theorists are writing essays, elaborating "Complete Schemes," and putting Royal Commissions in motion, the public is losing millions of pounds per annum in wasted time, and in the enhanced cost of transporting supplies of all kinds through the crowded streets of London. It has been estimated that at four only of the busy centres in London, namely, Cheapside, the Strand, Piccadilly, and the Tottenham Court Road and Oxford Street junction, the money loss mounts up to more than £2,000,000 sterling per annum. These figures may be multiplied many times before we can accurately gauge the cost of this traffic congestion to the community. In addition to the money lost, about eight thousand persons are injured and 150 killed every year in London through street accidents, these principally occurring where there is greatest congestion. Delay in giving the needed relief is alike dangerous and expensive. Those who have been called upon to solve the many difficulties, have consulted the greatest living experts on locomotion, and have presented, in various reports and investigations by Parliamentary and County Council Committees, all known information on modern transit. Added to this, they have the testimony of the ablest railway experts and engineers of England— men who have in many cases devoted their lives to the study of Metropolitan transportation. Back of all this they have at the present moment some of the strongest financial groups, representing both British and American capital with £50,000,000 sterling, ready and willing to take up, in conjunction with public authorities like the London County Council and Board of Trade, the fiscal and practical side of enterprises which will give immediate relief. Further than this, the proposals submitted at the session just closed—as will be presently shown—differ widely in character from those of former years.

The tube schemes were not short lines to be run under the most profitable thoroughfares, but systems taking in alike the fat and the lean, and planned with the ultimate idea of linking up into a network sufficiently comprehensive to give the needed relief and take the population out into the open. In a few cases only did these projects savour of the mere promoter, and the House of Lords Committee made short work of them. The time, in my opinion, has come for action in these matters, and not to still further hang them up. The suggestions of Lord Windsor's Joint Select Committee of the House of Lords and Commons were sensible and practical, and the procedure therein laid down has been fairly well carried out by the House of Lords Committee of the session of 1902, in dealing with the several underground or tube projects brought forward for decision. The London County Council, likewise, went carefully over the proposals of the session of 1900, and gave their views at considerable length on each proposed scheme, many of which they recommended as useful, and suggested that, subject to certain reasonable conditions, they should be proceeded with. Then the Board of Trade investigated the entire subject from its point of view, and submitted through its experts, a report which goes very thoroughly into the technical side of the question, and which makes demands in relation to construction and operation that have been accepted without a murmur by the promoters, but which nevertheless will in many cases prove very costly. In short, the public interests appear to have been exceedingly well protected.

III.—LET US BE JUST TO LONDON

Mr. Sidney Low and some other writers, who contend that London "is strangely behind the age" in facilities for transporting its multitudes, are apt to become a trifle too severe when they compare London with other cities of the world. In justice, we should bear in mind that while other cities are working up towards a thousand million passengers per annum, London has, with such methods as she possessed, provided for thirteen hundred millions of passengers, and must now find additional facilities for half as many, and perhaps for as many, more. There is such a thing as being on the ground too soon, and according to the following para-

graph, taken from Mr. Low's excellent article in the *Fortnightly Review*, this seems to have been the trouble with London: "We had begun, it is true, rather well thirty or forty years ago, or more. We were among the first of great towns to supersede oil lamps by gas, and so to render street traffic safe after dusk. We had for those times excellent steamboats on the Thames—fifty years ago—some of them, I believe, are there still. Railway enterprise, when England was leading the world in steam locomotion, instead of dropping mournfully behind, had given London facilities for suburban transit at a period when such things were hardly dreamed of in Paris, Vienna, or Brussels. There was a time — it sounds like a fairy tale, but I believe the statement is correct—when people would come a long way merely to see that forlorn edifice, the London Bridge Station of the South - Eastern Railway; and when the same company's railway to Deptford and Greenwich was deemed a marvel of enterprise and engineering skill. London, again, first grappled boldly with the problem of internal locomotion by the really striking conception of an underground railway; and the sulphurous and smoke-grimed tunnel between King's Cross and Paddington was for some years one of the sights and wonders of the Metropolis, like the Crystal Palace, and Rotten Row in the season. To our capital also belongs the credit of developing two excellent public vehicles—the hansom was long the best thing of its kind, and the neat, rapid, quaint little carriage, with its good horse and skilful driver, was the envy of foreigners accustomed to mouldy fiacres drawn by decrepit cattle. The omnibuses of London were regarded with natural admiration in an era when, in most continental and provincial cities, no equally cheap and convenient public conveyances were to be found."

All this is true, and more might be said of the old - time enterprise shown by the railways centring in London, in handling passenger traffic quickly and cheaply. Take, for example, the Great Eastern Railway, which handled last year the amazing number of 91,740,654 passengers in their four London stations — Liverpool Street, Bishopsgate Street, Bethnal Green, and Fenchurch Street; the North London Railway, which, on less than twelve miles of line carried forty-seven million passengers, about twenty-seven millions of which centred at Broad Street ; the London and South-Eastern and Chatham and Dover, which combined nearly reached an aggregate of sixty millions; the London Brighton and South-Coast, with nearly twenty-eight millions for London Bridge and Victoria ; the London and South-Western, which can boast of thirty millions of passengers to and from Waterloo last year; and the Great Northern system, which including season tickets, handles thirty-four million passengers annually. On that ever busy spot at the foot of Old Broad Street we find the combined number of passengers passing in and out of the Liverpool Street Station of the Great Eastern Railway, and the Broad Street Station of the North London Railway to have been 80,780,724. These are prodigious figures when applied to the steam railway, which is fast becoming a clumsy and cumbersome machine in the transportation of urban passengers.

That some of these railways have reached the point where they can carry no more passengers on existing tracks, or that the demands of the population have become so enormous that these millions can no longer converge and radiate is not surprising, and certainly the railway companies themselves are not to blame. The policy of both underground railways, I think, has been mistaken. If these two companies had absolutely amalgamated ten years ago, electrified their lines, and devoted their energy to feeding the outer systems of railway, instead of building and extending lines themselves, the situation might have been improved. It is not too late yet. The District Railway has fallen into capable hands, and those now in charge will be able to make the most of it. The Metropolitan is sure to follow suit, and in a few years the community of interest which now exists, will have changed into common ownership. Aside from delay in adopting modern methods, there has not been such avoidable delay as some claim, especially when we consider the numerous conflicting interests, and become conversant with the " how-not-to-do-it " peculiarities of British Departments and Public Bodies, through which railway enterprise must slowly drag its way. London, according to Mr. Low, first grappled boldly with locomotion by the striking conception of an underground railway. Compare the details of the first tube railway, the City and South London—

built, I think, only ten years ago — with the completed work on the Great Northern and City Railway, and it makes one rejoice that more of these tubes were not projected a decade ago. To begin with, the tunnels which contain the lines of the Great Northern and City Railway are of much larger size than have hitherto been made for any tube railway. Measuring 16ft. in internal diameter (at sideway stations 21ft., and at terminals 23ft.), they are some 8ft. bigger than the standard suggested by the Board of Trade for the numerous tube railways that have appealed to Parliament for powers this Session. The tunnels of the Central London are only 11ft. 8½ins., and those of the City and South London are still smaller. The consequence is that the Great Northern and City tunnels are capable of accommodating the ordinary rolling stock of any steam railway in this country, and coaches with side doors could pass through them if desired. It may not be necessary for other tube railways to follow these plans, but the House of Lords Committee paid a good deal of attention to these details at its sessions this year, and the public will be much better served in consequence. At the present moment there are only about twenty-two miles of tubular railway in actual operation, so that the new rules and regulations can be made to apply to the new lines, and to as many of the projected lines, as come before Parliament for additional time, changes in routes, and extensions of track.

The national love of the Englishman to grumble often leads him to complain without a cause. While we have some up-to-date electric traction in New York, the condition of the locomotion service of that city is as bad, if not worse, than London, and will remain so until after the subway has been completed. Even then the rapid transit problem will not have been solved. The elevated railways ought to have been electrified ten years ago, instead of which they are, like the London Underground, only now setting about the work. Horse cars still jog merrily over the very badly laid rails of New York cross streets. The Metropolitan Railway System, with its splendid cars and conduit system of traction, is the one bright and satisfactory spot in our rapid transit. Public opinion clamoured for fifteen years before it succeeded in getting the subway out of the air down to the solid road of fact. The subway will cost £7,000,000 to build, and probably £10,000,000 including equipment. There are at this moment several schemes knocking at the door of Parliament, and some already in progress of completion, for London, as big if not bigger than this. Mr. Yerkes and his group have planned to spend £5,000,000 more than this amount of money—if not considerably more. The scheme which passed the House of Lords under the clever management of Sir Clinton E. Dawkins for Mr. Morgan's English house, involved in its original form over £16,000,000 —twice the cost of the New York Subway. The London County Council has proposals, including its tramway purchases and its schemes for electrically equipping the London surface street railways, and its subway connecting the north and south tramway systems, equivalent to twice the cost of the New York Subway. Indeed, if all the proposed schemes had gone through the present session, the total capital involved nearly £55,000,000 sterling—more than five times the money to be expended on the Broadway and Harlem Subway. There are some stupendous locomotion projects just now in London, and before describing the several groups individually, and attempting to ascertain their relation to each other and to existing transportation systems of London, it may be well to find out if statistics will aid us in gauging the magnitude of the traffic in and around London.

IV.—THE MAGNITUDE OF LONDON TRAFFIC

It is comparatively easy to make an approximate estimate of the traffic of almost any city in the world, but London is an exception, and presents so many difficulties, that such an estimate is almost impossible. For the County of London—population, 1891, something under five millions—the following estimate of passengers carried during the year 1900 has some elements of probability :—

Railways (on basis of Mr. Kinnear Clark's estimate, in 1891, of seventy-five per head of population)	400,000,000
Omnibuses (estimated on basis of number of passengers carried per omnibus by the London General and Road Car Companies)	500,000,000
Tramways (estimated by deducting 10 per cent. from the actual total number of passengers carried by the London Tramway Companies)	300,000,000
Hackney carriages (estimated on basis of 6,000 passengers per annum for two-wheeled and four-wheeled cabs alike)	70,000,000
Steamboats	3,500,000
	1,273,500,000

The above figures are about equivalent to the number of passengers carried annually on the various street railways of Greater New York, including, of course, Brooklyn, the population being a million and a half less than London. The London passengers are carried in such a variety of ways, by such a network of railways and tramways and omnibuses; that it is necessary for a clear idea of the subject in hand, to understand something about the existing methods of transportation. To begin with, we have the important railways running into London, bringing passengers from all parts of the kingdom, as well as suburban passengers, to and from their business. These are as follows :—

TABLE II.—RAILWAYS RUNNING INTO LONDON (NORTH SIDE)

Railway.	Length of Lines within County (miles).	Number of Stations within County.
Great Central	2.37	1
Great Eastern	16.79	27
Great Northern	4.31	4
Great Western	4.75	4
London and North-Western	9.64	12
London, Tilbury and Southend	.62	1
Metropolitan	12.25	18
Metropolitan District	10.42	16
Metropolitan and Metropolitan District Joint	2.12	8
Midland	7.27	6
Tottenham and Hampstead Junction	1.92	6
Total	72.46	103

On the south side of the Thames we find the following railways :—

TABLE III.—RAILWAYS RUNNING INTO LONDON (SOUTH SIDE)

Railway.	Length of Lines within County (miles).	Number of Stations within County.
London, Brighton and South Coast	31.14	29
London, Chatham and Dover	26.22	33
London and South-Western	14.05	12
South-Eastern	37.86	27
London and South-Western and London and South Coast (joined)	.60	—
Totals	109.87	101

Making 182.88 total mileage, both sides of the River Thames, and 204 stations. This does not complete the list, for we must add to it the railways wholly within London, which I find to be as subjoined :—

TABLE IV.—RAILWAYS WHOLLY IN LONDON

Railways.	Length of Lines within County (miles).	Number of Stations within County.
Central London Electric	6.50	13
City and South London (Electric) ...	6.65	14
East London	7.22	7
Hammersmith and City	3.00	5
North London	11.19	18
Waterloo and City Electric ...	1.50	2
West London	2.30	2
West London Extensions	4.76	4
Whitechapel and Bow	3.00	4
Totals	46.12	69

Here, then, we have at the present time, within the 121 square miles of superficial area comprising the county of London, and including the tube railways in operation, a total length of line of 228.45 miles, and no less than 278 railway stations.

Before dealing with the new railways in course of construction, and those authorised at the recent Session of Parliament, in the hope of linking them up into one possible harmonious system, it is proposed to ascertain some facts about the extent of the tramways, which, according to our estimate, carried in 1900 above three hundred million passengers. Upon examination, I find that the London County Council and eleven companies, have running powers in the county of London. The total length of lines within the county, according to the latest available official report, is 115 miles, and the length of the line belonging to the companies which extends beyond the county boundary is nearly thirty - two miles. The London County Council owns seventy-two miles of line, forty-eight miles of which, situated on the north side of the Thames, is at present worked by the North Metropolitan Tramways Company, while the twenty-four miles on the south of the Thames, purchased January 1st, 1899, is worked by the Council itself.

That we may better understand the existing tramway systems of London the following table has been prepared, giving the names of the companies, the length of lines within the county, the length outside, and the total length.

So, without considering for the moment the railways and tramways outside the county of London, but quite within what we may call the area of metropolitan travel, we have in round numbers 348 miles of lines

TABLE V.—LONDON TRAMWAYS

Name of Tramway.	Length of Line within the County (miles).	Length of Line outside County (miles).	Total.
London County Council (worked by the Council)	24.16	...	24.16
London County Council (leased to North Metropolitan Company)	47.72	.48	48.20
Harrow Road and Paddington	1.93	.92	2.85
Highgate Hill	.49	.22	.71
London Bridge, Leyton and Walthamstow	.40	4.40	4.80
London, Camberwell and Dulwich	2.85	...	2.85
London, Deptford and Greenwich	6.33	...	6.33
London Southern	5.70	...	5.70
London United	4.32	12	16.32
North Metropolitan	.99	13.87	14.86
South-Eastern Metropolitan ...	2.46	...	2.46
South London	12.73	...	12.73
Woolwich and South - east London...	4.79	...	4.79
Totals	114.87	31.89	145.76

over which seven hundred millions, or more than half the total number of London passengers must annually pass. I am inclined to regard the estimate of four hundred million passengers conveyed by steam railways as too low. When I treat this division of the London traffic further on, the reasons for this belief will be given.

To the railways — surface, underground, and tubular—and the tramways, propelled alike by horse or electric traction, must be added the extensive omnibus service. These vehicles traverse the great lateral thoroughfares, beginning at such points as Shepherd's Bush and Hammersmith in the West, and so on up Oxford Street and Holborn to the Bank, and then to the East End; and on the north of Hyde Park, taking the Piccadilly and Strand route on the south side. They cross and recross the lateral thoroughfares at almost every available street, and join with the broad circle of the Metropolitan and Metropolitan District Railways, making connections which the tube railways, now in progress of completion and projected, will, it is hoped, bring about much more expeditiously. These omnibuses, slow and clumsy as they seem when compared with electric traction, carry, according to the above estimate, more passengers than either of the two other systems of London locomotion. The average number of omnibuses running must be fully 3,200, and the total number of passengers carried in Greater London—for they penetrate far beyond the county area—may be put at five hundred millions per annum, the two principal companies, namely, the General Omnibus Company and the Road Car Company, alone transporting in the neighbourhood of three hundred millions of passengers in the twelve months. To the omnibuses we must add nearly twelve thousand hackney carriages, or cabs—eight thousand hansoms, and the remainder four - wheeled vehicles.

Such then, in brief, is the locomotion service in London as we find it on the eve of an important change in methods of traction, a change which will, if we may judge from the success attending the first attempts to apply the new motor power, make it possible to utilise an unoccupied area beneath the surface of this intensely crowded space, for transportation purposes.

V.—The " Nether County " of London

An interesting writer on London locomotion has baptised this space below the surface as the " Nether County " of London, and thus picturesquely describes it: " But not many feet down below the surface of the county of London there are 121 miles of lateral space practically unappropriated, absolutely void of any kind of valuable property, and totally unpopulated, even by the dead. Under the county of London, as we know it, with all its life and stir and multiplicity of interests and conflicting forces, there is another county of London, an unknown land for the most part, a great void of silence and darkness in which there are absolutely no human interests to come in conflict, and in which the only force is *vis inertiæ*." But that this nether world can be turned to use in solving the locomotion question everyone of the passengers carried back and forth through the " Twopenny Tube" is fully aware. It is, moreover, true that, while horizontally we are dealing with a district of 121 square miles, vertically, when aided by the Greathead shields, by modern engineering, electric traction, and the invention of the vertical " lift," the space is practically unlimited. Through the tunnels, each six miles long, of the Central London Railway, built as it was without stopping the traffic, and penetrating valueless space, pass in comparative comfort fifty million passengers under some of the most congested streets of the

Metropolis. Referring to this enterprise, G. F. Millin, in a recent number of the *Contemporary Review*, says :—

" The two lines—the up and down—have been carried, sometimes side by side, and sometimes one above the other—along the Bayswater Road, Oxford Street, Holborn, right under the Fleet City Sewer, and the Holborn Viaduct and subways, along Newgate Street and Cheapside, and not a single omnibus has been stopped by the work. The full tide of traffic has rolled on the whole time. There has been a sectional break-up of the road in front of the Mansion House, but that has been necessitated, not by the deep tunnelling, but by the construction of a subway for foot - passengers just underneath the surface." The capacity of these railways for carrying passengers will undoubtedly be improved, and further attention given to the removal of atmospheric pollution, but the Central London Railway, in its infancy as it were, with a little over six miles of length, is showing excellent results. This company is now carrying over seven million passengers per mile, and if it had secured the Piccadilly route, it expected to increase the carrying capacity to over one hundred millions per annum, on a little over twelve miles of line. The Piccadilly route, for a railway of this sort, is even better than that of Oxford Street. The vehicular and pedestrian traffic during twelve hours, from eight o'clock in the morning to eight o'clock in the evening, was thus recorded (1890): At the Marble Arch, 10,974 vehicles and 21,080 pedestrians ; at Oxford Circus, 12,831 vehicles, 54,100 pedestrians ; Holborn Bars, 14,801 vehicles, 59,455 pedestrians. It was on that traffic the Central London Tube was built. By the Piccadilly route there passed during the same number of hours: At Knightsbridge, 18,874 vehicles and 37,036 pedestrians ; at Piccadilly Circus, 12,551 vehicles, 52,930 pedestrians ; at the Strand, 11,997 vehicles, 56,927 pedestrians. Summarily we find the two routes stand relatively to each other as follows :—

TABLE VI.—RECORDED DAILY TRAFFIC, PICCADILLY AND OXFORD STREET ROUTES

Traffic.	Piccadilly Route (1902).	Oxford Street Route (1890).
Vehicles	43,422	37,636
Pedestrians	146,898	134,635

It will be noticed that the census of the Oxford Street route was taken in 1890, and upon those figures the London Central was encouraged to go on with its scheme. The Piccadilly returns are for this year, and upon that showing we find four distinct groups of capitalists, including the Central London Company, willing to undertake a similar enterprise along this great east and west artery of London. Here we have a comparatively simple illustration of how the traffic problem of London must be studied by those who are prepared to invest their own fortunes and other people's money in rapid transit undertakings. A few more figures will also illustrate the amount of traffic per hour at points of greatest pressure. The following converging and radiating centres all have a pressure of over four hundred vehicles per hour at the busiest time of the day. The Bank, 774 ; Charing Cross, 692 ; Piccadilly Circus, 643 ; Oxford Circus, 627 ; Elephant and Castle, 597. These are points one must keep in mind in studying London locomotion. Table VII is interesting ; it records twenty-four points of London's greatest pressure.

TABLE VII.—CONVERGING AND RADIATING CENTRES WHERE THE NUMBER OF VEHICLES REACHES OR EXCEEDS FOUR HUNDRED PER HOUR

1. Bank of England.	13. London Bridge.
2. Charing Cross.	14. Liverpool Street.
3. Piccadilly Circus.	15. Piccadilly.
4. Oxford Circus.	16. Holborn.
5. "Elephant and Castle."	17. General Post Office.
6. Oxford Street.	18. Angel, Islington.
7. Oxford Street and Tottenham Court Road Junction	19. Edgware Road.
	20. Pall Mall East.
8. Strand.	21. Hyde Park Corner.
9. Regent Street.	22. Cheapside.
10. Marble Arch.	23. Ludgate Circus.
11. Victoria Station.	24. Parliament Street.
12. King William Street.	

It is not surprising, therefore, that the first comprehensive efforts to construct a new system of rapid transit, whether by subways or tubular railway, should tend towards these important centres, though in doing so, as will be shown hereafter, some of the most responsible promoters have by no means neglected the sound principles which should be the basis of such operations, namely, extensions beyond the congested area into districts where land is cheap, and comfortable homes can be obtained at moderate rentals.

VI.—UNITED STATES RAILWAY LEGISLATION

Having learned something about the extent of the traffic and its places of greatest density, we may pass on to a consideration of the principles which Parliament and the various governing bodies have laid down for the construction and operation of the railways.

In the United States it is undoubtedly easier to obtain concessions and franchises for light railways and tramways in new districts and towns not already supplied with such means of transit, than it is under similar circumstances in the United Kingdom. To begin with, except in the District of Columbia, which is the seat of Government, Congress has nothing to do with such matters. The laws relating to street railways differ in detail in almost every State and Territory. The constitutions and laws of some States limit the period of franchise to twenty-five years, as in New York, and even to ten years, as in Wyoming, while in Louisiana and Mississippi the limit is ninety-nine years. There are twenty States which seem to have "no limit," but "no limit" as to the State's power, may mean a short term in the case of the Municipality, for the fact that the State has a free hand in the matter does not mean that it will delegate that right to its cities and towns. It is within the power of some State Legislatures to grant rights direct to companies without the intervention or consent of the Municipality, and in a few cases this has been done. It is safer to say that each of the half-hundred States of the Union is a law unto itself in all questions appertaining to railways and tramways, whether steam, or electrical, or horse, that operate within its borders. In consequence of this, we find the laws varying greatly, and no promoter could tell what this procedure would be, until the statutes in the State in which he wanted his franchise, had been carefully examined. Permanent railway commissions have been created in several States, which have to hear all testimony, and are, subject to Municipal approval—and in some cases without—empowered to grant or refuse permits to build railways, in accordance, of course, with the general Act of the State relating to such undertakings. It is true that we point with pride to our twenty thousand miles of street railways, and to our £400,000,000 sterling invested therein ; and this is why our English friends say: "They do these things much better in the United States; we in England are sadly behind the times, and our laws are so cumbersome." Yet in a large city like New York, for example, rapid transit was most shamefully tied up for fifteen years by Special Commissions that accomplished nothing, and by political interference, State and Municipal, which blocked everything, until the public would stand it no longer. In instances where there is no conflict of interests, and little or no opposition, our laws are more flexible than yours, and our rules and regulations as to operating street railways, less stringent, but I am by no means sure that under like conditions we could have made more headway than you have done in solving the London problem. The crowded state of every means of conveyance in New York at the present moment, is not favourable to that assumption. It is true that works are in progress to connect the new subway with tunnels running under the Hudson River to Jersey City; and under the East River to Brooklyn and Long Island; but these much needed enterprises have only recently been inaugurated, and probably will not be completed sooner than the present schemes of a similar character, now in various stages of development, for the relief of congested London.

VII.—THE JOINT COMMITTEE'S REPORT

To obtain a fair idea of the supervision exercised, and the method of granting railway franchises for London, it is not necessary to go further back than a year, when the report of the Joint Select Committee of the House of Lords and the House of Commons on London underground railways, was ordered to be printed. That committee was appointed for the purpose of "ascertaining whether the lines of route for underground railways in and near London, proposed by Bills which have been, or may be, introduced during the present session, are best calculated to afford facilities for present and probable future traffic; and if not, what modifications of those lines of route are desirable." The Committee was furthermore instructed to consider what special provisions should be made for the protection of the owners, lessees, and occupiers of properties adjacent to underground railways from damage or

annoyance; also as to the conditions relating to construction and works, that should be imposed upon the promoters. Brief as are the above instructions, they seem to cover the entire subject, and the expert testimony, taken and published in full, shows conclusively that the committee performed its task thoroughly and intelligently, making a report that will become the basis for future legislation authorising these enterprises. A Royal Commission might have consumed more time, but could not have obtained more expert information, for all persons of experience in this sort of work; all persons financially interested; and all available experts; appear in the list of witnesses. If we examine this report of last year, and the testimony taken by the Lords Committee of the present year, we shall find that every possible phase of the London locomotion question has been touched. In a like manner, by the aid of the able cross-examiners — and they were numerous and most merciless, it seemed to me, in their questions — the strength and weakness of the several schemes were laid bare on the parliamentary dissecting table, in full view of the public and the legislators. Some of the proposals appear to have fallen by the wayside, for they are only to be found on stray maps. Others were speedily disposed of for lack of financial backing, and without even a discussion on their merits. Others went down, as it were, to avoid punishment, or were withdrawn. Still others passed, with limbs and branches, extending unfairly into fields already occupied, chopped off; while those strong enough to withstand the severe handling of the Committee, were so hedged around by the numerous little clauses suggested by the collective wisdom of the engineers and experts of the London County Council and Board of Trade, that it may fairly be assumed public and private interests of all sorts and kinds have been amply protected. No account has been taken of the important element of competition entering into the proceedings of both these Parliamentary Committees. True, these franchises were not put up for public auction at so much cash rental, but with four important groups of capitalists vigorously competing, for instance, for the through Piccadilly and City route, or, one might say, Hammersmith and City, *via* Piccadilly, it is fair to presume that the group securing the award, offered the most attractive scheme, including remarkably cheap through bookings, penny fares, and liberal concessions relating to the safety and comfort of the travelling public.

The test of all such enterprises should always be : What are the companies willing to give the public in safety, speed, rate of fare, comfort in travelling? and how great a responsibility will they assume, to ensure that the rights of others are not invaded? These points are essential, and in all the new Bills, and in Bills giving additional time and granting extension to existing railways, they have been well looked after by the Committee. Revenue for such privileges is of secondary importance, while final absorption by Municipal authorities is out of the question, unless, as in the case of the New York and Boston subway, the local authorities furnish the capital.

The Joint Committee, when it assembled in 1901, found the following deep - level undergrounds open for traffic or authorised :—

TABLE VIII.—LIST OF DEEP LEVEL LINES OPEN AND AUTHORISED

Open to traffic ...	City and South London	1884-7.
„ ...	„ „ (Clapham Ext.)	1890.
Works in progress	„ „ (Islington Ext.)	1893.
Open to traffic ...	Central London	1891.
„ „ ...	Waterloo and City	1893.
Works in progress	Great Northern and City ...	1892.
„ „	Baker Street and Waterloo ...	1893-5.
Authorised „ ...	Charing Cross, Euston, and	
	Hampstead	1893.
„	... Brompton and Piccadilly ...	1897.
„	... City and Brixton	1898.
„	... Great Northern and Strand ...	1899.
„	... North-West London	1899.
„	... Metropolitan District (deep level)	1897.

The Islington Extension of the City and South London has since been open to traffic, making in all nearly six miles, to which we may add a little over six miles of line for the Central London and a mile and a half for the Waterloo and City—a total of fourteen miles representing at the present time all the tubular railway open to traffic. The proposals for the session 1901 were as follows :—

Brompton and Piccadilly (extension).
Central London (two small extensions, west and east end).
Charing Cross, Euston, and Hampstead (two small extensions).
Charing Cross, Hammersmith, and District.
City and North-East Suburban.
Islington and Euston.

King's Road.
North-East London.
Piccadilly and City.
West and South London Junction.
Also two tubular railways, proposed by the Great Eastern Railway, from Liverpool Street to Stratford, thence diverging to Walthamstow north and Ilford almost due east.

The Joint Committee of 1901 decided, wisely I think, not to deal with the merits of these several proposals, but to leave them to take their course by ordinary Private Bill Committees in the session of 1902, and take up the broader question of the relation of the several schemes to the locomotion service of the Metropolis. Their decision on this phase of the inquiry was that the various railways open to traffic, in progress of building, authorised, and proposed, left considerable areas unprovided for, especially north of the river in the neighbourhood of East and West Ham, and south of the river between Greenwich and Dulwich. The committee suggested that possibly this may be accounted for by the fact that the subsoil is of such a character as to make the construction of underground railways very costly. In commenting on the ten above - named Bills, the committee referred to the difficulty in dealing with the question of the best routes, because, as we have seen, a great number of underground railways had already been authorised, while others have been partially constructed. In conclusion, this committee laid down under the modest title of " General Points," some suggestions that have, in a large measure, guided the action of Parliament in these matters during the present session, and which will probably have considerable influence on all future legislations relating to London underground railways.

This memorandum is of sufficient importance to submit a complete summary for future reference.

(1) Underground railways or underground tramways in London and its immediate suburbs, which can be hereafter extended if required, above or below ground, into the country, but from the termini of which passengers could, for the present, proceed by electric surface tramways, omnibuses, and so forth, appear to be the best mode of dealing with the present traffic, and the probable requirements of an increasing population.

(2) These underground railways or tramways should run from well-recognised centres of traffic to other like centres of traffic, or from centres of traffic to districts whence large numbers of people have to be carried daily to and from their work in London or the suburbs.

(8) It is desirable that Parliament should carefully investigate the circumstances under which those controlling authorised lines apply for an extension of time. The result of many of the authorised railways having remained in abeyance for a considerable number of years has been, in some cases, to prevent other companies coming forward to make lines along the same route. The renewal, therefore, of lapsing powers should not be granted without the most careful consideration as to the probability of a company, which has already failed to carry out its obligations to the public, being able by an extension of time to fulfil those obligations within a reasonable period.

These would seem to be safe and sound general principles. The committee then proceed to recommend that the London County Council shall have *locus standi* before Parliament to oppose all systems proposed by promoters, whether original or renewals. That the lines should be worked at the terminals on the shuttle system, or by a terminating loop; that confluent junction inside tubes should be avoided, and that stations should be so constructed as not to pour out passengers into crowded streets. Damage to the owners of property was also considered, and means adopted for insertion in Bills to provide against injury due to subsidence or vibration. In conclusion, the committee deliberated on the proposal that all these underground railways should be subject, within certain limits, to the control of a central authority, but, while agreeing that some such direct control might be desirable, it made no specific recommendation. An extension of the powers of the Board of Trade, and the adoption of some of the suggestions made by Colonel Horatio A. Yorke, expert of that department to Lord Windsor's Committee this session for extending the powers of inspection, will result in the needed reform. These proposals may be epitomised.

The company shall from time to time submit for the approval of the Board of Trade, plans, sections, and other details of their proposals with respect to (a) permanent way, tunnels, platforms, stairs, lifts, and other communications; (b) rolling stock; (c) lighting; and (d) ventilation. The railway rolling stock, and the other works shall be constructed, reconstructed, and maintained only in accordance with the plans, sections, and other details as approved by the Board of Trade. These proposals have met with no serious objection on the part of the responsible promoters, and some of the owners of routes already authorised, have expressed their willingness to modify their plans to conform with the more advanced ideas for the construction of these railways.

VIII.—THE LONDON COUNTY COUNCIL'S VIEWS

Parliament having laid down the general principles, and the Board of Trade having followed suit with these technical proposals for the safety of the public—the London County Council submitted a report on April 22nd, 1902, setting forth with considerable detail their views of the situation. Originally this body wanted some public control or supervision of the present and future tube railways in London—vested, I suppose, in the County Council itself. Parliament, however, decided that the hands of that body were already full with their numerous tramway and omnibus schemes, and that to go in for legislation, looking to this end, would only cause still further costly delay. Accepting this decision in good faith, the County Council very wisely took up the practical side of the question, and examined each of the proposed Bills. In doing this, however, the Council frankly said they did not seek to endeavour to obtain the insertions of any clauses in these Bills which would hamper promoters, and place difficulties in the way of carrying out their undertakings. They were willing to leave general structural questions to the Board of Trade, as well as clauses providing for payment of damage in cases of subsidence or vibration. They proposed to interest themselves before the committee in the matter of fares and ot workmen's trains, or specially reduced rates of fares for workmen. In addition to these they included more or less general requirements of their own, for the protection of sewers, thoroughfares, bridges, monuments, public buildings, and other details coming specially within the Municipal sphere of actions.

The decisions arrived at with regard to the individual schemes were grouped in this order :—

(1) Schemes which, subject to certain conditions, should not be objected to by the Council; under these we find the following Bills :—

(*a*) Baker Street and Waterloo.

(*b*) Central London Railway (new lines).

(*c*) Edgware and Hampstead Railway.

(*d*) Great Northern and City Railway.

(*e*) Great Northern Railway Bill, No. 2.

(*f*) Great Northern and Strand Railway.

(*g*) Islington and Euston Railway (suspended for session, 1901).

(*h*) North-West London Railway.

(2) Schemes which, subject to certain conditions, and to the attention of the Select Committee being drawn to the financial proposals contained therein, should not be objected to by the Council; under these come the following Bills :—

(*a*) City and Crystal Palace Railway.

(*b*) City and North - East Suburban Electric Railway Bills, No. 1 (suspended from session, 1901) and No. 2.

(*c*) North - East London Railway Bills, No. 1 (suspended from session, 1901) and No. 2.

(3) Schemes which, subject to certain conditions, might be considered satisfactory except for financial proposals which they contain, but which on that account require to be strenuously opposed by the Council, and which are the following Bills :—

(*a*) King's Road Railway Bill, No. 1 (suspended from session, 1901) and King's Road Railway Bill (Putney extension).

(*b*) West and South London Junction Railway Bill (suspended from session, 1901).

(4) Schemes which on general grounds are unsatisfactory, and which consequently should be opposed for the most part *in toto*. In this category we find these Bills :—

(*a*) Brompton and Piccadilly Circus (new lines and extensions) Bills.

(*b*) Charing Cross, Euston, and Hampstead Railway Bills, Nos. 1 and 2 (suspended from session, 1901) and No. 8.

(*c*) Charing Cross, Hammersmith and District Electric Railway Bills, No. 1 (suspended from session, 1901) and No. 2.

(*d*) City and Brixton Railway.

(*e*) London United Electric Railways Bill.

(*f*) Piccadilly and City Railway Bills, No. 1 (suspended from session, 1901) and No. 2.

As Parliament did not appear to be guided by these recommendations, it will not be worth while to go into the reasons advanced by the London County Council for the classification. The reproduction of the list, however, will aid us in understanding the part these several bodies — Parliament, the Board of Trade, and the County Council—take in solving the rapid transit question, and it also brings us face to face with the various tubular railway schemes as they exist to-day, and as they appear on the map for the session of 1902. In discussing the merits and demerits of these railways, whether open to traffic or in course of construction, authorised or before Parliament, it has been decided to take up first those proposals which are not allied—as, for example, the Yerkes schemes—with old systems of transportation. In a subsequent article the steam surface railways entering London will be considered, and with them the two Underground Railways, with their proposed new tubular feeders, electrical equipment, and other improvements.

IX.—The London Suburban Railway
(Plate II)

The most important and far - reaching new scheme for the relief of London street traffic of the session of 1902 was the project that will in future be known as the London Suburban Railway, and which, as it passed the House of Lords, was the combined undertaking of the London United Electric Railways and the Piccadilly, City, and North-East London. This venture, in its original shape, also included the City and North-East London Suburban, and in the form it assumed in the session, of this year, combined in one comprehensively arranged system of tubes and electric tramways, a number of railways that, under various names and separate promoters, had previously been before Parliament. That we may

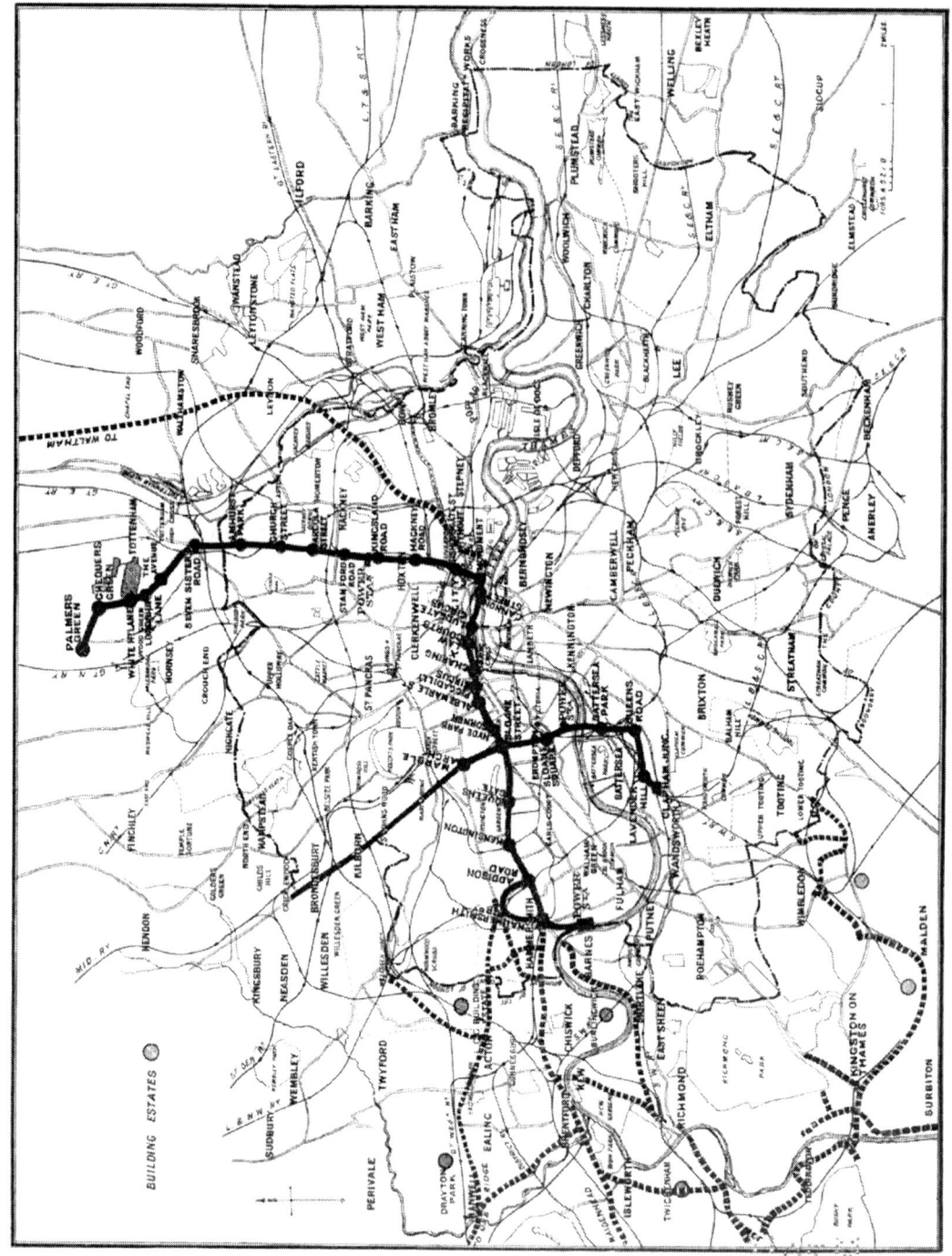

The London Suburban Railway, and the London United Tramways

UofM

better judge the magnitude of this enterprise, Plate II and Table IX have been compiled, showing the routes, the total capital asked for, and the estimated cost of each of the four lines amalgamated into one:—

TABLE IX.—CAPITAL AND COST OF LONDON SUBURBAN RAILWAY SCHEME

Name of Bill.	Shares.	Borrowing.	Total Capital.	Total Cost and Interest during Construction.
	£	£	£	£
London United Electric ..	3,750,000	1,250,000	5,000,000	4,671,494
North-east London ..	3,750,000	1,250,000	5,000,000	4,510,597
Piccadilly and City	1,500,000	500,000	2,000,000	1,764,316
City and North London Suburban	3,000,000	1,000,000	4,000,000	3,638,978
Total..	12,000,000	4,000,000	16,000,000	14,585,385

The enterprise tabulated above has been projected by Sir Clinton E. Dawkins, representing the house of J. S. Morgan & Co., and by J. Clifton Robinson and George White, and is known as the London Suburban Electric Railway. It is the largest entirely new proposal for tube railways ever submitted to Parliament. When complete, Mr. Yerkes' proposed scheme, with the District Railway as a nucleus, will require as much capital, but nearly all the important arteries of this system have already been authorised, while work on some of them, as will be shown in a subsequent article, is progressing. In its entirety the London Suburban Railway is by all odds the boldest enterprise of the kind ever pushed forward by thoroughly responsible financiers, and many of its proposals are far in advance of anything heretofore attempted. The main feature is a tube railway running to Hammersmith, where it will be fed by a general system of tramways, of which some seventy or eighty miles have already been sanctioned. The line takes the Piccadilly route to Charing Cross and Cannon Street, a north and south branch crossing at Sloane Street, and running from the Marble Arch south through Battersea, Lavender Hill, to Clapham Junction. From Cannon Street the north-east section of the railway turns almost direct north, taking a course through Highbury and Stoke Newington, and coming into the open at Tottenham. From there it becomes a surface railway, skirting the County Council estates for workmen's dwellings, and having a terminus at Palmer's Green. At this point the railway enters the field of the North Metropolitan Tramways Company, which, supported by the British Electric Traction Company, owns and leases from the London and Middlesex County Councils what is rapidly becoming a network of electric railways. The other branch of this important railway, the City and North-east Suburban, was withdrawn by the promoters for the purpose of changing its entrance into London, but it will, I am sure, be resubmitted next year, and should be authorised, in which event J. S. Morgan & Co. have promised to support it financially. The City and North-East Suburban—some four miles of tube and eleven miles out into the country—is the one tube railway which passes through the heart of the most crowded portion of London. It will afford great relief to the densely populated boroughs of Bethnal Green, Hackney, Shoreditch, and Stepney, taking the people of this cauldron of humanity in the East End into the country—Upper Clapton, Hale End to Walthamstow, Chingford, and ultimately to Battle Abbey and Epping Forest. There is no more desirable railway than this for the benefit of the people, but without forming part of a general scheme as above planned, and running into the Piccadilly and City, it could never be carried out.

Another important feature of this undertaking, which connects nine of the great working-class districts of the west and south-west—Southall, Drayton Park, L.C.C.'s building estate near Shepherd's Bush, Burlingwick, Twickenham, Hounslow, Hook, Malden, and Wimbledon—with two enormous working-class districts of the east and north-east, is the cheapness of the fares. These fares, be it remembered, are scheduled in the Bill, and become part of the contract or agreement; they are as follows:—

TABLE X.—THE SCHEDULE OF FARES ABOVE REFERRED TO

(1) HAMMERSMITH, SHEPHERD'S BUSH, AND PALMER'S GREEN (via CITY)

Either way between:—

Hammersmith and Charing Cross	...	1d.
Sloane Street and Monument	...	1d.
Hammersmith and Monument	...	2d.
Cannon Street and Stamford Road	...	1d.
Stamford Road and Seven Sisters Road	...	1d.
Seven Sisters Road and Palmer's Green	...	1d.
Cannon Street and Palmer's Green	...	2d.
Hammersmith and Palmer's Green	...	4d.

(2) MARBLE ARCH AND CLAPHAM JUNCTION (*via* SLOANE STREET)

Either way between :—

Marble Arch and Sloane Street ...	...	1d.
Marble Arch and Clapham Junction	...	2d.

(3) CANNON STREET AND WALTHAM CROSS (CITY AND NORTH-EAST LONDON SUBURBAN SCHEME)

Either way between :—

Cannon Street and Victoria Park	...	1d.
Victoria Park and Walthamstow...	...	1d.
Walthamstow and Chingford	...	1d.
Chingford and Waltham Cross ...	...	1d.
Cannon Street and Walthamstow	...	2d.
Victoria Park and Chingford	...	2d.
Walthamstow and Waltham Cross	...	2d.
Cannon Street and Chingford	...	3d.
Victoria Park and Waltham Cross	...	3d.
Cannon Street and Waltham Cross	...	4d.

Workmen's fares in each and every case are the single fare for the return journey. The rates of fare for the City and North-East Suburban are given because it hardly seems conceivable that Parliament will refuse, should it be asked for next session, an extension purely in the interests of the poorer class, giving them access into the country at phenomenally cheap fares. Both these north-east schemes received the endorsement of the London County Council and the Joint Committee of 1901 appointed to investigate the various proposed routes. They were both characterised as affording great facilities to crowded districts, and to districts where building is increasing and likely to increase. The pivot of this entire system, comprising nearly forty miles of tube and surface electric railway, is, naturally, the central line, enabling the traffic from these great north-eastern districts to move, not only to the City, but to be carried to the West End, and there distributed over the eighty miles of authorised tramways which are linking up this vast residential district of London. For the better performance of the work, arrangements have been made with the tramway system for through bookings on the combined undertakings. This will enable passengers to book to the City from Ealing, ten miles, for 4d. ; Hounslow, fourteen miles, 6d. ; and Richmond, ten miles, 4d. By workmen's trains those will be return rates of fare. The central idea of this scheme has been cheap travelling to the districts where there is plenty of room, at a less rate per mile

for a longer journey, instead of penalising the longer journeys. It is essential there should be cheap communication to the open country. We have here the first striking move in this direction. Mr. Yerkes, when his railways are fully connected up, will accomplish much the same end by other routes, not less important, but the London Suburban Railway penetrates new and unworked territory where no tubular railways have yet been authorised.

The Marble Arch and Clapham Junction section of this railway is quite important. From Clapham Junction, at the convergence of an immense network of railways, it crosses the river, goes up Sloane Street, and there will be an interchange station at the top of Sloane Street, into the east or west line. Thence the passenger can go further northward to the Marble Arch, where he comes immediately in contact with the Central London, and proceed to Shepherd's Bush or the City, that way, instead of to Hammersmith or the City by the Piccadilly and Charing Cross route. Beyond this is the North-West London, a tubular railway authorised from Hyde Park Corner, up Edgware Road, to Cricklewood, joining, as it were, the whole system of the Midland Railway and the London and North-Western Railway, coming in contact with these two main lines there. Links can easily be formed with the Hyde Park Corner and Cricklewood line when constructed, and new facilities will thus be given to large and important districts.

The linking up of this route is a matter of public interest, and by giving it now it will make it easier to understand the effect of all these schemes of London transportation when we attempt a general summary of the results. Beginning at Hammersmith Broadway, there will be the following interchanges with the London United Electric Tramways and the Metropolitan District. (1) Addison Road, next station east interchange with West London extensions. (2) High Street, Kensington, interchange with Metropolitan District. (8) Queen's Gate. (4) Sloane Street, interchange with north and south line, Marble Arch to Clapham Junction, and to North-West London to Cricklewood, when completed. (5) Hyde Park Corner. (6) Albemarle Street. (7) Piccadilly Circus, interchange with Baker Street and Waterloo, Brompton and Piccadilly. (8) Charing Cross, interchange with Charing Cross, Euston, and

Hampstead, and South-Eastern Railway. (9) Law Courts, interchange with Great Northern and Strand. (10) Ludgate Circus, interchange with London, Chatham, and Dover. (11) Cannon Street, interchange with Metropolitan and Metropolitan District Railways. (12) Monument, interchange with Metropolitan and City and South London. (13) Bishopsgate Street Without, interchange with North London and Great Eastern Railways. (14) Hackney Road. (15) Kingsland Road. (16) Stamford Road. (17) Arcola Street. (18) Church Street. (19) Amhurst Park. (20) High Road. (21) The Avenue. (22) Lordship Lane. (23) White Hart Lane. (24) Chequers Green. (25) Palmer's Green.

In addition to all these stations and connections taking the north and south section at Clapham Junction, interchange with the London, Brighton, and South Coast Railway, the London and South-Western, and other lines using Clapham Junction, might be made. As I have shown, when the north-west line to Cricklewood shall have been completed, connections may be also arranged between the Midland, and London and North-Western main lines. In short, it will touch nearly all the great centres of traffic. When the City, North-East, and Suburban shall have been added, it will penetrate the densest population of the East End on the one side, and carry the constantly growing population of the beautiful Thames Valley direct, without change, from their suburban homes, at less than half the steam railway rates, to and from their work in the City, bringing them in cars cleaner and nicer than the first-class carriages of existing railways.

Having ascertained the territories these railways tap, it is possible to estimate the probable number of passengers they will carry. Including the City and North-East Suburban, the seating capacity of the system will be 665,000,000, and the total estimated traffic, say at 40 per cent. of the capacity for the whole line, 252,000,000, distributed as follows: Hammersmith and Palmer's Green line, 138,000,000; Cannon Street and Waltham Cross, 92,000,000; Marble Arch and Clapham Junction 22,250,000. On eighteen miles of this railway, cars will run every two and a half minutes. On the outer lines the time will be every five minutes. These estimates

were made by J. Clifton Robinson, and have been severely criticised by Mr. Gooday, of the Great Eastern Railway, and others. It is nevertheless true that on sixteen miles of track Mr. Robinson is at the present moment carrying 40,000,000 passengers a year, and when his entire system, which, as authorised, amounts to nearly eighty miles, is finished, he expects to carry annually at least 200,000,000 passengers. Outside of Mr. Robinson's estimates, there are other facts which support the accuracy of these figures, and also of the estimates made for the system of tubular railways which Mr. Yerkes proposes to operate. I cannot do better, on this point, than quote a paragraph from remarks of Mr. Balfour Browne before Lord Windsor's committee.* This statement was in answer to a claim that, in order to make a certain tubular railway pay, they would have to carry the entire population of the district in the course of a year ninety-two times. Mr. Browne said: "My Lords, that is nothing in comparison with what is being done by tramways at the present time, as I will show you immediately from the statistics that are before you. These railways do pretty well. The North London Railway, according to Mr. Dunn, although, of course, it is not a through route, but a circular route around the north of London, carries 44,611,000. The Great Northern Suburban carries, according to Sir Henry Oakley and Mr. Grindling, 80,000,000 of passengers. The Central London—and here we come to something better—carries 45,000,000, and I believe, but this is only from Board of Trade statistics, that the Metropolitan Railway carries something like 81,000,000 of passengers in the year. But, my Lords, that is a bad service—a slow service with five or ten minutes intervals. On the Metropolitan and Metropolitan District, round London on the circle, there is only a ten-minutes service. That is nothing in comparison to what is being done with tramways to-day, as you heard from Mr. Robinson and other gentlemen. The North Metropolitan, the line we connect with at Tottenham, has sixty-four miles, which, of course, is a long mileage, but it carries 160,676,847 persons per annum,

---

* Pages 299 and 300, Minutes of Proceedings before the Select Committee of the House of Lords on the North-Eastern Railway (No. 1) Bill, May 14th, 1902.

and that is merely a horse tramway. When it is really worked by electricity, I have no doubt that it will be doubled, but it is 160,000,000 per annum, my Lords, on their lines. The London County Council have twenty - four miles, and, as yet, they are not electrically equipped, but they carry 118,281,820 people per annum. The South London, which is quite a small line, carries, practically, 18,000,000. Take the London United Tramways, which has only sixteen miles open, worked by electricity, you have the evidence that they carried last year 30,000,000 or 40,000,000 passengers. We know that when electricity is applied to the carrying of the whole population of a district, ninety - two times is nothing at all. Glasgow has a population of 762,000 people. It carried upon its tramways, which are forty-five miles in length, and some quite out in the suburbs, 132,557,724 persons. It carried its whole population, not ninety - two times, but 174 times. Liverpool has sixty - six miles of tramway, its population is 685,000, and it carried 98,776,881 passengers, or it carried its whole population 187 times. My Lords, these figures are really not so great when they are compared with what Philadelphia and some American towns do where they have had electric traction much longer, but I am content to take these figures as the basis. Are we not, therefore, sound in our estimate of seven million passengers per mile per annum, and will that pay, as we believe it will, and as we have given evidence to think it will? We have no doubt the cheap fares will induce an enormous traffic which does not at present find its way on any railway in London. The fares at the present time on the Metropolitan and Metropolitan District are very high indeed, and I venture to say that the fares on the Central London are for short distances too high, and for long distances too low, because no one who wanted to get into the City would hesitate to pay 3d., but anyone wanting to go from Oxford Street to another station near would hesitate before paying the present fare."

The history of these enterprises when conducted on the broad ideas of cheap and comfortable service, with every possible convenience for through booking, would likewise support the above estimates of the traffic, which will no doubt be realised. It should be remembered that through facilities such as here proposed between the tubes on one hand, and the tramways in the north and south-west of London on the other, are much more likely to create traffic than the circular routes. The lowness of the fare adopted by this scheme, it is thought, will prove especially attractive. By this route a person can get from Hammersmith to Sloane Street for 1d., or from Sloane Street to the City for 1d., and on the north to south line there would be a penny fare, which is lower than anything heretofore suggested. By touching these important territories the system will undoubtedly be able to make it pay. There are unquestionable advantages in the uniform fare, but until modern invention can still further reduce the cost of operation the risk will be too great for even such enterprising men as we find in this combination, to assume the responsibility of a uniform penny fare. An examination of these proposed rates shows a great improvement for long distance passengers over the prohibitive long haul rates that have heretofore been enacted.

X.—Central London (Plate III, Line A)

The present epidemic of tube railway promotions may be in a large measure attributed to the success of the Central London Railway, or Twopenny Tube, as it has been popularly christened. The Central London Railway was authorised in 1891 to run from Shepherd's Bush under the Uxbridge and Bayswater Road, Oxford Street, Holborn, Newgate Street, Cheapside, to the Bank—about six miles—with stations at Holland Park, Notting Hill, Queen's Road, Lancaster Gate, Marble Arch, Bond Street, Oxford Circus, Tottenham Court Road, British Museum, Chancery Lane, Post Office, and the Bank, where there has been built a large subway, access to which may be had from the converging streets at this, the greatest centre of traffic in London. The selection of this route was wise, because it runs through the very centre of London traffic, and converges at the Bank, where 774 vehicles pass each hour of the day. It passes under Oxford Street, which can boast more traffic—running 550 vehicles per hour —than any other street in London; and it has a station at Oxford Circus, which ranks fourth in the list of points of greatest traffic, Piccadilly Circus, Charing Cross, and

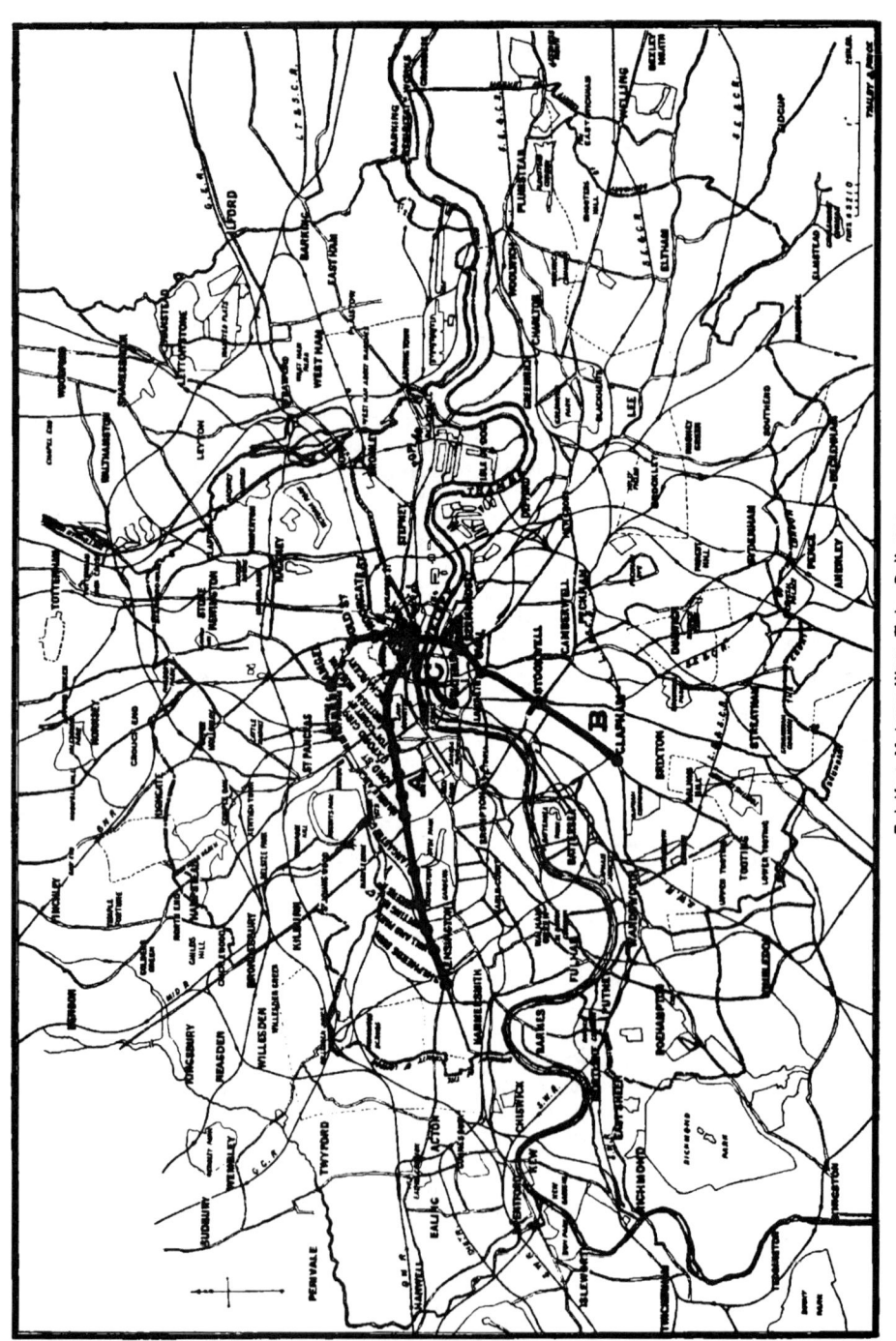

Existing Metropolitan Tube Railways

U of M

the Bank only exceeding it. The Central London has another station at the junction of Oxford Street and Tottenham Court Road, where five hundred vehicles pass per hour; also one at the Marble Arch, where it has the benefit of the Edgware Road and Marble Arch converging traffic, each exceeding four hundred vehicles per hour. At the time this tube was projected the thoroughfares under which it runs were found to be the routes of greatest traffic, and are probably so to-day. A more recent census — taken February of this year — of traffic, however, shows that what is called the Piccadilly and Charing Cross route from Hammersmith to the City has a greater traffic now than the Oxford Street route had ten years ago. The fact that the Piccadilly route is even a better one, together with a 4 per cent. dividend, after some two years of operation and a steadily increasing traffic, undoubtedly prompted the enterprising projectors of the Central London Railway to seek powers this session for an extension of their railway by the Piccadilly route, together with an important extension to Liverpool Street at the City end of the railway, and for some small lines at the west end of the line.

The new route proposed by the London Central Railway began at Shepherd's Bush, curved round to Hammersmith Broadway, then along Kensington Road, turning into the Park as soon as possible to avoid disturbing roads or house property, and continuing until it reached Hyde Park, when the proposed line crossed over and continued under Green Park, coming out again just by Walsingham House; then straight along Piccadilly, through Leicester Square and King William Street to the Strand, straight along the Strand and Fleet Street till it reached Bridge Street, Blackfriars. Here the question of St. Paul's came very prominently under consideration. To avoid this complication, the route was diverted nearer to the river. It was arranged there to go under the forecourt of the South-Eastern and Chatham Companies' station. This gave the tube a better curve, and put the railway in direct communication with that station. From thence it went round to Queen Victoria Street, along Cannon Street, passing the Bank, down Cornhill and Leadenhall Street, until it arrived at St. Mary's Axe. Passing to the left there, it

ran along St. Mary's Axe, turning round to the point where it should come out to Liverpool Street. Broadly speaking, the view the promoters had in mind was to give the City as much accommodation as they could, to avoid concentrating all traffic at a particular spot, and also to pick up the Great Eastern and North London at Liverpool Street. At this point, as is well known, about eighty million passengers per annum (Liverpool Street and Broad Street combined) converge, and the Central London proposed to be in constant readiness for any of these millions who might wish to be carried westward—by either the Oxford Street or Piccadilly route. The stations for this extension were, starting from Hammersmith: in the Broadway, then Addison Road, High Street Kensington, Albert Hall, Knightsbridge, Hyde Park Corner, St. James's Circus, Piccadilly, Charing Cross, the Law Courts, Ludgate Hill (at the foot of it), Cannon Street, Bank, St. Mary's Axe, and Liverpool Street. They had, in fact, five City stations, supplying the very core of the City business. It was an excellent scheme, and one that would have undoubtedly paid well at the uniform twopenny fare. If there had not been three other combinations competing for the same route—one of which offered more satisfactory terms in fares, a through service from west to north-east, and a larger tunnel construction—the London Central Railway would have obtained this valuable addition to its lines, and secured access to all the greatest traffic centres of London except the "Elephant and Castle." Last year the Central Railway carried forty-two million passengers, and this year they will carry forty-five, or probably fifty millions. Had this extension been approved it would have easily brought its passenger traffic up to a hundred millions, and that would have been the cream of the London traffic. The House of Lords Committee, however, decided that the company occupying the Piccadilly route must, in accordance with the general principle laid down in the Joint Committee's report of 1901, construct through the edge of the greatest traffic into the districts where land was cheap and rents lower. For this reason, I think, more than for any other, the Bill was thrown out. In deciding not to proceed with the Central London Bill, as far as relates to the proposed railway from Shepherd's Bush, *via* Hammersmith, to the Bank, the committee said they were prepared to consider the extension of the line beyond the Bank, and the small branch lines at the west end. The company afterwards, however, decided not to proceed with this portion of the Bill, so the whole matter has been postponed. Under the circumstances the House of Lords Committee could have hardly followed any other course, and the Central London Railway, in withdrawing all their proposed extensions are undoubtedly awaiting the final action of Parliament. The granting of a through Piccadilly route cannot fail to increase the traffic on the Central, and arrangements for joint working are almost sure to be effected before the new tube of the London Suburban Railway is open to traffic.

It was claimed before the House of Lords Committee, by both the Metropolitan and Metropolitan District railways, that traffic from both these lines had been diverted by the Central, and that the Tube was living largely upon stolen traffic. This may be good enough talk for Parliamentary committees, though in this case the committee very properly paid little heed to it. As at present managed, the underground railways of London are not entitled to much consideration. When they are once cleaned up, electrically equipped, and converted into up-to-date railways, the traffic will come to them — if not immediately, certainly as soon as the new authorised tubes have been coupled up as feeders. Meantime the Central will be kept busy taking care of the traffic it has legitimately won, and its entire capacity will be taxed to provide for the natural growth of this most important route.

XI.—CITY AND SOUTH LONDON (PLATE III, LINE B)

Sir Benjamin Baker, engineer to the City and South London Railway, in his testimony before the House of Lords Committee this session, gave some interesting facts in relation to the construction of the first London tube railway. The City and South London, now running from Clapham Common to the "Angel," Islington, was the pioneer line in the world of tube construction. Tube railways as experiments were, however, of earlier date than twelve years ago. The first one was a few hundred yards long; it was put down as a trial at the Crystal Palace, and demonstrated that in a 10ft. tube you could give the public better accommodation than you could in any of the omnibuses or cars then running. Four years later a similar experiment was tried, with same results, in New York. "Nothing whatever was done after that for seventeen years, in 1888, when Mr. Charles Gras Mott, the chairman of the South London Railway," said Sir Benjamin Baker, "came one day and told me that he proposed to go to Parliament for a tube railway from Stockwell to the City, under the Thames by London Bridge, now called the City and South London Railway. Undoubtedly the present state of the tube mania, as you may call it, dates from that time. I told Mr. Mott that there would be a tremendous Parliamentary opposition, because it was a novel affair; questions would be raised of damage to property, damage to London Bridge, and all the other things. And so it turned out; but, however, after great hesitation, the Act was granted. Mr. John Walter, of the *Times*, was the chairman of the committee, and I remember he told me the day after that he was so anxious about it, and about the danger of making these tube railways, especially as regards London Bridge, that he went at five o'clock in the morning and stood on London Bridge and pictured to himself London Bridge tottering, and then he thought, after a while, if this thing be a success it will lead to a great development, and he finally hardened his heart, and passed the City and South London. That is the origin of all these tube railways. English engineers are reproached for want of enterprise, but they cannot be reproached in this respect. That is solely a British idea. It is British developed, and it is British capitalists and shareholders that have lost largely in developing these railways. It is only at the last moment, when you get a railway with shares at a premium, that our friends on the other side of the Atlantic come over and offer to do the work for us."

It may be said of the City and South London that it felt its way along the subterranean darkness of the nether county of London, and its history may be studied to great advantage by those who are now projecting more pretentious schemes. It has demonstrated clearly that, with the exception of such routes as Oxford Street and Piccadilly, these tubes will not pay unless they really run somewhere—that is, unless they really move the traffic from one outer ring of London right away through the City into the open on the other side, in this way creating what may be termed a current of traffic. The South London was opened in 1890 as a short line from King William Street to Stockwell, with a tunnel 10ft. 6ins. in diameter, and cars to match. Two or three years afterwards the company found the limit of traffic on their small isolated three miles of track. They next determined to extend the line on the south to Clapham Common and on the north-east to Islington. The South London begins at Clapham Common, and has the following stations : Clapham Road, Stockwell, Oval, Kennington, "Elephant and Castle," Borough, London Bridge, Bank, Moorgate Street, Old Street, the "Angel," and, if the extension refused this session shall hereafter be allowed, additional stations at King's Cross, St. Pancras, and Euston. As the new sections were opened the stagnation of the traffic decreased, and it began to grow. The figures are worth studying. The maximum was substantially reached on the three-mile line in 1896, when it aggregated for the year about 6,600,000, keeping between 6,500,000 and 7,000,000 per annum until the end of 1899, just prior to the opening of the first extension. From that time to June 30th, 1902, there has been a steady increase of traffic, as will be seen by the following table :—

TABLE XI.—PASSENGER TRAFFIC, CITY AND SOUTH LONDON RAILWAY, 1899-1902

Half Year.				Passengers (exclusive of Season Ticket-holders).	Receipts (including Season Tickets).	Dividend Per Cent. Per Annum.
					£ s. d.	
June 30th, 1899	...	..	..	3,540,098	26,749 3 0	2½
December 31st, 1899	..	..	..	3,442,942	26,197 14 10	1½
June 30th, 1900	..	..	..	4,169,717	33,606 2 3	1½
December 31st, 1900	..	..	..	5,018,342	44,716 3 11	1½
June 30th, 1901	..	..	..	5,887,786	51,013 17 3	1½
December 31st, 1901	..	..	..	7,006,842	59,734 14 8	2½
June 30th, 1902	..	..	..	9,192,120	78,343 12 3	3

Since the opening of the line on December 18th, 1890, nearly ninety millions have been carried.

The opening this year of the Islington extension will still further improve the above figures, and this little railway, six and a quarter miles long, will soon be carrying twenty million passengers per annum. It has from the beginning paid the full dividend of 5 per cent. upon the preference stock, and is now paying 3 per cent. upon its ordinary stock. The company asked for its extension of less than two miles, from the "Angel" to Euston Station, for the purposes of coupling up with the London and North-Western, and thus taking passengers direct from Euston Station to London Bridge. It was strongly opposed by the Metropolitan, and the Bill was thrown out. On the other hand, both Mr. Harrison of the London and North-Western, and Mr. William Forbes of the London, Brighton, and South Coast, testified in favour of the extension, while other equally well-known traffic experts declared that such an extension would simply accommodate passengers at present unprovided for except by omnibuses or cabs. The experience of the South London is also interesting in relation to fares. It began on the uniform fare idea, which is almost exclusively in vogue in the United States, and I believe the fare was fixed at 2d. After trying this for a while penny fares were introduced, and, according to Mr. Mott, the chairman, are not likely to be changed. On this subject, Mr. Mott, at a recent meeting of shareholders, said : " Mr. Russell wants us to go back again to our old uniform fare. I thought I had explained that matter. I have gone into it carefully, and as far as I can make out, if we had adhered to the uniform fare you would not have had much dividend this half year. No doubt uniform fares are nice to the public in many respects, but they are unjust on a long line. It is unjust to a working man who only wants to go one mile to make him pay the same as the banker sitting by his side who wants to go six. If you extend your line much it is clear that a uniform fare cannot be maintained. I very much doubt, myself, whether the Central London will not alter their system in this respect before very long. We tried it for a number of years, and were forced to the conclusion that, although it might be necessary for a line three miles long, yet, when you got a line the length of ours—and now the Islington extension is opened it is longer than the Central London— it is not the right thing to do. I consider that a uniform fare would not answer, considering that there are tramways running all along our route, charging only ½d. and 1d. for short distances. I think, if we charged 2d. for those short distances, that we should lose a large number of passengers." Where the experience has been as limited as in the operating of tubes, it is well to note such an opinion as the one above quoted. As we shall see, Mr. Clifton Robinson, who has had

XII.—GREAT NORTHERN AND CITY

The next tubular railway open to traffic will be the Great Northern and City Railway, running from Finsbury Park to a station at

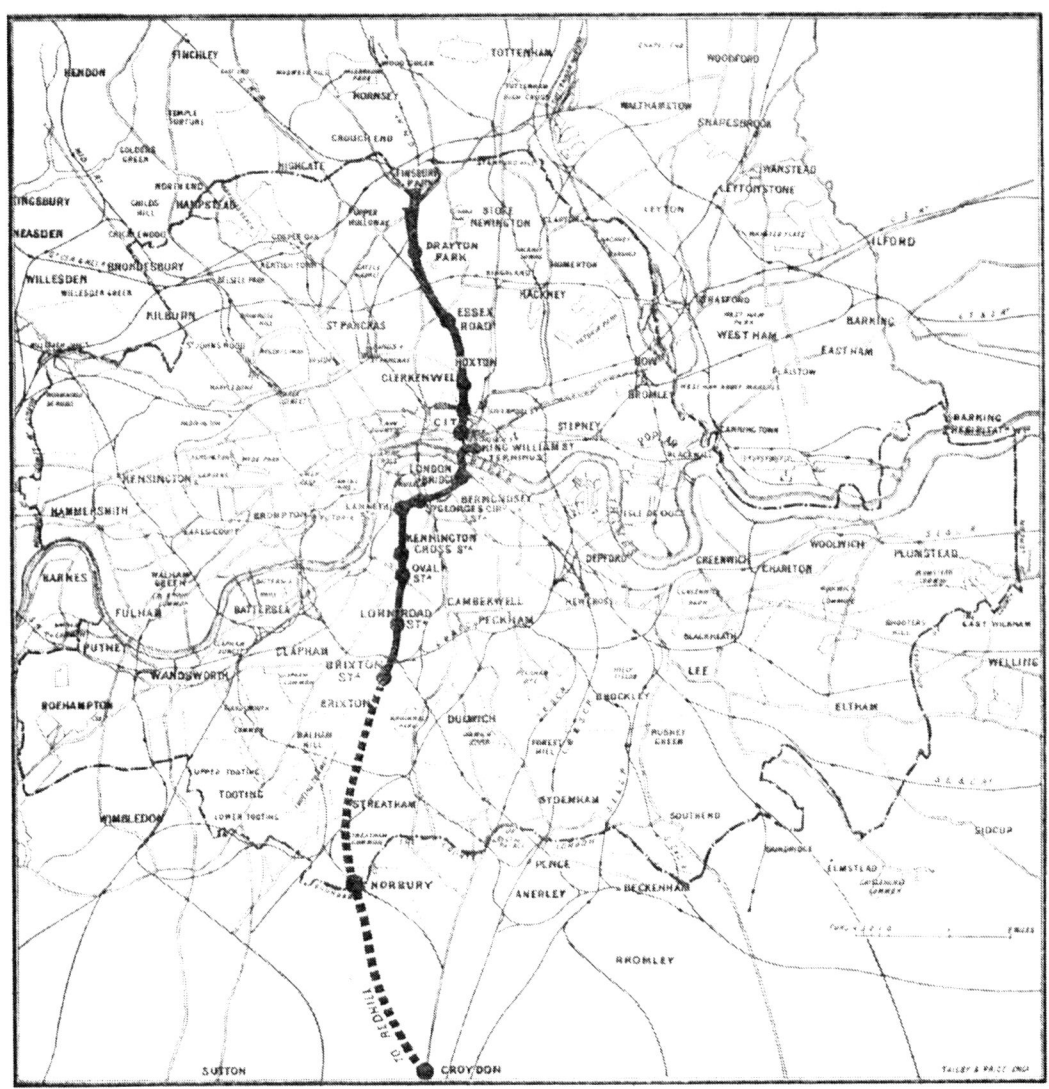

Plan Showing the Great Northern and City, and the City and Brixton, Tube Lines

considerable experience in tramways in the United Kingdom, makes a penny fare one of the factors of the London Suburban Railway, and is strongly of the opinion that these cheap short distance fares will be an important source of revenue.

the junctions of Moorgate Street, Princes Street, and Lothbury. This enterprise presents several features of interest in the transportation problem, not only by reason of the fact that it has been promoted by the representatives of two great railway systems, but because it has been so constructed that both tunnels, with a diameter of 16ft., will take the Great Northern Railway Company's heaviest suburban trains, consisting of eleven vehicles, with a seating capacity of five hundred passengers, from Finsbury Park and land them in the City. The chairman of this company, Sir Charles Scotter, one of the most experienced railway managers in the world, was largely a promoter of the Waterloo and City Railway, a small tube railway running from Waterloo Station, where the station is under the main terminus of the London and South-Western Railway, and is reached by inclined plane, to the Bank (Plate III, Line C). This tunnel, only a mile and a half in length, was the second of the kind open for traffic, and was designed for the purpose of taking the South-Western Railway Company's suburban passengers quickly to the City. It began by carrying three million passengers per annum, and has increased at about five hundred thousand per year; now they are carrying about five millions over this little railway. Every four minutes a train goes from Waterloo Station, taking just four minutes for the journey, and I am told this time, instead of the original time of five minutes, will be the permanent working of the railway throughout the day. At the Bank, owing to the Central London Station, there are five exits. We have here a quick way to get from Waterloo Station to Oxford Circus, by taking the Waterloo and City from Waterloo Station; changing at the Bank Station to the London Central Railway; and alighting at Oxford Circus or Bond Street Station. While the Waterloo and City seems to have suggested the Great Northern and City Railway, the original idea has been greatly improved on. In the first place, as I have shown in this article, the north-east part of the Middlesex county has become a great and constantly growing centre of residential population. Not only does the census prove this, but it is clearly demonstrated in the growth of suburban traffic on the Great Northern Railway. The suburban traffic of this splendidly conducted railway was in 1883 about 14,000,000; in 1886, 17,000,000; in 1891, 22,500,000; while at the present time it exceeds 30,000,000. There has been for many years an increase of nearly a million a year. This company pays both the

Metropolitan and North London enormous sums annually to transport its suburban traffic into the City. The new line, far from robbing these railways, will be made to pay by the increase of traffic, and, of course, its great advantage will be the direct route it takes from Finsbury Park to the City, and the few stopping places between. Unlike the Waterloo and City, the Great Northern and City will fill a double purpose, namely, that of furnishing the Great Northern Railway with a City terminus for its constantly growing suburban traffic, and of serving a large local traffic for the densely populated districts of Islington and Highbury, where the density of population ranges from 100 to 150 per acre. Originally planned for about three miles, the City extensions may increase it to nearly four miles.

The traffic of this enterprise may fairly be based on the local traffic of routes in this vicinity. Here are some figures:—

TABLE XII.—TRAM-CARS AND OMNIBUSES ALONG THE GREAT NORTHERN AND CITY ROUTE

	Per Mile per Annum.
The North London Railway Company carries	3,000,000
The season tickets issued by the company amount to the large total of 85,000, so that the actual passengers carried cannot be estimated at less than 6,000,000.	
The South London Electric Railway, with its small carrying capacity of ninety-six per train, carries over ...	2,400,000
The Central London Railway (with smaller tunnels than proposed by the Great Northern and City) estimates its local passengers at	7,000,000
The Metropolitan Railway (Moorgate Street to Paddington, about four and a half miles) in the first years after opening, carried (inclusive of season ticket-holders) at the rate of	5,500,000

Owing to extensions, separate figures for the above section of the Metropolitan Railway are not obtainable for recent years. Upon this basis, the Great Northern and City will carry 10,500,000, but with the additional conveniences, including the City Station near the Bank and the Highbury Station, the number will exceed these figures. The railway, as I have said, was originally planned to extend from Moorgate Street, where the station is opposite those of the City and South London and Metropolitan companies, to Finsbury Park, where the station will be under that of the Great Northern Railway, with which it will be connected by lifts and wide passages. The intermediate stations are at Old Street, where there is a connecting passage with the City and South London stations at Essex Road and Drayton Park. The journey is expected to be performed in thirteen and a half minutes. The tunnels, both up and down, are complete between Drayton Park and Moorgate Street, and the permanent way is being laid down, while preparations are being pushed on for work on the remaining portion between Drayton Park and Finsbury Park, which is to be made by the Great Northern under its existing lines, and leased to the Great Northern and City. By a Bill now before Parliament the company is seeking powers to construct an additional station at Highbury Corner, which has been specially asked for by the local authorities, and to build a short extension from Moorgate Street to Lothbury, in order to save its passengers the walk of about a quarter of a mile into the heart of the City. This Bill has passed its third reading in the House of Lords, and after passing second reading in the House of Commons has been considered by a committee, and reported back for third reading and passage. The new station will be constructed under the open space at the junction of Moorgate Street, Princes Street, and Lothbury, and will be formed on the model of that now existing in front of the Royal Exchange, with ample exits in every direction, so as to prevent any chance of congestion. There have also been alterations in the policy of the railway as regards its connection with the Great Northern Railway Company. The Great Northern will still use it as a means to get their traffic to the City, but will not run their own trains over as originally contemplated. The idea was to detach the locomotives and put on the electric motor at Finsbury Park Station, where the tubular trains would run in on level with the steam railway. In its final form, however, the Great Northern and City will be an electric railway from the City to Finsbury Park Station, where it will come in under the Great Northern Station, and passengers will be conveyed in a lift or by a plane to the upper station if they want to continue their journey.

The Great Northern and City will, in my opinion, when once put in operation, serve a wider purpose than its promoters originally had in view. At Finsbury Station, as well as at Old Street, it will have an interchange station with the City and South London Railway, thus enabling passengers to continue their journey on to London Bridge Station, or straight away through to the "Elephant and Castle," Kennington, on to Clapham Common. If the City and South London extension to Euston is ultimately granted, the Old Street Station will give an exchange to the "Angel" and on to Euston, coupling up with King's Cross, St. Pancras, and Mr. Yerkes' Great Northern and Strand, and Charing Cross and Hampstead systems. This is undoubtedly an important link in the tubular system, and as it will be the next railway of the kind open to traffic, considerable interest attaches not only to its construction, which will undoubtedly be discussed by other writers in TRACTION AND TRANSMISSION, but as to its possible traffic. From all accounts it will represent the most advanced work of the kind yet given the London public. From these existing tubular railways I shall pass on to the miscellaneous schemes proposed.

XIII.—MISCELLANEOUS PROPOSALS FOR TUBE RAILWAYS

The North-West London Railway, and West and South London Junction Railway, together with the proposed Victoria, Kennington, and Greenwich Railway, form, in conjunction, a line running from a northern point at Cricklewood, under the Maida Vale and Edgware Road, under Park Lane, Grosvenor Place, Vauxhall Bridge Road, under the Thames, around the Kennington Oval, under the Camberwell Road, and then east, *via* New Cross, to Greenwich. As to the economic importance of these three railways it is impossible to judge. The North-West London is the only one of the three authorised, and, as I have before said, it might make a valuable extension to the north and south branch of the London Suburban Railway, which runs from Marble Arch to Clapham Junction. The West and South Junction Railway crosses the Marble Arch and Clapham Junction branch of the London Suburban Railway at the Marble Arch, and goes from thence north-west to Paddington Station. An interchange at the Marble Arch would there enable passengers from Cricklewood district and from Paddington to have choice of routes either by London Suburban Railway to Clapham Junction, or by the West and South London Junction Railway through to Camberwell, or further east should the proposed Victoria, Kennington, and Greenwich Railway ever be taken from the list of proposed railways and receive Parliamentary sanction. These three proposals were withdrawn for this session, but will probably come up again next year. The King's Road Railway, suspended from session of 1901, came up again this session, and was thrown out. It sought authorisation to construct a tubular line from Victoria Station, via Eel Brook Common, to Putney. This line, I think, will also come up again, and, if properly financed, would prove useful. It is four miles long, passes through a very dense population, and will serve a district inhabited by clerks and people with moderate incomes. Running through Westminster, Chelsea, Fulham, and Wandsworth, under the King's Road, it will serve a very congested district—Chelsea and Fulham alone representing a population of a quarter of a million. There are two other schemes for this part of London, one extending across the river into East London, namely, the East London, City, and Peckham Electric Railways, with a terminus at Peckham Rye. The other proposal, which is of interest to South London, has for its basis the revival of the City and Brixton Railway. The company representing this railway, which was authorised in 1898, has not carried out its undertaking, and it is doubtful if the so-called City and Surrey Electric Railway will succeed much better. The plans for this railway are on a more pretentious scale, proposing to run parallel to the City and South London by another tunnel from the Borough Station into the City. From the Borough Station it will extend to St. George's Circus, thence to Lambeth, with stations at Kennington Cross, the Oval, Lorn Road, Brixton. From Brixton powers of extension will be asked next session to go via Norbury through Croydon, and thence, forking at Warlingham, to Westerham on the east, and Reigate and Redhill on the west. The aim, in this case, is to get out of the tunnel as soon as possible after leaving Brixton, and change it simply to an electric light railway. The length of the Brixton route is five miles. After then the

endeavour will be to make it a surface railway.

The above, however, were not the only schemes proposed for south-west and south-east London. There are two proposals for electric lines to Sydenham and the Crystal Palace—one a surface tram all the way, and the other a railway all of which will be in a tube. This line was to begin at the junction of Cannon Street and Queen Street in the City, and to pass under the river, through Bermondsey, Newington, Camberwell, Peckham, Dulwich, and Sydenham, to the Crystal Palace. The capital required was £5,000,000, and the territory it proposes to run through is a valuable one. The scheme was considered a reliable one by Mr. Garcke of the British Electric Traction Company. This company has leased an important tramway system from the Croydon Corporation, and are applying for extensions north and south; the northern extension, going to the Crystal Palace, would be in close proximity to the City and Crystal Palace Railway. The estimated passenger traffic of this proposed enterprise was placed at one hundred millions. The London, Brighton, and South Coast and South-Eastern and Chatham Railways strongly opposed the line, and declared the estimates absurd. There would seem to be a reasonable chance for a line in this direction if it were not too expensively constructed. The object, of course, is to serve those very congested districts which lie between Cannon Street and Sydenham, and, secondly, to serve the people who want to get conveniently and expeditiously to the Crystal Palace. It certainly does serve a district which at present is without good railway facilities, and which would, in my opinion, enormously increase its population as soon as a good railway system was established. The opposition tried to show there was no population for the railway, but that is no reason why it should not be built. The district is near London, and would soon fill up when the railway opened for traffic. The proposed line is seven miles long. It commences at Queen Street, and at that point could be joined to the City and North-East Suburban Electric Railway (which was withdrawn this session, but which will come up next session).

From Queen Street it crosses under the river, and there would be stations at Borough High Street, Old Kent Road, where it joins with Trafalgar Road, Peckham High Street,

Rye Common, Dulwich Park, Lordship Lane, Sydenham, and at Penge. It is a deep level railway throughout. Through much of the district which the Crystal Palace Railway passes the people object to surface trams and light railways, but at the same time need some rapid communication. For the present the scheme has been side tracked. This fact seems to have delayed the surface railway, though I believe the London County Council are agitating the idea of taking it up again now that the Crystal Palace Tube Railway has been refused. The House of Lords Committee did not regard the financial backing as sufficiently strong, and refused to consider it further. It, or the surface electric railway, will come up next session in some other form, as there is need of additional railway facilities in this part of London. The second scheme is the City, Wandsworth, and Wimbledon, but as the proposals have not yet reached the Parliamentary stage it is no use discussing them.

The foregoing list seems to be complete, at least, of tubular railways, including those open to traffic, in course of construction, authorised, and for the construction of which authorisation is being sought of Parliament, but excepting the lines of the Yerkes system, which I shall consider in a subsequent article in connection with the Underground Railways. Having once obtained a clear idea of these various proposals, and having eliminated therefrom those that are parallel to or overlap each other, it may be easier to form some general conclusions. It may even be possible, taking for a basis the railways already constructed, in course of construction, and authorised, to construct something akin to a harmonious system of underground locomotion for London. This, however, together with a discussion of the tramway and omnibus systems of London, must be left for another article.

(To be continued.)

THE GENEVA MUNICIPALITY

By A. ACHARD, Geneva

THE annexed Tables I to VII contain the results given in 1901 by the industrial services of the Geneva Municipality, and supplement my article* describing these services, and the results obtained in the four years from 1897 to 1900. The figures for 1901 were not available when I wrote the

administrators who had charge of superintending the new installations, and endeavoured by various means at each general election to prevent their being returned again to their official positions. The efforts of the Press were partly crowned with success on the occasion of the general election of May,

TABLE I.—WATER SERVICE AND HYDRAULIC POWER DISTRIBUTION

	1901.	
Volume of Water Distributed.	Cubic Metres.	Gallons (Millions).
Potable water	4,839,997	1,064.8
Water for industrial purposes	806,373	177.4
Water for motive power	11,430,205	2,516.6
Water restored to works	3,401,694	748.3
Water for the public service	6,905,814	1,453.3
Total	27,093,083	5,960.4
Capital involved	5,449,963frs.	£218,000
Cost.		
Working expenses	219,905frs.	£8,800
Three and a half per cent. interest	190,749	7,630
Sinking fund	301,352	12,054
Total cost	712,006frs.	£28,484
Giving an average cost of	2.63 cent. per cubic metre.	95/- per million galls.
Receipts.		
Potable water	432,074frs.	£17,283
Average selling price per cubic metre and 1,000 gallons	8.93 cent.	4d.
Water for industrial purposes	57,012frs.	£2,280
Average selling price per cubic metre and 1,000 gallons	7.07 cent.	3.21d.
Water for motive power	264,091frs.	£11,363
Average selling price per cubic metre and 1,000 gallons	2.48 cent.	1.13d.
Other receipts	73,413frs.	£2,936
Water for the public service — cost price estimation	164,040	6,561
Total receipts	1,010,630frs.	£40,423
Less participation of adjacent communes	5,500	220
Balance receipts	1,005,130frs.	£40,203
Profit	293,124frs.	£11,719
Percentage of profit on capital		5.38

TABLE II.—ELECTRIC POWER DISTRIBUTION

	1901.	
Kilowatt-hours	22,839,237	
Capital involved	6,760,819frs.	£270,433
Working expenses	329,018frs.	£13,161
Three and a half per cent. interest	236,629	9,465
Sinking fund	80,705	3,228
Total charges	646,352frs.	£25,854
Average cost per kilowatt-hour	2.83 cent.	.27d.
Gross receipts	704,781frs.	£28,191
Average receipts per kilowatt-hour	3.09 cent.	.29d.
Less participation of adjacent communes	48,076frs.	£1,923
Balance receipts	656,705frs.	£26,268
Profit	10,353frs.	£414

TABLE III.—ELECTRIC LIGHTING DISTRIBUTION

	1901.	
Kilowatt-hours	3,830,423	
Capital involved	3,011,109frs.	£120,444
Working expenses	520,345frs.	£20,814
Three and a half per cent. interest	105,389	4,215
Sinking fund	71,731	2,869
Total charges	697,465frs.	£27,898
Average cost per kilowatt-hour	18.26 cent.	1.75d.
Gross receipts	950,685frs.	£38,027
Estimation of Municipal lighting	64,785	2,591
Total	1,015,470frs.	£40,618
Average receipts per kilowatt-hour	26.58 cent.	2.55d.
Less participation of adjacent communes	17,140frs.	£685
Balance receipts	998,330frs.	£39,933
Profit	300,865frs.	£12,035

article in question, and in asking to place them now before the readers of TRACTION AND TRANSMISSION I may be allowed to add the following remarks.

The Genevese Government of 1882 submitted with very bad grace, and not without mental reservations, when the Municipality obtained the concession that was sought after by the private company whose interests the Government Authorities were desirous to serve. A portion of the Press commenced thereupon furiously to attack the Municipal

1898, when a few members of the opposition were elected to the Municipal Council. Aided by the discontented members of the staff, these opposition councillors made every attempt to disorganise the industrial services. They succeeded, by dint of bickering, to bring about the resignation of Mr. Turrettini, who had started these services and had placed them on a good footing, and also that of Mr. Butticaz, his principal assistant. They had an idea that something was wrong in the manner in which the stores

---

*See TRACTION AND TRANSMISSION, Vol. IV, page 154.

accounts were kept, and they proposed that the matter should be placed before experts. When this was decided upon, they succeeded in arranging that the audit, instead of bearing on these accounts alone, should include the whole organisation of the industrial services.

The report of the experts was handed in last April. As regards the secondary matter it concluded to introduce certain alterations in the stores account keeping; on the main point, however—the one which the opposition councillors had chiefly in view—the report

TABLE IV.—WATER SERVICE, ELECTRIC POWER AND LIGHT DISTRIBUTION

	1901.	
	Frs.	£
Capital involved	15,221,891	608,877
Receipts (after deduction of participations) ..	2,660,165	106,404
Cost	2,055,823	82,236
Balance profit	604,342	24,168
Percentage		3·97

TABLE V.—GAS LIGHTING AND GAS HEATING SERVICE

	1901.	
	Cubic Metres.	Cubic Feet.
Volume of gas supplied	8,189,060	289½ millions.
Capital involved	5,850,198 frs.	£234,007
Working expenses	1,608,672 frs.	£64,347
Interest at 3½ per cent. ..	204,757	8,190
Sinking fund	143,355	5,734
Total expenses	1,956,784 frs.	£78,271
Average (per cubic metre and per 1,000 cubic feet)	23.35 cent.	5s. 3¼d.
Gross receipts	2,194,708 frs.	£87,788
Municipal lighting (estimation)	91,403	3,656
Total receipts	2,286,111 frs.	£91,444
Average (per cubic metre and per 1,000 cubic feet)	27.92 cent.	6s. 4d.
Less participation of adjacent communes ..	27,280 frs.	£1,091
Balance receipts	2,258,831 frs.	£90,353
Profit..	302,047 frs.	£12,082
Percentage of profit		5.16

decided absolutely against the said councillors, and concluded that the industrial services had been organised on a most irreproachable basis.

This verdict, which was unexpected by the opposition councillors, did not prevent the elections of May, 1902, from resulting in their favour. The first step had been taken in this direction at the previous elections, and at the present time the majority in the Town Council belongs to the party which is hostile to the former directors. This change will perhaps cause the tension between the Government and the

Municipality to cease — temporarily, at all events—but it will be fatal to the Municipal finances, and the tax-payers will suffer greatly by it, for it places the industrial services in the hands of men who are anxious to work them, not for the benefit of the budget, but for political ends.

The reflection from all these facts is very clear. In the countries in which suffrage is a wide one, but especially in those in which "universal suffrage" is the rule —as in Switzerland, for instance—political questions intervene in Municipal elections

TABLE VI.—WATER SERVICE, ELECTRIC POWER, ELECTRIC LIGHT AND GAS DISTRIBUTION

	1901.	
	Frs.	£
Capital involved	21,072,077	842,884
Receipts, after deduction of participations ..	4,918,996	196,737
Cost	4,012,607	160,507
Profit	906,389	36,250
Percentage of profit		4.30

TABLE VII.—ABSTRACT OF THE MUNICIPAL BUDGET ACCOUNTS

	1901.	
	Frs.	£
Receipts from industrial services	2,111,889	84,475
Other receipts	1,715,702	68,633
Total receipts	3,827,591	153,108
Charges on debt	1,938,566	77,542
Other expenses	2,355,460	94,218
Total outlays	4,294,026	171,760

quite as much as in other elections. It follows, as a consequence, that the municipalising of an industry is attended with bad results, for the reason that political interests must needs invade a department outside which they should most certainly remain. Politics in Municipal matters lead to failure.

But even were Municipal interests alone to direct the course of Municipal elections, there is yet another danger which the countries above referred to have to contend with. The industrial services of Geneva give employment to a numerous staff. All the members of this staff have a vote in the elections, and contribute to nominate their chiefs, under whose orders they will have to work. The directors of the industrial services are therefore, to a degree, appointed by their subordinates, and, under these conditions, it is impossible that perfect discipline—a necessary feature for the successful carrying out of all industrial undertakings—be not more or less compromised.

ELECTRICAL POWER AND INDUSTRIAL PROGRESS

AMONG the industrial developments fore-shadowed at the present, certainly none is so far-reaching in the extent of its influence on the progress of this country than that afforded by the possibility of obtaining an almost unlimited supply of cheap power—the *sine quâ non* of a manufacturing community. This problem of cheap power is now being solved by the formation of electric supply companies, the object of which is to furnish power from generating stations to the large industrial centres for operating machinery in shipyards, mills, factories, steel works, and, indeed, to all classes of manufacture requiring power for operating their plant. The aim of these supply companies is to replace the power now produced in isolated plants, and which too often are of an obsolete and inefficient type, and therefore costly to maintain. The principal objection to renewing an old and imperfect plant is most frequently the heavy capital expenditure that would be involved by the change. In the majority of the large industrial undertakings, however, and apart from a few which have been constructed on modern designs, such a capital expenditure would rapidly show a very handsome return through saving in maintenance, coal, and wages, and through increased efficiency. The advent of the central power companies will render it possible for manufacturers to take advantage of such economies while incurring a minimum of capital expenditure. Supply companies, by concentrating in one large generating station the production of power required for a whole district, and by means of electrical distribution, are able to employ large engines, driving generators of the most efficient type. They can thus supply power at a rate that will compare favourably with the cost of power when generated by the manufacturers individually in isolated plants, even when the latter are on a large scale. The difference will be still greater in the case of small power users. They will save largely in actual cost by taking their power from supply companies, and,

at the same time, they will be spared the cost for maintenance and extra supervision incident to a self-contained power plant. The great benefit from the introduction of cheap power likely to accrue to the small power user is certain, and many who now, by force of circumstances and on the grounds of expense, are obliged to rely entirely on hand or crude mechanical power, will grasp the opportunity afforded them, and take advantage of this new source of supply. The direct result will be an increase in their output and a reduction in their cost of production. This phase of development may well be so far-reaching in its results as to be compared to the extraordinary growth of the cotton industry that followed the introduction of the power loom.

The history of the development of many industries has demonstrated the fact that a material reduction in the cost of any manufactured article has almost invariably been attended by an increased demand; in some cases, indeed, the increased demand could only be partially met at first, notwithstanding the resources placed at the disposal of the manufacturer by improvements which rendered a reduction in cost and increased output possible. This is most strikingly exemplified in the case of the power loom just referred to; this invention, as everyone knows, completely transformed in a comparatively short period of the world's commercial history, the industrial and social conditions of an entire class of people, and the demand for cotton goods and textile fabrics generally is now such as to give employment to hundreds of thousands of hands, and to millions of capital. If this has been obtained in one industry, it is not unreasonable to expect as great a result, if not a greater, from the introduction of cheap power, one of the most important factors in the advancement of all the manufacturing industries.

Another result likely to accrue from the distribution of power electrically at a cheap rate, and on a large scale, will be the expansion of industry from the areas where power is available, and the gradual formation of new industrial centres. Fresh enterprises seeking outlets for capital to extend existing industries, will erect factories where cheap power is available, transport facilities good, and the value of land comparatively small. These conditions will probably tend, even within the next few years, to transform barren districts at present included in the areas of the electric supply companies, into manufacturing centres, by the removal of part of the existing factories from congested towns to the country beyond, and by the growth of industries. The workers would naturally follow the work, and this would indirectly tend to hasten the solution of that serious social problem, the housing of the working classes. As a factor in industrial progress, the solution of the problem of cheap power, may possibly have a widespread influence in inducing the manufacturer, when considering the adoption of the new methods of operating his machinery, to consider at the same time whether the machinery itself could not with advantage be replaced by appliances of an improved type. Could this be attained it would undoubtedly be one of the greatest benefits that had ever resulted from commercial enterprise.

It is often stated, and not without reason, that this country, the birthplace of all the leading manufacturing industries, is fast being eclipsed by others in the struggle for the commercial supremacy of the world, in the very industries which we have created and held for many years as monopolies. The manufacturer who argues that methods and machinery that enabled his predecessors to amass considerable wealth are good enough for him (an argument which is often seriously advanced against any capital expenditure on new and improved machinery), and who shuts his eyes to the progress due to applied sciences and improved methods of production, must expect to be driven out of the market, and to find himself unable to compete with those who, taking advantage of all the improvements industrial advancement offers, are enabled to produce at a minimum of cost a maximum of quantity. English conservatism and apparent over - caution, coupled with restrictive legislation, have caused us to be satisfied with the triumphs we have gained in the past as the pioneers of industry, while other and younger countries, taking advantage of our former initiative

and experience, have been rapidly advancing to the leading position. Drastic reforms are needed in almost every branch of our staple industries, and these reforms involve the abandonment of obsolete machinery and methods. They will necessarily entail a loss at first, in the shape of first cost for new types and processes, but if the necessary steps had been taken gradually as improvements presented themselves, the change would not have been so heavy. It is only by introducing the latest methods into our systems of production, and by acquiring commercial enterprise, that we can be firmly reinstated in our former position as leaders of the manufacturing world. The effort necessary to attain this will involve a vast increase in the capital now invested in industrial undertakings, but provided the change is effected with due regard to economy and the results to be obtained, the prosperity which will attend the reformation will produce a good return both on the new capital invested and on that which was necessarily written off as the depreciated value of the superseded plant. This has actually been the history of some of the largest manufacturing companies in the world, and serves to show what enterprise, coupled with energy and efficient commercial organisation, can effect. Never, it is safe to say, was the law of the survival of the fittest exemplified in a higher degree than in the modern struggle for commercial supremacy ; probably, never was the standard to be attained so high, but, given the necessary qualifications, the opportunities and facilities for attaining that standard have never been so great as they now are. It should therefore be the first interest of the manufacturer that he should adopt cheap power and re-model obsolete machinery.

As an indication of the advantages to be gained in this direction, it may be of interest to note a few of the results obtained by the operation of the Newcastle-on-Tyne Electric Supply Company's power scheme, the first of the large power companies to be in commercial operation. This was described and illustrated in detail in one of our former issues.* We hear that the company have recently applied for an extension of their area.

As will be remembered, the electrical

---

* See TRACTION AND TRANSMISSION, Vol. I, page 290.

equipment of the generating station, and of the works, was carried out by the British Thomson-Houston Company, Ltd., of Rugby, to whom a large measure of credit is due for the success that has attended this, the pioneer undertaking of its class.

With reference to the advantage to the user in obtaining power from the company in this manner, the evidence of Mr. Thomas Miller, of Sir William Armstrong, Whitworth & Co., given before a Committee on Private Bills in the House of Commons on March 12th last, affords striking testimony.

675. Your firm, I think, commenced to take power from the Supply Company in the beginning of last year?—Yes, in the month of May last year.

676. And, I think, you have now running 420 horse-power motors from their system?—That is so.

677. And you have also an extensive electric lighting installation?—We have.

678. I think, already the majority of your machinery is being driven by electricity?—It is.

679. And you are gradually replacing all other forms of motive power by electricity?—We are.

680. The energy is transmitted from the Neptune Works to your works, and transformed at your works to the pressure you require?—It is.

681. The Supply Company provided the installation?—Yes, they did.

682. In your opinion are the terms upon which you get your electric power very favourable?—They are.

683. Have you observed the ability and activity of the Supply Company?—I have.

684. And, in your opinion, has the district benefited very considerably by their energy and enterprise?—Decidedly.

685. And so far as your experience has gone, has the supply to you been eminently satisfactory and reliable?—It has.

686. At what price does your company obtain the electric power?—1.161d. per unit.

687. Is it within your knowledge that other large firms are being supplied at an equally low rate?—It is.

688. Now, with your knowledge and experience of this company, is it your opinion that the company would supply the extended area and very reliably?—I think so.

691. Could you give us an idea how much you save per annum by the use of the electrical energy instead of steam or other motive power?—About 40 per cent.

692. What is it 40 per cent. on?—On the actual amount of money we have expended in coal and attention to machinery and so forth.

693. You are not in the extended area at all?—Not at all.

694. Elswick Works, where the power is taken, is on the River Tyne?—I am at the Walker Works.

695. They are on the River Tyne?—Yes.

696. And close, therefore, I take it, to the generating station of the Supply Company?—About a mile from the generating station.

697. Have you got any electrical installation of your own?—We have a small one.

698. How many horse-power?—I should think it does not exceed 30 horse-power, but we are taking that out; we are getting the whole of our power from them.

699. Manufactured on a small scale it does not pay?—No.

702. I leave you there. I should have asked you one thing. Is there, besides this payment of 1.161d., a dead rent?—No.

703. Nothing at all?—Nothing at all.

704. That is the total?—Yes.

The following prices, which may be taken as typical, are charged by the Neptune Bank Power Station to some of their customers:—

	Price per Unit.
Sir W. G. Armstrong, Whitworth & Co., Ltd., Walker Shipyard	1.161d.
The Northumberland Shipbuilding Company, Howden	1.141d.
Wigham, Richardson & Co., Ltd., Walker-on-Tyne	1.218d.
The North-Eastern Marine Engineering Company, Wallsend	1.083d.

The testimony given above is, of course, reliable, and shows the results that can be effected by supplying the needs of a large area from one central power distributing station, and confirms the remarks made above with reference to the advantage that would be so gained.

Central power stations, of which that at Newcastle may be regarded as a pioneer, will soon be at work in various parts of the country, and the changes they will effect will be followed by the construction of other stations, till the industrial situation in Britain will be largely modified. Thus, the Midland Power Distribution Company (Messrs. Kincaid, Waller, Manville, and Dawson, consulting engineers) has commenced its supply of power. The great station at Cardiff (Messrs. Bramwell and Harris, engineers), is under construction, and the Yorkshire Central Power Station (Mr. H. F. Parshall, consulting engineer), will shortly be commenced.

MUNICIPAL TRADING*

(t) By ROBERT DONALD
Editor of the *Municipal Journal*

IN my opening article to your series of papers on Municipal trading, I described certain principles affecting public ownership. I do not propose to go over the same ground, but would like to supplement some of the remarks which I then made. First I would point out how Municipalities are handicapped in their trading enterprises as compared with private companies — a fact which your contributors overlook. I think the local authorities have quite as much reason to complain of legislative restrictions and conditions as companies have. Take, for instance, the case of electricity supply works. A Municipality has to begin paying interest as soon as it borrows the money. Not only so, but it must begin within the year its sinking fund to redeem its loan at the end of twenty-five years—in the provinces. If the works take two years to start—not an unreasonable period—the interest and sinking fund forms a very heavy charge which there is no revenue to meet. Naturally, there is frequently a loss on the first year's trading. Investors in companies do not expect interest while the works are being constructed, although it is sometimes paid out of capital. They are quite ready to wait for the first year. Municipalities have not only to pay back the whole of the borrowed amount on the plant in twenty-five years—which is quite right, as it will not last that time—but they have also to pay back the money on the buildings and land. Sound Municipal finance would also make provision for emergencies in the way of a depreciation fund, although depreciation is not necessary to the same extent as in the case of companies, as the sinking fund in a way takes its place. The system assumes, however, that the buildings will be useless at the end of twenty-five years, while the land, as it were, has to be written off the face of the earth. These conditions as to loans seriously handicap Municipalities,

---

*See TRACTION AND TRANSMISSION, Vol. I, pages 205 and 244; Vol. II, pages 20, 90, 160, and 222; Vol. III, pages 15, 91, 153, 237; Vol. IV, pages 41, 100, and 220.

and it is only fair to make allowance for the first year in working.

In some respects Municipalities are handicapped for their good. They have, for instance, to conduct their affairs publicly, and maintain a higher standard of business morality than companies. It is quite right that they should do so, although it is very noticeable that the representatives of companies who live in glass houses seize the opportunity to throw stones at Municipalities as soon as there is the slightest suspicion of favouritism about their transactions. During the last year or two the code of Municipal morality has been raised to such a height in some cases that the rule absolutely becomes detrimental to the town. The Manchester resolution, for instance, that no one interested in a public company as a shareholder should sit on the Council or its committees if the company had direct or indirect trading relations with the town, is carrying purity rather too far, as it might deprive the Council of the services of some of the most public spirited men.

The Municipality as trader is handicapped in several other ways. A minority always compels it to incur heavy expenditure in connection with Bills. At a public inquiry, for instance, over a loan for electric lighting, an envious or interested company — as happened recently at Hendon — may add greatly to the expense. In other ways Municipalities are themselves to blame. Some authorities pursue a short - sighted policy which handicaps themselves. One of your contributors has pointed out that they grudge fair salaries for professional services. They maintain the market rate for wages, but not always for salaries. I am glad, however, to find that this parsimonious policy is changing. The assumption is that local authorities must manage industrial concerns better and more in the interest of the public than companies can do. It is folly, therefore, to try to save money in organising ability and in professional skill. To substitute a system of Municipal collectivism for private enterprise requires the application of a better organisation. Municipalities should be able to tempt the best men to enter their services. As it is, there are a large number of men employed by Municipalities, such as city engineers, accountants, electrical engineers, who could sell their services to private undertakings for much more any day. Naturally, some of them are tempted to do so. The majority, perhaps, belong to a type which our excellent Civil Service system has created—men who find Municipal work and the promotion of the public welfare more congenial than the more remunerative field of private trading. Small towns should always retain the services of consulting engineers just as a small company does, as their undertakings are not large enough to justify paying a first-class resident engineer.

I will now deal with some of the main points raised by my critics. Your contributor "Civis," in an able article, raises some important points. He deals with my statement that it is preferable that local authorities should not make profits, but should provide a cheaper commodity to the community. This is a matter of more theoretical than practical interest for the time being, but is important as a principle of Municipal ownership. "Civis" says :—

> If this is to be considered as a proposal for the solution of the difficulties of the question, it cannot be considered as satisfactory, for it binds over as security the property of the whole community for the benefit of a particular class, the consumers of that commodity; and further, when the principle of profit-earning is absent, the stimulus which leads to good management and careful supervision of expenditure is removed, and the probability is that loss is incurred.

I do not think that "Civis" is justified in separating a particular class from the community at large, as the benefits from Municipal ownership are in some cases widespread. Take, for instance, Municipal tramways, baths, and wash-houses. The chief consumers of electric current and gas may rarely use the tramways or baths; still, they would not deny that both cheap travel and cheap baths promote the general welfare of the community. If, as is proved to be the case up to now, Municipalities can supply better and cheaper gas, and cheaper electric current, than companies, the benefit is not confined to the chief consumers of these articles, who are not, of course, the whole community. The same applies to gas and to other articles which have more restricted use. We must regard all the Municipal undertakings in the light which

Mr. Chamberlain has done, when he likened a Municipality to the directorate of a company in which every citizen was a shareholder, and the dividends were paid in the increased health, comfort, happiness, and welfare of the community. "Civis" fears that if the profit-earning element is absent, the stimulus which leads to good management and careful supervision, will be removed. But in the case of Municipal ownership the stimulus of good management, for its own sake, must always be present, otherwise the system would not be justified. I think, however, that it is equally true of Municipalities as it is of companies, that the presence of large surpluses is more likely to lead to extravagance than to economy.

"Civis" assumes a case in which a city receives power to set up a cold storage plant, which will be run at a loss, made up from the rates, and says this means that "the lawyer, the teacher, the chandler, the house decorator, etc.—none of whom had the slightest need for cold storage—are being taxed for the benefits of those particular trades in which cold storage is a necessity." Taking this hypothetical case, I think everyone would benefit by cold storage. Cold stores are a necessary part of slaughter-houses. It is in the interest of health that the slaughter-houses should be in the public hands and regarded as part of the great sanitary system. It is done so, much more largely on the Continent than in England, with beneficial results. Cold storage is a necessary part of the system, and in Continental cities meat must remain a certain number of hours in the cold store before it can be removed and put on the market. Cold stores are used in this country to maintain meat in a wholesome state, which is in the interest of the lawyer, the teacher, the chandler, the house decorator, and everybody else. It will be seen, therefore, how difficult it is to create sectional interests in Municipal affairs, the whole object of local government being to promote the welfare of the community as a whole. While I consider that the best Municipal policy in the end is to spread the benefits of Municipal ownership over the largest possible number of people, the practice is not largely carried out. I do not see how it can be while opposing interests are at work, seeking to turn the balance of profit into loss, and while the present muddle of local taxation remains.

"Civis," for instance, points to the great profits which the Manchester Corporation raises on its gas and electric lighting. This is probably rendered indispensable in Manchester, because of the heavy subsidy which has to be paid to the Manchester Ship Canal. The rates are made to appear less than they really are. I doubt whether the people of Manchester think that the subsidy of a 1s. 4d. rate to the Ship Canal is really lost, as that great enterprise was carried out, not for the benefit of the people who use it, but for the welfare of the whole city. It has undoubtedly the effect of increasing the trade of Manchester, and in so doing of raising the rateable value of property.

This leads me to point out how the extension of Municipal trading does not mean an increase of rates, even when surplus profits are not used to relieve them. The case of Glasgow, with which "Civis" deals, illustrates my point. In Glasgow, as in other Scotch cities, the object has always been to reduce charges for water, gas, etc., rather than relieve rates from surplus profits. In his review of Municipal work in Glasgow from 1896 to 1899, Sir David Richmond, the Lord Provost, gives a table of rates levied in the city since the year 1855. I find that the Municipal rates amounted, in 1866, just before Municipal trading began, to 2s. 7d. in the £. Ten years later they were 2s. 4½d. ; in 1886, 2s. 6d. ; in 1896, 2s. 10d. ; and in 1900, 2s. 11d. In the meantime, owing to Municipal ownership, the water rate had fallen from 1s. 1d. to 5d. ; the poor rate had decreased from 1s. 7d. to 10⅝d. ; the School Board rate, which was first imposed in 1873, had, of course, increased. Yet during this period of great expansion in Glasgow, many new impositions had been made, including a public health rate in 1874, a Municipal buildings rate in 1878, roads and bridges rate in 1884, sewage rate in 1891, and new improvements rate in 1898. The total rates in 1866 were 5s. 3d., without any school rate ; in 1890, with 11½d. school rate, they were 5s. 2d. This includes the period of the great expansion of Municipal trading in Glasgow. The explanation is, of course, to be found in the good government of the city, the cheapening of commodities, the lowering of the death rate, and the rise in rateable value.

"Civis" is much concerned about the finances of the Glasgow tramways department. If he will look at the last accounts he will have no reason to complain, as the department, after lowering fares, increasing wages, paying the city a mileage rate, etc., etc., has renewed the whole of the track in eight years, written down the horse equipment to nothing, and started its new electric system almost entirely unburdened by any expenditure connected with the old.

"Civis" raises another important point as to the tendency of Municipalities to apply for powers to manufacture certain articles in connection with their gas and electricity departments. As a rule, they only seek power to provide, sell, and hire such fittings, but not to manufacture them. A Municipality should certainly have power to repair fittings, and to regulate them, otherwise it would be placed at a disadvantage in comparison with companies carrying out similar functions.

In the course of the discussion we have heard a great deal of invidious comparisons being made between England and America as to tramways and electric lighting, and the blame is put on Municipalities for checking British enterprise. I do not admit the comparison. In America tramways were laid down as the towns were built. The illuminant, in many cities, was electric light to begin with. They have not the problem of old settled communities to deal with. As Sir W. H. Preece said in an address before the Society of Arts, on November 20th, 1901 : "The use of arc lamps for street illumination in the United Kingdom is not to be compared with the practice in the United States, but the difference is due to the universal presence of cheap gas here, and of no—or dear—gas in the States." In few departments of industry can we compare with the United States. Municipal trading does not interfere with printing, yet from personal experience I find I can get printing done cheaper, better, and quicker by sending it to New York than by getting it executed in London. Municipal trading cannot be blamed for allowing Americans to encroach on our boot-making industry, bicycle industry, and in almost every sphere of engineering enterprise the comparison is always in favour of America.

Nor do I accept as a true analogy a comparison with Continental cities. In Germany, companies have to exist under much severer conditions than in England. See for, instance, Mr. Dawson's article in

Traction and Transmission on the electrical undertaking and tramway company in Berlin. Yet the use of electricity is much more extended in Berlin, although it is sold at a higher price than in any English city.

One of your contributors, Mr. W. Valentine Ball, has magnified the difficulties of another problem which Municipalities have to face, viz., the working of tramways outside their borders. He admits that the working of tramways within their own borders is a legitimate enterprise for local authorities, but he suggests that, as the more extensive field for important electric enterprises lies beyond the areas of local authorities, they would get out of the difficulty by giving up their own tramways. This system would certainly relieve a town of its difficulty—also of its undertaking. On this principle there would be no Municipal tramways at all. There are certainly difficulties as to working in the way, but I do not see why they should not be just as easily adjusted by a little experience, as has been the supply of water, gas, and electric lighting, by one Municipality to its smaller neighbours. Some towns supply larger communities with water outside, than within, their borders. The Salford Town Council trade in gas with twenty-eight independent authorities outside. The only difference between tramways and gas, electricity, or water, is that the problem is newer.

Mr. Ball exaggerates the effects of the Public Authorities Protection Act, which protects local authorities from harassing or vexatious litigation in the performance of their public duties. Seeing that so many attempts are made to exploit public authorities in a way which would not be done were they private concerns, this Act is very necessary, and up to now its powers have not been abused.

Mr. Dixon Davies had a formidable sounding article—more rhetorical than argumentative. Some of his arguments I anticipated in my first article, and he deduces no facts in support of the strongest statements which he makes. For instance, he says :—

Suppose at the beginning of the nineteenth century this Municipal craze had obtained, who can doubt that all the canals would have been in the hands of the authorities? The proposal to introduce a new means of transport would have

been met with the same brutal, ignorant, and uncompromising opposition that the gas-owning Municipalities have dealt out with all the force of their political power to the introduction of electricity.

What would have happened to the railways had the canals been owned by Municipalities is purely conjectural. What has happened to canals under private ownership is notorious. They have been bought up by railway companies, not for the purpose of using them, but of destroying their utility in order to consolidate the railway monopoly. In fact, the railways have pursued a "brutal, ignorant, and uncompromising" policy towards canals. People are now beginning to see how our opportunities for transport by water have been wasted. Mr. Davies's statement about gas-owning Municipalities cannot be supported by facts. The Municipalities which have owned the gas-works have been the keenest and the earliest to introduce electricity themselves. Few of them who own gas have allowed private companies to introduce electricity. Having experienced the benefits of public Municipal ownership of gas-works, they were naturally anxious to extend it to electricity. Birmingham is, perhaps, the most noticeable exception, but I do not think that Mr. Davies's strictures are applicable to the Midland capital. There have been far more examples of Municipalities starting electricity works in competition with gas companies which were over-charging the public. We have had an excellent example of this in the fight between a wealthy gas company and the Municipality in Liverpool, the result of which was that the Municipal authority acquired the electric lighting works.

Mr. Davies devotes a great part of his paper to railways. I am quite ready to discuss the advantages of the State ownership of railways, but it does not come into the field of Municipal trading. Our railways have little to boast about in comparison either with private enterprise in America or State ownership on the Continent, as exemplified in Prussia, Austria, and Belgium, or in our own colonies of Natal and Cape Colony. I should have liked Mr. Davies to have dealt more with Municipal conditions, instead of theorising about what might have been. To argue that Anglo-Saxons do not require Municipal trading is a waste of space. Municipal trading is here. It has

ELECTRICITY SUPPLY

FINANCIAL AND OTHER EFFECTS OF MUNICIPALISATION

ELECTRIC LIGHTING (see page 43)

	LEEDS.		SHEFFIELD.		BIRMINGHAM.		LIVERPOOL.	
Purchased by Municipality in year	1898		1898		1899		1895	
Capital spent by company ...	£217,420		£124,472		£219,000		£264,711	
Capital paid by Municipality for undertaking	£370,580		£272,398		£420,000		£436,474	
Financial Results	Last Year under Company. Year 1897.	Most Recent under Municipality. Year 1901-2.	Last Year under Company. Year 1897.	Most Recent under Municipality. Year 1900-1.	Last Year under Company. Year 1899.	Most Recent under Municipality. Year 1900-1.	Last Year under Company. Year 1895.	Most Recent under Municipality. Year 1901.
Capital outlay	£161,009	£505,029	£123,023	£433,016	£269,366	£543,657	£264,711	£1,187,622
Units produced	833,280	3,055,165	747,063	2,381,708	2,252,692	3,040,822	1,185,964	20,018,142
Receipts, all sources	£18,405	£45,332	£16,245	£41,939	£43,246	£55,409	£35,414	£168,489
Working expenses	£5,212	£13,255	£4,769	£15,110	£18,799	£28,175	£12,041	£83,187
Gross profit	£13,193	£32,077	£11,476	£26,829	£24,447	£27,234	£23,373	£85,302
Percentage to capital ...	9.90	7.35	10.92	6.94	9.44	5.31	9.04	7.63
Provided for depreciation and sinking fund	£5,439	£10,889	Nil.	£6,030	£6,137	£6,597	£7,657	£30,903
Net profit	£7,754	£21,188	£10,268	£20,799	£18,310	£20,637	£15,716	£54,399
Working expenses per unit ...	1.50d.	1.04d.	1.53d.	1.52d.	2.00d.	2.22d.	2.44d.	1.00d.
Average price charged for current per unit... ...	4.68d.	3.56d.	4.60d.	3.83d.	4.38d.	4.20d.	6.86d.	3.60d.

come to stay. It may extend or it may not, but we cannot get rid of what exists, and have to discuss it on its merits.

Mr. Davies argues that the absence of heavy polls on Municipal Bills means the apathy of the people. One might just as well conclude that it signifies their complete confidence in the measure and in their Government. If there was that general hostility to Municipal trading which Mr. Davies assumes to exist among rate-payers, they would take the trouble to attend a meeting and vote against the measures which, according to him, are so detrimental to their individual and collective welfare. Mr. Davies, however, has a radical remedy for limiting Municipal trading. He would impose the New York limit for borrowing money. He would limit the debt of a town to 5 per cent. on its capitalised assessment, leaving it, however, an opportunity to promote Bills under conditions which would give little chance of their success. There is not much good in making such a proposition. It is locking the Municipal stable door after the individualistic horse has gone. Mr. Davies could have pictured what might have happened had the New York limitations suggested

been in force throughout the century. I could also imagine what might have been—I think a state of anarchy and social chaos would have existed. The limitations would have meant that our cities could not have made adequate provision for the poor, could not have built sufficient schools, libraries, technical institutes, nor carried out their sanitary reforms, nor provided parks, as the capital for the educational, charitable, and sanitary purposes of cities, would have far exceeded the suggested limit.

Many comparisons have been made between Municipal and company electricity supply works. None of them I consider are fair. Towns of similar character should be selected. The nearest I can get to similar conditions is in the case of Aberystwith (company) and Llandudno (Municipal)—two Welsh resorts like each other in most respects. The advantage should be in favour of the former, as the works are one year older :—

	Capital.	Units Sold.	Gross Profits. Per Ct.	Average Price per Unit. Pence.
Aberystwith, 1900 ...	£19,205	78,815	2.19	5.76
Llandudno, 1900-1 ...	£28,057	241,271	9.06	5.04

The Municipal undertaking, on a third more capital, sold three times as many units, and made four times as much profit at a lower price. As very frequently happens, public lighting is being retarded by the exorbitant charges of the company —4.73d. per unit in Aberystwith as compared with 1.96d. in Llandudno.

A better comparison, however, can be made between Municipal and company ownership in the same towns. The cities of Leeds, Sheffield, Birmingham, and Liverpool acquired the undertakings of the companies at enormous cost rather than permit the full length of the Provisional Order to run. Notwithstanding the high premiums paid to the companies' shareholders, municipalisation has been justified, and has proved stimulating to industry and beneficial to the city. The Table on the preceding page is an excellent proof of the efficiency and economy of Municipal management of electrical undertakings.

In the case of Leeds, Sheffield, and Birmingham, the undertakings only supply current for power and light, the tramway system having separate generating plant in Leeds and Sheffield. In the case of Liverpool the undertaking has benefited enormously by electric traction, but before the electric tramways were established the benefits of municipalisation had been proved. The company in its last year paid a dividend of 6 per cent., and 1895 was by far its best year; 1896 was a six-months year, both as regards the company and the Municipality, and, therefore, not comparable. I find, however, that by 1897 the Municipality had increased the units sold by over a million. It at once reduced the price. The receipts increased from £85,414 to £51,722, and after the payment of all charges, interest, and sinking fund, there was a surplus of £3,015. The advantage was equally as marked in the case of other cities after the first year of municipalisation. I invite the opponents of Municipal trading, who are always harping on the incompetence of electric lighting committees, as compared with boards of directors, describing them as mere amateurs who are always changing office, to study the figures in the foregoing table carefully. I doubt whether many companies which had to face such an increase of capitalisation could show better or as good results.

Hastings, Eastbourne, and some other towns have more recently acquired undertakings of companies at very great cost, and have had the temporary disadvantage of beginning their Municipal working when coal was exceptionally dear. It is likely, however, that municipalisation in these cases will, in the end, also be justified, as in the case of the larger cities.

Some of your contributors seem to regard Municipal accounts with suspicion, and they do not think that the trading enterprises are charged with the full quota of service, rates, taxes, etc. In the smaller towns the service of a town clerk or a solicitor cannot always be put against the electricity or tramway accounts, but in the larger cities this difficulty does not arise, as the trading departments are self-contained. The rating is perfectly fair in every case, and trading departments contribute their full quota. In England the rating authority is not the same as the Municipal authority.

There is one set of controversialists who have been largely represented in your discussion whom I am not inclined to take seriously. It is the class who represent companies rather than industrial interests. There is a wide field for difference of opinion on the ultimate benefit, or otherwise, of Municipal trading. It is a great economic and industrial problem, which should be discussed on the broad basis of public policy and national interests. Some of your contributors, however, are men whose positions prevent them from taking but one view. Their contributions are tinged with prejudice and, in some cases I fear, sullied with self-interest. I do not blame the writers. It is their business to make money by the absence of Municipal trading; public welfare is a secondary consideration. The progress of the electrical or any other industry is not the paramount interest of their lives. They seek to limit Municipal trading in order to widen the field for company promotion. They are quite right to fight hard for their own. I admire their industry. But I want to see them avow their purpose openly; to proclaim frankly their position. They are the kind of antagonists whom no amount of statistical proof or any kind of argument can possibly induce to change their views. There is another reason why I need not trouble myself much about their contributions. They are generally so thoroughly misleading that they answer themselves. They can only influence those who do not know who the writers are, or what interests they represent, and can only mislead the ignorant. Just to show how thoroughly they can misrepresent obvious facts, and twist statistics to suit their own purpose, I will allude to the contributions of one or two of the class whom I indicate.

Take, for instance, that by Mr. Sydney Morse, the gentleman who is a solicitor to forty or more tramway and electric lighting companies. He is trying to answer the impartial introduction to your discussion, and, to meet the statement that in the case of the supply of gas, electricity, and tramways, these can be better provided by the Municipalities than by companies, he quotes statistics submitted to the committee on Municipal trading with regard to gas, which show that Municipalities charge less and earn almost the same gross profit. He omits the important statement that Municipalities supply much better gas — on an average three-candle power higher than the companies—which necessarily costs more to produce. Next, he makes a comparison between the profits earned by the St. Pancras electric light undertaking and the St. James's and Pall Mall Company, selecting, be it observed, for his Municipal comparison a wide-spread residential district, largely inhabited by the poor, and for his company a rich and compact West End area. Referring to tramways he quotes a report about a trade union representing some of the London County Council's tramways employees. The Council seems to have refused to consider grievances where apparently none existed, but Mr. Morse, as the champion of labour, says : " What would not County Councillors have said if these allegations had been made against their company ? " But what would Mr. Morse not have said if the County Council had given in to the men's demands ?

Another contributor was Mr. T. C. Elder, who begins his article like a professor of political economy, as follows :—

Political economy is a science which affords such a favourable field for the exercise of pure reason and common sense, to the exclusion of all sentiment, that to arrive at a satisfactory conclusion on such a question as Municipal trading, should be as exact a process as the working out of a mathematical problem. The main difficulty lies in the fact that one of the most important factors in the problem is the somewhat elusive and volatile influence of human nature, which forces itself into the discussion with most disturbing effect.

I endorse this dictum, and it is the " disturbing effect " of this "elusive influence" which I find in Mr. Elder's article that prevents me taking him seriously as an exponent of political economy. I must, therefore, summarily dismiss Mr. Elder from the discussion. Mr. Elder can never forget that he holds a brief as an official of the first electric power distribution company, and its numerous progeny,* which has manufactured more companies than it has distributed current in the brief period of its existence. When, for instance, Mr. Elder says that Hornsey District Council was utterly neglectful of the benefit of the consumers, that it insisted on starting a Municipal undertaking when " a perfectly sound and powerful company offered to supply current at 3½d. per unit," he did not mention that " the perfectly sound and powerful company " was the North Metropolitan Electric Power Company, which he represents. It may be " perfectly sound," but it has never been in a position to supply Hornsey, or any other North Metropolitan district with current. It has only two small stations, many miles away from Hornsey. It has tried to be "powerful," but powerful as an obstructive force. During two years it has done what it could to block local authorities anxious to promote electric lighting in the district, and while it has been pursuing these tactics the "short-sighted" and despised Hornsey has laid down electricity works, and is almost ready to begin supplying. Yet Mr. Elder refers to the action of Hornsey as " that monumental decision," which almost induces him to end his remarks on the "internal merits of Municipal businesses."

Another contributor belonging more than ever to the same category is Mr. Emile Garcke, who lays down a definition of local government to his own complete satisfaction. He makes a number of plausible and misleading statements, but what interests me most in his article is his great concern that local authorities are overburdening themselves by the multiplicity of their responsibilities.

---

* Since taken back to the bosom of its overburdened parent.

The London County Council, for instance, has actually twenty-six committees, and he is much afraid that the members of this authority and others cannot give the necessary time to conduct their operations, "which demand constant attention, expert knowledge, and practical supervision." Mr. Garcke, in making these statements, is no doubt influenced by the desire to relieve these overburdened Municipalities of many of their responsibilities. He is himself a chairman of only twelve companies, managing-director of a large number of others, and on the Board of only forty—a member, consequently, of many more committees than of Boards, being, perhaps, the greatest pluralist. director in the country. Still, so great is his desire to see Municipal trading get on to a true basis that he is no doubt perfectly ready to relieve a few more towns of their responsibilities, to say nothing of their profits.

It is possible that Mr. Garcke and his colleagues of the British Electric Traction Company may be animated by the best of motives—primarily to confer benefits on the public. I think, however, that great public dangers inevitably accompany a huge national organisation of this kind, which wields enormous power, confers directorships on men of local influence, or gets them interested financially in its numerous concerns. It is impossible that the system can improve public morality.

Many of the company's undertakings may yet be great successes and will serve the public well, but its recent policy, and the quarrels which it has provoked seem to suggest that it has pegged out more claims than it can thoroughly develop. The appetite for starting new concerns on the part of the parent company has become so voracious that it has recently taken to vary the pleasing and profitable pastime of company promotion by the process of absorbing some of its own children — an experiment in industrial cannibalism undertaken, no doubt, with the charitable purpose of saving the unfortunate children from a more painful fate.

I welcome the chastened tone in which Mr. Porter writes in your last issue. I agree with much which he says, and only call attention to one or two points. No doubt he represents the American view about uniform fares, but I contend that for London and other English cities what we want is cheap fares for short distances. The traffic on the London Central Railway is chiefly a long-distance traffic. On the tramways, omnibuses, and the Metropolitan Railway it is mainly short distance. The average fare on the London County Council Tramways is about $\frac{3}{4}$d.; the average on the Metropolitan Railway, where the fares vary from 1d. upwards is 1$\frac{3}{4}$d. Mr. Porter's defence, "from information received," as the police say, of the Chicago tramways would, if pursued, open up a long and romantic story, but I need only say now that I quoted figures from one of the numerous official reports issued by the Municipal authorities under Mayor Carter Harrison. Mr. Porter's system of reckoning every free transfer as another fare is a novel one, and if applied to tramways in Continental cities—in Düsseldorf, for instance, where, by the way, the fares have not been doubled, but only increased one-third on some of the long-distance routes—would bring the average fare down to less than $\frac{1}{2}$d.

Mr. Porter shows admirable discretion in saying nothing about that excellent review article of his of a few years back on Municipal progress in England. He then became thoroughly intoxicated over what he called the "Municipal spirit in England," and now, five years later, when he could have had a much bigger draught of that spirit, he becomes a prohibitionist, and tells us that we should stop at water!

Mr. Porter recognises that our town councillors rank higher in point of character and ability than in the United States. "Men of affairs, professional men, retired capitalists, and men of active business in England, take an interest in, and have been found willing to give their time to, Municipal work, and to this fact may largely be attributed its success." Quite right—that is the secret of our success. We have men who devote their time, energy, and abilities to public life without getting anything out of it. So far from getting anything out of it many of them make great sacrifices to serve the public. I do not admit that the supply of such men is running short because Municipal work increases. There is a possibility that the supply will not keep pace with our needs, but that crisis is not in sight at present. It is just where the duties are hardest that the strongest and best men are found. In the days when there was no democratic local government, no Municipal trading, our councillors were corrupt, our officials venal. Not until local government was democratised and Municipal trading began could we get rid of jobbers in London. Direct trading and direct employment checks or altogether destroys jobbery. I do not admit that the London County Council has altered its ideals, or has lost some of its best members because of increased work or altered policy. The men on this Council, as on others, who complain of the hard work are those who do least. The London County Council has lost men, but they have died on the field of honour. Mr. Bottomley Firth, Mr. Haggis, and Mr. Charles Harrison wore themselves out at the Council's work. They were martyrs to duty. Other men have sacrificed their business interests that they might serve the people. Where can we get finer examples of public men than in the present heads of our two greatest Municipalities—London and Glasgow —Sir John McDougal and Mr. Chisholm? The former might have lived in quiet retirement after an active business life. He preferred the turmoil and greater activity of Municipal life, only for many years to be misrepresented, and suffer much obloquy. Mr. Chisholm has remained a small trader instead of becoming a large one because he gave half his time to the service of the city. Both men were always animated by noble impulses —fanatics they were called on some things— but ever ready to put public service before private interest. It is because we have such men that we are able to develop Municipal Government in industrial fields. It is in places where apathy exists that companies and private interests reap their richest harvests. It is in cities where company rule obtains, that grit gets into the Municipal machine to corrode and corrupt. It is in these cities where it is most difficult to get the best men on the councils. Naturally so ; it is only an ideal that can call forth the higher qualities of men. The Municipal ideal is the impulse which leads to self-sacrifice. We cannot always attain it. Insidious influences may hold it in check. Self-interested men may get on councils and destroy it, but it always comes up again.

Some people may think that the public-spirited citizens who advocate Municipal trading are wrong in their policy, but, as a rule, no one can impugn their motives. So long as we have men stimulated by a desire to serve the community, influenced by the noblest of altruistic motives, believing that public ownership leads to social well-being, the progress of Municipal trading will not be arrested.

ELECTRIC CRANES

THIRD ARTICLE

By PHILIP DAWSON

Coal and Ore Handling, etc. — When dealing on a large scale with the transportation of coal, ore, or material of a similar nature, it is customary to employ a type of crane specially designed for the purpose. Such cranes are usually either of the gantry or cantilever class, or else a combination of gantry and cantilever. Some manufacturers have given special attention to the design of electric apparatus for transporting material. Such are the Temperley Transporter Company, in England; the Benrather Maschinenfabrik on the Continent; and the Brown Hoisting and Conveying Company in the United States of America. The work done in this direction has already revolutionised the methods of handling coal, ore, etc., in the steel industry.

Brown Hoisting and Conveying Machinery. —There is probably no firm that has done more towards the development of coal and ore handling plant than the Brown Hoisting Machinery Company, of Cleveland, Ohio. They first designed and used these machines on the shores of the great lakes of America, the first plants being erected some twenty years ago at Cleveland, Ohio. At the present moment machines put in by this firm handle about 90 per cent. of the entire lake coal and ore traffic, which in 1899 amounted to about 20,000,000 tons. This company now builds several different forms of conveying and hoisting apparatus which may practically be divided into three main classes: Bridge tramway plants; cantilever plants; and what the Brown Hoisting Company call "fast plants"; that is to say, plants whereby the storage on the dock, of coal and ore, is entirely avoided, and which consist of a number of separate machines spanning two or more railway tracks, with arms or cantilevers extending over these tracks, giving room for from six to eight cars to stand under each machine for loading or unloading purposes. Besides these three types of machinery

they have also constructed a special type of charging apparatus which has been designed for use in blast furnaces. The earlier machines were, of course, operated by steam, but at the present time electricity is rapidly superseding this method, and it is only with the electrically driven machinery that this article will deal. Several illustrations of the different types of plant mentioned above are given, and are more or less self-explanatory.

A typical form of bridge plant of the very latest design is shown in Figs. 1 to 3, page 48. This type of apparatus generally consists of three or four standard bridges mounted side by side on suitable rails, each machine working into one hatch of the boat which is being unloaded. The bridge girders are built up of steel, and are designed to give maximum strength with a minimum weight of material. The various members are made and arranged in the trusses, so as to offer the least resistance to wind pressure, which, owing to the exposed locations where these machines are generally used, is a very important factor. The Brown Company build sizes to meet any requirements, but the two most generally used, have 180ft. span, with 80ft. aprons, which can be lowered down above the vessel; cantilever extensions are added, capable of reaching from 80ft. to 104ft. beyond the back pier. The second type has 192ft. span, with the same sized aprons and cantilever extensions. These bridge plants are made in such a way that, if desired, they can be put in at first without cantilever extensions, these being added later. This is illustrated in the drawing, Fig. 1, where the cantilever extension is shown in dotted lines. The bridges are often built in a slightly different way from that shown in the diagram, with single front piers of "A" frame construction, mounted on wheels, and running on a single line of rails. Each bridge is connected to the front

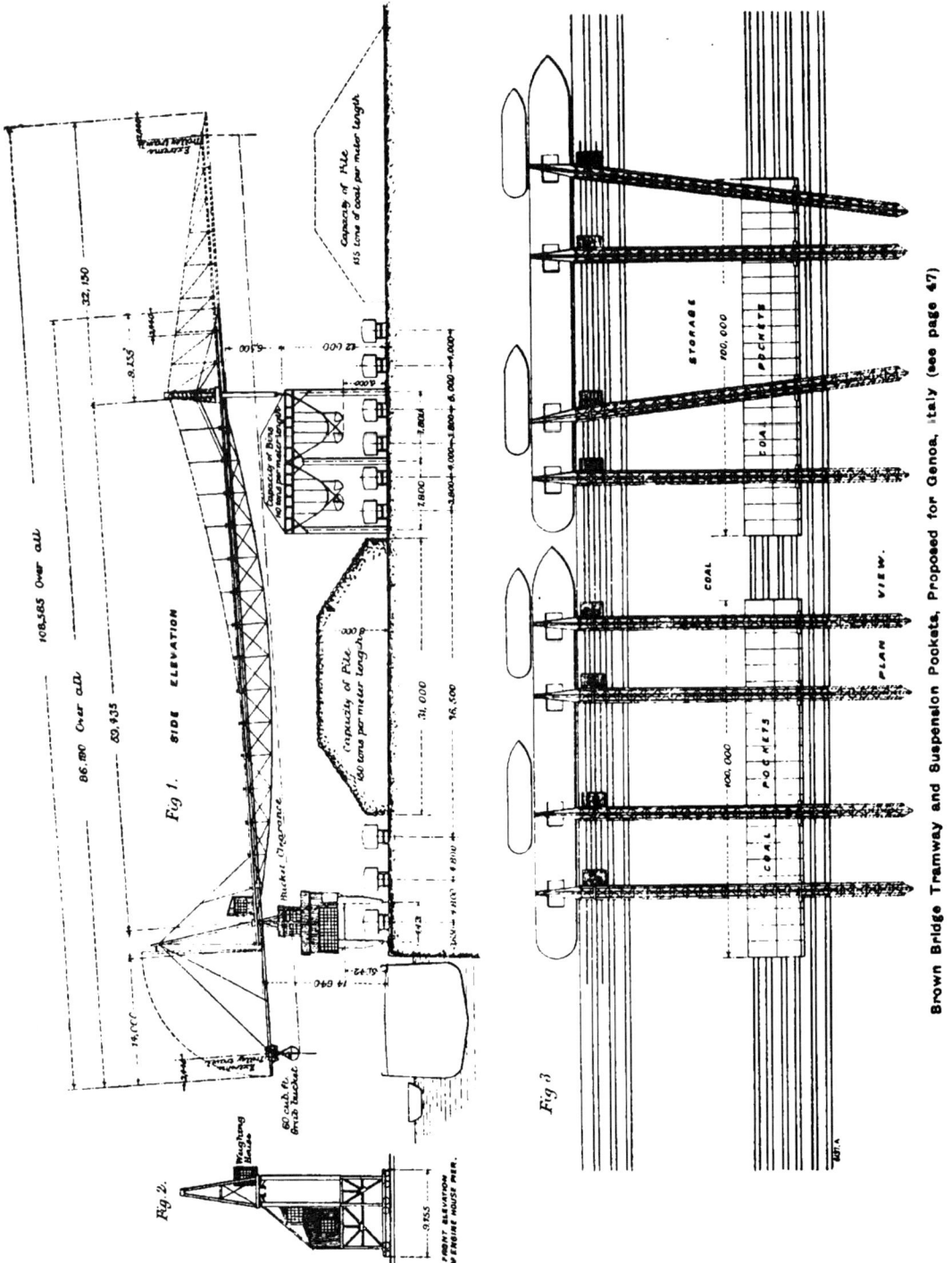

Brown Bridge Tramway and Suspension Pockets, Proposed for Genoa, Italy (see page 47)

Plate IV

Fig. 5.—Brown Double Cantilever Travelling Wharf Crane, Philadelphia and Reading Railway

Fig. 6.—Brown Storage and Re-handling Plant, Marioupol, Russia

ELECTRIC CRANES

UofM

Fig. 7.—Brown Coal Transporter at Alexandria. Egyptian State Railways

Fig. 8.—Brown Conveying and Hoisting Apparatus, Carnegie Steel Works, Pittsburg

UorM

M to U

and back piers in such a way as to allow the front end of the bridge to be moved sideways to suit the hatches of the vessel, and without having to move the back pier. The latter are usually mounted on wheels, moving on two sets of tracks. The hinged apron can be lowered over the vessel underneath the line on which the trolleys or buckets travel, and, when not in use, they can be raised into the vertical position out of the way of passing vessels, thereby keeping the front of the pier entirely free and unobstructed. The operator's house is fixed either at one end or under the crane, and from it all the various movements can be controlled. The hoisting machine (which is also called the trolley) runs along tracks suspended from the bridge between the girders. This trolley, together with the bottom block and hook, is attached to the hoisting or pulling line, and is controlled from the operating house. Various forms of buckets, automatic dumping-tubs, and crab-buckets, can be used with this apparatus. These conveyors can also be supplied with weighing scales, so that every load as it passes a given point can be weighed and recorded. One man only is required for each bridge, and controls all movements. The buckets are lifted and hauled to their destination by power, and when they have been emptied they return to the hold of the ship by gravity. By this apparatus the loads can be taken from the dock or car and conveyed and emptied into the hold of the vessel, either from the trolley, or when lowered to the bottom of the hold; or materials can be taken from any point under the bridge and delivered to any other point under the bridge. In the type illustrated, for instance, it is possible to unload from the ship directly into the trucks shown alongside; or on to the coal piles shown; or into coal-pockets from which trucks can be filled; or else directly into the trucks on the other side of the pockets. Coal can be taken either from the piles or the pockets and loaded into the vessel. As mentioned before, these plants were first applied to handle ore on the American lakes, and it has been found that an installation consisting of three bridges will easily hoist and unload on to the dock 1,200 tons every ten hours, at an average distance of 150ft. to 200ft., if the filling of the buckets and hooking on are attended to with reasonable despatch. A much greater load could be handled if it

were possible to fill buckets and hook them on to the machine as fast as it could take care of them. It has been found that a complete cycle can be made from hold of the vessel to the extreme end of the cantilever extension and back again, in one minute. As regards the cost of operation, this, of course, is very variable, and depends on the quality of material handled, and on the cost of labour and of power. The following figures are the results obtained when operating three 180ft. tramway bridges by steam during seven months at the New York, Pennsylvania, and Ohio docks at Cleveland, Ohio :—

Three drivers, seven months at $50 ...	$1,050
One fireman, seven months at $65 ...	455
One man on the dock, at $30	210
Fuel (1 ton of coal for every 1,000 tons of ore)	262
Repairs (average for two years) ...	123
Total	$2,100

If the machines could have been worked for the whole year round, instead of for only seven months, it is estimated that the cost per ton would have worked out as follows :—

Labour	$.01
Fuel	.002
Repairs	.0012
Total	$.0132

The results obtained on the lakes of America by this method of handling the ore are certainly surprising. The vessels can, of course, be unloaded faster, the larger the number of hatches, since one conveyor can work into each hatch. The number of hatches varies generally from three to thirteen, and the number of tons handled per hour in unloading each vessel, varies according to the number of hatches available and the number of bridge plants which can be used in connection therewith, from 182 tons to 592 tons per hour. The diagram, Fig. 4, (see page 50) is very interesting. It shows the increase in the tonnage of ore handled, and the decrease in the price of freights, between 1883 and 1899, in the Lake Superior iron ore district. The decrease in cost of freight rates shown is largely due to the handling appliances installed by the Brown Hoisting Company.

Fast Plants.—Fig. 5, Plate IV, and Fig. 7, Plate V, are examples of what the

Brown Hoisting Company designate "fast plants." Fig. 5 represents a coal wharf of the Philadelphia and Reading Railway, whilst Fig. 7 shows a combined bridge and fast plant, used at Alexandria for the Egyptian State Railways.

Every operation of a fast plant is adjustable independently, so as to fit the hatches of the vessel, and each machine only requires one man to work it. The trolleys, hoisting apparatus, etc., are similar

practically automatic in their working, and their operation is extremely easy. Each bucket takes about a 5 - ton load. Such plants will handle from 1,500 to 2,000 tons of ore a day, and can be operated by one man. At Marioupol there are two standard bridges, driven by electric motors. A complete installation of a tipping and hoisting plant is illustrated in Fig. 8, Plate V, and comprises a bridge tramways car-tipping plant and blast furnace loading

LAKE SUPERIOR IRON ORE SHIPMENTS [GROSS TONS] AND FREIGHT RATES FROM 1883 TO 1899.

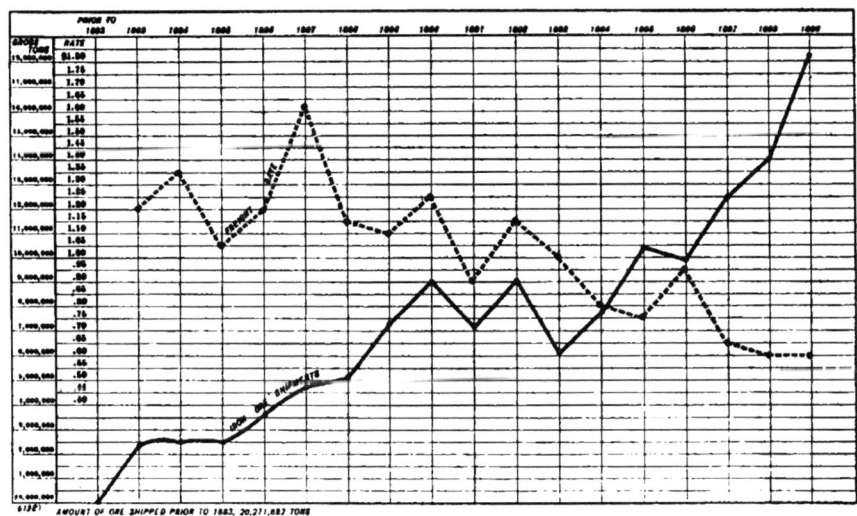

Fig. 4.—Diagram showing Increase in Material Handled and Corresponding Decrease in Cost (see page 49)

to those used in the bridge plants, described later. It will be seen from the illustration that there is very little pier space taken up by these plants. All the machinery, motors, etc., are situated in the engine house, at the top of the machines above the track. Fig. 10, Plate VI, illustrates the type of electric hoisting engine used by the Brown Company.

In connection with the first type of coal and ore handling apparatus already described, there are several other mechanical details which have been brought to a very high pitch of perfection, such as grabs, shovels, buckets, car-tipping and hoisting plants. An illustration, which indicates the operation of the shovel buckets, is given in Fig. 6, Plate IV, which represents a storage and rehandling plant lately installed at Marioupol, Russia. The special shovels used are

plants. It is one of the latest types installed, and is situated at the Carey Furnaces of the Steel Company of America, near Pittsburg.

Car-tipping Machines.—There are several types of car-tipping machines in existence for transferring coal, either from cars into ships, or from cars into storage tanks. The chief difficulty met with in designing a satisfactory machine of this type is the important question of not breaking up the coal. The type of apparatus illustrated in Figs. 9 and 11, Plates VI and VII, and applied at the Carnegie Works, has been specially designed with this object in view. It is essential in such a machine used for loading vessels, that the ship should be kept on an even keel while loading; that the entire cargo should be put on board without moving the ship; and that the loading should be per-

Fig. 9.—Brown Electric Blast Furnace Charging Apparatus, Carnegie Steel Works, Pittsburg

Fig. 10.—Brown Electric Winding Engine, used on Cautilever Cranes

UorM

Fig. 12.—Temperley Transporter, Electric Engine

Fig. 13.—Temperley Transporter, Two-speed Electric Engine

Fig. 11.—Brown Coal Tipping Holst, Carnegie Steel Works

Mアol

formed as rapidly and as economically as possible. It is very important to do away with the locomotive for moving loaded and empty coal trucks, and to let the tipping wagon take care of all this part of the work, as well as of the lifting and tipping work. The car-tipping device consists of a cradle, into which the truck is lowered and clamped; the whole device then turns over with the car, and discharges its contents into transfer tubs or tub cars. The tubs are then handled by an overhead travelling crane, which takes them from the trucks and lowers them into the hold of the ship. When the cradle is in its lowest position the loaded coal truck is pushed into it by an automatic car-pushing device, which rests in a pit between the tracks when not in use, so that the trucks can pass over it. When once in the cradle, which is fitted to hold any size of coal truck from the largest to the smallest, the car is clamped on the top and sides by clamping bars, and the cradle slowly turned over till the car is upside down. This operation is shown in Fig. 11, Plate VII. During the process of turning, the coal has rolled, not fallen, from the car into several hopper compartments attached to the cradle, and these hoppers each enter the transferring tub. The hopper compartments have doors which are automatically released on touching the bottom of the tubs, and when the cradle has returned to its original position, the load of the truck is left in the transfer tubs in which it has been carefully placed without having been dropped or broken. The oblong tubs in which the coal has been placed are designed in such a way that they can be lowered by cranes into the holds of the ships. When the cradle has been returned to its first position, the empty coal truck is pushed out by the next loaded truck as it comes along, and runs by gravity to tracks set aside for empty trucks. During this time the truck which contains the tubs which have just been filled is pulled away by the man who operates the device, and a new truck containing empty tubs is substituted for it.

A specially designed crane can often take the tubs, lift them, bring them over the hold of the vessel, and lower them into the vessel. When the bottom is reached the doors of the tub are opened, and the coal gently rolls out as the tub is pulled away. One car-tipping machine with two overhead cranes to lift the tubs can handle between 400 and 500 tons per hour. The tipping device can handle double that amount if necessary, and if it were possible to work at such a speed, one tipping machine with four cranes would have a capacity of about 1,000 tons an hour. The following figures are taken from a recent report of Mr. Ferris, the general manager of the Toledo and Ohio Central Railway Company, and apply to one car-tipping machine and to the working during nine months from April to December, 1898 : " During this time 253 vessels were unloaded, 882,000 tons of coal were handled in a total working time of 449 hours, at a total cost, including repairs, of $.0849 per ton. The men necessary to work the crane, car-tipping device, etc., were four engineers, two firemen, and thirty to thirty-eight coal trimmers." This number varies with the size of the vessel, and according to the ease or otherwise with which the coal can be trimmed. The number of coal trimmers given includes all the men employed in connection with the machine, except the engineers and firemen. To give an incentive to rapid unloading, the engineers and firemen, in addition to their ordinary fixed salaries, receive a premium of $\frac{1}{4}$d. per ton for all coal handled in excess of 2,500 tons per day and 1,800 tons per night.

Temperley Transporter Company.—This firm has done a great deal to popularise the use of transporting and hoisting apparatus in the United Kingdom, and has also had a considerable experience in the same class of work abroad and in the colonies. The type of apparatus which they manufacture serves the same purpose as that built by the Brown Hoist and Conveying Company. It can be used for handling coal in a similar way to that already described, and also for handling goods in warehouses. The illustrations give a good idea of the different purposes for which this apparatus can be used. Figs. 12 and 18, Plate VII, illustrate the electric engines employed, while Figs. 14 to 17, page 52, show the transporter as supplied to the Smelting Corporation of Cheshire at Ellesmere Port. It is used for taking the ore from ships and transporting it to a series of bins, from which it is taken by trucks and conveyed to the furnaces. The transporter is of the traveller type; the table and diagram (Fig. 18) on page 58 which refer to it, give the standard dimensions of this form as constructed by the Temperley Transporter Company.

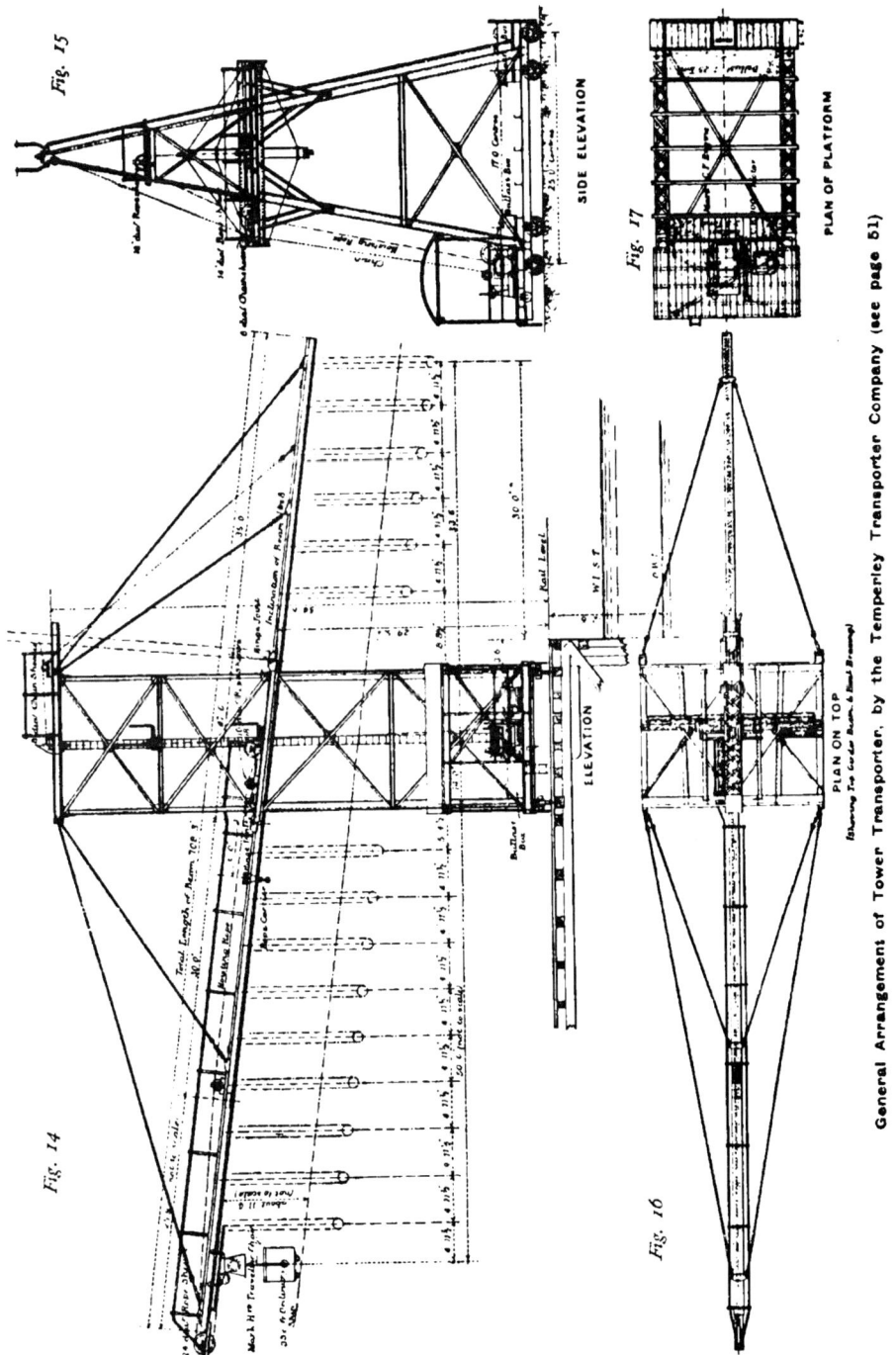

General Arrangement of Tower Transporter, by the Temperley Transporter Company (see page 51)

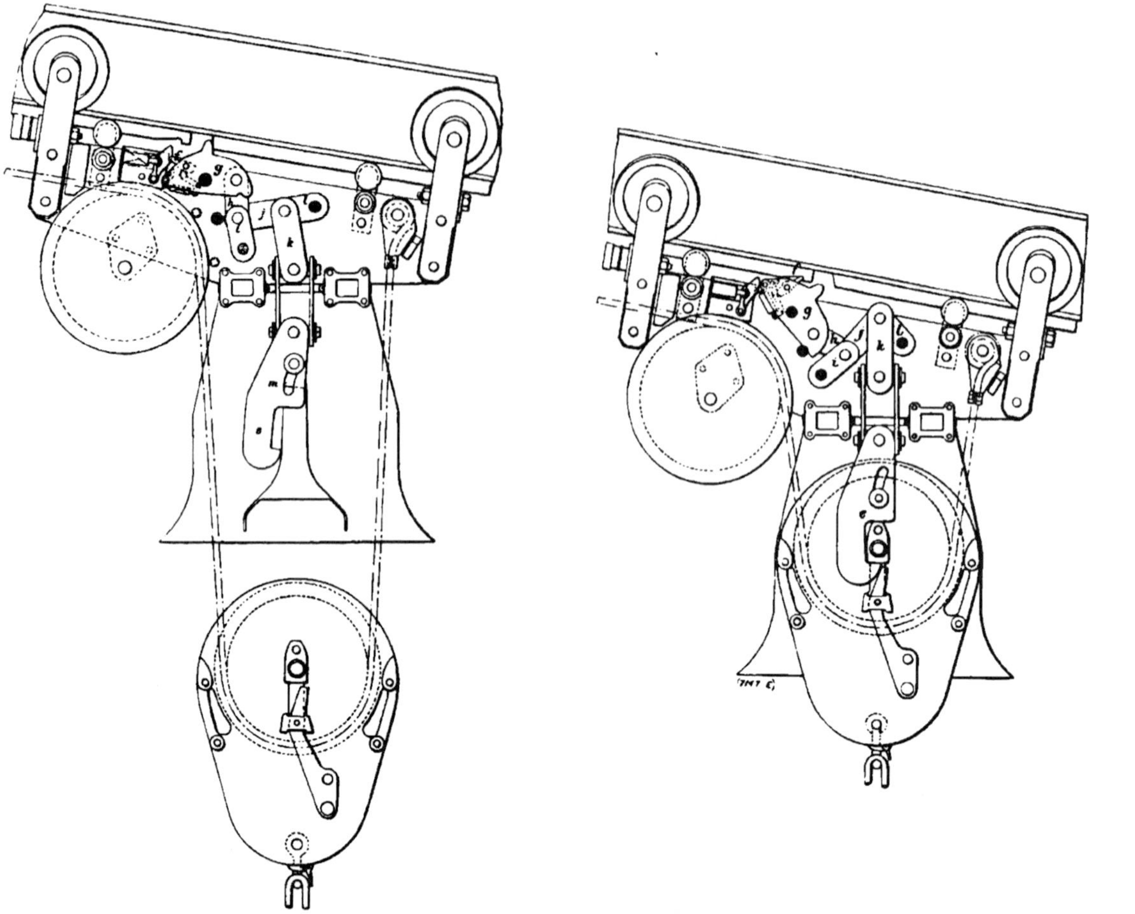

Plate VIII

Figs. 19 and 20.— Details of Temperley Transporter

Fig. 21.—Temperley Transporter at Savigliano

ELECTRIC CRANES

The transporter beam is provided with stops or notches at intervals of 5ft. throughout its entire length, and the load may be lifted or lowered at any of these points at the will of the driver. The operation is as follows: As soon as the loaded skip has been hung on the lifting hook the driver starts the engine lifting at full speed (about

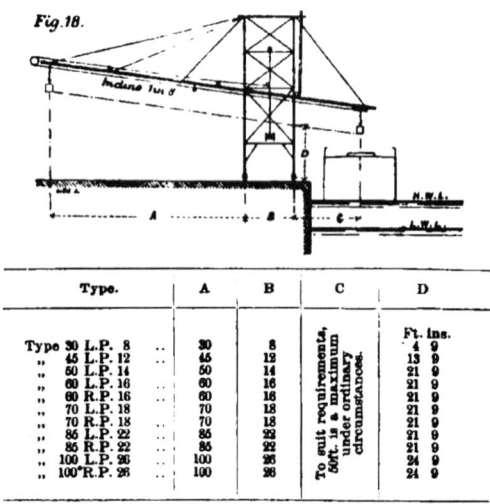

Fig.18.

Incline 1 in 8

Type.	A	B	C	D
				Ft. Ins.
Type 30 L.P. 8	30	8	To suit requirements, 50ft. is a maximum under ordinary circumstances.	4 9
„ 45 L.P. 12	45	12		13 9
„ 50 L.P. 14	50	14		21 9
„ 60 L.P. 16	60	16		21 9
„ 60 R.P. 16	60	16		21 9
„ 70 L.P. 18	70	18		21 9
„ 70 R.P. 18	70	18		21 9
„ 85 L.P. 22	85	22		21 9
„ 85 R.P. 22	85	22		21 9
„ 100 L.P. 26	100	26		24 9
„ 100 R.P. 26	100	26		24 9

Fig. 18.—Standard Type and Dimensions of the Temperley Transporter (see page 51)

800ft. a minute) until the fall block approaches the bell of the traveller, at which point the speed is decreased. As soon as the fall block has entered the bell of the traveller (see Figs. 19 and 20, Plate VIII), it becomes engaged, and is hung on sustaining hooks, the whole strain of the load being taken off the lifting rope. At the same moment the traveller becomes released from the beam, and the engine, being put to full speed, draws the traveller, with its load, along the beam at a speed of from 700ft. to 800ft. a minute. On arriving at the point where the load has to be dropped, the driver stops the engine and throws the hoisting drum out of gear. The traveller then commences to run down the beam, which, as seen from the drawing, is on an incline, and engages automatically with the first stop which it encounters. This stop fixes the traveller to the transporter beam, at the same time releasing the fall block from the bell of the traveller, and, by continuing to pay out the rope, the skip is

lowered by means of the brake. On commencing to lift, the bucket is automatically upset, and discharges its contents. The empty skip is then hauled up until it again engages in the bell, and, the hoisting drum being thrown out of gear, the traveller, with the empty skip, runs down the beam, being controlled by the brake, at a speed of from 800ft. to 1,000ft. a minute. On arriving at the bottom stop, the traveller automatically disengages, and, by continuing to pay out the rope, the skip is lowered into the hold of the vessel. The complete operation of lifting the loaded skip from the vessel, transporting it to a distance of 170ft., lowering it to the ground, emptying, and returning back into the hold of the ship, is stated to be performed easily in one minute. The transporter is generally constructed to carry a load of 30cwt. The hoisting gear, by which all the different motions are controlled, can be worked by one man. The hoisting drum runs loose on the shaft for lowering, but is put into gear for hoisting by means of a friction cone. An overhauling or tail rope is attached to the traveller, and connected to a set of counter-weights, which prevent the traveller over-running the hoisting rope should the driver, when reducing speed, do so too suddenly. The electric motor usually supplied for operating one of these machines, and lifting 1 ton of coal at a time with a hoisting speed of 300ft. a minute, is generally rated at about 40 horse-power. Under ordinary circumstances the length of the arm which projects over the vessel, and which is arranged so as to be hinged up when not in use, does not exceed 50ft. in length. An exceedingly ingenious adaptation of this transporter is shown in Fig. 21, Plate VIII, and Figs. 22 to 25, page 54, representing a coal depôt at Savigliano, in Italy. In this case one travelling tower is used to fill a very large shed, a series of tracks being installed in this shed, along each of which, at choice, a transporter can be run. Fig. 26, page 54, shows in diagrammatic form another application of this transporter for unloading barges into trucks or into warehouses in a similar manner. In this case one transporter beam can be used to unload into any portion of the shed. For work of this kind the transporters are often built to lift 25cwt. at a speed of 100ft. a minute, travelling along the beam at a speed of from 500ft. to 600ft. a minute. With a complete length of run, aggregating 200ft. from the barge to the end of the shed, from fifty to sixty complete runs an hour can be made. As in the first transporter described, notches are situated every 5ft., with which the traveller can be automatically engaged.

the hoisting point to which they have to be stored. In some cases the loads are conveyed above the main girders supporting the roof, so that the ordinary construction is not interfered with. Fig. 27, Plate IX, shows a Temperley transporter installed at Ellesmere Port, and Fig. 28 is another at the

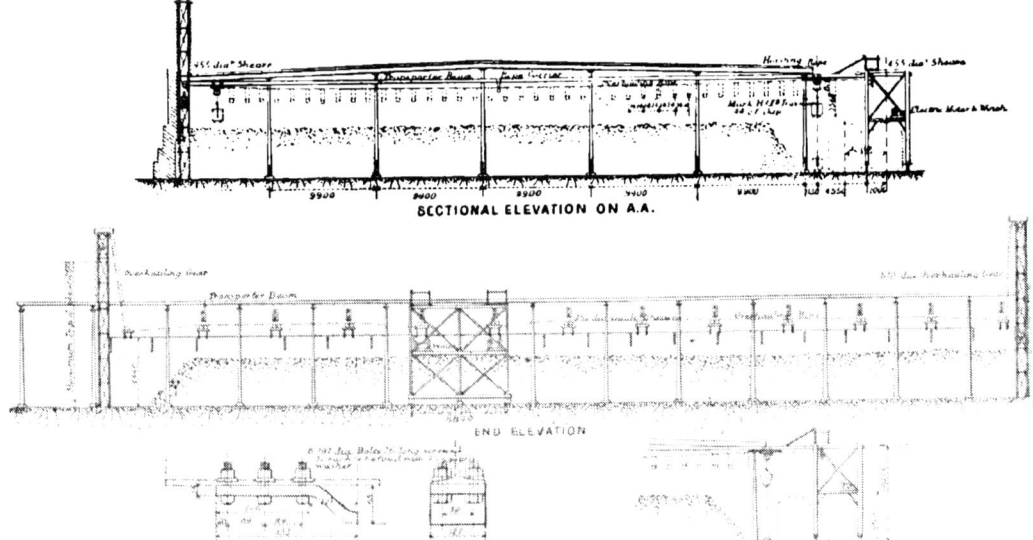

SECTIONAL ELEVATION ON A.A.

END ELEVATION

Figs. 22 to 25.—Horizontal Temperley Transporter at Savigliano (see page 53)

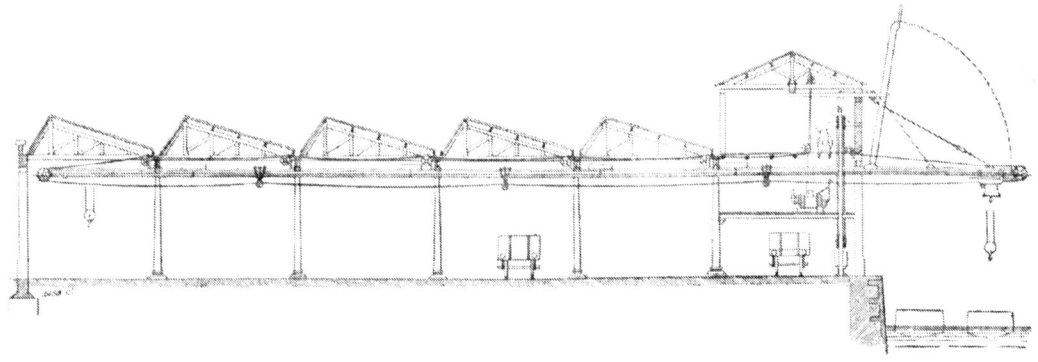

Fig. 26.—Temperley Transporter for Unloading Barges (see page 53)

Rope carriers are supplied which support the hoisting rope at intervals of about 50ft. The transporter can be used for lifting sacks, or goods in any other shape. In designing transporters for this class of work, sufficient headway should always be allowed, so that the materials can be delivered above

Willesden Electric Lighting Station of the Metropolitan Electric Supply Company.

Union Elektricitäts-Gesellschaft Coal Transporters. — The Benrather Maschinenfabrik, in connection with the Union Elektricitäts-Gesellschaft of Berlin, have carried out a large number of very interesting coal conveying

Plate IX

Fig. 27.—Temperley Transporter at Ellesmere Port

Fig. 28.—Temperley Transporter at Willesden Electric Lighting Station

M 90

Fig. 30.—Coal Handling Plant at Rheinau, Benrath and the Allgemeine Elektricitäts - Gesellschaft

U of M

Fig. 31.— Coal Handling Plant at Rheinau, Benrath and the Allgemeine Elektricitäts-Gesellschaft

U of M

plants. The one shown diagrammatically in Fig. 29, is an installation carried out for the Rhenish Westphalian Coal Syndicate at Rheinau on the Rhine, near Mannheim. Continuous current of 550 volts is used for operating this plant. The length of the conveyor, or travelling gantry, is 120 metres (394ft.); it works over tracks 700 metres (2,296ft.) in length, and can serve a floor space of 84,000 square metres (904,200 square feet.) The functions of this apparatus are numerous. As will be seen from the diagram, there are two tracks on the top of the travelling bridge, on which run two electric locomotives, each one of which hauls two trucks containing 700 kilogrammes (1,540lbs.) of coal. The gauge of the tracks is 60 centimetres (28.6ins.), and the speed at which the trains run is about 10ft. per second. Each electric locomotive is fitted with series-wound motors of 6 brake horse-power. On the top of the bunkers, which in turn unload into the trucks; the locomotives then return with their empty train. The trucks, when loaded, are weighed.

One man can fill, weigh, and operate the trains. The locomotives are controlled by means of an electro-magnetic device. The two locomotives together have a maximum capacity of 700 tons per day of ten hours, and two cranes are necessary to handle the coal from the ship to the conveyor. A screen for separating the finer from the coarser coal is located at the end of the bridge nearer the vessels, and is worked by a 18 horse-power shunt-wound motor, which consumes 147 watt-hours per ton of coal screened. The whole bridge generally changes position about twelve times a day. It is lighted by ten arc and twenty incandescent lamps. The gantry is used principally for loading from the coal pile into the railway trucks, whilst the electric trains unload from the ships on the coal piles. For this purpose two hoppers

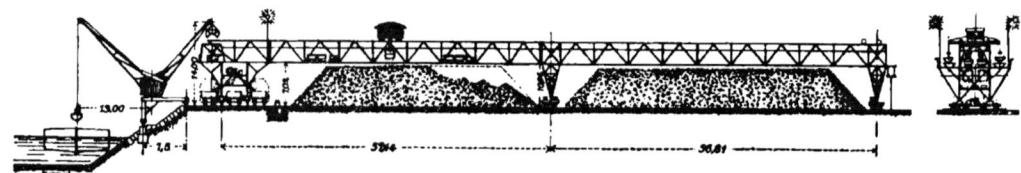

Fig. 29.—Coal Conveying Apparatus, by the Benrather Maschinenfabrik

framework circulates a travelling gantry which carries two hoppers, each of which can contain 1,600 kilogrammes (3,520lbs.) of coal. One series-wound 35 brake horse-power motor, running at 275 revolutions, is fitted on this gantry for lifting purposes, the hoisting speed being at the rate of 68ft. per minute. A 10 horse-power motor is also fitted, which propels the gantry along the bridge at a rate of 10ft. a second. The gantry is operated from an enclosed cage at the top, in a similar way to the ordinary cranes. It is capable of loading 40 tons from the coal pile into the railway truck per day of ten hours. The bridge can be propelled laterally at the rate of .2 metre per second (nearly 40ft. per minute). This is done by means of five shunt-wound motors, two on the front, two in the middle, and one at the back of the bridge, each motor being rated at 12 brake horse-power. While the small electric locomotives are travelling along the bridge the cranes are unloading the ships into are fitted to the end of the bridge into which the buckets carried by the gantry unload their contents, and from which the railway trucks under them are filled. By this means ships can be unloaded and the coal screened simultaneously, in which case the coal is conveyed to the pile by means of the electric trains. Or the coal can be unloaded directly into the hoppers carried by the travelling gantry, and thence into railway trucks or on to the coal piles. It can also be unloaded from the ship into the railway trucks, either direct or by means of the hoppers already described.

Figs. 30 and 81, Plates X and XI, illustrate a coal-handling plant, supplied by the Benrath Company and the Allgemeine Elektricitäts-Gesellschaft to Frederick Becker, who has a large coal storage ground on the Rhine, at Rheinau.

Fig. 30 shows the whole plant, and Fig. 81, a more detailed view of the handling apparatus and crab, which serves to unload the coal barges either into the railway trucks or on to the storage ground. The side movement of this crane is performed by electric motors fixed to the pillars from which the crane is supported. The motors in this case are three - phase. It will be observed that this type of crane is similar to some of the apparatus, already described, as manufactured by the Brown Hoist Conveying Company. The enterprise of the Benrath Company, and the great extensions which it has made within the last few years may be inferred from the fact that the factory itself was only started less than ten years ago.

Fig. 32, Plate XII, shows a coal-handling plant erected at the Moabit central station of the Berlin Electricity Works, which the writer described fully in an article in TRACTION AND TRANSMISSION, on page 26, Vol. III. This apparatus serves to bring coal from the Spree to the power house, and also to the coal stores. There are electrically operated suspended tip cars, from which the coal passes direct into the boiler bunkers. The cranes themselves were constructed by Bleichert & Co., of Leipsig, and the motors used are three - phase. Another type of coal-handling plant, which is very similar to that manufactured by the Temperley Transporter Company and by the Brown Hoisting and Conveying Company, is shown in Fig. 33, Plate XIII. The electrical portion was supplied by the Allgemeine Elektricitäts - Gesellschaft, and consists of three-phase motors. The cranes

themselves were manufactured by Bleichert, of Leipsig. These cranes belong to the North German Coal and Coke Syndicate of Hamburg, and are installed on the India Quay.

Two other types of coal-handling cranes are shown in Figs. 34 and 35, Plate XIV. The former was built by Jessop & Appleby, and the latter by the Brown Hoisting and Conveying Company. The crane shown in Fig. 34 is of a locomotive type, with derricking motion, and serves to unload barges.

Fig. 35 is a fixed crane with variable radius, built by the Brown Hoisting and Conveying Company, and is also used for unloading ore and coal.

A general description has now been given of most of the types of coal-handling cranes in use. Electricity has also proved very satisfactory in working turn - tables and traversers in goods yards and locomotive sheds.

Experience has shown that electrical power is eminently suited for every class of operation in large railway goods yards, whether for cranes, traversers, turn-tables, capstans, or coal-handling apparatus of every description. In this and in the two preceding articles a general description of the most frequent applications of electricity to cranes of every description has been given. In the next article some of the detailed apparatus, such as controllers and motors required to operate such cranes, will be considered.

Fig. 32.—Coal Conveying Crane at the Moabit Power Station, Berlin

Fig. 33.—Coal Handling Plant at Hamburg, by the Allgemeine Elektricitäts-Gesellschaft and Bleichert

UorM

Fig. 33.—Coal Handling Plant at Hamburg, by the Allgemeine Elektricitäts-Gesellschatt and Bleichert

U of M

M to U

Plate XIV

Fig. 34.—Revolving Travelling Crane, with Blackwell Trolley, by Jessop & Appleby

Fig. 35.—2½-ton Brown Swivelling Crane with Variable Radius

ELECTRIC CRANES

THE ELECTRICAL POWER SUPPLY OF THE CITY OF MEXICO

THE electric power scheme of the Compania Explotadora de San Ildefonso, supplying electricity for lighting and general power purposes to the city of Mexico, is one of the most remarkable and complete long-distance transmission systems in the world. It is worthy of particular attention, owing to the unusual methods which have been successfully adopted, whereby the energy available supplies of high-tension current as generated at the various power stations. The usual conditions of high-tension transmission systems are reversed. Instead of power being generated at one large main generating station, and being distributed to several small sub-stations, power is generated at several small main generating stations and is collected at one large sub-station.

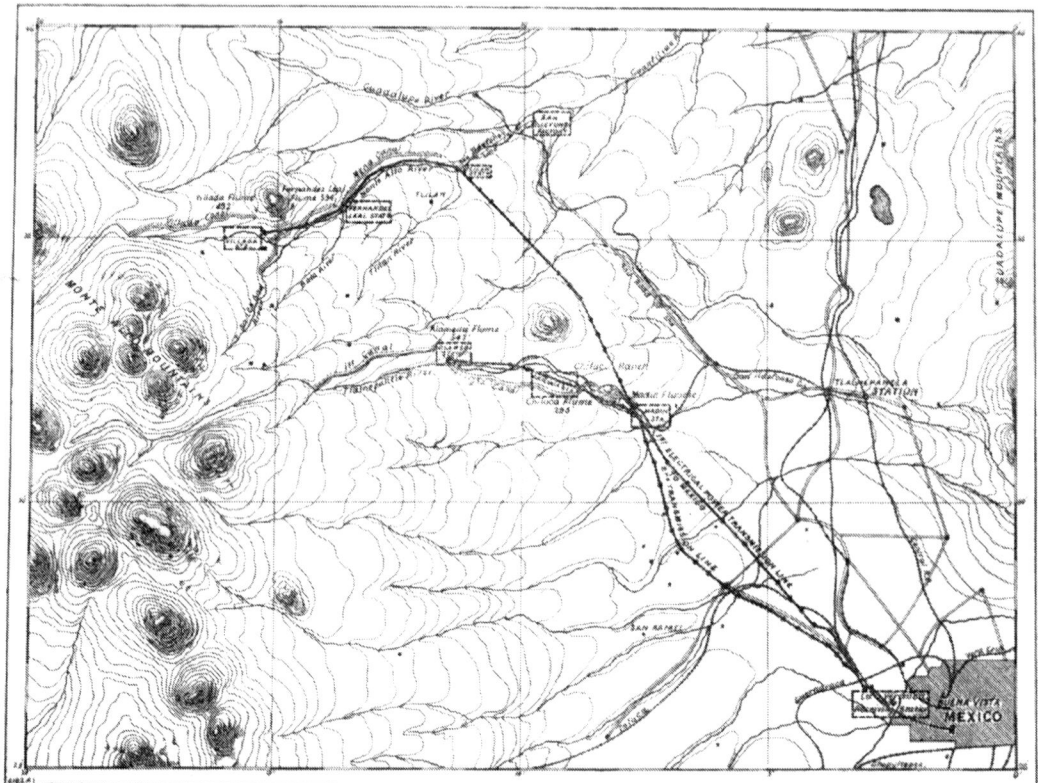

Fig. 1.—Map showing Power Stations and Transmission Lines to the City of Mexico

at several comparatively small, widely separated centres of natural power has been collected and brought together in one power house for distribution throughout the city. The problems involved in this unique undertaking were mainly those dealing with the actual transmission of the water power between the natural sources and the power houses, and the handling and control of the different

Power is derived from two mountain streams— the Tlalnepantla and the Monte Alto. Three power stations, at Alameda, Chiluca, and Madin, receive their power from the former; whilst two others, at Villada and Fernandez Leal, draw their supply from the Monte Alto River. The accompanying map (Fig. 1) shows the courses of the rivers, the respective positions of the power stations, and also the position of the city of Mexico, near which is indicated the receiving sub-station at the suburb of La Veronica.

The difficulties which had to be overcome in the construction of the hydraulic part of the scheme were, as may be supposed, very considerable. The waterways between the rivers and the power houses are of lengths of from two to eight miles, and pass over mountainous ground. Each waterway required open canals, tunnels, aqueducts, and pipe lines. In the case of the canals and tunnels, some parts of the cuttings were in hard volcanic rock of a sufficiently close nature to require no linings; in other cases, retaining walls of masonry were required where light clayey soils were met. The aqueducts across the numerous small valleys and ravines are of masonry, supported by wrought-iron or stone pillars set on stone foundations. A pair of wrought-iron girders between the pillars, with sheets of corrugated iron between the lower flanges, support the duct. In one case, where a valley too wide and deep for the practical construction of an aqueduct was encountered, another method was adopted. This consisted of a syphon connection between the two sides of the valley. The steel pipe which dips down into the valley is carried on a masonry bridge, the ends being rigidly anchored in massive stone blocks. Where pipe lines were required, steel tubes about 4ft. in diameter have been put down. In straight lengths the pipes have simply been laid along the hill sides, every other pipe length resting on a brickwork pedestal, but where bends occur, they are securely fixed to substantial blocks of masonry.

In the case of the Monte Alto River power stations, that of Villada is the higher of the two. The intake of the canal for the supply of this station is high up in the mountains, some seven and a half miles distant. The flow of the river at this spot averages about 21,000 cubic feet per minute, and the fall at the power station is about 430ft. The canal starts from behind a masonry dam, thrown at right angles across the stream. Two strong iron grills or gratings in the mouth of the canal, placed one behind the other, serve to arrest the entrance, during flood times, of drift-wood and other floating *débris*. The canal terminates in a reservoir on the brow of a steep hill immediately above the power station. The reservoir is built in two parts. The first is practically a settling tank, and is connected with the second by a brickwork canal about 35ft. long, in which further straining gratings and a sluice gate, are fixed. The second basin is 28ft. long by 23ft. wide by 20ft. deep. The bell mouth of the pipe line enters through the lower part of the wall of this reservoir. The tail race from the power station below, discharges back into the Monte Alto River at a point just above the second dam, from behind which the water supply for the lower station, Fernandez Leal, is drawn. This second canal is about five miles long, and is of similar construction to the first. At about one mile and a half from its

commencement it receives a tributary which raises its final flow to 25,500 cubic feet per minute, the available head at the power station being about 394ft. The syphon arrangement mentioned forms a part of the tributary duct of this water-way.

On the Tlalnepantla River the water power schemes are arranged in a similar manner. At Alameda the available fall is 520ft., and at Chiluca and Madin the falls are 275ft. and 185ft. respectively.

With regard to the generating plant, it was resolved that the power stations should all be equipped with turbines, dynamos, transformers, and accessory apparatus of exactly similar types and sizes, the only difference at the several stations being in the number of units installed in each case according to the power available. The advantages secured by this arrangement are many. The risks of a total or serious breakdown of the generating plant are very remote; very few spare parts require to be stocked, and all are interchangeable; the best possible conditions for parallel running are gained; the transport of the power plant over the rugged country could be more easily undertaken with the machines built in small units and of comparatively light parts. There are in all nineteen main generating sets. Five of these are installed in each of the power houses of Villada and Fernandez Leal; four in La Alameda station; three in Chiluca station; and two in the Madin power house. Each set consists of a Westinghouse two-phase alternator, yielding 225 kilowatts at a pressure of 440 volts when running at a speed of 430 revolutions per minute. The generator is direct connected by a Raffard coupling to a Picard & Pictet water turbine. Two exciting sets, consisting of Westinghouse direct current generators, direct coupled to Pelton wheels, are installed in each power station. Each exciter set is capable of furnishing the whole current for all the main generators in the one station, working at full load. The pressure of the exciting current is 125 volts, and the power required for exciting each alternator is equivalent to about 2 per cent. of its maximum output. The transformers, of which there are twenty-two altogether in the power stations, are each of 225 kilowatts capacity, and serve to transform the two-phase 440-volt current, as generated, into three-phase current at a pressure of 22,000 volts for the transmission lines. The arrangements of the transformers and high-pressure apparatus at Chiluca power station are shown in Fig. 2, Plate XV.

It may be mentioned here that a pair of transmission lines interconnect the power stations along the one river, and a pair also connect those of the other river, the four combining at the Madin Works, from which a pair of lines run direct into La Veronica; thus any generator at any station may be connected to either or both the transmission lines. The switchboards at the power stations for this class of service must necessarily be very complete and somewhat unusual in their apparatus and arrangement. The main switchboards at the power stations are built up of exactly similar panels, the only difference being in the actual number of the panels, which in each case is proportional to the number of generators, etc., installed. Fig. 3 is a diagram of the connections of the board. The switchboard is of standard Westinghouse construction, consisting of a uniform series of white marble panels, mounted on an angle-iron framework, supported at a convenient height on substantial cast-iron legs. Starting from the left the first is the exciter panel, followed by three generator panels, a load panel, and a transformer panel.

The exciter panel carries the instruments, regulators, and switches for the two 15-kilowatt exciters installed, there being two ammeters, two voltmeters (one on the swinging arm), two field rheostats, and two main switches connecting the machines direct to the exciter bus bars, as shown

together. This interchange of current is often sufficient to blow the fuses before the machines can correct each other and recover, after a moment, to run in perfect synchronism, as they would normally do. Hurried paralleling would only be required in cases of emergency, and fuses, under such circumstances, certainly increase considerably the risks of serious breakdown. Further, the opening of the armature circuit of a Westinghouse alternator under conditions of very heavy overload is more likely to produce damage to the machine than is the presence of the overload itself.

The load panel carries two indicating wattmeters, which give indications of the total output of the station. They are coupled one in each phase of the 440-volt bus bars, between the machine main end and the feeder or transformer main end, the series coils being supplied from series transformers, ratio 1,500 amperes to 5 amperes, whilst the pressure coils are direct across the bus bars. These wattmeters are admirable

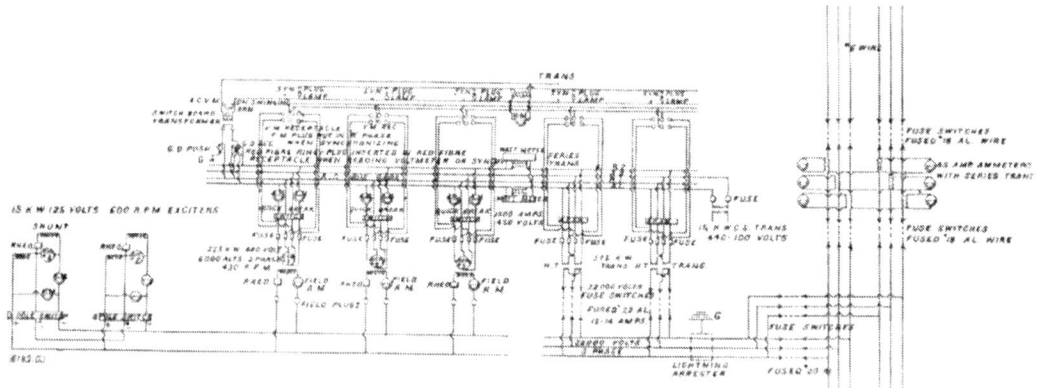

Fig. 3.—Diagram of Switchboard at Chiluca Station

clearly in the illustrations. Each generator panel carries two main ammeters—one for each phase—and a field ammeter, a field rheostat, a three-pole quick-break main switch, a two-way set of voltmeter plugs, and a pilot lamp. The alternate current main and machine voltmeters are carried on the swinging bracket outside the exciter panel. It will be seen that fuses have been shown in the machine main circuits; this is not in accordance with general practice, and is not to be recommended. They were only introduced in connection with this scheme under protest, because they were particularly called for by the power company. As a matter of fact, Westinghouse alternators, which have inductive armatures, are easily capable of withstanding very high overloads without suffering the slightest damage. When hurried or careless paralleling of the machines occurs, there is always likely to be an excessive interflow of current between two machines if they are not very nearly in step before connecting

guides as to the economical phase conditions of the working plant, the sum of the machine ammeter readings, multiplied by the bus bar voltmeter reading, giving the apparent power generated, which, compared with the readings of the wattmeters, gives the power factor of the supply. The exciting current of the generators can be adjusted to bring this ratio as near unity as possible, and the economy of generation thereby maintained maximum.

The transformer panel carries the two four-pole quick-break main switches for the two sets of main current step-up transformers. These switches are of 600 amperes capacity each. The equipment of this panel also comprises voltmeter and synchroniser plug contacts and lamps. These are necessary in connection with the feeders, owing to the unusual arrangement of this power scheme, the station as a unit requiring to be synchronised with the circuit of the transmission line, which may be already in circuit with one or more of the other power stations. If no generators are actually running at the power station, then the step-up transformers may be switched on to the three-phase, 22,000 - volt transmission line by the high-tension circuit breakers provided, and the four-pole switches on the switchboard may also be closed, thus putting the two-phase low-tension current direct on to the main switchboard 440-volt bus bars. The machines can then in turn be run up to speed, paralleled with the bus bars and switched into the supply circuit, in the usual manner, as required. But should the generators be running first, then it becomes necessary to parallel them as a whole with the transmission line circuit. For this purpose the three - phase high-tension circuit breakers are closed on one bank of transformers, which thus act as pressure reducers and introduce a 440-volt two-phase pressure on to the outside contacts of the open four-pole

Ammeters are placed in each transmission main, whereby the attendant at the station can read at a glance the load already placed on the lines by the other power stations, and so, if necessary, select the one suitable for his portion of the load, thereby avoiding overloads on either of the lines. The ammeters are all fed from series transformers, and they can be isolated by high - tension circuit breakers, which are placed in the main circuit at each side. It should be mentioned that the attendant at Chiluca has switches so arranged that he has the power to divert the supply of the Alameda station above him to either or both of the transmission lines, or to cut it off altogether.

The high-tension circuit breakers used are of the "fused" type (see Figs. 4 and 5). It will be seen that they are mechanically simple, and depend on an exceedingly long break for effectively

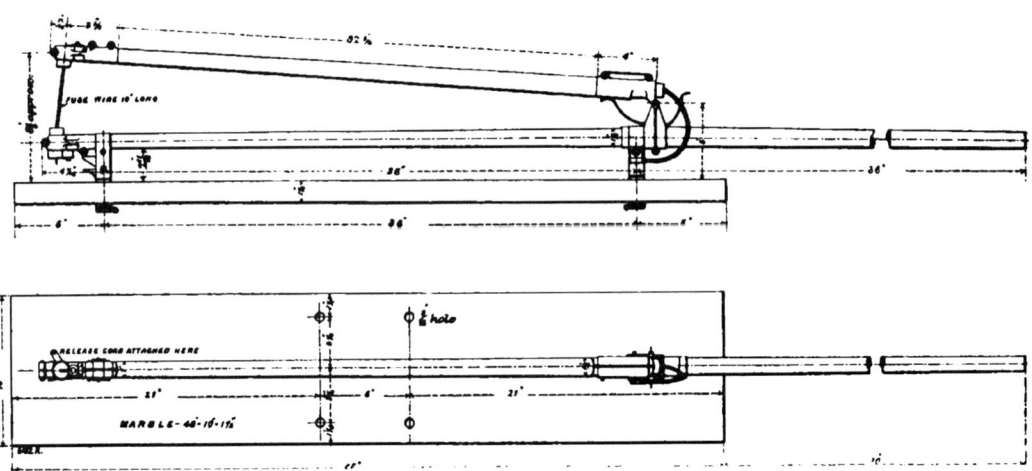

Figs. 4 and 5. - High-tension Circuit Breakers

transformer switch. The bus bar pressure is already at the inner contacts, and therefore the two circuits at the extremes of the switch simply require to be brought into parallel and the switch closed. The synchronising of the two is carried out in the usual manner, the pressures being balanced by working in the bus bar circuit, the generators connected with which are regulated as a unit by means of the rheostat in the exciter shunt-field circuit. The panels are fitted with the usual pilot lamps, ground detectors, and lightning arresters.

These last are fitted in connection with the three-phase, high-tension bus bars, that is, between the high-tension circuit breakers on the transformer side and the high-tension circuit breakers of the transmission line feeders. The intermediate stations, as at Chiluca, have additional switchboards, through which both the transmission lines pass.

opening the circuit. This type of circuit breaker consists of two hardwood sticks or poles, the shorter one of which is hollow, and is hinged to the centre of the longer one, so that their upper ends are in line. The upper extremities are fitted with copper sleeves bearing hollow carbon cylinders, which practically form the contacts of the switch. The two hinged contact rods, or the switch proper, are easily detachable from the marble panel into which the terminals, in the form of spring copper jaws, are fitted at a distance apart corresponding to the height between the hinge and the upper contact of the long rod, the rod at these points being fitted with blades on the contact pieces corresponding to the fixed terminals on the board. The switch is thus removed entirely from the panel and its live terminals for the purpose of re-fusing. A length of 10ins. of aluminium wire forms the fuse, which

Plate XV

Fig. 2.—Chiluca Power Station: Arrangement of Transformers, etc.

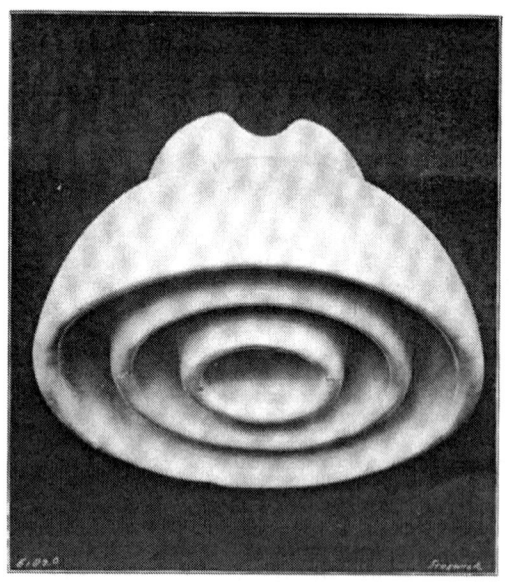

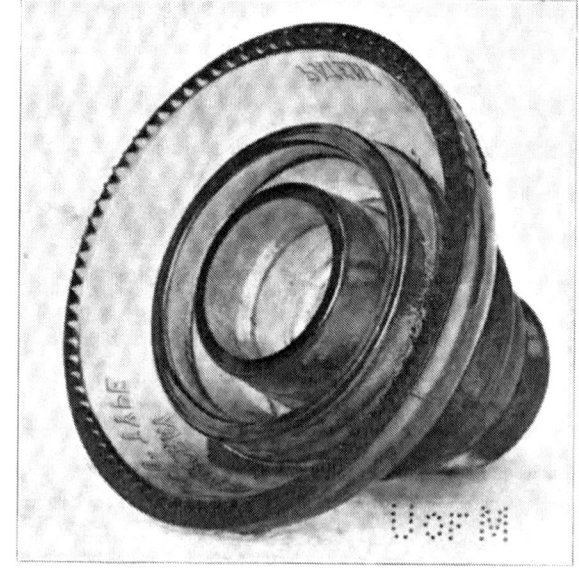

Figs. 7 and 8.—Insulators for High-pressure Transmission Lines

ELECTRICAL POWER SUPPLY OF THE CITY OF MEXICO

MtoU

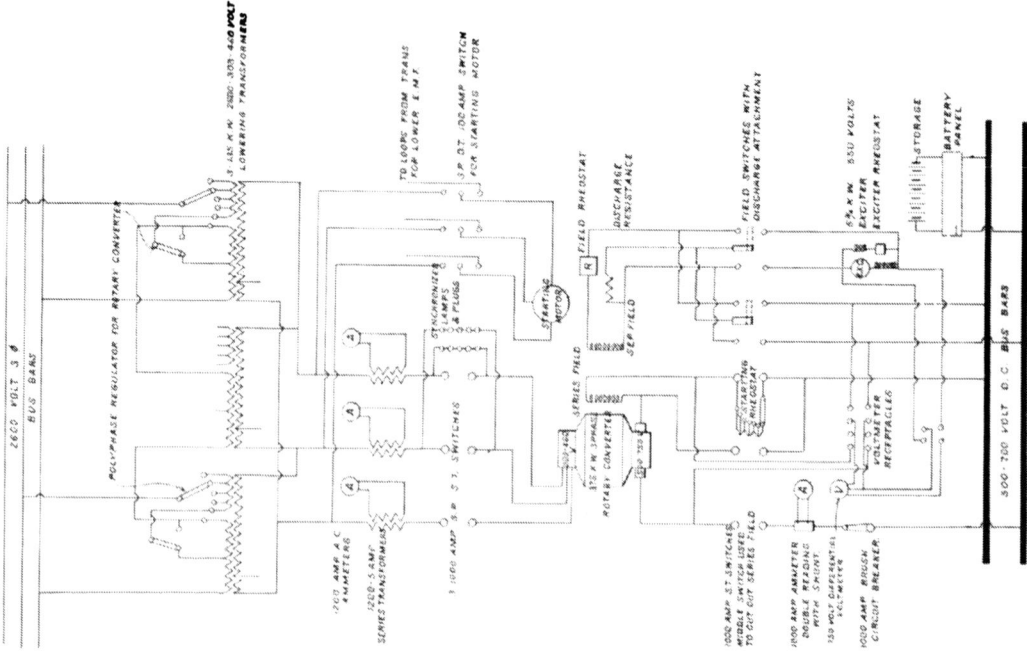

Fig. 11.—Diagram of Switchboard Connections, La Veronica Sub-station

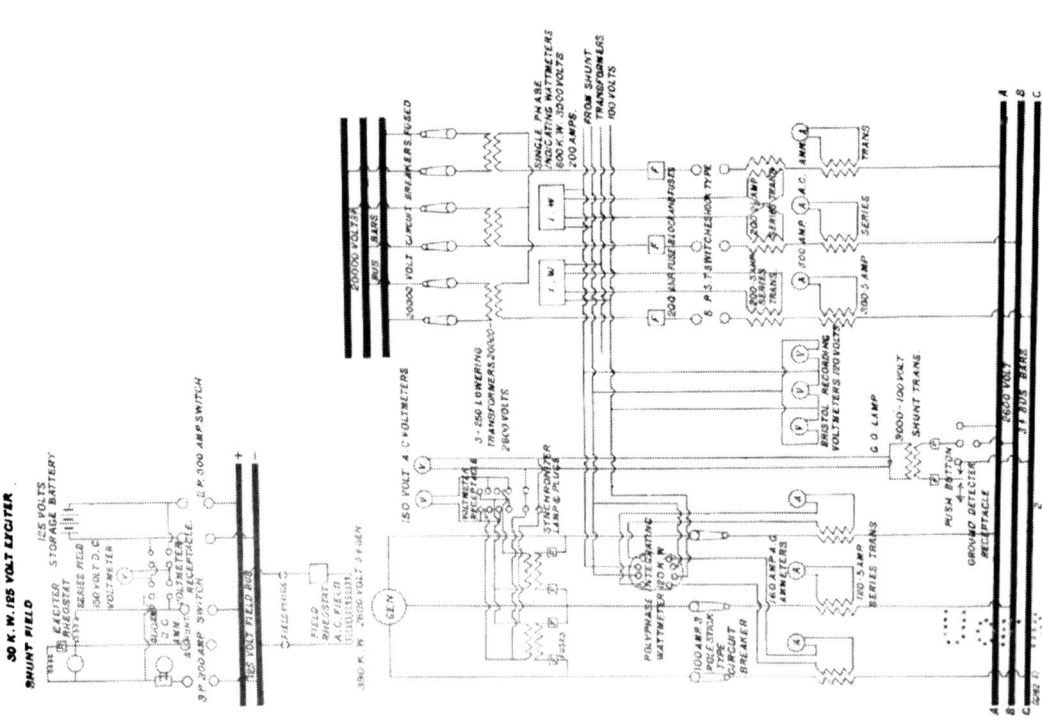

Fig. 10.—Diagram of Steam Generator Connections

MたoU

is held in tension between the carbon contact ends of the switch. The switch is set by taking the long rod with the attached arm away from the panel, passing the fuse wire through the hollow carbon end of the shorter rod, and securing it by screw and washer to the copper end; the aluminium wire is then passed through the hollow carbon of the corresponding contact of the longer rod, the hinged arm being drawn up against the resistance of the flat spring, until the carbon ends are 10ins. apart, and the wire secured in a special cam clamp. The clamp holding the fuse wire is divided, so that it can be opened easily by means of the length of cord attached, and the device may therefore be used either as a simple switch or as an automatic circuit breaker. The long rod is pressed into position in the panel terminals; the hinge terminal is connected to the upper extremity of the short rod by a flexible conductor, which passes up through the centre of the rod; the circuit breakers are separated from each other by large asbestos-covered wooden barriers. The lightning arresters used are of the well-known Wurts type; each one is mounted on a separate marble panel, the set of spark gaps occupying the front of the board, the choking coils being fixed to the rear.

The main switchboards at all the power stations are similar to those of Chiluca just described; there are, however, at Madin additional switchboard arrangements required, because it is there that the two duplicate transmission lines from the other generating stations are brought together, and connected to feed either, or both, of the high-tension transmission lines running direct to the sub-station at La Veronica. Of course, synchronising arrangements are required. These are of the usual form, and identical with those used for paralleling alternators. A series of wattmeters is arranged in all the circuits, so that the actual state of load and its distribution amongst the several mains can be seen at a glance.

In all cases, single-phase wattmeters—whether indicating or integrating — are used in connection with this system; two single-phase instruments being required to give the total power or energy of the three-phase circuit. Figs. 6 and 7 are diagrams of the connections of two single-phase indicating wattmeters, as arranged to give an indication of the true power of a three-phase circuit. It will be seen that the wattmeter current coils are supplied from the ammeter series transformers, of ratios of 100 to 2½ and 100 to 5 amperes; whilst the pressure coils are supplied by shunt transformers of 20,000 to 100-50 volts ratios. The two single-phase wattmeters, coupled as shown, will each indicate half the total power of the circuit, in the case of a balanced load on each phase, and in the event of the loads per phase being uneven, the sum of the two readings will give the true total power. That this is so can readily be proved. In the diagram Fig. 7 the phase relations of the three-phase circuit are given. Lines O A, O B, O C, represent the currents in the wires A, B,

and C, respectively. Take, then, the first single-phase wattmeter D. Its current supply is drawn from the two series transformers A and B, whose secondaries are coupled in parallel. The current supplied to wattmeter D is therefore represented by the resultant of O A, and O B, and is equal to A B. The pressure coil of wattmeter D, is supplied direct from the extremes of the shunt transformer across mains A and B, and is therefore in phase with the current A B. In the case of wattmeter E, the current supply is drawn from the single series transformer C, and is proportional to, and in phase with, O C; the pressure coil of E is coupled across the shunt transformer,

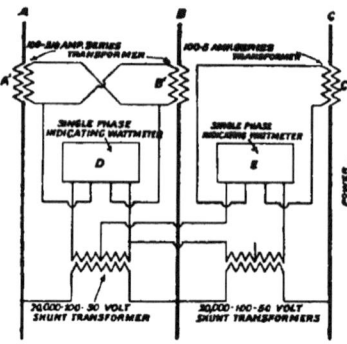

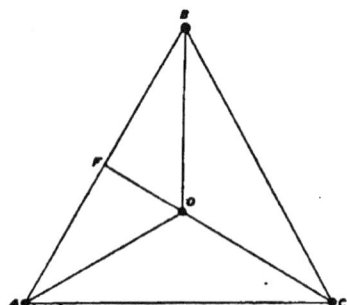

Figs. 6 and 7.—Diagrams of Wattmeter Connections

between B and C, and also spans half of the secondary of the first transformer—that between A and B. Assuming the load to be non-inductive, the pressure circuit will be in phase with the current O C, and will be represented by C F. Having now got the exact relations and proportions between the phases and valves of the currents in the series, and pressure coils of both wattmeters, one can easily work out an actual example. Although the scales of the wattmeters are marked to indicate the actual powers of the circuits, both the pressure and the current coils are supplied through reducing transformers; the former having a ratio of 200 to 1, the latter a ratio of 20 to 1, exciter, with the instrument switches, etc., is given in Fig. 11, Plate XVI.

There is also in the sub-station a direct current system of 500 to 700 volts pressure. This is obtained by means of a Westinghouse rotary converter, receiving a three-phase current at pressures of from 303 to 460 volts, supplied by a set of reducing transformers between it and the 2,600-volt bus bars. During periods of heavy load advantage is taken of this rotary converter to help the A C supply. A storage battery has been installed for this purpose, and serves to drive at such times the rotary converter as an A C generator. There are in all seventeen white marble panels in the switchboard of the La Veronica station; these serve for the control of the whole of the plant, including the exciter, alternator, A C side and D C side of rotary, storage battery, and feeders. The large range of the secondary pressures of the reducing transformers supplying the rotary converters are secured by bringing out several loops from the secondary windings (see Fig. 12, Plate XVI). The range of pressure is necessary, so that the storage battery may at any time be either charged by the rotary, or discharged into the rotary, without interfering with the three-phase main supply. The rotary converter is supplied with the usual alternate current starting motor, and also with a separate special exciter, to ensure a close automatic regulation when the rotary is supplying the current from its A C sides.

The distribution throughout the city of Mexico is by 2,600-volt three-phase feeders. In the suburbs the distribution is by means of overhead wires, and in the central portions of the town underground mains are used. There are in all eleven miles of overhead work, and some thirty-one miles of underground work, installed for the primary distribution, which is undertaken by seven distinct feeders, four of which are used for power purposes, and three for general lighting.

The secondary house-to-house supply is installed on a four-wire two-phase system, the pressure being 240 volts. The lighting is arranged as single-phase on a three-wire system, with 120 volts on each side. In the city there are three distribution centres, each receiving current at a pressure of 2,600 volts by underground mains. One feeder which connects all three of these transformer centres together is kept separate from the rest, and serves to supply power for the larger sized motors only, the object being, as far as possible, to keep the lighting supply pressure steady and independent of the fluctuations caused by the starting and stopping of motors of larger sizes than 5 horse-power each. At the same time the additional feeders put down serve always as reserves in case of emergency. All underground mains are steel armoured, and laid direct in the ground.

The price per unit charged for lighting purposes varies. It is arranged on a sliding scale and averages about 7d. per kilowatt-hour. The price is less for power purposes, varying from 2d. to 7d. per kilowatt-hour. A very large number of motors are run from the circuits, some of these being of over 75 horse-power capacity each. The demand for energy, both for lighting and power, is increasing at a very rapid rate, and already work in connection with large extensions of the system is being forced quickly forward.

THE PATHS OF PROGRESS

A MONTHLY REVIEW

THE MEASURE OF PROSPERITY

He is a wise and happy person who knows when he is well off. For it is unfortunate that the attainment of such knowledge is dependent upon the temperament as much as upon the reason. Let a man's assets be never so large, let his liabilities be never so well covered, if, notwithstanding, he is of over cautious habits, or of worrying disposition, he will find no lasting satisfaction in his auditor's report, and will regard every ascending step as the approach to a precipice from which he may possibly be flung headlong to ruin. Within certain limits the practice of self - searching and the cold-blooded analysis of one's financial or social position, are useful and salutary ; but carried to excess such introspection becomes a curse and a disease. There is no man so placed that he cannot provide for himself disappointments or forebodings if he sets his mind on the unpleasing task. One can always find trouble if one looks for it.

We are justified in extending this rule to communities and nationalities, and it is therefore with uneasiness that some of us observe the rather unhealthy public interest shown of late in the commercial position of this country. When otherwise wholly estimable citizens take to spending their leisure in the pursuit of statistics, and when the whole press raises, morning and evening, weekly and monthly, the cry of " Trade in Danger " ; when the subject of industrial decline is actually discussed in the comic papers, the matter becomes serious indeed. Yet it is difficult to resist being somewhat amused at the laborious efforts of the conscientious Englishman to ascertain, by the study of columns of figures, whether he is or is not prosperous. Free indulgence in trade statistics is not good for the average man. Like the patent medicine advertisements, they give him an attack of " symptoms," and tend to produce the imaginary disorders which alone they are

capable of curing. The truth is that the masses of figures and facts served up for him in blue-books, newspapers, and magazines, are beyond the understanding of all but advanced economic students. What the plain man wants is a clear balance sheet that will show him the financial position of the nation, just as his private accounts reveal the profit or loss on his own business. Nothing of the kind exists, however. The Budget and the Board of Trade returns afford a mass of interesting information, which is used for all manner of controversial purposes with equal and impartial effect. We may ascertain whether certain departments of our trade are advancing or declining. We may form an opinion as to the economy with which the government of the State, and of local areas, is carried on. But whether the British Empire, Limited, is paying dividends out of revenue, or is living on its reserves, or is mortgaging its future, are perplexing questions that seem to produce much anxiety among certain thoughtful citizen shareholders.

Yet, to assure ourselves of our present prosperity as a community, it is surely only necessary to accept the evidence of our senses, and decide the question upon our perception of the comparative degree of comfort, luxury, and leisure, enjoyed by the inhabitants of this and other States. We know that in our latitude and our climate such things are only to be obtained by mental or physical exertion, either on our own part or that of our forefathers. England is not a land flowing with milk and honey, and it can only be made decently habitable for so many millions of human beings with civilised appetites, by persistent labour and fertile invention. When we find, then, that the average Englishman is more bountifully blessed in his supply of luxuries, in his holidays and hours of ease, than the natives of other lands, and that he pays £87,000,000 a year in income tax, we are forced to the conclusion, either that the Englishman's work is specially productive, or that his environment is specially favourable. If we take first the so-called "working man," we observe that he is better paid, and that he has more playtime, than the foreigner, who, according to agitators—that would compel all men to be brothers by measures of drastic severity—is his "comrade," but who, in many instances, might more fitly be termed his competitor. At a recent conference of the Garden City Association, established to promote human harmony by the abolition of the landlord, there was something like an uproar when Mr. Lever complained that the great advance in the cost of building was entirely due to the higher remuneration and less laborious exertions of the bricklayers. This is a subject that may be discussed in these columns hereafter; for the purpose of the present notes it is sufficient that the bricklayer is flourishing like most other British working men.

Amongst other classes, the fruits of our observation are essentially the same. There are hard workers here and there, but the ordinary "busy man" is more or less a fraud. There is no country in which it is easier to earn a comfortable living, and there are few signs of strenuous effort, or of what the evolutionists call "struggle for life." There is a "housing question," no doubt; but this is due to some of the towns being suddenly swamped with immigrants, for whose convenient accommodation no provision had been, or could be, made at short notice.

SUCCESS PAST AND PRESENT

Somehow or other, the result has been arrived at that the British people have gained for themselves by far the largest stake in the prosperity of the world. It has been attributed, by foreign critics, to such "accidents" as the discovery of rich coal deposits, the invention of the steam engine, the aloofness of the country from European wars and political upheavals, and partly to certain racial characteristics—in short, as has been said by some patriotic orator, to "British pluck and British luck." The native excellencies of the people themselves, which are somewhat reluctantly admitted and under-valued by the said foreign critics, are advertised by the fact that similar results have been achieved in greater or less degree by settlements of Englishmen in far distant colonies. It was not coal mines that

conquered India; and it was not Stephenson or Watt who prevented Napoleon from becoming Emperor of Europe. Cromwell did not overawe the Continent by the sight of smoky factory chimneys, and there was not a single Belleville or Scotch boiler in the fleet that chased the Armada. English arms and English commerce were a power long before the Steam Age, and it is most illogical to argue that our predominance depends solely on our supply of coal or any such material support. If we cease to be a conquering race, cheap coal will not help us very powerfully in industrial competition. Yet there are many people who ignore national virtues as a commercial asset. They will idolise the British soldier, and anathematise the British workman, who is the same person in another suit of clothes. The English are not like the Zulus and the Matabele, a purely military race, who scorn productive labour. On the contrary, we have been for centuries an industrial people first, and a martial people afterwards. Recently we have had considerable trouble in overcoming a small nation in warfare; at the same time, in trade competition, the equivalent of industrial Boers have inflicted several "regrettable incidents" upon us. We conquered the Transvaal by weight of numbers, but in the commercial struggle we have no such advantage. Our competitors are more numerous, and they have a far greater extent of territory. The coast line of Great Britain is not an elastic band, and we cannot hope to find room for as many workers as the United States. One British working man cannot produce as much as three Americans, even if his trade union would allow him to try. At present our manufactured exports are three times as large as those of the U.S.A. But prosperity is not to be reckoned by mere totals of imports and exports. Trade is the *exchange* of commodities, and there are two sides to a business transaction. So long, therefore, as the representative average Englishman receives all the necessaries of life, and many luxuries that are denied to less fortunate foreigners, and so long as he does not pay for them by parting with his birthright, or, in other words, by disposing of his capital, so long the nation will rightly be termed prosperous. There is, indeed, so little opening for disputation on this subject, that the whole discussion turns on the question whether we are buying our enormous imports too dearly—whether we are enjoying a merry but short life, like a nation of prodigal voluptuaries. A manufacturer would not be prospering if he had to purchase imported raw material by pawning part of his machinery; and a householder could not be said to be growing rich who paid for his dinner by selling the table. The allegation that the British people are squandering accumulated wealth, therefore, deserves careful attention.

CHAMPIONS OF COMMERCE

Let us see first what the average Briton actually does purchase, and how he pays the greater part of the price. The following table shows the annual imports per head of the population averaged over quinquennial periods :—

	United Kingdom.	France.	Germany.	United States.
	£ s. d.	£ s. d.	£ s. d.	£ s. d.
1875-79	9 10 4	4 6 7	4 6 1	2 2 5
1880-84	9 15 4	5 1 4	3 8 3	2 15 7
1885-89	8 14 2	4 6 10	3 9 5	2 8 11
1890-94	9 7 3	4 8 0	4 2 2	2 11 11
1895-99	9 17 2	4 4 9	4 6 10	1 19 11

And here are the average annual exports of home products :—

	United Kingdom.	France.	Germany.	United States.
	£ s. d.	£ s. d.	£ s. d.	£ s. d.
1875-79	6 0 0	3 3 0	3 3 0	2 16 3
1880-84	6 13 2	3 13 5	3 8 8	3 5 11
1885-89	6 3 8	3 9 3	3 5 6	2 11 10
1890-94	6 2 11	3 11 4	3 2 9	2 19 0
1895-99	5 19 5	3 14 8	3 7 2	2 18 4

It was only in 1899 that the Board of Trade included among exports the item of new ships and their machinery, which is not taken into account above. In 1899 the value was £9,200,000, or, on a population of forty millions, about 4s. 7d. per head, raising the total figure from £5 19s. 5d. to £6 4s. By our insular labour we sent forth from our shores some £260,000,000 worth of what the Board of Trade terms " domestic produce " in 1899, and, as is shown by the preceding tables, the Englishman is so far ahead of his competitors in production per head of population as really to form a class by himself.

His claim to the world's championship cannot be challenged, and although it is naturally difficult for England to keep pace, in respect of aggregate production, with a country like the United States, with nearly double the number of workers, it is obviously the proportion of exports to population which is the real test of the industrial fertility of a nation, and of the prosperity of its inhabitants.

We return now to the " balance of trade." Old-fashioned commentators on such statistics judged the prosperity of a nation by the crude method of subtracting the imports from the exports, and regarding the difference as profit. On such a basis of calculation only America has made any material progress of recent years, and in the case of England there is an adverse balance of trade year after year, the figures per head of population being :—

			£ s. d.
1875-79	...	...	... 3 10 4
1880-84	...	...	... 3 2 2
1885-89	...	...	... 2 10 6
1890-94	...	...	... 3 4 4
1895-99	...	...	... 3 17 9

That means that in the whole twenty-five years, Englishmen lost £81 7s. 1d. per head on foreign trade, or a trifle of some £2,885,000,000 for thirty-five million people. Did we grow poorer in the meantime ? On the contrary, we are now more blessed with the world's goods than ever.

We have already seen that the value of shipbuilding and naval machinery added £9,200,000 to the 1899 exports, raising the average per head to £6 4s. There still remains a " balance of trade " for that year amounting to £3 18s. 2d., which had to be provided for, as it is not possible to give interminable I.O.U.'s for international debt. And this difference is made up from three main sources :—

(1) Interest on investment of British capital abroad.

(2) Profits on the collection and re-exportation of foreign merchandise not included in the foregoing tables either as imports or exports.

(8) Profits on the ocean carrying trade.

BRITISH GOLD

Opprobrious terms, intended to rouse envy, hatred, and malice, have always been readily invented by Continental enemies of this country to denounce the most powerful weapon employed by our statesmen in foreign affairs. The wealth of Great Britain has had a commanding influence on the world's wars and the world's commerce. Farther than from Greenland's icy mountains to India's coral strand, almost the whole earth is sprinkled with British capital. In foreign and colonial government securities; in the railways of North and South America and India; in the mines of Africa, America, India, and Australia; in banks, in land, in mortgages; in numerous other departments of trade and finance; there are thousands of millions invested, much of which is as unproductive as if it were at the bottom of the Atlantic, but the remainder of which yields an enormous income to this country. In the national balance sheet this would form a valuable item, yet no exact statement is in existence showing the amount invested and the interest received. On the London Stock Exchange, foreign and colonial bonds, stocks, and shares, to the nominal value of about £5,500,000,000 are officially quoted, out of which probably more than half are held in this country, and there are other investments, especially in mines and other speculative business, which are not in the list.

Secondly, we have to consider the profits on the great distributing trade of the country. Immense quantities of goods are collected from abroad and re-shipped at a profit to the merchants who undertake this class of business, which is, of course, greatly beholden to our maritime pre-eminence, for if the carrying trade were to pass to other countries, England would cease to be so favourably situated as an *entrepôt* for such merchandise. The commercial grandeur of Venice in the Middle Ages was mainly, if not entirely, due to its position as a distributing centre, with command of the means of transport, and Holland, at the present day, thrives by its position astride the direct route of Anglo-German trade. So long as British vessels ply to all the ports of the earth, England remains the centre of the world's sea-borne trade, and profits apace like many other middlemen. The foregoing figures from the Board of Trade returns do not take into account these re-exports, except that they are deducted from the value of the imports.

SECOND THOUGHTS ON THE ATLANTIC COMBINE

A third source of income is the carrying trade itself. It is obvious that when our imports and exports are transported in our own craft the "balance of trade" is disturbed; for the value of imports at our coast represents the value at the port of shipment plus the cost of freightage; while, on the other hand, we, as a nation, take toll from the purchaser of our exports by charging him with the carriage. In other words, the exchange value of commodities imported is thereby reduced, and the exchange value of commodities exported is enhanced, as between England and the other countries. It is true that, as consumers of the imports, we pay the cost of shipment; but we pay it to our own country, which also receives the corresponding charges paid by the foreign consumers of our exports. It is this consideration which has apparently such an important bearing on the expropriation of our Atlantic liners and other departments of our shipping industry. On the face of it the sale of a number of second-hand ships for a high price is an item of export trade on which we may congratulate ourselves. But the dubious character of the bargain from a national point of view lies in the future use which the purchaser may make of the industry. If it remains in its present state, simply as it has been created by British enterprise, and if the British vendors draw, in the shape of interest on the purchase price, a sum equal to what they would have received if the ships had been retained, there does not seem to be any great harm done. But the purchasers have also acquired the opportunity for future development, and if they can, by expansion and improvement, cultivate this section of the world's carrying trade for their own profit, it would certainly seem that the amount of that profit will represent a loss to the British Commonwealth, because then the exchange value of our imports from America will be increased by the charges of the American shippers, and the exchange value of our exports will be diminished in like manner. We shall be paying toll both ways to the United States.

This is indeed the turning point in the present essay. Recognising that we are the most prosperous of nations, and that our prosperity is largely the fruit of past, rather than present, industrial activity—for we are incontestably paying for a proportion of our imports out of the accumulated and invested profits of former periods—can we hope to remain prosperous if we are not able to retain our position in respect of what are apparently the industries to which we owe so much of our past success? To put an extreme case, we may suppose that the whole nation is living "on its income"—that after a century of amazing industrial progress, we have been able to invest so much capital all over the world, that we do not need to export anything whatever. Should we then be assured of permanent prosperity? On the contrary, we should be in a somewhat precarious condition, for if the working nations did not flourish, our interest would fall into arrears; while, in the other event, if they did enjoy commercial progress, they would soon be able to repay our capital, just as in the past year or two large quantities of United States railroad bonds and stocks have passed from British to American ownership, because the latter have become possessed of the profits of industry in sufficient measure to require such investment. While, therefore, our accumulated funds are a present help, it is obvious that the future of the country depends on intelligently directed labour, and not on mere money changing, and it is not an unreasonably alarmist view that any breach in the fabric of our "industrial system" is a more or less serious menace to the welfare of the general population. The alienation of our mercantile marine, the wastage of our fuel, the failure to keep our hold on the iron and steel trade, though not necessarily fatal, when taken singly, to England's future progress, cannot be contemplated without grave misgivings, and it is, for example, an ugly feature of the Board of Trade return, prepared by Sir Alfred Bateman, that we have of late years shipped enormous quantities of the product of our best coal mines in return for imports of which a large proportion consists of pure luxuries. Even less advantageous, from a national point of view, is it to sell a branch of our shipping industry in exchange for "scrip."

THE EFFECTS OF OVER PROSPERITY

A nation which has practically "retired" from business, and which is in receipt of an enormous income gained without hard work, is obviously running the risk of going out of training. Men of science tell us that the individual or species adapts itself to its environment—or perishes; and a community that, after long struggling, adapts itself to difficult circumstances, will, in the process, develop strength, address, and endurance, as they are required, for necessity is the mother of many other children besides invention. Yet, there are more dangers in the victory than in the battle. It is possible to be over successful, and over prosperous, which condition may lead to sluggishness, self-complacence, and false security. For that reason it is a matter for congratulation that the challenge to our industrial supremacy has come before England has carried the "go easy" policy too far, and before her people have become demoralised. So long as the term is unjust, it is doing us a real kindness to describe this country as effete and "played out," and thus turn our thoughts to the direction in which we may be tending. Similarly, an occasional period of bad trade, whatever regrettable hardship it may inflict on the individual, has a strengthening influence on a nation that has not dissipated its powers of recuperation.

The Board of Trade Memorandum as to the comparative progress of Great Britain, the United States, France, and Germany in recent years, comes as a very useful reminder to our politicians that they must be careful not to impose further restrictions on native enterprise. The publication shows fairly conclusively that we cannot hope to produce quantities of goods equal to the output of the United States, owing to the difference in population and other causes, but in respect of quality and value there is no such limitation, and it is to be hoped that these politicians, who voluntarily concern themselves with the national welfare, will take careful note of the fact, and will guide their actions accordingly. It is customary for Parliament and the press to attempt to use the manufacturer as a scapegoat. But obviously, the prosperity of the country is not the manufacturer's business, as a manufacturer. His business is with his factory, not with the nation, and if he is doing profitably the country has nothing to reproach him with. If, on the other hand, his revenue declines, or his expenditure increases to such a degree as to threaten his peace and comfort, he will "wake up" without any exhortation; and will exert once more those personal and racial qualities which enabled his predecessors or himself to attain commercial eminence. If the Imperial Government confines its attention to the question of conserving England's general advantages as a site for industrial enterprise, and if the local authorities will recognise a similar duty in respect of the areas over which their jurisdiction extends, they may safely leave the rest to the incentive of self-interest.

THE NORTH-EASTERN PLUNGE

Analogous to the relationship between Great Britain and foreign manufacturing competitors, is the new situation in the railway world produced by the development of railroad traffic. The upstart rival in both cases is, in the interests of self-preservation, necessarily more alert and progressive, and consequently orders go abroad in the one case, and suburban passengers, in the other, are captured. In both cases, also, it would seem the sounder policy to anticipate the risk of adversity rather than await all consequences with unshakable self-confidence. The North-Eastern Railway Company, for example, is, of course, still a prosperous corporation. Directors and shareholders have reason to be well satisfied with the present position of the undertaking. To be satisfied with good, however, does not preclude all thoughts of better and worse, and when they observe that their company has evidently not quite risen to its occasions and possibilities in the matter of popular travelling facilities; and that other companies have, by means of electric traction on the public roads, annexed a goodly portion of the North-Eastern local traffic, and considerably added to the value of the capture by enterprising management; the North-Eastern proprietors are divided between regret for their lost opportunities and uneasiness as to their further vulnerability.

The directors have decided to face the situation, not to turn their backs upon it. And the prompt decision to electrify the North Tyneside system is to be followed by proportionately prompt execution, for the specification demands that the work shall be completed in twelve months. Technical details have been commented upon in *Engineering* and other journals, and are not within the province of these notes, the intention of which is to deal with economic tendencies. Of such is the much debated action of Mr. Merz, who is in control of the work, in inviting all sorts and conditions of tenders for its accomplishment, instead of confining manufacturers within the limits of his own conception. Controversy has arisen as to whether Mr. Merz should dictate more or less rigid conditions, or merely announce that here is a railway system to be electrified, and that the field is open to all comers. It would appear that, in taking what is tantamount to the latter course, Mr. Merz is constituting himself a public examiner in technical education. He gathers together a number of electrical manufacturers eager to show their proficiency in the conversion or adaptation of railways to electric traction, and he puts the question to them as earnest students: "State what you know about electric traction on heavy railways, and give examples."

The answer is rather an expensive matter for the manufacturers, and must lead to some delay, but it should surely be a gain to science if it produces any novel schemes or important modifications of existing systems of electrification. Will it do so? Mr. Merz evidently does not attach much importance to the Inner Circle arbitration, and perhaps he is right in refusing to regard that decision as the last word on the subject. But whether it is fair to manufacturers that they should have to undergo a similar contest every time a railway company begins to consider electric traction is another question. Designing the system and making the machinery are different departments, and for some reasons it is advantageous to keep them distinct, leaving the manufacturer simply to construct machinery ordered from him according to an exact specification prepared by an engineer who has studied the special requirements of the case. As it is, each company willing to tender will have to go over the whole ground for itself, which, if, as has been conjectured, a benefit to the scientific community, is nevertheless rather trying to the firm, which would prefer to specialise as a manufacturer and turn out just what machinery was ordered.

TRAINS AND TRAMS

The actual working of this electrified local system on the north of the Tyne will, needless to say, be watched with intense interest; but there is one result which may safely be anticipated, namely, that with low fares and with short trains of one or two cars departing so frequently as to give almost a continuous service, this busy district will certainly produce a large amount of additional passenger traffic on the line. For nearly all its length it will have to compete with parallel lines of electric tramways, either the Newcastle Corporation, or the Tyneside, or the Tynemouth to Whitley routes. Somewhat unreasonably the latter system has been singled out for sympathy. It runs along the sea coast, and serves a substantial settled population, besides the summer holiday makers. Many residents thereabouts will shortly be in the happy position of having an electric tramway at the front door, and an electric train at the back door, and at times they will be in danger of resembling the proverbial donkey, which is reported to have starved owing to its inability to choose between two equally appetising bills of fare.

To take the train or the tram will become a matter of habit, and the tramway company has the first opportunity in directing the formation of that habit. Its other advantages are that it can stop whenever required, and that it is more convenient to reach, inasmuch as houses have been built along main roads rather than along main railway lines, or even round stations. On the other hand, having once boarded the train, the passenger will be transported to another station twice or three times as fast as if he made the journey by tram-car, and it is a fair general conclusion that when it is necessary to travel three or four miles, and the stations are convenient, the train will have superior attractions. To compensate for any injury they may do to the tramway companies on the route, these electric suburban railways will unquestionably open up new fields for tramway development. It is in the open districts beyond the suburban railway station that the tramway will be most useful to the public, when other companies have followed the North-Eastern's example, and it is the Municipal or company city and suburban tramway that will feel the competition.

Undoubtedly, the combination train and tram journey, which whisks the City man from the Bank to Shepherd's Bush in twenty minutes, and then leaves him free to board a tram-car and arrive home a few minutes later, is the coming system in the neighbourhood of all large towns, with the exception that "tubes" will not always be necessary. At present, millions of unfortunate passengers annually travel in all weathers by the London County Council tramway to the southern suburbs. After crawling about five miles in an hour, they are even then not out of the crowd. The Council is, at enormous expense and great public inconvenience, electrifying the lines on the conduit system; but the result, of course, will not be to increase the speed through these busy streets, or to make Tooting and Streatham more habitable. What is wanted, and what will be obtained in time, is a twenty minutes electric and railway journey to places like Sutton, Epsom, and tramways beyond in various directions.

The opening up of these outer circles of suburbs is the joint undertaking of the railway and tramway companies, and the electrification of the former, offering the attractions of frequency, speed, and cheapness, must benefit those larger schemes of tramway enterprise which, in this country, are mainly associated with the names of the British Electric Traction and London United Companies.

RAILWAY ECONOMICS

By the Hon. Robert P. Porter

V.—LONDON LOCOMOTION *(continued from page 32)*

XIV.—The Oldest Underground Railways

In the previous article on London locomotion, the various tubular railways, and proposals for railways, were dealt with, and it is now proposed to consider the two oldest underground railways — the Metropolitan and Metropolitan District. Within the county of London the Metropolitan Railway operates about twelve and a quarter miles of line, and the Metropolitan District about ten and a half miles, but as both of these railways own and operate three or four times the mileage outside the county of London area, comparisons of this sort are of little value. In their best days, before the opening of the Central London, and establishments of tramways, the Metropolitan Railway carried annually well on to one hundred million passengers, and the Metropolitan District in the neighbourhood of fifty millions. The last reports of these companies show considerable diminution from these figures. The managers of both of these properties have awakened to the necessity of doing something to put their respective railways on a paying footing. While the Metropolitan still manages to pay a small dividend on its ordinary stock, the District has long since relinquished the luxury of a dividend, and of later years has defaulted part of its dividend on the 4 per cent. guaranteed stock. It is hoped that electric equipment and more progressive management will bring these properties up again, and both companies are vigorously pushing forward the electrification of their lines. The District Railway Company, under the able management of Mr. R. W. Perks, M.P., have recently shown great energy, and, in a position of much difficulty, have displayed unexpected resource. They have — as we shall see—in partnership with the Tilbury Railway recently opened eastern extensions from Whitechapel to Bow. They intend next session to submit to Parliament a scheme for further railway extension in the East End of London. Nor is this all. They have raised the capital for electrically equipping their line and for building their power house. Their allies—the Brompton and Piccadilly Company—have also raised the money to proceed with that important tributary line. And all this in face of the fact that the shareholders for many years have had no dividends; that the railway has had to bear the heavy strains of costly Metropolitan improvements; and, more recently, the opposition and competition of the Central London Railway. This is a good showing, and one that does Mr. Perks great credit. In view of all this the District Company contend that a new railway from Hammersmith to the City is not needed; and they urge, further, that to sanction a new railway along the Strand, Fleet Street, and Cannon Street, parallel with the District Railway, with stations, in many cases, only a few yards away from District stations, would be a grave injustice. This seems the point of difference between the District group of financiers, with Mr. Perks and Mr. Yerkes as the moving spirits, and Sir Clinton Dawkins, with the house of J. S. Morgan & Co., as financial sponsor. The plea of the District Railway, mainly *ad misericordiam*, in spite of the facts that there are some points that command a certain amount of sympathy, would hardly seem strong enough to justify the throwing out of such an important scheme as that of the London Suburban Railway. The London *Times* thus summarises the situation :—

The District Railway was hardly treated by Parliament, which imposed onerous conditions when the construction of the line was sanctioned. On the other hand, it must be presumed that the projectors did not then think the conditions too

The Metropolitan District System

M of U

severe, since in that case they would have abandoned the scheme. The interest of projectors are not always identical with those of the shareholders, who ultimately find, or become responsible for, the money; but the District Railway is by no means the only undertaking whose shareholders suffer for this unfortunate divergence. London must not be indefinitely deprived of relief from intolerable congestion merely because some set of promotors made a bad bargain with Parliament on behalf of the District Railway. Most people hold that it has not made the best of its position, and its belated electrification — under American direction, since so much is made of the American element in the Tube scheme—does not confer the right to bid all rival schemes stand still until it has made its leisurely experiment to show whether it can meet a pressing want. When we consider how little effect it has produced upon the traffic in the Strand, and how difficult it is to deflect traffic by ever so little from its accustomed route, we may well doubt whether the District Railway, however improved, can ever give the public exactly what they want. It has its own sphere, which it will keep and enlarge, but the main part of the business of the projected through line would be new business, which the District Railway has not created and is not in a position to attract.

This would seem to be a fair statement of the case, and one to which the strong-headed business men now controlling this property can hardly object.

XV.—THE METROPOLITAN DISTRICT SYSTEM
(Plate XVII)

The scheme which has the support of J. S. Morgan & Co.—described in a previous issue of TRACTION AND TRANSMISSION—and has been engineered so ably by Sir Clinton E. Dawkins, Mr. Clifton Robinson, Mr. George White, and Sir Douglas Fox in Parliament, involves the planning and building of nearly forty miles of new railway, tubular and surface. On the other hand, the comprehensive scheme of Mr. Charles T. Yerkes, Mr. R. W. Perks, M.P., supported by Speyers & Co., of London, and the Old Colony Trust Company, of Boston, deals with the linking-up and completion of various schemes, some of which have lain dormant for many years. Mr. Yerkes comes to London somewhat in the *rôle* of an assembler of railways, and his first venture was the purchase of the franchise of the Charing Cross, Euston, and Hampstead Railway; this was followed almost immediately by the acquirement of the Metropolitan District Underground Railway, a property

which sadly needed electric traction and good business management. Mr. Yerkes is an expert in building up and making profitable street railways which have heretofore not been profitable, or those which have not been worked to their full capacity. He made an excellent reputation and a good deal of money at this business in Chicago, and gave the people a much better system of locomotion than they had before his advent. A glance at the map of London shows that, including the running powers of the Metropolitan District Railway, the system now controlled by Mr. Yerkes extends in a good many directions, and will command an important share of London traffic.

To begin with, in the District we find the newly completed Bow terminus gives an East End connection with the London, Tilbury, and Southend Railway, and carries the toilers of those districts to the "Coney Island" of London, a business capable of enormous development by good service and cheap fares. South-east there is a branch extending through Shadwell, Wapping, Deptford to New Cross, and connecting with the London, Brighton, and South Coast. South west we find important tentacles of the District System branching south from Earl's Court through Walham Green, Parson's Green, Putney, Southfields, and thence on to Wimbledon, joining the London and South-Western; and another leaving the main line at Turnham Green, *via* Gunnersbury, Kew Gardens, to Richmond, where it likewise connects with the London and South - Western. Penetrating Chiswick Park, the District makes a fork at Mill Hill Park, southward to South Ealing and Hounslow, and northward to North Ealing, and, ultimately, to South Harrow. This latter extension is now being equipped with electric traction. The tubular branches of the District Railway have still to be accounted for. They consist of three north and south lines, all crossing Holborn or Oxford Street, and under the Metropolitan tracks on the Euston Road. The first of these branches is the Great Northern and Strand, coming down from Finsbury Park, *via* Holloway, Randells Road, and King's Cross to Strand, with a projected short extension to the Temple Station of the District; the next, the Charing Cross, Euston, and Hampstead, takes a northern course from Charing Cross, *via* Euston Road to Camden Town, where it forks, the eastern branch going, *via* Kentish Town, as far as "Archway Tavern," and the western *via* Hampstead Heath to Golder's Green. Beyond this will be a line right away up to Edgware. This is a line which is to carry out a suggestion of the Joint Committee of 1901, and has an important bearing in dealing with the connections for bringing people out from London.

The idea of the scheme is, jointly with the Charing Cross, Euston, and Hampstead authorised railway, to make a connection with them, so as to work from the Strand east and west through London, enabling the people from Edgware, Hyde, Hendon, and Brent Bridge to get into London—in fact, to open up a new district, which is ripe for building purposes, and which, though it is within six or seven miles of Charing Cross, is, as to parts of it, two miles from a railway station. The third branch of this system begins at that important focus of traffic—the fifth great centre of London, only the Bank, Charing Cross, Piccadilly Circus, and Oxford Circus out-reaching it—the "Elephant and Castle," where, as I have shown, nearly six hundred vehicles pass per hour. From the "Elephant and Castle," on the south side of the Thames, the Baker Street and Waterloo Railway passes under the river near Charing Cross, under the Metropolitan and District tracks, and the Brompton and Piccadilly, under Oxford Circus, up Baker Street, under the Metropolitan Railway, when, turning westward by Regent's Park, it crosses under the Edgware Road, and ends near the terminus of the Great Western Railway at Paddington. About three-quarters of this railway is finished, only a mile and a half remaining to be done. The fourth link to this system is the Brompton and Piccadilly, which, as originally authorised, begins at Piccadilly Circus, running under Piccadilly to Hyde Park Corner, and thence, *via* Knightsbridge, Brompton Road, under the District track to Earl's Court. Three extensions were proposed to this branch this session, one towards Putney to Parson's Green, one from Piccadilly Circus to Bloomsbury, and another to the Charing Cross Station of the District. These extensions were thrown out by the House of Lords Committee. Such, then, is the Yerkes-Perks scheme, as authorised at this present moment. It covers important territory, and, in conjunction with the Morgan schemes, will add greatly to the passenger

transportation of the Metropolis. With the important exceptions of the authorised tube above Piccadilly, it does not come in conflict with the London Suburban Railway, and if the latter is authorised, some arrangement will undoubtedly have to be made which will obviate the necessity of constructing two lines under Piccadilly until it has been demonstrated that one will not do the work.

In the northern routes Mr. Yerkes couples up with the Great Northern and gets to Hornsey, with its seventy thousand inhabitants; to Wood Green, with thirty-five thousand; to Palmer's Green, where the other line stops; to Enfield, to Barnet, to Muswell Hill, the Alexandra Palace, to Highgate, to Finchley, and to Edgware. There is also an enormous interchange at Finsbury Park, and there it has been agreed, with the Great Northern Railway, to build a very big station under the Finsbury Park Station of that company, for purposes of interchange. By the Baker Street and Waterloo there will be an exchange station at Piccadilly Circus. Here a passenger will be able to take a train down to Waterloo Station, and by the Brompton and Piccadilly Circus Railway he can get from Sloane Street to Waterloo Station in ten minutes. He can get up to the Great Central Station, Marylebone Road, for exchange also. South from Waterloo to the "Elephant and Castle" this tube will be in immediate proximity with the City and South London, going to the Oval and other places in South London.

This comprehensive scheme, extending as it does far to the east and west, with four branches south of the River Thames, terminating respectively at New Cross, "Elephant and Castle," Wimbledon, and Richmond, and three branches spreading out as far north as Finsbury Park, "Archway Tavern," and Golder's Green, covers about sixty miles of route, exclusive of the Metropolitan Railway, over which it has running powers. The total capital represented by the existing railways is £12,500,000, while the various tubular branches and the cost of electrically equipping the District will amount to £17,000,000, a total of about £30,000,000. This total is made up, roughly speaking, in the following manner: Cost of Chelsea Power House, £1,250,000; Brompton and Piccadilly Circus Railway Company, £3,233,000; Baker Street and Waterloo Railway, £3,260,000;

Great Northern and Strand, £3,200,000; Charing Cross, Euston, and Hampstead Railway, £5,768,000; making a total required capital of £16,611,000. It is not improbable that, with the proposed minor extensions yet to be asked for of Parliament, and the increased cost of such work, that the financiers engaged in this undertaking will be called upon to furnish in the neighbourhood of £20,000,000 before all the work planned is equipped and ready for operation. An amount equivalent to one-quarter of this has been furnished jointly by American and English banking firms. This fund of £5,000,000 is to be used as a reserve fund for contingencies. This fund will be used to guarantee 4 per cent. interest to the public. It is the intention of the promoters to secure the whole of the capital for these undertakings from the British and American public. These gentlemen regard their position as a very strong one.

There has been no reliable estimate as to the number of passengers to be carried. The District Railway, on its own lines, at the present time is carrying about forty millions annually, but the change to electric traction should increase this at least to one hundred millions. By its own lines I mean merely the District from Ealing to the City, joining the Metropolitan, including about twenty-six miles of line. The new connections in the north—the Baker Street and Waterloo, and the southern tube tapping the important "Elephant and Castle" traffic centre, will naturally add many millions more. Then, as I have shown, there is the extension to Bow open this year, and the new arrangements with the London, Tilbury, and Southend Railway. The mileage of the system is the District proper, about twenty-six miles—the District including railways leased, in all 39.96, say forty miles of existing line; the Charing Cross, Euston, and Hampstead Railway, eight miles; Brompton and Piccadilly Circus, and Great Northern and Strand, another eight miles; and the Baker Street and Waterloo, five miles; in all, as I have said, about sixty miles. It is a little difficult to give the exact mileage of this system, because it includes such a variety of arrangements. For example, the District owns, I think, about thirteen miles; it jointly owns the City lines; leases and works the Richmond extension, Acton curve, Hounslow and Harrow

sections—in all about fifteen miles more, which, added to the thirteen, makes twenty-eight miles. The company has leased, at a fixed rental, a share in the East London Railway, and it is a joint owner of the Whitechapel and Bow. To these we must add and link up the new tubes, in order to complete the combination, which seems to involve every imaginable shade of railway contract or agreement for operation from joint ownership and consolidation, to that more modern plan of "community of interest." Of course, as Mr. Yerkes has repeatedly remarked, his object in getting together this system was that it might be a good thing for the four tubular railways, three of which, as I have shown, run north and south, to empty their passengers and connect with the District Railway. If these connections can be made, and interchanges of passengers effected for the tube railways to the Underground without too much loss of time, it may ultimately become one harmonious system, profitable to the shareholder, and affording accommodation to the public. Mr. Yerkes is therefore counting on two causes to help in improving this profitless property—the economy and quicker and more comfortable service resulting from electrical equipment, and the reviving influence of these new lines of connection. The weak part in Mr. Yerkes' well-digested scheme—one which he has been so far unable to control—is that it does not include the Metropolitan Company. The original conception of the Inner Circle as a line devoted to general and mutual communication has been greatly impaired, and the public badly served, by reason of the senseless want of harmony that has characterised these two companies in their relation to each other. A glance at the map of the Metropolitan (see page 76) and Metropolitan District (Plate XVII) systems, as they exist at the present moment, shows very clearly that they have been trying to convert, each its own particular section, into a terminus of suburban traffic lines. In the attempt to do this they have practically wrecked both the properties. Mr. Yerkes' ultimate idea must be to bring these properties back to their original moorings, put the whole Inner Circle under one management, worked by electricity, with frequent trains, and interchange stations at the places where they have now confluent junctions. On this point I quote Sir Alexander R.

Binnie, chief engineer of the London County Council :—

I believe that even now the fortunes of those two companies (Metropolitan and Metropolitan District Railways) might be very much retrieved. If the Inner Circle were worked as an electric railway with two-minute trains, and forming those present confluent junctions into interchange stations, a great deal would be done to facilitate

understanding between the two interests, and before the work of electric equipment has been completed there may be a "community of interest" arrangement if closer relations shall prove impracticable. There will naturally be considerable economy in working this system together, comprising as it will the Metropolitan District Railway and its running powers, and the four new tubular

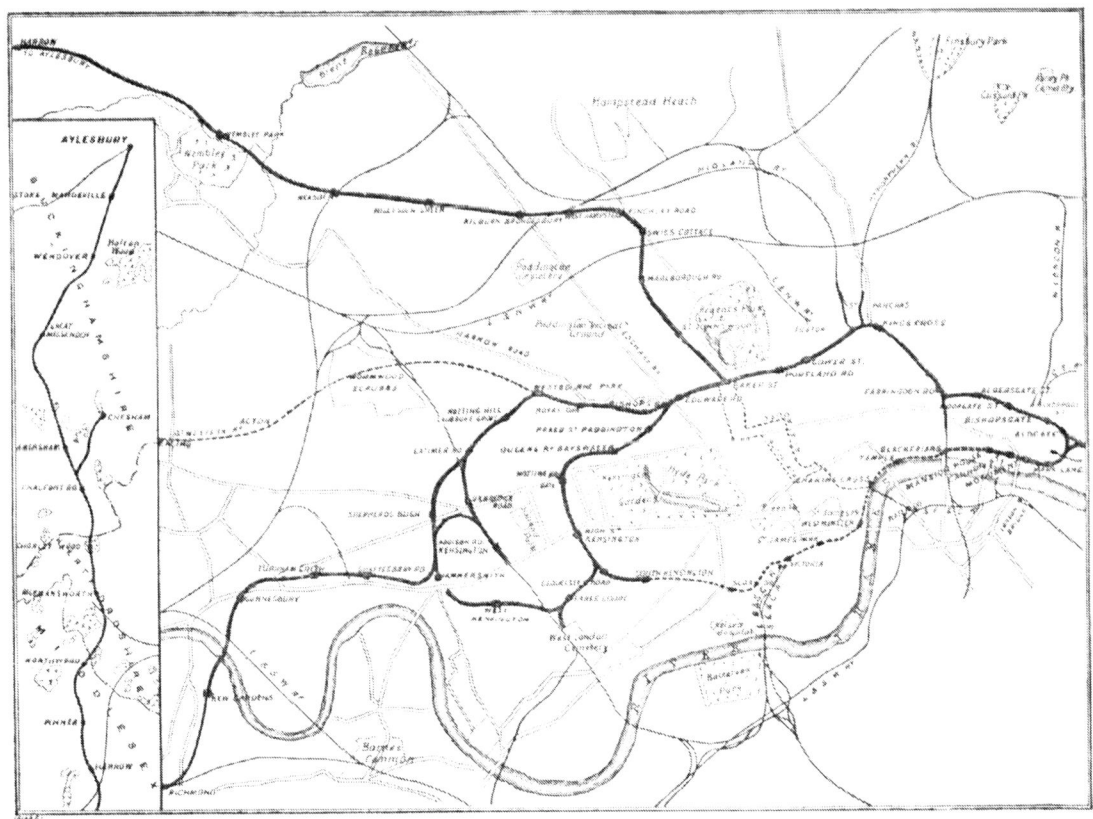

Map of the Metropolitan Railway (see pages 77 and 78)

the traffic in London, and, at the same time, to help the companies a little out of their present troubles.

Mr. Yerkes has got hold of one side of the problem, and has made the Metropolitan Railway an offer for its part of the Inner Circle, which may be in time accepted—an offer which, in my opinion, combined with electrical equipment, would put both properties on a paying basis. Anyhow, there are indications of a better

railways—Brompton and Piccadilly, the Charing Cross, Euston, and Hampstead, the Baker Street and Waterloo, and the Great Northern and Strand. If to this could be added the Metropolitan Railway and its running powers, with a great central power distributing station, still further reduction in cost of running could be effected. The larger the "load factor" in electrical plants the cheaper the power. The power and the generating station, or power house, for this combination will be the largest in the world. The Central London is about 5,000 horse-power. The Yerkes power house will be about 60,000 horse-power. The authorised lines of the Yerkes scheme will, therefore, when coupled up, make an extensive system. On the deep level of the District Railway—for this railway has the right to construct tubes under its own route—the new company will go to South Kensington, from South Kensington to Piccadilly Circus, on by the Brompton and Piccadilly route. From here they wanted to go to Charing Cross, with a spur and a short branch to Bloomsbury, coupling up as they went along with the Baker Street and Waterloo, the Charing Cross and Euston, and the Great Northern and Strand. That scheme, if it should ultimately pass, would couple north - east London, north-west London, and central London. The coupling up process was thus explained by Mr. Littler, attorney for these interests :—

In the north-west we couple up with the Hampstead and Charing Cross line, the North-East London couples up at the Mansion House and Charing Cross, by which we get two routes to north-east London. Then, coupling up everything on the Hampstead and Charing Cross line, coupling up everything on the Baker Street line, and going on, as I say, to the extreme west, and there effecting junctions again, and effecting junctions at Victoria with the London, Brighton, and South Coast ; at Charing Cross with the South-Eastern ; at Ludgate Hill, quite conveniently near to the Chatham and Dover ; at Cannon Street with the South-Eastern ; then, at Bishopsgate, an interchange station, by subway, with the Great Eastern ; then, going on to the Great Eastern at Bishopsgate ; it is only just across the road to the North London ; and then, in the other direction, we communicate with the Great Northern, the Midland, the London and North-Western, the Great Central, and the Great Western ; so that, in point of fact, it couples up the whole of the railways which run north and south of the Thames.

The Morgan and Yerkes schemes, taken together, with the various linking ·up of existing railways, make a fairly harmonious beginning in these tubular railways for London, and one which would be difficult to improve upon unless it were possible to begin, as I have said, with a clean white sheet of paper, and plan an entire new system.

XVI.—Metropolitan Railway System

An excellent map (see page 76) from which one may learn the extent and connections of the Metropolitan Railway, accompanies this article. This company is also very sensitive in relation to the facilities from Hammersmith, and also from Kensington, Addison Road, and all adjoining districts to Farringdon Street, the City, Liverpool Street, and to Aldgate, and, now that the Whitechapel and Bow is open, right away on to Tilbury and Southend. Like the District, it is opposed to another route from Hammersmith to the City. The Metropolitan claims to have lost considerable traffic through the London Central Railway, but will try and gain it again when the schedule for working by electricity is in operation. It is hoped then to make the schedule time slightly lower than the Central, especially when the delay occasioned by the lifts is taken into consideration. The Metropolitan has been especially liberal to working men, carrying them from South Kensington to the City for 2d. return journey. The Metropolitan does not come forward with any new schemes for extensions, nor is it exploiting any of the new tubes. Its management, however, has earnestly set about the work of improving and strengthening the existing property, and the capable manager, Mr. A. E. Ellis, is hopeful the work will be completed by the end of 1903. Contracts were let early this year to the British Westinghouse Company for the supply of the complete installation of the power house at Neasden. They have undoubtedly profited by the experience, and, possibly, the mistakes of others, and it is believed the system will be a very perfect one. The best possible form of carriage has been adopted, and the accommodation will be excellent in every respect. Two, instead of three, classes will, it is thought, be sufficient. When all this is finished, the managers look forward to renewed prosperity for the Metropolitan. The opinion of the chairman of the Metropolitan — Mr. J. J. Mellor—in relation to some of the London locomotion schemes previously described, may be gathered from the following remarks :—

No doubt they had read with more or less interest the reports which had appeared in the Press of the struggle going on between the two groups of tube railways. Two American magnates were fighting for supremacy on English ground. In their anxiety to secure the necessary Parliamentary sanction for their rival schemes, the promoters were making reckless promises as to the rate at which they were prepared to carry passengers. In some instances that rate was as low as a penny for eight miles. He could only say that if Parliament sanctioned such schemes, and if such railways were made—bearing in mind the enormous initial expense of these undertakings, with their elaborate and costly system of lifts— he would be sorry for the people who invested their money in them. They would not be all "Central Londons," with a route presenting exceptional advantages. Meanwhile, the Board were watching these schemes with the greatest vigilance, and if the Metropolitan Company's interests were threatened, the utmost would be done to protect them. He wished to repeat that the directors of this company would be no parties to any financial engagements in connection with those multitudinous tube schemes, the financial results of which became every day more and more doubtful as they learned the ruinous terms on which some of them, at least, were proposed to be worked. They still had confidence in the Metropolitan Railway. They believed that bedrock had been touched in the traffic decreases. Indeed, increases had already set in, and when the locomotive was banished from their underground system it was only reasonable to expect that these increases would receive a great impetus. No one could say that the state of the company's tunnels during the recent hot weather was altogether agreeable, but had the line been "electrified" those tunnels would have been the coolest and pleasantest thoroughfares in London. It was, therefore, only reasonable to expect an increase in the popularity of the company's routes, and a consequent development of traffic, the extent of which only the future could reveal.

It is evident the Metropolitan will do its utmost to oppose all tubular railways. Yet, as a matter of fact, every north and south tube railway will add to its traffic, and bring additional money to its treasury.

XVII.—The North London Railway

In referring to the North London Railway, which closes the account of existing London railways, I cannot do better than borrow a few facts from an instructive article—"IV.—Economics of Railways," by Mr. James Dredge—which recently appeared in TRACTION AND TRANSMISSION. Mr. Dredge contends that this railway is a striking example of the type of rapid transit much favoured by Londoners. Its length is

only twelve miles, but it has so many connections with other lines that it possesses a very large collecting area, focussed at the Broad Street terminus. In the year 1900 it carried 38,882,728 passengers, exclusive of season ticket holders, and nearly all of these favoured the lower rates, as the following figures show:—

First class	...	...	...	...	641,313
Second class	...	...	...	...	3,152,403
Third class	...	...	...	...	34,589,012
			Total	...	... 38,382,728

In addition to these, 89,075 season tickets were issued, which, allowing five hundred journeys per annum for each ticket, would represent 44,537,500 more passengers. This puts up the North London passenger traffic to over 82,750,000 per annum, indicating the immense carrying capacity of twelve miles of line if only located within the county of London. This railway seems to be fairly prosperous, and we hear nothing of a change from steam to electricity. The electrification of some of its important connections, however, may make it necessary. It is, as Mr. Dredge points out, an important factor in London locomotion.

XVIII.—County Council Tramways
(Plate XVIII)

The tramways of London are so closely bound up with the work of the London County Council that the story is best told by a study of what that body has accomplished, and is intending to do, in this branch of London locomotion.

While there undoubtedly exists in the minds of many, a serious question as to the wisdom of the London County Council operating either omnibuses, tramways, or tubular railways, the ability and energy that body has devoted, during the last ten years, to the London locomotion problem, deserves nothing but unqualified praise. It has put to work some of the ablest engineers on the subject, has carefully examined every proposed scheme, and, in the main, the influence of the Council has been exerted in harmonising and systematising the spasmodic efforts of private enterprise, which, under conditions existing in England, naturally sought the locations where traffic was densest, and quick returns most easily

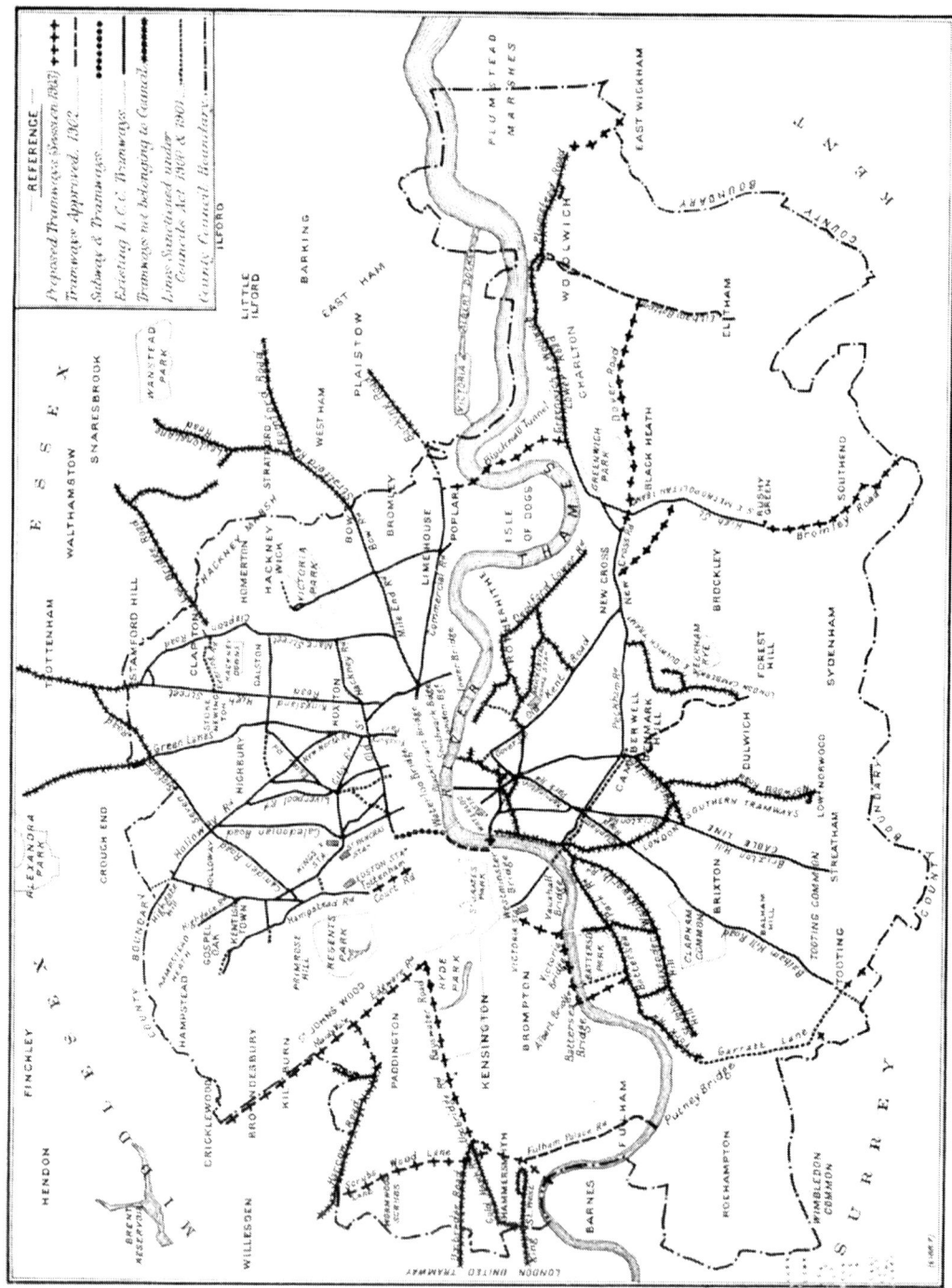

Map of the London County Council Tramways

obtained. In very much of this work, though perhaps not in all, the County Council has fulfilled the functions of a legislature thoroughly imbued with the highest form of Municipal enterprise. As to whether the results of its labours in this direction would have been more beneficial to the community had it kept within these functions, and not descended into the area of competition as a promoter of profit-making enterprises, there naturally exist wide differences of opinion, a discussion of which would be entirely out of place here. With regard to the London County Council's policy in tramways, the present majority of that body contends that the main policy of the Council has been to provide cheaper and better facilities of transit. At first it kept up the profit-making on the same lines as the company, and, its advocates claim, did exceedingly well, and justified its position as manager of a tramway undertaking. Its first year's working, it is said, will bear very favourable comparison with the last year of the company in South London. The work of the London County Council will be treated as impartially as I have endeavoured to treat the labours of all other bodies—public or private—that have had to do with solving the problem. In the scientific and statistical reports, including several valuable inquiries made abroad by members and engineers of the County Council, may be found useful information that throws light on almost all phases of London locomotion. In the same way we find, in the testimony before Parliamentary committees on this and on all kindred subjects, such as displacement of population, density of population, centres of greatest traffic, workmen's trains, the housing of the working classes, experts of the County Council, like Sir Alexander Binnie, Mr. Edgar Harper, the able statistician, and many others, taking a front rank in supplying information, and elucidating the difficult questions with which the problem abounds.

Eight or ten years ago the London County Council recognised the importance of this work, and the first comprehensive attempt to bring together the facts was made by that body in a return issued in 1895. This return formed Part 1 of a series of the reports, and embraced tramways, workmen's tramways, omnibuses, and steamboats. This inquiry was important to the Council in respect of (a) the means of intercommunica-tion between different parts of London for business and recreative purposes; (b) the housing of the working classes; (c) the carrying out of street improvements to be charged upon the whole county; (d) the provision of cheap and satisfactory means of transit of food and other products from extra London counties to the London market. The subjects undoubtedly have a common ground, but each of them has special features which must be considered apart. These reports have never been completed on the scale as originally planned, but from time to time reports have been made and maps published by the Council that have proved of considerable service in the preparation of this article. For example, their first map, showing the tramway and omnibus routes, formed one of these reports, and, though considerably modified now, was the basis of the preliminary work which will end in giving London a very fair tramway system. The Council has not yet given us all it promised in relation to the local distribution of traffic and the movement of population. There have been several short reports on the relationships of the locomotive service to the residences of the various industrial classes and the chief places to which they have to travel; these, when dove-tailed together, have thrown statistical light on the question with which we are dealing. It is still to be hoped that the Council will undertake a complete and detailed report on this entire subject, and one which will bring all data up to date, with maps showing how far the various systems of tramways, tubes, and light railways are being linked up into a harmonious system of locomotion for the metropolis.

The various investigations conducted by the County Council have resulted in that body taking up, in a practical way, the tramways of London, and if the present policy is adhered to, in a few years the county of London will be the undisputed owner of all tramways within its border. Not only is it the policy to absorb existing tramways, but to operate them, and at the present moment we have the interesting experiment in Municipal trading in South London of a tramway system owned and operated by the county authorities, while in North London a larger system, owned also by the county of London, has been leased to a private concern—the North

Metropolitan Tramways Company — until 1910. Sufficient time has not elapsed to show the result of these two experiments, but the fact of the two methods of dealing with the transit question having an opportunity to work out for a period of ten years side by side, will give students of economic questions an opportunity to study the two plans under like conditions. It may be that at the end of the lease the North Metropolitan Tramway Company will have paid the county such a goodly share of the profits that administrators will be glad to renew the lease for another term of years, and perhaps lease the other tramways also to private companies. On the other hand, the Highways Committee may have shown such ability in the tramway business that the public will favour the operation of all lines within the county of London by the Council.

The proofs of this article were submitted to a well-known economist, who favours Municipal trading, and believes in the wisdom of the County Council. On this point he writes as follows :—

Here you touch upon one of the principles which the County Council has adopted. There has been a little change of policy on this point. As you no doubt know, the first Council had great difficulty in getting the necessary majority of Councillors in the chamber to authorise the taking over of the tramways. The original policy of the Moderate party was to leave the tramways absolutely alone, and not to exercise the option under the Act. A resolution was, therefore, passed, in which the Council declared that it would buy the tramways, but not work them—a decision which was very soon reversed; and one of the main objects of Progressive policy is that the Municipality shall not only own, but operate. The amount of profits which the leasing system may give would not lead them to depart from their principle, as the main object is to provide the cheapest possible means of rapid transit. The tramways must, of course, always yield a profit — and a substantial one—but profit-making is not the main element of Municipal operation in London. Mr. Spensly, of the Statistical Department of the London County Council, puts it very well when he says :—' The people who use the tramway system are the people who pay for it, and they should receive any advantage from that use.' That is the reason why the profits from tramways should not go to the relief of rates, as they have partly done up to now; but they should go towards cheapening the service, and building up reserves. The effect in London would be to draw profits from the cheapest class in the community in the poorest districts, and, in spreading

them all over London, also help the West End boroughs and the City, which will not have tramways at all. In other words, the poorest classes of the people would be relieving the wealthy tradesmen and the ground landlords of the West End.

These two systems may be left to work out their own salvation in their respective ways, and I will pass on to a consideration of existing tramway connections as applied to all London, and the various proposals of the Council for the coupling up and completing the system. To whatever cause it may be attributed, the growth of the tramway in London proper has not, during the last ten years, been what it should have been. I have shown in this article that two large systems of tramways, under capable company management, are developing in North and West London outside the county jurisdiction. One of the most serious difficulties the Council has had, and will have, to overcome in completing its tramway system, is the fact that it, like all local authorities, can go so far and no further. Beyond the boundary of the county of London it meets with other ambitious Boards and other local authorities alike jealous of their rights and privileges, and with whom it will be found more difficult to deal in matters of this sort than with private companies. In such cases it may be found advisable for both sets of local authorities — as is the case both in North and West London — to lease to private companies, thus ensuring uniform fares, through bookings, and harmonious service. It is a situation, in short, where " community of interest " may be so strongly impressed upon both sides that the lion of Municipal trading may be willing to lie down side by side with the lamb of company enterprise, so that both may be preserved.

Again my friends representing the County Council object, and their objections may be best stated in the language of one of the ablest of their spokesmen :—

The dominant party in the London County Council, who are responsible for its policy, would not admit the justice of your comparison. They would point to the cheapened fares, to the provision of uniforms for the conductors, etc., the neater appearance of the vehicles, as well as to the increase of wages, the shortening of hours, etc. They have also sacrificed a considerable revenue from advertisements, which I think is quite right. The business of tramways is to carry people, and not to act as movable advertisement hoardings. All these concessions and improvements should be put to the credit of the Council. Moreover, as regards enterprise, the County Council has deserved more credit than the North Metropolitan Tramway Company. Until the Council was established there were no all-night services. When the Council announced its decision to run the night services, the North Metropolitan began. These cars probably serve a small number of people, but they are exceedingly useful. I do not know whether they have been profitable. Then the Council put on an excellent service of halfpenny 'buses. The Council's halfpenny 'bus was certainly the best vehicle of the kind ever seen in London. It was more roomy, neater, and cleaner than the old 'buses. The conductors were in neat uniforms and were polite. They were not the unwashed, unkempt, and badly clothed conductors we usually find on London omnibuses. As you know, the House of Lords stopped the Council running 'buses, and the public has suffered.

It is also set forth by the County Council's friends that I am "not quite correct" in the statement that Municipalities can go so far and no further, and that local authorities are jealous of their rights and privileges.

Although (says my critic) the London County Council is not likely to get power to go beyond its boundaries, you are no doubt aware that the Manchester Corporation, Glasgow, and many other cities, work tramways a long way beyond their own borders, for which, of course, they require a special enactment. The county authorities outside London are far from being jealous of their rights and privileges in the same sense as the London County Council is. The Middlesex Council, for instance, which is the chief one concerned, is a somewhat moribund body. There is extremely little interest in its elections; it is being cut into by District Councils becoming Municipal Corporations; it has less to do than any other county in the country; no Municipal trading works, and, unlike all other counties outside London, has not control of the police. The Middlesex County Council is therefore a rather apathetic body, and one of its chief characteristics is a strong dislike to the London County Council.

I am in no way prepared to endorse this view of the Middlesex Council. The fact that it has no Municipal trading works would rather commend it than otherwise, but it is interesting in a study of this sort to take into consideration various views. Only by so doing can one arrive at approximately accurate conclusions.

From the only available statistics, I am

able to construct the following table, showing the growth of tramways in London over a period of ten years :—

Tramways.	1890.	1899.
Length of lines open (miles) ...	132	141
Number of passengers conveyed...	196,914,890	294,002,749
Total capital expended	£3,787,543	£4,074,736
Total receipts	£1,048,124	£1,376,148
Total expenditure	£843,870	£1,086,386
Profits	£204,254	£197,158

Whatever may be the causes, the business side of the above budget is not entirely satisfactory. There has been an increase of 50 per cent. in traffic, and of about 88 per cent. in receipts, while the increase of expenses has been sufficient to absorb profits, which are not only less in 1899, relatively to the investment and passengers conveyed, but actually less in amount by about £7,000 than in 1890. It is not worth while to linger on the above figures, for they are probably only approximately correct, and have been introduced more for the purpose of showing the tendency and condition of the tramway business when the County Council took it actively in hand—that is, when the County Council began its work of absorption.

Under the Tramways Act, 1870, the County Council is empowered to purchase, either compulsorily, under Sect. 43, at the expiration of twenty-one years from the passing of the Authorising Act, or by agreement, under Sect. 44, any tramways undertaking within the county of London. Under this Act the Council's northern tramways were purchased by the Council and were leased to the North Metropolitan Tramways Company until Midsummer, 1910. Under the same Act the whole of the London Tramways Company's undertaking, comprising about twenty-five miles of line, all (except one short length in Vauxhall Bridge Road) of which are located south of the Thames, was acquired by agreement. Some of these lines became purchasable in 1898. In the annual report of the proceedings of the Council for the year ended March 31st, 1901, I find the following reference to this transaction :—

The London Tramway Company's undertaking was transferred to the Council on January 1st,

1899; and the Council having decided itself to work the lines, the whole of the employees of the company, including the clerical staff, were, with a very few exceptions, taken into the Council's service. At that time certain financial matters in connection with the purchase remained outstanding between the Council and the company. On October 12th, 1899, however, the final payments were made to the London Tramways Company, and the conveyance to the Council of a company's undertaking and property was completed. The total amount paid by the Council to the company by way of purchase money was £876,594 18s. 6d., including the sum of £22,872 under the award of Sir F. J. Bramwell in respect of the two and one-eighth miles of lines and depôts which formed the first portion of the system coming under the operation of the purchase clause. Including incidental expenses, the total cost of purchase was £882,043 1s. 8d. The Council has since expended £14,101 14s. 1d. on capital account of additional horses, rolling stock, etc., and the total capital outlay in respect of the undertaking up to March 31st, 1902, was therefore £896,144 15s. 9d.

The traffic receipts of the year 1900-1 amounted to £438,941, as compared with £439,230 in the previous financial year. The balance of profit from the working of the tramways, after payment of capital charges, interest on loan, and all other outgoings, during the year 1901, was about £14,000. The total receipts from the undertaking last year (March 31st, 1902), amounted to £462,133 5s., while the working expenses were £409,623 3s. 1d., showing a profit on working of £52,510 1s. 11d. Out of this, however, had to come interest and sinking fund, and the balance left was only £9,062 0s. 1d. The number of passengers carried during the year (1902) on the Council's southern system of tramways was 119,880,559; the average per passenger was .88d.

The accounts in connection with the Council's northern tramways system for the year ended March 31st, 1902, are of equal interest. The total capital expenditure in respect of the undertaking is £848,884 16s. 1d. The receipts for the year 1901-2 from the North Metropolitan Tramways Company, the Council's lessee, by way of rent of the lines, depôts, buildings, etc., have amounted to £55,788 15s. 2d.; the percentage on excess of the gross receipts of the company over those of 1895 amounts to £18,697 11s. 4d., and percentage on extensions to £2,354 19s. 6d., so that the total rents received from the company were £76,841 6s. 8d; while rents amounting to £284 4s. 9d. were received from tenants of properties belonging to the Council in Parkhurst Road. Thus the total receipts from all sources in respect of the undertaking have amounted to

£77,125 10s. 9d. The charge for interest on debt (less income tax) was £22,486 3s. 1d., and for sinking fund £14,905 7s. 5d., while ground rent, insurance, repairs to premises, and other incidentals have amounted to £577 14s. 6d., making the total expenditure £37,969 5s. The balance of receipts over expenditure is, therefore, £89,156 5s. 9d.

Speaking roundly, we have here two investments, one (the southern system) representing a capital investment of about £900,000, operated by the Council, on which the net returns this year were about £9,000, and the other (the northern system) leased to a company representing a capital investment of about £850,000, on which the net return to the Council exceeded £89,000. It should be stated, however, that the Council has reduced the hours of labour of its employés, and somewhat increased the wages, and incurred other expenditures which they put forward as an offset for the reduction of profits. The result of the working of these two undertakings may decide the future policy of the County Council. If the county of London can continue to secure the same service and more profits out of the leased lines than out of the operated lines it will hardly be worth while to conduct an enterprise that requires so much experience and such an infinitude of detail to carry out successfully.

Here, again, I am asked by my County Council friends to state some of the difficulties that body has encountered in the course of of its tramway legislation, and most willingly I comply. It is impossible to do better than state what these obstacles are in the words of one of the experts, who has been kind enough to look over the proofs of this article. He says:—

In this part of these articles, you have not dealt with the great delay of the Council in electrifying its lines and extending its system. I hope you appreciate the peculiar position in which the Council is placed. It is the tramway authority, without being the street authority. There are, therefore, endless difficulties with the local authorities who are the street authorities. Long disputes over street widenings have arisen, as to the proportion to be paid by the Council and the Borough Councils. Some of the authorities have been absolutely hostile to tramways, as you know; and then the Council has met with great opposition in Parliament. I think its Bill for getting the tramways over Westminster Bridge — that is, making a connection between the north and south of the river — has been defeated four times. I am sure that you appreciate these difficulties; still, at the same time, I have always held that the Council delayed far too long over its scheme for electric traction, because I feel that if it had been pushed on faster, and only got a five-mile track laid, the success of the electric cars would have been so great, and the object-lesson so convincing, that the effect would have almost destroyed the future opposition. Then the Council deserves credit for getting rid of the overhead trolley system in London.

There is so much of truth in all this that, in fairness to the County Council, I am pleased to fully set forth their views of the situation. The obstacles, however, which this body has encountered have equally to be met and overcome by private companies, because the English laws relating to tramways and street locomotives have seriously retarded all undertakings of the kind.

XIX.—SUMMARY OF COUNCIL'S UNDERTAKINGS

Meantime the Council is going ahead with the purchase of tramways as fast as the several lines still owned and operated by private companies fall under the Act of 1870. Not only this, but new powers have been sought and obtained from Parliament by the Council for the purpose of connecting its various lines, and extending the system. I have divided these several classes of operation into six classifications, as follows:—

Miles.

Section 1.—Tramways owned and worked by the Council 24

N.B.—The whole of this is south of the river, except a short length in Vauxhall Bridge Road.

Section 2.—Tramways owned and leased by the Council 48½

N.B.—The whole of this is north of the river.

Section 3.—Lines still in the hands of companies :—

London, Deptford, and Greenwich ... 6½
Woolwich and South-East London ... 4¾
South London 12½
London Southern 5¾
London, Camberwell, and Dulwich ... 2¾
London United (lines within county only) 4
Harrow Road 2
South-Eastern Metropolitan 2½
Lea Bridge ... ... ½
Highgate Hill ... ... ½
Total ... ... — 42

N.B.—The first four of these systems are about to be taken over by the Council, and the whole of the remainder, except Lea Bridge, will fall in before 1910.

Section 4.—Tramways which Parliament has authorised the London County Council to construct. These are entirely short extensions and connecting links.

Section 5.—Tramways now under consideration by Parliament :—
Hammersmith to Putney 2
Camberwell Green to Dulwich 2½
Woolwich to Eltham... ... ... 2¾
Theobald's Road to Westminster, about ... 1¼

N.B.—The Embankment portion of this scheme has been thrown out by the House of Lords.

Section 6.—Further schemes now under consideration by the Council, and which will be submitted to Parliament, Session 1903.

For the convenience of the reader I append the following summary, which shows the estimated amount of the expenditure on tramway account which will be involved in respect of each proposal:—

Route of Proposed New Tramways.	Approximate Length of Proposed New Tramways.	Estimated Cost of Construction of Tramways, of Paving of Track, and other Works in connection therewith.	Estimated Cost of Cars and Car-sheds.	Estimated Proportion of Cost of Street Widenings to be Charged to the Tramways Account.
	M. F. C.	£	£	£
(1) Hampstead Road Tramways terminus to a point in Tottenham Court Road near Oxford Street..	0 5 9	27,000	..	
(2) Edgware Road to Harrow Road, via Sutherland Avenue	0 5 5	25,000	5,200	
(3) Hammersmith Broadway to and across Hammersmith Bridge	{0 2 4 / 0 1 1 Single}	16,000	..	No street widenings required.
(4) Greenwich to East India Dock Road, via the Blackwall Tunnel..	2 2 0	69,500	13,000	
(5) Westminster Bridge Road to the Victoria Embankment ..	0 2 7	16,500	15,600	
(6) Harlesden to Hammersmith Broadway	2 7 7	121,050	10,400	21,400
(7) Shepherd's Bush Road to a point near the Marble Arch	{2 6 5 / 0 3 3 Single}	113,200	39,000	7,683
(8) Marble Arch to Cricklewood	3 5 6	136,000	45,500	35,333
(9) Deptford to Herbert Hospital, Woolwich	3 3 5	133,000	20,800	4,500
(10) New Cross to the South-Eastern Metropolitan Tramways, in the Lee High Road	1 3 5	55,000	19,500	8,500
(11) Battersea Park Road to a point near the "Grosvenor Hotel," via Chelsea Embankment, Commercial Road, and Buckingham Palace Road	2 4 9	97,600	20,800	10,867
(12) Tooting Broadway to Tooting Junction Station	0 5 3	24,000	6,500	14,900
(13) Garratt Lane, Wandsworth, to the county boundary, via Wimbledon	0 1 7	7,500	..	1,766
(14) Bushey Green to Bromley Hill, via Bromley Road ..	2 3 5	90,500	13,000	10,050
(15) A point near the terminus of Woolwich and South-East London Tramways to the county boundary, via Wickham Lane ..	1 1 2	39,600	..	12,166
	26 2 6	971,450	209,300	127,165
		£1,307,915		

A glance at the County Council map of the London tramways will not only show the location of existing tramways, but of those authorised and proposed, together with the subway between Theobald's Road and Wellington Street, which will ultimately be extended to the south side of the river and link the northern and southern system together. Both north and south, and outside the county boundary east and west, these tramways are rapidly forming an important network, which, with electric traction, will be decidedly improved. The important proposals for the next session are largely in the western part of the county. No 1, for instance, comes down Tottenham Court Road from Euston Road to Oxford Street; No. 8 from Cricklewood down to Marble Arch, where No. 7 connects, and, turning sharply westward via Bayswater Road, High Street Notting Hill, Holland Park Avenue, Richmond Road, Westwick Gardens, to Shepherd's Bush, where it connects with the United Electric Tramways system, already described; No. 6 runs from Harlesden (near the county boundary) via Scrubs Lane, Wood Lane, Shepherd's Bush Road, and Brook Green Road to Hammersmith Broadway. Nos. 2 and 8 are also in the west, the first linking up the proposed Edgware Road tramway, via Sutherland Avenue, with the Harrow Road tramway terminus, and the second coupling Hammersmith Broadway, via Bridge Road, to and across Hammersmith Bridge. Until these branches were proposed, including also No. 11, from Battersea over the bridge, along the Chelsea Embankment, and Chelsea Bridge, and Commercial Road, the entire county west of Hampstead Road north of the river was without tramways. It will be interesting, therefore, to see what Parliament will do with these proposals of the County Council to push its tramways to the western boundaries, where it will meet Mr. Clifton Robinson and his eighty or ninety miles of line authorised, under construction, or already open to traffic.

From West London let us glance eastward, and we find Nos. 4, 9, 10, 14, and 15 are important links for the East End. No. 4 runs from Trafalgar Road, Greenwich (London County Council Tramways), via Blackwall Lane and Blackwall Tunnel to the Council's (northern) tramways in East India Dock Road; No. 9 from Deptford (London County Council Tramways), via Blackheath Road and Hill, and Shooter's Hill Road to Herbert Hospital, Woolwich; No. 10 from New Cross Road (London County Council Tramways), via Lewisham High Road and Laom Pitt Hill and Vale, to the South-Eastern Metropolitan Tramways (London County Council lines); No. 14 to Bushey Green (London County Council, late South-Eastern Metropolitan Tramways terminus), via Bromley Road, to the county boundary near Bromley Hill; and No. 15 from High Street, Plumstead (near terminus of Woolwich and South-East London Tramway Company's line), via Wickham Lane, to the county boundary.

These will all undoubtedly meet the approval of Parliament, but to what extent the tramway is to encroach upon the West End of London is more a matter of speculation. The House of Lords threw out the Victoria Embankment proposal for a tramway, and that, as I have shown, has been met by the County Council with a proposal further west for one along the Chelsea Embankment; while No. 5, as will be seen by reference to the map, is a proposal for a tramway from Westminster Bridge Road, across Westminster Bridge, to the Victoria Embankment. These must ultimately be allowed, or the value of the County Council subway (which must also extend from the Strand to the Embankment, under Wellington Street, coming out on the Embankment level) will be impaired. Around this locality, and possibly on the Chelsea Embankment, will be fought the next battle between Parliament and the London County Council. A tramway along Hyde Park to Shepherd's Bush may also meet with opposition. Nevertheless, from a utilitarian point of view, they are greatly needed, and will do no harm.

In assembling all these tramways, the County Council is undoubtedly acting wisely, for, with proper connections, they will certainly be made to pay. The outlay, however, will be considerable before the several routes are properly linked together and equipped, as they must be, with electrical traction. The purchases already made, those in course of negotiation, and the improvements authorised, and for which power will be sought next session, amount to a total of nearly eight million pounds sterling, and in the course of time the Council will own the entire tramway system of London. The

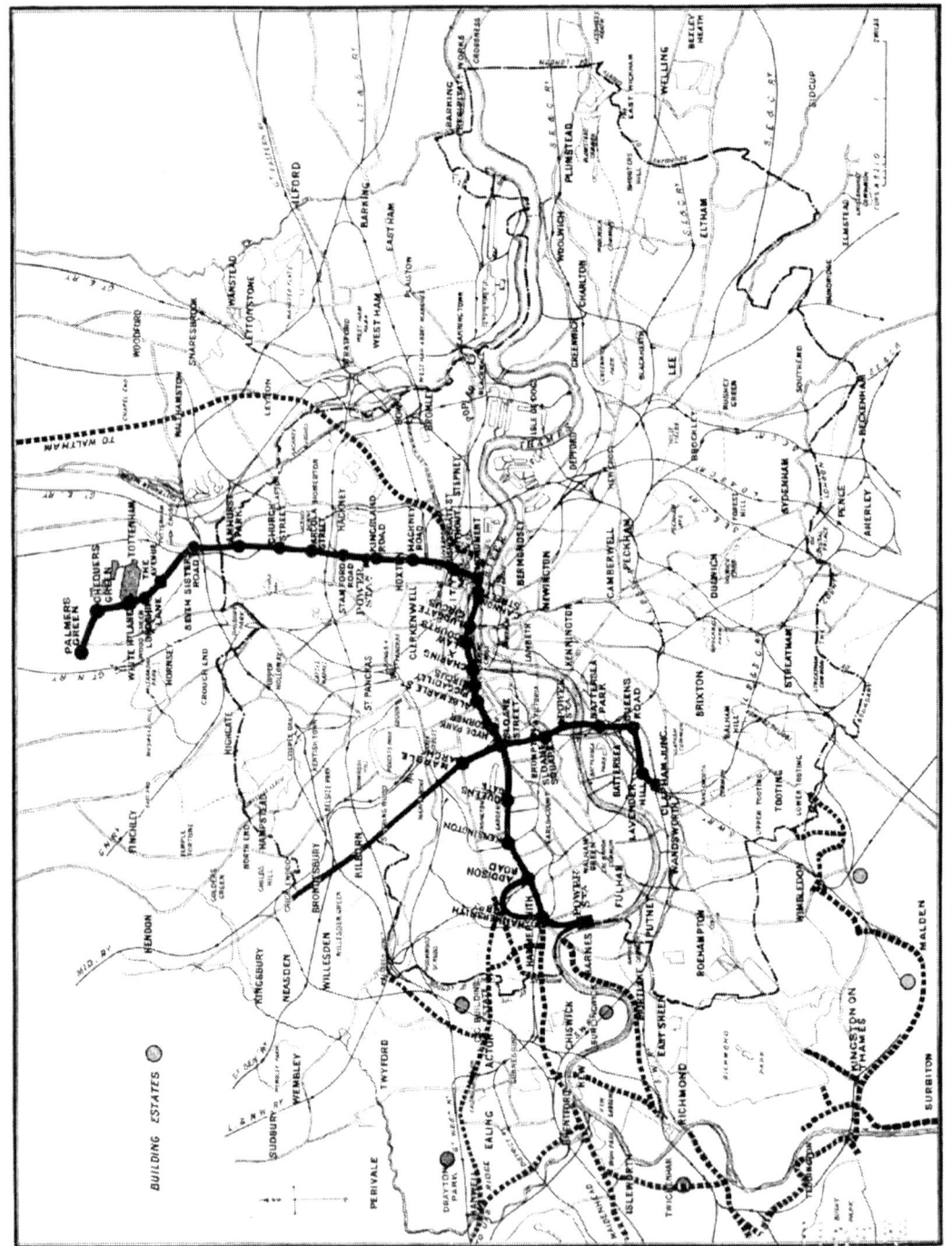

Map of the London United Tramways (Showing Lines of the London Suburban Railway)

BUILDING ESTATES

Finance Committee, which recently considered these undertakings from a financial point of view, recommended that, as a whole, they might be accepted ; that, with the exception of the line from Hammersmith Broadway to Harlesden, " there will be no serious deficit ; to that extent the objection to them on financial grounds is diminished, and some of them seem to promise very satisfactory financial results."

At the same time, the committee utters the following note of warning :—

We may point out to the Council that the proposals already approved or now before the Council in regard to the conversion to electric traction of the tramways on the south side of the river, including extensions and smaller undertakings about to be purchased, and the necessary generating station, involve an aggregate expenditure of about £5,500,000. The present tramways debt amounts to £1,750,000. In addition to this, there will be the expenditure on the proposed generating station at Pimlico, and for the conversion of the northern system and extension on that side of the river. While we are satisfied, on estimates which have been before us, that the large capital outlay involved in the development of tramways in London will be ultimately remunerative, we think it well to prepare the Council for the possibility that while these large works are in process of execution the tramways undertaking may occasion a charge on the rates. A great deal will depend, of course, upon the manner in which the various operations are carried out and the period during which expenditure remains unproductive. We believe that the Highways Committee are alive to this point, and are shaping their proposals accordingly.

Let us hope the committee recognise this danger, and that the administration of these important undertakings will be wise. It is further to be hoped that the Council's attitude towards private companies ready to invest millions of pounds in other forms of transportation, such as tube railways, will not be that of a competitor scrambling for part of the profits, but rather that of a public-spirited legislature, anxious to give the community better and cheaper transportation. There is room enough for all in this stupendous field if only good judgment is used in carrying out the several schemes, and capable management accorded them after they shall be open for traffic.

XX.—LONDON UNITED TRAMWAYS
(Plate XIX)

A map is given of the extensive tramway systems which are spreading wherever towns are growing and population settling in the north and west suburbs of London. Special mention of these tramways has been made in connection with the London Suburban Railway scheme, because one of the strongest features of this tube is the fact that it taps both these systems of tramways. Whatever may or may not be done about locomotion within the administrative area of London, and whether the County Council decides to take over the operation of all the tramways or not, these two systems must remain an important factor in London transportation. Extending, as they do, into areas outside of the county of London, and dealing, as they do, with other local authorities — many of them unwilling to come under the authority of the London County Council—contracts have been brought about which will practically keep these systems intact for twenty-five years, and, in some cases, for a longer period. If, therefore, good business judgment continues to be shown in handling these properties — and both enterprises are just now in most capable hands — we may reasonably expect two of the largest tramway systems in the world, probably each carrying in the neighbourhood of five hundred million passengers annually. It may be advisable to examine the reason for this belief. First take the London United Tramways, Ltd., and we find the following mileage :—

	Miles.	Fur.
Authorised lines	40	0
Extension, session of 1901	14	7
Proposed extension	21	6
Proposed extension — Hammersmith Bridge, Barnes, Mortlake, Richmond ...	3	5
Total route length ...	80	2

The authorised line extends from Shepherd's Bush, where it connects with the Central London Electric Railway, and goes straight away along the Uxbridge Road, north-west to Uxbridge. At or near Acton, a north branch has been planned to Willesden, where it couples up with the London and North-Western junction. At Hammersmith another main line, running in a slightly south-westerly direction, will penetrate Chiswick, Kew, Isleworth, Cranford, and so on right through to Maidenhead. These two main arteries will be connected by a north and south line between Hanwell and Kew. At Hammersmith two lines cross each other like the letter X, and at these points the Uxbridge main line passengers may be carried over to the Hammersmith Station of the London Suburban Railway and taken to the City *via* Piccadilly and Charing Cross. Maidenhead line passengers may be carried over to Central London Station at Shepherd's Bush and taken to the City *via* the Marble Arch and Oxford Circus. From what I have termed the Maidenhead main line there are to be several important branches, including two forks—one extending to Hounslow, the other south-west to Hanworth and thence beyond to Kempton Park. From Hanworth these tramways begin to run eastward again to Twickenham, and thence to the little gaps at Richmond, Kew, and Barnes, where the river must be crossed, back to the main Maidenhead line, joining it at Kew and forming connections on the Barnes side with the London United Railway at Hammersmith Broadway.

Following the Hanworth line, with its V-shaped connections at Kew and Hammersmith, we again branch off, just below Twickenham, almost due south, skirting Hampton Park and following the river around by Thames Ditton and Surbiton to Kingston, where these tramways will pass through Malden, and then back north-east to Wimbledon, and end at Upper Tooting. From this point it would seem that a connection, either by surface or tube, may be easily made through Wandsworth with the Clapham Junction Station of the London Suburban Railway. This connection will give quicker and easier access to the City for all the south-western territory covered by the London United Tramways. This masterly planned system of tramways, on its present sixteen miles of operated route, carries 40,000,000 passengers annually. The estimate is 300,000,000 when the entire system has been completed—an estimate, in my opinion, far below the realisation when a quick, cheap, and up-to-date electric traction railway has been installed. A glance at the map of London and its environs shows that these eighty miles of tramway run through some of the most picturesque and healthy districts around London, and, while here may be

found delightful residential towns for well-to-do people, there is also a vast area which may be easily converted into building sites intended to relieve the densely populated working-class districts of the Metropolis. Under existing circumstances, no better means could be planned than this network of tramways for the relief of the congested districts and for the encouragement of long distance travelling at cheap fares. It is in line with the best work of this kind in Continental Europe and the United States, while the myriad obstacles which the promoters have been compelled to overcome have been multiplied by the numerous towns and villages, and Municipalities, and local divisions, through which they have passed. It has, indeed, been a task for individual effort and the highest order of enterprise, for it is well known that the Acts which hedge around tramway and light railway enterprise in England are many and arbitrary, and tend to discourage rather than encourage the construction of the more comprehensive systems of transportation. In this surface traction, where travelling is made attractive by well-built cars, a large traffic is created, which, in such districts as the London United Electric Tramways run through, is bound to increase, not only relatively to the mileage, but at a far greater ratio. On the other hand, the tubular and steam railways merely draw the legitimate traffic; that is, passengers who must go to and from their business, or who want to go from one place to another on business. No one takes a tube ride—after the first novelty is over—for pleasure, and few people, for a similar purpose, commit themselves to the very grimy and close carriages of a steam railway. The electric tramway, when the country through which it passes is beautiful and historic, and the fares within the reach of the plain people, cannot be judged by the ordinary standard applied to passenger traffic. The possibilities, therefore, of this system will in all probability be, when completed, nearer 500,000,000 than 300,000,000. It has been admirably planned by such experienced men as J. Clifton Robinson and George White, who combine a knowledge of the tramway business, as we understand it in the United States, with an intimate understanding of the peculiarities of the British travelling public.

Map of the North London Tramways

XXI.—North London Tramways
(Plate XX)

Turning from the southern end of the county of Middlesex, from Surrey, Buckinghamshire, and Berks, let us glance at the situation in North Middlesex, Hertford, and Essex, and see what is going on there in this important business of carrying the ever-restless population of London. Here we come into the territory of the North Metropolitan Electric Tramways Company and their co-labourers the British Electric Traction Company—the largest and strongest electric tramway company in England, and one of the most important industries of this kind in the world. Before taking up in detail the lines of the great north-eastern tramway systems of London attention is directed to the map of this system showing the sweeping connection made by the proposed London Suburban Railway. The scale of this map lends itself to a comprehensive showing of the six great central points at which the passengers from the districts covered by the North Metropolitan Tramway Company may enter London. Dipping into the tube at Tottenham they may come direct to the City or alight at any station along the Strand and Piccadilly between the City and Hyde Park Corner, and from there go north to the Marble Arch, west to Hammersmith, and connect with the London United Electric Tramways; or they can, at Hyde Park Corner, turn south to Clapham Junction. On this map the London Suburban Railway looks like a great pair of ice tongs, or the letter X with a small top and enlarged lower half. The lines worked by the North Metropolitan Tramway Company greatly exceed those of the London Electric Tramway Company, but as the latter system is built up, the two systems will probably have equal capacity and length of lines. The work of the North Metropolitan has been more like the work of Mr. Yerkes, and that system, when once crystallised and operated entirely by electricity, will have been assembled from many fragments of railways and secured by a variety of arrangements. To better appreciate this we may ascertain of what it now consists. Here is a list of its several component parts :—

NORTH METROPOLITAN TRAMWAY SYSTEM

Name of Tramways.	Miles.
(a) Tramways in the county of London leased to the North Metropolitan Tramway Company by the London County Council	48¼
(b) Tramways in the county of Middlesex *owned* by the North Metropolitan Tramway Company, purchasable by the local authorities under the Tramways Act of 1870 in 1925	7½

The above two sections are now worked by horse traction. The tramways under section (b) will shortly be purchased and worked on the overhead system under powers obtained this session.

(c) Light railways in the county of Middlesex fully authorised, but not yet constructed, to be leased to the company by the Middlesex County Council when the construction is completed	15½
(d) Light railways in the county of Middlesex sanctioned by the Light Railway Commissioners, but not yet confirmed by the Board of Trade, when constructed to be leased by the Middlesex County Council to the company	18
(e) Light railways in the county of Middlesex applied for in May of this year by the Middlesex County Council, which, when constructed, will be leased as the light railways (c) and (d)	16¼
(f) Light railways in the county of Hertford, passed by the Light Railway Commissioners, but not yet sanctioned by the Board of Trade, to be leased by the Hertfordshire County Council to the company when constructed ...	9¼
(g) Tramways in the urban district of Watford, authorised, but not yet constructed, over which the company will have running powers	2
(h) Light railways in the urban district of Walthamstow, sanctioned by the Light Railway Commissioners, but not yet confirmed by the Board of Trade, over which, when constructed, the company will have running powers	3
Total owned, operated, and authorised ...	120

Here, then, we have a total route mileage as now proposed of about 120 miles, fifty-six miles of which are being worked. The system, as planned, will comprise both tramways and light railways, so-called and constructed, I suppose, because of the advantages of organising under the Light Railway Act, but all will ultimately be operated by electric traction. The operating lines of this company now carry annually 165,000,000 passengers, a number which will be easily doubled when the entire system is completed and electric equipment substituted for horse power. The field of operation of the North Metropolitan Tramway Company may be seen from a map especially prepared (Plate XX). On this map the leased lines of the London County Council are shown separate. The map shows an intricate network of trams in the Metropolis, serving centres of dense population, such as St. Pancras, Islington, Finsbury, Shoreditch, Hackney, Bethnal Green, Whitechapel, Stepney, and Tower Hamlets. The County Council lease expires eight years hence. There are also two small systems in Middlesex (purchasable 1925), and Essex (already under notice of purchase), serving in the one case, roughly speaking, Hornsey, Tottenham, and Edmonton, and in the other, Stratford, and East and West Ham. But there has been devised a plan for a large system of electric tramways or light railways, lying to the north and west of the Middlesex Tramways, embracing lines already authorised or for which applications for authorisation are pending. These light railways are owned by the counties of Middlesex and Hertfordshire respectively, and extend from various points of the boundary of the county of London Willesden, Edgware, Hendon, Stanmore, to Bushey, Watford, Hornsey, Finchley, Barnet, Wood Green, Southgate, Enfield, Tottenham, Edmonton, Waltham Cross, and Cheshunt; they are to be worked by the overhead trolley system, so that when completed they will form a network of electric railways in direct connection with the tramways owned by the county of London. The County Council has a plan by which it will, through a subway (partly authorised this session of Parliament), connect its northern tramways, operated by the North Metro-

politan, with the County Council southern systems of tramways (about twenty-five miles, running through the most densely populated district of South London), operated by the County Council, and there will be formed an interchange between the two sides of the river. It will enable the workers in the great Westminster, Kennington, Walworth, Newington, and Camberwell districts to have full access north-east, far beyond the administrative limits of London. The North London tramways will, when completed, stretch beyond Watford on the west, and to the border of Epping Forest, Woodford, Wanstead, Manor Park, and East and West Ham on the eastern extremity. North they extend *via* Enfield, Waltham Abbey, Cheshunt, and, as light railways, probably to Hoddesdon. It is a well-planned scheme, and has behind it some of the ablest tramway and light railway financiers and managers— among them Mr. James Devonshire, general manager—and the influence of the British Electric Traction Company, comprising Mr. Emile Garcke and his strong group of financiers and able corps of assistants. Such, then, we find the two big tramway and light railway schemes which do now, and will in the future, cut an important figure in London locomotion. The London County Council estimated that in 1901 some 300,000,000 passengers were carried on the tramways inside the administrative county of London. If electric tramways continue to develop along the lines here marked out, and extend into districts beyond the area of Greater London, in ten years, when the systems are coupled up and have interchange stations with the two great London tube railway schemes, these instruments of locomotion will be carrying in the neighbourhood of a thousand million passengers.

(To be continued.)

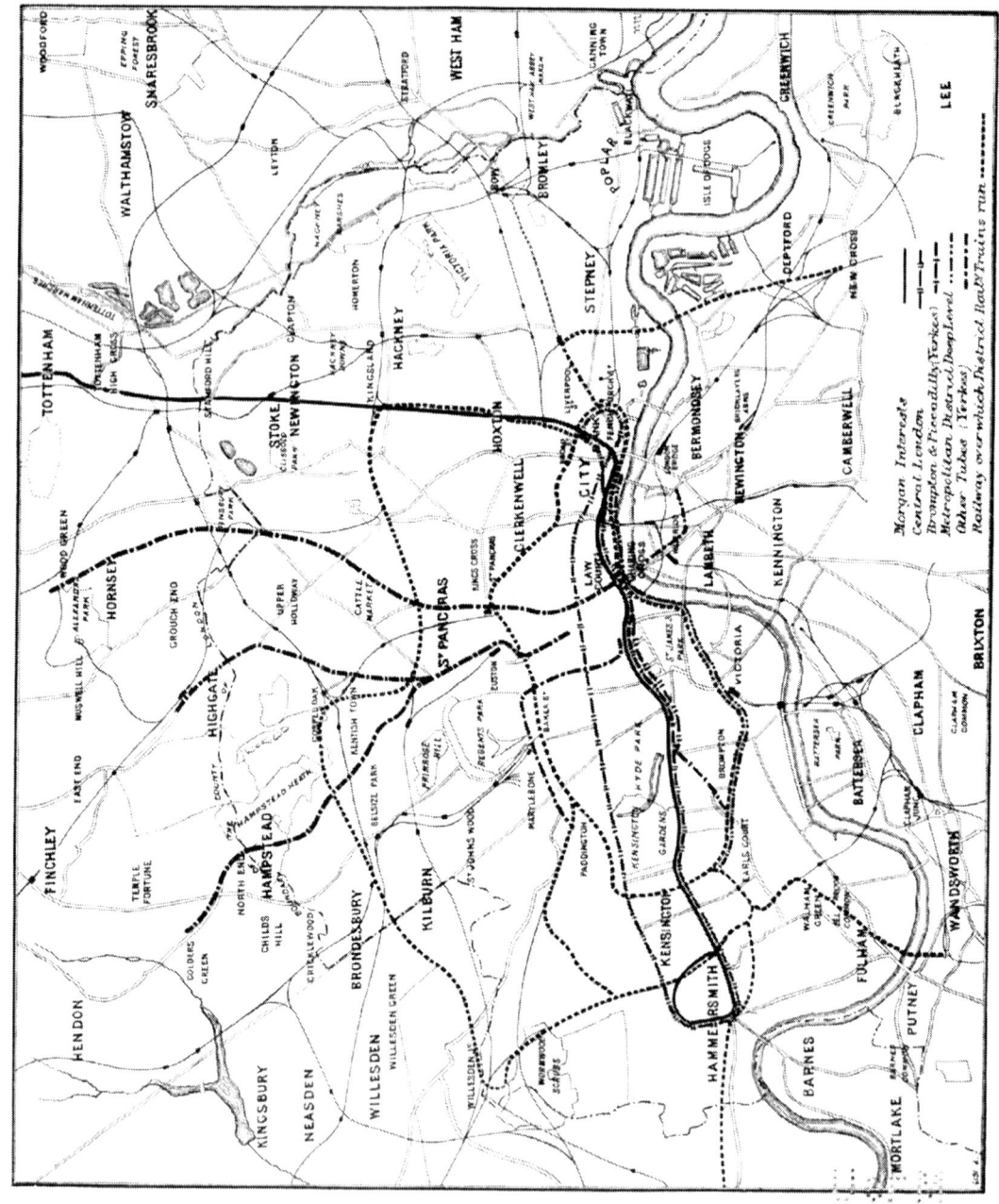

Map showing parallel Tube Schemes

THE FIGHT FOR UNDERGROUND LONDON

By Philip Dawson

In the last, and current, numbers of TRACTION AND TRANSMISSION there are two admirable articles by the Hon. Robert P. Porter, in which he considers, among other schemes, the systems of surface and tube lines which are being jointly promoted in Parliament by the London United Tramways and the Morgan interests. Maps of the systems are given showing the various districts which will eventually be connected by these proposed lines, should they be sanctioned by Parliament.

The Morgan scheme, though the most comprehensive, was not the only proposal before Parliament this Session, and as it may be of general interest to criticise the various

of the New York "Rapid Transit" subway, seem to have impressed both him and Mr. Morgan with the possibility of improving the transportation facilities of London. Probably the confidence shown by such an experienced and successful expert in traction matters as Mr. Charles T. Yerkes, and the way in which he is rapidly creating a rational and united system out of various disjointed interests, including the District Railway, contributed largely towards the appearance of the Morgan group in the fight for Underground London, though it must be admitted that these interests do not enjoy the advantage of a great practical experience like that possessed by Mr. Yerkes.

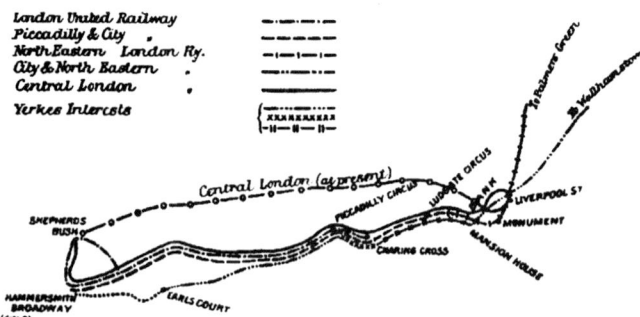

Diagram of Competing Tube Schemes

tube schemes as a whole, the other existing and proposed lines are also shown in the map which accompanies this article (see Plate XXI).

It will be seen from this map that, to a large extent, the proposed Morgan lines are paralleled either by lines for which franchises already exist, or by lines which are being promoted in other interests.

To understand the situation clearly, it must be remembered that when the various tube schemes were first before Parliament last Session, Mr. Morgan (through his English representative, Sir Clinton Edward Dawkins) had no apparent interest in them. But Sir Clinton E. Dawkins's visit to the United States last year, and the study he there made

The general condition of affairs when Mr. Morgan and his followers entered the Parliamentary arena is shown by the accompanying diagram.

There existed at that time a number of proposals, which, as a glance at the diagram will show, paralleled each other over a large portion of the routes.

(1) THE LONDON SUBURBAN INTERESTS, promoting a tube from Hammersmith Broadway and Shepherd's Bush, via Piccadilly, to Charing Cross.

(2) THE PICCADILLY AND CITY RAILWAY, promoting a tube from Hammersmith Broadway, via Piccadilly, to Ludgate Circus.

(3) THE NORTH-EAST LONDON RAILWAY, promoting a tube from Ludgate Circus, via Liverpool Street, to Palmer's Green.

(4) THE CITY AND NORTH-EAST SUBURBAN RAILWAY, promoting a scheme from the Mansion House, *via* the Bank, to Walthamstow.

(5) THE CENTRAL LONDON RAILWAY COMPANY, promoting an extension from their terminus at Shepherd's Bush to Hammersmith, and *via* Piccadilly and Charing Cross, Ludgate Circus, back to the Bank, with a loop to St. Mary Axe and Liverpool Street, and back to the Bank.

The Yerkes party already had a Bill, and were commencing work on a tube from Earl's Court, where there is to be a physical junction with the District Railway (of which one line came from Hammersmith) *via* South Kensington, Knightsbridge, and Piccadilly, to Piccadilly Circus, and from South Kensington, under the District line, as far as the Mansion House. They were also promoting a tube to connect Piccadilly Circus and Charing Cross with a junction at the latter place with their other tube, which would thus control traffic direct to the Mansion House.

Besides the foregoing, they promoted another tube to connect Piccadilly with the line already in their possession (which runs from the Strand to Finsbury Park) at the point where it crosses High Holborn.

At this period, powers were being sought to construct three separate lines of two tubes each under the Strand and Kensington Road, while under Piccadilly one road was on the point of being constructed, and powers were being sought to build three more.

As matters then stood, it was quite evident that the only proposals which had a fair chance of being considered by Lord Windsor's Committee, were those of the Central London Railway and Mr. Yerkes's junction line, powers to construct which he was seeking so as to complete his system.

It was at this moment that the Morgan groups and the London Suburban interests joined hands, and put before the Committee a joint proposal constructed from the following three schemes :—

(1) THE LONDON SUBURBAN, who maintained their proposals from Shepherd's Bush and Hammersmith Broadway to Hyde Park Corner, but dropping the line to Charing Cross.

(2) THE PICCADILLY AND CITY RAILWAY (belonging to the Morgan interests), who maintained their lines from Hyde Park Corner to Ludgate Circus, but dropping the line from Hyde Park Corner to Hammersmith.

(3) THE NORTH-EAST LONDON RAILWAY (controlled by Mr. Morgan), which joined it at Ludgate Circus and went on to Southgate *via* the Mansion House, Monument, and Liverpool Street.

To show the position of affairs at this time, the various competing lines proposed have been added to Mr. Porter's map of the London Suburban group, and this clearly shows the three main competing schemes before Parliament. All the tube schemes were held back last Session, and were brought forward again this year. The chief reasons for the postponement were vibration troubles and the uncertainty of the legislation which might be enforced to obviate any danger from this cause. The various schemes commenced their career in the House of Lords, which rejected several of them, during which process, as already stated, a large number of independent interests were amalgamated.

It is interesting to go back a few years and follow the history of some of the various promotions, starting with the Central London Railway, which (after the City and South London) was the pioneer tube line of the world, and which, although built later, owing to its great financial success from the very beginning, was the real pioneer tube from a commercial standpoint.

In Session 1897 various gentlemen interested in the Central London Railway promoted the City and West End Railway Bill, which proposed a line from Hammersmith to the City, *via* Piccadilly, the Strand, and Fleet Street. This Bill, together with the Brompton and Piccadilly Circus Railway Bill, which proposed a line from South Kensington, along the Brompton Road and Piccadilly, to Piccadilly Circus, was considered by a Committee of the House of Commons, with the late Mr. Woodall as chairman, and was rejected, the Brompton and Piccadilly Circus Bill, now controlled by Mr. Yerkes, being passed.

In November and December, 1900, the same gentlemen published the newspaper notices, and deposited plans, etc., for practically the same line from Hammersmith to the City. The Bill, if it had been proceeded with, would have been called the City and West End Railway Bill, 1901. It was abandoned, however, in view of the difficulties which had arisen owing to vibration on the Central London Railway, which was opened on July 30th, 1900.

The Central London Railway Company, in Session 1901, applied to Parliament for power to construct two loops, one at either end of their existing line. This Bill, together with the numerous other tube railway Bills of the same Session, was referred to a Joint Committee of both Houses of Parliament (Lord Windsor, chairman) which sat in Session 1901. The City and West End Bill, not having been deposited, was, of course, outside the scope of the Committee's inquiry.

The following were the Bills before that Committee affecting the route from Hammersmith to the City, *via* Piccadilly and the Strand :—

(1) Charing Cross, Hammersmith, and District Railway, from Hammersmith, under Kensington Road, Hyde Park Corner, the Green Park, and the Mall, to Charing Cross.

(2) The Piccadilly and City Railway Bill, commencing in Piccadilly Circus, thence taking practically the same route eastward to the City as the City and West End Railway of 1897, and terminating in Cannon Street.

(3) The North-East London Railway, commencing in Cannon Street, thence passing along Gracechurch Street and Bishopsgate Street, northwards to Tottenham, with a branch to Walthamstow.

There was also before the Committee the City and North-East Suburban Railway Bill, which commenced at Gracechurch Street, and thence went under Bishopsgate Street and Hackney Road out to Waltham Abbey.

The Committee reported that there ought to be one through line from Hammersmith, along Piccadilly, to Piccadilly Circus and the City. They also reported that there could be no objection to the proposed loop at the western end of the Central London Railway, but that there was more difficulty with respect to the proposed loop at the eastern end, and they recommended that the Central London Railway Bill should be referred to a Parliamentary Committee in the ordinary course. With reference to terminal loops generally the Committee, in their report, made the following remarks :—

The underground lines may be worked at the termini on the shuttle system, or by means of terminal loops; which system should be adopted in each case, is a question for the Parliamentary Committee to which the Bill is referred. But while the advantages to the working of the line by loops are obvious, and in outside districts there can be no objection to them, the Committee think that very great caution should be exercised in sanctioning them in the heart of the City, on the ground of the large amount of space occupied, to the possible exclusion of future railways. They have the less hesitation in making this recommendation, as the multiple motor system, by which much time is saved in shunting at terminal stations, appears likely to be adopted in future.

After the Committee had made this report, which was not presented until late in the Session, all the Tube Railway Bills of 1901 were suspended until the Session of this year.

In Session 1902, the Central London Railway Company did not proceed with their Bill for the terminal loops, but they deposited another Bill for a line from Hammersmith to the City, *via* Piccadilly and the Strand, forming junctions at each end with the existent Central London Railway, and thus making a circular route.

The Piccadilly and City Railway promoters deposited a new Bill for a line from Hammersmith, *via* Piccadilly to Charing Cross.

The North-East London promoters deposited a new Bill for a line from Ludgate Circus, under Bridge Street, Blackfriars, Upper Thames Street, and Queen Victoria Street, to their line formerly proposed at Cannon Street.

The Charing Cross, Hammersmith, and District Railway promoters deposited a new Bill for variations of their 1901 line at the Green Park and Charing Cross.

The City and North-East Suburban Railway promoters deposited a new Bill to meet the recommendations of the Committee of 1901, from Fenchurch Street, under Whitechapel Road, and through East London to their 1901 line at Leyton.

The Brompton and Piccadilly Circus Railway Company (controlled by Mr. Yerkes) had a Bill in Session 1902 for (*inter alia*) a short line from Piccadilly Circus to the Metropolitan District (deep-level line) Railway at Charing Cross.

During this Session a group of gentlemen interested in the London United Tramways deposited the London United Electric Railways Bill, which proposed a railway from Hammersmith, along Kensington Road, Knightsbridge, Constitution Hill, and the Mall, to Charing Cross, with a large loop at the west end, along Holland Road to Shepherd's Bush, and thence southwards to the Broadway, Hammersmith.

All the above mentioned Bills, with others not affecting this route, and the suspended Bills of 1901 were referred to a Committee of the House of Lords, of which Lord Windsor was again chairman.

The Piccadilly and City Railway, the

North-East London Railway, the City and North-East Suburban Railway, and the London United Electric Railways, as already mentioned, formed a combination, and by taking portions of the lines included in each of their Bills, while abandoning others, they presented to the Committee a continuous line from Hammersmith, through Piccadilly, the Strand, and Fleet Street, to the City, and thence to Tottenham.

After hearing the parties, the Committee rejected the Charing Cross, Hammersmith, and District Electric Railways, the City and North-East Suburban Railway, and the new lines proposed by the Central London Railway Bill, as well as the line proposed by the Brompton and Piccadilly Circus Railway Company from Piccadilly Circus to Charing Cross, and that line proposed by the London United Electric Railways promoters along Holland Road, and thence southward to the Broadway, Hammersmith. They, however, passed the line proposed by the combination, from Hammersmith Broadway, *via* Piccadilly, the Strand, and Fleet Street, to the City, and onwards to Tottenham.

As things stand at present, the extensions sought by the City and South London Railway have been thrown out, as well as that which was sought by the Central London Railway, although, in all probability, both these extensions will re-appear in Parliament next Session.

The following list of Bills considered by Lord Windsor's Committee, and their fate, may be of use for purposes of reference :—

(1) Baker Street and Waterloo Railway (extension of time)	Granted.
(2) Brompton-Piccadilly Circus Railway (extension of time)	Granted.
(3) Brompton-Piccadilly Circus Railway (Charing Cross Extension)	Rejected.
(4) Brompton-Piccadilly Circus Railway (Holborn Extension)	Sanctioned.
(5) Brompton-Piccadilly Circus Railway (Parson's Green Extension)	Rejected.
(6) Central London Railway (Shepherd's Bush - Hammersmith - City)	Rejected.
(7) Charing - Cross Euston and Hampstead Railway (Golder's Green Extension)	Sanctioned.
(8) Charing Cross, Hammersmith and District Railway	Rejected.
(9) City and North-East Suburban Railway	Withdrawn.
(10) City and South London Railway (Euston Extension)	Rejected.
(11) City and Crystal Palace Railway	Rejected.
(12) District Deep-level Railway (Earl's Court to Mansion House) (extension of time)	Granted.
(13) Edgware and Hampstead Railway	Sanctioned.
(14) Great Northern and City Railway (Lothbury Extension)	Sanctioned.
(15) Great Northern and Strand Railway (extension of time)	Granted.
(16) King's Road Railway	Rejected.
(17) King's Road Railway (Putney Extension)	Rejected.
(18) London United Electric Railway (Hammersmith to Piccadilly)	Sanctioned.
(19) London United Electric Railway (Marble Arch to Clapham Junction)	Sanctioned.
(20) London, Tilbury and Southend Railway (powers to run by electricity)	Granted.
(21) North-East London Railway	Sanctioned.
(22) North-West London Railway (extension of time)	Granted.
(23) Piccadilly-City Railway	Sanctioned.
(24) West and South London Junction Railway	Withdrawn.

At the present moment the fight rages hot between the two American interests represented by Mr. Yerkes and Mr. Morgan, and in this connection we may quote from the remarks on this subject made by Mr. Perks, the chairman of the Metropolitan District Railway Company, at the last half-yearly meeting of this company :—

We think that it is rather unfortunate that a combination, with which Messrs. Morgan's house is so closely identified, when they come into the Metropolis and try to seize possession of one of its main routes, to knock the bottom, if they can, out of the revenue of the District Railway, and other railways, which have been endeavouring, to the best of their ability, to meet the requirements of the public, should instruct their counsel to say to a Parliamentary Committee that they are our deadly competitors. We shall do our very utmost to persuade Parliament that their railway is not required, and that it will be, as we honestly believe it will be, a great financial fiasco should it be sanctioned. Of course, it is entirely a matter for Messrs. Morgans to consider whether they will offer to the London public and to the American public fifteen or twenty millions of capital, and take the responsibility of inducing small investors, and even large investors, to put up their money into such a project as they have fathered, particularly in view of the very absurd rates at which Mr. Clifton Robinson has agreed to carry the public from Hammersmith to the City and from Hammersmith to Charing Cross. Mr. Clifton Robinson, who was the chief witness, and, I suppose, the chief financial adviser, so far as rates go, has undertaken to carry people from Hammersmith to Charing Cross at the low fare of 1d. Now, we know that with regard to the Central London Railway, which is carrying from forty millions to fifty millions of people a year, that it costs them 1d. to carry people over one of the most crowded and most popular routes in London. In face of that experience, Mr. Clifton Robinson has entered into an undertaking, which has been scheduled in his Bill, to carry people all the way from Hammersmith to Charing Cross over a route which cannot be compared with that of the Central London, for 1d. I think that Messrs. Morgans and their financial colleagues should use a little more polite and courteous language to the District Company, and should not allow their counsel to go into the Committee-room and make these extraordinary allegations against us.

With this introduction we will proceed to consider what were the reasons that influenced the decision of the Committee.

In doing this any evidence which, although not essential to the present discussion, may be of general interest, will be touched upon. The easiest way will be to take the case as put forward by each proposer separately, and the evidence brought to bear on the different schemes, both for and against, and then discuss, as far as possible, the merits of the competing schemes in the light of the evidence given. The order in which they will be taken is :—

(1) The Central London Railway proposal. (2) The Morgan Amalgamated Scheme. (3) The fight of the Yerkes interests against both, but principally against the Morgan proposals.

Before commencing it is necessary to consider the evidence of Colonel Yorke, the Board of Trade adviser on railway matters, who has given special attention to the subject, having, by Board of Trade instructions, reported on the shallow tube electric lines of the Paris Metropolitan Railway. This consideration is very necessary, as the opinions expressed by him, although in many cases not agreeing with the views held by such experts as Sir Benjamin Baker, nevertheless carried great weight with the Lords Committee. Colonel Yorke stated that he strongly objected to junctions in tube railways, and that they should be avoided. Dangers from fires, he thought, could be easily obviated by omitting as far as possible all woodwork construction in the neighbourhood of motors, cables, and electrical machinery of locomotives or motor carriages, and the abandonment, as far as possible, of flexible couplings, these being

replaced by rigid conductors, protected by non-inflammable insulating material. Wood should be abandoned in the construction of platforms, and wooden sleepers in tubes, if used, should not be creosoted, as in case of fire they give out suffocating smoke. The carriages should be designed in such a way as to enable passengers to alight in case of emergency, and to pass between the tube and the carriages. It would be advisable, if possible, to have a uniform diameter of tubes, which as proposed varies from 11ft. 6ins. to 16ft. Personally he would advise no tube to be smaller than 13ft. 6ins. The tunnels between stations should be lighted, so as to prevent panic in case of accident or breakdown. The Central London Railway Company, of their own accord, had provided for lighting their tunnels, and he thought great credit was due to them for this. The Board of Trade had not got sufficient power as regards supervising construction of tube lines, and he suggested that the companies should be obliged to submit, for the approval of the Board of Trade, plans, sections, and other details of their proposals with respect to :—

(a) Permanent way, tunnels, platforms, stairs, lifts, and other communications,
(b) Rolling stock,
(c) Lighting,
(d) Ventilation,

and that the railway rolling stock and other works shall be constructed only in accordance with the plans, sections, and other details as approved of by the Board of Trade.

We may now consider the case for the Central London, as put forward by Sir H. Oakley, its chairman, who was for many years general manager of the Great Northern Railway Company. The Central London Railway was incorporated by the Act of 1891. The authorised capital of the company is £3,000,000, of which £2,000,000 has been paid up. The borrowing powers are £926,000, and of the total borrowing powers and authorised capital there remains as balance £258,000 unexpended. The line was opened for traffic on July 30th, 1900. For the first five months, from the opening to the end of December, 1900, the number of passengers carried was 14,916,922; the next half year the total was 20,885,789; the last half year of 1901 was 20,802,650—the average up to December 31st, 1901, gives seven million passengers per mile of route per annum. As regards earning capacity, the working of the first five months earned $2\frac{1}{2}$ per cent.; that of the next six months, 4 per cent.; the next six months 4 per cent.; and the six months of the first half of this year earned 4 per cent., a considerable balance being laid aside for contingencies. The amount carried forward beyond dividends paid amounted to £16,000.

At the Bank Station of the railway there are five lifts, each capable of accommodating eighty passengers; at the Post Office there are five lifts, four of them carrying fifty and one eighty passengers. From Chancery Lane to the Marble Arch every station has four lifts, each with a capacity of fifty passengers. From the Marble Arch westward there are three lifts in each station, each with a capacity of fifty passengers; but at Shepherd's Bush, in consequence of the rush which attends on Saturday afternoons and Sundays, there are seven lifts, each with a capacity of fifty passengers. As regards service, the trains begin to run from Shepherd's Bush at five o'clock in the morning, and from the Bank at 5.20; the last train runs from Shepherd's Bush at twelve midnight, and from the Bank at 12.30. Between 5 a.m. and 7.30 a.m., thirty-two trains are run; from 7.30 onwards the trains run at intervals of from two and a half to three minutes. This goes on till eight o'clock at night, and the result is that at present 333 trains are running every day in each direction. The average number of passengers carried per day amounts to 130,000. As regards maximum numbers which have made use of the Tube, the following figures are interesting :—

On C.I.V. day (October 27th, 1900), 190,975 were carried.

On October 29th, 1900, 235,720 were carried.

On the occasion of the late Queen's funeral, 217,000 were carried.

The standard locomotive train has seven cars. The experimental motor car train had only six cars, because the two motor cars used were not equipped with sufficiently powerful motors. The seating capacity of the ordinary seven-car train is 266 passengers —that is thirty-eight to each car—but in the rush hours, morning and evening, forty and fifty are frequently carried in each car.

Last year the Central London applied for a loop, and a Bill was deposited to this effect, but the Lords Committee did not view with favour the proposed City loop, although they thought that one at Shepherd's Bush might be granted, and this Bill, as well as all other Bills deposited that year, were adjourned to the present year. Lord Windsor's Committee of last year stated that they thought a line should come from Hammersmith to the City, and this induced the Central London Railway Company to alter their proposition. This was not done without grave thought and careful consideration, and consultation with their engineer, Sir Benjamin Baker, their electrical engineer, Mr. H. F. Parshall, and their land valuer. Before deciding this, they took a census of the surface traffic in Piccadilly as compared with Oxford Street, and found that it was heavier in the latter street. The lines which were thus proposed were eight and a half miles in length. They began at Shepherd's Bush, and went thence to Hammersmith, along Hammersmith Broadway, under Kensington Road, turned into the Park as soon as possible, up to Hyde Park Corner; then crossed under the Green Park, coming under Piccadilly at Walsingham House; then along Piccadilly and Leicester Square to the Strand, along the Strand and Fleet Street until Bridge Street, Blackfriars, was reached. To avoid damaging St. Paul's Cathedral, the route turned towards the river, and arrangements were made with the South - Eastern and Chatham Company to run under the forecourt of their station; thence round by Queen Victoria Street, along Cannon Street, down Cornhill and Leadenhall Street to St. Mary Axe, and so on to Liverpool Street. The general object was to avoid concentrating all the traffic at any particular spot, and to tap the Great Eastern and North London traffic at Liverpool Street.

The North London Railway carries 26,500,000 passengers in and out of Broad Street, and the Great Eastern fifty-three million passengers. As regards workmen's trains, up to 7 a.m. return tickets are issued at a single fare, and workmen are not required to return the same day they take their tickets. The average number of workmen carried per day through the month of January was 15,533, or $12\frac{1}{2}$ per cent. of the total number of passengers. The total number for the month was 419,000. Sir Henry Oakley held very strongly that the proposition made by his company was the very best method of running trains, that a great deal of time would be saved, and that as regards finance the Lords Committee last year pointed out that they did not want any waste in finance or otherwise, and in this particular the Central London would have a peculiar advantage, besides which, their existing plant would only have to be slightly enlarged. The tunnels were lit by electricity, which could be turned on from any station, and which was entirely independent from the line current. Sir H. Oakley, from his experience of working railways for fifty years, thought that it was possible with a circle to give a very much better service than with a railway worked on the shuttle system. He further stated that the main stream of the traffic would be from Hammersmith to the City. The moment you got away from these two extremities, the needs of conveyance were much less, except during particular hours in the morning and evening; this has been found to be the case on all railways with through trains running out into the country. To keep the busy part of the City supplied it would be necessary to run a continuous service into the outskirts all day, and by this means put themselves to a very serious loss, and commit a great extravagance. The busy part must be kept going all day, and in order to do this the Morgan lines would have to keep the semi-idle part also busy. The true and economical method of working in the present instance would be to work in two sections. The requirements of both would be met by the closed system proposed by the Central London, because it would afford the man in North London an opportunity of going the way he desires, and, *vice versâ*, the man in the country, who wanted to go to the Strand or Oxford Street, could at the end of his journey into London decide which way he would go.

The Central London Railway, as pointed out by Mr. Fitzgerald, was the pioneer of tube success, and it was only after the line had been worked sufficiently to show that it was a financial success, that Mr. Morgan came in. The Central London Company showed the way, and on that ground they certainly would appear to be entitled to reap their reward.

Sir H. Oakley stated that, as regards raising capital, after having most carefully considered the matter, and consulted with Sir Ernest Cassel and Messrs. Glyns, the bankers, they were assured that they could raise the necessary capital on a commission of $\frac{1}{4}$ per cent. to $\frac{1}{2}$ per cent. The Central London Railway Company proposed to work a continuous circle system as opposed to a shuttle, or to a system with confluent junctions.

In confirmation of the opinion held by the Central London directors, that this was the best system of working, and that the line they proposed would best fill the requirements of the public, several general managers of important railway companies were called.

Mr. Fred Harrison, general manager of the London and North-Western Railway, stated that he considered the extensions sought by the Central London would be very convenient for relieving the traffic, and that he considered the method proposed by them for working would be absolutely the most convenient way, and much to be preferred to the shuttle system.

Mr. J. F. Gooday, general manager of the Great Eastern Railway, stated that he thought the new Central London Bill was very good, and that, being a circular railway, and all in tunnel, it was less liable to delay and accidents than any other system; there being no lines in the open was a most important feature in its favour, as it avoided any trouble due to fogs. He also stated that he, as well as any railway manager who had any experience, would be in favour of the system proposed by the Central London Railway.

Mr. Vincent Hill, general manager of the South-Eastern and Chatham Railway, stated that, after the most careful investigation, he considered that the Central London was the best scheme, and that his company had arranged for an exchange station with it. He also agreed with Sir H. Oakley and the other managers that a train which works continuously round and round, without a single crossing, and without a junction, was, for punctuality and safety, as near perfection as any railway could be. He gave some interesting figures as regards through bookings, and stated that, for the year 1901, the through bookings from the South-Eastern to the Midland were 38,370; from the Midland to the South-Eastern and Chatham, 72,924; from the South-Eastern and Chatham to the Great Northern, 112,424 and from the Great Northern to the South-Eastern and Chatham, 144,822.

Mr. Thomas Jenkins, general manager of the City and South London Railway stated that a circular line was much the safest, and that with it the same traffic could be worked with fewer trains.

So much for the chief arguments brought forward for the Central London Railway Company by the promoters, all of which will bear the most careful examination. Summing up, they practically amounted to the following:—

(a) The Central London was the pioneer of successful tube railways.

(b) The scheme which was put forward this year was one that had been specially studied, so that it might fulfil the wishes expressed by Lord Windsor's Committee last year in Parliament.

(c) The Central London was a going concern, and would be able to raise the necessary money for the extensions at an exceedingly low rate, certainly not more than ½ per cent.

(d) The system proposed, viz., a complete circle system without junctions of any description, was the best suited to rapid transit and to handling large crowds.

We may now consider the arguments brought forward by the Morgan interests in favour of their proposed lines.

Mr. Clifton Robinson, general manager of the London United Tramways, gave evidence in favour of the amalgamated Bill. He suggested fares of 2d. from Acton to Charing Cross—at present passengers pay 1d. from Acton to Shepherd's Bush, and he stated that at the present moment the London United Tramways carried forty million passengers a year, and when the tramways were completed would carry two hundred million passengers. On Bank Holiday, the maximum number of passengers carried in one day over sixteen miles of route on the London United Trams was 250,000. For the tubes, he proposed to have, from 5 a.m. to 7.30 a.m., a five-minute service of workmen's trains, and from 7.30 a.m. to 9.30 p.m. a two and a half minute service, with the exception of Walthamstow and Epping Forest, where there would be a five-minute service. From 9.30 p.m. to 1 a.m. he would have a five-minute service, and from 1 a.m. till 5 a.m., on the whole system, a half-hour service. He estimated the annual maximum carrying capacity of the Hammersmith and Southgate line at 345,000,000 passengers; of the Cannon Street and

Waltham Cross line, 231,000,000; and the Marble Arch and Clapham Junction line, 89,000,000; the total capacity of the tube lines of the system being thus 665,000,000. He stated that from his experience, 252,750,000 passengers should be carried on the thirty-eight miles of line, which amounts to about 40 per cent. of the seating capacity of the train. He estimated that five-sixths would be ordinary passengers at 1½d., and the rest workmen at ¾d., giving a total income of over one and a half million pounds sterling. Taking the ratio of operating expenses to receipts at 50 per cent., the estimated profit would amount to 4.7 per cent., and the capital outlay to £16,000,000. The average receipts on their tramways were 1½d. per passenger. He stated that the London County Council returns showed that there were thirty-eight omnibus routes which converged from Hammersmith to the Strand, on which seven hundred omnibuses were running, while from Hyde Park Corner towards the Strand, there are twenty omnibus routes with 890 'buses. Mr. Robinson stated that on the former route nine thousand passengers per hour were being carried; on the latter, five thousand passengers per hour. The total length at present worked by the London United Tramways was sixteen miles of route, but when the sanctioned lines were completed, it would be eighty miles.

Sir Clinton Dawkins (senior partner of the firm of J. E. S. Morgan & Co. in London, and who was Mr. Goschen's private secretary for three years, while he was Chancellor of the Exchequer), in the absence of Mr. Pierpont Morgan, guaranteed to find the whole capital for the undertaking from Hammersmith up to North Southgate; at the same time, they would not be required to do so, as they were working with the London United Tramways. He also stated that he had agreed to take half interest with the London United in the line from Shepherd's Bush and Hammersmith to Charing Cross, beyond which point, however, it belonged exclusively to the Morgan group.

The line between Charing Cross and Hammersmith was to be promoted jointly, and the capital to be found jointly—a through rate of fares being proposed, not merely on the railway, but also on the tramways.

By an agreement entered into between Mr. G. White, of Bristol, and the promoters of the London United and Sir C. E. Dawkins, C.B., on the part of Messrs. Morgan & Co., and by agreements which were put before the Lords Committee, it was arranged that a clearing house should be established to divide the money received in through fares between the various companies, and the schedule of fares either way were set out as quoted by Mr. Porter (see page 21, ante).*

It is evident from looking at the map which accompanies this article, that the greatest opposition to this amalgamated scheme of the Morgan interests would come from the Yerkes group, as it was their anticipated traffic which the Morgan group hoped to acquire, and it is therefore not surprising that every possible effort to oppose the Morgan schemes was made by the Metropolitan District and the Yerkes interests.

Sir Ralph Littler pointed out the importance of the Yerkes proposition, which was to make the District Railway part of a group of lines. At Earl's Court the District branch had two directions, and there was a series of lines belonging to it which ran south through Fulham, on to Putney and Wimbledon. Another set ran to Ealing, and branched off from there to Hounslow. At Ealing there was a most valuable junction with the North-Western Railway, and before getting to Ealing there was a branch connecting up with Richmond. North of the Great Western there was the District line round to South Harrow, which was now being continued on to Uxbridge. This system formed an admirable means of access to the whole of what might be called the River End and south-western district of London, taking the passengers in many cases without change straight to and from the City. Besides this, there would be the Great Northern and Strand, which would bring people from Finsbury Park and King's Cross to the Strand. To give an idea of the traffic, it might be stated that there were four hundred trains a day on the Great Northern running into Finsbury Park. The tube station under Finsbury Park would give accommodation to the Edgware branch of the Great Northern, to the Finchley and High Barnet branch, to the Alexandra Palace and Muswell Hill branch, and to the main

line of the Great Northern passing over Wood Green to Hatfield. With all these lines authorised, the problem which Mr. Yerkes attempted to solve was so to use and connect them, as to make them useful to the whole of London, and to create a system which would be a nucleus of a more extended network hereafter. The necessity of constructing the tube lines contemplated by the Morgan group and the London United, would appear questionable.

There was already a connection between Hammersmith and the City both north and south. The Metropolitan Railway had a line running from Hammersmith. The Metropolitan Company was a partner in the Inner Circle with the District from South Kensington. Through High Street, Kensington, the Metropolitan had their own line. There were four tracks passing through High Street, Kensington; from there they went past King's Cross to Farringdon Road, Aldersgate Street, Moorgate Street, Bishopsgate Street, and Aldgate. From Aldgate there was a line which was the joint property of the two companies, called the Inner Circle completion, which came round to the Mansion House. From the Mansion House the lines belonged to the District, and ran through Charing Cross to High Street, Kensington. There were other lines which belonged to the District entirely, and which involved the traffic going out of Earl's Court. There was, therefore, a very effective system between Hammersmith and Moorgate, and also from Hammersmith, via Earl's Court, to the Mansion House and the Monument. From Aldgate there was another system running to Whitechapel, which for a certain distance was the joint property of the two companies. From there a new line had just been opened which connected on to the Tilbury and Southend Railway, and which was called the Whitechapel and Bow line. With these lines there was a through connection for the District Railway from Uxbridge down to Tilbury. From Earl's Court there was another line, which ran up to Addison Road by Latimer Road to Westbourne Park. This was worked by two companies—one from Addison Road to Aldgate, and the other from Addison Road, round by Gospel Oak and Kentish Town, to Broad Street. The two companies were the London and North-Western and the North London, of which the London and

* This amalgamated scheme is now known as the London Suburban Railway.

North-Western were two-thirds owners. The introduction of electric traction to these routes would enormously expedite the service. These existing lines gave very good access from Hammersmith to practically all the business parts of London. By means of the tube lines authorised, over which Mr. Yerkes presided, it would be possible to connect up the enormous districts of Uxbridge and Harrow on the north, to Wimbledon on the south, and by means of an exchange station at Earl's Court, to Hyde Park Corner and Piccadilly. By the extensions and junctions now sought it would be possible to continue on to Charing Cross, and by means of another deep level line from there, on to the Mansion House. From Piccadilly a line ran to Holborn, and then, by means of a connection, on to the Great Northern and Strand and to Finsbury Park. By this means there would appear to be a very complete connection provided between east and west, south-west and north-west, and north-east, with a comparatively small expenditure of money. With these lines already granted, the expenditure which was proposed to be made by the Morgan group would seem very doubtful as regards earning capacity.

Sir Ralph Littler also pointed out that several of the 'bus lines which had been mentioned never went to Hammersmith at all; but Mr. Clifton Robinson could not be shaken in his estimate of fifty-three million passengers per annum between Hammersmith and Charing Cross. It was shown, however, that these estimates were based on the assumption that the District Railway would not improve its carrying capacity between Hammersmith and Charing Cross on the introduction of electricity.

It was stated that the average fare on the District Railway per passenger carried was 1.49d., and on the North London, 1.84d., and that the North London were carrying passengers a distance of twelve miles for 2d. It was also stated that the North London Railway, by all the facilities that it gave, and even having penny-in-the-slot machines for tickets, only got 49,500,000 passengers, whereas Mr. Clifton Robinson estimated the traffic on the proposed Cannon Street and Waltham Cross line to be 77,000,000 ordinary passengers, and 15,500,000 workmen, or a total of 92,500,000 passengers.

Sir Ralph Littler clearly pointed out that at this stage the whole matter had assumed an entirely different aspect to what it did at the beginning, when the Bills were originally considered by Lord Windsor's Committee. Then there were four western schemes, which, if considered individually, very likely the Committee would have thrown out, whereas they had been welded into a whole by Sir Clinton Dawkins amalgamating with the London United. It was also pointed out by him that the London United would only give through tickets to the City by their own tube, and that this could not be called healthy competition, as there would be no through tickets issued either by the Central London or the District lines.

To prove the statement made that the traffic anticipated by the Morgan interests was excessive, expert evidence of great weight was called.

Mr. Charles Mott, director of the Great Western Railway, and chairman of the City and South London Railway, stated that the latter line had been working for nearly twelve years, and was now carrying sixty thousand passengers a day. He stated that, in his opinion, the traffic as estimated by Mr. Clifton Robinson was grossly exaggerated; that Mr. Clifton Robinson had evidently calculated as if all the lines he proposed would have the same traffic as the three or four miles in the centre part of the City, whereas really on the other portions of the line he would not get one-third as much.

As regards finance, it was pointed out by several witnesses that both the Yerkes and the Central London interests were in a much more favourable position to raise money than the Morgan group.

Sir Clinton Dawkins had already admitted that it would cost them 10 per cent. to raise their money as compared to $\frac{1}{4}$ or $\frac{1}{2}$ per cent. in the case of the Central London Railway. Sir Clinton Dawkins would have to find the money to build the road, as the public would not be willing to subscribe to a new enterprise, and this would cost, as admitted, £2,500,000 sterling over and above the cost of construction.

The Central London would be in a very much better position. The position of Mr. Yerkes, as shown by Mr. Fitzgerald, was entirely different from that of Mr. Morgan. Mr. Yerkes found a number of schemes in existence authorised by Parliament which the British public would not adopt. These were the Brompton and Piccadilly, the Baker

Street and Waterloo, the Charing Cross and Euston, and the Great Northern and Strand. These Mr. Yerkes put his money into, anxious to make them a success. Mr. Morgan's position is entirely different; he has only come forward "to grasp the golden apple when he finds out that it is of gold."

The advocates of the Morgan group stated that they proposed, and expected to get, an average speed of twenty miles an hour on their tube line. This would seem to have been proved by the evidence to be commercially impossible, in which case the number of trains on the Morgan schemes, as well as the working expenses, would have to be increased, and the receipts would, therefore, be smaller.

There were other points also in which the proposals of the London United and Morgan interests seemed to be impracticable. Thus, Mr. C. Robinson proposed to collect fares and issue tickets on the cars, and not, as is the practice on the Central London, to have a universal fare paid over at the booking office. Mr. T. Jenkins, the general manager of the City and South London Railway demonstrated that it would be impossible to collect and examine tickets while the train was travelling. With the average speed of twenty miles an hour proposed by the Morgan interests, the actual travelling time between two stations would be about one minute, and from actual experience on the City and Waterloo Railway, where the travelling time is four and a half minutes, it was found that in the latter case during busy hours, with two collectors in each car, it was difficult to issue or collect tickets.

As regards the question of speed, Mr. C. T. Yerkes stated that at his request the General Electric Company of America had carried out separate tests on their experimental lines at Schenectady, and they had found that, with an average distance of 2,500ft. between stops, the maximum average speed which was obtainable with comfort to passengers was sixteen miles an hour, and that with a greater speed the wear and tear on the contact shoes, brake shoes, and wheels, and the vibration, was excessive, as well as causing discomfort to passengers, owing to the rapid acceleration and retardation. This evidence was confirmed by Mr. Chapman, the electrical engineer of the District Railway, who has had a very large amount of experience in electric traction,

both on tramways and on main line railways in the United States. He stated that the average speed of sixteen miles an hour was the maximum obtainable in tubes, a statement which contradicted that made by Sir Douglas Fox, who had estimated on twenty miles an hour.

As regards this same question of speed, Mr. Parshall, the electrical engineer of the Central London Railway Company, stated that the average speed between stations on that line was 18.8 miles an hour. Under those conditions it was found that brake shoes lasted five weeks, and third rail shoes three weeks, and that from the great experience he had in this connection he stated that his deliberate opinion was that the average speed of twenty miles an hour, suggested by Messrs. Morgan & Co., with the distances that obtained between stations, was contrary to all precedent, and that sixteen miles an hour was the maximum obtainable.

Sir H. Oakley, in summing up his evidence, stated that, after most carefully considering the Morgan proposal, he was of the opinion that they had created very great difficulties for themselves both as regards finance and operation. The idea of graduated fares as suggested by Mr. C. Robinson was impracticable. He had found that, with a universal fare, double the number of passengers could be booked than could otherwise have been handled. The views of Mr. Yerkes and his adherents on the amount of traffic which would be handled were diametrically opposed to those of Messrs. Morgan & Co.

The London Suburban estimated they could carry with their tubes and trams 250,000,000 passengers, but Mr. Yerkes did not think that they could ever carry more than 200,000,000. Out of thirty-eight miles of the London Suburban, sixteen miles ran more or less in the open country. The District at present carries on its own lines 40,000,000 passengers, and Mr. Yerkes estimates that when it is entirely electrified it will carry 100,000,000. He stated that Messrs. Morgan & Co. had never worked any railways in America. The length of the District is twenty-six miles, and it was on this mileage they calculated carrying 100,000,000 passengers. The present service on the District Railway from Hammersmith to the City is six trains an hour each way. There are also six trains an hour from the City to Hammer-

smith each way on the Metropolitan. Of
the six trains on the District, there are two
to Ealing, two to Acton, and two to Richmond. At Earl's Court, these are joined by
four trains coming from Wimbledon and
Putney, and two from the London and
North - Western from Addison Road, per
hour each way, and there are, therefore,
twelve trains from Earl's Court to the City
each way per hour.

Mr. Perks proposed to put on the high
level lines, when electrified, six trains from
Harrow, six from Ealing, six from Hounslow,
and six from Richmond per hour each way,
making twenty-four trains per hour running
on a two and a half minute headway. As
all these trains passed through Hammersmith,
this would give a two and a half minute
service from Hammersmith to the City, and
a five-minute service from Wimbledon and
Putney to the City. Mr. Perks was confident
that they could run on a one and a half minute
headway, and it was suggested to run a five-
minute service on the Circle instead of, as
at present, a ten - minute service. The
present seating capacity of the trains from
Hammersmith to the City on the District
is 29,500,000 passengers. The new service
will be a seven-car train, having a seating
capacity for 330. This will give an annual
seating capacity from Hammersmith to the
City of 57,000,000. The trains on the Yerkes
tube line will be composed of six cars,
with a seating capacity of 284 passengers,
and it is proposed to run a two - minute
service from Earl's Court to Piccadilly on
the Tube, and then a two or four - minute
service between Piccadilly Circus and Finsbury
Park, and a two or four - minute service
between Piccadilly Circus, *via* Charing Cross,
to the Mansion House. With tube lines
there will be a two - minute service for
twenty hours and a fifteen - minute service
for the remaining four hours per day. The
carrying capacity of the Great Northern and
Strand, and the Brompton and Piccadilly
combined, will be 180,000,000 per annum.
and it is expected that they will carry
86,000,000, of which 12,000,000 will be
workmen at one penny fares. The deep level
is proposed to be worked at present from
Earl's Court, but could be worked as far as
Hammersmith, the trains coming up on the
District line at Earl's Court. The line from
South Kensington to Charing Cross, if constructed, would probably be worked on the

shuttle system. At Piccadilly Circus there
would be a divergent junction, from which
trains would be run through to the Mansion
House or Finsbury Park. Mr. Perks stated
that they calculated the average fare to be
1.89d. per passenger.

The North-Western contributed £100,000
to make the piece of railway to the
Mansion House, and in consideration of that,
they had a right to run four trains an hour
to the Mansion House, and have a separate
bay of their own.

Mr. Perks, M.P., stated that the opening
of the Central London had been disastrous
to the District—the preference dividend had
never been large, but it had disappeared
entirely, and the 4 per cent. guarantee on
£1,250,000, which was raised for the purpose
of finding half the shares of the City line,
disappeared gradually, and last year the
directors were able only to pay a nominal
dividend on a stock which had paid regularly for thirty years.

Mr. Perks said that the junction of
the Brompton-Piccadilly line at Piccadilly
Circus with the Finsbury Park and Mansion
House line, would be a physical one. He
also stated that at Baker Street Station
there was a change of passengers on the
Metropolitan line of from forty to fifty
millions a year. He testified that the
distance on the proposed Morgan tube line
from Hammersmith to the Mansion House
will be six and one-eighth miles, as compared to the District six and a half miles,
but that it would be possible to run quicker
on the open District than in the tubes.

Mr. Gooday, the general manager of the
Great Eastern Railway Company, stated that
he thought Mr. Clifton Robinson's views as
regards realising $1\frac{1}{2}$d. per passenger carried
were absolutely illusory. The reason he gave
for this was that, on Mr. Robinson's basis,
he carried one passenger in every six miles
in each seat, at an average fare of $1\frac{1}{2}$d.,
workmen going half - price. Taking his
average at $1\frac{1}{2}$d. per mile, his two lines would
have to carry 115,200,000 passengers per
annum, equal to 315,600 per day, to earn
4 per cent. on the capital. His experience
was that two-thirds of the total traffic were
carried between 6 a.m. and 10 a.m., and
between 5 p.m. and 9 p.m., and on this
basis to carry the passengers which Mr.
Robinson calculated on, every morning and
evening he would have thirty - five trains

per hour over each line and in one direction. Comparing Mr. Robinson's calculations of the proposed Walthamstow line with the experience of the Great Eastern, they found that the total passengers carried by the latter were 21 per cent. of their seating capacity, whereas Mr. Robinson calculated on carrying 40 per cent. He stated that the greatest number of passengers ever carried by the North London was 236,000—on C.I.V. day.

Mr. J. Holden, locomotive superintendent of the Great Eastern Railway, stated that his locomotives could give an acceleration of 12ins. per second per second, with a train weighing 192 tons, thus attaining a speed of twenty miles at the expiration of thirty seconds. Mr. F. Dunne, general manager of the North London, stated that they had twelve and a half miles of railway belonging to them, but they worked over one hundred miles. Five miles of their line was a four-track route, and the remainder a double route. In 1901 they carried 46,992,442 passengers, and of these 46,500,000 used Broad Street Station. Between Broad Street Station and Dalston there were 632 trains a day, taking both directions, and return tickets were issued at 2d. for twelve miles.

The average passengers, per mile of line operated, were four millions per annum. He stated that for the North London alone to earn 4 per cent. on £5,000,000 capital they would have to earn 1.88d. per passenger carried; he thought the maximum they could expect would be 1d., and to pay 4 per cent. on their capital they would have to earn £482,713 per annum, as against the North London's £312,000—this latter figure including all docks, warehouses, and goods charges—they would have to carry 55,289,000 passengers at an average fare of 1.88d., and he did not think that was possible, and if they took the average receipts of 1d. they would have to carry 120,000,000 passengers, whereas the whole North London did not carry more than 47,000,000.

Having so far examined the evidence given before Lord Windsor's Committee by what we may call the three competing systems, taking them in the order of existence, viz., the Yerkes interests, the Central London, and the Morgan group, we will try and sum up the situation by examining the probable traffic, as well as the expenditure,

and see whether the competition between these lines will serve the public welfare or not. It is also interesting to endeavour to fathom the reasons which induced Lord Windsor's Committee to throw out what was really a very important section in each of the three propositions, viz., the Central London Railway Extensions, the connecting link asked for by Mr. Yerkes to connect up his Brompton and Piccadilly line to the already sanctioned deep-level lines at Charing Cross to the Mansion House, and the loop asked for by the Morgan interests to connect up Shepherd's Bush to their underground line from Hammersmith to the City.

Taking the amalgamated groups first, we can tabulate as follows :—

Name.	Mileage of Route.	Share Capital.	Borrowing Powers.	Total Capital.	Capital per Mile.
		£	£	£	£
London United Tube	10.33	3,750,000	1,250,000	5,000,000	481,900
North-East London :—					
Tube	7 }	3,750,000	1,250,000	5,000,000	579,700
Open	4 }				
Piccadilly and City	2.25	1,500,000	500,000	2,000,000	880,200
City and North-East Suburban :—					
Tube	4.50 }	3,000,000	1,000,000	4,000,000	505,590
Open	11.33 }				149,500
					Average per Mile.
Total in round figures	39.41	12,000,000	4,000,000	16,000,000	401,900

The interest, reckoned on a basis of 8 per cent., for two years on the total capital which would be utilised during the construction, is estimated at £825,900, and the balance over estimated cost and interest, all of which would certainly be required for financing, in the case of the Morgan schemes is £1,410,800. These figures are from the revised estimates presented by the Morgan interests. As an idea of the changes made, we may mention that the London United interests dropped four Bills, and diminished the capital expenditure proposed from £4,213,047 to £3,677,074.

The Piccadilly and City Railway reduced its proposed expenditure from £1,409,284 to £892,517.

The Piccadilly and City (No. 2) Railway dropped three lines, and reduced its estimates from £2,971,088 to £1,055,432.

The North-East London dropped five lines and a generating station, and reduced its estimates from £3,562,029 to £2,219,578.

The City and North-East Suburban dropped four lines, and reduced its estimates from £1,950,000 to £371,798.

The City and North-East Suburban (No. 2) dropped two lines, and reduced its estimates from £2,703,388 to £2,161,205.

The capital of the old Central London Railway was £8,000,000 shares and £1,000,000 borrowing powers, total £4,000,000, and to construct the new lines it was proposed to double this capital, making a total of £8,000,000.

It will be interesting to consider what the Yerkes systems are capitalised at, and what it will cost to transform the Metropolitan District.

It may be estimated in round figures that the cost of transforming the Metropolitan and District into an electric system, including the necessary sub-stations, rolling stock, signals, transmission, and lighting, will not fall short of £2,000,000. The capital of the Charing Cross, Euston, and Hampstead is £2,136,000 in shares, and £712,000 borrowing powers, or a total of £2,848,000.

The capital of the Brompton and Piccadilly stands at £1,000,000 in shares, and £888,000 borrowing powers, or a total of £1,888,000.

The capital of Baker Street and Waterloo is £1,725,000 ordinary shares, £660,000 preference shares, and £794,000 borrowing powers, or a total of £3,179,000.

The Great Northern and Strand has an authorised capital of £2,400,000, and loans to the extent of £800,000. Adding to this the capitalisation which will be required for the various connecting lines which were being sought by the Yerkes interests, the total capital of the joint undertakings, including that required to electrify the Metropolitan District line, will not run short of £16,000,000. In addition, the capital required to build the City and Brixton Railway, the powers for which have already been granted, and including the shares and loan capital of £1,200,000, and adding the City and South London, who have a share capital of £1,680,000, with a loan capital of £518,000 ; and the Waterloo and City with a share capital of £540,000, and loan authorised of £180,000, we find that the grand total of capital either already authorised, or which will be authorised within the next couple of years, is in the neighbourhood of £45,000,000. Besides this is the capitalisation of the West London Tramways, the Croydon Tramways, and those controlled by the County Council, so that the total proposed investments in rapid transit facilities for London, leaving out the existing railways and omnibus lines, will be over £50,000,000 sterling. The omnibus lines can be for the present neglected, as where either electric, overhead, or underground roads compete, the horse omnibus has to give place. This fact has been proved over and over again in England. The same thing cannot be said of the railway companies entering London, who have a vast capital locked up in lines which can only be utilised for handling suburban traffic, and who in the near future will be bound to work this traffic electrically unless they are prepared to abandon the field.

Adding the capital of the Metropolitan and Metropolitan and District, London, Tilbury and Southend, North London, East London, West London Extensions, and that portion which the railways entering London have practically invested in lines only suitable for handling suburban traffic, the additional capital invested will not fall short of another £50,000,000, which means that at the present moment there is practically a capital of over £100,000,000 sterling invested in Greater London for the purpose of handling urban and suburban traffic—an amount nearly equal to the capital invested in Greater New York in rapid transit. From a comparison in the article of Mr. James Dredge on the "Economics of Railways," page 189, Vol. III, of TRACTION AND TRANSMISSION, it was clearly demonstrated that London is not as mobile as New York, and it is shown that in New York the total population is carried once a day. It is not probable that we shall obtain in the near future a greater traffic in urban and suburban passengers than exists in New York to-day, and a little arithmetic will suffice to show the enormous traffic which will have to be secured if anything like a fair interest is to be paid on the capital already expended or proposed to be invested.

From a careful examination of the evidence before the Committee of the House of Lords, as well as from an investigation of the facts and figures, it would seem to be impossible that the two systems of Morgan and Yerkes could find sufficient traffic to make any adequate return on the money expended.

The position of Mr. Yerkes is a very much better one than that of the Morgan group, in that the District Railway will be electrified, as well as several of the Yerkes tubes, before the Morgan group can possibly have finished their lines, and it is also certain that whenever passengers can utilise a shallow line such as the District, when it is operated electrically, and when the foul air in the tunnels is done away with, they will use it in preference to the deep tunnel line. It is also to be expected that the speed on the District system will be greater than on the Morgan deep tunnel line. Furthermore, from the vicinities of Ealing, Acton, Uxbridge, Harrow, Wimbledon, Richmond, passengers from the District will be able to go through to the City without changing, which travellers could not do by the proposed Morgan lines.

Mr. C. Robinson stated that he expected to carry over 250,000,000 passengers a year on his system when completed, and that would be sufficient on his estimate of average fares (which the evidence would seem to show to have been too optimistic) to justify the large capital expenditure proposed.

The Yerkes group of lines would have to carry at least as many passengers, that is to say, that the two lines which practically compete over most of their territories, would have to jointly carry five hundred million passengers. It is quite possible that this service may increase the population and the district served to such an extent that in the future such a traffic might be reached, but the present position does not seem to justify the capital expenditure proposed by the Morgan group, in addition to the money which has already been expended by the Yerkes system.

The Morgan lines would doubtless greatly reduce the receipts which the Yerkes group anticipate, but it is not probable that they would secure the traffic they count on, which appears excessive, because the average fare on which the estimates are based is higher than the circumstances warrant. Had the old *régime* which once ruled the Metropolitan District been still in force, it could have been easily understood, but with such a pushing American as Mr. Yerkes, very heavily interested in the success of the District, and under the guidance of their present chairman, Mr. Perks, it does not seem that any fear need have been entertained that the policy of the District would be to block other enterprises unreasonably.

As regards the proposals of the Central London, the case was a very different one. Here was a scheme proposed and backed by the highest railway authorities; it was an extension of an existing system which has proved eminently successful, and it would have been carried out under the best possible auspices. The evidence given by the railway managers of the main lines entering London, and by all those who had any practical experience in tube lines, was so strongly in favour of the Central London proposal, and the financial arrangement was so sound and satisfactory, that it came as a surprise to everyone that this excellent Bill was thrown out by the Lords Committee.

There have been several deep tunnel lines authorised in the past, which, up to the time that they were bought out by Mr. Yerkes, were blocked for lack of funds, and had it not been for the great enterprise shown by our American cousins, these Bills would still have been in the hands of the original promoters, and would probably have lapsed. It is most desirable that public confidence in the stability of railway undertakings should not be upset, and it is on this account that one could have wished that Parliament had taken different views about the Morgan proposals. The public are very anxious for new methods of transportation, and the promoters, in their eagerness to produce new schemes, may very likely defeat their object by causing tube lines to get such a bad name that the prudent investing public will have nothing to do with them.

There used to be a time when Parliament never sanctioned any new line which for a great part of its length closely paralleled an existing one, and till recently it has shown a benevolent interest in the schemes which it has already sanctioned, and declared to be of use and for the general good. Competition is no doubt necessary to ensure the public getting the best service, but there may be such a thing as too much competition, which will make it impossible for the rival railway companies to earn any dividends. The public has to find the money for the undertakings in the long run, and if they realise that within a given district, provided good service is given, Parliament will not protect them against new and parallel competing lines, this class of investment will be discredited. This is not a state of affairs to be desired either by the engineer or by the general public.

ELECTRIC MOTORS: THEIR THEORY AND CONSTRUCTION*

FOURTH ARTICLE

By H. M. HOBART

"SPACE FACTOR"

THE ratio of the total cross section of copper in an armature slot or field spool to the cross section of the total available space is termed the "space factor." It is a very variable quantity, and depends not only upon the normal voltage and output of the motor, and upon the shape of the slot or field spool, but—and very largely—upon the care and skill employed in the winding and insulating, and upon the insulation tests to which the motor is subjected. Many manufacturers prefer to subject the apparatus to very severe insulation tests, with a view to reducing to a negligible percentage the number of subsequent breakdowns. Others reason that such large factors of safety are unnecessary, and that for a given expenditure a motor of inferior qualities in other respects must be the result of such lavish insulation. The writer is of the opinion that the very highest factors of safety which it has yet been customary to employ in any country in the design of the insulation of electrical machinery are none too liberal. The subjecting of electrical machinery to severe insulation tests does not as a rule lead to any undue sacrifice of space to insulating purposes, but rather to a careful study of the properties of insulating materials and their correct treatment. The skilful use of high grade and durable, though relatively thin, insulation, will go further towards producing a motor capable of undergoing severe insulation tests than lavish space allowances less skilfully utilised. The properties of magnetic and conducting materials entering into the construction of the motor have been carefully investigated with a view to their economical use, but although a very great deal of

experimental work has been carried out on insulating materials, the results are not yet accessible in such form as to permit of their ready and correct application in motor construction, and the choice and treatment of the insulating materials are hardly given the attention they deserve, even by the very largest manufacturers.

A consideration of the relative proportions

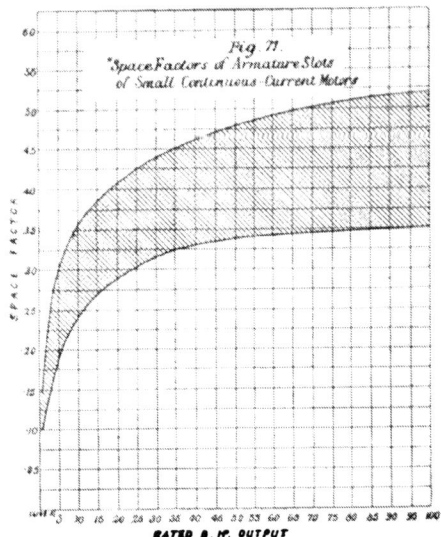

Diagram showing Space Factors of Armature Slots

of the winding space, devoted respectively to copper and insulation, emphasises the importance of a study of the question of a better use of insulating materials.

In Fig. 71 are given two curves limiting a shaded area within which the "space factors" of the armature slots of small motors lie. The range of voltage is from 100 to 600 volts. The values approach the lower limit, or even fall below it, the higher

*See TRACTION AND TRANSMISSION, Vol. IV, pages 76, 135, 206.

the voltage, the greater the number of slots, and the less the skill and knowledge employed in the processes of winding and insulating, and in the selection and testing of materials. Under fair conditions the lower limiting curve for 600 volts, and the upper for 100 volts, and for motors of the ranges of speeds corresponding to the data of Figs. 67 to 70 (Vol. IV., page 219,) should be consistent with subjecting the motors to the following insulation tests :—

Rated Voltage.				Guaranteed Insulation Test from Copper to Iron at 60degs. Cent. for One Minute.
100	...	...	...	2,000 R.M.S. volts.
600	...	...	...	3,600 R.M.S. volts.

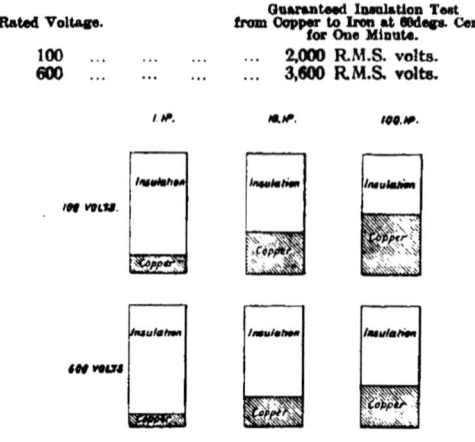

Fig 72. Graphical representation of relation between total slot area and total copper cross section in small Motors

Diagram showing Proportions of Slot Area and Copper and Insulation

In Fig. 72 the shaded portions of the six rectangles show the proportions of the total slot area occupied by copper and insulation respectively. These results are extremely significant. The art of insulating, in motor manufacturing, is still extremely crude, and there is every reason to look for great improvements. In cable manufacturing* it is well understood that the cost of the copper is, for all but the lowest voltage, but a small part of the cost of the complete cable, and the design and construction of the insulation is reduced to a science, whereas in motor building the insulation is regarded as one of the less important details. But the diagrams of Fig. 72 show that the

possible gain, either in decreased dimensions of motors or in increased output (which amounts to nearly the same thing), is not a matter of a few per cent. merely.

The lower the voltage and the larger the capacity, the greater is the percentage of the total insulation devoted to insulating the conductors from the armature core. In small motors for the higher voltages, on the other hand, the greater part of the insulation space consists in the coverings of the individual wires. Hence, in spite of the increased cost of insulation, it often, in very small motors, becomes economical to employ silk-covered wire. A great deal of the space lost in these smaller sizes for higher voltages is due to the multiplicity of wires required. Hence, two-circuit windings should be employed wherever these small sizes are built multipolar. The mistake should, furthermore, never be made of using two wires in parallel in small motors for high voltages for the purpose of using the same slot as for the lower voltages of the same size.* If the same slots must be used for all voltages, then the size should be chosen with due regard to the high voltage requirements. The choice of width and depth, and number of slots also, of course, have a great influence upon the "space factor."

In field spools, higher "space factors" may generally be used, but this varies even more with the nature of the design. Thus, for a given rating a motor with many poles requires relatively few turns of relatively large cross section, as compared with a machine for the same output at the same voltages and speeds with few poles. The former has, consequently, a high, and the latter a low "space factor." Moreover, the field-spool "space factor" is of much less importance than the armature slot "space factor," because space on the field poles is less restricted. The following example (Table III) of the application of a method for calculating a spool winding, proceeds from the standpoint of an assumed "space factor," and has the advantage of bringing out clearly the bearing of this factor on the result, and the consequences in relation to weight of copper

---

* Much of the information on insulating materials contained in the paper, by O'Gorman, on " Insulation of Cables," *Proceedings of the Institute of Electrical Engineers,* 1901, Vol. XXX, page 608, could be employed to great advantage in the design of dynamo electric machinery.

* Such mistakes are, nevertheless, constantly being made, and this is the result of a widespread failure to appreciate the proportions actually existing between amounts of insulation and copper, even when employed to the best advantage possible, in the light of the experience at present available.

employed and watts required in excitation, of changes in the "space factor," or in the overall spool dimensions :—

TABLE III.—TABULATED CALCULATIONS FOR SPOOL WINDINGS FOR 25 BRAKE HORSE-POWER MOTORS FOR 100, 200, AND 400 VOLTS

	Voltage.		
	100	200	400
Internal diameter of spool (centimetres)	13	13	13
Depth of winding (centimetres)	5	5	5
External diameter of spool (centimetres)	23	23	23
Mean diameter of spool (centimetres)	18	18	18
Mean length, one turn (metres) (a)	.565	.565	.565
Ampere-turns per spool (b)	4200	4000	3800
a × b	2380	2260	2150
.000176 × a² b²	1000	900	810
"Space factor" (s)	.45	.40	.35
Axial length of spool (centimetres)	13	13	13
Cross section spool winding (t) (square centimetres)	65	65	65
Total cross section copper in spool (m = s × t) (square centimetres)	29.3	26.0	22.8
Cubic centimetres copper in spool (100 a s t)	1660	1470	1290
Weight copper in spool (kilogrammes) (1 cubic centimetre of copper weighs .0089 kilogramme)	14.9	13.1	11.5
Watts per spool at 60degs. Cent. (w) Watts = .000176 × a²b² / kilogrammes	67.5	69.0	70.5
Square decimetres of external cylindrical surface per spool	9.4	9.4	9.4
Watts per square decimetre of external cylindrical surface	7.20	7.35	7.50
Number of poles	4	4	4
Volts per spool (v)	25	50	100
Amperes per spool (i = w/v)	2.70	1.38	0.705
Turns per spool (n = b/i)	1560	2900	5400
Cross section copper per turn (m/n) (square centimetres)	.0188	.0090	.0042
Current density in amperes per square centimetre	144	153	168
Watts in all spools	270	276	282
Kilogrammes copper in all spools	59.2	52.4	46.0
Diameter bare spool copper (millimetres)	1.54	1.07	0.73

This 25 brake horse-power motor is designed for the three voltages, 100, 200, and 400, on the plan of employing somewhat lower magnetic densities the higher the rated

external dimensions shall not require appreciably more energy for excitation, and hence shall not have a greater temperature rise. Since the magnet frame is the same for all three voltages, this requires either the adoption of higher speeds for the motors with the higher rated voltages, or else the employment of armatures of greater strength as expressed in armature ampere turns per pole piece. The latter plan is disadvantageous, since one encounters in the armature design the difficulty that the "space factor" of the armature slot is also much lower the higher the voltage. In view of these facts it is more consistent to widen the magnetic system, and in some cases to decrease the number of field poles for the higher voltage motors, and thus use less armature ampere turns. This leads to extremely practical results, since the width required for the commutator is, for a given output, almost in inverse proportion to the rated voltage. In machines designed on this plan, not only may due regard be paid to the variations in the "space factors" of both armature slots and field spools, but the commutators may be given proportions suited to the duty required of them. The overall dimensions are precisely the same for all voltages ; in fact, all essentially mechanical parts — base, stands, bearings, and shaft — as well as distance between bearings—are entirely independent

TABLE IV.—PARTICULARS OF 110, 220, AND 525-VOLT MOTORS (see Fig. 73, page 107)

(DIMENSIONS IN MILLIMETRES)

Number of Poles.	Brake Horse-power Output.	Revolutions per Minute.	Voltage.	A	B	C	D	E	F	G	H	I	J	K	L	Length of Laminations between Flanges.	Number of Ventilating Ducts.	Width of each Ventilating Duct.	Effective Length of Armature Laminations.	Diameter of Magnet Core.	Radial Length of Magnet Core.	Number of Armature Slots.	Width of Slot.	Depth of Slot.	Number of Commutator Segments.	Thickness of Segment and Surface (excluding Insulation).	Thickness of Segment from Commutator Connection to outer end of Commutator	Armature Conductors per Slot.	Height of Armature Conductor.	Width of Armature Conductor.
6	100	500	110	1366	1650	1300	740	610	1325	340	690	620	330	215	1350	125	3	10	80	155	190	60	16.2	28.0	240	7.2		290	8	11.1	2.7
6	100	500	220	1366	1650	1300	740	610	1325	390	610	620	430	250	1350	170	3	10	190	170	190	96	10.4	29.5	384	4.2		190	8	12	1.2
6	100	500	525	1366	1650	1300	740	610	1325	420	580	620	500	400	1350	282	6	10	200	225	190	162	11.5	19.0	516	3		120	10	6.3	1
8	120	460	110	1585	1900	1500	900	710	1450	370	730	715	395	190	1470	125	3	10	80	130	210	102	14.5	30.0	408	4.7		315	8	12.3	2.3
6	120	460	220	1585	1900	1500	900	710	1450	420	680	710	470	260	1470	165	3	10	104	175	216	108	11.8	30.0	432	4.4		230	8	13	1.6
6	120	460	525	1585	1900	1500	900	710	1450	460	610	710	550	420	1470	248	6	10	168	232	216	114	11.4	22.5	570	3.2		160	10	8	1.2
8	150	420	110	1813	2210	1740	1070	790	1650	395	875	730	370	200	1660	125	3	10	80	152	235	112	14.0	30.0	336	6.7		350	6	11.7	3.1
6	150	420	220	1813	2210	1740	1070	790	1650	445	825	730	460	300	1660	160	3	10	95	195	235	130	11.6	30.0	390	5.6		250	6	11.7	2.1
6	150	420	525	1813	2210	1740	1070	790	1650	485	785	720	560	435	1660	220	6	10	141	235	235	166	10.6	25.0	624	3.1		170	8	8.6	1.2
8	180	380	110	2114	2470	2030	1200	840	1735	390	940	770	350	275	1740	125	4	10	77	154	250	120	14.0	32.5	360	6.9		400	6	12.2	3.7
6	180	380	220	2114	2470	2030	1200	840	1735	450	880	770	475	300	1740	160	4	10	95	165	250	144	12.0	33.6	576	3.7		275	6	12.5	1.8
6	180	380	525	2114	2470	2030	1200	840	1735	500	830	770	580	330	1740	220	6	10	126	235	250	168	11.4	26.0	672	3.2		170	8	9	1.4

voltage. This is done in order that, with the lower field spool "space factor" of the higher voltage designs, spools of the same

of the voltage, so that the same drawings, patterns, and castings are used for all voltages, the patterns being constructed to be adjust-

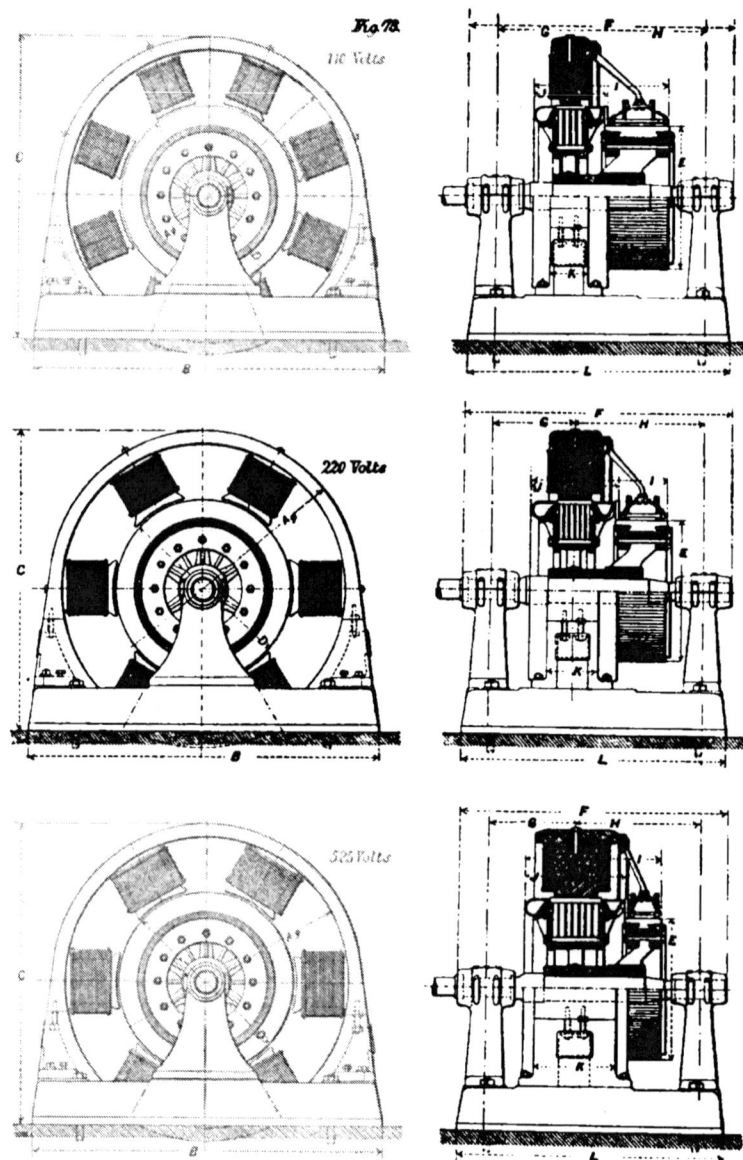

Diagrams of Motors for 110, 220, and 525 Volts

able in width to the extent necessary for the different voltages. The diameters of magnetic yoke, whose dimensions must be chosen with reference to mechanical, as well as magnetic considerations, and of armature and commutator, are the same for all voltages, and the magnetic yoke could, in many cases, be made the same section for all voltages, different magnet cores in number and section being used, according to the voltage of the motor.

In Fig. 78 are given outline drawings for a group of machines designed by the writer on this plan. The machines were originally designed for generators. Their ratings for normal output, speed, and voltage as motors, and their dimensions, are set forth in Table IV* (page 106).

In the field spools of machines with many poles the volts per spool become relatively low, and also the volts per turn, thus permitting of but a thin layer of insulation on the conductor. This materially increases the "space factor," but requires that additional care be taken in winding. In the interests of a high "space factor," field spools should all be connected in series.†

Series spool windings and low-voltage shunt windings may be constructed from thin strip, wound on the thin edge, and in many cases such construction leads to a much higher "space factor" than can otherwise be obtained. Thus "space factors" of 0.75 are sometimes obtainable in the series spools of moderate sized machines‡ by this construction. There is the additional advantage that the heat is readily conducted, by the continuity of the solid copper, to the exterior surface of the spool, where the circulating air currents quickly dissipate it. Thus, in this type of spool winding, higher values may, for a given temperature increase, be permitted for the "watts per square decimetre of external spool surface." It is of some further advantage to leave the edges of such edge-wound conductors bare, merely insulating between adjacent conductors. When the surface is then polished, the general appearance of the machine is greatly improved.

HOPKINSON METHOD OF TESTING MOTORS

Motors are generally tested in pairs, one running as a motor from the supply of power, and driving the second as a generator, the current from the latter being returned

to the source of supply. By this means a considerable saving is effected, since only sufficient power is required to supply the losses in the two machines. This method of testing was first devised by Hopkinson, and is generally designated as the Hopkinson method, although numerous modifications have subsequently been devised by Kapp, Swinburne, and others.

It is diagrammatically represented in Fig. 74, in which A and B are the armatures of the two machines to be tested, F and G

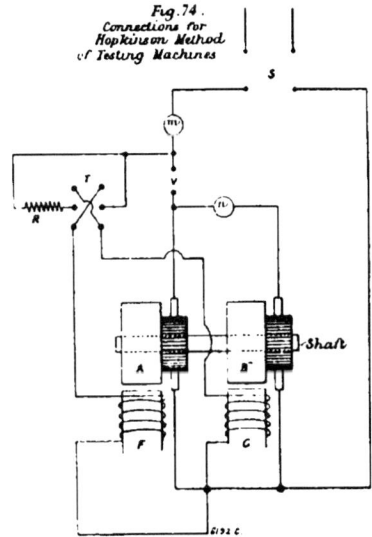

Hopkinson Method of Testing Motors

representing their field magnet systems. The two machines are mounted upon the same shaft, or otherwise directly coupled together. S is the main switch leading to the source of supply, and T is a double-pole, double-throw switch leading to the field circuits, and V is merely a single-pole switch, inserted for the purpose of enabling the field circuits to be excited independently of the armature circuits. As is shown, T is so connected to the field circuits of the machines A and B, that when it is thrown down, a suitable resistance, R, is inserted in the field circuit of machine A, and when thrown up, the resistance is in B's field circuit. When switches S, T, and V are closed, the machine having the resistance, R, in its field circuit, runs as a motor, its counter electromotive force being the least, and the other, thus

---

* The designs shown in Fig. 73, and in Table IV, are adapted from a paper on "Modern Commutating Dynamo Machinery," published in the *Journal of Proceedings of the Institute of Electrical Engineers*, 1901, Vol. XXXI, page 170, where this plan of designing is discussed in much greater detail.

† In machines with many poles, but for low voltage, the thickness of the insulation on the conductor may exert but a negligible influence on the "space factor," and a more convenient size of conductor may occasionally, in such cases, be obtained by a series parallel connection of the field spools.

‡ This is too high a figure to be attained in motors of less than 100 horse-power rated capacity, unless of very low speed or voltage.

PLATE XXII

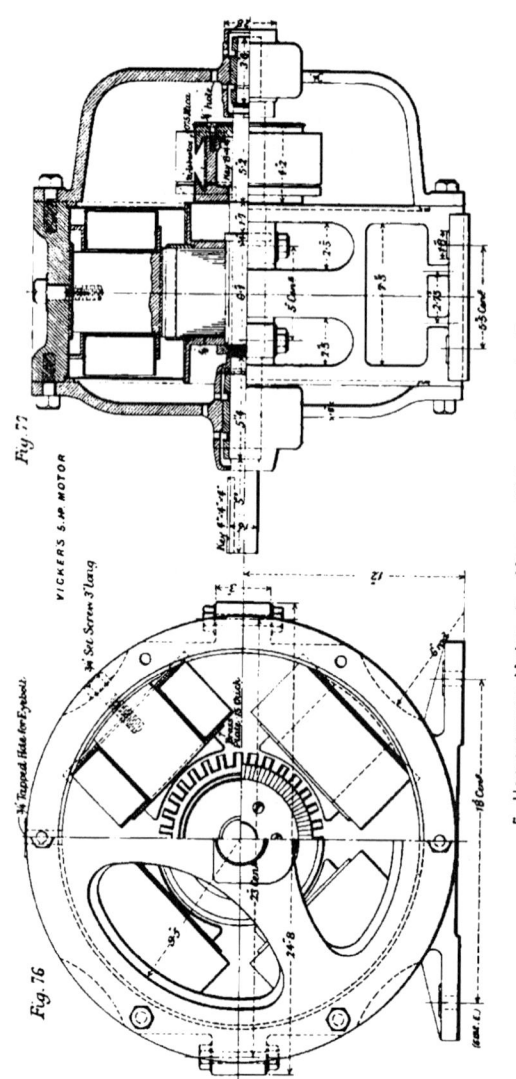

Fig. 77

VICKERS 5 H.P. MOTOR

Fig. 76

5 Horse-power Motor by Messrs. Vickers Sons & Maxim

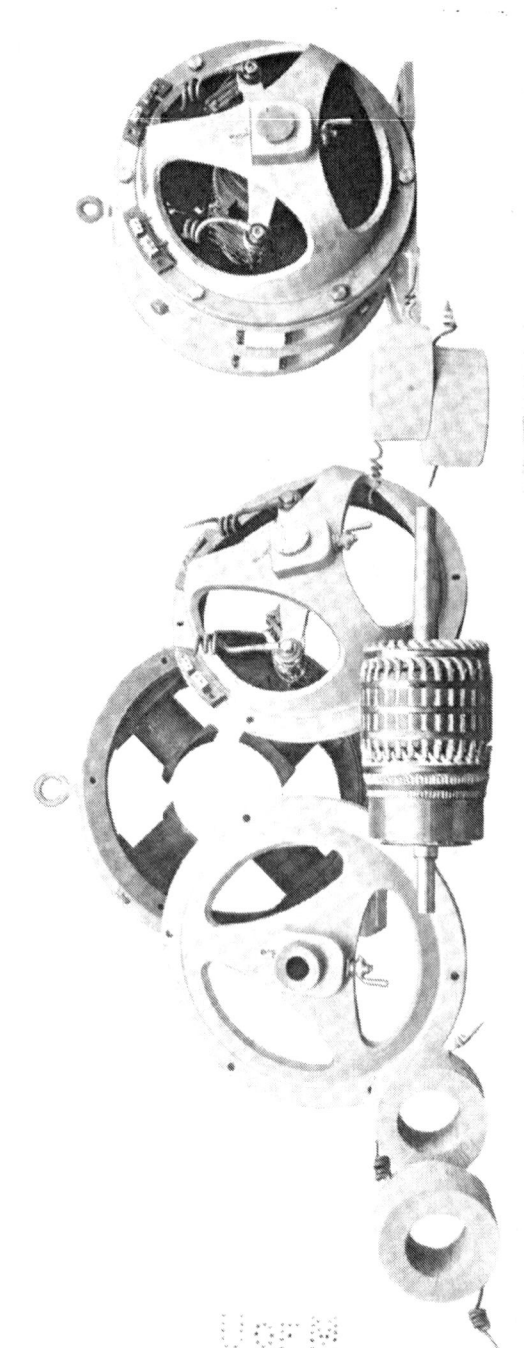

U of M

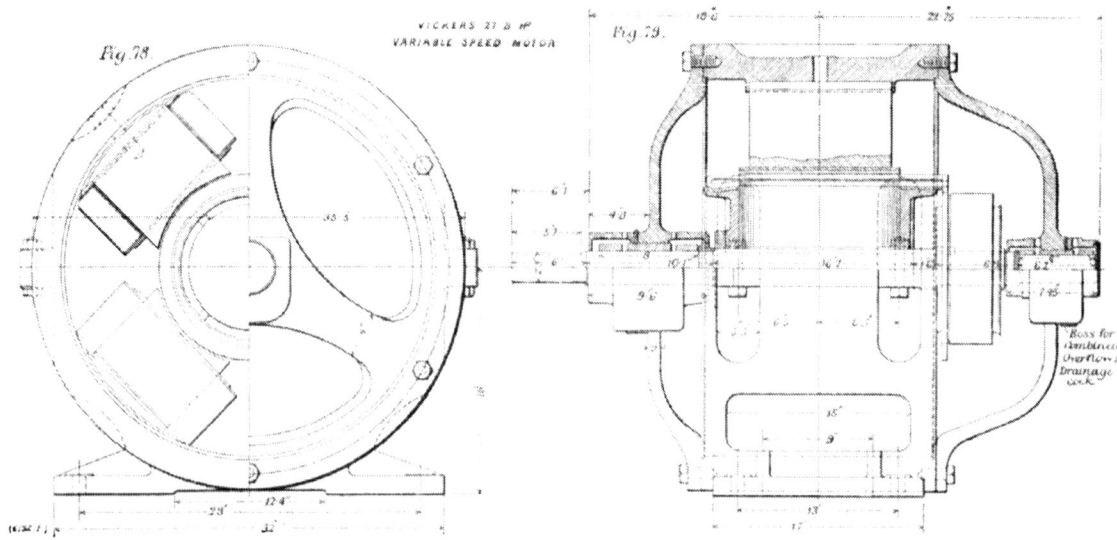

Fig. 78.

VICKERS 27.5 HP
VARIABLE SPEED MOTOR

Fig. 79.

Boss for
Combined
Overflow &
Drainage
Cock

27.5 Brake Horse-power Variable Speed 220-volt Motor

driven mechanically, acts as a generator in virtue of its higher excitation and electromotive force, and returns to the line as electrical energy, a portion of the electrical energy absorbed by the motor, this energy having thus undergone a double transformation, first by the motor into the mechanical energy transmitted by the shaft to the generator, and by the latter into electrical energy delivered from its commutator.

It is customary during a heat run to reverse switch T at, say, half-hour intervals, so that both machines are equally subjected to motor and generator loads, for the motor armature winding is more heavily, and its field winding more lightly, loaded than the generator's.

Ammeter m measures the current supplied to the system to cover the losses, i.e., a current equal to the motor current minus the generator current. Ammeter n measures the motor current when switch T is in the "up" position, in which case the generator current equals $n - m$; and in the "down" position of switch T it measures the generator current, and the motor current is then $n + m$. The generator current is sometimes designated the "circulating current."

Mr. A. D. Williamson has kindly furnished the writer with the results of such a test on two 5 brake horse-power motors of his own design. The results of

the Hopkinson test, together with the observed temperature increase, are given in Tables V and VI.

TABLE V.—TEST OF TWO 5 BRAKE HORSE-POWER, 600 REVOLUTIONS PER MINUTE, 220-VOLT, SHUNT-WOUND, STANDARD, VENTILATED, ENCLOSED VICKERS MOTORS. (HOPKINSON CONNECTIONS)

Revolutions per Minute.	Volts.	Auxiliary Current Amperes.	Circulating Current Amperes.	Brake Horse-power.	Square of Efficiency.	Efficiency.
683	220	6.5	19.5	5.75	.751	.866
690	203	5.7	19.0	5.17	.770	.877
685	204	4.3	15.0	4.10	.777	.881
681	204	4.2	14.0	3.82	.770	.877
665	203	3.4	10.0	2.72	.747	.864

TABLE VI.—TEMPERATURE RISE AFTER FIVE AND A HALF HOURS' RUN ON FULL LOAD

Date of test, July 21st, 1902. Temperature of engine room, 32degs. Cent.

	Ultimate Temperature. Degrees Cent.	Rise in Temperature. Degrees Cent.
Commutator	73	41
Core	68	36
Shunt coils	61	29

These motors were designed and built by Mr. Williamson for Messrs. Vickers Sons & Maxim. An engraving of this 5 horse-power motor, assembled and in parts, is given in Fig. 75, and the general arrangement is shown in the drawings of Figs. 76 and 77, Plate XXII. The machine may be used up to its full rated capacity as a reversible motor, the commutation being excellent at that load, with the brushes in the neutral position.

Another interesting machine by the same designer is shown in the drawings of Figs. 78 and 79 (page 109). It is rated as a 27.5 brake horse-power variable speed 220-volt motor, and gives 25 horse-power at a range of speed from 800 to 1,000 revolutions per minute on shunt excitation, and 30 horse-power from 300 to 800 revolutions per minute. The motor is quite reversible up to about 800 revolutions per minute at 27.5 horse-power, *i.e.*, it operates satisfactorily under these conditions with the brushes in the neutral position.

The following test results (Table VII) of one of these motors are of interest :—

TABLE VII.—TESTS OF WILLIAMSON MOTOR

Date of test, May 7th and 8th, 1902.

Speed.	Volts.	Total Current.	Shunt Current.	Brake Horse-power.	Efficiency.
324	224	96.5	4.72	24.65	.862
386	222	103.0	3.48	26.75	.88
498	224	101.5	2.78	26.70	.884
502	227	168.7	2.37	45.60	.882
718	221	100.7	2.10	25.73	.872
750	227	123.5	1.20	32.55	.875
950	222	106.3	0.97	26.80	.863
960	222	96.5	0.97	24.85	.875
960	222	106.7	0.97	27.30	.869
970	230	109.4	0.97	28.80	.868

The three runs at different loads, giving the following results, were each of six hours' duration :—

TABLE VIII.—RESULTS OF SIX HOURS' RUN

Date.	Speed. Revolutions per Minute.	Field Current.	Mean Current.	Mean Voltage.	Mean Brake Horse-power.	Temperature Rise of			
						Commutator Degrs. Cent.	Field Coil. Degs. Cent.	Armature Core. Degs. Cent.	Armature Winding. Degs. Cent.
May 12th, 1902..	349	3.54	97	222	25	36	42	48	38
May 13th, 1902..	353	3.32	118.8	221.4	30	52	42	65	54
May 14th, 1902..	610	..	118.8	221.4	30	43	42	54	—

Further data of these two machines is set forth in Table IX :—

TABLE IX.—GENERAL DATA OF 5 HORSE-POWER AND 27.5 HORSE-POWER MOTORS

	5 Brake Horse-power.	27.5 Brake Horse-power.
Speed	600	300 to 900
Voltage	220	220
Weight in lbs.	840	3470
Material of yoke	Cast iron	Steel
Material of poles	Steel	Steel
Type armature winding ...	2 circuit	2 circuit

Armature Dimensions :—

External diameter...	9ins.	15ins.
Axial length core between flanges	4.75ins.	13ins.
Effective length core between flanges	4.5ins.	12.5ins.
Number of ventilating ducts ...	None	None
Depth slot	1in.	.96in.
Width slot	.33in.	.35in.
Number of slots	31	47
Internal diameter laminations ...	2ins.	3ins.
Height of bare conductor ...	} .072in.	.4in.
Width of bare conductor... ...	} diameter	.06in.
Number of conductors per slot ...	30	6
Slot, "space factor"	.37	.33

Magnet Core :—

Length of pole, face parallel to shaft	4.75ins.	13ins.
Length of pole arc	5.5ins.	9ins.
Radial length of magnet core ...	5ins.	7ins.
Diameter of magnet core... ...	4.3ins.	—
Length of air-gap	.15in.	.25in.

Commutator :—

Diameter	8ins.	11.8ins.
Number of segments	93	141
Length of segment from external end to commutator connection	2.8ins.	3.7ins.
Thickness of brushes	.75in.	1in.
Width of brushes	1in.	1in.
Number of brushes per set ...	2	3
Number of sets used	2	2
Ampere turns per armature pole	1140	1900
Shunt ampere turns per spool...	3150	7300*
Weight copper per shunt spool ...	15.5lbs.	83lbs.
Core loss	170	450*
Shunt loss	210	944*
Commutator loss	50	300*
Armature C² R loss	230	750
Bearing friction loss	80	250*
Mean length one armature turn...	28ins.	56ins.
Armature turns per segment ...	5	1
Mean length one spool turn ...	19ins.	40ins.

* At 300 revolutions per minute.

CHOICE OF NUMBER OF ARMATURE SLOTS

The choice of the number of armature slots is a matter requiring comment. In the first place, the use of the two-circuit winding, which, as has been explained, is especially desirable for small motors, limits the available numbers. Table X gives, for the case of the plain two-circuit single winding, the number of conductors or sides of coils (groups of conductors) which are possible per slot for motors with from four to sixteen poles.

TABLE X. — DATA FOR APPLYING TWO - CIRCUIT SINGLE WINDINGS FOR DRUM ARMATURES

Number of Poles.	Possible Numbers of Conductors or Groups of Conductors per Slot, for Symmetrical Windings.							
4	1	2	...	6	...	10	...	14	—
6	1	2	4	...	8	10	...	14	16
8	1	2	...	6	...	10	...	14	—
10	1	2	4	6	8	...	12	14	16
12	1	2	...	...	...	10	...	14	—
14	1	2	4	6	8	10	12	...	16
16	1	2	...	6	...	10	...	14	—

Other numbers of conductors per slot can be used. For instance, four conductors, or groups of conductors, per slot in a four-pole motor, by the device of having one "dummy" coil, that is, one coil not connected to the winding or the commutator, or a space block in its place. But this, while often employed, introduces, in the writer's opinion, a very undesirable lack of symmetry, and should only be used where the sparking constants are very conservative. All limitations relating to the possible numbers of groups of conductors per slot, lead to difficulties in employing the same punchings for windings for different voltages. Frequently, in spite of the lower "space factor" and other undesirable properties for small motors, multiple-circuit windings, which are free from these limitations, are used for some voltages, in order to use one standard punching for all voltages. The use of conductors of rectangular cross section sometimes enables a given slot to be filled up more efficiently when employed for a winding of a different voltage, speed, or rating from that for which it was designed. Most manufacturers, however, prefer to use round wires for small motors, and on page 818 of the *Electrotechnische Zeitschrift* for April 11th, 1901, Rothert * describes some novel types of winding. In one of these, with six groups of conductors per slot, and four conductors per group—see Fig. 80—the conductors may lie four wide and six deep, there being twenty-four conductors per slot. In another —see Fig. 81—with four groups of conductors per slot, and four conductors per group,

* See also Rothert's U.S.A. patent, No. 660659.

the width of the slot would correspond to three conductors, and the depth to six, this arrangement corresponding to sixteen conductors per slot. The more customary, and, of course, the most effective arrangement corresponding to these two cases would be those shown in Figs. 82 and 83, where, however, the slots are rather deep. The

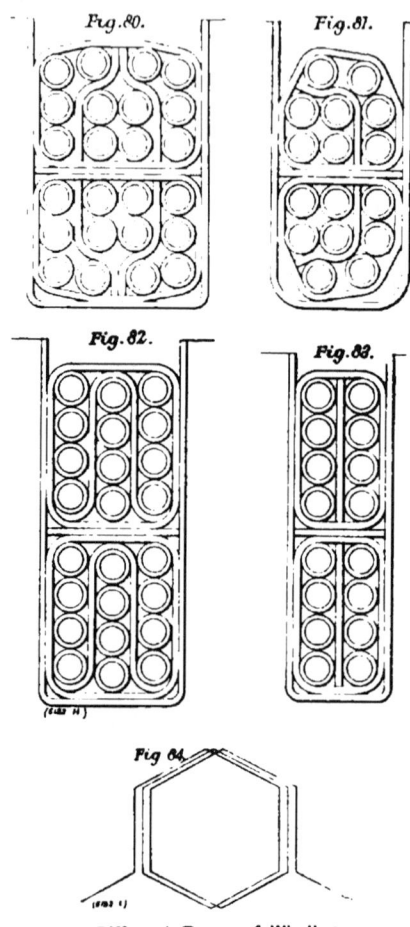

Different Types of Winding

arrangements suggested by Rothert are capable of considerable extension, and increase the flexibility of the two - circuit winding, and, indeed, of slot-type windings in general. The ideal from the manufacturing standpoint is, of course, to have one standard punching suitable for as many windings as possible, and while a too close adherence to this plan of procedure leads to sacrifices much greater than the advantage striven for, it is, nevertheless, well to give careful consideration to all methods leading to reduction in number of standard punchings.

Thus, the cases shown in Figs. 80 to 83 may be taken as representing four arrangements for a motor requiring, with a given

It will be seen from Table X that, generally, for four or eight poles, Figs. 80 and 82 would be the most suitable with three commutator segments per slot, whereas Figs. 81 and 83, with two commutator segments per slot, are suitable for six or ten poles. None of them would do for twelve

Fig.85. 4.Pole, 2-Circuit, Single Winding of the formula C=ny = 2m(162=4=41-2=1)
with every 2ⁿᵈ and 3ʳᵈ segment omitted.

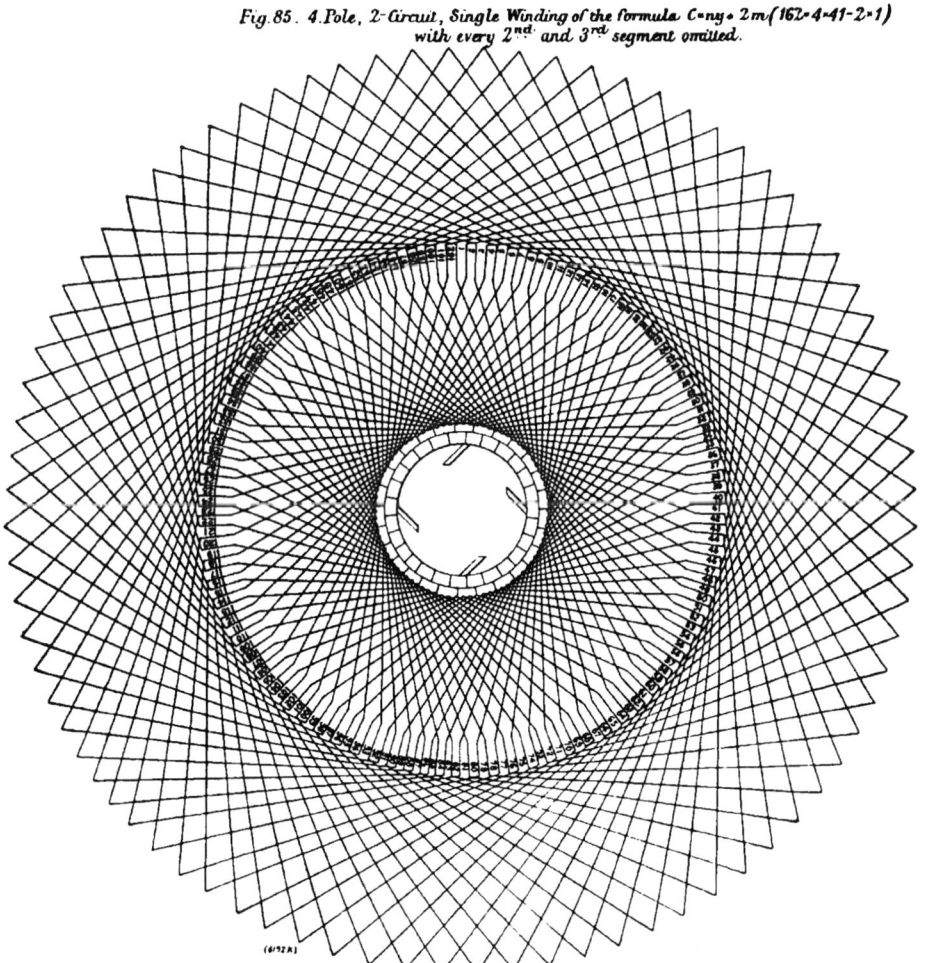

Single Winding for Four-pole Two-circuit Motor (see page 113)

total number of conductors, four turns per commutator segment, of the size wire shown in the figures. By adopting the arrangement shown in Fig. 80, a certain number of slots would be required. The use of the arrangement shown in Fig. 81 would require 50 per cent. more slots.

poles (for a symmetrical two-circuit single winding), and any one of them could be used for fourteen poles. The choice between Figs. 80 and 81, as against Figs. 82 and 83, would be greatly influenced by the sizes of slot found most suitable for designs for other rated voltages for the same motor.

Wherever at all practicable, the writer prefers bar to coil windings, in spite of the greater number of connections to be made. Thus, for a four-pole machine with three turns per commutator segment, there would generally be employed a coil winding with three turns per coil. This could be diagrammatically represented as shown in Fig. 84, page 111. For some sizes of slots, and especially for small conductors, this would be the best arrangement, but there often arise cases, even with conductors of fairly small cross section, where it would be preferable to arrange the winding as shown in Fig. 85, page 112. The total number of conductors, and the number of commutator segments, remain

even when the conductor is fairly small, and —other considerations aside — more readily wound into a coil. For the case chosen for the illustration the "space factor" is 8 per cent. lower for the bar winding.

The diagram in Fig. 85 represents the case of a two-circuit four-pole winding, with 162 face conductors and 27 segments, the equivalent of a three-turn coil winding. The pitch y equals 41, and the winding is a two-circuit single winding, conforming to the formula $C = n\,y + 2$ $(162 = 4 \times 41 - 2)$.

There could be numerous other forms of this winding; thus every fifth turn could be connected to a segment, corresponding to a five-turn coil winding, or the winding

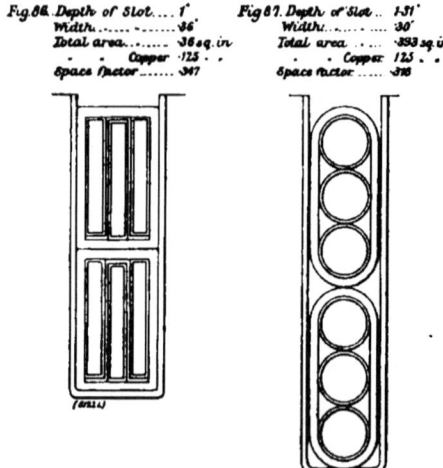

Fig. 86. Depth of Slot.... 1˝.
Width........ ....36˝
Total area....... .36 sq. in.
. . Copper .125 . .
Space factor...... .347

Fig. 87. Depth of Slot .. 1·31˝
Width... ....30˝
Total area . .... ·393 sq. in.
. . Copper .125 . .
Space factor ..... ·318

Methods of Winding

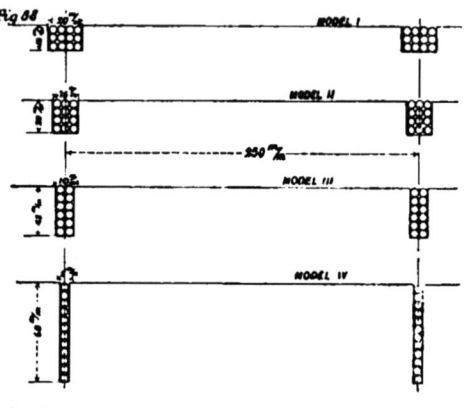

Depth of Iron laminations - 50 cms. (7˝ insulation between laminations)
Mean Length of turn (for all cases)= 134 cms.
Free length per turn . . - 78 ˝
Embedded length per turn . - 56 ˝

Models of Slot Dimensions

unchanged, but the dimensions of the slot, and of the conductors, and their arrangement in the slot, are as shown in Fig. 85, whereas the coil winding would be arranged as shown in Fig. 86. The coil winding requires at the front (commutator) end of the armature, not only space for the end connections of the individual coils, but also further space for the conductors interconnecting these coils. The other arrangement is very much better, where each conductor is sufficiently large to consist of a rod of rectangular cross section, and especially where the dimensions preferred for the slot require a conductor of such a cross section, since such conductors are less readily made up into coils. The superiority in orderliness should often make the winding preferable,

could have six poles and still have every third, fifth, or seventh turn connected to commutator segments. In general for this winding, every $(n+1)$th pair of conductors, —n being any even number—has a corresponding commutator segment.

WIDTH AND DEPTH OF SLOT.—The chief disadvantage of wide slots is that they lead to eddy currents in the pole faces, if the latter be solid, due to the rapid local changes in the magnetic flux distribution caused by the successive passage of tooth and slot by a given point in the pole face. This has led in many cases to the adoption of laminated pole pieces, although, unless the slot is very wide and the air-gap short, high resistance, cast-iron pole faces suffice to reduce the pole face loss to very moderate proportions. Wide slots, when there are but very few slots per pole, also sometimes lead to noisy running, which can be best remedied by lengthening the air-gap, or chamfering, or otherwise shading the pole pieces. These are troublesome and uncertain remedies, and it is desirable on this account not to choose too low a number of slots per pole. In the case of tramway, or crane, or other motors operating in the midst of greater noises, this is not a point requiring to be taken into account. There is some slight advantage in wide and shallow slots from the standpoint of decreased inductance of the embedded portion of the winding, best expressed in c.g.s. lines per centimetre of length. The extent of the influence upon this value, of the width and depth of the slot, may be seen from Table XI, where the values experimentally observed on models with the slot dimensions shown in Fig. 88, page 113, are given.

TABLE XI.

Model.					Lines per Centimetre of "Embedded Length."
I	...	...	...	...	2.8
II	...	...	...	...	3.2
III	...	...	...	...	4.2
IV	...	...	...	...	7.5

There is, however, the consideration to remember, that the deeper and narrower the slot, the shorter may be the end connections and the less their total inductance. The armature I^2R loss and the dimensions of the armature are also decreased by deep slots, so that they cannot at once be set aside as unsuitable, but must generally be taken into consideration in the case of the preparation of each design, and the relative advantages compared. Mechanically and thermally, it is much better to have wide and shallow slots, and several commutator segments per slot.

When several coils are thus to be grouped in one slot, it is generally more economical to wind them at one operation from several reels of wire. Another and very interesting way has been described by Rothert, in the article already once referred to (*Elektrotechnische Zeitschrift* for April 11th, 1901).* He describes it by the aid of a diagram reproduced in Fig. 89. The wire is wound in the winding form about the points *a b c d e f* as many times as there are to be turns per segment. The wire is then

* See also Rothert's U.S.A. Patent 660659.

continued out about the points *g h*, and the turns corresponding to the next spool are wound again about the points *a b c d e f*, and a loop is again brought out about the points *g h*, and this is repeated till all the wires of the combined spool, whose two sides are to lie in a given pair of slots, have been wound. Then, either before or after assembling the winding on the armature core, the loops are cut between *g* and *h*, and the six ends (supposing this to have been a case of winding with three segments per slot) are connected to the six corresponding segments.

Two methods of arranging the slot insulation are shown in Figs. 90 and 91. In

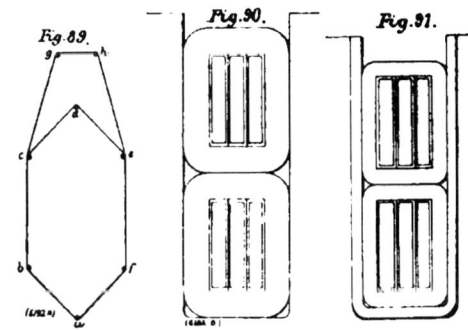

Methods of Winding (Rothert)

the former (Fig. 90) the general plan of procedure is to have sufficient insulation in wrappings of braid impregnated with varnish, and to dispense with an additional insulation at the sides and bottom of the slot. In the latter (Fig. 91) there is less insulation upon the coils, the space thus saved being taken up by a U-shaped lining to the slot, which serves more to protect the formed coil from abrasion when being put in place, than as insulation. This latter method has the additional advantage that the end connections may be insulated practically to the same specification as the slot portion, and still not employ any more space at the ends of the armature than is required for their suitable protection and insulation.

A six-pole, semi-enclosed, compound-wound "Castle" motor, for 25 brake horse-power, at 720 revolutions per minute, is illustrated in Figs. 92 and 93, Plate XXIII. The writer is indebted to Messrs. J. H. Holmes & Co., of Newcastle, for permission to publish a description of this motor, which is one

Plate XXIII

Fig. 93.

CASTLE. MOTOR. MULTIPOLAR TYPE
28 B.H. 720 REVS.
SCALE 1⅛ᵗ LFT.

Fig. 92

Figs. 92, 93 and 95.—Motors by Messrs. J. and H. Holmes & Co., Newcastle

they have manufactured extensively, often for operating printing presses. The drawings are of a 220-volt motor, which differs from the 460-volt motor of the specification in Table XII chiefly in number of slots, winding, length of commutator, and in being plain shunt wound.

TABLE XII.—DESCRIPTION OF "CASTLE" MOTOR

Number of poles	6
Speed	720 r.p.m.
Terminal voltage	460 volts
Full load current...	45 amperes
Armature diameter	15ins.
Gross length armature laminations between flanges	7ins.
Width ventilating duct in laminations ...	⅞in.
Effective length of armature laminations ...	6ins.
Inside diameter of laminations	7.75ins.
Number of slots	91
Depth of slot	1⅛ins.
Width of slot	0.27in.
Type of armature winding	2-circuit single
Pitch	61
Turns per commutator segment	2
Commutator segments per slot	2
Total number of face conductors	728
Total number of commutator segments ...	182
Commutator diameter	11.25ins.
Active length commutator segment	3.5ins.
Commutator segment made from strip of 1.125ins. × .163in. × .1242in.	
Brushes of carbon 1⅛ins. wide and ⅝in. thick	2 brushes per set
MAGNETIC CIRCUIT — magnet core cross section	21.64 sq. ins.
Pole pieces are of steel and in one casting, with yoke	
Cross section of yoke	13.25 sq. ins.
Length pole face...	6.75ins.
Length pole arc	5.13ins.
Cross section of air-gap at pole face ...	34.5 sq. ins.
Diameter of bore of pole faces... ...	15 ⅜ins.
Depth of gap	⅜in.
Full load armature ampere turns per pole ...	1370

After four hours' run at full rated load, the temperatures by thermometer were as follows :—

	Temperature Increase above Surrounding Air in Degrees Cent.
Magnets	32
Armature core	24
End connections	24
Commutator	30

Temperature of surrounding air = 18degs. Cent.

The arrangement of the conductors in the slot is shown in Fig. 94, drawn to a scale of 4 to 1.

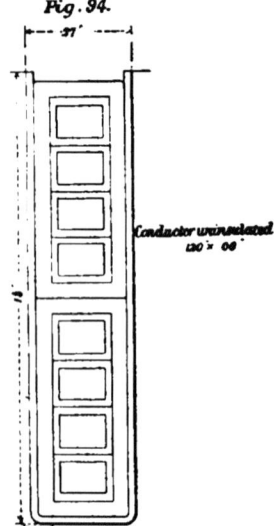

Fig. 94.

Conductor uninsulated 120 × 08

Arrangement of Conductors, "Castle" Motor

There are eight conductors per slot, and each conductor measures (bare) .12in. × .08in.

The "space factor" is therefore 0.816.

The shunt winding has 8,100 turns per limb, and the resistance of the six spools in series equals 880 ohms when warm.

An open-type six-pole motor of the same firm, and of about the same capacity as the motor just described, is shown in the engraving, Fig. 95, Plate XXIII. The set is for running a printing press, and the small auxiliary totally enclosed motor at the left is employed at starting in order to obtain a small current. It is subsequently. at the desired speed, automatically disconnected from the shaft by a toothed clutch, the work being taken over by the main motor.

THE
WESTINGHOUSE APPRENTICESHIP COURSE

By Walter M. McFarland, Pittsburg

THE proper training of the young men who are to fill leading positions in the manufacturing industries, has never been of greater importance than at the present time. It will be remembered that there was an extended series of letters in the columns of *Engineering* some time since from various engineers, discussing the questions of technical education, shop experience as articled pupils, etc., and great diversity of opinion was expressed as to what method is productive of the best results. The glamour which the achievements of the past are apt to throw, and a knowledge of the limited advantages possessed by the famous engineers who carried out great undertakings, are apt to mislead us unless we consider the question very carefully. Those older engineers did their work before the days of technical education, and it was, indeed, the experience gained by them, and its records in the proceedings of the engineering Societies, that formed the basis of the technical education of to-day. Because these men of genius were able to do splendid engineering work without technical education, there are some who are disposed hastily to jump to the conclusion that the same method of training which had to suffice for them, would answer to-day.

It seems to the writer that this is a very mistaken view, and it brings to mind a story told of a conversation between President Lincoln and one of the Union generals whom he had called to the chief command. In this conversation the President told him of certain well-recognised faults which he possessed, and then said: "It is not on account of these, but in spite of them, that I have appointed you." The same would seem to be true of the great engineers of the past; their successes were not on account of the lack of good technical training and the opportunities of to-day, but in spite of it.

There is, however, a side of the question of engineering training on which there is a difference of opinion, and on which the practice of the Westinghouse Manufacturing Company, of Pittsburg, sheds a very useful light, namely, the practical, or shop, side of the training, as distinguished from the class-room work. Of course, in these days, every well-organised technical school has workshops more or less efficiently equipped with typical tools, and all the students are required to spend a considerable time in these shops learning the use of both power and hand tools, and acquiring thus a very moderate manual dexterity. This experience is of great value, and certainly makes the young engineer on graduation a better equipped man than if his training had been entirely in the class-room. The fact remains, however, that in almost all school shops the work done is only typical, and is entirely free from the pressure of commercial requirements. Indeed, without frequent changes in the instructing staff, and its recruiting by people brought directly from manufacturing establishments, it would be difficult to have instruction keep pace with the latest developments of manufacturing progress.

For the very best results, and in order that the young engineer may be thoroughly grounded in the profession, the school course must be supplemented by actual practical acquaintance with shop work under manufacturing conditions where considerations of organisation and equipment to secure a profit, are the controlling factors. This means, in general, that the college graduate with a degree must go into the shop and gain his experience there under practically the same conditions as those which would obtain for an apprentice who is learning the trade. There is, of course, the important difference that the college graduate comes with a mind immensely broadened, and with faculties trained for observation and analysis, or, in other words, he is in condition to appreciate the reasons for everything that is done, and to acquire the necessary acquaintance with particular details of the work in a very much shorter time than the lad five or six years younger, and with only an ordinary school training.

The Westinghouse Electric and Manufacturing Company, under the guiding spirit of its distinguished head, Mr. George Westinghouse, found when it began business in 1886 that there were scarcely any men available with experience in electrical machinery, and that it must, therefore, train its own men. Accordingly, from the very beginning, what has been known at different times as the "Students' Course," the "Special Course," and the "Apprenticeship Course," was established, the idea being to take engineering graduates from colleges, preferably those who have been trained in electrical or mechanical engineering, and give them by actual experience in its shops, for a period of two or three years, that intimate practical acquaintance with all the details of the manufacture of electrical machinery, which would fit them for occupying higher positions with the company.

The number of young men enjoying these advantages varies from time to time, but there are usually about 150 going through the course. The pay is only nominal, and the work is regarded both by the company and by the young men themselves, as a post-graduate course to their college career.

The vice-president of the company, who is in charge of manufacturing operations, has the general control of this course, but it is especially looked after by one of the company's younger engineers, himself a graduate of the works, who lays out the order in which the apprentices shall go through the different sections of the factory; the length of time to be spent in each; and who exercises general supervision over their attention to work and proficiency. While the length of the course was, until recently, nominally three years, the growth of the electric business has become so rapid that it has been found necessary in many cases to put specially bright men through in a shorter time, so as to obtain their services at an earlier date.

To illustrate the correctness of this policy, it may be stated that almost the entire force of designing engineers of the company consists of graduates of this apprenticeship course; among them may be specially mentioned such well-known electrical engineers as B. G. Lamme and C. F. Scott. The graduates of the course are also utilised in the construction department, which looks after the installation of plants, in the selling, and in the correspondence departments. Indeed, in a concern with such a large business and of such an extremely technical nature, it can be appreciated how much more valuable men in the correspondence and the selling departments are, who have received a theoretical engineering training in the colleges, and have then gone through this apprenticeship.

As might be expected, in spite of the inducements which the company can offer, some of the able men who have gone through this training prefer, when they have gained some reputation, to start business for themselves as consulting or contracting engineers, and some of the most prominent consulting electrical engineers in America to-day have been graduates of the Westinghouse Company.

It should be clearly understood that the work done by these young men while going through the shops is the regular commercial work, and is not in any sense mere experimenting to give them a general idea of the business; they take their places at the various tools just like any of the other workmen. It will be understood at once, that with their theoretical training, such men become exceptionally valuable in the testing department, and that when they have the other necessary qualifications they also make excellent foremen. As a matter of fact, one of the leading engineers of the company was for a time a principal foreman in charge of large work.

It will be of special interest to British readers to know that some sixty young Britons have been for the past two years going through this apprenticeship course in the Pittsburg shops of the Westinghouse Company, to fit them for positions in connection with the British Westinghouse Company, whose great shops at Manchester are now completed and, indeed, at work. Many of these young men had not only completed college courses, but had filled positions of some importance in electrical work before taking up the apprenticeship course at Pittsburg.

The following reprint of the circular

THE
WESTINGHOUSE APPRENTICESHIP COURSE

By Walter N. McFarland, Pittsburg

The proper training of the young men who are to fill leading positions in the manufacturing industries has never been of greater importance than at the present time. It will be remembered that there was an extended series of letters in the columns of *Engineering* some time since from various engineers, discussing the questions of technical education, their experience as articled pupils, etc., and great diversity of opinion was expressed as to what method is productive of the best results. The glamour which the achievements of the past are apt to throw, and a knowledge of the limited advantages possessed by the famous engineers who carried out great undertakings, are apt to mislead us unless we consider the question very carefully. Those older engineers did their work before the days of technical education, and it was, indeed, the experience gained by them, and its records in the proceedings of the engineering Societies, that formed the basis of the technical education of to-day. Because these men of genius were able to do splendid engineering work without technical education, there are some who are disposed hastily to jump to the conclusion that the same method of training which had to suffice for them, would answer to-day.

It seems to the writer that this is a very mistaken view, and it brings to mind a story told of a conversation between President Lincoln and one of the Union generals whom he had called to the chief command. In this conversation the President told him of certain well-recognised faults which he possessed, and then said: "It is not, on account of these, but in spite of them, that I have appointed you." The same would seem to be true of the great engineers of the past; their successes were not on account of the lack of good technical training and the opportunities of to-day, but in spite of it.

There is, however, a side of the question of engineering training on which there is a difference of opinion, and on which the practice of the Westinghouse Manufacturing Company, of Pittsburg, sheds a very useful light, namely, the practical, or shop, side of the training, as distinguished from the class-room work. Of course, in these days, every well-organised technical school has workshops more or less efficiently equipped with typical tools, and all the students are required to spend a considerable time in these shops learning the use of both power and hand tools, and acquiring thus a very moderate manual dexterity. This experience is of great value, and certainly makes the young engineer on graduation a better equipped man than if his training had been entirely in the class-room. The fact remains, however, that in almost all school shops the work done is only typical, and is entirely free from the pressure of commercial requirements. Indeed, without frequent changes in the instructing staff, and its recruiting by people brought directly from manufacturing establishments, it would be difficult to have instruction keep pace with the latest developments of manufacturing progress.

For the very best results, and in order that the young engineer may be thoroughly grounded in the profession, the school course must be supplemented by actual practical acquaintance with shop work under manufacturing conditions where the organisation and equipment are the most...

other words, he is in condition to appreciate the reasons for everything that is done, and to acquire the necessary acquaintance with particular details of the work in a very much shorter time than the lad five or six years younger, and with only an ordinary school training.

The Westinghouse Electric and Manufacturing Company, under the guiding spirit of its distinguished head, Mr. George Westinghouse, found when it began business in 1886 that there were scarcely any men available with experience in electrical machinery, and that it must, therefore, train its own men. Accordingly, from the very beginning, what has been known at different times as the "Students' Course," the "Special Course," and the "Apprenticeship Course," was established, the idea being to take engineering graduates from colleges, preferably those who have been trained in electrical or mechanical engineering, and give them by actual experience in its shops, for a period of two or three years, that intimate practical acquaintance with all the details of the manufacture of electrical machinery, which would fit them for occupying higher positions with the company.

The number of young men enjoying these advantages varies from time to time, but there are usually about 150 going through the course. The pay is only nominal, and the work is regarded both by the company and by the young men themselves, as a postgraduate course to their college career.

The vice-president of the company, who is in charge of manufacturing operations, has the general control of this course, but it is especially looked after by one of the company's younger engineers, himself a graduate of the works, who lays out the order in which the apprentices shall go through the different sections of the factory, the length of time to be spent in each, who exercises general supervision over attention to work and proficiency. the length of the course w nominally three years. electric business has has been found n put specially brigh time, so as to earlier date

To ill rate it may ich for the

consists of graduates of this course; among them may be tioned such well-known as B. G. Lamme and C. graduates of the course are the construction department after the installation of selling, and in the ments. Indeed, in a large business and of technical nature, it can be much more valuable men in and the selling received a theoretical the colleges, and have this apprenticeship.

As might be inducements which some of the able men this training some reputation selves as consulting and some of the electrical engineers, been graduate of the

It should work done by through the work, and is menting in business take will be ther consul

motor rrent for or lighting. locomotive 3.8 miles per m the accumulice, however, the motor armatures of ninety-six cells n, and through four ation of the fields is is regulated by the tential difference at the at 500 revolutions (corresponding speed of sixty-four miles an medium energising of the fields, ; the normal current which the can take in constant working reaches eres; the effective power of one of otors at the above speed is approximately 300 horse-power. The electrodes each cell on the locomotive weigh 280lbs. the useful output at an average rate of scharge of 500 amperes, is put down at 500 ampere-hours. The locomotive weighs 4.5 tons, of which 12.5 tons are on the front axle, and 16 tons on each of the two driving axles.

The storage battery van is carried on four axles, the wheels of which are 3ft. 3ins. in diameter. The two end axles are 23ft. 4ins. apart, and have a lateral play of .04in., the lateral play of the middle axles being .67in.;

issued by the Westinghouse Company, shows some further details of the system :—

AGREEMENT

At the expiration of the first three months of service the engineering apprentice shall execute with the company a regular form of agreement covering the entire term of the course.

Each applicant, upon entering the course, distinctly releases the company from all liability for any injury which may be sustained by him during the entire term thereof.

RULES

Engineering apprentices will be expected to faithfully observe all shop rules, and must not be absent from work unless sick or excused by the head of the department or section in which he may be employed.

DISCHARGE

The company reserves the right to discharge an engineering apprentice at any time for misbehaviour, inattention to duty, or if, in the opinion of the company, he is not qualified to pursue successfully the work undertaken.

APPLICATION

Application for admittance as engineering apprentices must be made by letter in the handwriting of the applicant, stating :—

Date of birth.

School education, and where received.

Name of university.

Course pursued.

Degrees received.

Reference to professors or others.

Statement of any practical experience which applicant may have had.

Name and address of father, or of mother if father is deceased, or guardian in case both parents are deceased.

COURSE FOR ENGINEERING APPRENTICES

This course has been arranged for graduates of universities and technical schools.

The company desires to train a skilled force of engineers, upon whom it can draw for assistance in the various branches of its industry.

Approved applicants will be given the opportunity of entering the works of the Westinghouse Electric and Manufacturing Company, in order that they may become familiar with the various manufacturing operations and the general construction and working of the apparatus produced. The engineering apprentices will be afforded, in the various departments of the works, actual shop and engineering experience, both mechanical and electrical, and the work of the technical school will be supplemented by the practical training thus afforded. Upon the completion of the course, it is expected that the engineering apprentice will have prepared himself for filling satisfactorily a position in some department of the company's service. Preference in compensation and position will be given to those who prove their worth by aptitude and diligent attention to duty during the apprenticeship period, and by an intelligent appreciation of the work.

DURATION OF COURSE

Engineering apprentices will be expected to remain two years on the work thus outlined, or a total period of 5,616 hours. The regular working period is fifty-four hours per week.

COMPENSATION

The engineering apprentice will be paid 16 cents per hour during the first 2,808 hours, and 18 cents per hour for the second 2,808 hours. Where called called upon to work overtime or holidays, due credit will be given therefore, and the rate will be one and one-half time for such overtime work.

EXPERIMENTAL ELECTRIC LOCOMOTIVE; PARIS - LYONS MEDITERRANEAN RAILWAY

By Daniel Bellet, Paris

The engineers of the Paris - Lyons Mediterranean Railway Company have been seriously considering the question of electrifying several of their lines in the South of France. Before, however, carrying out any extensive changes in the substitution of electric for steam traction, and incurring the heavy outlay that would be involved in laying down central stations and conductors for a number of tracks, they decided to ascertain, consistent with the possibility of obtaining useful data as cheaply as possible, what would be the comparative results that might be expected. To this end they constructed, for experimental purposes, an accumulator locomotive, longitudinal and transverse sections of which are shown in Figs. 1 and 2, Plate XXIV.

Electric traction by storage batteries—the method they chose for the trials—is evidently a safe system, but, as might have been expected, the engineers in charge of the tests soon discovered that this method would not yield all the information they wanted to obtain.

A few data concerning the locomotive in question will be found of interest. It has been designed for half the power of one of the company's standard express engines. It carries a few storage batteries; the main driving battery is contained in a van coupled to the locomotive. The locomotive is carried on three axles, two driving and one trailing; the latter has inside bearings, the axle-boxes allowing a lateral displacement of .59in. each way. Both the driving and trailing wheels are 3ft. 7ins. in diameter. The two driving axles are rigid, with outside bearings; they are independent one of the other, and are 7ft. 3ins. apart from centre to centre. The distance between the two end axles is 19ft. 8ins.

There are in the locomotive five separate compartments: (1) The driver's cab, which contains all the apparatus for working the electric connections, the wheel for the handbrake, and the valves for the compressed air brakes. (2) A compartment in front of the cab, the roof of which is made sloping; this contains an air compressor, worked by a 5 horse-power electric motor, for supplying the air brake, the whistle, and the starting apparatus. (3 and 4) Two side compartments, 3ft. 3ins. high, containing each nine cells; and (5) a central compartment, 4ft. 3ins. in height, which contains a liquid rheostat.

The eighteen cells, when coupled in series, ensure the exciting of the motor fields and supply the necessary current for working the air compressor and for lighting. They also serve for driving the locomotive at a reduced speed, 1.9 to 3.8 miles per hour, when it is detached from the accumulator van. In normal practice, however, the current is supplied to the motor armatures by the storage batteries of ninety-six cells each, fitted in the van, and through four cables. The excitation of the fields is independent, and is regulated by the rheostat; the potential difference at the motor brushes at 500 revolutions (corresponding to a speed of sixty-four miles an hour), with medium energising of the fields, is 360 volts; the normal current which the armature can take in constant working reaches 700 amperes; the effective power of one of the motors at the above speed is approximately 300 horse - power. The electrodes of each cell on the locomotive weigh 280lbs. and the useful output at an average rate of discharge of 500 amperes, is put down at 1,500 ampere-hours. The locomotive weighs 44.5 tons, of which 12.5 tons are on the front axle, and 16 tons on each of the two driving axles.

The storage battery van is carried on four axles, the wheels of which are 3ft. 3ins. in diameter. The two end axles are 23ft. 4ins. apart, and have a lateral play of .04in., the lateral play of the middle axles being .67in.;

there is no righting device. The electrodes of each one of the 192 cells weigh 198.4lbs. The van complete weighs 45.8 tons, divided equally over the four axles. The cells have a useful capacity of 1,000 ampere hours, at an average rate of discharge of 500 amperes.

The motors are two-pole continuous current machines. The armature is keyed direct on the axle. Each motor is with two commutators. The field consists of two large horse-shoe magnets (Fig. 1, Plate XXIV), made of mild steel, placed one in front and one in the rear of the axle, the pole pieces encircling the greater part of the armature outside surface. Extensions which end in head pieces with cushions, the latter surrounding the inside journals on the axle, between the commutator and the wheel boss, Figs. 5 and 6, Plate XXIV, start from the yoke of one of the magnets; while from the yoke of the other magnet start extensions ending in a kind of half-collar, concentric with the journal and with the outside part of the former extension. A system of rods, levers, and spiral springs firmly hold the half-collars on the opposite head-pieces. The cushions above referred to exert no pressure on the axles, there is therefore practically no friction. The electro-magnets are held in place by two vertical rods, fitted at the ends of a horizontal balance lever (Figs. 3 and 4, Plate XXIV); the latter is suspended to the frame by a rod which bears on a spiral spring. The top part of this rod is threaded and provided with a nut for regulating the position of the field magnets. In this manner the field polar pieces remain always exactly centred on the armature, notwithstanding the oscillations of the axles; these oscillations do not entail any appreciable shifting of the centre of gravity of the field magnets, the result being that the axles have but very slight reactions to withstand.

The armature is of the Brown type, with enclosed conductor. The iron laminations are fitted on a gun-metal sleeve, which is keyed on the axle, the whole forming a cylinder 27ins. in diameter and 21ins. long, with a smooth outside surface. The leads, which are under induction, consist of solid copper bars, elliptic and .10 square inch in section, enclosed in vulcanite tubes; the latter are placed in a hole cut in the armature near the outside surface. These leads are 150 in number. A steel-bar commutator is placed on each side of the armature. Four systems of carbon brushes, two for each commutator, serve to transmit the current to the armature. The lower part of the motors is protected by a brass sheet cover. The motors were built by Messrs. Sautter, Harlé & Co., of Paris, from the designs of Mr. Auvert, electrical engineer of the Paris-Lyons Mediterranean Railway Company.

The accessory apparatus installed are the following: A hand brake, an automatic brake, a regulator brake, and a whistle, which work by compressed air. The electro-mechanical devices consist of a reversing gear, a starting rheostat, an automatic cut-out, a main switch, a coupling switch, and starting rheostat for the air pump. The locomotive is further provided with an ammeter giving the total current intensity passing through the armatures. One voltmeter shows the pressure at the motor terminals, another the pressure at the terminals of the van batteries, and a third that at the terminals of the locomotive batteries. An ammeter gives the intensity of the current supplied to the pump motor.

The reversing gear is worked from the lever, A (Fig. 1), which can take up three positions. When at the end of its travel in front, it presses on the spindle of the valve, b, which supplies compressed air to two cylinders of a mercury pneumatic switch, and the field exciting current is established in the required direction. When, on the other hand, the lever is brought completely back to the rear, it presses on the spindle of another valve, and the exciting current is established for reverse motion. When the lever is vertical the cylinders of the pneumatic switch are clear, and the exciting current is cut off. The pneumatic switch is shown on Figs. 7 and 8, page 121. Fig. 9, page 122, illustrates the starting gear. As its action is a very quick one, special precautions have been taken to prevent short circuiting the locomotive battery, which would occur were the lever to be brought too rapidly from one extreme position to the other; an electric latch, placed on the lever guide, and supplied with current from the field magnet terminals, prevents the lever from crossing the vertical position until the exciting current is cut off.

The electro-pneumatic rheostat is inserted in the motor armature circuit; it consists of a wrought-iron rectangular tank, BB (Fig. 1), of 70.6 cubic feet capacity, carried in a central

Plate XXIV

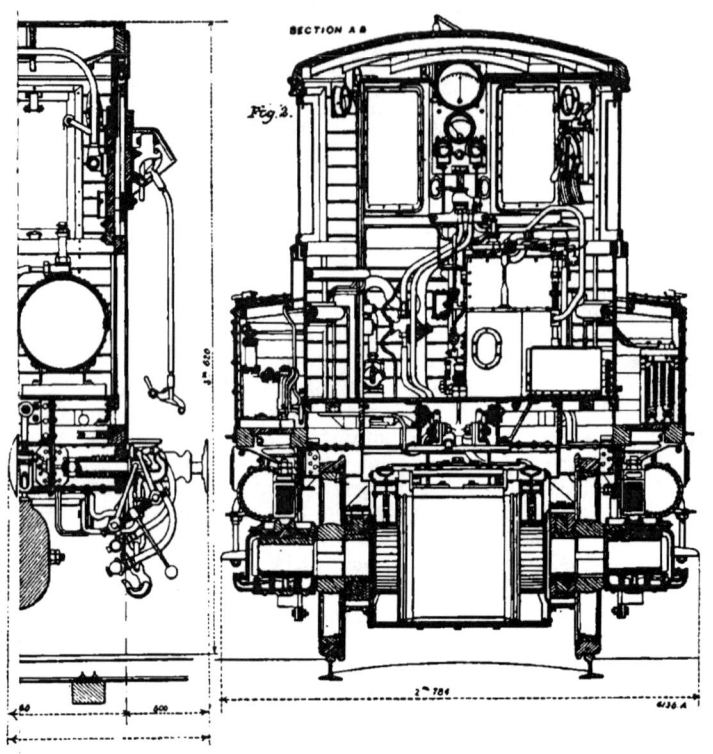

SECTION A B

Fig. 3.

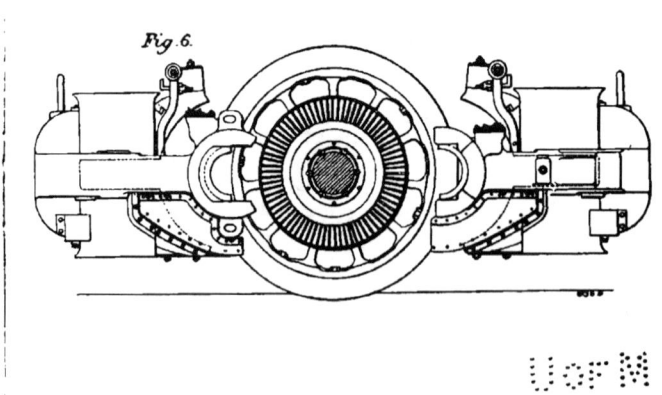

Fig. 6.

U of M

ELECTRIC LOCOMOTIVE; PARIS-LYONS MEDITERRANEAN RAILWAY

compartment in front of the driver's cab, on wood and indiarubber supports, which serve to insulate it. It contains twenty lead plates, placed vertically, like the electrodes of a storage battery, and 3.9ins. apart. Ten of these plates are connected to each other and with one of the sections of the circuit, the ten others being in connection with the other circuit. A wrought - iron

on the latter valve is pressed down, and the three-way cock lever is in the horizontal position, the rheostat receiver, CC, communicates with the compressed air receiver, and the solution is driven up in the tank, establishing the current. When the solution arrives near the top of the plates above referred to, it comes in contact with a float, and effects the closing of a local circuit, the

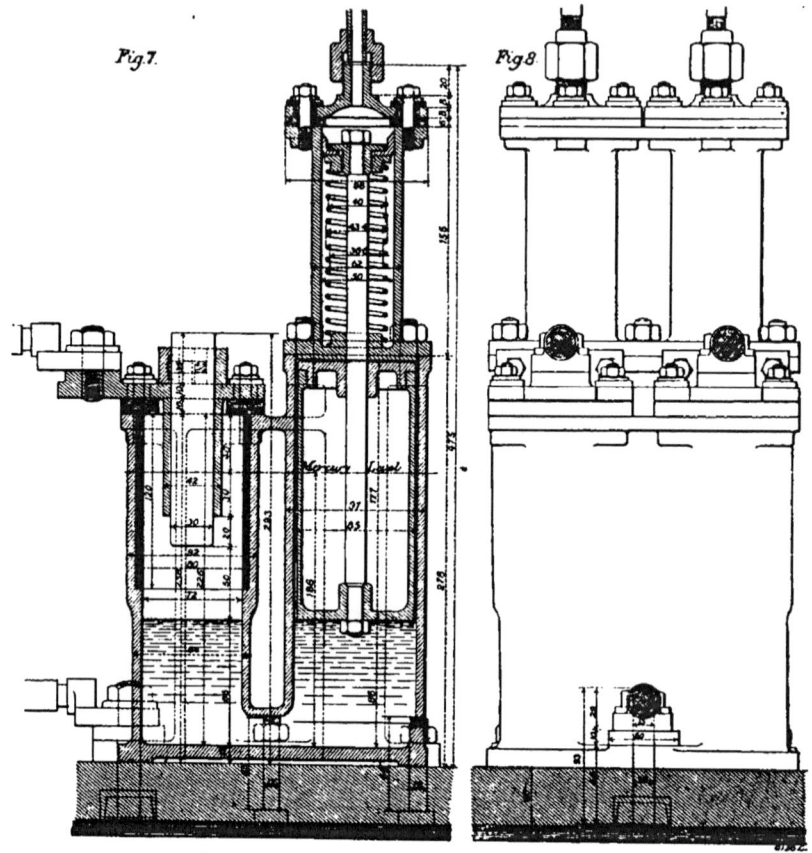

Pneumatic Switch (see page 120)

receiver, CC, is suspended underneath the tank, below the frame, and is insulated; it communicates with the tank by two pipes, D, 5.9ins. in diameter. The receiver contains a solution of carbonate of soda in water, which covers also the bottom of the tank above. The receiver is provided with a three-way cock, E, by which it is opened to the atmosphere or put in communication with a valve, F. When the handle

current flowing through which works a special apparatus which short circuits the two sets of lead-plates and lights a lamp, by which the driver sees that the tank is full and that he must release the valve handle. For cutting off the current the lever of the three-way cock is placed vertically; the air in receiver, CC, escapes and makes place for the solution. Besides being used for starting and stopping, the action of the rheostat can be resorted to also—but with a certain loss of energy—for regulating the current intensity; this is done by maintaining the level of the solution at a given height.

The automatic cut-out prevents the current supplied by the batteries in the van from reaching a too great intensity through an excessive load on the locomotive, or through a mistake on the part of the driver.

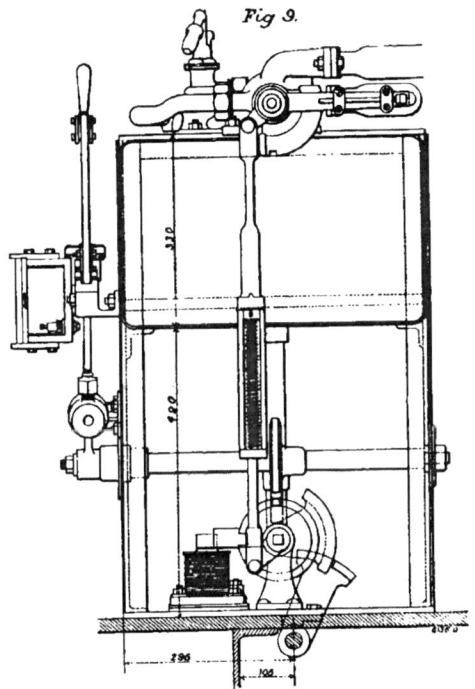

Fig 9.

Starting Gear (see page 120)

An electro-magnetic relay, G, regulated by a spring, is inserted in each of the cables connecting the van with the locomotive; when the current intensity reaches 1,200 amperes in any one of the cables, the relay closes the circuit of a tubular quick-acting electro-magnet and armature. This action disengages a spring valve which normally closes the orifice of a pipe, branched on the conduit joining the rheostat receiver to the three-way cock; the air in the receiver then escapes, lowering the level of the solution in the tank, and also the current intensity. When the automatic cut-out has thus operated the driver causes it to resume its former position by pressing on a foot lever.

The main switch is simply a large two-way switch, for supplying the motors both with current from the batteries on the locomotive and from those in the van. It is operated by the handle, H; when this handle is forward, the armatures are supplied with current from the van batteries only, and when thrown back, with current from the locomotive batteries alone. The coupling switch serves to connect the motors and the van batteries in various ways. It is operated by the lever, K, which can take up three positions. In the first, the two batteries in the van are coupled in parallel, and the two motors in series; in the second, the two batteries are in series, and the motors also; and in the third, the two batteries are in series and the motors in parallel. The shunt-wound motor which drives the air pump is governed by a small rheostat; this serves for starting the pump and regulating its speed. The various levers and switches for starting and reversing are provided with inter-locking arrangements.

The storage batteries consist of impregnated wood cells, lined with lead and celluloid; they were manufactured by the Fulmen Company. The negative electrodes are in perforated celluloid cases; the positive electrode cases are lined inside with asbestos cloth. The electrodes are held apart by celluloid rods, and the cells are uncovered to facilitate inspection.

The first thing the driver does when the locomotive is to be put in service is to set the air pump working, in order to obtain a pressure of 85lbs. to 100lbs. per square inch in the air receiver; the pump continues working to maintain this pressure practically constant. The accumulator van being coupled to the locomotive, and the necessary connections being established between the two, the main switch is placed on the forward position, and the lever of the coupling switch in the notch which corresponds with the required speed. When starting on a gradient, the lever of the coupling switch is not placed immediately in the third position, as the maximum draw-bar pull would be at a low figure, and starting would not be rapid. The reversing gear lever is also placed in the forward position; the three-way cock handle is laid horizontal, and the magnetic intensity of the field magnets is allowed to reach its highest value by placing the rheostat handle to the right-hand side of the index, on the word "Maximum."

The engine is then started by moving the handle of the starting valve until the total current ammeter shows an intensity of about 1,000 amperes, the coupling switch lever being in notch 1; the intensity is about 800 amperes when the lever is in notches 2 or 3. The engine travels forward, and has a tendency to increase its speed, this causing a decrease in the current intensity; but the decrease is negatived and the current intensity raised by still moving the starting-valve handle until the lamp signal above referred to is lighted. The handle is then released, and the magnetic field intensity is gradually brought to correspond with the speed required by moving the rheostat handle towards the left. In order to keep the actual speed within narrow limits of the normal speed, corresponding with a given position of the coupling-switch lever, it is sufficient to act on the magnetic field of the field magnets by working the rheostat handle. But if it is required to vary the speed within large limits, it is necessary to alter the position of the coupling-switch lever; the three-way cock handle is first placed vertical, and when the ammeter shows the current to have fallen to zero, the coupling-switch lever is set in the position for the required speed, the three-way cock handle is horizontal, and the starting-valve handle is pressed down. In order to stop or slow down quickly, the stop-valve handle is set vertical, and the brake is started. To prevent the current intensity from exceeding the limit, the driver first increases the exciting current, and if this is not sufficient he places the handle of the three-way cock momentarily vertical, which inserts a fast increasing resistance in the motor armatures. Should the current increase nevertheless, the automatic cut-out, which is regulated for an output of 1,200 amperes per battery, would open the special valve, the effect being the same as that produced by the working of the stop-valve. When the engine works alone, without the van, the main switch handle is thrown back, and that of the coupling switch in notch 1 if a 1.9 mile speed is wanted, and in positions 2 or 3 for a 4.5 to 5 mile speed.

With a train load of 147 tons, including the weight of the engine and of the van, the motors being coupled in series, the speed obtained is twenty-eight miles per hour. When the motors are coupled in parallel, and when the engine is running on a level, with a 100-ton load, a speed of sixty-two miles is easily obtained. The motors act well, and a still higher speed could be reached were the useful potential difference at the accumulator terminals not to decrease in a marked degree. The motors can easily withstand a 700-ampere current in constant working at 500 revolutions, corresponding approximately to sixty-two miles an hour. Should the engine be supplied from an outside conductor, it could, therefore, absorb 500 kilowatts in round figures. The motor armature efficiency being slightly above .90, the effective power of the engine is 611 horse-power. The rolling friction is low—it does not exceed 9.9lbs. per ton at a speed of fifty-six miles.

THE MILAN-CERESIO RAILWAY

By Nicola Romeo, Milan

THREE years ago the two principal Italian railway companies commenced experiments with electric traction on two of their lines—the Lecco-Colico-Sondrio line* of the Adriatic system, and the Milan-Varese-Porto Ceresio line of the Mediterannean Company.

These are the only two railways in Italy where the tractive energy produced in a power station is transmitted to the cars by one or more conductors. Experiments have been made with traction accumulators on two other lines — those of Milan - Monza and Bologna - San Felice, but these are of little interest because of their restricted application. Of the two lines, Lecco-Colico-Sondrio and Milan - Porto Ceresio, it may be noted that the former runs for nearly its whole length through a mountainous district, skirting for a certain distance the beautiful Lake of Como; it is a line much frequented by tourists. The Milan-Ceresio Railway, on the other hand, crosses the most industrial region of Italy, and forms at the same time a line of communication between Milan and the Lakes Maggiore and Lugano. Up to the present time the electric trains run only from Milan to Porto Ceresio (see Fig. 1), while the sections Gallarate - Laveno and Gallarate-Arona are still worked by locomotives; these sections will, however, soon be adapted for electric traction.

Fig. 1 shows a plan of this railway. From Milan to Rho the rails are common to the electric trains and to the locomotive trains that run to Turin. Between Milan and Gallarate there is a double track, reduced to a single line in the branches Gallarate-Porto Ceresio, Laveno, and Arona. From Milan to Gallarate the gradients are almost level, and the route nearly straight, but between Gallarate, Varese, and Porto Ceresio, there are several curves and somewhat steep inclines. As already said, the Milan-Porto Ceresio line traverses an industrial area, which is also a favourite residential district. Increased

* See Traction and Transmission, Vol. II, page 213. Descriptions of the Milan-Ceresio Railway appeared elsewhere at the date of opening the line. The following article has been written after a year's working.

travelling facilities were urgently needed both for freight and passenger traffic, the latter to enable men of business to go to and from Milan every day. The change from steam to electric traction had, therefore, two ends in view—increased speed, and a greater number of trains per day. The employment of the third rail as a conductor was then necessary to get the best results, and notwithstanding all the objections raised on

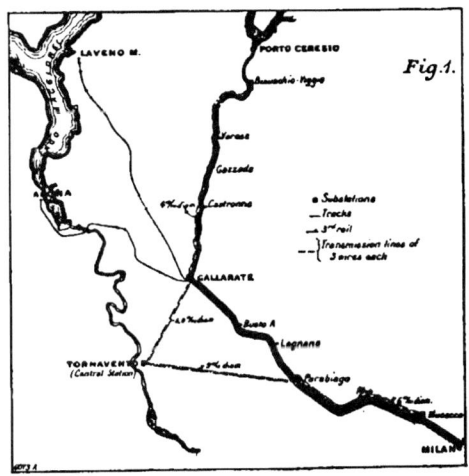

Plan of the Milan-Ceresio Railway

many sides to the adoption of such a system on a line intersected by many level crossings, the third rail was adopted, and has given full satisfaction. On the other hand great difficulties are met with on the Lecco-Colico-Sondrio line, where three-phase traction has been adopted, though possibly, as the line is only now in complete working order, opinions should be suspended for the moment. Very great importance attaches to the Milan-Gallarate Railway, the first Italian electrical line, from the fact that while waterfalls are numerous in Italy, coal has to be imported, and is, therefore, costly. Before describing the central power station, the line, the sub-stations, and the third rail, something may be said about the route. The maximum

Fig. 2.

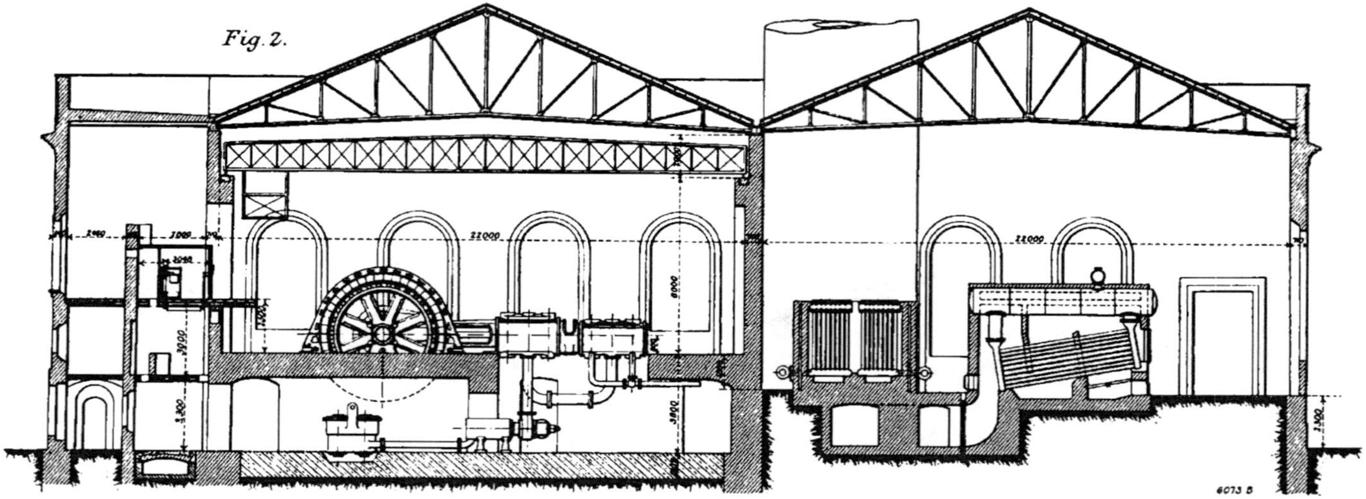

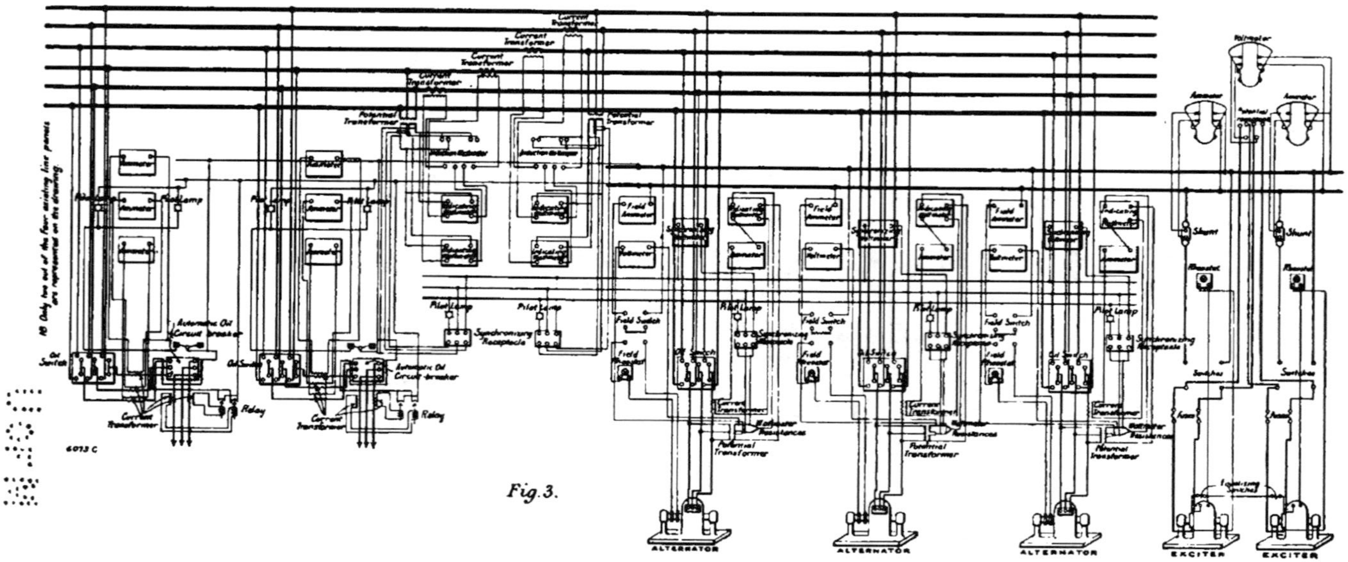

Fig. 3.

Power Station at Tornavento

UofM

gradient is 2.1 per cent., and the minimum radius of curves is 300 metres (984ft.). Such gradients and curves are to be found at different parts of the line between Gallarate and Porto Ceresio. The distance between Milan and Gallarate is 24.8 miles, while the three branches that lead to Porto Ceresio, Laveno and Arona, are respectively 20.5, 19.8, and 16.1 miles in length. The greatest speed the trains acquire between Milan and Gallarate is sixty miles an hour, and 48.5 miles between Gallarate and Porto Ceresio. There are three classes of trains:—

(1) Express trains composed of an auto-motor car weighing 43 tons, and one trailing car. The total weight of the loaded train is 73 tons.

(2) Fast trains.

(3) Omnibus trains, which, besides the special cars, have one or two ordinary wagons used on the steam railway, coupled on.

In preparing the traffic plan of the Milan-Gallarate-Porto Ceresio railway, it was assumed that the trains would work on a ten-minutes headway. This schedule, however, has not yet been adopted. During the summer the traffic is relatively very heavy. Sixty-four trains run every day between Milan and Gallarate; forty-six between Gallarate and Varese, and twenty between Varese and Porto Ceresio. On the Milan-Gallarate section thirty-two trains run from Milan towards Gallarate, distributed as follows: Thirteen omnibus; ten fast; nine express. Of the thirty-two trains running every day from Gallarate towards Milan fifteen are omnibus; ten are fast; seven are express. The heaviest traffic occurs between eight and nine o'clock in the morning, and between four and five in the evening. The maximum number of trains in motion at the same time between Milan and Gallarate is now six.

Of course the great economy in working such a line must be obtained by the use of hydraulic power, which is furnished by the Ticino River. The hydro-electric central station was to have been installed at Tornavento, but difficulties not yet surmounted have made it necessary to erect a temporary steam central station which will eventually be used as a reserve.

(1) POWER STATION.—The central station does not present any special features; it is illustrated by Figs. 2 and 3, Plate XXV. There are three compound tandem steam engines, each of 1,400 horse-power, supplied by F. Tosi, of Legnano; eight multitubular boilers, which may work at 12 atmospheres; and three batteries of economisers. Each boiler has 3,121 square feet of heating surface, and is composed of 114 steel tubes and two steam drums. The weight of each engine fly-wheel is 86 tons, and the working speed is 94 revolutions per minute. As this central station is only to serve as a reserve, triple expansion engines have not been used, nor have the boilers been furnished with superheaters, so that under existing conditions the cost of production of energy is rather high. The consumption of coal per kilowatt-hour is, on an average, 3.96lbs. What has no small influence on the cost is the difficult communication between Gallarate and Tornavento, where the central power station is placed.

The three engines are direct coupled to three alternators of 750 kilowatts each, and giving a voltage of 13,200. The inductors have thirty-two poles, so that with a speed of 94 per minute there results a frequence of 25 cycles per second. This frequence has been adopted in view of the rotary converters to be fed in the sub-stations. The alternators are built to carry an overload of 25 per cent., and a momentary overload of 40 per cent., without overheating. To excite the alternators there are two compound vertical steam engines of 85 horse-power each, which are direct coupled to two six-pole dynamos of 75 kilowatts each, at 125 volts. One of these can excite two alternators. The switchboard includes nine compartments, of which, three are for the three alternators, one for the two exciters, one totaliser compartment, and four line compartments. Each engine has a registering wattmeter and a hand-oil, three-pole circuit breaker. Four power lines leave the central station—two of them carry their energy towards Gallarate, and two towards Parabiago (Fig. 1); each is provided with an automatic oil circuit breaker. No fuse has been employed either on the engines or on the lines. The automatic circuit breakers are specially constructed with six contacts, two for each pole; the opening of these contacts is done in oil so as to avoid sparks. The circuit breaker would tend to remain open through the action of gravity on the movable parts, but this is prevented by a catch, which can be closed by pressing a button on the controlling lever of the circuit breaker in the front of the switchboard, or which automatically closes when the intensity of the current increases in one of its phases. Two current transformers are in connection with two wires of each line. The induced current in the secondary of these transformers passes through two coils, which have an iron core terminating in a brass cone. If an intense current crosses one of these relays the keeper is attracted, and closes the circuit of one of the coils placed on the bus bars of the excitation; it is this coil which frees the catch that closes the circuit breaker. It is evident that it was not necessary to have recourse to the continuous current by causing the secondary current of the transformers to pass through the coil, but by the use of the coil crossed by the continuous current the circuit breaker is disengaged from any point of the engine room by simply pressing a button. The lines are protected by Wirt's lightning arresters.

(2) TRANSMISSION LINES.—From the central station of Tornavento run two separate lines, one in the direction of Gallarate, the other towards Parabiago (Fig. 1). At each of these places sub-stations are installed. The lines extend, one as far as Bisuschio, the other to Musocco. Each of them is composed of six wires, disposed in groups of three, arranged in equilateral triangles. The distance between Tornavento and Parabiago is about thirteen miles, and between Tornavento and Gallarate, 7.5 miles. Each wire of the first line has a diameter of 9 millimetres, and of the second, 5.8 millimetres, while between Gallarate and Bisuschio, and Parabiago and Musocco, the wires have a diameter of 4.6 millimetres. Gallarate and Parabiago are now to be united by another line of six wires, so that if any damage is sustained by one of the lines the service can be maintained. Fig. 4 (page 127) shows the form of insulator employed for the high tension, and Figs. 5 and 6 are sections of the double track. The supporting poles are of wood, and carry two cross-pieces, on the first of which are fixed four insulators, and on the second, the other two. The high-tension line is divided into sections by means of blades, supported by cross-pieces placed on four poles. Lightning arresters, placed on top of the poles, serve to protect the line from atmospheric discharges.

(3) SUB-STATIONS.—The first sub-station beyond Milan is that of Musocco, distant 8.7 miles. Eleven miles beyond is the sub-station of Parabiago, and at similar intervals are those of Gallarate, Gazzada, and Bisuschio. Between the latter and Porto Ceresio, which is at the end of the line, the distance is only three miles. The sub-stations of Musocco, Parabiago, and Gallarate are in all respects similar. Each of them contains seven single-phase transformers (one of which is a reserve) of 180 kilowatts each, with a ratio of transformation from 12,000 to 420. Cooling is obtained by means of two centrifugal ventilators, each driven by a small asynchronous motor. Beyond the seven transformers are two reacting coils (R RC, Fig. 7, Plate XXVI), and two converters of 500 kilowatts each. Fig. 7 shows the scheme of the circuits of the Parabiago sub-station. The double high-tension line, coming from Tornavento, enters a turret, and thence goes on towards Musocco. In the turret are twelve knife switches, L, which serve to insulate either the double line coming from Tornavento or the one going towards Musocco. The switchboard of the sub-station contains six bus bars, from which are taken two lines running towards Musocco after having crossed two three-pole oil circuit breakers, o f. There is also a third circuit breaker in parallel. The blades, L, and the three circuit breakers o f, serve to ensure the service in case of any damage between Parabiago and Musocco, or at any of the circuit breakers, o f. If any damage happens in the left circuit breaker, o f, by closing the circuit breaker in parallel the two transmission lines can be still utilised. Before going to the two bus bars to which the transformers are connected, two automatic circuit breakers, O K, like those at the central station, are inserted. Here, however, the continuous current that moves the coils, C C, which disengage the automatic circuit breaker is arrested by a small battery of accumulators charged by the current coming from the bus bars on the continuous side of the converters. The battery consists of few elements, and the voltage of 650 volts of the converters is reduced by means of resistances formed by lamps. Before passing to the primary of the transformers a compensator is met with, which serves to reduce the tension from 12,000 to 6,000 volts, so as to put the converters in motion.

These latter are compound, and on the frame of each are shunts which are used to

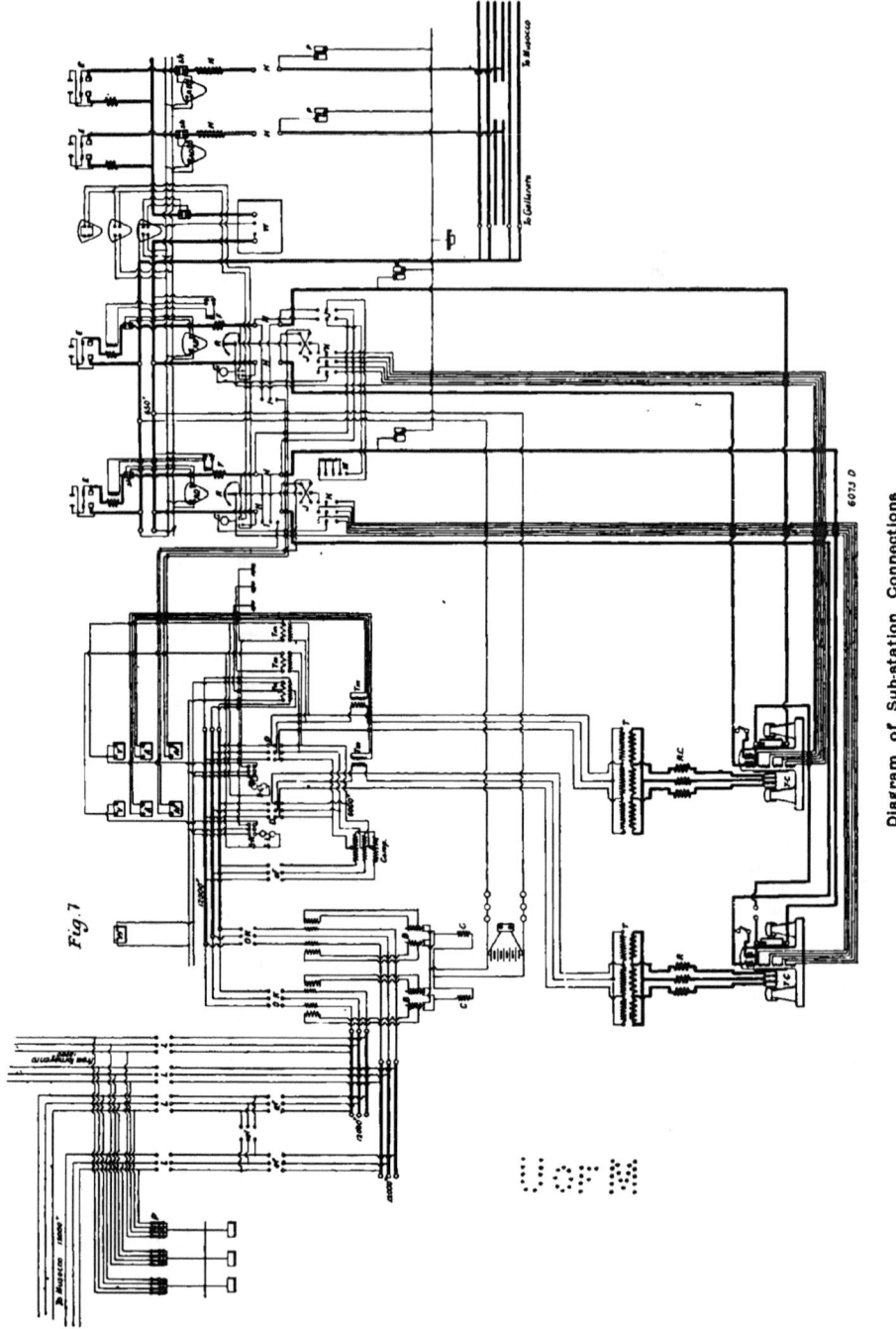

Fig. 7

Diagram of Sub-station Connections

MℛU

vary the degree of compounding, the reacting coils, R RC, serving to render such a compounding effective. In this way a constant voltage is obtained from the continuous side. A starter operates the converters from the continuous current side, and a polarised relay disengages the continuous automatic breaker placed in the circuit of the converter, should this latter absorb the current of the third rail, and act as a motor. (Of course, this could happen if the alternating current were

stations of Gazzada and Bisuschio contain only one converter of 250 kilowatts, with four transformers of 90 kilowatts each with oil coolers. In each of these are two batteries of accumulators of 333 elements, with a capacity of 300 ampere-hours. The charge of the battery is worked by a booster. At present a third battery of 500 ampere-hours at Musocco is being installed.

(4) THE THIRD RAIL.—This is composed of Vignoles rails of 45 kilogrammes per

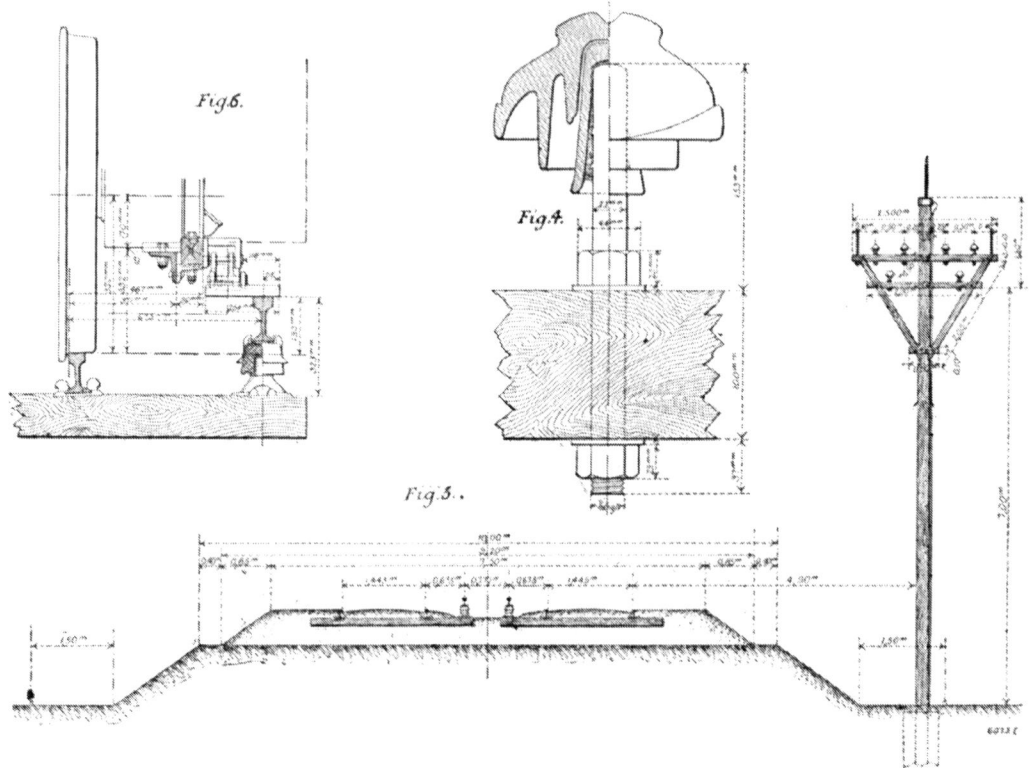

Fig. 6.

Fig. 4.

Fig. 5.

Details of Permanent Way (see page 126)

interrupted.) The third rail is fed direct, and it is possible at Parabiago either to break or put on the current towards Gallarate or Musocco. We have spoken of the sub-station of Parabiago as equal to that of Gallarate and Musocco. It contains two converters of 500 kilowatts each. One only of these ensures the normal service; the other, while it serves as a reserve, works when the traffic becomes intense, which happens in summer during certain hours. The sub-

metre (90.7lbs. per yard), laid in lengths of 12 metres (39ft. 4ins.); they are carried at intervals of 18ft. by special insulators, which are illustrated in Fig. 6. They are made with iron hexagonal projections, having each two ears placed diagonally, and which embrace the bottom of the rail, leaving it free to slide; these are attached to granite insulating blocks, which have excellent electrical and mechanical qualities. There is finally an iron tripod, fastened by three screws to the wooden cross ties. The third rail is 675 millimetres (26.57ins.) from the nearest track rail, and is elevated 7.59ins. above them. The track rails were already in place; therefore to place the insulators of the third rail it was necessary to displace the sleepers, which were adjusted to allow the rail an even bearing on all the insulators. The laying of the third rail was done as follows: The sleepers on which the insulators were to be fixed were removed, and after being planed to reduce them to the right thickness, the insulators were fixed on them, and turned so that the distance between the two ears holding the sole of the rail (measured normally to the axis of the track) should be greater than the sole. The rail was then laid on the sole-plates, and the distance from the track rails was regulated with a gauge, displacing the insulators more or less; the tripods were then screwed on to the sleepers. Two consecutive rail lengths were mechanically connected by means of one fish-plate, with two bolts. Under this fish-plate was placed the bond, which has a section of 200 square millimetres. At every tenth rail an expansion joint was formed, and at these points the rails are electrically joined by means of a flexible connection, which can expand for about 4ins. At these points two fish-plates are placed, fixed to only one of the rails by means of a bolt. The flexible connection was formed by two copper plugs, connected by two copper plates, bent so as to be lodged under the fish-plate.

In the section between Milan and Gallarate the track is double, and the two supply rails are laid between the two tracks, and are electrically connected by bonds of 11 millimetres diameter. At level crossings the continuity of the third rail is secured by an underground cable of 200 square millimetres section. The ends of this cable are stripped to the copper for a certain length, then for a short distance the insulation is left attached to the copper, and finally only the external wrapper is removed. An insulator having a hole through it enlarged in the top is threaded on the cable. A cover is then screwed on, and the projecting part of the copper is forced into the web of the rail. Fig. 8, Plate XXVII, is a detail of this arrangement; the end of the cable passes up from the ground through the insulator, and thence to the metal cap

on top, from a socket in which a rigid bar connection is made to the web of the third rail.

The third rail is divided into sections by means of switches enclosed in boxes. The formula $\frac{1.64}{p}$, in which p is the weight of the rail per metre, gives us the electrical resistance in ohms per kilometre, the resistance of the bonds included. In this particular case $\frac{1.64}{45} = 0.086$. For the track rails that weigh 72.5lbs. per yard we have $\frac{1.64}{2 \times 36} = 0.023$.

The total resistance per kilometre, deduced from the formula, is 0.059. Observations have been taken to calculate the practical electric resistance; these are completed on the Bisuschio - Porto Ceresio section. The extremity of the third rail was limited to the running rails, and Fig. 9, Plate XXVII, indicates the circuit; in this C is the converter, R is a liquid resistance, A an ammeter, V and v two voltmeters. The values found out are: $A = 265$, $V = 600$, $v = 525$, $E = 77$, instead of 75. The resistance of the third rail and the track rails, r, is taken as 0.29, on a length of about 4,600 metres. The resistance per kilometre is, therefore, according to this experiment, $\frac{0.29}{4.6} = 0.063$, or slightly superior to the calculated resistance. The insulation of the third rail was found most satisfactory, notwithstanding its numerous supports; the rail is of steel, but from the point of its electrical resistance, it would be better if made of iron.

In the stations and near the level crossings the third rail is protected by boards nailed on rectangular wooden frames set in the ground, or attached to iron plates. The latter have been used in the stations where wood would have worn out too quickly. In places where the feeding rail is interrupted it is bent towards the end, so that the shoe may resume contact without violent shocks. In places where the train passes very rapidly the gradient of the third rail is slight, and therefore long. For the first 2ft. the slope is 15 per cent., while for the next 30ft. it is only 0.75 per cent. At crossings, and where the train passes more slowly, the slope is steeper and shorter, so that the interruption of the light and of the current to the motors may not last too long. During the last winter neither snow nor rain gave rise to any inconvenience. The greatest inconvenience is the formation of

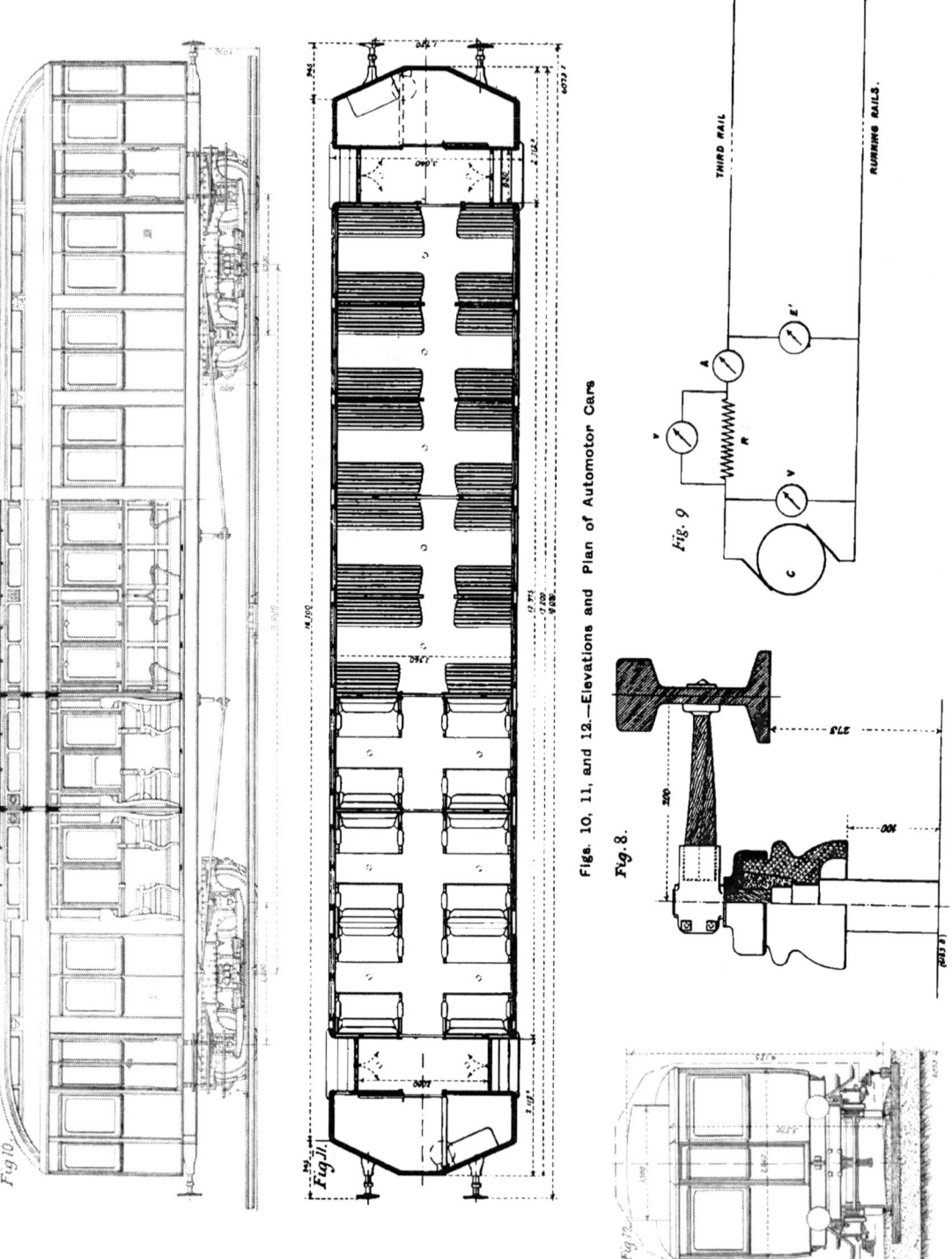

Figs. 10, 11, and 12.—Elevations and Plan of Automotor Cars

Fig. 8.

Fig. 9.

Fig. 9.—Diagram of Testing Resistance

Fig. 8.—Third Rail Connection at Level Crossing

ice on the rail-head, which might insulate the shoe.

(5) ROLLING STOCK.—Figs. 10, 11, and 12, Plate XXVII, illustrate the automotor cars that contain two classes, first and third, only. They are carried on two trucks with double elastic suspension, and can carry seventy-five passengers, of which twenty-four are first class and the rest third class. The electrical equipment of the cars comprises four motors (GE-55), capable of giving a speed of 100 kilometres an hour with rapid acceleration. Two series parallel controllers regulate the running, and the circuits are protected by an automatic circuit breaker which yields at a little over 1,000 amperes. It can be cut out by the motor-man if necessary. The carriage is fitted with a hand-brake and a Westinghouse compressed-air brake, worked by a motor and compressor of 4 horse-power. The cars are heated by Blackwell electric heaters placed under the seats, and lit by incandescent lamps connected with the shoe, an arrangement which has the inconvenience of putting out the lamps at the level crossings. The current shoe is fixed by means of springs to a wooden cross piece attached to the axle-boxes. Each car is fitted with four shoes, united by a cable. The weight of the automotor car is 43 tons with its full load. The motors alone weigh 10 tons; the trailer is of the same construction as the automotor, and its weight with load is 30 tons; it can carry ninety passengers. The goods trains are hauled by a locomotive of the usual Thomson-Houston type, also fitted with four motors of 16 horse-power each.

(6) TRACK RAILS.—These were laid prior to the electrification of the line, and are of Vignoles section, weighing 72.6lbs. per yard. They are electrically connected by ordinary rail bonds. Trials have been made with Blackwell plastic bonds, Edison Brown type; these bonds are put under the fish-plate, and are, therefore, not liable to be detached and stolen, especially as their value in copper is very small.

We will consider the cost of the equipment, exclusive of the central station and the line, as these are of no interest except for this special application, and the total outlay might be much increased if, for example, the central station be far from the line. The prices quoted, of course, relate to Italy. The following figures per kilometre will be found exact:—

					Lire.
Third rail, 45 tons at 250 lire per ton...				...	11,250
Fish-plates and bolts	...	...	...	...	216
Bonds of all kinds	...	...	...	...	522
Bonding track rail	...	...	...	...	1,730
Insulators	...	...	...	...	1,750
Accessories	...	...	...	...	300
Labour	...	...	...	...	500
Miscellaneous	...	...	...	...	462
		Total ...	...	...	16,730

Or £1,070 per mile.

(7) COST OF SUB-STATIONS. — We may take a sub-station containing two converters of 500 kilowatts each; this is the case of the Musocco, Parabiago, and Gallarate sub-stations.

	Lire.
(1) Seven single-phase transformers 180 kilowatts each (one is for reserve), 25 cycles with the ratio 12,000/420ᵛ, two reacting coils, two compensators, and two ventilating motors	70,000
(2) Two converters, 500 kilowatts each, six poles, 25 cycles, and one armature for reserve ...	90,000
(3) Switchboard	20,000
(4) Connection between the high-tension line and the transformers, the converters, and the switchboard	8,000
(5) Miscellaneous	15,000
Total	203,000 = £8,120

(2) Sub-station containing only one 250-kilowatt converter :—

	Lire.
(1) Four 90-kilowatt transformers (one for reserve), 25 cycles; transforming ratio 12,000/420ᵛ, one reacting coil, and a compensator	29,000
(2) One 250-kilowatt converter and one armature for reserve	35,000
(3) Switchboard	12,000
(4) Connections between the high-tension line and the transformers, the converters, and the switchboard	5,000
(5) Miscellaneous	10,000
Total	91,000 = £3,640

The total cost for the equipment and mounting in the five sub-stations is then approximately :—

$$3 \times 203,000 = 609,000 + 2 \times 91,000 = 791,000 \text{ lire} = £31,640.$$

The overhead line from Milan to Porto Ceresio being 73 kilometres (45.3 miles) long, the expense as regards material per kilometre is :—

$$\frac{791,000}{73} = 10,835 \text{ lire} = £697 \text{ per mile.}$$

For the third rail, the bonds of the track rails, and the electric equipment of the sub-stations, it follows that the cost per kilometre was about 27,000 lire, or say £1,700 per mile.

In conclusion, it may be noted that the amount of passenger traffic has increased threefold since the electrification of the line.

ELECTRICAL INDUSTRIES IN NORWAY AND SWEDEN

By J. S. Egstrom

A LARGE electric central station, operated by water-power, was put in operation some time since at Kvarnsveden, near the iron-works of Domnarfvet, in Central Sweden. The station is owned by the Stora Kopparsberg Bergslags Aktiebolag, and is situated at a waterfall on the Dalelfven. The available fall has a height of 13 metres (42½ft.), and the amount of water varies from 100 to 2,000 cubic metres per second. During nine months of the year 200 cubic metres are available, which, with 20 per cent. loss in the turbines, corresponds to 25,750 horse-power on the turbine shafts. At present 10,000 horse-power are installed, divided into eight units—a ninth unit serves as reserve (Figs. 1 to 6, Plates XXVIII and XXIX). Each unit consists of a double turbine; four of these work the machinery of the Kvarnsveden Mills, and four are coupled to electric generators. The turbines were built at the Dayton Globe Ironworks, at Dayton, Ohio; each has a diameter of 915 millimetres (36.02ins.), and develops about 1,200 horse-power at 225 revolutions per minute. The hydraulic efficiency is guaranteed to be 84 per cent. The four electric units generate alternating three-phase current at a pressure of 7,000 volts; this energy is used partly at the paper mills of Kvarnsveden, but is also transmitted to the iron mills of Domnarfvet, a distance of about 4.5 kilometres (2.8 miles). At both these mills step-down transformers are arranged, which reduce the current to a pressure of 520 volts, when it is used direct in alternating current motors for the iron mill at Domnarfvet. At Kvarnsveden a secondary station transforms the alternating into direct current, which is used for lighting and driving motors, and for operating an electric railway about five miles long.

The alternators in the large power station at Kvarnsveden (Figs. 7 and 8, Plate XXX) have an outer diameter of 3,200 millimetres (10ft. 6ins.). They are connected direct to the shafts of the turbines by flexible couplings.

The exciters are coupled direct to the shafts of the generators, and develop current at 600 amperes and 30 volts. The switch-board is built of iron and marble slabs, and is fitted with the necessary instruments for high tension. The electric machinery, as well as the lines and step-down transformers, at Kvarnsveden and Domnarfvet, were supplied by the Oerlikon Co., of Zurich, Switzerland.

Another large central station is in operation at Hafslund, in Southern Norway. This station is situated on the largest river in Norway, the Glommen; the available fall is 18.2 metres (60ft.). The channels are made for a water supply of 127 cubic metres per second, corresponding to a total efficiency of 22,240 horse-power.

Part of this water is used to drive the old mills at the fall; another part is employed in the central station; while some of the water is not as yet utilised.

In the central station two smaller units, each of 200 kilowatts efficiency, and six larger ones, each of 800 kilowatts, are installed. Jonval turbines, from the Rieter factory in Winterthur (Switzerland), are used. Each of the six larger ones produce 1,200 horse-power on the shaft, at 143 revolutions per minute. Alternating current is generated at a pressure of 6,000 volts.

The electric energy is used, partly near the fall for the operation of a carbide factory and a railway from the falls to the seaport, but it is also transmitted to the city of Fredrikstad, a distance of about 10 kilometres, where it is used for lighting and power.

The railway has a length of track of 4.4 miles, with a ruling gradient of 8 per cent., and minimum curves of 150 metres (500ft.) radius. The gauge is 1.435 metres (4ft. 8½ins.). Two locomotives are in operation, each driven by four motors of 30 horse-power; the weight of the locomotives is 22 tons.

The electric equipment of this central station and railway was furnished by the Schuckert Company of Nuremberg.

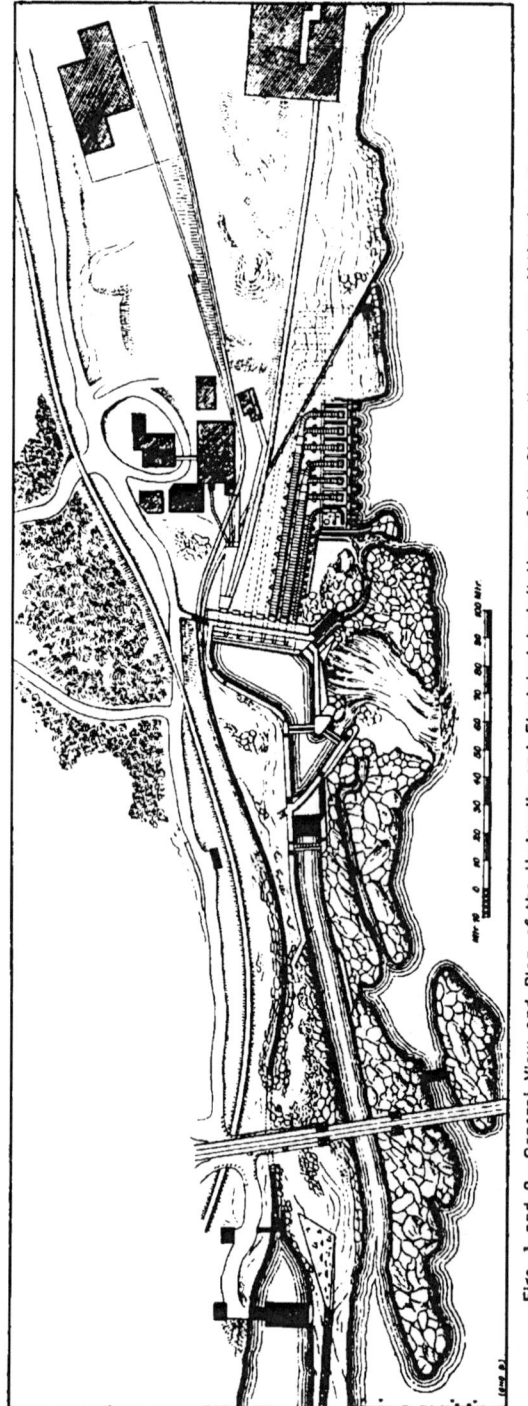

Figs. 1 and 2.—General View and Plan of the Hydraulic and Electrical Installation of the Stora Kopparsberg Aktiebolag, Sweden

MをU

Plate XXIX

Fig. 5.

Fig. 6

Fig. 3.

Fig 4

U of M

MnoU

Plate **XXX**

Fig. 7.—Interior of Power Station

Fig. 8.—7,000 volt Three-phase Alternator, by the Oerlikon Company, Zurich

ELECTRIC INDUSTRIES IN NORWAY AND SWEDEN

Plate XXXI

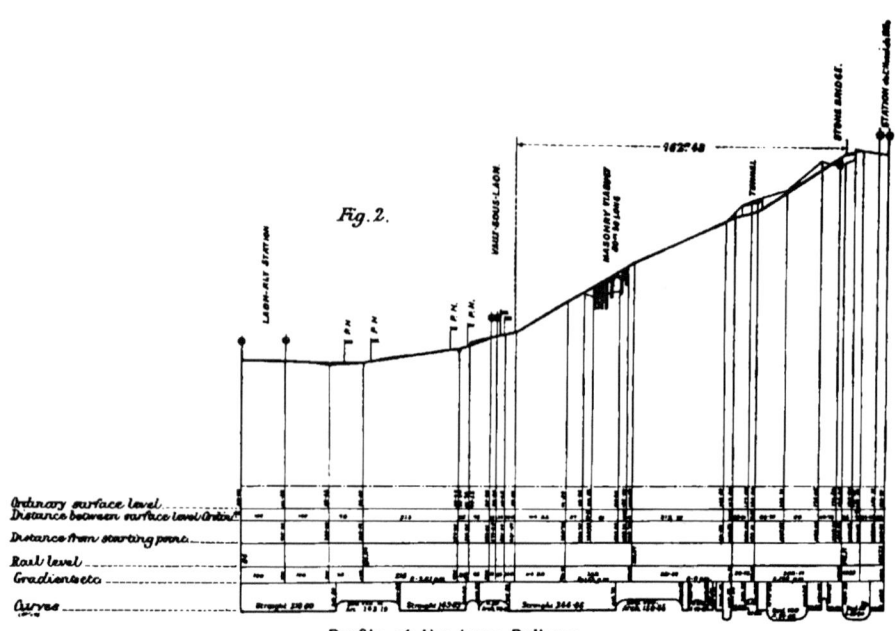

Profile of the Laon Railway

Fig. 3.—General View of the Laon Railway

THE ELECTRIC RAILWAY OF LAON

THE ELECTRIC RAILWAY OF LAON

Laon is the chief town of the Department of Aisne, to the north-east of Paris, on the Northern Railway of France; the railway station is on a junction of five lines, with an annual traffic of eight hundred thousand passengers. Laon is an important commercial centre; the distance by the main road from the town to the railway station is one and a quarter miles; the principal part of the town is on a ridge 100 metres (328ft.) high. Fig. 1 and Fig. 2 (Plate XXXI), are respectively a plan and a profile of the line. It was decided to build an electric railway for taking the traffic between the railway station and the town

the electric railway. The first part of the work presented but few difficulties, the track being practically level; this portion calls for no special comment. The steep gradient commences at a distance of 621 metres (2,037ft.) from the railway station, and from that point to the interior of the town, a distance of 750 metres (2,460ft.), the gradient is such that it was intended to use a rack. In this portion the gradients reach 112, 122, and 129 in 1,000, the latter having a length of 200 metres (656ft.). The inclines are connected by curves 200 metres (656ft.) in radius;

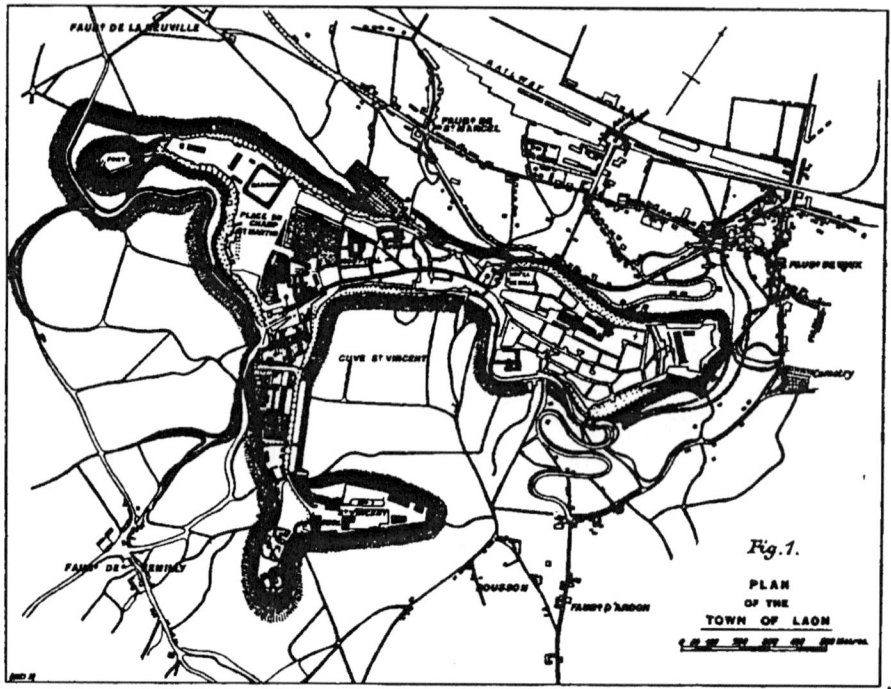

Plan of the Laon Electric Railway

and the town; the line was designed by Mr. Bourquelot, engineer of the Ponts and Chaussées, and was built by the French Thomson-Houston Company. The line starts from one of the platforms of the Northern of France Railway Station. On leaving the station it describes half a circle through the neighbouring plain and runs up to the town. It is 1,479 metres (.9 mile) in length, and the rise is 95.53 metres (313ft.). At the railway station a siding has been provided, which runs into an old carriage depôt of the Northern Railway Company, which has been transformed into a station for the passengers who travel from and to the town by

the curves have a minimum radius of 50 metres (164ft.) in the flatter, and of 120 metres (394ft.) in the steeper, portions. The line runs over a six-arch masonry viaduct, part of which is straight and part curved to a radius of 195 metres (640ft.); on the viaduct the line has a gradient of 122 in 1,000, and owing to this the centre piers had the same strength as the abutments. The viaduct is built on concrete foundations laid on sandstone. There is a tunnel of about 45 metres (148ft.) in length, with round arch of 3.80 metres (12ft. 6ins.) in diameter, and 4.05 metres (13ft. 3ins.) high. Part of the tunnel is straight, and part on a curve 130 metres (426ft.) in radius. In the tunnel the line has a gradient of from 52 to 129 in 1,000. Over part of its length the line is in cutting, while other portions are carried on a wall, which separates them from the main road. Where the line runs between two walls, one on a bank and another in a cutting, the walls have been strengthened underneath the track by masonry abutments. At several places the foundations of the line had to be laid on earth-banks. As these settled down crevices were found, but these gave no further trouble after they had been once filled up with cement. Effective means have been taken for the running off of rain water.

The line is 1 metre (39⅜ins.) gauge; the rails weigh 20.4 kilogrammes per metre (41lbs. per yard), fixed to oak sleepers 1.80 × .18 × .14 metres (6ft. × 7ins. × 5½ins.), placed .90 metre (3ft.) apart from centre to centre.

A rack on the Abt system was provided on a portion of the line, although the Thomson-Houston Company had guaranteed that this was not necessary. This rack has now been removed, it having been found that the chains working the rack-wheel absorbed a large amount of power, and that the cars could easily ascend, at a speed of 12 kilometres (7½ miles) and with ordinary adhesion, the 90 metres (295ft.) of track, which lie at a gradient of 122 in 1,000, and on a curve of 120 metres (394ft.), the motors being connected in multiple, and the consumption of current reaching 160 to 180 amperes, corresponding to 108 and 122 horse-power. This power of climbing is not due to any magnetic effect of the rails, for the trials were quite as successful when they were carried out with the return through a special cable.

Adequate means have been taken to prevent all sliding action of the track down the heavy inclines; to this effect, the masonry work and abutments have been brought in contact with the rail flange, and some of the sleepers are embedded in the masonry. Besides this, where the line runs between two walls, old rails placed transversely to the line have been built in the walls, in the rear of the sleepers and in contact with them. Means have been provided for joining the rails of the line to the old rails in the masonry, should this be found necessary. The return circuit being through the rails, the joints are fitted with Chicago rail-bonds, of copper, 60 square millimetres (.093 square inch) in section.

The power plant belongs to the Northern Railway Company; it had been put down for electric lighting, and has been enlarged, but not to a great extent, for the amount of current it was capable of producing was in excess of that required for lighting purposes. The Electric Railway Company, which has a capital of 250,000frs. (£10,000), purchases the necessary current from the North of France Railway Company.

The power station comprises three semi-tubular boilers, each with 150 square metres (1,615 square feet) heating surface; the steam pressure is 7 kilogrammes (99.560lbs. per square inch). Artificial draught is supplied to the boilers by Meldrum blowers. The two steam engines are vertical, on the Corliss system, each of 200 brake horse-power at a speed of 160 revolutions per minute, and ⅓ admission. Regularity in the working is ensured by a fly-wheel weighing 8 tons; a coupling boss on the engine shaft works a similar one on the dynamo shaft, both being joined by Raffard coupling with rubber rings, which break when there is a short circuit in the dynamo, thus preventing accident. The dynamo has ten poles, and at a speed of 160 revolutions per minute generates a current of 1,200 amperes at 115 volts (188 kilowatts). The voltage is raised to 500 or 550 volts by means of boosters. Each booster has a double wound armature with six poles, and runs at 400 revolutions per minute. One winding takes a current of 115 volts, the other supplying a current of 200 amperes at 500 volts. The total efficiency is about 80 per cent. Current is supplied to the cars by an aerial line, formed of a copper wire 8¼ millimetres (₁⁶/in.) in diameter, carried by means of flexible suspensions on poles of the ordinary type, or on horizontal brackets fitted to lattice posts. The line is fitted at each end with a lightning arrester, and a section switch at the starting point. A feeder 650 metres (2,132ft.) in length has been laid down, its section being the same as that of the trolley line.

There are two 45 horse-power motors for each car, which work the two axles by gearing, the armature being made with four windings per coil. Each motor takes up 80 amperes at 500 volts; it can work at 100 amperes, but at this intensity the circuit breaker opens and cuts off the current. By opening the circuit breaker and by reversing the motor, the motors work as generators, and the car is made to stop almost instantaneously, on the steepest gradients. Each car is fitted with two lightning arresters.

There are thirty-two to thirty-six journeys each way daily, each journey taking seven minutes. Starting at the termini and at the various stoppages takes up 60 to 80 amperes, equal to 30 or 40 kilowatts. On the steep declivities the current varies from 120 to 180 amperes, according to the gradient. The daily power consumption from six in the morning to midnight averages from 350 to 375 kilowatt-hours. The line cost 445,000frs. (£17,800).

THE PATHS OF PROGRESS

A MONTHLY REVIEW

MENTAL ENGINEERING

MOST of the multitude who lift up their voices on the subject of education prove most convincingly their own want of it. What is called the "education question" in politics is, indeed, merely the struggle of sects for the right to peg out claims in the infantile mind for future dogmatic development. The British Association and the Church Congress have papers read to them of learned length and thundering sound. The Nonconformist Conscience, which exists as much for the purpose of striking as for being stricken, stoutly defends the traditions of sectarian freedom. Meanwhile our children do not adjourn their birth until a settlement has been arrived at as to what shall be done with them, and in the midst of this clash of arms they are a countless crowd of babes in the wood, with none to offer them guidance.

Every year there are born unto the nation so many thousand souls, so many thousand brains, so many thousand pairs of hands, and the nation knows not what to do with them. Yet, if he will but take the trouble to reflect, every thinking man will see what is the right end to aim at, although he may not perceive the means to that end. The objective is, of course, to develop these children into industrious, moral, and patriotic citizens; but when one contrasts this desired consummation with the general environment of the average child, one recognises at once that in existing circumstances that child can only become a good citizen by accident. In the main, it has been British policy to trust to such accidents rather than to design, and, on the whole, results have perhaps justified this faith. But in the course of the advance of civilisation and international competition or co-operation, it becomes more and more necessary for even Great Britain to husband its human and other resources, and to systematise the development of the coming generation on scientific principles.

It is, unfortunately, customary to discuss "technical," "elementary," and "secondary" education, as if they were independent subjects. Rightly speaking, there can only be one education, which is the cultivation of the natural powers and talents of the child and the man to the end that he may worthily occupy the fittest position for him as a specialist in society. In so far as the individual powers are undeveloped, the education is defective. What is termed "technical education" is intended to signify, in its simplest sense, the teaching of the handling of tools, and the conscious skill of labour; and it is supposed to begin when the "elementary" stage is past. In reality, however, technical education, to be most effective, must start much earlier, by directing the growth of the mental powers and manual readiness, to be afterwards utilised in a special career of labour. It is obviously the first duty of the schoolmaster to teach his pupils how to think, and in order to do so it is necessary to give them something to think about, which he generally does soon enough.

The curriculum of a good elementary school should include the subjects of attention, observation, reflection, calculation, and expression, of which the three R's are merely sub-sections. Obviously, cultivation of the above recited list of mental qualities must precede any really satisfactory course of "technical" education. The schoolmaster is too often only a stoker of the mental apparatus. He shovels in fuel, and sometimes stirs it up more or less violently, but it is to be feared that he does not usually treat the intellect as the engineer handles a complicated set of machinery. Consequently, when the day comes for the beginning of what is called technical education, it frequently happens that, while the professor is learned enough, the laboratory or tool shop admirably fitted, the pupil is a being with five thumbs on each hand, and a muddled brain. Anyone whose elementary education has been bungled must necessarily be a most refractory subject for the technical "finisher."

On the other hand, if the young are early taught to think, all other things may be easily accomplished, so far as they lie in the natural bent of the individual.

In the bringing up of young Britons, the leakage of efficiency is in the elementary period, when they are almost entirely dependent upon their elders for guidance. Reaching their later "teens," there is awakened in them the consciousness of their personal responsibilities, and they are able themselves to recognise the need for technical training. If this awakening does not come, that is but another proof of the failure of the system of elementary education.

THE THREE PROFESSORS

We cannot fairly say that Professors Dewar, Perry, and Armstrong, who all lectured on education at the British Association Congress, did more, in effect, than what so many other public men and newspapers do; they "called attention" to the subject. With all respect to these distinguished men, that is not a very difficult or a very useful achievement. It would be more to the point if they would draw up a specification from which the general public might learn exactly what is wanted, how much it will cost, and what the tax-payer will get in return for his money. Professor Dewar, for example, gives us a comparison between the numbers of trained chemists employed in German and in British factories, and he tells us that there exist in the Fatherland chemical industries worth fifty millions sterling, largely founded upon the researches of Englishmen. *Primâ facie*, therefore, we have lost £50,000,000 by neglecting to develop these industries, which opportunity has been lost, according to Professor Dewar, through the lack of chemists trained and employed in the commercial application of scientific discoveries. We had the men of science, we had the capital and the raw material, but we allowed the industries to settle undisturbed in Germany. Professor Dewar might, however, admit the possible reason that we may have been too busy; that we cannot carry on the whole of the world's manufacturing business in this little island; and that the instinct of self-preservation impelled Germany to develop either the chemical or other industries at a time when we had no such incentive. It is more likely

that the "trained chemists" are the product of the industry than that Germany owes her commercial success in this department to her system of technical education. If we produced these trained chemists they might have to emigrate in order to get a living.

We are on firmer ground when we discuss with Professor Perry the education of the engineer, because there is, and will continue to be, home employment for British engineers. "To utilise the forces of nature, to combat nature, to comprehend nature as a child comprehends its mother—this," says Professor Perry, "is the pleasure and pain of the engineer." The literary critic may object to the jumble of metaphors, urging that a child does not combat its mother in well-ordered nurseries, much less does it comprehend her, which even its father generally fails to do.

But the meaning is clear, and Professor Perry's endeavour to widen the philosophical horizon of the average engineer is undoubtedly of educational value. He is not, apparently, enamoured of German technical drill systems, since in allusion to his own training at the feet of Lord Kelvin and Professor James Armstrong, at Queen's College, he declares that "a course of five years at a German Polytechnic would not do him so much good as one month's contact with one of these men." And he demands that, instead of copying Germany, we should strive to construct a system peculiarly suitable to the British boy, who is, after all, unique in many respects, and should be treated accordingly.

Professor Armstrong, on somewhat similar lines, deplores the dearth of imaginative power in contemporary art, literature, and science. Both of these gentlemen would aim at abolishing or diminishing the drudgery of education. They would prompt and cajole the youth of the country to search after knowledge with as keen interest as if they were engaged in trapping rabbits.

THE EVASIVE SYSTEM

But the British Association meets and parts, and we have still to seek the method. It may be true, as Professor Perry says, that "we learn mathematics in such a fashion that we hate the sight of an algebraic expression all our lives"; but how are we to make these figures and symbols more picturesque?

Professor Perry, I see, denounces Euclid as responsible for many weary hours which might be better spent. But for the present writer the short stories of this genial geometrician had nearly always a happy ending to a mildly exciting plot. The information conveyed might perhaps be imparted with less circumlocution sometimes, but, as mental gymnastics, there is a good deal to be said for the " Elements." Mechanics can, of course, be made more interesting, as introducing more or less familiar objects which have excited the youth's curiosity. But a general scheme for making the whole education process enjoyable is probably an unattainable ideal. The conversion of a young savage into a civilised adult must be to some extent a painful and wearisome operation, for there is certain evidence to support the theory that the child passes in the course of its growth through those successive evolutionary stages which the race has collectively left behind, and to teach a boy of ten or eleven to appreciate the mystic charm of mathematics is almost as forbidding a task as to explain the money market to a full-grown Zulu.

In the meantime there is undoubtedly an appalling quantity of ignorance on every side, which is more especially dangerous, one would think, in a democratic country. Political ignorance is not so glaring in Great Britain as it is in the United States and certain colonies, but the consequences of a national blunder are more serious. Professor Perry has made the noble suggestion that £1,000,000 should be granted by the Government to encourage men of science to find means of increasing the efficiency of engines and economising in the matter of fuel. A worthy object truly, and well worth many millions. But the design of a national education machine is of even more importance to the future welfare of Britain, and it should be made worth the while of our professors and doctors, moralists and politicians, to combine their efforts and construct a system which will realise the mental and physical assets of the nation to the greatest individual and common advantage.

THE PARLIAMENT OF LABOUR

Spasmodic demands for technical education, even at Trades Union Congresses, are of little avail in the absence of a comprehensive national system of elementary instruction. And without wishing to imitate those glib commentators who find it so easy to "score" off the trade unionists and their crude methods of procedure and immature opinions, one wonders whether there is a genuine demand on their part for greater skill, or whether the cry of England's backwardness in technical education is not raised merely in order to create class prejudice by the implication that the Government ignores the claims of labour. It is, however, certainly not the wage-payers who would throw obstacles in the way of the ambitious young artisan; and it is significant that the unions which profess to be interested in technical education actually make it a rule to handicap superior proficiency and to discourage personal ambition amongst their members. Just when it is of vital importance that the young workman should be inspired to educate himself, and to take advantage of the means provided, he is confronted with the veto of his trade union, exercised in the direction of preventing him from improving his material welfare by the superiority of his hands and brains.

It would be a sorry outlook for England if the members of the trade unions were not possessed of more common sense than their leaders, who, in most cases, exhibit something like the symptoms of intoxication when elevated to the platform. In their mutual jealousy and rivalry there is naturally a disposition to compete in violence of language, in extravagance of denunciation, and in the enticing promises of their proposed reforms. Such men fatten on grievances, and general contentment among the working-class would not suit their interest. Therefore they manufacture grievances, and concoct fearful and wonderful resolutions of protest. Even then, so serious was the deficiency of plausible subjects for their invective at the recent congress, that they found it necessary to place the Boer War on the agenda as a subject for discussion.

In their impatience with the worst aspect of trade unionism, many people utter dismal predictions of national decline and final doom, which may only be checked by the breaking down of labour organisations. One manufacturer has £10,000 on offer as a contribution towards the construction of a machine for smashing the unions. There is no question of the feasibility of such a scheme in the present state of the world's commerce. Capital has at once greater range and mobility than labour, and any general hostile movement on the part of merchants and manufacturers would be irresistible; it would destroy the "new unionism" in a few months, if not in a few weeks. It is more statesmanlike, however, to recognise that, if developed on sensible lines, the organisation of labour should be productive of national advantage. That the craftsman should go through his day's employment with some sort of pride in his work, with the consciousness of having taken his part in keeping the world moving, and that he should recognise his position in the sphere of public usefulness, is surely more politically desirable than that he should simply be driven through his diurnal toil like a blinkered 'bus horse.

At present trade unionism is going through an educational transition. Naturally, the first thought of any such organisation is to secure a larger share in the wealth of the country. There is a good deal of human nature in people, as some philosopher has observed, and the working man has his share. It is perfectly reasonable that he should desire to attain a higher standard of comfort. What he does not see, owing to faulty education, is that such material gains as he covets are not to be obtained at the expense of another class. A struggle against capital is civil war of most injurious effect on both sides. The true economic course of trade unionism is to improve the life conditions of the worker by enabling him to produce more cheaply and with greater ease. A mere demand that he shall have a bigger share in what is already produced is a demand for stagnation in industry.

MUNICIPAL AND OTHER SOCIALISM

Acting on the natural first impulse of the imperfectly educated human or other animal to grab all good things within reach, the Labour Party and the Socialists have sought to acquire wealth for their adherents by capturing the machinery of local governments and applying it to the multiplication of what are vulgarly known as "soft jobs." The result is, of course, an amazing increase in Municipal expenditure. What takes place is, in reality, that the local committees raise a certain amount by taxation, and distribute

it amongst a number of their constituents who are sufficiently pertinacious to make their demands effective. The *Times* correspondent on the subject produces ample evidence of the evils caused by such successful attempts to subsidise labour out of the rates, or, more correctly speaking, to grant public pensions to able-bodied workmen. No particular blame attaches to the recipients—most people rather prefer pensions and high salaries and short hours. But it is surprising that anyone can be found to defend such a system as if it were a sound and permanent basis for Municipal and national progress, and it is more than surprising that so many persons belonging to the prosperous classes should be subject to these delusions. The very party whose pet principle is that "all wealth is produced by labour," have in the same breath persuaded not only themselves but many worthy burgesses, that the country will flourish to an amazing extent if a Socialist system is adopted under which everyone is to be assured of a comfortable livelihood without irksome exertion. One would think that the corollary of "all wealth, etc.," is "the more labour the more wealth"; but it is the avowed policy of the party to endeavour to accelerate the train by putting on the brake and even reversing the engines. Assuming for the moment that this labour clap-trap is sincere, we require it to be demonstrated that there is more than sufficient wealth produced at present to support the whole population in the enjoyment of three Bank Holidays every week before we can accept any further proposition. The real truth is that labour of itself is almost helpless in these latitudes. It is not what these people call "labour" that of itself enables forty million mouths to be fed in Great Britain. By far the greater part of the productiveness of the country is traceable to the inventions of comparatively a very small number of men. Stephenson, Watt, Arkwright, Bessemer, and others, are the great wealth producers of the United Kingdom, not the man with the pick-axe. Mere physical labour is absolutely unprogressive, and has been ever since Adam delved and Eve spun.

Yet the basic principle of Municipal Socialism is not even that one man is as good as another, but that the manual labourer is a great deal better than anyone else, that his word should be law, and that the whole world is his and the fulness thereof. By concentrated political manoeuvring, an attempt is actually being made to give practical effect to such pestilential doctrines in our Municipalities, and in several cases the result has been to cause the town to make marked "progress" in the direction of insolvency.

RAILWAY CRITICISM

While decrying private enterprise, the Municipal Socialists have it in their power to make it more and more difficult to earn profits. The railway company and the manufacturer have to suffer the mortification of seeing their property pledged as security for public debt, from the expenditure of which they derive no benefit, but sometimes positive injury. The rates paid by railway companies are increasing at such a pace as to suggest that in the not far distant future nearly the whole of the net revenue, after meeting working costs, will be collected by the tax gatherer, so that virtually the Municipality will own the railway.

In the meantime, the railway director is held up to public obloquy or ridicule because he is not able to convey us all over the country at excursion fares in punctual express trains, starting every ten minutes, and furnished with all the luxuries and conveniences of a first-class hotel. The *Daily Mail* suggests that the directors are too old; that a board of patriarchs are not likely to be "hustlers." But, curiously enough, the financial critics maintain that the capital account of our railways is being recklessly inflated, which symptom of unsound management would more likely be displayed by hot-blooded youth than by timorous senility. Is it possible that our railway directors are too young?

There is no secret about it—our railways are unsatisfactory in many ways; but the main cause is to be found in physical and political conditions. Taking these conditions into account, the record of railway management in this country is one that may be regarded with a good deal of admiration and exasperation. Is it not amazing to read, sixty years after the first faltering steps in railway construction, this vigorous outburst of indignation and dismay in the *Daily Telegraph*?

England taught the world the use of railways, and is now paying the penalty for so doing. We have almost, if not quite, the dearest railways in Europe. If George Stephenson had only repressed his inventive genius, and the people of this country had waited until Germany, France, or America had yoked the iron horse, we might have learnt from their errors, instead of committing specimen blunders for all the rest of the world to avoid. Fearful parliamentary costs, monopoly prices for land, and fancy charges for construction, have made the railway tariff in this land—the mother of railways and of parliaments—heavy and grievous to be borne.

True it is that our railways were expensively constructed, and that parliamentary costs were "fearful," and land was sold as if worth its weight in gold. But if we had waited till to-day these conditions would be precisely the same. No possible advantage could have been gained by postponing our period of railway construction until America and the Continent had shown us the way. On the contrary, land would in the interim have advanced in value considerably. A large part of the Great Central property only dates from the end of the nineteenth century, yet that company is one of the least prosperous. If George Stephenson had "repressed his genius," and these other strange things had happened, the press would certainly have contended that our expensive railway rates, etc., were due to our backwardness in allowing France, Germany, and the States to take a long lead in construction.

If more lines had been laid years ago we should be, not in a worse condition, as the *Telegraph* argues, but in a much better condition, as the traffic manager of any company having a terminus in London would at once admit. Construction was carried out with some want of foresight, although it is perhaps unreasonable to expect railway directors to anticipate and provide for the extraordinary growth of some of the great towns. Now that they are faced with the problem, Parliament carefully makes it as costly as possible to widen the lines and enlarge the stations, by such enactments as that compelling the companies to re-house persons whose dwellings are swept away by improvements of immense advantage to the general population.

In respect of goods traffic many unfair comparisons are drawn between British and foreign railways, and it is urged upon our directors that they should rush to imitate American practice, and effect the necessary changes out of revenue. America is a country of long distances and homogeneous loads, as contrasted with our short hauls and more mixed freight. In nearly every department of industry it would be more seemly for the lay press to take it for granted that British business men generally have some reason or some excuse for their system of management and results obtained, than that the said press should attribute every apparent shortcoming to the lack of intelligence or enterprise. English railway government is not perfect, but there is quite as much in it deserving of praise as of blame, and its variations are in the direction of continual improvement.

THAMES TRAFFIC

Even a good word may be said for the Thames Steamboat Company, which is now, like certain professional ladies and gentlemen, "resting." But it is no part of the purpose of these notes to defend lost causes, and as the company has thus retired, there is more profit in taking a fresh view of the river as a highway than in retelling the sad story of the Thames fleet. One fact, however, ought to be set down as a curiosity in traffic management not hitherto published, namely, that it is claimed that Mr. Hills might have made a profit, instead of a loss on his enterprise if he could have overcome his temperance scruples and developed the liquor department on board. Just as the whisky and beer duties, as distributed by the Government, are in part allocated to meet the expenses of technical education, so that every tippler contributes towards increasing the industrial efficiency of the nation, so from the same source might come a subsidy to solve the interesting engineering and financial problem of conveying penny passengers at a profit on the Thames.

Mr. J. Bull, M.P. for Hammersmith, has propounded a scheme for a service which includes such items as " the whole river lit with large arc lights," " cheap refreshments, papers and tobacco, etc.," " bootblacks on board," and " shaving shops on piers and steamers." The boats are to be " powerfully engined, easily steered, and well lighted," and Mr. Bull believes in a 2d. fare from Hammersmith to the City, with halfpenny stages.

Now, it is not to be doubted that, if we had cheap and swift steamers, comfortably fitted, if it was no trouble to get on board, and if we were fairly certain of reaching our destination at or near the appointed time, many people would travel by this route—in fine weather. Mr. Bull thinks that the capital required would not be more than a million, which is rather a severe back-hander for the London County Council scheme, estimated to cost £400,000. When one reflects that it costs a million to construct less than three miles of tube railway, there is certainly something fascinating in the prospect of taking possession of ten miles of riverway cutting through the centre of London for the same amount of money. Paradoxical as it may sound, the venture is more likely to pay dividends on a large capital than a small one ; for after all this disappointment the people of London will not be tempted to the river brink by any cheap and shabby expedient ; and to construct and run boats, competent to overcome the natural difficulties of the tidal Thames, is no light task.

Very fairly Mr. Bull enumerates these difficulties, which London County Council Progressives at any price overlook ; but he declares his conviction that there would be a profit, after two or three years of dividendless patience.

A few summers such as that from which we have now happily escaped, would undoubtedly be a sore trial to the shareholders, unless, as was darkly hinted above, the refreshment department was cunningly contrived to produce a cheerful spirit among the weather - beaten passengers. There is much money invested in less promising speculations than this designed by Mr. Bull.

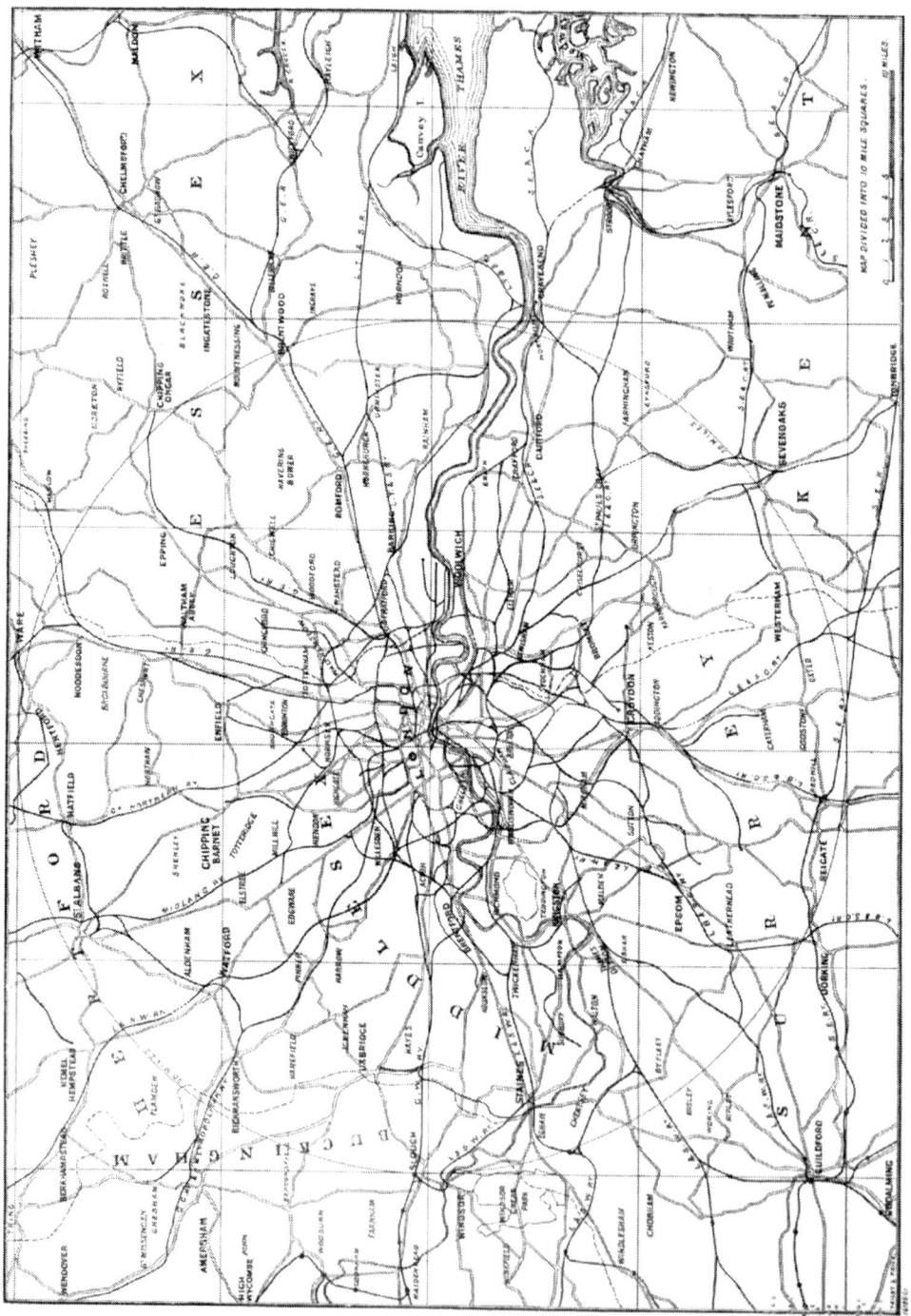

Fig. 1.—Map of Railways Converging on London

RAILWAY ECONOMICS

By the Hon. Robert P. Porter

V.—LONDON LOCOMOTION *(continued from page 88)*

XXII.—Railway Systems Centring in London

Take a pair of compasses and a good map of London and the surrounding country, and draw a circle of twenty miles radius. Within this circle you will find three important boundaries: (*a*) the city of London; (*b*) the county of London, and (*c*) the area of the Metropolitan Police District. A more comprehensive idea of the great steam railway systems which enter London from all points of the compass may be obtained by an outer circle of ten additional miles, making, in all, a radius of thirty miles around London (see Plate XXXII). A glance at the top of this map, between the twenty and thirty miles radius, will show that we have included Hatfield, on the Great Northern system; Hertford, reached by both Great Northern and Great Eastern; Chipping Ongar, Chelmsford, and Brentwood, all on the Great Eastern; Pitsea and Southend, on the London, Tilbury, and Southend Railway; Rochester, Strood, and Chatham, on the London, Chatham, and Dover; Sevenoaks and, just beyond the thirty miles radius, Tonbridge, on the South-Eastern; Redhill, Reigate, Dorking, and Horley, on the London, Brighton, and South Coast; Guildford, Woking, Pirbright, and Ascot, on the London and South-Western; Windsor, Taplow, Maidenhead, and Henley, on the Great Western; the Chenies, Great Missenden, and Aylesbury, on the Great Central; Tring and Leighton, on the London and North-Western; and St. Albans and Hemel Hempstead, on the Midland, where we arrive at our starting point, and meet the Hatfield spur of the Great Northern which joins the Midland at St. Albans. In our circle we have gone completely around London, and roughly mapped out (see Fig. 1, Plate XXXII) the field of the eleven railways which enter the City at the following main stations:—

1. Great Northern	King's Cross.
2. Great Eastern	Liverpool Street.
3. London, Tilbury, and Southend ...	Fenchurch Street.
4. London, Chatham, and Dover	London Bridge, Cannon Street,
5. South-Eastern	Charing Cross, Victoria, etc.
6. London, Brighton, and South Coast	London Bridge and Victoria.
7. London and South-Western	Waterloo.
8. Great Western	Paddington.
9. Great Central	Marylebone.
10. London and North-Western	Euston.
11. Midland	St. Pancras.

Within the twenty miles radius it is more difficult to keep these great systems separated. By the aid of the North London Railway, the Metropolitan, the Metropolitan District, the Hammersmith and City (Great Western and Metropolitan Joint), Metropolitan and Metropolitan District Joint, Tottenham and Hampstead Junction, West London (Great Western and London and North-Western Joint), Tottenham and Forest Gate (Midland and London, Tilbury, and Southend Joint), East London Joint, London, Brighton, and South Coast and London and South-Western Joint, and sundry other extensions and connections, these steam railways, after breaking through our outer ring, cross and recross each other in such a complex network of lines, that they all become hopelessly merged into one system, handling together more than five hundred millions of passengers annually. In this tangle of lines, with several hundred stations, all within the limits of the county of London, the most we can expect to do is to become familiar with the trains of the district to which we belong. It is equally impossible to make anything like a correct estimate of the traffic. A letter addressed to the managers of the several railways running into London, and to the managers of the railways which have a separate existence within the Metropolitan area, has brought an estimate of the passengers arriving and departing at the important stations. These estimates, however, are misleading, because some of the larger systems —notably the Great Eastern, South-Eastern and Chatham and Dover, London, Brighton, and South Coast, and London and South-Western—handle their own suburban passengers to a larger extent than others. On the other hand, the Great Northern, the London and North-Western, Midland, and Great Western convey passengers by through trains over the North London and Metropolitan into the City, whilst vast numbers of others, by exchange stations, enter the City by these subsidiary railways. Then, again, some of these totals include estimates for season tickets, and some do not. It is assumed that the journey value of season tickets is about five hundred journeys each ticket per year. The following table may give some idea of the traffic, but only a rough estimate of the relative proportion carried by each railway company :—

Name of Railway.	Number of Passengers taken in and out of London, 1901.
1. Great Northern	34,000,000
2. Great Eastern	91,741,000
3. London, Tilbury, and Southend ...	14,250,000
4. London, Chatham, and Dover	29,159,000
5. South-Eastern	28,645,000
6. London, Brighton, and South Coast	27,262,000
7. London and South-Western ...	30,000,000
8. Great Western	
9. Great Central	
10. London and North-Western ...	18,000,000
11. Midland	
Total	273,057,000

XXIII.—SUBSIDIARY LINES

Here we have a total of nearly 275,000,000 without the important steam and electric railways within the area of London. To add these two totals together would, of course, result in duplication, but the number of passengers transported in 1901 by the principal lines is indicated at the head of the next column.

The traffic of the smaller subsidiary railways and joint lines is not recorded separately, but is included in the reports of the traffic of the several railways operating them. How many of these passengers are

APPROXIMATE NUMBER OF PASSENGERS ON CITY LINES, 1901

Name of Railway.	Number of Passengers Conveyed in 1901.
Metropolitan Railway	90,000,000
Metropolitan District	40,000,000
North London*	47,000,000
Central London	45,000,000
City and South London...	16,000,000
East London Railway	7,000,000
Waterloo and City	5,000,000
Total ...	250,000,000

conveyed all the way to and from their homes by the railways within the London area, and how many are fed from the greater railway systems to these minor lines and thence into the City, it is impossible to even estimate. A glance at the maps of the Metropolitan lines and connections of each of these great railway systems will give some idea of the exact field occupied by each railway, and of the never ceasing endeavours of each to cover, in some way, as much as possible of the field which geographically belongs to the neighbouring railway. These maps certainly show how keen is the existing competition.

Looking, for example, at Fig 2, Plate XXXIII, the map of the Great Northern Metropolitan lines and connections, it will be seen that from Finsbury and King's Cross it makes connections *via* the North London and Tilbury Railways, with Broad Street, Stratford, Bow, Poplar, Blackwall, and Tilbury on the east, and on the west it runs to Willesden and, *via* the Metropolitan, to Paddington and then around the Inner Circle.

When its new tubes—the Great Northern and City and the Great Northern and Strand (leased to the Yerkes syndicate)—are open, the Great Northern will be able to land its passengers at the Bank, at Charing Cross, and at Waterloo Station. The map also shows that it now connects with the southern system of railways *via* the Metropolitan and Chatham and Dover, and *via* the District at Victoria.

XXIV.—THE GREAT EASTERN

Curiously enough, the Great Eastern map of its Metropolitan lines and connections Fig. 3, page 141, is much more compact, keeping almost strictly within its own

---

* Season tickets bring this total up to over 80,000,000.

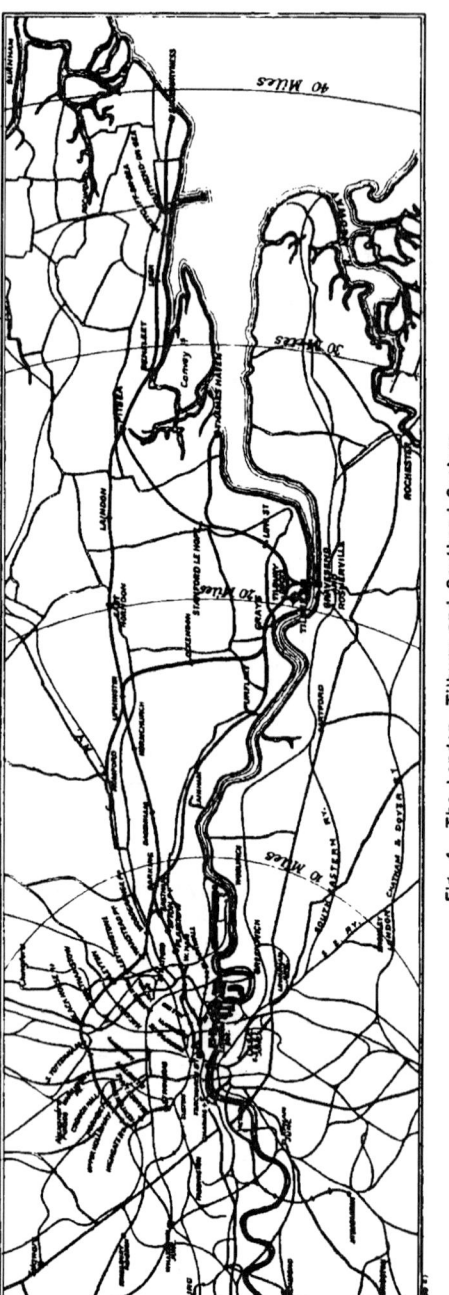

Fig. 4.—The London, Tilbury and Southend System

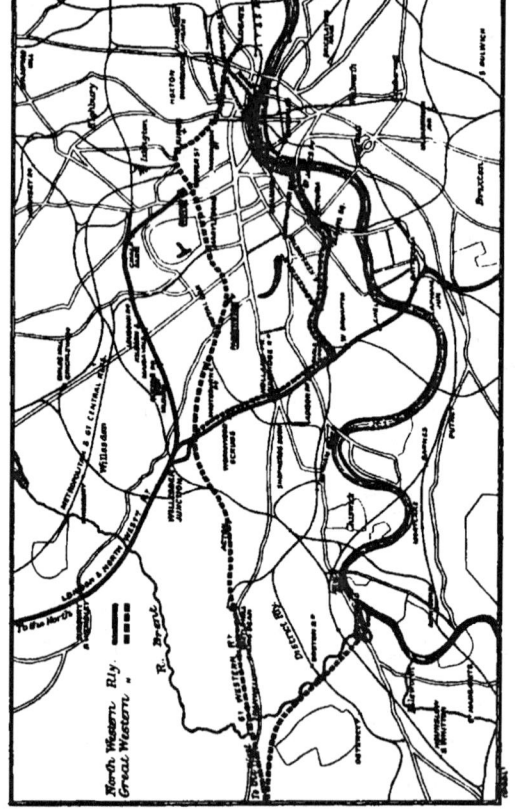

Fig. 8.—The Great Western and London and North-Western Suburban Systems

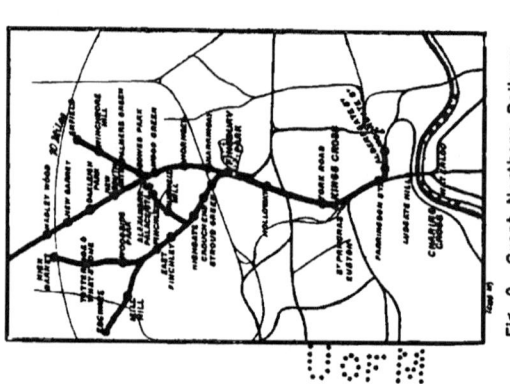

Fig. 2.—Great Northern Railway Suburban System

UofM

territory; yet this company literally pours passengers into London at its four Metropolitan stations — Liverpool Street, Bethnal Green, Bishopsgate Street, and Fenchurch Street. Before long this railway, which has prospered under the astute guidance passengers from Woolwich, Barking, Romford, Epping, and all the new towns along the east length of the Forest. West of the Forest, it extends to Chingford, running through Walthamstow, Hackney Downs, and London Fields to the City. There are two

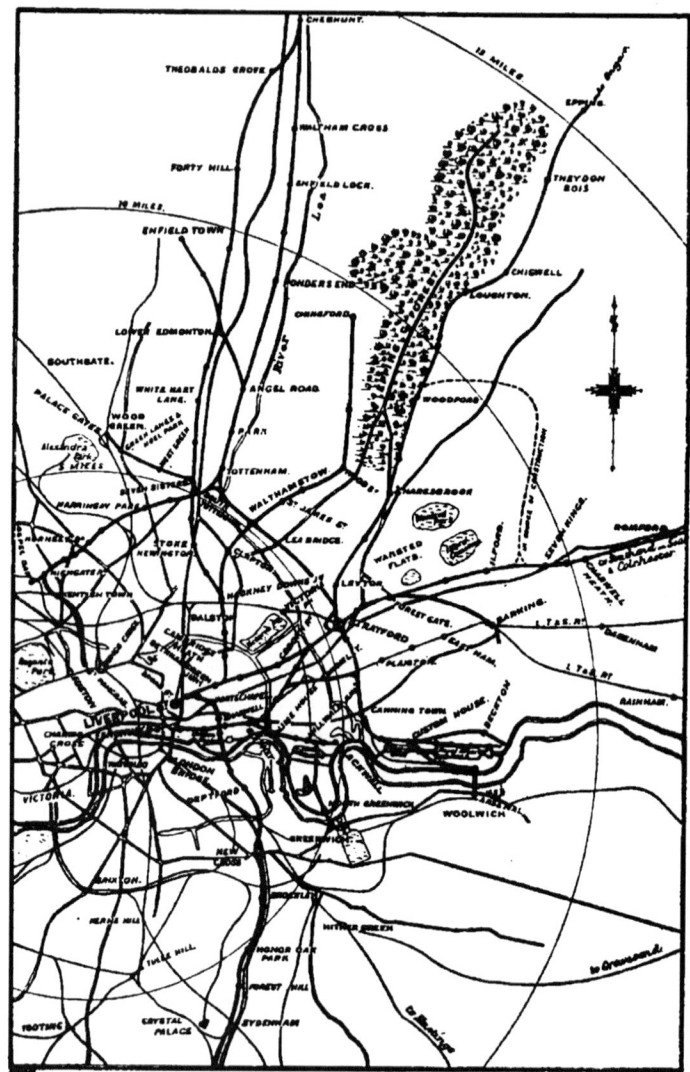

Fig. 3.—Great Eastern Railway–Suburban System

of Lord Claude Hamilton and the able management of Mr. Gooday, will handle one hundred million passengers in and out of London annually. Beginning at North Greenwich, the Great Eastern brings branches following the River Lea, the Tottenham section, close to the river, to Enfield Lock, or Waltham Cross to Cheshunt. The Enfield section, connecting with the Tottenham branch at Seven Sisters, and again at

Lower Edmonton, merges into one line at Cheshunt. There are no more thickly populated districts in London than those through which the Great Eastern penetrates.

The London, Tilbury, and Southend Railway map (Fig. 4, Plate XXXIII), begins at Shoeburyness, thence on to Southend-on-Sea. At Pitsea it dips towards the River Thames *via* Stanford le Hope, where a branch runs eastward to Thames Haven, as the line continues on to Tilbury Docks, and thence, *via* Grays, Purfleet, Rainham, to Barking, where it joins the upper line and enters London by several different routes, namely Great Eastern to Fenchurch Street, Forest Gate and Tottenham Joints, and the District Railway.

Charing Cross, Waterloo Junction, St. Paul's, Ludgate Hill, Holborn Viaduct, "Elephant and Castle," and Victoria. With these important entrances into London, the South-Eastern and Chatham Railway skirts South London, running through Battersea, Wandsworth, Brixton, Stockwell, Denmark Hill, Peckham Rye, Lewisham, and Blackheath, coupling up with New Cross and Greenwich, and going eastward to Woolwich, Plumstead, Abbey Wood, Belvedere, and to Barnehurst, where the upper line connects with the Blackheath, Kidbrooke, and Bexley Heath branch. There are two eastern lines south of these, one *via* Sidcup and Crayford, and the other *via* Chislehurst

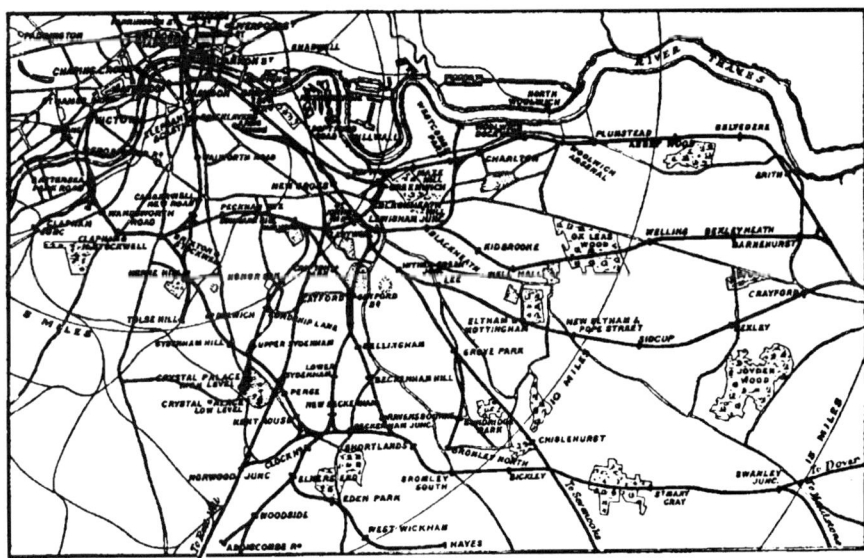

Fig. 5.—South-Eastern and Chatham Railway—Suburban System

XXV.—THE SOUTH-EASTERN AND CHATHAM

The South-Eastern and Chatham Railway have a joint arrangement; hence the suburban lines and stations of both are shown on one map, Fig. 5. Like the Great Eastern these railways, with their sixty million passengers, are confined strictly to their south-eastern territory, and cut no figure on the north side of the Thames. As in the case of the Great Eastern they jointly enjoy many important London stations, namely, London Bridge, Cannon Street,

and Swanley Junction, to Margate. Branches of these two railways run in all directions, through the Crystal Palace, Sydenham, Penge, Dulwich, also to Croydon, Beckenham, and Bromley. In fact, the South-Eastern and Chatham Railway is (theoretically) to southeast London exactly what the Great Eastern is to north-east London. Both of these systems have reached the limit of their passenger-carrying capacity, and the only way for them to keep ahead of the times will be to build electric railways. If they do not, such railways will be started by independent companies.

XXVI.—The London and Brighton

Another clearly defined system of Metropolitan suburban lines and connections is that of the London, Brighton, and South Coast Railway, as seen on Fig. 6. A little to the west of the South-Eastern and Chatham, the lines of the London, Brighton, and South Coast run almost due south, keeping within

Junction and beyond, while the south-easterly branch goes through Upper Warlingham on to Oxted and Limpsfield. Community of interest rather calls for joint operation of all three of these south-eastern railways. They would, if consolidated and aided by good electrical connections for entering London, form a nucleus for the efficient working of this territory, especially

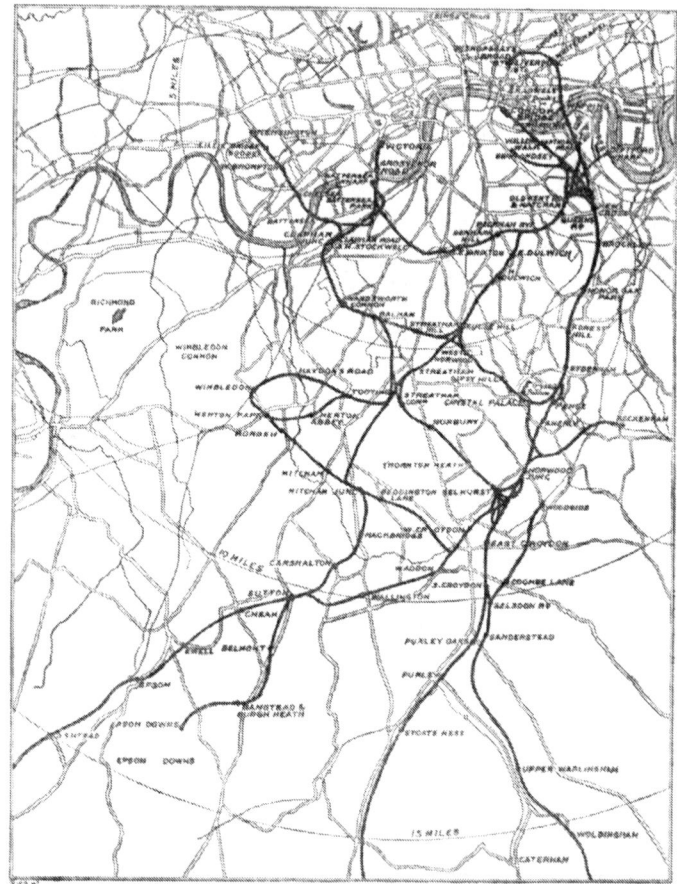

Fig. 6.—London, Brighton, and South Coast Railway—Suburban System

a compact territory with Penge, Anerley, Norwood, and East Croydon on the east, and Wimbledon, Wallington, and Sutton on the west. From this point the line takes a south-westerly direction to Epsom, Leatherhead, and Dorking. The two other branches diverging at South Croydon extend, in the first case, almost due south to Redhill

as the condition of the soil of this part of London makes tubular railways more expensive than in the north, while the districts, as shown in a previous article, are not as thickly populated. With better suburban railway facilities, however, population would seek these pleasant and healthy districts. As it is, the traffic of these three railways will soon reach one hundred million passengers per annum—a beginning capable of very great development.

XXVII.—THE SOUTH-WESTERN

The London and South-Western Railway, as it appears on its London District Map Fig. 7, is comprised of a vast number of circles, and squares, and oblongs, and triangles,

the well-known Metropolitan and Metropolitan District Circles, we have a rather blunt triangle, with Clapham Junction, Putney, Barnes, and Mortlake for a base, and Willesden Junction for its apex. Then we have a case of looping the loop, starting at Waterloo *via* Brixton, Streatham, Tooting, Wimbledon, back to the City *via* Somers Town, Clapham Junction, Queen's Road, Vauxhall, and Waterloo. Looping the loop

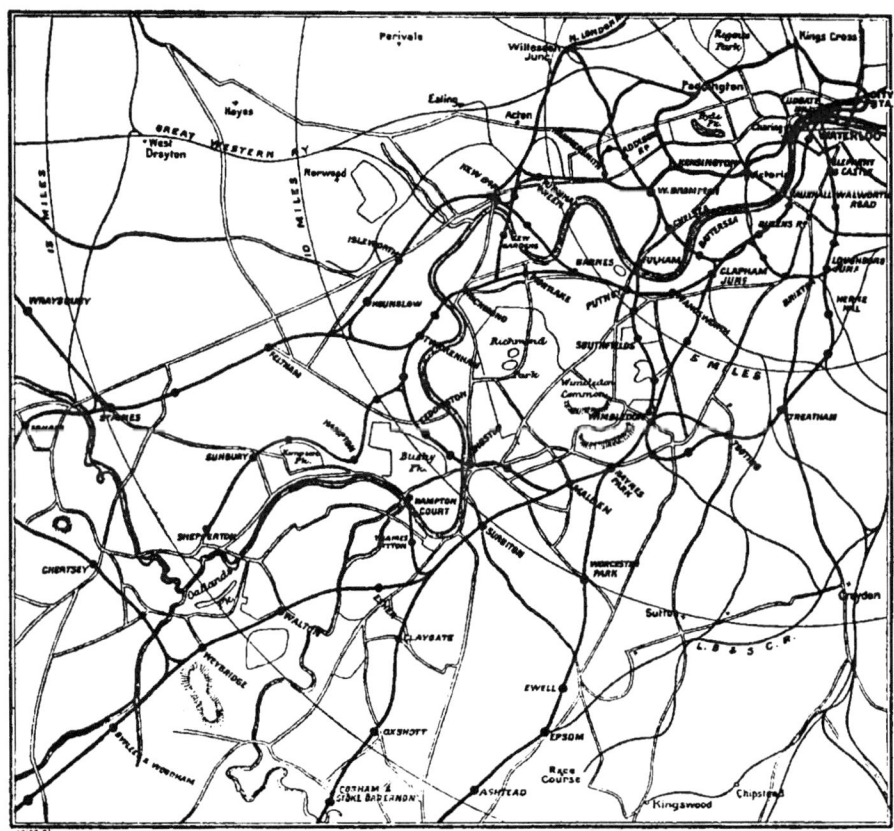

Fig. 7.—London and South-Western Railway—Suburban System

and loops, and queer shapes that would baffle Euclid to describe.

Now and then the lines of this railway seem to end, as at Shepperton, while the Staines and Datchet line appears to drop you into Windsor Park; but, as a rule, the trains of the suburban divisions must be whirling round in circles and loops, with a fair chance, if they keep on long enough, of arriving at the point of departure. Without counting

seems to be performed at Merton Abbey, Merton Park, Wimbledon, Haydon's Road, back to Tooting. Again, the South-Western literally forms a circle around Richmond Park, Wimbledon Common, Wimbledon Park, and Combe Woods. Beginning, say at Clapham, one could go, *via* Putney, Mortlake, Richmond, St. Margaret's, Strawberry Hill, Teddington, Hampton Wick, Kingston, Norbiton, Malden, Raynes Park, Wimbledon, Wimbledon Park,

Somers Town, Wandsworth, and back to Clapham. Or, to extend the circular tour, one could branch off at Twickenham, *via* Feltham, Ashford, Staines, Egham, around by Virginia Water, Chertsey, Addlestone, and Weybridge, back to London, *via* Walton, Long Ditton, Surbiton, Malden, and so on to Waterloo. A longer route might be taken by starting from London, or the last described route continuing from Weybridge to Woking, thence to Guildford, and back *via* Clandon, Effingham Junction, Leatherhead, Raynes Park, and thence, *via* Wimbledon, back to Waterloo. It is not surprising that Mr. J. Clifton Robinson's tramways give the South-Western some anxiety. These electrical cars dodge in and out all around, very much as the South-Western Railway seems to do, but they perform the work more easily, and with greater comfort to the traveller. Those who have had to study the time-tables of these complex railways, with their innumerable trains, and their countless City connections, know something of the joys of a tram-car ready at your door every few minutes. Is it surprising that forty million passengers are carried on sixteen miles of tramway, many of them drawn from within the shade of the bridges and viaducts of the South-Western Railway? The management of the South-Western is superb and up to date, but a steam railway is too cumbersome to make these quick turns, to run around circles, and for the more modern device of looping the loop.

XXVIII.—OTHER RAILWAYS

The Great Western, Fig 8, Plate XXXIII, unlike the railway system we have just discussed, sends most of its suburban passengers to the various parts of London by the Metropolitan, the Metropolitan District, the North London, and other minor railways, over some of which its own carriages are run. The map shows the river district of the railway, and its close connections with the three most important subsidiary lines. When the Great Central through line is completed, and it ceases to use the tracks of the Metropolitan Railway to Aylesbury, it will follow the example of the Great Western in the disposition of its suburban traffic.

On the two remaining railways, the

London and North-Western (also shown on Fig. 8, Plate XXXIII) and the Midland, Fig. 9, the same plan is in a measure adopted, though the London and North-Western handle at Euston about seven million passengers annually. At Willesden Junction it uses the North and South London junction for its south-western traffic, and the West London Railway and West London extension to reach Clapham Junction and make its southern and south-eastern connection. The aim of this railway appears to be more in the direction of looking after its valuable through connections from the north and north-west than to figure largely in suburban business beyond that which naturally comes within its own territory. The Midland map of London and district shows a similar endeavour, except that it is invading the Great Eastern territory by the

Fig. 9.—The Midland Railway Suburban System

aid of the north-east connections, and may be found in the thickest of the business around the Victoria and Albert docks. Here, however, we enter the field of freight, which is altogether another story.

XXIX.—BATTLE OF THE RAILWAYS

The last of these eleven railways to secure an entrance into London was the Great Central at Marylebone, and prior to that the Midland, more than a generation back. It seems almost inevitable that the suburban systems of these railways will be operated by electricity, if the companies propose to increase or even retain their present traffic. The simplest way to have managed this would have been for the steam railways to have absorbed the subsidiary railways, such as the Metropolitan, Metropolitan District, North London, and so forth; to have electrically equipped them, and formed a comprehensive system in conjunction with their own suburban systems. In addition to this, these railways, following in the footsteps of the Great Northern Railway and London and South-Western, should themselves have promoted the tubular railways. Instead of this, we find the Metropolitan and Metropolitan District dictating arbitrary terms to the great companies, playing one company against the other, and generally standing in the way of improvement and progress. It has undoubtedly been a case of the tail wagging the dog, and not the dog wagging the tail. In the interest of preserving or increasing their suburban traffic, a community of interest arrangement between the important railways would have easily been possible, and the railway systems wholly within the county of London, together with those in process of completion, with up-to-date electrical equipment, should have been utilised to bring about the result. A central power distributing company would materially reduce the cost of operation, and a cheap uniform fare become practical and profitable. The electrical distributing railways should have been built to run underneath the tracks of the principal railway stations, as at Waterloo, and the Finsbury Park Station of the Great Northern. The Boston Central Station perhaps may be suggested as a good model for the combination of steam and electrical traction. There are, of course, some exchange stations now in existence, but they are mostly old-fashioned and inconvenient, while the stations of the subsidiary railways in the vicinity of large railway stations are difficult to get at, and involve great loss of time. Nor is this the worst of it. The battle of big railways is constantly being fought over the lines of these minor railways, resulting in all sorts of annoyance to the public, both in rates of fare, and in lack of through booking. It was shown before the House of Lords Committee this session that in some cases, owing to the squabbles between the companies about the through communications, the more frequently the unhappy passenger booked, the cheaper he could travel. From Richmond to the City, for example, a distance of less than ten miles, in order to come up and return for, say a shilling, it is necessary to book three times. The failure on the part of the great railway companies to unify and harmonise the suburban traffic at least ten years ago, and to introduce electric

traction, is the real cause of reduced receipts from suburban traffic. The lamentation of the railway chairman over the loss of passenger traffic which may be found in nearly all the annual reports, though attributed to electricity, and competition, and the perversity of modern enterprise, and goodness knows what else, is in reality due to not looking the situation squarely in the face; to that British trait of sitting tight and doing nothing. For a time this policy may work, but in the long run never. The great railway companies have simply been appearing to nibble at modern devices for working suburban traffic, when they should have long ago adopted them.

XXX.—The Railways and Electric Traction

It is interesting in this connection to note what some of these gentlemen have to say on the subject. Here, for example, is Lord Claude Hamilton, chairman of the Great Eastern Railway, a company that has done good work in cheap rapid transit, calling attention to the fact that their suburban traffic was "threatened by the multifarious projected tube railways." In his speech in January last he stated that the policy of the directors, as regarded increased facilities of traffic on their suburban system, was to consolidate and develop to the full the company's existing resources and accommodation before coming to any decision as to further capital expenditure on the new lines or the "electrification" of existing lines. They had since then, by means of widened carriages and additional trains, provided such extra accommodation that there were more seats in any one hour in their trains than there were passengers travelling. Passengers would, however, rush for one particular train, and, as an instance of this, he might mention that, in order to relieve the 6.33 p.m. train from Liverpool Street to Chingford, which was overcrowded, they recently put on a new train at 6.27 p.m. This train was now overcrowded, while the 6.33 p.m., which used to be overcrowded, and also a preceding train at 6.23 p.m., now ran with about five hundred empty seats, because passengers preferred to travel by the 6.27 p.m., so that, of three trains running within ten minutes, one was crowded and two were comparatively empty. Similar illustrations occurred at other times, arising from like causes. Mr. Vreeland of the Metropolitan Street Railway, of New York, could give precisely the same experiences, resulting from his endeavours, during the rush hours, to spread the traffic of the crowded Broadway, Madison and Sixth Avenue cars, to lines not carrying their full quota, by means of free cross-town transfers. These efforts have been only partially successful, because passengers seem to prefer hanging on the steps to riding even a block or two, without additional cost, out of their way. The Great Eastern Company's officers were also considering, and had reported to the directors, on improved traction, both by means of steam locomotives and by the "electrification" of a portion of the line. These were matters which were receiving the constant attention of the Board, but they had not yet come to any decision as to the method that ought to be adopted. The new decapod locomotive of exceptional power, which they were building as an experiment, was not yet completed, and they could not find, in America or elsewhere, any railway working by electricity, trains of thirteen carriages, capable of conveying 656 passengers, equal to a total weight of 210 tons, at a two minutes' interval, which was what they required. It was doubtful whether a railway working such trains would, with the existing knowledge of electrical tractive power, be commercially successful, which, of course, was the principal point to be considered, although there was no doubt that it would be possible to work the traffic in the manner indicated. As to existing electrical railways which conveyed much lighter trains, there was by no means unanimity of opinion as to the best mode of working, etc. The Central London Railway had been opened only two years, and yet the Board of that company had decided on an alteration of their system of working. The shareholders would remember also the different opinions expressed at the inquiry before the Board of Trade as to whether the Ganz or the multiple unit system should be adopted for the "electrification" of the Metropolitan and District railways. Again, before the Lords Committee on the tube railways this session, one expert said that Parliament made a mistake in allowing the Central London Company to build an 11ft. 6in. tube. Another expert, on the contrary, argued that the Central London Tube was quite sufficient, and that a larger tube would prevent many undertakings from being a financial success. Lord Claude Hamilton alluded to other differences between experts, and said that the Board did not, therefore, consider that they ought at present to bind themselves down to any particular system, even in order to prevent the extension of the tube lines into the company's district. One tube scheme through Leyton and Walthamstow to Waltham, had been withdrawn, but the promoters announced that they would bring it forward again next session, while another, the North-East London scheme, which would compete with the Great Eastern line for its Tottenham and Edmonton traffic, had been passed by the Lords Committee. To enable them to pay a dividend of $8\frac{1}{2}$ per cent. on the ordinary shares, the promoters of the last mentioned scheme estimated that they would carry 68,888,000 passengers per annum, which was equal, making the usual allowance of 25 per cent. for Sunday traffic, to 194,000 passengers per day. This was a number which, in practical working, could not be carried over a double line of railway; while the whole of the traffic carried by the Great Eastern, the North London, and the Great Northern Railways, from the district proposed to be served by the North-East London Tube, was only 27,215,147 per annum, or equal to 88,482 per day.

XXXI.—Co-operation Needed

These views are interesting and important, representing as they do the opinion of such capable and practical railway experts as the men who have built up the largest steam railway suburban traffic of London. The testimony, however, before the House of Lords Committee shows beyond question the terribly crowded condition of the Great Eastern carriages—a condition so bad that it was claimed by some, that churches and public halls had been opened in the East End of London to shelter the work girls and others who were obliged to come to the City hours ahead of the time they were admitted to the shops and factories employing them. I have no doubt the Great Eastern has done its best to take care of the increasing traffic from London over the border, but its managers should bear in mind that a new town of a quarter of a million souls springs up here every decade. Between 1891 and 1901 over 260,000 persons added to the population an increase of 60 per cent., as against the increase in London proper of 10 per cent. The united population of Liverpool, Manchester, Birmingham, Leeds, and Sheffield increased during the same period 255,000, or an average of 12 per cent. Surely this part of London can sustain additional transportation facilities. Long before it is in operation, the population will be ready to use it, and the Great Eastern will never know the difference. Lord Claude Hamilton and his able manager, Mr. Gooday, should co-operate with Sir Clinton Dawkins and J. S. Morgan & Co., rather than oppose them. Both systems are needed.

XXXII.—Signs of Enterprise

The London, Tilbury, and Southend Railway, the nearest geographical neighbour of the Great Eastern, seems awake to the necessities of the present situation. The Whitechapel and Bow Railway was open to traffic July 1st, this year, and was carrying a large number of passengers. Their capital expenditures, Mr. Henry D. Brownes, the chairman, said, are not at an end. If they were to make the undertaking successful they must give full and fair facilities to the public. They had, therefore, got powers to double their line between Bromley and East Ham, which would not involve the company in very great expense. They had also the Bill which was now awaiting the royal assent, taking power to "electrify" their railway. In regard to that matter they proposed to adopt a prudent policy. They wished to see the result of the work of the Metropolitan and District Companies, who were engaged in "electrifying" their systems, before doing anything. The Board had, however, taken some trouble in the matter of electric traction. They had sent one of their staff out to America to see what was being done there, and they had also got one of their colleagues, Mr. Stride, to join the Board of the District Railway. In conclusion, he said that if they went on as they were going, and did not waste their money in foolish and unprofitable extensions, he did not see why the company should not maintain their present position, and continue to be a useful and lucrative

investment. This company will undoubtedly fall in with the work now in progress, because, while it has less than a mile of line within the county of London, it is, to all intents and purposes, a London suburban railway. And then, does it not lead direct to what was once known as the "Trippers' Paradise" —Southend ? "Whitechapel by the sea," we are told, is slowly and surely losing its old reputation, and it only needs quick electric service to make it distinctly fashionable after its kind. At any rate, it has possibilities of becoming the "Coney Island" of London. Not that Southend will ever desert the East End crowd who brought it prosperity, we are assured by a recent writer. Indeed, it has repaid them to the full, giving them everything that can help to make their sparse holidays happy ; but the Corporation are going much further. They want to create a suburbia for Southend, and people it with a West End population, such as brings lasting prosperity in its train. This is a matter in which an excellent train service, good and cheap houses, and accessible pleasures will be the determining factors. The principal advantage that Southend offers to this newer scheme is its proximity to town. Westcliff is thirty-five miles by rail from Fenchurch Street, and it is possible to leave town and reach Westcliff in forty-seven minutes. The London, Tilbury, and Southend, Great Eastern, and Midland lines have an excellent service, but business men still ask for more trains in the early morning. The existing service will be much facilitated in the near future by the new District extension to East Ham. When that is complete, it will be possible to book right through from Victoria to Southend, which means that the West End of London will for the first time be opened up, and it may be that, as explorers from Bethnal Green, Stepney, and Bow discovered and established Southend years ago, West Enders will rediscover it, and bring the desire of the Corporation, the railway companies, and residents to fulfilment. The Corporation of Southend, as at present constituted, seems to be one of the most ambitious in England. The Highways and Works Committee of the Town Council are recommending to the Corporation the expenditure of £340,000 for the purpose of improving the Marine Parade. It is proposed to reclaim eighty acres of the foreshore for the formation of a marine drive, gardens, and a huge marine lake. The present width of the Marine Parade (27ft.) is to be made 140ft. The proposal now under consideration, if carried out, will doubtless have an important effect on the future of the town. There is also a scheme on foot whereby permanent quarters may be secured at one of the largest hotels in the town for £100 per annum, including railway ticket. This figure comprises full catering for week-ends, and, naturally, breakfast and dinner every day, and this in a town which boasts two yachting clubs, golf links, fishing, amusements to meet all tastes, and a Corporation which has taken its place among the most go-ahead bodies in the kingdom. In talking with Mr. Chapman, the experienced American engineer and general manager of Mr. Yerkes' group, I gathered that he appears very hopeful of Southend and its railway possibilities, and the company that opens the first electric railway there will undoubtedly secure the traffic.

XXXIII.—ELECTRICITY AND OIL CONSIDERED

The South-Eastern and Chatham Railway is also feeling the necessity of doing something to counteract the effect of tubes and tramways, as will be seen from the report of Mr. H. C. O. Bonser, the chairman. In his report, he referred to the growth of the first and second-class passenger traffic, although he pointed out that there had been a decrease in the number of third-class passengers carried. The suburban traffic had been affected by the tubes and tramways. There was, however, a continuous growth outside, but the most satisfactory increase was in the season tickets, of which, he thought, they issued a larger number than any other line in England. The Board had had before them other forms of motive power—electricity and oil. The directors watched with the greatest interest the improvements which were being made in the development of electricity for drawing trains, and as soon as they could see that it was applicable to any portion of the railway, the directors would ask the shareholders to adopt it. As to oil, this matter had been brought before them very frequently during the past six months, but at present it did not compare favourably with coal, but should the price fall sufficiently the directors would welcome it.

"Access to London," rather than "Tube and Tramway" competition seems to be the key-note of the Chatham portion of the amalgamation. The delay between London Bridge and Cannon Street must be overcome. The three southern systems can do much to improve their time and access to London. The South-Western built the Waterloo and City Tube for this purpose, and that little railway will soon be a very good paying investment. Mr. J. S. Forbes, once chairman of the London, Chatham, and Dover, thus criticises these three railways: He (Mr. Forbes) used to spend a good deal of his time at Folkestone, and that service had no stronger critic than he himself was at the time. He held that opinion until he went to live near Petworth, on the Brighton system. Dover was bad, Folkestone was much worse, but Petworth was worse still. The South-Western Railway was perfection as compared with these railways, but at the same time he had been late when travelling on the South-Western Railway. The fact was that the access to London was the dominating factor, and access in their case was even more difficult than it was on the Brighton or the South-Western lines. They must, of course, do all they could to remove these impediments to the public service, and no one could be more anxious to improve the undertaking than Mr. Hill had shown himself to be. He had been much gratified in hearing the congratulations which had been bestowed on that gentleman from time to time in connection with the great reforms he had so rapidly introduced on the South-Eastern and Chatham Railway.

XXXIV.—THE SOUTH COAST AND ELECTRIC TRACTION

Since the advent of Mr. William Forbes as general manager, a spirit of enterprise has been awakened in the London, Brighton, and South Coast, and it is reasonable to expect, before long, the inauguration of electric traction on certain parts of this system. On this point I may quote a paragraph from Lord Cottesloe's last half-yearly report :—

The high figure at which Parliamentary expenses stood, represented the necessary cost of opposing the hostile schemes referred to in the report, about one-half of the charge being the expense connected with the proposed electric railway to Brighton. There were other schemes, mainly tramways and the "tube" railways in the suburban area, which the Board thought it right to oppose, and although the company's interest had been safeguarded, and undue invasion of their territory prevented, the activity of promoters would, in all probability, compel the company to act on the defensive for some time to come. The possibility of checking such schemes by improvements and extensions of the company's system, and particularly the advisability of establishing electric traction on some of their lines, were seriously engaging the attention of the Board, and the proprietors might be assured that no stone would be left unturned in seeking means for preserving to the company the traffic to and from those districts which their railways now served.

The first part of this paragraph is quoted as a fair example of the sort of opposition which all new schemes for London locomotion must meet. Of course we cannot blame a company for defending its territory against invasion, but my contention is, there has been far too much of this in the London field. The spirit of harmony would have accomplished far better results, cost less money, and served the public better. The second part of Lord Cottesloe's remarks may be cordially endorsed. That the possibility "of checking such schemes by improvements and extensions," and especially by "establishing electric traction," has really become part of the policy of an English railway system, is a matter over which we may well rejoice. Surely light is streaming through the grime-covered windows of London Bridge Station! Improvements, extensions, and electric traction! That is the surest way to check the invasion of your district by outsiders and of increasing your receipts. Let the good work go on.

XXXV.—SOUTH-WESTERN v. TRAMWAYS

The recent evidence of Mr. C. J. Owens, general manager of the London and South-Western Railway, before the Commons Select Committee, I read in a daily journal, shows why English railways are now so bitterly opposing every extra-urban traction scheme. Mr. Owens said that since the opening of the West London electric tramways the gross receipts of his line between Kew Bridge, Brentford, Isleworth, and Hounslow had fallen from £1,516 to £524 in the half year. Mr. Owens estimated that the opening of an electric tram-

way from Wimbledon to Malden would mean a loss of £6,000 a year to his company. Mr. Pember, K.C., said that the railway had lost £10,000 a year by the opening of electric tramways in London and the suburbs. In this the South-Western Railway is sharing a common experience. Reports from the Midland show that, wherever it is possible for people to go from point to point for a few miles by electric cars, they prefer them to railways. We have heard all this before, and shall continue to hear it. Now let us see what Mr. Owens proposes to do in order to keep his suburban traffic from further inroads on the part of Mr. Clifton Robinson and his London United Electric Tramways, which more than any other system has invaded Mr. Owens' territory. I notice that in the last half-yearly report of this railway, reference was made to the proposals of the Metropolitan and District Railway Companies for equipping those portions of this company's system over which they had running powers for working by electricity, on the same system as that on which they proposed to work their own lines. The directors were arranging an agreement by which this equipment should be carried out by this company themselves, but on such terms as would secure an adequate return on the capital they might expend, and also give them the right to use the equipment for electrical working should they at any time decide to do so. The Board would watch the working of these branches very closely, in order that in the proper time they might see how far it would be possible for the company to adopt electrical working for their own suburban traffic. They offered a strenuous opposition to the proposals of the London United Tramways Companies for extending their lines in this company's system; but it was difficult in these days to get Parliament to decline to pass any proposals which were held to give increased facilities to the public, whether these proposals were detrimental to other vested interests created under the authority of Parliament or not. This looks like a move in the right direction, and the refrain of the London, Brighton, and South Coast Railway "improvement scheme and electric traction" to check the encroachment of tubes and tramways, is respectfully recommended to the directors of this up-to-date and well-managed railway. Keep and increase your own traffic, and do not waste time blocking other enterprises, is sound advice. Earl Cawdor, for the Great Western Railway, in the 184th half-yearly report, gave particulars of various important works, almost all for improvement of suburban traffic, which are being carried out on different parts of the company's system, and mentioned that, under the provisions of the Metropolitan Railway Acts of this Session, the Hammersmith and City Railway, owned by the Great Western and Metropolitan Companies, jointly, was to be adapted for working by electrical power, as was also the portion of the Great Western line intervening between the Hammersmith and City Railway and the Metropolitan Railway at Bishop's Road. The cost was to be borne by the two companies in such proportions as might be agreed, or settled by arbitration.

The Great Central Railway is fully alive to the problem of suburban traffic, and when its own line into London is completed, will take up the question in the spirit of its enterprising neighbours above mentioned. For the moment the Great Central Railway is practically dependent upon the Metropolitan Railway, which, owing to its own complications with other systems, has not been over anxious to serve the Great Central, except on through traffic.

XXXVI.—An Interesting Experiment

Sir Ernest Paget, chairman of the Midland Railway, gave some extremely interesting views on the subject of electric traction, and although they do not especially apply to the London district, they are of value in this connection as showing the attitude of this important and enterprising company on the question we are endeavouring to elucidate. The matter came up when he informed the shareholders that their sanction would be sought for the promotion of a light railway between Burton-on-Trent and Ashby-de-la-Zouch. The Light Railways Bill of 1896 provided that its powers were not to be used in the promotion of lines to compete with existing railways, and in these circumstances the Light Railway Commissioners felt bound to throw out the scheme which was being locally promoted, but at the same time expressed their regret that they were obliged to do so, because they thought that in the interests of the public the railway

in question ought to be constructed. The local promoters approached the Midland directors, and the latter, in view of the opinion expressed by the Commissioners, now proposed to build the line themselves. Here we have displayed the modern spirit of enterprise. The reason of the improved condition of American railways may be largely attributed to the quickness with which they have made the same solution of these problems which the Midland Railway Company seems to have done in this case. It will be carried out on such lines, Sir Ernest Paget tells us, as would not interfere with the legitimate Midland traffic, and he believed that it would be of considerable utility to the neighbourhood. It would certainly be an interesting experiment, for it was quite new for the Midland Company to hold a light railway. The line would be worked by electricity, the capital would be £160,000, and the length of the line would be eleven miles four chains. A lady shareholder who had expressed herself as too modest to address the chair, had written to him asking him whether it was the intention of the directors to electrify—she believed that was the word in use—the whole or part of the Midland system. His answer to that question was " No "; at present it was not their intention to do so. At the same time it should be explained that, so far as the Midland was concerned, there was really no part of the line which would lend itself particularly to this mode of traction. He dared say his fair questioner, and other shareholders, had seen that it was the intention of the North - Eastern Company to electrify a portion of their line in a district in which they suffered very great competition from existing tram lines. In a case like that electricity might be used with economy, and altogether for the benefit of the company. Although the Midland directors had no present intention of doing anything in this direction, he believed that engineers generally considered that electricity would in future be the means of traction, but when he could not say. Whenever it did happen it would be gradual. For instance, the Midland Company owned 2,700 locomotive steam engines, and those engines had cost between five and six millions sterling, and they could not possibly contemplate the scrapping of such a large number of locomotives all at once. Three or four hundred engines, as they came into the works for renewal, would have to be renewed as electric motors, and a certain portion of the line would have to be adapted to their use. That process would have to go on until the whole line was electrified, but it must take some time. This half year ninety-five engines had been renewed, and on that basis it would take something like fifteen years to get rid of these locomotives. If ever they came to the conclusion that it was the right thing to do, it could no doubt be accomplished quicker than that. There was, by the way, one portion of the line— or, rather, a portion of the line in which they were interested, namely, the Cheshire lines—on which he thought they might use electricity with good result, and that was the portion from Manchester to Liverpool. The Cheshire lines belonged to three companies—the Great Northern, the Midland, and the Great Central, and it would be a useful object lesson to those companies to electrify the portion they had mentioned, and watch the result, before dealing similarly with their own systems. An excellent idea, and one, let us hope, that will be carried into effect.

XXXVII.—INCREASE OF LOCAL TAXATION

Lord Staleybridge, in the last London and North - Western report, gave more attention to arrangements between his competitors, the Midland and Great Northern, on northern traffic than on London suburban. He did, however, touch upon a subject of general interest to railways, though not to be discussed in this series of articles, namely, the hardship of Municipal trading. Here is the substance of his remarks :—

The item of rates and taxes was a very important one, and it showed an advance of £23,262, of which at least £18,000 was attributable to the increased rate in the pound, over which their officers had no control whatever. All the assessments were most carefully looked at, and everything possible was done to keep down the amount, which represented more than 1 per cent. on their dividend. As the proprietors were aware, the company paid rates to maintain the roads over which their rivals, the tramway companies, ran without any cost whatever. They also helped to keep up the Manchester Ship Canal—a deadly rival of theirs— and in other ways they had to pay rates in connection with matters in which they had very little interest.

Nor is this the only complaint we hear on this danger, which I venture to assert will soon grow to far greater proportions than at present. The chairman of the South-Western, Lieutenant - Colonel Hon. H. W. Campbell, practically declares that he looks for the increase in rates and taxes as calling for more serious comment than any other. The additional amount paid by the company in the past half-year was no less than £12,529, and but for this the directors could easily have recommended an additional $\frac{1}{4}$ per cent. dividend on the ordinary stock. From a statement made to him, he found that in twenty-eight parishes on their system the company paid from 50 per cent. to 80 per cent. of the total rates, and in twenty-three parishes they paid from 40 per cent. to 50 per cent., while they had no voice whatever in the control of the expenditure in these or other parishes. He might state that the amount paid in rates and taxes by thirty - nine railway companies in Great Britain rose from £2,142,956 in 1891, to £3,729,528 in 1901, an advance of 73.45 per cent. During those ten years the capital of the same companies only increased 20.72 per cent., and their gross receipts by 26.37 per cent. In the decade 1889 to 1899, the whole rates paid in England and Wales rose by 39 per cent. Much of this increased taxation goes to establish rival enterprises.

Lord Allerton, of the Great Northern, also took the ground in his last report that the question of rates and taxes was one of growing urgency, and came home to all of them. Of the increased sum which they were called upon to pay, more than two-thirds was due, not to increased assessment, but increased poundage, i.e., the rates had gone up in the pound. Some remarkable instances had been supplied to him. In the adjacent parish of Islington the rates had increased in the last three years by 1s. in the pound, and they now stood at 6s. 8d. In seventy of the largest parishes on the line the rates had increased in the last year by an average of 9d. in the pound. In the urban districts of Edmonton and Barnet, the rates had increased by 1s. 4d. and 1s. 5d. in the pound respectively, and now stood at 8s. in the pound in one case, and 7s. 8d. in the other. In East Retford the rates had increased by 1s. 10d., and in Spalding from 5s. 7d. to 7s. 5d. These were alarming figures, and suggested the question whether our local governors were not going a little too fast. Public luxuries were very well, but the bill would have to be paid, and he could not help thinking there would be such a public outcry if this went on that there must be a check put on it. Here we have a just reason on the part of railways for not going ahead with expansion improvements.

XXXVIII.—Enterprise of the Great Northern

In the previous article mention was made of the Great Northern and City Railway, and elsewhere I speak of the Great Northern and Strand. Both of these important enterprises emanate from Lord Allerton's well-managed railway, the Great Northern, and that gentleman, in his last half-yearly report, referred to these enterprises in the following manner :—

As regards the Great Northern and City Railway, the work was in the hands of well-known and responsible contractors, and was proceeding vigorously. With reference to the Great Northern and Strand Railway, the contract for the work had been let, and this company was doing everything possible to give them possession of the necessary land, and he was sure the work would progress as fast as it was possible to do. When those two lines were finished they would have an outlet for suburban passengers which would be second to none in London.

Of the wisdom of this action on the part of the Great Northern we shall soon have an opportunity to judge. I strongly suspect these tubular railways will not only serve the purpose of an access into London for Great Northern passengers, but will both become paying investments.

In this connection, it is interesting to note that the first movement in favour of adopting electric traction on the part of a steam railway company comes from the North, where the tramways seem to be reducing suburban passenger receipts. It has been officially announced by the North-Eastern Railway that, the revenue from passenger traffic in the neighbourhood of Newcastle having suffered from the competition of tramways, the directors have carefully considered what action should be taken to meet this competition. They consider that the best method of meeting it is to increase the train service on the lines

affected by the competition, and as they are advised that this can best be done by using electric traction, they have decided to seek tenders for the electrical equipment of the lines extending from Newcastle Central to New Bridge Street, *via* Tynemouth, including the Riverside Branch. As the tenders are asked for in October, we may hope within a reasonable time to have this experiment fully tested.

The views of railway managers have been thus touched on at length, because only by so doing can we ascertain the many obstacles which these gentlemen have to face in attempting to bring about the changes which many of them now see to be inevitable, in order to retain their suburban traffic. It is not likely these great interests centring in London will follow the recent example of a Scotch railway company, and simply abandon the field. It is much more likely that the good results of electric traction will soon become so apparent in the locality under discussion that those now hesitating will follow suit, and, by improving their methods, hold their own fields against invaders, and secure additional profits by the continued increase in the population of the metropolis and the important surrounding districts.

XXXIX.—The London Omnibus

In the changes of London locomotion, it is surprising to find how well that typical London vehicle, the omnibus, holds its own. The great railway systems may increase their carrying capacity, tramways may multiply north and west, electrical tubular railways may carry their millions annually underneath the routes followed by the London 'bus, but that conveyance jogs along apparently undisturbed by what is taking place in all directions. The best available estimate gives a traffic of five hundred million passengers annually for the various lines of London omnibuses, on a basis of 1,500,000,000 passengers for the entire metropolitan districts. The omnibus comes in, at least numerically, for its full one-third, though, of course, the short-distance travellers avail themselves more particularly of this method of locomotion. It is impossible to foretell the effect of the proposed penny fares of the London Suburban Railway, nor of the still lower proposed fares of the London County Council tramways, for it will be some time before these become operative on an extensive scale. Meantime, the omnibus continues on the even tenour of its ways, in undisturbed possession of a fair share of the passenger traffic of the metropolis and surrounding districts. Nor is the average paid on the omnibus per journey the lowest. The North London Railway has that distinction, .98d. Next the tramway system, 1.08d., and then the omnibus, 1.33d. Indeed, if we take the two leading companies we find that within the area of the county of London the number of passengers carried shows a fairly good increase for the last six years.

PASSENGERS CARRIED

Year.			London General.	London Road Car.
1894—5	...	...	...	135,131,902	44,610,220
1895—6	...	...	...	144,077,267	46,999,743
1896—7	...	...	...	158,541,458	54,087,013
1897—8	...	...	...	173,436,410	57,768,638
1898—9	...	...	...	184,984,711	57,179,774
1899—1900	...	...	...	195,692,926	65,326,150
1900—1	...	...	...	202,024,222	67,919,537

This continued growth in omnibus traffic undoubtedly indicates that the new facilities for transportation have not, up to the present, kept up with the annual increment of London passenger traffic. The discomforts of the underground lines are greater to many people than those on the top of a bus on a rainy day, while in fine weather, the outside of an omnibus has many compensations. Ultimately, this means of conveyance will give way to some sort of traction, whether tramway or road motor. The latter, I think, are remote, as the tramway, aided by the tubular railway and electrified steam lines, will meet the present requirements even of London traffic. When the outer terminus of each " tube " is the starting point of an electrical tramway—as in the case of the United Tramways or the North Metropolitan Tramways—or an electrified suburban railway, reaching far out into the country, you have a combination that will be difficult to improve on for some time to come. But the general deductions, resulting from a study of these several systems of locomotion, must be reserved for the next, and concluding, article of this series.

(To be continued.)

ELECTRIC MOTORS: THEIR THEORY AND CONSTRUCTION*

By H. M. Hobart

FIFTH ARTICLE

The Union Elektricitäts Gesellschaft of Berlin has kindly furnished the writer with

volts at 950 revolutions per minute. In Figs. 96 to 107 are given drawings of this

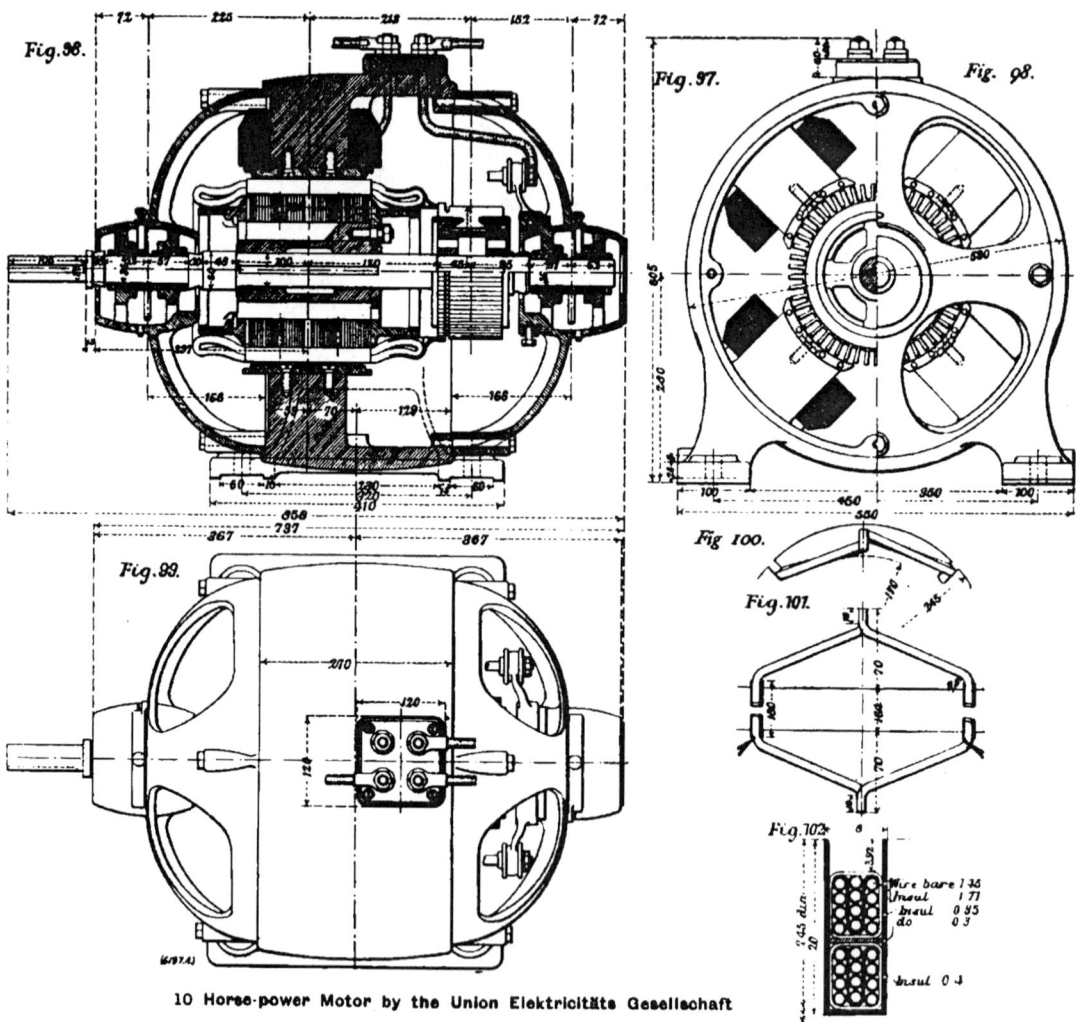

10 Horse-power Motor by the Union Elektricitäts Gesellschaft

full particulars of its latest 10 horse-power, semi-enclosed shunt-wound motor for 500

* See TRACTION AND TRANSMISSION, Vol. IV, pages 76, 135, 206; Vol. V, 104.

motor, and Fig. 108, Plate XXXIV, is a view of the next larger size of the same line of motors. All these small motors have the same number of slots, and the same

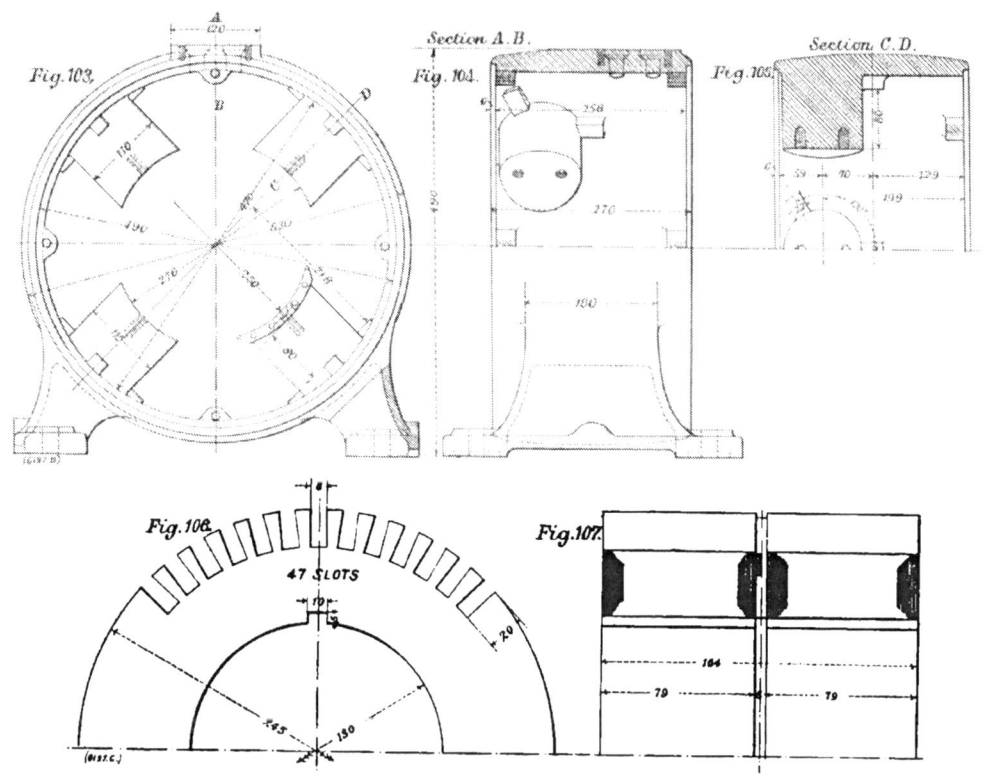

10 Horse-power Motor by the Union Elektricitäts Gesellschaft

commutator segments for all voltages, this corresponding to the minimum number considered to be required to give satisfactory results for the 500-volt motor, the length of the segment being determined by the permissible heating for the lowest rated voltage.

TABLE XIII.—DESCRIPTION OF THE UNION ELEK-TRICITÄTS GESELLSCHAFT'S SEMI-ENCLOSED MOTOR

Number of poles	...	...	...	...	4
Rated output	...	...	...	...	10 B.H.P.*
Rated voltage	...	...	...	...	500 volts
Rated speed	...	...	...	...	950 revs. per min.
Amperes input at full load	...	...	...	17.0 amperes
Amperes input at no load	...	...	...	1.5 „
Watts input at no load	...	...	...	740 watts

Armature :—

External diameter	...	...	...	...	245 millimetres
Axial length of winding	...	...	...	304 „
Internal diameter of laminations	...	...	130 „
Effective length of laminations between flanges	...	...	...	...	142 „

* The continental horse-power = 736 watts (75 kilogrammetres per second).

Armature (continued) :—

Length occupied by ventilating duct	...	6 millimetres
Axial length occupied by thickness of insulating varnish on laminations	...	16 „
Gross axial length of core between flanges	164 „
Thickness of each lamination	...	...	0.5 „
Number of slots	...	...	...	47
Depth of slot	...	...	...	...	20 millimetres
Width of slot, as punched	...	...	...	8.3 „
Width of slot, as assembled	...	...	8.0 „
Width of tooth at root, as stamped	...	5.4 „
Average width of tooth, as stamped	...	6.7 „
Width of tooth at armature face, as stamped	8.1 „

Magnet Core :—

Effective length of pole face parallel to shaft	...	155 millimetres
Effective length of pole arc	...	...	147 „
Thickness of pole shoe at centre of pole arc	...	13 „
Radial length of the magnet core	...	80 „
Diameter of cross section of magnet core	115 „
Radial depth of air-gap	...	...	3 „
Ratio of effective pole arc to pitch	...	0.75

Magnet Yoke :—

External diameter of yoke	...	...	530 millimetres
Internal diameter	...	...	...	470 „
Thickness	...	...	...	...	30 „
Axial width	...	...	...	...	270 „
Radial thickness of pole seat	...	...	17 „

TABLE XIII (continued)—

Commutator :—

Diameter	175	millimetres
Number of segments...	141	
Thickness of a segment at periphery	3.2	millimetres
Thickness of the insulation between segments	0.7	„
Effective length of segment	70	„

Armature Winding :—

Conductors per slot	24
Type of winding	2-circuit single
Size of wire	1.45 mm. diam.
Size of insulated conductor	1.71 „
Current per conductor	8.5 amperes
Current density in armature conductor ...	510 amperes per sq. centimetre
Armature slot " space factor "	0.25
Number of turns in series between brushes	282
Mean length per turn	77 centimetres
Resistance of winding from + to – at 60degs. Cent.	1.30 ohms
C R drop in armature winding at full load	22.0 volts
C R drop at brush contact surfaces ...	1.4 „
Total induced voltage at full load ...	476.6 „

Calculation of Reactance Voltage :—

Peripheral speed of commutator	8.7 m. per sec.
Length of arc of brush contact	14 millimetres
Frequency of commutation $=\frac{1000 \times 8.7}{2 \times 14}=$	313 cycles per sec.
Width of segment at periphery (including insulation)	3.9 millimetres
Maximum number of coils short-circuited under a brush	4
Turns per coil (q)	4
Maximum number of simultaneously commutated conductors per group (r) ...	32
" Free length " per turn (s)	49 centimetres
" Embedded length " per turn (t)	28 „
Lines per ampere turn per centimetre of " free length " (u)	0.8
Lines per ampere turn per centimetre of " embedded length " (v)	4.0
Lines per ampere turn for " free length " (u × s)	39.2
Lines per ampere turn for "embedded length " (v × t)	112
Lines per ampere for " free length " $\left(\frac{r}{2} \times u \times s = o\right)$	625
Lines per ampere for "embedded length " (r × v × t = p)	3580
Total lines linked with short-circuited coil per ampere (o + p)	4205
Inductance per segment $\left(\frac{q \times (o+p)}{10^8}=l\right)$ ...	.000168 henrys
Reactance per segment (2 π n*l)	0.33 ohm
Current per conductor at full load... ...	8.5 amperes
Reactance voltage at full load	2.8 volts
Average voltage per segment	14.2 „
Armature ampere turns per pole at full load	1220

Magnetic Circuit Calculations :—

Full load internal voltage (E)	477
Turns in series between brushes (T) ...	282
Periodicity in cycles per second (N) ...	31.8
Flux entering armature per pole at full load (M)	1.33 megalines
(E = 4 T N M × 10⁻⁸)	
Leakage factor (assumed)	1.20
Flux generated per pole full load	1.60 megalines

*n = number of complete cycles per second.

	Cross Section (Square Centimetres).	Kilolines per Square Centimetre.	Magnetic Length (Centimetres).	Magnetomotive Force in Ampere Turns per Centimetre.	Magnetomotive Force in Total Ampere Turns.
Armature core below slots	106	12.6	12	8	100
Flux-carrying teeth ...	71	18.3	2	130	260
Pole face	228	5.8	0.3	4650	1400
Magnet core	104	15.4	10	35	350
Yoke	150	10.7	20	10	200
Total ampere turns per spool					2310

The motor at 17 amperes and two segments backward lead runs at 980 revolutions per minute, and takes 0.45 amperes in field.

Each field spool is wound with 2,400 turns of single cotton-covered wire of 0.60 millimetre diameter (bare), and 3,500 turns of 0.55 millimetre diameter (bare), a total of 5,900 turns per spool, at 60degs. Cent. the shunt current is 0.45 ampere, the resistance being 1,120 ohms for the four spools in series, as determined by resistance measurements.

Ampere turns per spool = 0.45 × 5,900 = 2,660 as against the calculated value of 2,310.

Energy for excitation = .45 × 500 = 225 watts, or 56 watts per spool.

Taking the average depth of the spool winding as 5 centimetres, the external circumference is 6.75 decimetres, and the equivalent external cylindrical radiating surface may be taken as 5.5 square decimetres, thus giving about 10 watts per square decimetre.

The temperature increase, as determined by *resistance* measurements, is 40degs. Cent. at the end of a 4.5 hours' run at full load, or 4degs. Cent. per watt per square decimetre.

TABLE XIV.—CALCULATION OF ARMATURE LOSSES AND THERMAL CHARACTERISTICS

Armature resistance at 60degs. Cent. = 1.30 ohms.
Armature C²R loss = 17² × 1.30 = 380 watts.
The core loss, as measured, was 325 watts, which, by chance, agrees exactly with the core loss as calculated by means of the curve of Fig. 21 on page 137 of TRACTION AND TRANSMISSION, Vol. IV.
Total armature loss = 705 watts.
Cylindrical radiating surface, 23 square decimetres ∴ 31 watts per square decimetre.
Temperature increase at end of four and a half hours' run at full load, as determined from resistance measurements = 41degs. Cent.
Temperature increase per watt per square decimetre = 1.32degs. Cent.

TABLE XV.—CALCULATION OF COMMUTATOR LOSSES AND THERMAL CHARACTERISTICS

Length of brush contact arc	14 millimetres
Width of brush	19 „
Contact surface per brush	2.67 sq. cm.
Number of brushes per pole	1
Total number of positive brushes ...	2
Contact surface of all positive brushes ...	5.34 sq. cm.
Current density at contact surface ...	3.2 amperes per sq. centimetre
I²R loss in watts per ampere*	1.4
Total I²R loss...	24 watts.
Peripheral speed of commutator	8.7 m. per second
Friction loss in watts per ampere* ...	1.7
Total friction loss	29 watts
Total commutator loss	53 „
Cylindrical radiating surface	3.9 sq. decimetres
Watts per square decimetre cylindrical radiating surface	13.6
Observed temperature increase	33 degs. Cent.
Temperature increase per watt per square decimetre...	2.4 „

TABLE XVI.—EFFICIENCY AT 60 degs. CENT.

Core loss	330 watts
Armature copper loss	380 „
Brush contact I²R loss	20 „
Brush friction loss	30 „
Bearing and air friction loss ...	160 „
Shunt winding I²R loss	220 „
Total of constant losses ...	740 „
Total of variable losses ...	400 „
Total of all losses	1140 „
Output at full load	7350 „
Input at full load	8490 „
Commercial efficiency at full load	86.5 per cent.
„ „ 1¼ „ · ...	87.0 „
„ „ ¾ „ ...	85.0 „
„ „ ½ „ ...	81.2 „
„ „ ¼ „ ...	70.0 „

TABLE XVII.—WEIGHTS AND COSTS OF NET EFFECTIVE MATERIALS

	Weight in Kilogrammes.	Assumed Cost in Pence per Kilogramme.	Total Cost in Shillings.
Armature copper ...	6.2	24	12.4
Commutator copper ...	9.5	24	19.0
Field copper	31.0	24	62.0
Armature laminations ..	29	3.6	8.7
Magnetic circuit portion of cast steel frame...	115	4.5	43.0
Pole shoe laminations	10	3.6	3.0
Commutator mica ...	1.8	24	3.6

Total cost of net effective material ...	151.7 shillings
Total cost per horse-power rated output	15.2 „
Weight of motor, complete, without pulley or belt-tightener	310 kilogrammes

Figs. 109 to 115 (see page 159) are a series of curves plotted from test results of this machine.

* See Table XIV.

COMMUTATOR DESIGN

The commutator must be proportioned with regard both to heating and to the avoidance of sparking. It may be assumed that in a well-proportioned motor, current

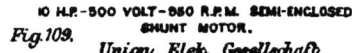

Fig. 109.   10 H.P.-500 VOLT-850 R.P.M. SEMI-ENCLOSED SHUNT MOTOR.
Union Elek. Gesellschaft.

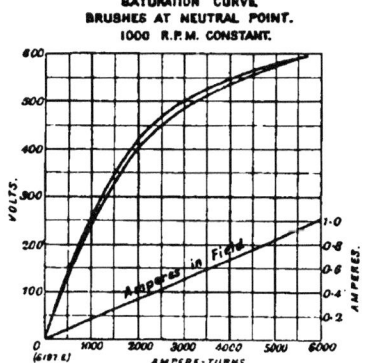

SATURATION CURVE BRUSHES AT NEUTRAL POINT.
1000 R.P.M. CONSTANT.

Fig. 110.   10 H.P.-500 VOLT-850 R.P.M. SEMI-ENCLOSED SHUNT MOTOR.
Union Elek. Gesellschaft.

SPEED CURVES.
0-45 AMPERES IN THE FIELD.

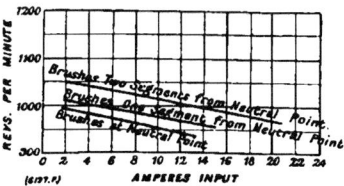

Fig. 111.   10 H.P.-500 VOLT-850 R.P.M. SEMI-ENCLOSED SHUNT MOTOR.
Union Elek. Gesellschaft.

FIELD CHARACTERISTIC AS GENERATOR.
1140 R.P.M. - 550 VOLTS CONSTANT.
BRUSH LEAD - ONE SEGMENT.

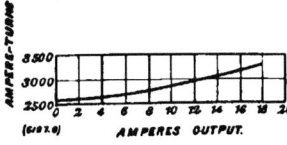

in the short-circuited coils, and sparking, are so minimised that the heating may be considered as due entirely to the ohmic resistance of the brush contacts, and to the brush friction. Very complete investigations have been carried out by Arnold and others * to determine the value of the brush contact resistance, and its dependence upon the peripheral speed, the current density at the brush surface, the brush pressure, and the material of the brush. While the brush contact resistance has been shown by these

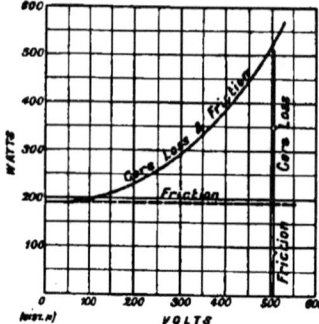

Fig. 112.

10 H.P.-500 VOLT-950 R.P.M. SEMI-ENCLOSED
SHUNT MOTOR.
CORE LOSS & FRICTION.
Union Elek. Gesellschaft.
1000 R.P.M.

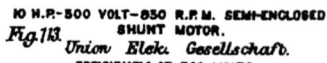

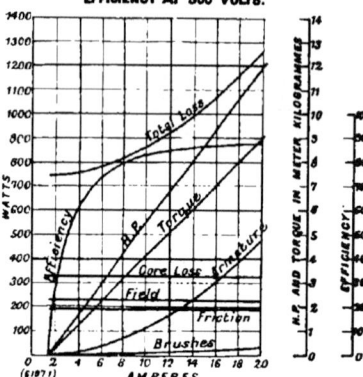

Fig. 113.

10 H.P.-500 VOLT-950 R.P.M. SEMI-ENCLOSED
SHUNT MOTOR.
Union Elek. Gesellschaft.
EFFICIENCY AT 500 VOLTS.

the surfaces of contact. Copper brushes, now rarely employed, have an extremely low contact resistance (less than one-tenth that of carbon brushes), and were their use practicable, the length of the commutator could be very greatly reduced, because of the greatly decreased losses due to brush contact resistance and to brush friction. The employment of copper brushes for motors was almost entirely abandoned in favour of carbon brushes many years ago, because it was found that carbon brushes permitted of

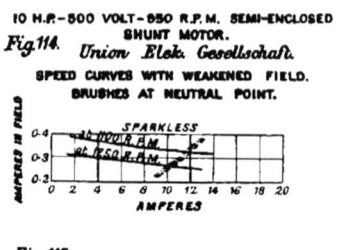

Fig. 114.

10 H.P.-500 VOLT-950 R.P.M. SEMI-ENCLOSED
SHUNT MOTOR.
Union Elek. Gesellschaft.
SPEED CURVES WITH WEAKENED FIELD.
BRUSHES AT NEUTRAL POINT.

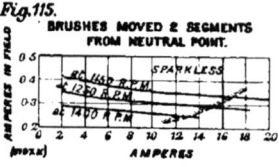

Fig. 115.

BRUSHES MOVED 2 SEGMENTS
FROM NEUTRAL POINT.

sparkless running in motors which would have sparked undesirably with copper brushes. It is probable that with the general improvement in design as regards commutation, it would now be much more practicable to employ copper brushes in many cases, but no such brush has yet been produced which compares at all favourably with the carbon brush as regards the small amount of attention required, and the great durability. The carbon brush is also superior with respect to operation where the direction of rotation is frequently reversed. While the specific resistance of a carbon brush is some four thousand times that of copper, the *contact* resistance is only ten to fifteen times greater. Different grades of carbon and graphite brushes vary widely in specific resistance (resistance between opposite faces of a cubic centimetre of the material), but the contact resistance is much less, and may, for practical calculations, be taken at 0.2 ohm per square

investigations to vary considerably with variations in each of these factors, by far the greatest influence is exerted by the quality of the brushes, and the current density at

* *Die Gleichstrommaschine*, Vol. I, 1902, by E. Arnold, page 476, gives a useful summary of much experimental work on this subject. Also Parshall and Hobart's " Electric Generators," pages 271 to 280.

centimetre of bearing surface,* at a current density of 4 amperes per square centimetre, and decreasing at values for higher current densities rather more slowly than in proportion to the increase in current density. Graphite and carbon brushes should, in the interests of good commutation, preferably not be run at higher current densities than from 4 to 7 amperes per square centimetre, although it is claimed for some qualities that densities much higher than these values may be employed. Better satisfaction will be obtained with the lower values, although at the expense of increased loss due to mechanical friction.

Measurements of the specific resistance *of the material* of the brush are misleading. The chief consideration is that the brush *contact* resistance shall be low, and that the material and method of manufacture of the brush shall be such as to ensure smooth, quiet running, and to maintain a hard, clean, glazed commutator surface.

Table XVIII shows at a glance that the general order of magnitude of these two components of the total loss is the same, hence it is not very necessary in the interests of a minimum total loss † to make any departure from the values found from other considerations to be the most desirable. These other considerations relate to commutation.

As we have already seen, commutation will, in general, be better the greater the number of segments per pole, and the less the average voltage and the reactance voltage per segment. From this point of view the com-

---

* Arnold, on page 481 of *Die Gleichstrommaschine* (1902), gives the following table of values for different qualities of carbon brush, which are based on the assumption that the brush contact resistance is inversely proportional to the current density :—

Le Carbone (quality X), softest quality ...	0.45 to 0.6 volt
Ordinary soft quality... ...	0.7 to 1.0 „
Harder quality	1.0 to 1.2 „
Very hard quality	1.2 to 1.5 „

At a current density of 4 amperes per square centimetre, this would give the following contact resistances, expressed in ohms per square centimetre of bearing surface :—

Softest quality, about ...	0.13 ohm per sq. centimetre	
Ordinary soft quality, about...	0.21	„ „
Harder quality, about ...	0.28	„ „
Very hard quality, about ...	0.34	„ „

† The total loss is a minimum at that load at which the two component losses are equal.

TABLE XVIII.—ESTIMATION OF COMMUTATOR LOSSES WITH CARBON BRUSHES

Current Density in Amperes per Square Centimetre.	Sum of Volts Drop at Positive and Negative Brushes, or Loss in I²R at Brush Contact Surface Expressed in Watts per Ampere.			Friction Loss at Positive and Negative Brushes, Expressed in Watts per Ampere at following Peripheral Speeds in Metres per Second (Brush Pressure = 0.1 Kilogrammes per Square Centimetre, and Friction Coefficient = 0.3).									
	A	B	C	METRES PER SECOND.									
				8	10	12	14	16	18	20	22	24	26
3	1.6	1.4	1.2	1.6	2.0	2.3	2.7	3.1	3.5	3.9	4.3	4.7	5.1
4	1.6	1.6	1.6	1.2	1.5	1.8	2.1	2.4	2.6	2.9	3.2	3.5	3.8
5	1.6	1.8	2.0	0.94	1.2	1.4	1.6	1.9	2.1	2.4	2.6	2.8	3.1
6	1.6	2.0	2.4	0.78	0.96	1.2	1.4	1.6	1.8	2.0	2.2	2.4	2.6
7	1.6	2.2	2.8	0.67	0.84	1.0	1.2	1.3	1.5	1.7	1.9	2.0	2.2

For A the brush contact resistance is taken as inversely proportional to the current density.

For B the brush contact resistance is taken as decreasing less rapidly than in inverse proportion to the current density.

For C the brush contact resistance is taken as having for all current densities the value of 0.2 ohm per square centimetre.

B would generally be a safe value to use, A giving in practice rather too low, and C too high results for the customary working densities of from 4 to 7 amperes per square centimetre.

A brush pressure of the low value of 0.1 kilogramme per square centimetre can only be obtained with the best types of brush holders and in stationary motors. For tramway motors, the specific pressure must be at least 50 per cent. greater.

---

mutator should be permitted, where desirable, to have rather high peripheral speed, thus being proportioned of large diameter and short. It is, however, well to decrease the friction loss to the extent permissible by the choice of fairly high current densities— say, in small motors, up to 6 or 7 amperes per square centimetre—for the brush friction loss is a constant loss at all loads, and in the interests of high efficiency at light loads it should be made as low as is consistent with good commutation. The commutator should be no longer than is necessary for obtaining the required radiating surface, and to obtain the necessary brush bearing surface the arc of brush contact should be increased rather than the length of the commutator. When, however, with fairly high current density at the brush contact, the arc of brush bearing surface is large, additional care must be taken to so fit the brush to the commutator surface that there shall be good contact at all parts. These are the best lines on which to construct the commutator. If, with the intention of obtaining a reduced total loss by low peripheral speed, by a long commutator of small diameter and relatively few segments, the friction loss is materially reduced, there will in all probability be introduced an additional loss much greater than the saving sought, and this loss will be in sparking, not necessarily so severe as to be destructive to the commutator, or even very noticeable, but representing a dissipation of energy,* which, if determined and allowed for in the efficiency, would condemn the design of the motor. With good mechanical construction of commutator, shaft, and brush gear, much higher commutator peripheral speeds than are at present customary may be used with entire success. Indeed, shortness of commutator is an essential element to rigidity, and the larger the diameter the shorter need it be for a given radiating surface. The slightly increased labour involved in building up a commutator of many segments is, in view of the great gains thereby obtained, altogether negligible, and, with suitable design, the rigidity is in no wise impaired. The surface wears and remains more truly cylindrical, the greater the subdivision. This may be illustrated by Fig. 116,

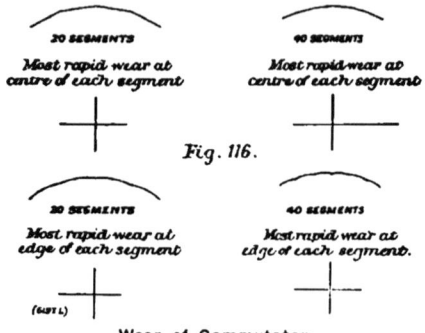

Fig. 116.

Wear of Commutator

which shows portions of the surfaces of two commutators with twenty and forty segments respectively, which are assumed to have a tendency, due to sparking or to the quality of the mica or the copper, to wear, in the one case more rapidly at the centre, in the other case at the edge of the segment.

Care should, of course, be exercised in selecting a soft and uniform quality of mica for the insulation between the segments. The quality of the copper segments should also be uniform, but there is no sufficient reason why its *conductivity* should be specified, as is often done, for it is the *contact* resistance which is of importance, and not the resistance of the copper itself. Copper brushes have given way to carbon brushes with four thousand times as great resistance, which carry the current continually, but the com-

mutator segments, which carry the current intermittently, and but for an exceedingly small fraction of the time, are often specified to be of the highest electrical conductivity. It has, in fact, never yet been demonstrated that copper is the most suitable material of which to construct commutator segments.

The use of Table XVIII for determining the commutator loss, may be illustrated by the case of a 110-volt 30 horse-power motor, whose commutator runs at a peripheral speed of 14 metres per second, and with brushes proportioned for a current density of 5 amperes per square centimetre.

$$\text{Ampere input} = \frac{30 \times 746}{110 \times .89} = 230.$$

Commutator I²R loss in watts per ampere	... 1.8
Commutator friction loss in watts per ampere	... 1.6
Total I²R loss at commutator = 230 × 1.8	= 413 watts
Total friction loss at commutator = 230 × 1.6 = 367 watts	
Total commutator loss =	780 watts

Had the motor been of the same capacity, but for 440 volts, the watts per ampere would still have remained 3.4 (1.8 + 1.6), but the amperes would have been but one quarter as great (57.5 amperes) and the total commutator loss but $\frac{780}{4} = 195$ watts. Hence, while for the customary temperature increase of 40degs. Cent., the 110-volt commutator would have required a total cylindrical radiating surface of $\frac{780}{50} = 15.6$ square decimetres (based on a temperature increase of 0.8deg. Cent. per watt per square decimetre), the 440-volt motor would require but $\frac{15.6}{4} = 3.9$ square decimetres for an equal temperature rise.

Now, with a limited number of segments, it is relatively easier to design a 110-volt motor for few segments without having sparking, than a 440-volt motor. Hence the latter, to find room for a sufficient number of segments, should have a relatively large diameter. But as it requires but small radiating surface, it should be very short. The 110-volt motor, however, in order to have the four times greater radiating surface for its commutator without the latter being too long, should also have a large commutator diameter. Such a 30 horse-power motor works out most satisfactorily with the same diameter of commutator for all voltages, but of lengths more or less proportionate to the greater current, *i.e.*, inversely as the rated voltage.

Motors of 10 horse-power capacity and

---

* See TRACTION AND TRANSMISSION, Vol. IV, No. 16 (July, 1902), pages 139 and 140, and Figs. 23 to 25, where these extra losses are considered.

less will have, even for the lowest voltages, when designed on these lines, such short commutators that it is hardly worth while varying them in length with the voltages. It *is*, however, a great advantage, and in the interests of giving a group of machines a high rating to which those of all voltages will comply equally satisfactorily (*i.e.*, in using a minimum of material most effectively), to vary the number of segments with the voltage, even in these small motors,* and for motors from 15 horse-power or 20 horse-power upwards it is decidedly economical to employ active lengths of segments inversely proportional to the rated voltage, widening the armature core, as in the case of the motors of Fig. 73,† for the higher voltages, and keeping the same overall length for all voltages.

Segments are often made of considerably greater radial depth than was required for mechanical stability, the additional depth being for the purpose of allowing for wear and for occasional turning down of the commutator. Any considerable allowance for wear should not be necessary in a well-designed motor. Radial depths of from 2 to 4 centimetres, according to the capacity of the motors, are nevertheless necessary from considerations of the mechanical design, and, for segments of any considerable axial length, even greater radial depth is sometimes required in order to avoid any outward bending due to centrifugal force.‡

---

* An exception is to be made in the case where manufacturers find it expedient to employ in 500-volt motors such a large number of segments as to ensure thoroughly satisfactory commutation at that voltage, *and to employ this same number*—then, except for 500 volts, unnecessarily high—for the lower voltages. On this basis it is not difficult to arrange, for the lower voltages, windings corresponding to this large number of segments. The only trouble is that, on this plan, the manufacturer will be inclined to adopt rather less than the most satisfactory number of segments for the 500-volt motor. It is highly probable that even in small motors the greatest economy is, in the end, attained by using for each voltage the number of segments and the winding best adapted to that voltage. All attempts in the other direction involve sacrifices in quality in many ways only fully appreciated by the designer.

† For Fig. 73, see TRACTION AND TRANSMISSION for October, page 107, Vol. V.

‡ The centrifugal force at the periphery is conveniently calculated by the following formula :—

    Centrifugal force = 0.00000559 Dn^2 kilogrammes per kilogramme, in which—

        D = diameter in centimetres,
        n = revolutions per minute.

In motors of from 10 to 100 horse-power rated output, present constructions require about 8 kilogrammes of copper per square decimetre of external cylindrical radiating surface, measured from the joint of the connection of the armature winding with the commutator segment, to the outer end of the commutator segment. With really good ventilation through the inside of the commutator spider, and light brush pressure, the temperature increase need not exceed 0.8deg. Cent. per watt per square decimetre, hence 50 watts per square decimetre may be permitted. At 1s. 8d. per kilogramme the cost of commutator copper is $\frac{1.7 \times 3}{50}$ = 0.10 shilling per watt dissipated at the commutator. By means of this value, and of the constants of Table XVIII, using Column B for the I^2R losses, there has been calculated, for Table XIX, the cost of the commutator copper per ampere for various peripheral speeds.

TABLE XIX.—COST OF COPPER COMMUTATOR SEGMENTS (AT 1s. 8d. PER KILOGRAMME) IN SHILLINGS PER AMPERE, AT FOLLOWING PERIPHERAL SPEEDS

Current Density at Brush Contact in Amperes per Square Centimetre	METRES PER SECOND									
	8	10	12	14	16	18	20	22	24	26
3	.30	.34	.37	.41	.45	.49	.52	.57	.60	.64
4	.26	.29	.32	.35	.38	.40	.43	.46	.49	.52
5	.23	.26	.28	.30	.33	.35	.38	.40	.42	.45
6	.21	.23	.26	.28	.30	.32	.34	.36	.38	.40
7	.20	.22	.24	.26	.27	.29	.31	.33	.34	.36

This table is very instructive, and is useful in preliminary estimates. While the cost of all the other conducting and magnetic material in the motor is a function of the horse-power rated output and speed, the commutator segments fall into an entirely different category. The commutator serves to collect the current, and its cost is practically independent of the voltage. For this reason the cost of the commutator segments constitutes a greater percentage of the total cost of effective material in the motor, the lower the rated voltage. For similar reasons it forms also a greater percentage of the total cost, the higher the speed of the motor in revolutions per minute, since the current to be collected remains unchanged. In fact the commutator tends then to be more expensive, since rather higher peripheral speeds (and, consequently, higher friction losses) must be employed in order to find room for the required number of segments; the mechanical construction must also be more solid, and the larger segments must be of somewhat greater radial depth to resist bending outward under the greater centrifugal force.

The component cost of armature copper, field copper, and of magnetic material, cannot be tabulated in this manner, since, for thoroughly satisfactory designs, these components may be very greatly varied. Thus, one designer may prefer an outlay of 50

been shown in Fig. 73, page 107, *ante*, and Table IV, page 106, *ante*.

The total of these costs, *i.e.*, field copper, armature copper, and effective material in the magnetic circuit, may, for ordinary semi-enclosed shunt motors, be taken roughly, as shown in the curve of Fig. 117. For the two curves of Fig. 118, for 500-volt and 100-volt motors, the cost of the commutator segments is included. These curves show very clearly that while there would be scarcely any economy in using different lengths of segments for the different voltages

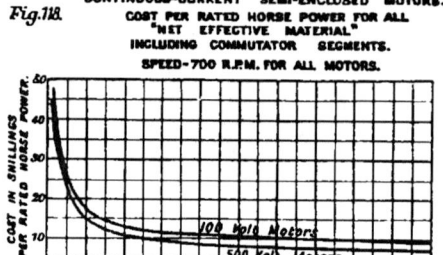

Fig. 117.

CONTINUOUS-CURRENT SEMI-ENCLOSED MOTORS.
COST PER RATED HORSE POWER FOR ALL
"NET EFFECTIVE MATERIAL" EXCEPT COMMUTATOR COPPER.
These costs include Field & Armature Copper:
Net Laminations, Magnet Cores & part of Frame
required for Magnetic Circuit.
SPEED-700 R.P.M. FOR ALL MOTORS.

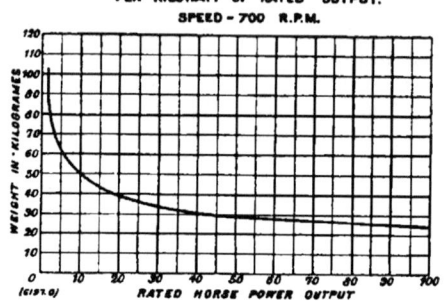

Fig. 119.

CONTINUOUS CURRENT SEMI-ENCLOSED MOTORS.
CURVE OF TOTAL WEIGHT
PER KILOWATT OF RATED OUTPUT.
SPEED - 700 R.P.M.

Fig. 118.

CONTINUOUS-CURRENT SEMI-ENCLOSED MOTORS.
COST PER RATED HORSE POWER FOR ALL
"NET EFFECTIVE MATERIAL"
INCLUDING COMMUTATOR SEGMENTS.
SPEED-700 R.P.M. FOR ALL MOTORS.

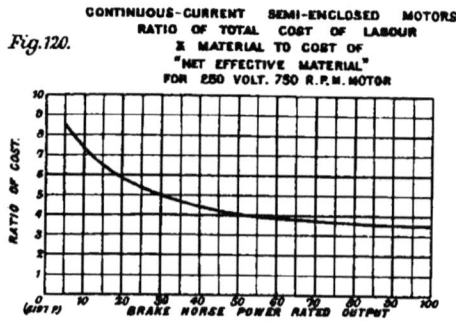

Fig. 120.

CONTINUOUS-CURRENT SEMI-ENCLOSED MOTORS
RATIO OF TOTAL COST OF LABOUR
X MATERIAL TO COST OF
"NET EFFECTIVE MATERIAL"
FOR 250 VOLT. 750 R.P.M. MOTOR

for field and armature copper, and 50 for magnetic material, where another would devote but 25 to copper and 75 to magnetic material. The writer's own preference is based on the consideration that the percentage of cost of field and armature copper to cost of total "effective material," exclusive of commutator copper, should be higher the lower the rated voltage, because the amount of insulation associated with the use of each kilogramme of copper is very much less the lower the rated voltage. These considerations, in their full application, lead to such proportions for different voltages as have

for motors of less than, say, 7½ horse-power, the difference in cost of net effective material is at 30 horse-power already some 15 per cent., and rapidly increases with higher capacities. This margin amply provides for the greater cost for insulation and for the labour of winding the many turns of fine wire in the higher voltage motors, and for motors of more than 15 horse-power capacity the higher voltage motors should cost the least.

All such figures must necessarily be only

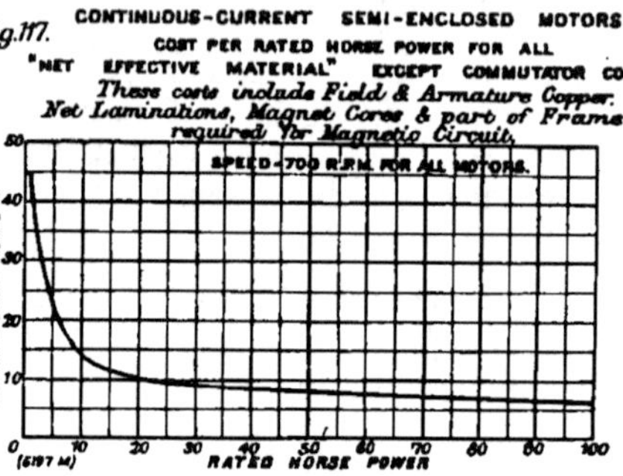

very rough estimates, but the important point to be understood is the influence of the cost of the commutator segments upon the basis of design.

The curve of Fig. 119 gives, for 700 revolutions per minute, semi-enclosed shunt motors, the approximate weight per rated horse-power. The weights vary considerably with different manufacturers, and, of course, the manufacturing costs vary to a still greater extent, but the values given in Fig. 120 give a rough idea of the range of variation in the ratio of the total cost of labour and material to the cost of net effective material for 250 - volt, 700 revolutions per minute, semi-enclosed motors.

The amount by which such motors must be rated down, in order not to exceed permissible temperature limits on continuous running as totally enclosed motors, depends mainly upon the ratio of the "constant" and "variable" losses, as already explained on pages 82 to 86 of TRACTION AND TRANSMISSION, Vol. IV. Motors of different manufacturers at present vary greatly in this respect, although all employ undesirably and needlessly high values for this ratio, and hence such totally enclosed motors are, for a given output, either needlessly expensive, or else they run undesirably hot.

STANDARDISATION OF ELECTRIC MOTORS

The *Verband Deutscher Elektrotechniker* has this year issued a set of standardising rules for electrical machinery. While these may be taken as setting forth the limits within which manufacturers in Germany, and probably also fairly generally in Austria, Switzerland, Belgium, and Sweden, will undertake to guarantee their apparatus, it does not necessarily follow that they will deem it expedient to take full advantage of the rather high temperature limits permitted, the extremely low prescribed insulation tests, and the rather vague requirements in regard to commutation. In fact, the writer's observations have shown him that, while this machinery is rated higher than conforms to the more strict requirements of English and American practice, the ratings are generally considerably more conservative than would be indicated by the rules adopted by the *Verband Deutscher Elektrotechniker*. So far as they relate to continuous current

motors, the standardising rules are in substance as follows :—

Motors are divided into three classes—

A.—For intermittent work, where the periods of work and rest alternate every few minutes, as for cranes, lifts, tramways, etc.

B.—For work lasting for such a short time that the final temperature corresponding to continuous running at full load is never reached, and where the pauses are sufficiently long to permit the temperature to fall to approximately that of the surrounding air.

C.—For continuous running, where the working period is sufficiently long to cause the motors to reach a constant temperature.

For Class A the rating of the motors should be that output which, maintained for one hour, will not cause a greater temperature increase than that specified in the clause relating thereto.

For Class B this same temperature increase must not be exceeded when the motor is operated continuously for the specified time at the rated load.

For Class C the rating must not exceed that. giving the permissible temperature increase when the motor is operated at its rated load until the attainment of constant temperature or until the expiration of ten hours.*

TEMPERATURE INCREASE. — When the temperature of the surrounding air does not exceed 35degs. Cent., the increase in temperature above the air shall not exceed the following amounts :—

For windings on moving parts—

	Degs. Cent.
Where cotton insulation is employed ...	50
Where paper insulation is employed ...	60
Where mica or asbestos insulation is used	80

For windings on stationary parts the temperature increase may be permitted to be 10degs. Cent. higher than the above values. For the iron in which windings are embedded, the same temperature limits as for the windings themselves are permitted.

For commutators the temperature increase must not exceed 60degs. Cent.

For field spool windings the temperature increase is to be determined by resistance

---

* The temperature may still be increasing at the end of ten hours.

measurements on the assumption of an increase of resistance of 0.4 per cent. per degree Centigrade.

For all other parts the temperature increase is to be determined by thermometric measurements.

Where insulations are made up from more than one of the above described materials, the lower limiting temperature shall not be exceeded.

For tramway motors the temperature increase shall not exceed the values specified in the following :—

The windings and iron of both moving and stationary parts :—

	Degs. Cent.
Where cotton insulation is employed ...	70
Where paper insulation is employed ...	80
Where mica or asbestos insulation is used	100
Commutator	80

COMMUTATION.—With the brushes well fitted and set in the most favourable position, the motor must run at all loads with sufficient freedom from sparking not to require treating the commutator with sand-paper or its equivalent more than once per twenty-four hours.

OVERLOADS.—In practical operation motors shall only be required to carry overloads for so short a time, or when at such temperatures that the permissible temperature increase shall not be exceeded. With this limitation they shall be capable of sustaining the following overloads :—

25 per cent. overload for one half-hour.
40 per cent. overload for three minutes.

The commutation at these overloads shall be such as not to require any departure from the conditions specified in the preceding general clause relating to commutation.

Motors required to run at various speeds by field regulation shall not be required to withstand overloads.

INSULATION.—Continuous current motors are to be tested for one half-hour, when warm from windings to frame, with twice normal voltage. When these tests are made with an alternating current, the R.M.S. voltage need be but 1.4 times the normal continuous current voltage of the motor.*

The recommendations of the American Institute of Electrical Engineers are, in most particulars, rather more exacting. So far as they relate to continuous current motors, they are, in substance, to the following effect :—

RISE OF TEMPERATURE.—The temperature of field and armature, as determined by resistance measurements, should, with rated full load, not exceed an increase of 50degs. Cent. above that of the surrounding air; that of commutator, by thermometer, 50degs. Cent.; and that of bearings and other parts of motor, by thermometer, 40degs. Cent.

When a thermometer applied to a coil or winding indicates a higher temperature elevation than that shown by resistance measurement, the thermometer indication should be accepted.

In the case of apparatus intended for intermittent service, the temperature elevation which is attained at the end of the period corresponding to the term of full load shall not exceed 50degs. Cent. by resistance in electric circuits.

INSULATION (Insulation Resistance).—Insulation resistance tests should, if possible, be made at the pressure for which the apparatus is designed. The insulation resistance of the complete machine must be such that the rated voltage of the apparatus will not send more than $\frac{1}{1,000,000}$ of the full load current, at the rated terminal voltage, through the insulation. Where the value found in this way exceeds one megohm, one megohm is sufficient.

DIELECTRIC STRENGTH.—The dielectric strength or resistance to rupture should be determined by a continued application of an alternating electromotive force for one minute, and should be made from

---

* In the *Elektrotechnik Zeitschrift* for October 3, 1902, page 839, Dettmar explains that these rules of the *Verband Deutscher Elektrotechniker* correspond only to the highest permissible rating, and that the quality of electrical machinery manufactured in Germany is not surpassed by that of other countries. He states that " All good German firms give much higher guarantees than those prescribed by the *Verband Deutscher Elektrotechniker*, and the following specification is almost universally complied with :—

" 25 to 30 per cent. overload for three hours without harmful sparking or heating.

" Thermometrically determined temperature increase of not over 35degs. to 40degs. Cent.

" Ability to withstand momentary overloads of 100 per cent. without harmful sparking or heating.

" Constant brush position for all these conditions.

" In many cases still higher guarantees are undertaken, and the machines are, as a rule, considerably better than required by the guarantees."

windings to frame at the following R.M.S. voltages:—

Rated Terminal Voltage.	Rated Output. B.H.P.	Testing Voltage (R.M.S. Volts).
Not exceeding 400 ...	Under 15	1,000
Not exceeding 400 ...	15 and over	1,500
From 400 to 800 ...	Under 15	1,500
From 400 to 800 ...	15 and over	2,000

OVERLOAD CAPACITIES.—Motors should be able to carry a reasonable overload without self-destruction by heating, sparking, mechanical weakness, etc., and with an increase of temperatures not exceeding 15degs. Cent. above those specified for full loads.

The following overload capacities are recommended:—

25 per cent. for one half-hour,
50 per cent. for one minute,

except in railway motors and other apparatus intended for intermittent service.

More severe requirements than those recommended by either of these two associations, are often exacted both in England and America, and serve a good purpose in keeping up the standard.

The writer—in the interests of sound construction—considers the following insulation tests to be desirable for continuous current motors:—

Rated Voltage.				Guaranteed Insulation Test from Copper to Iron at 60degs. Cent. for One Minute.
100	...	...	...	... 2000 R.M.S. volts
200	...	...	...	... 2400 ,, ,,
400	...	...	...	... 3000 ,, ,,
600	...	...	...	... 3600 ,, ,,

As to temperature rise and sparking, these points may, in the writer's opinion, be briefly and yet satisfactorily covered by the following guarantee:—

Twenty-five per cent. overload during one half-hour, without harmful sparking or heating. Thermometrically measured temperature increase not over 50degs. Cent. above surrounding atmosphere during continuous operation at rated load. No harmful sparking or heating with momentary overloads of 50 per cent. Fixed brush position for all these conditions.

As already stated, the basis of rating of railway motors—independently of the recommendations of associations—has become

quite generally that the determined thermometric temperature rise of the hottest accessible part, as tested on a testing stand for one hour at the rated nominal capacity, shall not exceed 75degs. Cent. above the surrounding air.*

It is necessary to keep in mind these methods prevailing in different countries, in order to draw any intelligible conclusions in comparing the weights and costs of different motors.

In Fig. 121 are reproduced curves of weights of continuous current motors as given by others. Curve A is taken from the *Zeitschrift für Elektrotechnik*, Vol. XIX (1901), page 246, from an article by Seefehlner. Curve B is from page 910 of Vol. XVIII (1901), of the *Transactions of the American Institute of Electrical Engineers*, and was

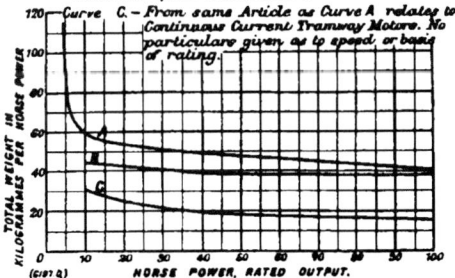

Fig. 121. CURVES OF WEIGHTS OF CONTINUOUS-CURRENT MOTORS.
Curve A.–Zeit. für Elek.–Vol. XIX. (1901) p. 246,– Article by Seefehlner. Represents average of many Continuous Current Shunt motors from 15 manufacturers in several different countries. Speeds not stated.
Curve B.– Transac. Am. Inst. Elec. Eng.– Vol. XVIII (1901) p. 910, Communication by Goldsborough & relates to moderate Speed Shunt Motors.
Curve C.– From same Article as Curve A relates to Continuous Current Tramway Motors. No particulars given as to speed, or basis of rating.

communicated by Goldsborough. In both cases the authors were comparing the weights with those of corresponding induction motors, and consequently were justified in not stating the speeds corresponding to the motors in question. This, nevertheless, detracts from from the usefulness of the curves. Curve C, also from Seefehlner's article, gives similar data for tramway motors.

* On standardising rules, see also *Proceedings of the American Institute of Electrical Engineers*, Vol. XV (1898), pages 3 to 32; Vol. XVI (1899), pages 255 to 268; TRACTION AND TRANSMISSION, Vol. I, No. 1 (1900)—article by Mr. Parshall on "Standardisation of Electrical Apparatus"; *Elektrotechnik Zeitschrift* (1900), page 727—Dettmar on "Standardisation"; *Elektrotechnik Zeitschrift* (1900), page 1,058—Oelschlager on the subject of the rating of intermittently loaded machinery; *Elektrotechnik Zeitschrift* (1901), page 499—Dettmar on "Standard Tests for Electrical Machinery."

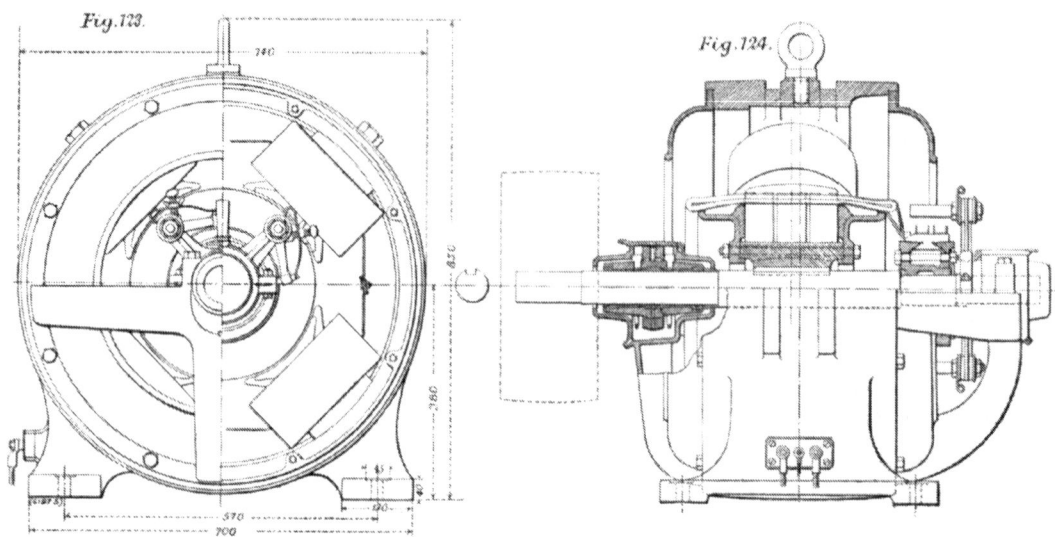

120 Horse-power Shunt Motor, designed by A. V. Clayton, Ludvika, Sweden

In Fig. 122 will be found a curve giving the weights of continuous current 500-volt tramway motors in kilogrammes per rated horse-power, reduced to the uniform basis of 500 revolutions per minute of the armature, which is about the speed generally employed for geared tramway motors at their full load rating. The basis of the rating is that given above.

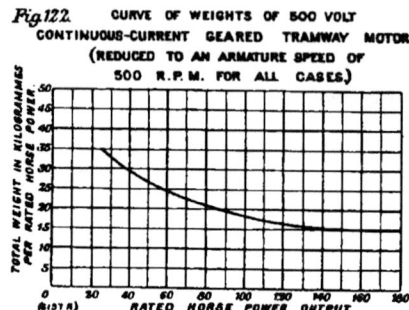

Fig.122. CURVE OF WEIGHTS OF 500 VOLT CONTINUOUS-CURRENT GEARED TRAMWAY MOTORS (REDUCED TO AN ARMATURE SPEED OF 500 R.P.M. FOR ALL CASES.)

The illustrations, Figs. 123 to 129 (see Plate XXXIV), are of a four-pole 20 horse-power shunt motor, for 700 revolutions per minute and 500 volts, built by the Elektriska Aktiebolaget Magnet of Ludvika, Sweden, from the designs of Mr. Aubrey V. Clayton, who has kindly permitted the writer to publish the particulars of the machine.

These have been arranged by Mr. Clayton in the form of the calculation set forth in Table XX.

TABLE XX.—SPECIFICATION AND CALCULATION FOR FOUR-POLE, 20 HORSE-POWER, 700 REVOLUTIONS PER MINUTE, 500 - VOLT DIRECT CURRENT SHUNT-WOUND MOTOR

Core, diameter (outer)	340 millimetres
Core, diameter (inner)	155 ,,
Number of slots	83
Conductors per slot ...	12
Style of winding	2 circuit single
Turns in series	$\frac{6 \times 83}{2} = 249$
Flux (480 internal volts) (M) ...	2.08 megalalines
	$(480 = 4 \times 249 \times \frac{700 \times 2}{60} \times M \times 10 - 8)$
Full load current input	33 amperes
Armature ampere turns per pole	$\frac{248}{2} \times \frac{33}{2} = 2050$
Size of conductor, bare ...	2.2 millimetres diameter
Size of conductor, D.C.C. ...	2.52 ,,
Density in conductor	$\frac{33}{2(2.2^2 \times .7854)} = 430$ amperes per sq. cm.
Size of slot	7.3mm. × 20mm.
Ratio of depth and width ...	.365
Width of tooth at face ...	5.6 millimetres
Width of tooth at root ...	4.0 ,,
Mean width of tooth ...	4.8 ,,
Ratio of tooth width to slot width	.66
Average length of pole arc ...	187 millimetres
Effective length of armature laminations	145 ,,
Average density in teeth ...	$\frac{2.08}{16(4.8 \times 145)} = 18.7$ kilolines per sq. cm.
Length of arm between flanges	145 × 1.10 (insulation) plus 2 air-ducts 6 mm. wide each = 170 millimetres
Density at pole face	$\frac{2.08}{187 \times 170} = 6.5$ kilolines per sq. cm.

TABLE XX *(continued)*—

Density at magnet core (cast steel) ... ... $\dfrac{2.08 \times 1.12}{147^2 \times .7854} = 13.8$ kilolines per sq. cm.

Density at magnet yoke (cast steel) ... ... $\dfrac{2.08 \times 1.12}{2(110 \text{sq.cm})} = 10.6$ kilolines per sq. cm.

Density at armature core ... $\dfrac{2.08}{2(145 \times 72.5)} = 10.0$ kilolines per sq. cm.

Calculation of Field Ampere Turns :—

		Length.	Density in Kilolines per Sq. Cm.	Ampere Turns.
Armature core	... ...	9 cm.	10.0	55
Armature teeth	... ...	2 cm.	17.8 (corrected value)	320
Air-gap in centre	... ...	3.5 mm.}	6.5	2050
Air-gap at pole tip	...	7.0 mm.} Aver. 4 mm.		
Magnet core ...	... ...	15 cm.	13.8	240
Magnet yoke ...	... ...	25 cm.	10.6	200
Sum ...	... ...	...	...	2865
Further allowance	...	...	...	300
Calculated total ampere turns		...	...	3165

Field Spool Calculation :—

Permissible loss for excitation = 1.7 per cent. of output = 250 watts, or $\dfrac{250}{4} = 62.5$ watts per spool.

Therefore amperes $= \dfrac{250}{500} = 0.5$; and turns per spool $\dfrac{3165}{0.5} = 6330$.

Resistance per spool must be $\dfrac{500}{0.5} \div 4 = 250$ ohms when warm, or, allowing for 40degs. Cent. rise, 215 ohms at 20degs. Cent.

On the assumption that 8.5 watts can be radiated per square decimetre of the outer cylindrical surface of the spools, $\dfrac{62.5}{8.5} = 7.4$ square decimetres are required. The magnet core diameter is 147 millimetres, and adding to this 5 millimetres for insulation, and 70 millimetres for winding, gives an outer circumference of

$$\pi (147 + 5 + 70) = 700 \text{ millimetres,}$$

hence the winding space must be $\dfrac{74000}{700} = 105$ millimetres long.

As 1 cubic centimetre Cu has, at 20degs. Cent., a resistance of .00000174 ohm, area of copper in winding will be

$$\dfrac{.00000174 \times 6330 \times \pi(147+5+35)}{215} = 0.03 \text{ sq. millimetre.}$$

Wire 0.65 millimetre diameter, with an area of 0.033 square millimetre, may be taken. This has a diameter of 0.77 millimetre single cotton covered, and can be wound in forty-six layers of 142 turns each, the space required being 115×38 millimetres. The measured resistance of spool is 208 ohms at 20degs. Cent.

Commutator and Commutation Calculation :—

Diameter ... ... 200 millimetres
Number of segments ... 165°

Average volts per segment $500 \div \dfrac{165}{4} = 12.2$

Breadth of segment at face $\dfrac{\pi \times 200}{165} - 0.7$ (insulation) $= 3.1$ mm.

Breadth of brush face on arc 11 mm. (brush is 10 mm. thick)

To explain the basis of the calculation of the frequency it is necessary to mention that the brushes short circuit three coils. Therefore the time required for complete reversal of the current is that taken by any segment to move across the brush face until it leaves the opposite brush corner; or the time required for a given point on the commutator to travel the distance of the brush arc, plus the thickness of one commutator segment. Hence, frequency in cycles per second is,

$$\dfrac{\frac{1}{2}}{\dfrac{11+3.1}{200\,\pi \times \dfrac{700}{60}}} = \dfrac{200\,\pi \times 700}{2 \times 14.1 \times 60} = 258$$

Coils short circuited per brush	...	3
Turns per coil	... ...	3
Conductors in each group simultaneously undergoing commutation		18
Flux set up per ampere turn, per centimetre of gross length	...	9 c.g.s. lines
Gross length	... ...	17 centimetres
Flux set up per ampere turn	...	153 lines
Flux per ampere	... ...	$18 \times 153 = 2750$ lines
Linkage per ampere	... ...	$3 \times 2750 = 8250$ lines
Inductance	... ...	.0000825 henrys
Reactance	...	$0000825 \times 2\,\pi \times 258 = .134$ ohm

But this is the reactance of the short-circuited coils when four sets of brushes are employed. With this motor but two sets of brushes were used, and the reactance was hence that of two coils in series, or .268 ohm.

Amperes per conductor ...	...	16.5
REACTANCE VOLTAGE ...	...	$16.5 \times .268 = 4.4$ volts
Brushes per spindle	...	2 of 25mm. × 10mm.
Average density at brush face ...	...	6 amps. per sq. cm.
Resistance at positive and negative brushes	...	.074 ohm
I²R loss at positive and negative brushes		$33^2 \times .074 = 80$ watts
Peripheral speed of commutator	...	7.3 metres per sec.
Watts lost in friction	... ...	22
Assumed stray watts	... ...	10
Total loss in commutator...	...	112 watts
Effective length, commutator	...	75 millimetres
Watts per square decimetre of commutator surface	...	23

The machine with three segments backward lead of brushes stands 25 per cent.

---

* In one of the slots there is only one coil connected, the ends of the other being insulated, and the coil used only as a dummy or filler.

Plate XXXIV

Fig. 126.

Section G.H.

Section E.F.

Section C.D.

Fig. 125.

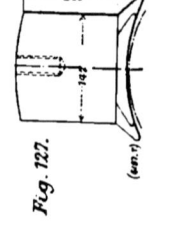
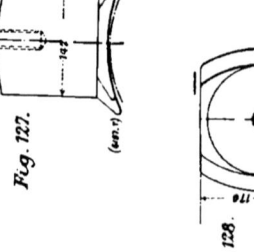
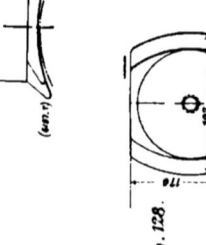

Fig. 127.

Section K.L.

Fig. 128.

Figs. 125 to 129.—20 Horse-power Shunt Motor,
designed by A. V. Clayton, Ludvika, Sweden

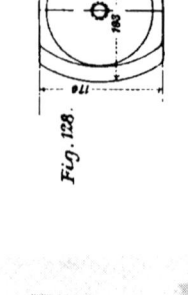

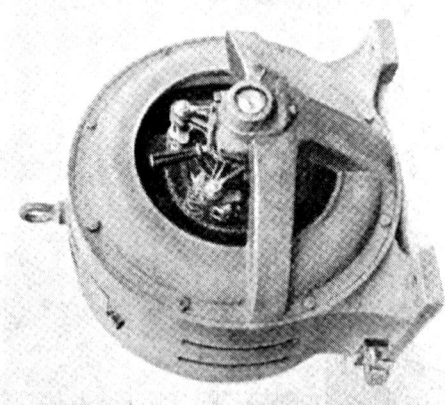

Fig. 129

Fig. 108.—Semi-enclosed Shunt Wound Motor by the Union
Elektricitäts Gesellschaft

Fig. 130.—35 Horse-power Four-pole Motor, designed by A. V. Clayton

overload without sparking, no movement of the brushes being required from no load up to 25 per cent. overload.

After six hours' run as generator, with 80 amperes output, at 740 revolutions per minute, the following final temperatures were observed by thermometer :—

Heating :—

					Ultimate Temperature in Degs. Cent.		Degs. Cent. Rise.
Field spool	...	...	...	...	39	...	23
Magnet yoke	...	...	...	...	32	...	16
Pole face	...	...	...	...	40	...	24
Armature	...	...	...	...	42	...	26
Commutator	...	...	...	...	37.5	...	21.5
Bearing (pulley side)	...	...		...	39	...	23
Bearing (commutator side)	...		...	36	...	20
Room temperature	...	...		...	16	...	—

These low values were in large measure due to the ventilation afforded by the ducts through the magnet yoke, which secured a very thorough circulation of air.

Efficiency :—

	Watts.
Measured no load losses (core loss, brush and bearing friction, and windage)...	700
Armature I²R (resistance measured 0.58 ohm at 20degs. Cent.) 33² × 0.65	710
Field losses	245
Commutator I²R and stray losses (calculated) ...	90
Total losses	1,745
Total output, 20 × 736* = ...	14,720
Total input...	16,465

Commercial efficiency at full load, 89.5 per cent.

The four-pole, 35 horse-power, 950 revolutions per minute, 440-volt shunt motor shown in the engraving, Fig. 180, Plate XXXIV, is developed from the 20 horse-power motor just described, the same yoke, press flanges, bearings, and shaft being used. The bearings and brackets are also the same as for the firm's induction motors. The heating constants are higher, but this is offset by the better ventilation afforded by the higher speed.

---

* The continental horse-power = 736 watts.

In the next article the specification and calculations will be given of a 35 horse-power, 220-volt machine, also designed by Mr. Clayton.

TRACTION AND TRANSMISSION IN SOUTH STAFFORDSHIRE

By R. N. Tweedy and P. J. Pringle

FIRST ARTICLE

It is now more than two years since the question of supplying electrical energy over extensive areas from one or more large power stations, generating current at high pressures, was placed before the general public by sheer force and doggedness in such a way as to create a keen and lasting interest. It will be appropriate to the purpose of this article if we briefly review the causes which led to the crisis in 1900, and the effects which have materialised since.

The causes are very ancient history; a history which, however, should be known intimately by everyone interested in the supply of electricity, and they should be recorded, for the average memory is but short.

As stated by Mr. Madgen in his paper on the "Power Bills of 1900 and After," the reasons for the lamentable backwardness of electric supply in England are the Tramways Act of 1870, and the Lighting Acts of 1882 and 1888, together with the disastrous action of the Municipal authorities.

Till the Light Railways Act of 1896 it was impossible for private enterprise to develop tramways; on the other hand, the Municipalities, who had every facility, were content to let things slide. But the passing of the Light Railways Act was followed immediately by a rush to do what ought to have been done years before; it acted towards capital like the opening of sluice gates on a dam, and since the Municipal authorities have been shown by private pioneers that, with intelligent and specialised management, electric traction is a paying business, they have proved themselves belatedly eager to supply the public with this means of cheap transit.

The Electric Lighting Act of 1888, while not a brilliant example of equity, increased the purchase period from twenty-one to forty-two years, and was followed by increased private activity. Almost since the advent of the incandescent lamp, optimists have proclaimed that, in a few years, electricity would become the poor man's light—in other words, they insisted that the cost of production could be so reduced that the selling price would be appreciably lower than the price of gas. Now, under general existing conditions it is evident that the electric light is still a luxury and a forbidden thing to the vast majority of the inhabitants of this island. In places where there is an electricity supply the reason is either that the price is too high or that the cost of supply would make a really extensive system of mains an economic impossibility. In places where there is no supply at all the reason is either that the local authority is sitting on its lighting order, or that the small district or the widely scattered population would not remunerate a private company for its outlay. It has been clearly demonstrated of late that the cost of supply is reduced whenever the "diversity factor" is improved, and this factor improves as the area of supply is extended.

We have heard occasionally of local authorities trying to agree to live happily together, and share each other's profits; we have also heard of most enlightened schemes for amalgamating districts, but, practically in every instance, the schemes have not fructified, and have indeed been doomed to failure from the start by reason of the incompatibility of temper of the proposed allies. Taking the country with which this article will deal, can anyone who knows the district imagine that Wolverhampton, Dudley, Birmingham, and Walsall—four busy towns forming the corners of a densely populated "hive of industry"—would combine with each other and with the central districts, to erect one huge station, located in the most favourable spot, which would supply all with power and light for much less cost, and at a lower price, than could be done when each has its separate stations, only one of which, and that the third in size, is really modern? A company brave enough to aim at the supply of such an area, and endeavouring to obtain powers by the Provisional Order method under the main Act of 1882, would be sure of an expensive and trying time, and never would be granted powers to compete against any district already possessing a supply station, although the Act expressly states that it is not intended to annihilate competition.

Every local authority has to be treated diplomatically and approached carefully, till it has been brought to the desired frame of mind; and, as the number of authorities to the square mile is rather high in some parts of England, this game wastes much valuable time and money. The actual root of the evil lies not so much with the local authorities as in the delimitation of their boundaries, which becomes more of a hindrance and an anachronism every day. Quoting again from Mr. Madgen, there occurs a most apposite passage in his pamphlet on "Industrial Redistribution," which reads as follows:—

We are confronted with the fact that our system of local government rests upon what may be a very convenient boundary system in relation to the social order and common duties of the inhabitants, but, when viewed in the light of modern political science and industrial progress, is, in many cases, an extremely inconvenient and uneconomic delimitation of districts. These boundaries were fixed at various periods with reference to the jurisdiction of ecclesiastical authorities, School Boards, sewage commissioners, and general local administrators. Sometimes the areas coincide; very often they do not. They have no natural reference whatever to such matters as industrial development; and they were certainly not designed for the purpose of plotting out the most suitable areas for the economic distribution of water, or gas, or electricity, or for the provision of mechanical means of transport. Our forebears, who settled upon those boundaries, had, of course, nothing of the sort in their minds. They decided that a certain area was conveniently compact for the administration of a Poor Law authority, and that to another might conveniently be allotted an administration of its own; and in this way districts have grown up. And, to this day, notwithstanding all the developments of science, so great in the inertia of independent thought, that we still find our Legislature complacently ministering to the view that, because a certain area has a local government system, therefore it is fitted for an electrical supply system.

Instead of ignoring the boundaries so far as they obstruct the progress of industry, Parliament actually attempts to pack the latest developments of electrical science within limits which were intended simply for purposes of ecclesiastical, or magisterial, or public health jurisdiction. If a survey were made nowadays to determine the boundaries of districts in relation to their industrial development, the Commissioners would not decide that because a town has a mayor and council, and a board of guardians, therefore it should have a light railway system of its own.

The worst of it is that the Legislature will not move to break down this tyranny of geographical boundaries. Meantime every cot, hamlet, village, parish, borough, or urban district, is governed by men, for the most part well-intentioned, sincere, and upright; who, as the result of long years of circumscription, are capable of thinking only in terms of their own limited boundaries, instead of in the grander range of national interests.

A move in the right direction was made when Parliament, in 1898, appointed a select Committee of both Houses to report on the supply of electrical energy, and recommended that powers be given to companies to supply over areas including the districts of numerous local authorities, and that the power of provisional veto given to these authorities by the Acts of 1882 and 1888 should be dispensed with. Although no more encouragement than this unsupported recommendation was given, Bills for large power schemes were drafted immediately, and by the session of 1901 Acts had been passed which studded Great Britain with prospective supply stations.

No better proof of the requirements of the country can be given than the statement that, within two years of the passing of the first power Bill, further Bills had gone through, authorising the raising of capital to the extent of eleven millions, with borrowing powers of one-third. That these schemes were not merely the work of promoters is evidenced by the fact that strict inquiry was held in every case into the financial *bonâ fides* of the proposed undertaking, and by a glance over the names of the promoters themselves, in many cases the wealthiest manufacturers in the districts.

The map recently published * shows the

* See TRACTION AND TRANSMISSION, Vol. IV, Plate XXXI.

areas covered by these schemes. As might be imagined, they are, almost without exception, placed on the coal-fields—the real vital centres of Britain.

The eight largest of these schemes embrace within their areas no less than 7,500 square miles, the most extensive covered by any one concern being the 1,800 square miles of the Yorkshire Company.

Forming close networks in the already densely populated manufacturing centres, the mains of these companies will be sent out on all sides into the more open country, to tempt or to follow the employer who finds himself confined beyond the possibility of expansion in the crowded town, and whose manufacturing costs will be reduced enormously by lessened rates, cheap land, healthier workmen, lighter workshops, and cheap power, and by the exchange of the antiquated and wasteful machinery he was too conservative, temporising, or timid to scrap while he clung to his old shops. Thus will the density of factories per square mile, and the density of workers per cubic foot, be reduced, to the benefit of the whole community, and it will be no longer the first inquiry of the prospective employer, " Where is the site best served by a river or canal, by a colliery, and by a railway ? " The latter will be a necessity always, but the first two considerations will not enter into his calculations.

It is well within the bounds of possibility that these power schemes, and others that will follow, will assist very materially in solving three problems, of which we hear so much nowadays—the maintenance of the supremacy of British trade; the overcrowding of towns and depopulation of the country; and the smoke nuisance; the health of the whole community being affected most deeply by the last two.

When the first Electric Lighting Bill was passed, electrical engineering was in an undeveloped condition. In those days the distribution of power outside very restricted limits was not practicable, and a separate electricity works for every town forward enough to welcome the new illuminant was as necessary as the local gasworks. Now, the generation, control, and distribution of electricity, have been developed to such an extent that small independent stations are recognised as being economical absurdities

Until power can be supplied at, or below, $1\frac{1}{4}$d. per unit the incentive to a manufacturer possessing a fairly economical steam plant is not enough to induce him to change, and it is well known that neither local companies nor local authorities will offer such terms save in a few exceptional instances. That local authorities cannot be expected to improve in this respect is foreshadowed by the frank statement recently made by the deputy - chairman of the Wolverhampton Lighting Committee, to the effect that the total profit of those Corporations that had been successful was £80,148, and the total loss of those that had not been fortunate was £79,853. If from the profit a fair amount for depreciation and administration was deducted the credit balance of £800 would be turned into a heavy loss.

Our only hope, then, is in these large power schemes, whose cost of production may be reasonably expected to be under $\frac{1}{2}$d. per unit. To take an actual example, the cost of generation at the Wallsend station of the Newcastle-upon-Tyne Company for the first few months of this year reached .48d. per unit, and has been reduced since to .87d. per unit, with the certainty of further immediate reduction. At this rate a handsome profit would be made on a selling price of 1d. to 1.25d. per unit.

While all the schemes rising out of the special Act have received considerable public attention, the Midland Electric Corporation for Power Distribution, Ltd., which was conceived almost before any other, has been favoured with scant acknowledgment during its lengthened period of construction. This was chiefly because it is the only company that gained its area by means of separate Provisional Orders for each district within that area. In this respect it served a useful purpose as a warning to others about to enter the field, for no procedure can be more irritating, lengthened, and expensive, than this.

The promoters of the project were Messrs. J. F. Allbright, Edmund Howl, Thomas Parker, and Macbean; but the gentleman who appears to be mainly responsible for the inception of the idea was Mr. G. L. Addenbrooke, who was for some time consulting engineer for the scheme, and is now so closely associated with some of the other large power companies.

Mr. J. W. Swan and Lieutenant-

Colonel Crompton were both in full sympathy with the proposals of the promoters. Mr. Addenbrooke has favoured us with the copy of a letter to Mr. Swan and a memorandum, both dated in 1896, in which the area and the prospects of the scheme are outlined. Calculations were based on coal being delivered to the boilers at 3s. per ton, the total cost of generation being under ¼d. per kilowatt-hour, with delivery to consumers within half a mile radius at ½d. per unit, and up to four to five miles radius, including supply and upkeep of motors, at 1d. per unit, with lower charges as the undertaking grew. It was considered possible that the scheme would include Birmingham, Wolverhampton, Walsall, Dudley, Stourbridge, and Oldbury, which, with the other towns in the area, held a population, in 1891, of over 1,200,000. Mr. Addenbrooke suggested the possibility of the local bodies undertaking the distribution of energy supplied to them in bulk. He referred to the extensive tramway systems which were worked there, with one small exception, by steam locomotives, but which, he foresaw, would be reconstructed and extended if cheap power was available. He believed that the supply of power to manufacturers would form the most remunerative part of the undertaking; for them current could be generated on the same lines, and as economically as at the great power station at Niagara. He stated that there was no likelihood of the coal supply falling off for fifty years, and that there were unworked seams which would last for another century at least. In the memorandum, Mr. Addenbrooke pins the greatest faith to the actual South Staffordshire district, comprising Wolverhampton and Walsall on the north, and Dudley, Oldbury, and West Bromwich on the south, an area containing, then, about 520,000 people, but he recognised that though Wolverhampton and Walsall, which then owned stations, would be unwilling to foster competition, they might take power in bulk. Without these two towns the population of the proposed area was about 355,000.

At this time the amount of coal raised annually in South Staffordshire was fairly constant at 10,000,000 tons; while the annual output of ironstone was about 40,000 tons. Much iron ore is imported, and the annual production of pig-iron is given as 300,000 tons; the output of the various furnaces and mills, in the shape of rails, girders, boiler-plates, sheets, and iron of every description, was, in 1894, 375,000 tons.

As showing how enormously diversified are the trades in the district, the following by no means exhaustive list of manufactures is given:—

Anchors, axle-trees, bedsteads, buckets, boilers, chandeliers, coach and harness furniture, cables, chains, and shipping tackle, electrical machinery and fittings, files, girders (iron and steel), gasholders, iron gates and hurdles, railway carriages and wagons, spurs, stirrups, sanitary fittings, springs, steel pens, telegraph materials, umbrella frames, art metal, bits, buckles, bolts and nuts, cooking ranges, cycles, edge tools, fire-irons and fenders, galvanising of all kinds, locks, rails, roofs, rolls, rivets, saws, screws, safes, scales, stampers and piercers, spades and shovels, stoves and grates, tin-plates, tanks, wire ropes, tubes, vices and anvils.

This list does not include the Birmingham trades, and does not mention the large chemical, glass, fire-brick, blue and red brick works, for all of which South Staffordshire is noted.

The enumeration is tedious, but instructive. These diversified industries are included in an area of about one hundred square miles, and it is not to be wondered at that Mr. Addenbrooke and the promoters of the Midland Electric Corporation thought that great things might be accomplished amidst such surroundings. The whole area is practically one huge town. From Birmingham to Wolverhampton, and from Stourbridge to Walsall, it is hardly possible to say where one town begins and another ends.

It was, of course, out of the question to obtain powers in Wolverhampton, Dudley, or Walsall, where stations already existed, but West Bromwich, Oldbury, and Stourbridge appear to have refused to give their ratepayers the chance of cheap light and power without risk to themselves. The authorities of West Bromwich, indeed, have run up a petty station, from which they started to supply light at 4½d. for one hour and 1½d. after, and power at a flat rate of 1d.! This has resulted, very naturally, in a heavy deficit, and the proposed raising of prices to a level corresponding to the size of the station.

Of the other two towns, Oldbury is the more considerable, and has been sitting on its Lighting Order since 1898; while Stourbridge has been blocking progress vigorously by passive action only since 1899. It is a fairly significant fact that both authorities own the local gas-works. Wolverhampton is past sighing for, but it would have helped the load factor of the central power station. The Corporation began supply in 1895, and this year the first "profit" of £500 has been made. The station is full of antiquated plant. The price charged for lighting is 6d. for the first one and a half hours, and 3d. after, in winter; 6d. for the first hour, and 3d. after, in summer; and for power, 2d. for the first two hours, and 1d. after.

In Dudley, supply was commenced in 1899, under very favourable conditions; as, before a house service was put in, the station was running on a full tramway load, for the Corporation insisted on supplying energy within their area to the Dudley, Stourbridge, and District Tramways. The price for light and power to ordinary consumers is 6d. for two hours, and 1½d. after. The price to the tramways was fixed by arbitration at 2d. up to 150,000, decreasing by .1d. for each additional 50,000 units to 400,000, anything over being at 1d. The actual cost for the last year was just over 1½d. per unit, while we have proof that a power company will supply a consumer at from 1.25d. to 1d. per unit; the saving of over ¼d. being sufficient to make all the difference in a balance sheet.

However, without these barred districts, the area over which the Midland Electric Corporation have powers to supply, is sufficiently inviting. The relative productiveness and general prosperity of any part of the country may be estimated from the amount of smoke, or from the number of chimneys, if the smoke will permit the numbering; and, assuredly there are few smokier districts than this part of the Black Country. The number of works requiring power in the area served by the Midland Electric Corporation is about two thousand, taking an estimated horse-power of 250,000.

The wasteful and barbaric conditions under which a large part of this energy is produced, are almost incredible. We will take one example of many. In one of the largest iron and steel works in the district there is a line of Lancashire and Cornish boilers—all exposed to the weather—attended by a gang of men more than twice as numerous as is economically required, simply because the firm owns its own collieries, and has to burn the fine slack-coal and screenings for which there is no market. It has got to burn this stuff, and it does burn it, partially, on ordinary steam-coal grates, without the aid of anything in the way of draught more than heavily overloaded chimneys. As for the introduction of an economiser, or some other feed-heating arrangement, we doubt if the men responsible for this deplorable state of things, would regard such devices in the light of anything but capital-consuming fads.

A veneration for antiquities is one of the most marked traits of a highly civilised race, and is laudable enough in the archæologist; but, when we see it take the form of clinging to mechanical ruins, and in the continued use of balloon, haystack, or vertical egg-ended boilers, which would be in danger of bursting if pressure was raised to 20lbs.; and to engines which were truly wonderful in the time of Watt; then we feel that the charges of industrial decay, brought against us by our foreign rivals, are not without foundation. Mechanical conservatism means deficiency of progress, and its stronghold is in the Black Country, where nothing in the shape of feed-heaters, forced draught, superheating, or condensers seems to have been heard of. The flue gases go straight from the boilers to the stack, and the exhaust steam direct to the atmosphere. All over acres of works are dumped down steam engines of all sizes fed by hundreds of yards of badly covered, or totally uncovered, steam piping so that the engines are driven more by hot water than by steam. Doubtless much of this isolation of small engines is quite unavoidable, and one is not exacting enough to ask that each of these engines should be provided with a condensing plant; but the point is, that while a works has been paying its way, its proprietors have been perfectly contented to preserve the machinery and tools used by their grandfathers with astonishing success.

To a certain extent a change has been going on in the Black Country for some time, and it may be that out of decay will come salvation, for there is a tendency to merge the smaller works into large concerns.

Some interesting examples of antiquated plants still working, or until recently worked, in the South Staffordshire coal area, will illustrate our criticism (see Figs. 2 to 17, Plates XXXV to XXXIX). It will be seen that the beam engine is chiefly in

Plate **XXXV**

Fig 1.--Light Railway, Kinver

Fig. 2.—Nelson Pumping Engine and Balloon
Boilers

Fig. 3.—Nelson Pumping Engine, showing
Subsidence of Chimney

UorM

TRACTION AND TRANSMISSION IN SOUTH STAFFORDSHIRE

Plate XXXVI

Fig. 4.—Valve Gear of Old Engine

Fig. 5.—Mine Chain Haulage

Figs. 6 and 7.—Rastrick Boilers Fitted with Mechanical Stokers

evidence. The majority date back to the early part of the nineteenth century; of the Nelson pit pumping engine, and Messrs. Cochrane's collieries near Brierley Hill, we know that the new (?) iron beam replaced a wooden beam in 1841, and that the engine has been at work for over one hundred years. The illustrations of this engine house and the boilers are particularly interesting; in the first place because the engine still works quite comfortably in a house which is so much out of the perpendicular that a stranger to the district would be particularly courageous if he passed it on the side to which it leans. This phenomenon is due to the getting of coal from under the house, but we shall refer to such subsidence effects more fully later on (see Figs. 2 and 3, Plate XXXV).

A special interest attaches to these illustrations because the type of boiler in sole use is one of the oldest in existence. This is the "balloon" boiler. The bottoms of these boilers are dished inwardly. They are under-fired from a square grate, embracing the whole area of boiler; and they carry a maximum pressure of 5lbs. per square inch. Sometimes the boiler tops are covered with bricks, more with the idea of protecting them from the weather than with the object of minimising radiation, and, in rare instances, some kind of lagging protects the steam pipes. Any sort of shed to cover the boilers seems to be regarded as a superfluity. The particular engine of which we have been writing has a steam cylinder 6ft. in diameter, and allows a piston stroke of 8ft. The number of complete strokes per minute varies between five and six. The steam pressure at the time of our visit was 2½lbs., and the vacuum 20ins. As a matter of fact, there was something wrong with the condenser at the time, for the vacuum is generally over 24ins. In any case the condenser is a most important factor in the driving of the engine, and, with this type, as one might expect, a condenser is found as a rule. It consists essentially of an air pump and the condensing chamber. The air pump is driven direct from some point on the beam, and every double stroke (the engines are mostly single acting) a tappet on the air-pump rod opens a valve to admit water to the condenser. Similar tappets actuate the steam and exhaust valves, and these are connected with levers, so that the engine can be started and stopped by hand. Fig. 4, Plate XXXVI, gives a good

idea of the valve gear in current use. Engines of any size run into three storeys, much to the disgust of the photographer. It is needless to say that most of these enormous engines, weighing hundreds of tons, and involving costly buildings, could be replaced by a 50 horse-power motor which could be put, with all its gear, on the ground floor of the existing houses.

Another illustration of interest is that showing mine haulage by means of iron chains wound in a flat helix (see Fig. 5, Plate XXXVI), and the fearful and wonderful train of gears added to an engine used originally for pumping, to drive the machinery in a brickworks by bevel gears on a vertical shaft (see Fig. 8, Plate XXXVII). The construction of the chain seen in Fig. 5 is very peculiar, consisting as it does of three ordinary round iron chains connected in parallel by means of hard wood wedges driven through the links. This method of hauling is seen but seldom, but was in general use before the advent of the steel rope. As may be imagined, the chain works anything but silently. Efforts appear to have been made to lessen capital expenditure by omitting the engine house, and we give illustrations (Fig. 14) of the combination of a beam engine with the driver's shelter containing the operating mechanism. Messrs. Foster's ironworks at Pensnett, near Dudley, are full of interest to the mechanical antiquarian, and it is through the courtesy of the manager, Mr. Cook, that we were enabled to roam over the works and take some of these photographs. Quite the most interesting objects, however, are the boilers shown in Figs. 6 and 7. These have been disused for some years, but are greatly superior to the majority of boilers still working in the district. They are of the Rastrick type, are fitted with mechanical stokers, and, in part, with revolving grates, both by the inventor of the boiler. Coal was delivered from standard gauge trucks above the boilers into inclined shoots ending in hoppers. It was then crushed mechanically, and spread over the grate by sprinkling fans geared to revolve in opposite directions. The revolving grates are constructed very solidly, and appear to be still in excellent condition. Power to drive both the stokers and the grates was transmitted from bevel gears on the main shaft of the large blowing engine to which the boilers supplied steam. This engine supplied hot blast to a row of antiquated furnaces. In this connection it may be said that the gases therefrom are used, as a general rule, for heating the blast and for generating steam in boilers, but there is still enormous waste going on, and the use of the gas engine is practically unknown. Further illustrations of antiquated engines and boilers, either still in regular use or only recently abandoned, are given in Figs. 8 to 11, Plates XXXVII, and Figs. 12, 13, and 14, Plate XXXVIII.

Not only is the production of steam power lamentably behind the times, but there are actually in operation at the present day some pits from which minerals are lifted to the surface by horses, and even by men, operating winzes or jennies. An illustration of this is given in Fig. 15, Plate XXXVIII.

We are indebted to Mr. G. R. Jebb, chief engineer to the Birmingham Canal Navigations, for the interesting photograph and drawing of one of the oldest engines in the world, Figs. 16 and 17, Plate XXXIX. This engine is in the possession of the Birmingham Canal Navigations, and was constructed by Boulton & Watt in 1777. It was not only designed by Watt, but the drawings were prepared by him, and it was constructed under his control at a period prior to his invention of the crank, sun, and planet movement, governor, or parallel motion. It is recorded that the basement of this engine was a favourite resort for mechanical discussions of Watt, Smeaton, and Murdock, and it was on it that Watt tried his first indicator. It is a single-acting beam engine, with chains at each end of a wooden beam. The cylinder is 32ins. diameter by 8ft. stroke, developing about 90 effective horse-power; the engine was installed at the Canal Company's pumping station at Rolfe Street, Smethwick. For 120 years it worked regularly, and it was only in 1898 that it was removed to the Canal Company's station at Ocker Hill, to be re-erected and preserved as a relic of what can be done by good management when dealing with machinery of undoubted quality. The world is indebted to Mr. Jebb, primarily, for the preservation of this unique engine. It is visited by many engineers from all parts of the world, and very large sums have been offered, without avail, for it. It is still connected to a boiler, and is set to work now and again

to keep it in order. The actual removal, re-erection, and maintenance of the engine was entrusted to Mr. J. Robinson, Mr. Jebb's assistant, to whom we are indebted for various kindnesses and much information. It is worthy of remark that the old firm, under the title of James Watt & Co., have erected recently at the Walsall pumping station of the Canal Company, two triple-expansion engines of 240 horse-power, with a capacity of 12,750,000 gallons per diem. In its early days the firm seems to have enjoyed the monopoly of steam engines, for its order book shows that, between 1777 and 1828, engines aggregating nearly 70,000 horse-power (effective) were turned out of the works. Nineteen of these engines went to the Birmingham Canal Company, and the remainder seem to have been dispersed over the canal systems from Fort William to Gloucester; one was sent in 1806 to Holland.

There are, of course, a few brilliant exceptions to a bad rule. For instance, Sir Alfred Hickman's works are largely driven by gas-generated electricity; the Patent Shaft and Axle Tree Company has a complete installation of three-phase plant; and the Sandwell Park Colliery does its hauling, ventilating, and lighting by means of its own three-phase machinery. Mr. Herbert W. Hughes, who is the engineer for this large colliery, among others, considers that there is a vast field for electricity in the industries of the Black Country, and now that competition is becoming keener day by day, and we may hope that manufacturers are beginning to recognise that the last penny has to be saved, there is a very bright prospect before the Midland Electric Corporation in this district. It may still take a little while to educate the blind to appreciate their lack of sight, but it is an old saying that men are very much like sheep, and it only needs a few of the more enlightened to change their leaky steam pipes and engines for modern motors; the lagging majority are sure to follow.

The first client of the Midland Electric Corporation was the Wolverhampton District Tramways, Ltd., one of the promising offspring of that most prolific parent, the British Electric Traction Company, and as the whole of South Staffordshire is ramified by lines owned by this company, a short description of the systems will not be amiss.

Five years ago the only electrically

Fig. 8.—Old Engine and Boiler still in Work, showing
Power Transmission

Fig. 9.—Balloon Boiler at Nelson Pumping Station

Fig. 11.—Battery of Balloon Boilers still Worked
at 3lbs. per square inch

Fig. 10.—Battery of Balloon Boilers

Figs. 12 and 13.—Old Deep Mine Pumping Engines

Fig. 15.—Ancient Mode of Hoisting Ccal still in Operation

Fig. 14.—Old Deep Mine Pumping Engines (1802-1805)
still at Work, Dudley Collieries

U of M

Figs. 12 and 13.—Old Deep Mine Pumping Engines

Fig. 15.—Ancient Mode of Hoisting Ccal still in Operation

Fig. 14.—Old Deep Mine Pumping Engines (1802-1805)
still at Work, Dudley Collieries

U of M

Plate XXXIX

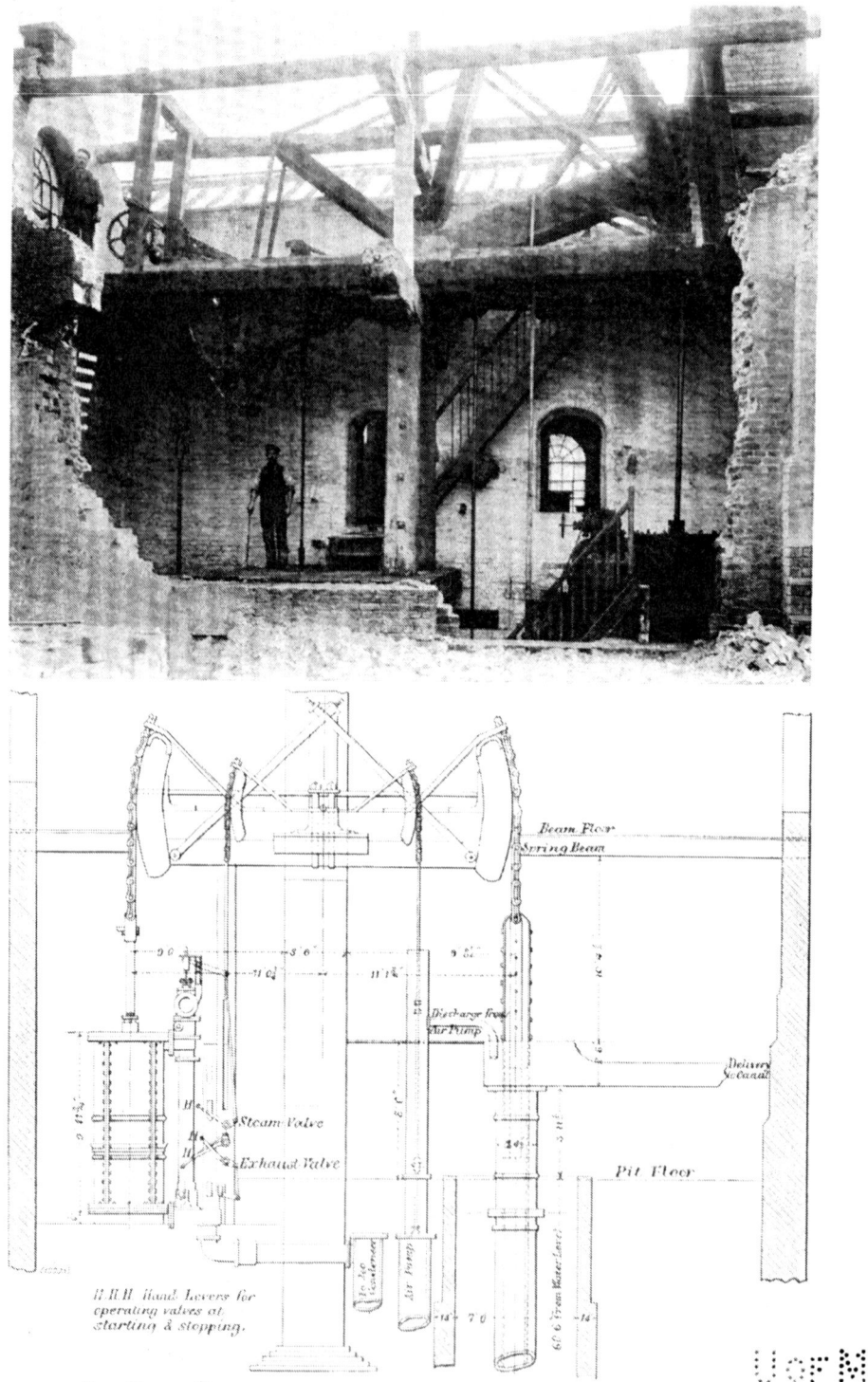

U of M

Figs. 16 and 17.—Boulton & Watt Pumping Engine (1777) at Smethwick

TRACTION AND TRANSMISSION IN SOUTH STAFFORDSHIRE

operated line in the South Staffordshire district was about eight miles long; it was owned by the South Staffordshire Tramways Company, Ltd., and connected Walsall, Wednesbury, Bloxwich, and Darlaston. That line was opened in 1893, and was one of the first overhead trolley systems in England. Owing to uncertainty of tenure, the original construction still stands, and the old cars still run, and run well. The power station is equipped with three 120 horse-power horizontal tandem compound condensing engines by Musgrave, and their smooth running, after so many years' continuous and heavy work, speaks well for the makers and the engineers. Most American engines would have been scrapped, or would have required re-bored cylinders long ago. These engines are coupled by rope drives to 90 - kilowatt E.C.C. bipolar dynamos. They were shunt wound originally, but series turns have been added recently, greatly improving the regulation of voltage. The line voltage is only 300, and, as the motors of the old cars are all open bipolar machines, exposed to a considerable extent to dust, wind, and water, the low voltage is probably quite sufficient for the peace of mind of the engineer. The cars are an interesting survival, and are well worth inspection; they are equipped with crudely simple controllers with open resistance coils below. Series parallel control was not known in the days when these cars were built, so we find two motors permanently in parallel, run up to speed on resistances which are cut gradually out of circuit.

The overhead construction is on the side-running bracket system throughout, with one wire only, except at loops, where there are spring switches at each end. The poles and arms seem so light as to be almost dangerous after the eye has become accustomed to modern work. Perhaps they are too light at curves, but we are sure that, as a whole, they are better proportioned than much of the newer work, which, especially for bracket arms, is often grotesquely heavy, helping to give point to the frequent remarks on the unsightliness of the trolley system. Mr. Alfred Dickenson must be credited with this pioneer work. The line was constructed before the Board of Trade had thought of electrolysis as a possible danger with an insufficient rail return, so that the bonding of joints was performed by securing 16-gauge iron wire, or something equally absurd, under

a fish-bolt, or in the web of the rail by means of a drift pin. Since the awakening of the Board of Trade all this has, of course, been altered.

The remainder of the company's lines, about fifteen miles, is operated by steam engines. The only reason for their continued existence is to be found in the action of some of the local authorities, with whom it appears to be well-nigh impossible to come to terms. Indeed, Walsall has practically elected to forego the manifest advantages offered by the continuance of the company's service in the nature of specialised management, through services and through intercommunication, and profit without risk; having decided to buy out the company under the Tramways Act, and isolate itself by working independently.

The southern boundaries of the system touch Birmingham and Dudley. The latter town has become within the last three years an important tramway centre, being fed from no less than seven diverging routes, of which four are electric. On the east the Birmingham and Midland Tramways Company, practically owned by the British Electric Traction Company, join Dudley to Birmingham by a route eight miles long. This is still worked by steam cars; but, all negotiations with local authorities having had a happy issue, it will be converted to electric traction very shortly. Power for this line, and for extensions which have received the sanction of Parliament, will be obtained from a central station at Smethwick, from which station the company will also supply light and power as contractors under the Lighting Order owned by the Smethwick Corporation.

Prior to 1899 the only line entering Dudley from the west was the steam operated track from Stourbridge, five and a half miles away. When the old company was bought up by the British Electric Traction Company, it was converted immediately to electric traction, and powers were obtained to build new lines, till, at the present time, the route mileage owned by the company has increased four - fold. Not only do the new lines tap densely populated and grimy districts such as Netherton, Cradley Heath, and Lye; they have catered also for the rural district of Kingswinford by joining it both to Stourbridge and Dudley; and they have opened up one of the lungs of the Black Country by building a real light railway from Stourbridge to Kinver, a spot widely famed for its beauty (see Fig 7, Plate XXXV). All the other routes are used purely for business, but this line is first and last a line of pleasure. Previously, extortionate and tardy wagonettes conveyed holiday hundreds from a smoke-laden atmosphere and grim surroundings to pure air and an unequalled view; while now, so much has the popularity of the ride, and the resort, increased, that, not only is it impossible on a Bank Holiday for the cars to cope with the multitude, but the attendance of horsed vehicles has actually increased. The area now served by the lines of the Dudley, Stourbridge, and District Company, had a population of over 180,000 at the 1891 census.

Power for these lines is obtained outside the Borough of Dudley, from a private generating station situated near Brierley Hill, with which is combined a large car shed. Here, in contradistinction to the South Staffordshire Company's station, where everything is British, all the generating plant except the boilers is American. It consists of three 170 horse-power tandem compound condensing horizontal Ball & Wood engines, coupled direct to six-pole General Electric (U.S.A.) generators. The boilers are 30ft. by 7ft. 6ins. plain Lancashire type by Danks, of Netherton, the economiser of 192 tubes by Green, and the surface condenser plant by the Wheeler Company.

The generating plant has been augmented lately by a Tudor battery of 810 ampere-hours capacity, installed at the junction of the Kinver and Kingswinford lines with the main line. This battery is rendered really effective as a producer of a high load factor and correspondingly lower generating cost at the power station, by the provision of a Crompton automatic reversible booster, whose function it is to keep the load on the main engines constant, and as near the most efficient load as possible, by discharging or charging as the line load increases or diminishes.

As previously mentioned, the Dudley Corporation supply the lines running within their boundary, and in the case of the Cradley Heath line, which receives current entirely from their station, some way outside. The station is quite modern, and contains one 500 - kilowatt Ferranti E.C.C. set, and

three 200 - kilowatt and one 100-kilowatt Westinghouse sets, all condensing during a portion of the day. Part of the exhaust steam is shunted through a Boby feed-heater, giving a constant temperature of 212degs. Fahr. There is an additional feed-heater in the shape of a Green's economiser. Jet condensers are used, combined with a Worthington natural draught cooling tower. The boilers are all Babcock & Wilcox, with Vicars mechanical stokers, and Scotch furnaces. Superheaters have been fitted recently. As the station is situated in a hollow, it has been possible to run coal - trucks right over the coal - bunkers, which are built in front of the boilers, and discharge on the firing level. It is not often that so little handling can be arranged, and at such small cost. The coal comes straight from Lord Dudley's collieries at Himley, and the trucks are weighed automatically as they pass over one of Avery's machines at the entrance.

Turning to the north of Dudley, we re - enter a district in which the British Electric Traction Company has created great interests. When the company obtained the controlling influence in the old Wolverhampton Tramway Company, it did so with the evident intention of turning one of the most decrepit tramway properties in England, into an up - to - date, well - served concern. They were fully prepared to rip up the whole line from Dudley into Wolverhampton, and to replace the tottering steam vehicles with smart electric cars in a few months. In this design they were barred by the Wolverhampton Corporation, who refused to grant a lease or running powers to the company after their tenure lapsed under the Act.

During negotiations, the line from Dudley to Sedgley has been reconstructed, and was running, and when it was seen that Wolverhampton held to its policy of isolation, reconstruction of the remainder of the line to the Wolverhampton boundary proceeded immediately, and service began last January.

The result of this policy has been that for two years and more, people have been brought to the Wolverhampton boundary by the company's cars, and have then had to walk one and a half miles to the centre of the town, or to ride in a badly preserved omnibus, drawn at four miles an hour. On other routes in the town, the Corporation has adopted a surface-contact system, which had to be tried in actual service. The trolley was said to be dangerous and unsightly; on the other hand the trolley was cheap. But in spite of the fact that the whole ot the lines outside the Municipal boundary, serving an area of nearly two hundred square miles, were already, or were to be, equipped with the overhead system, the Wolverhampton Corporation have already built ten or eleven miles on a plan which will make it impossible, except at enormous expense, for the company to carry passengers into the town without a change.

Disgusted, but not disheartened, by the action of the Wolverhampton Corporation, the British Electric Company proceeded so well with their new lines to the north of Sedgley and east of Wolverhampton, that in May last about seven more miles were opened for traffic. The remainder, bringing the total owned by the Wolverhampton District Company to seventeen miles, will be complete very shortly. These lines place the Wolverhampton District system in communication, both at Moxley and Willenhall, with the extensive lines of the South Staffordshire Company. On the other side they touch the Wolverhampton boundary at two points.

It should be said that the Dudley-Stourbridge Company work the lines of the Wolverhampton District Company under arrangement with that company. The former company controls, therefore, the largest system of electric trams in that part of the country, consisting of nearly forty miles of route, operated by about one hundred cars.

From the last report of the British Electric Traction Company we gather that the number of passengers carried during three years over their lines in the district was as follows :—

1899	...	...	...	... 20,157,839
1900	...	...	...	... 25,883,783
1901	...	...	...	... 29,425,603

The last year given does not include any electrically worked line on the Wolverhampton District system, except that from Dudley to Sedgley, so that the rate of increase for 1902 should be considerably above the normal. Then, when we consider that there are still thirty-four miles of route unconverted, and that further extensions in several directions are contemplated, it will be seen what an enormous business is in question.

Birmingham is pictured usually as a particularly black and uninviting city. So far as that portion which is given up to manufacture goes, this is undoubtedly, though not necessarily, true; but there are large areas which are relatively beautiful.

There is one short overhead trolley line, which was referred to in TRACTION AND TRANSMISSION for August, 1901, but this ends inconveniently, some way from the centre of the city. There is also a three miles stretch of cable route, which is quite disconnected from any other system; but the whole of the lines running from the suburbs and the Black Country through the city are worked by steam.

At the present time, a spirited controversy is in progress as to whether or no the whole of the tramways within the city bounds shall be municipalised, and one of the arguments in favour thereof which recurs most often is that the company are not entitled to the confidence of the public because they have not swept the steam cars from the streets. Councillors themselves hurl this reproach with great show ot indignation; yet the Council itself has, most consistently, made it impossible for the company to remove the cause of the reproach. The company has pressed the Council for years for permission to reconstruct the lines on the trolley system. This it was willing to do without extension of leases, but the Council, after much apparent consideration, decided that the trolley system would so mar the beauty of the streets that it could not be permitted. If the company wanted to better the public service it must put down the conduit system. This meant enormous capital outlay, which obviously could not fructify, even if it could be raised, unless the rapidly expiring leases were lengthened; but this the Council refused, and have continued to refuse to grant.

Meanwhile, the British Electric Traction Company has purchased the controlling interest in the City of Birmingham tramways at a heavy premium. It has control, therefore, over practically every line entering the city, and it may now be hoped that complete, uninterrupted, and cheap intercommunication with the outlying districts shall be ensured by the continuance of the leases within the city, which suffers as much as any town in England from the inconvenience and dangers inseparable from an overcrowded population.

THE SERPOLLET AUTOMOBILE

By Daniel Bellet, Paris

THE progress that has been made ot recent years in France, in the construction of automobiles, is largely due to the enterprise of M. Serpollet, the well-known French manufacturer. As far back as 1895 we called the attention of our readers to the Serpollet steam cars, as they were built at that comparatively early stage of automobilism.* Since then they have been much improved in every detail, and have achieved great success. The present description applies to the latest types now in use, and which are styled "Gardner-Serpollet Automobiles."

As an illustration of the high speed that can now be obtained from steam-propelled cars, we may mention that, at a recent race for the Rothschild Cup, at Nice, for cars weighing 1,430 to 2,205lbs., carrying at least two passengers, a Serpollet steam car ran a flying kilometre in 29⅖secs., equal to slightly less than 75 miles per hour. Four years ago a Bollée car ran at a speed of 1 kilometre per minute (37¼ miles per hour), this rate of speed causing at the time general amazement. Last year a Serpollet car ran a flying kilometre in 35⅔secs., equal to 100½ kilometres (62¼ miles) per hour. A 40 horse-power Jenatzy electric car took 35⅔secs.; and a 40 horse-power Mercédès petroleum car, 35⅔secs., a speed equal to that of the Serpollet car; while a 20 horse-power Darracq car took only 35⅓secs., giving a speed of 64¾ miles per hour.

In a steam car, built for speeds up to seventy-five miles an hour, the most important part is the boiler. As is well known, M. Serpollet introduced some years ago, a type of generator almost instantaneous in its action; it contained a thick serpentine tube, flattened down in such a way that the inside of the tube was reduced to a very narrow slit. The water that flowed in the tube through this narrow slit was rapidly converted into steam, the latter being supplied direct to the motor. This could be considered, for all practicable purposes, an inexplosible boiler; it had withstood pres-

sures up to 2,205, 3,675, and 3,985lbs. per square inch. The steam-producing power was a very high one; thus, for a boiler 405 cubic decimetres (14.305 cubic feet) in capacity, measured from the ash-box to the base of the chimney, the evaporation was .162 kilogramme per cubic decimetre (10lbs. per cubic foot) of the boiler capacity, per hour, for a fuel consumption of 1.215 kilogrammes per square decimetre of grate area (24.6lbs. per square foot) per hour. The boiler, therefore, took up but little space in comparison with its duty, and seemed admirably suited for automobile service, especially as it required no supervision. As originally designed, however, it contained several disadvantages, among which may be mentioned the rapid choking up of the flattened tube, even when using distilled water; the irregularity in the steam pressure; and the too high superheating of the steam.

In order to do away with these disadvantages, while maintaining the characteristic features of his boiler, M. Serpollet has designed a new type, which he now uses on his high-speed cars. This boiler is shown in Figs. 1 to 8, pages 181, 182. The flattened down serpentine tube of the original design has been replaced by three sets of special shaped coils, made of small diameter tubes, fitted one above the other. The arrangement of the upper set of coils is that of a continuous tube, bent as shown in Fig. 1 to form a number of horizontal layers. Fig. 2 shows two such layers placed in position, one above the other. The second, or middle set of coils, is formed of tubes bent as shown in Fig. 3; these tubes are of the same outside diameter as those forming the upper ⌐t of coils, but their wall is thicker, and their junction curves smaller in radius. Figs. 4 and 5 show the lower coil; this is of rectangular shape, and is made of tubes of similar section to those of the middle set of coils. The general arrangement of the boiler is shown in Figs. 6 to 8, Figs. 7 and 8 being vertical sections through the centre of the boiler. The arrows show the direction of circulation; water is

---

* See *Engineering*, Vol. LX, pages 471 and 499.

Plate XL

Fig. 14.

TOOL
BOX

A

Q

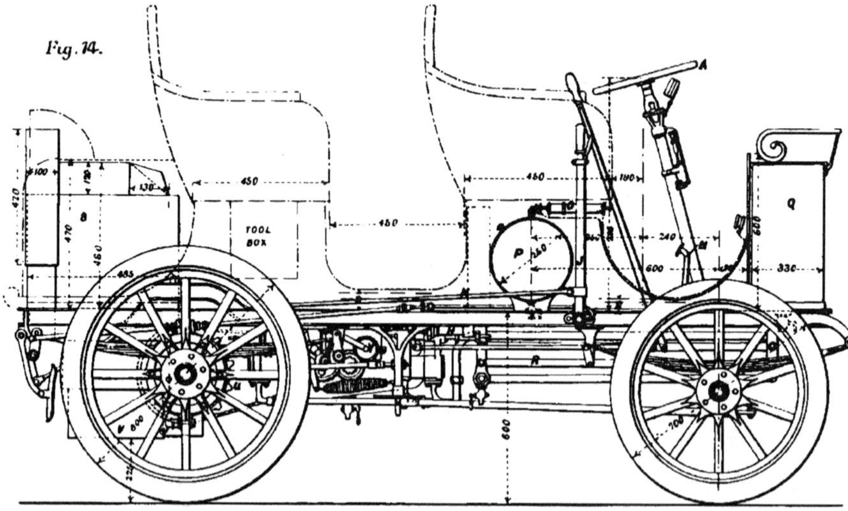

Fig. 15.

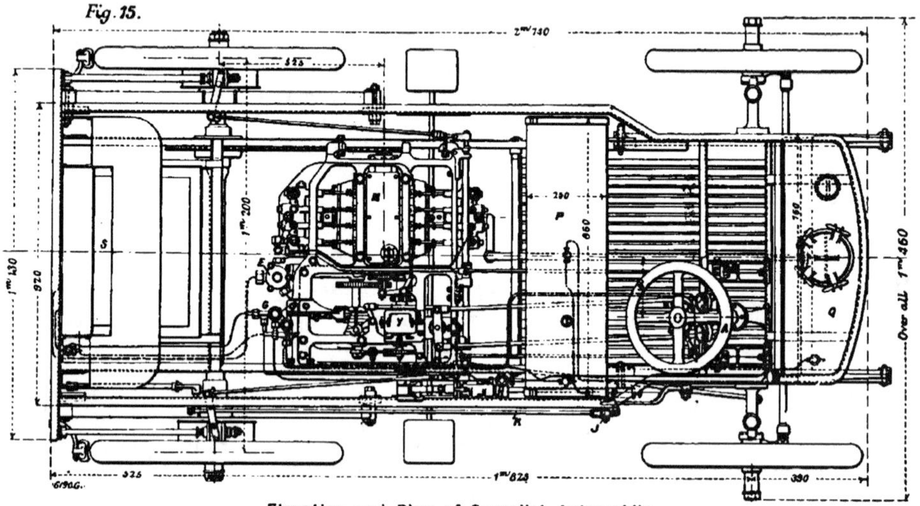

Elevation and Plan of Serpollet Automobile

Fig. 16.

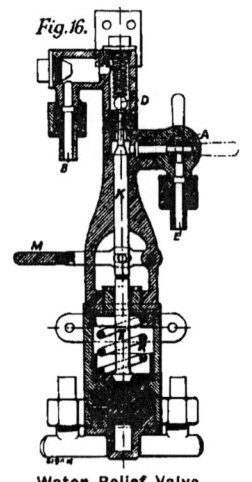

Water Relief Valve

Fig. 19.

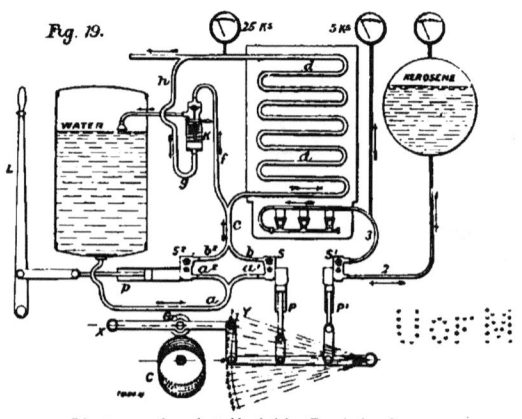

Diagram showing Variable Feed Device

THE SERPOLLET AUTOMOBILE

supplied from a tank or a feed pump, and enters at *a* (Figs. 6 to 8), at the top part of the upper set of coils ; it flows through tube *b*, and is led down through the tube *c* to the lower coil of thick tubes. It enters this coil at *d*, leaves it at *e*, and arrives at *f* in the middle set of coils ; it leaves this set at *g*, and rises through pipe *h* to

a manner that, should one get damaged, it could easily be removed for repair. The outside shell is built up of steel plates ; the various parts are held together at *w* and *y*, and in order to remove a layer of tubes, the corresponding joints are unscrewed, and plate *x* is lifted off.

The smoke-box is illustrated in Figs. 9 and

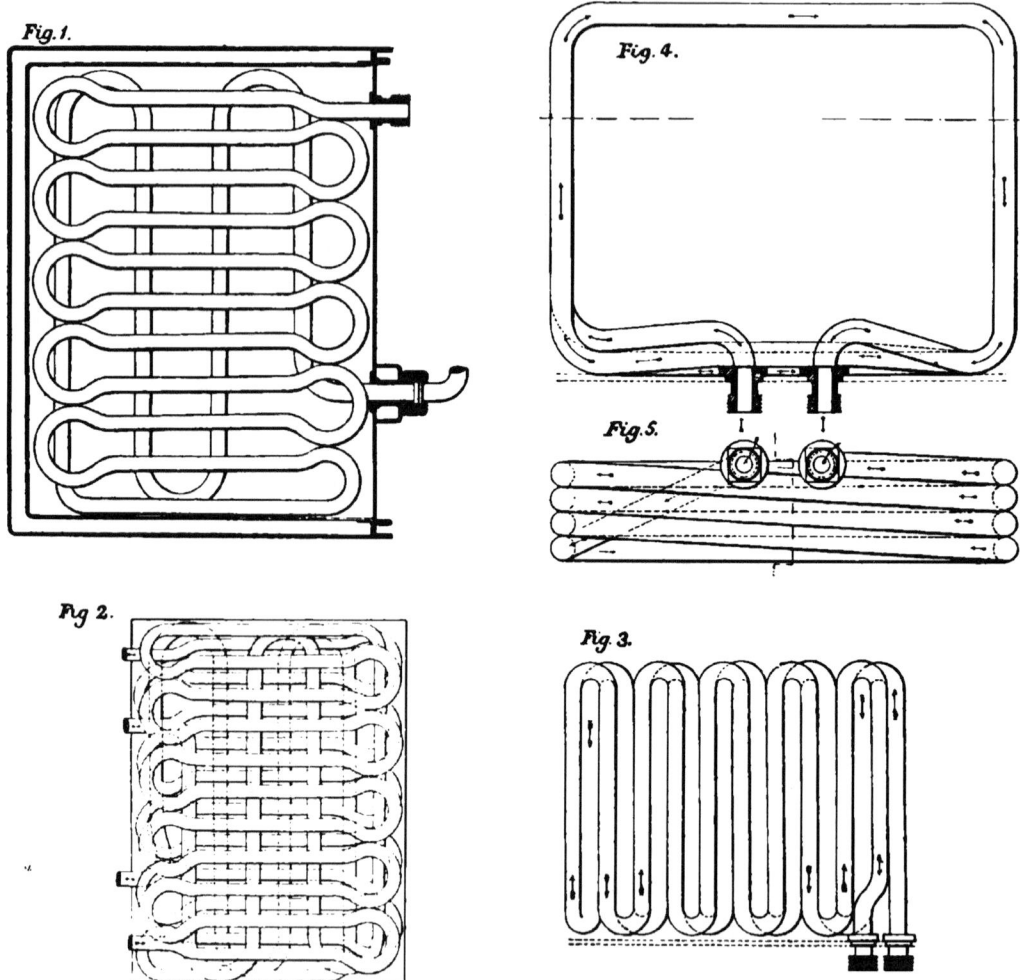

Details of Serpollet Boiler

re-enter the top set of coils, which, as will be remembered, is formed of tubes having a larger internal section. It ultimately leaves this set at *u* as steam.

The layers of tubes forming the coils are grouped together two by two in such

10, page 182. In order to prevent a down draught, a vertical pipe, *b*, square in section, is fitted on the horizontal outlet, *a*. The vertical pipe is open in the rear, at *c*, and is protected by a screen, *d*. An alternative arrangement for the smoke escape is illustrated in Figs.

11 and 12. Fig. 13 shows the air inlet to the burner and the gas escape.

chiefly used is kerosene. This, on being led down to the burners, gets volatilised,

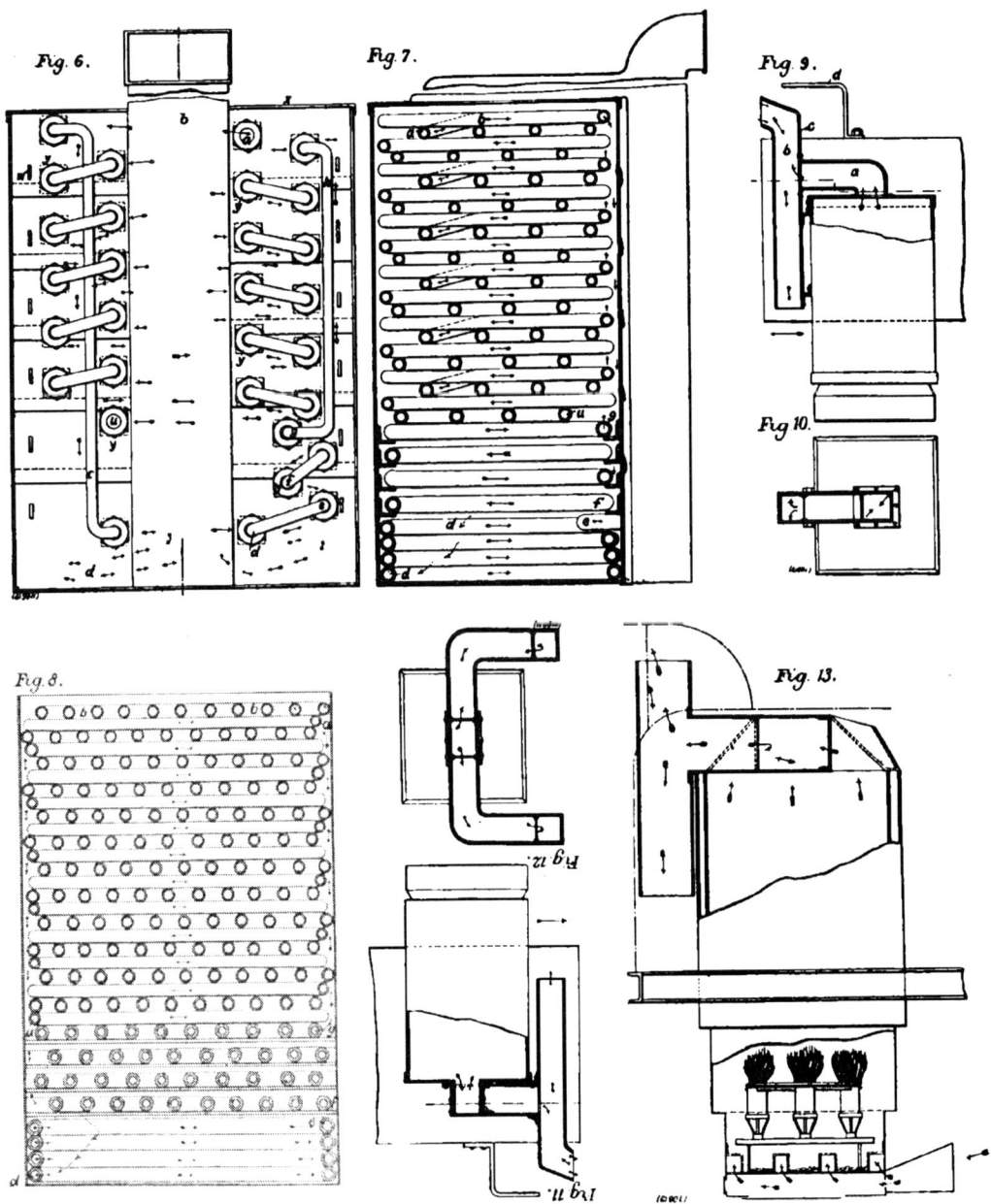

Fig. 6.

Fig. 7.

Fig. 9.

Fig 10.

Fig. 8.

Fig. 13.

Details of Serpollet Boiler, Furnace, and Smoke Box

Although recent experiments made with alcohol have given good results, the fuel

the vapour jets burning when coming in contact with the air, in a device similar to that of the Bunsen burner. The heating of the boiler tubes is proportioned to the steam output, and to the supply of feed water to the boiler, and although super-heating is always ensured, as well as evaporation, the tubes are never carried to a dangerous temperature.

The frame and mechanical parts are shown in Figs. 14 and 15, Plate XL. The kerosene is contained in the receiver marked P; this is on the forward part of the frame, and under the front seat when the car is built to carry four persons. A certain pressure can be created over the kerosene surface, when required, by acting on the small horizontal pump marked O. The automatic kerosene pump is marked F on Fig. 15, and the automatic water pump, G. These pumps are worked by levers, carefully designed to ensure proper proportion. The starting pump is marked H; it is worked from a lever placed on the right-hand side of the driver, and by which water is injected in the boiler while the car is at a standstill, and pressure given for starting. The boiler S is in the rear. On leaving the boiler, the steam enters the obturator, or steam valve E, which is worked by the foot lever D. The closing of the obturator is absolutely automatic; the action of the foot on the lever allows the steam to flow from the boiler to the motor, and the steam is cut off when the action of the lever ceases. This is important, both with a view to ensure a quick stoppage of the car, and its remaining at a standstill when all the passengers have alighted. It is true that the driver must have his foot constantly on the lever when the car is running, but this he can do without any trouble or fatigue. When in the open country, the steam inlet is allowed to remain fully open by the driver, the changes in the speed being obtained by variations in the feed. For temporary slowing down, in populous districts, for example, the steam admission to the motor can be made to vary by pressing more or less on the foot lever. The brake action can also be combined with the wire-drawing of the steam. The steam passes from the steam valve to the motor M. At the same time it flows, as described further on, through a branch pipe to a needle valve, illustrated in Fig. 16. The exhaust steam from the motor is directed first to a collector, provided with a diaphragm, in which the oil is deposited, and is allowed to run out

through a special orifice. The steam then flows to the condenser R (Fig. 14). This consists, according to the power of the engine, of a greater or less number of straight copper tubes. From the condenser, in which the steam is almost completely condensed, it is delivered at the top of the tank marked Q. Before it is used again for feed the condensed water is made to flow through a strainer.

The car is steered by means of the hand wheel A. This acts on the front axle through a system of gearing that ensures smooth and safe working, without any reaction. Underneath the hand wheel are two small handles, one, B, to the right, which works the pump rod to vary the supply of water and of kerosene, and one, C, to the left, which acts as a reversing lever. The hand brake is worked by the lever J, and the rod K. A double-acting brake can also be set by the foot lever N. Lubrication is ensured by a Serpollet lubricator, marked Y, which supplies oil to every part requiring it. The chain-wheel is shown at U; the burners are at V. Pressure gauges show the pressure of the kerosene and of the steam at the steam valve.

Fig. 17, Plate XLI, reproduced from a photograph, shows a Gardner-Serpollet motor. It has four single-acting cylinders, in two opposite groups. The design of the cylinders is that followed for ordinary petroleum motors. One of the main objects aimed at in this construction has been to do away with the stuffing-boxes, as these generally cause a large amount of trouble. In this particular motor the connecting rods are joined direct to the pistons, the tightness of the latter being ensured by four segments. Distribution is effected by valves. These are practically under no wear and tear, as they are not exposed to shocks, the eccentrics that work them following them in the whole of their action and preventing them from falling hard on their seat. The series of eccentrics that work the valves are cut on a shaft. The action on the valves for starting, stopping, or backward running, is obtained by shifting the eccentric shaft laterally by means of a small handle which the driver holds in his left hand. At the dead point the cylindrical portions of the eccentric shaft are in contact with the rollers at the end of the valve rods. To start the motor the eccentric shaft is driven back in one direction, when one valve at least, but generally two, are on admission, while a third, or generally the two remaining ones, are on exhaust. The admission of steam by one valve only is sufficient to start the motor, when the working regulates itself. When running there are always two valves on admission and two on exhaust alternately. If the eccentric shaft has been driven back the other way the action is reversed, and the car is made to run backwards. The whole mechanism runs in oil in a tight casing. The steam distribution device also allows of various degrees of cut-off at will. To obtain this it suffices, when the motor is started, to displace the eccentric shaft laterally more or less, by acting on the small handle above referred to, the eccentrics being set in a way to ensure various degrees of cut-off. The action of the motor is transmitted direct to the rear axle by means of a single chain, protected from mud and dust inside the frame, which joins the motor pinion to the driving wheel of the balance - gear drum. M. Serpollet prefers this system of transmission on account of reduced friction, and believes that to this, among other arrangements, is due the efficiency of his cars, these, although of only 6 and 12 horse-power, working better than many other automobiles of 20 and even 35 horse-power. Thus, at runs made in Austria, September, 1901, on a gradient of 4 in 100, six miles long, a number of 6 horse-power Serpollet cars maintained an average speed of twenty-six miles an hour, giving a much better performance than 12 and 20 horse-power petroleum cars.

One of the characteristic features of the Serpollet car is the proportional feed device, by which the steam production is made to vary to meet constantly the need of the motor without it being necessary to attend to the working of the burners. It will be remembered that variations in the steam production of the Serpollet boiler depend entirely upon variations in the feed of the boiler. The feed pump has a variable stroke, and is connected to a lever worked by a non - continuous cam, formed by the fitting together on a shaft of a series of eccentric discs, which can be displaced to coincide in turn with the roller on the pump lever. The device is shown in Fig. 18, Plate XLI. The disc marked 0 is concentric with the shaft; the one marked 1 is brought out of the centre by 2 millimetres compared with the 0 disc; that marked 2 is out of the centre by 2 milli-

metres compared with that marked 1, and so on. The stroke, and consequently the output of the water feed pump, increases in proportion with the eccentricity of the disc which comes in contact with the roller on the pump lever. The working is further illustrated in diagram Fig. 19, Plate XL, which shows the discs and various positions taken up by the pump lever. As it is necessary that the heat produced should increase in proportion with the increase in the water supply, the lever also works the kerosene pump, as shown in the diagram. The connecting levers operating the two pumps, and the difference in surface of the two pistons, have been calculated upon the quantity of water that can be practically transformed into superheated steam by a litre of kerosene. The kerosene pump, therefore, delivers to the burners a quantity of liquid fuel which is in constant proportion with the quantity of water injected by the water feed pump. The driver never needs to inquire into the intensity of the flames, as it corresponds always with the required steam production. In Fig. 19 the automatic water feed pump is marked P, and the kerosene pump P1. The respective pump valves are shown at S and S1. The starting pump is shown at p; it is worked by the hand lever L, and its valve is marked S2. The eccentric discs are shown at C; the roller and lever above referred to, are marked respectively G and X Y. The arrows in the diagram show the circulation of water and hydrocarbon.

The latter arrives under pressure in tube 2, and is driven to the burners through tube 3; it passes over the burners, and is vaporised. The pressure gauge shows at what pressure it is supplied to the burners. The feed water, according to whether it is delivered by the starting hand pump, or, in normal working, by the automatic pump, passes through a^2 and b^2, or through a^1 and b, after flowing, in both cases, through pipe a. It then rises through tube c and is delivered partly in the boiler $d\,d$, and partly, should there be any excess, to the needle valve, K, through pipe f. The object of this valve is the following: The water which has been fed in the boiler gets vaporised; most of the steam flows to the motor, but a certain quantity flows also through h and g, to the lower part of the needle-valve piston. The needle valve, as will be seen, communicates with the water tank, and all excess in the

Plate XLI

Fig. 17.—The Gardner-Serpollet Steam Motor

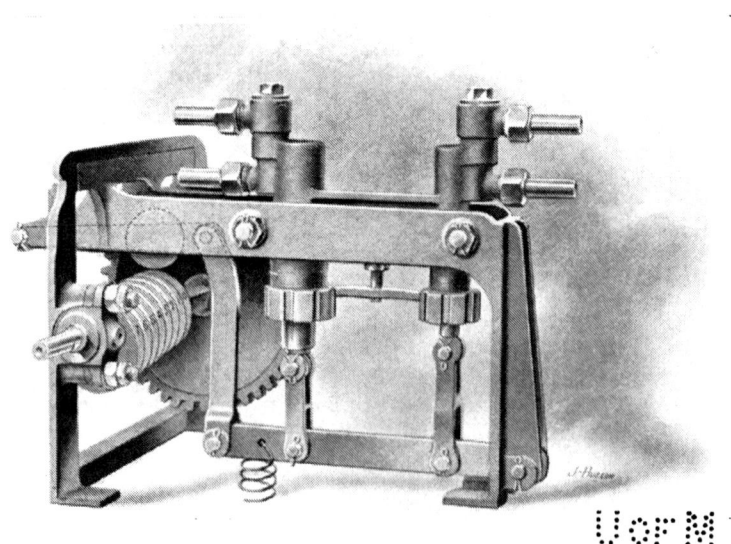

Fig. 18.—Water Feed Regulating Device

Plate XLII

Fig. 23.—Frame and Mechanism of Serpollet Steam Car

Fig. 24.—Serpollet Steam Car, for Long Distance Travelling

THE SERPOLLET AUTOMOBILE

Plate XLIII

Fig. 25.—Serpollet Steam Car, Latest Type

Fig. 26.—High-speed Serpollet Steam Car

M moll

feed water is thus made to flow in the tank. The references in the view (Fig. 16) of the needle valve are the following: P, piston on which the steam pressure acts; the piston is fitted with a rod, T, and is loaded by the antagonistic spring R. The rod T acts on the spindle K, which lifts the spherical valve D. The top part of the valve D is under the pressure of part of the water which comes from the feed pump through the orifice B. The spindle K is fitted with a handle M, within reach of the driver, and the strength of the spring R is so calculated that until the steam pressure reaches a certain limit, the valve D remains in its seat, and all the water from the feed pump enters the boiler. As soon as this limit is reached, the valve D rises and part of the feed water, the overflow, is delivered to the water tank through the pipe E. The pressure in the boiler then gets lowered, the valve D falls back on its seat, and the feed water flows exclusively again to the boiler. When it is required to empty the boiler, the handle M is raised by hand, and all the water in the piping and in the boiler flows to the tank. It occasionally occurred, at first, that the spherical valve did not close hermetically, when part of the feed water always ran to the tank, this meaning a loss of power and the defective working of the system. M. Serpollet has devised a means to obviate this leakage, by placing a two-way cock A (Fig. 16) on the return pipe to the water tank. This shows whether there is a leakage or not, and eventually the valve is inspected and regulated.

Another interesting device which forms part of the mechanism is the auto-starting device, or accumulator, the main object of which is to do away with the working of the hand pump. It would prevent, also, the rapid and untimely emptying of the boiler by the raising of the needle valve, caused by a sudden increase of the boiler pressure, due to the car coming to a standstill, in the congested part of a town, for example. Fig. 20 is a diagram showing the device in question, which consists of a vertical cylinder A, in which travels freely a piston B, covered with oil to prevent the parts under friction from getting oxidised, to facilitate the action of the piston and increase its tightness. The top part of the cylinder is connected to a metallic receiver C, and to a pressure gauge D. The lower part of the

cylinder is in communication with the feed, through a stop-cock, E, placed within reach of the driver. The apparatus is charged with air, or carbonic acid gas, through the cock F; it is in working order when the top of the cylinder A, and the receiver C, are filled with air or gas at a pressure of about 300lbs. per square inch. This is arrived

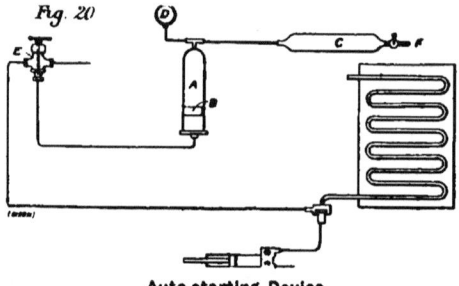

Fig. 20

Auto-starting Device

at without difficulty, as carbonic acid gas bottles can readily be obtained, failing which an ordinary automobile air-pump for inflating the tyres would meet the case. The system remains under pressure for weeks at a time. The cock E is open when the car is running; it is closed by the driver every time a stoppage has to exceed a few minutes. The device acts as follows: When it is under the full air or gas pressure, the piston B is at the bottom of the cylinder. The motor can then be started in two different ways. In order to start rapidly, the boiler is filled with water by means of the hand pump, the stop-cock E is opened, and the water pressure is allowed to rise in the boiler to 600lbs. per square inch. This boiler pressure acts on the lower surface of the piston, and drives the latter to the top of the cylinder; the air, or gas, is compressed, its volume is reduced by one half, and its pressure is doubled, giving thus an available reserve of 90 or 180 cubic inches—according as the car is of 6 or 12 horse-power—under a pressure of 600lbs. per square inch. Before starting, the cylinders are warmed by means of the hand pump, and in order not to waste the water from the auto-starting device, the latter is isolated for a time by closing the stop-cock E. On starting with the stop-cock E open, the pressure in the boiler will drop and the piston B will force in the boiler tubes the reserve of water contained in the auto-starting device, thus giving time to the automatic feed pump to ensure the feed in proportion with the steam consumption. The second manner of starting demands no preparation; the operation is carried out as though there were no accumulator; the cylinders are warmed by means of the hand pump; the feed hand lever is opened out full, and the motor starts in the usual way, care being taken to open the stop-cock, E. The accumulator thus gets charged automatically. When running, the feed hand lever is placed at the suitable notch.

The following examples show the important part played by the auto-starting device: When the car is running normally, at a pressure of, say 220lbs. per square inch, and that, by reason of an impediment on the road, it is necessary to slow down, the steam valve is closed by the driver releasing the foot lever, the pressure rising rapidly to, say 440lbs. and 580lbs. per square inch. The piston B (Fig. 20) rises in its cylinder, and gives place to a quantity of water, which increases should the car continue to remain at a standstill.

When the driver comes to a gradient, he charges the accumulator in advance, by letting the boiler feed increase slightly more than is necessary, and by causing the steam to be wire-drawn on its passage through the steam valve. To do this he releases the foot lever slightly. The steam produced not being all used, the steam pressure rises, and the accumulator is charged. The gradient can thus be mounted with a reserve of energy. When the car has to remain at a standstill for any length of time, the device is also made to act in the same way, but in this case the driver closes the stop-cock E before leaving the car, and he feeds the boiler by a few strokes of the hand pump, before using the pressure in the device on opening the stop-cock when resuming the run. When the car has completed its service, and the fires are to be put out, the accumulator is charged to its maximum, and the stop-cock, E, closed.

The lubricator is shown in Figs. 21 and 22. It is worked from the motor or from any part of the car mechanism, and stops therefore when the car is at a standstill. It can be regulated to work under pressures varying from 15lbs. to 375lbs. per square inch. It consists of an oil receiver, which contains the spindle worked by a ratchet wheel; and of a hollow piston, fitted with a cam, in which are cut suction and delivery

ports. The flow of oil is regulated, for pressure, by acting on a piston weighted by a spring, the quantity distributed

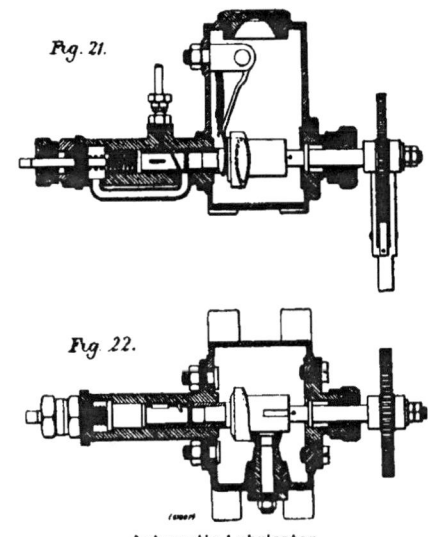

Fig. 21.

Fig. 22.

Automatic Lubricator

depending, as usual, upon the speed of the ratchet wheel.

A new Serpollet steam car, or one that has been out of use for some time, is started working in the following manner: The burners are first heated for about five minutes by burning a small quantity of alcohol that has been poured round them, and when the pressure over the surface of the kerosene in the kerosene tank has been raised to about 1lb., the hydrocarbon is led down to the burners. No smoke is discharged when the burners have been suitably heated. The driver then takes his seat and presses down the foot lever which works the steam valve, giving a few strokes with the hand pump, to warm the cylinders and start the motor. He continues to feed the boiler with the hand pump until the car has reached a certain speed, by reason of the automatic feed coming into play. The handle which regulates the working of the feed pumps is then placed in the notch corresponding to the rate of speed required. Slowing down, as above mentioned, can be obtained by wire-drawing the steam to the motor; or the steam valve foot lever is released and the brake set. The boiler valve is weighted for a pressure of 375lbs. per square inch; this comparatively low pressure for a Serpollet boiler is due to the caution of the French Government authorities. All the levers and instruments are within easy reach, or within sight, of the driver. When the car is running the pressure in the kerosene receiver is maintained constant—from 1.5lbs. to 8lbs.—by a few strokes of the special pump above referred to, in order to obtain the right utilisation of the fuel. The driver has always to use the hand feed pump sparingly, as it does not deliver water to the boiler in proportion as kerosene is supplied to the burners.

The Serpollet cars are not free from mishaps any more than those of other systems. The burners may work badly; the water feed may be insufficient, and the needle valve may remain open, causing water to flow to the tank; pipe joints may get loose and pump valves fail to act. But all these defects can easily be made good, and as the car is provided with hand as well as automatic feed, a run can always be completed should the automatic device get out of order. The high speed obtained with the Serpollet cars is due to the fact that the amount of steam produced is always that required by the motor; this enables them, as stated, to master steep gradients without difficulty.

As the use of methylated spirits for fuel is gaining ground rapidly every day, the results given by a Serpollet car, the boiler of which was fitted up specially for burning methylated spirits, will be found of interest. The car in question, apart from the boiler, was of the usual type, of 12 horse-power, to seat four persons; but besides the condenser, it carried also a ribbed radiator. With two persons, the average speed works out at 35¼ miles per hour; on a level the speed often reached 52 miles. The total water consumption for a run of 81¼ miles was 41.8 pints, showing that the car could run 310 miles without having to renew the feed water supply. The consumption of methylated spirits, including two experiments for lighting the burners, amounted to 96.8 pints. A pint of methylated spirits, costing 1.9d., the cost works out at 2¼d. per mile. With ordinary kerosene, costing 1.7d. per pint, the consumption is 1 pint per mile (1 litre for 8 kilometres), equal, therefore, to 1.7d. per mile. The higher expenditure of methylated spirits is explained by the fact that high racing speeds were maintained.

We illustrate in Figs. 23 and 24, Plate XLII, and in Figs. 25 and 26, Plate XLIII, various views reproduced from photographs, and showing respectively the frame and mechanism of a Serpollet steam car; a Serpollet steam car for long-distance travelling; and the latest type of high-speed Serpollet steam cars.

ELECTRIC CRANES*

By Philip Dawson

FOURTH ARTICLE

CRANE MOTORS

For general work, the continuous current series wound traction type of motor is the most suitable for operating cranes, and we will, therefore, first examine the various classes of this form as usually adapted to the special purpose. In unloading ships it is essential that at first the movement should be very gradual, so as to prevent the wrenching of ropes, or the shaking loose of sacks or cases, which may form the load of a sling. This necessitates a practically constant acceleration from first starting, until the maximum speed has been attained. It is also necessary to have absolute control of the lifting and turning speeds, as well as to be able to start and stop very rapidly when at high speeds. In other words, there must be perfect regulation and control, and this must be effected by as simple an operating device as possible. In order to attain the greatest efficiency, and to reduce wear and tear, the gear clutches should be as few, and transmission as simple, as possible. The motors and controllers must be so designed as to resist continuous wear, and they must be enclosed in such a way as not to be affected by dust or moisture. In this application, as in many others, the qualities which the crane motor has to fulfil are identical with those required in traction work. The efficiency, of course, must be as high as possible, so as to reduce the energy consumption to a minimum. The arrangements for lifting and slewing should be commanded by only a few regulating handles; there should certainly be not more than two such levers, and, preferably, only one, so as to allow the operator to give his undivided attention to what is going on below, and to enable him to rapidly execute the necessary manœuvres. The braking arrangements should always be absolutely under his

command, and there should be safety devices arranged in such a way that it is impossible for the load to drop accidentally. The demand on crane motors differs from those for traction in that power is only required for short periods; the energy consumed varies with the loads lifted; the driving apparatus should be such as only to need energy during the period of lifting or slewing; when loading or standing still, there should be no losses or leakage of power. It is also essential that the lifting speed should be highest with no load, that it should decrease until the maximum load is reached, and that this should be ensured automatically and without loss. Electricity is the only motive power which fulfils these numerous requirements.

In some electric cranes all the movements are effected by means of one motor, and speed regulation and variation depend on gearing; others have two or more motors—one for each motion—in these the speed regulation and reversing are done electrically.

In the first case the motor is generally shunt wound, and runs at full speed all the time, whether the loads are being lifted or not. In the second, the motors are generally series wound, and only take current when doing actual work.

Cranes are sometimes, with advantage, supplied either with two series wound motors for lifting purposes or with one series wound motor with a double armature winding. This is particularly convenient when they are used both for lifting loads which can only be raised at a comparatively slow speed, such as long rails or baulks of timber, and for handling cases or sacks that should be rapidly lifted. The crane which is thus equipped has the advantage of two economical speeds at which it can be run, that is to say, with two motors in series, or with two motors or armatures, in parallel. Theoretically, it is quite possible, either by the use of shunt motors or three-phase motors, to turn the current into the line when the load is being lowered, but

* See Traction and Transmission, Vol. IV, pages 145 and 247; Vol. V, page 47.

practically there is little or no advantage to be gained by this; the same experience has been found to apply in traction-work.

In the cases where it is necessary to work where the temperature is high. Slow speed motors are to be preferred, as, by their means, rope drums of large diameter can be used without introducing an excessive amount of

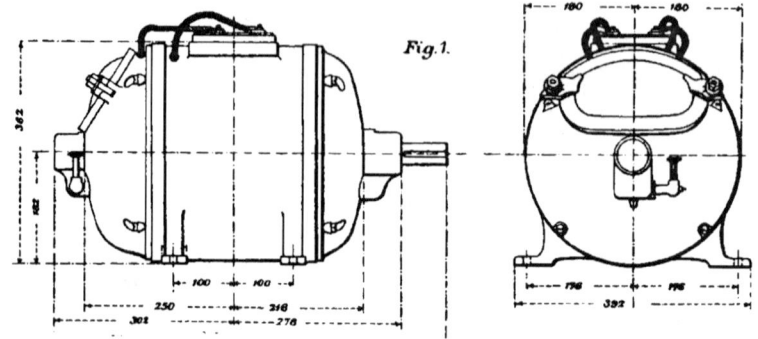

U.E.G. 2.5 Horse-power Gearless Motor, 110, 220, 500 Volts—Type W.D. 2/750 (see Table I)

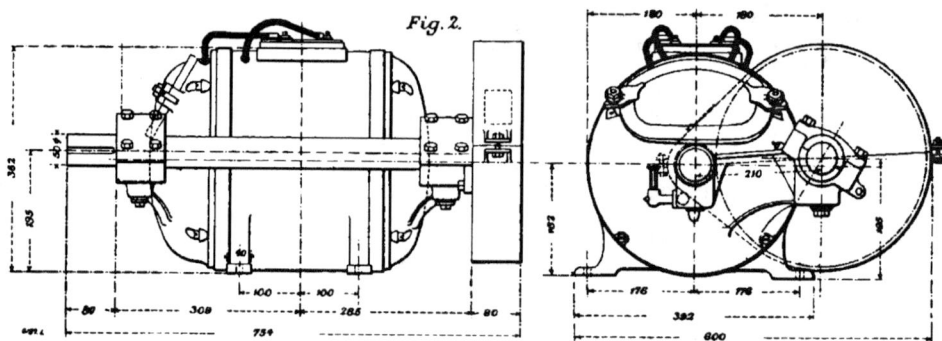

U.E.G. 2.5 Horse-power Direct Acting Geared Motor, 110, 220, 500 Volts—Type W.D. 2/750 (see Table I)

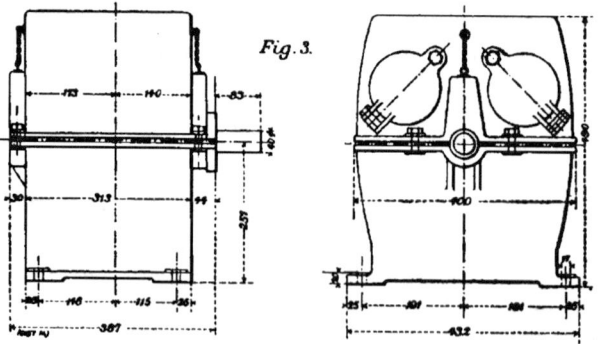

U.E.G. 5 Horse-power Gearless Motor, 220 and 500 Volts—Type W.D. 5/400; 7 Horse-power, 775 Revolutions—Type W.D. 7/700 (see Table I)

the crane rapidly and at a large number of cycles per hour, the motors should be larger than for general work. This also applies where the motors have to work in places

gearing. Furthermore, the starting period is shorter, and the strain on the motors is therefore lighter.

Crane motors should be of the enclosed

traction type, the mechanical parts, as mentioned before, being, if anything, stronger than for traction work. The motor cases are generally made in halves, so that the armatures can be taken out, the joint of the casing being made in such a way as to be absolutely water and dust proof. The motors have carbon brushes, and, when

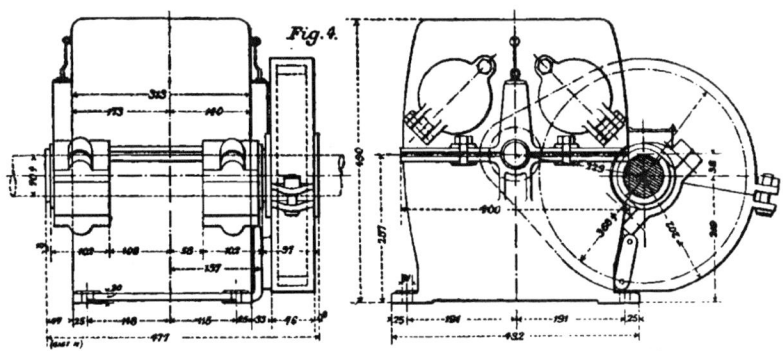

U.E.G. Geared Motor, 220, 250 Volts, 5 Horse-power—W.D. 5/400; 7 Horse-power—W.D. 7/700 (see Table I)

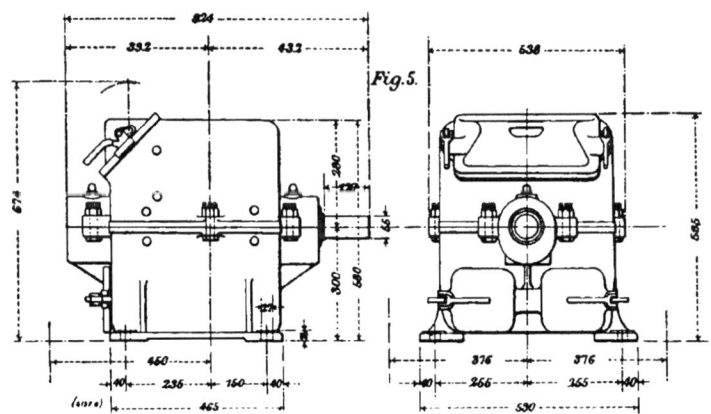

U.E.G. 16 Horse-power Gearless Motor, 750 Revolutions, 110, 220, 500 Volts—W.D. 16/600 (see Table I)

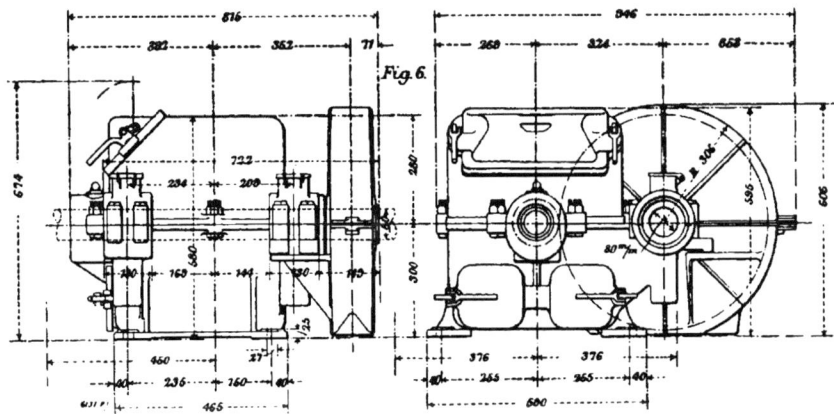

U.E.G. 16 Horse-power Geared Motor, 110, 220, 500 Volts—W.D. 16/600 (see Table I)

properly designed, there is no trouble with the commutators, which require practically no attention. This fact has already been abundantly proved in traction work.

To illustrate the foregoing general principles I have made a large selection of standard types by various manufacturers, and on the following pages give diagrams

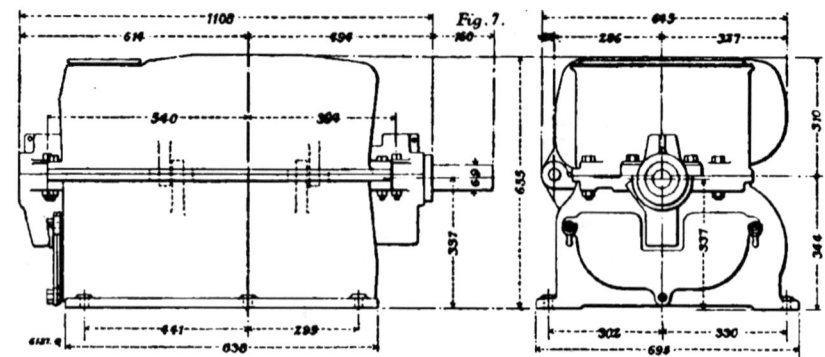

U.E.G. Gearless Motor, 110, 220, 500 Volts; 24 Horse-power, 250 Revolutions; 35 Horse-power, 340 Revolutions; 52 Horse-power, 530 Revolutions (see Table I)

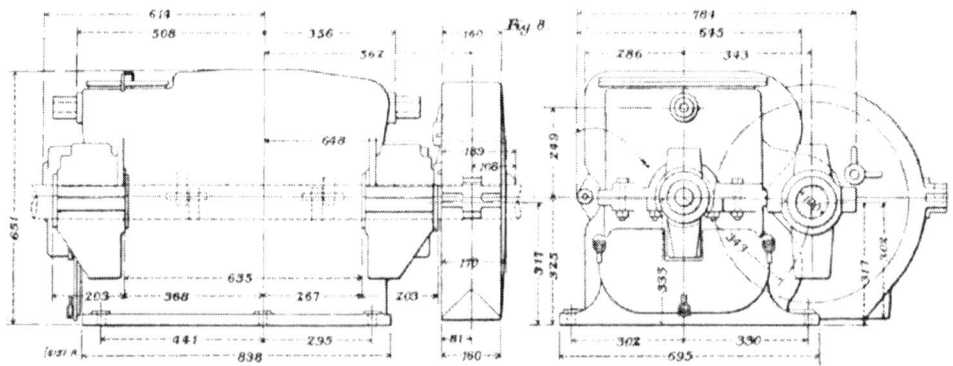

U.E.G. Geared Motor, 110, 220, 500 Volts; 24 Horse-power, 35 Horse-power, 52 Horse-power (see Table I)

TABLE I.—U.E.G. CONTINUOUS CURRENT CRANE MOTORS

(See Figs. 1 to 8, pages 189, 190, and 191)

Type.	Rated Brake Horse-power.	Speed in Revs. per Min. at Rated Load.	Torque at Rated Load.		Kilowatts Supplied at Rated Load.	Efficiency per Cent. at Rated Load.
			Metre-kilo-grammes.	Foot-pounds.		
W.D. 2/750	2.5	800	2.24	16.2	2.25	81.9
W.D. 5/400	5.0	525	6.82	49.2	4.64	79.5
W.D. 7/700	7.0	775	6.48	46.8	6.34	81.2
W.D. 8/400	8.0	400	14.35	103.5	7.36	80.9
W.D. 12/700	12.0	875	9.80	70.9	10.70	82.6
W.D. 16/600	16.0	750	15.25	110.5	14.50	81.1
W.D. 18/350	18.0	400	32.20	233.0	16.20	81.7
W.D. 26/450	26.0	540	34.50	249.0	23.00	83.25
W.D. 24/200	24.0	250	68.7	496.0	22.00	80.03
W.D. 35/275	35.0	340	74.0	535.0	33.00	78.10
W.D. 52/450	52.0	530	70.3	508.0	45.00	85.1

and data of the most advanced electric crane motor practice. A series of types of continuous current motors specially designed by the Union Elektricitäts-Gesellschaft of Berlin for crane purposes are illustrated in Figs. 1 to 8, pages 189, 190, and 191; particulars of these will be found in Table I. Figs. 9 and 10, pages 192 and 193, with the accompanying Tables II, III, and IV, on the same pages, give the sizes and weights of the standard types of crane motors built by the Lahmeyer Company, of Frankfort.

Figs. 11 and 12, page 194, show two types of crane motors as manufactured by the British Thomson-Houston Company, while Fig. 13, page 193, shows the characteristic curves of a motor built by the same firm.

Figs. 14 to 18, page 195, are the characteristic curves of crane motors of the Westinghouse Company, ranging from 2 to 20 horse-power rated capacity; other diagrams, and some ot the motors to which these curves refer are illustrated by the outline sketches given in Fig. 21, page 195, and Figs. 19 to 23, Plate XLIV.

Figs. 24, 25, and 26, page 196, are

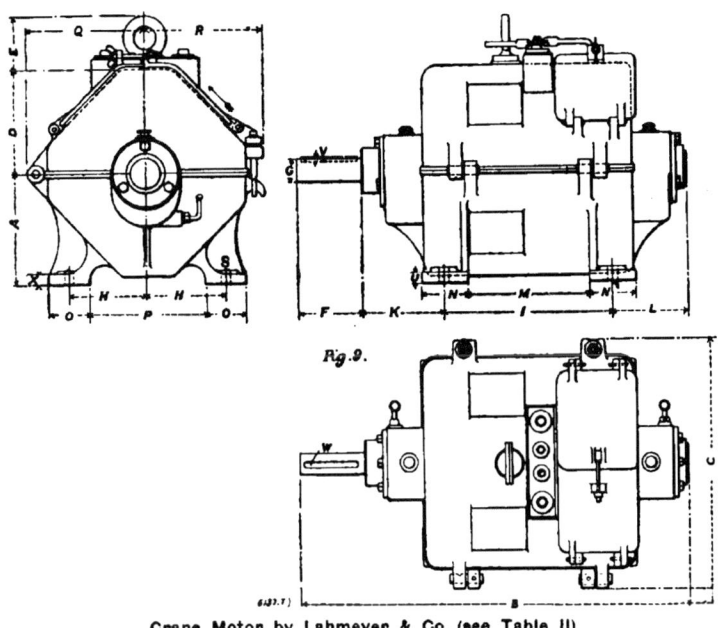

Fig. 9.

Crane Motor by Lahmeyer & Co. (see Table II)

TABLE II.—TYPES OF GEARLESS CRANE MOTORS BY LAHMEYER & CO., FRANKFORT (see Fig. 9)
(Dimensions in Millimetres)

Type.	A	B	C	D	E	F	G	H	I	K	L	M	N	O	P	Q	R	S	T	U	V	W
Tr. 2/900	165	580	352	145	80	70	28	120	220	144	146	150	60	60	175	175	177	16	20	16	3	12
Tr. 4/800	195	617	436	185	82	85	32	152	305	122	105	215	80	70	225	218	218	16	25	20	3	12
Tr. 7/700	245	780	545	230	100	100	40	145	390	155	135	300	90	90	200	275	270	20	25	20	3.5	15
Tr. 10/600	280	938	614	260	112	150	50	182	380	220	188	275	105	105	260	306	308	23	30	25	4	18
Tr. 15/525	300	1068	666	280	140	175	55	220	460	230	203	330	130	115	325	336	330	27	40	30	4	19
Tr. 20/450	335	1158	734	310	172	190	60	240	570	215	183	440	130	130	350	372	362	30	45	35	4.5	20
Tr. 25/400	370	1266	810	345	172	220	70	260	620	230	196	480	140	140	380	415	395	35	45	40	5	22
Tr. 35/320	410	1442	928	402	172	245	80	290	740	250	207	590	150	150	430	460	468	40	55	45	5.5	25

TABLE III.—LAHMEYER CRANE MOTORS

Type.	B.H.P.	Revs. per Minute.	Kilowatts at Terminals.	Weight in Kilo-grammes.
Tr. 2/900	2.5	900	2.55	90
Tr. 4/800	5.0	800	4.7	165
Tr. 7/700	6.0	500	5.4	300
Tr. 7/700	8.5	700	7.6	300
Tr. 10/600	12.0	600	10.6	400
Tr. 10/600	14.0	750	12.4	400
Tr. 15/525	18.0	525	15.6	600
Tr. 20/450	25.0	450	20.5	800
Tr. 25/400	30.0	400	25.5	1,100
Tr. 35/320	40.0	320	35.0	1,500

characteristic curves of motors manufactured by the Electric Construction Company of Wolverhampton.

Messrs. Siemens Bros. make a special type of motor adapted for cranes. The frame is of cast steel, rectangular in shape, with cast-iron bearings supported on large circular seats bolted to either end of the frame. The lugs for the holding-down bolts are in recesses at each corner of the frame, and so do not increase the over-all space required. The circular seats of the bearing enable the motor either to be placed upon

Plate XLIV

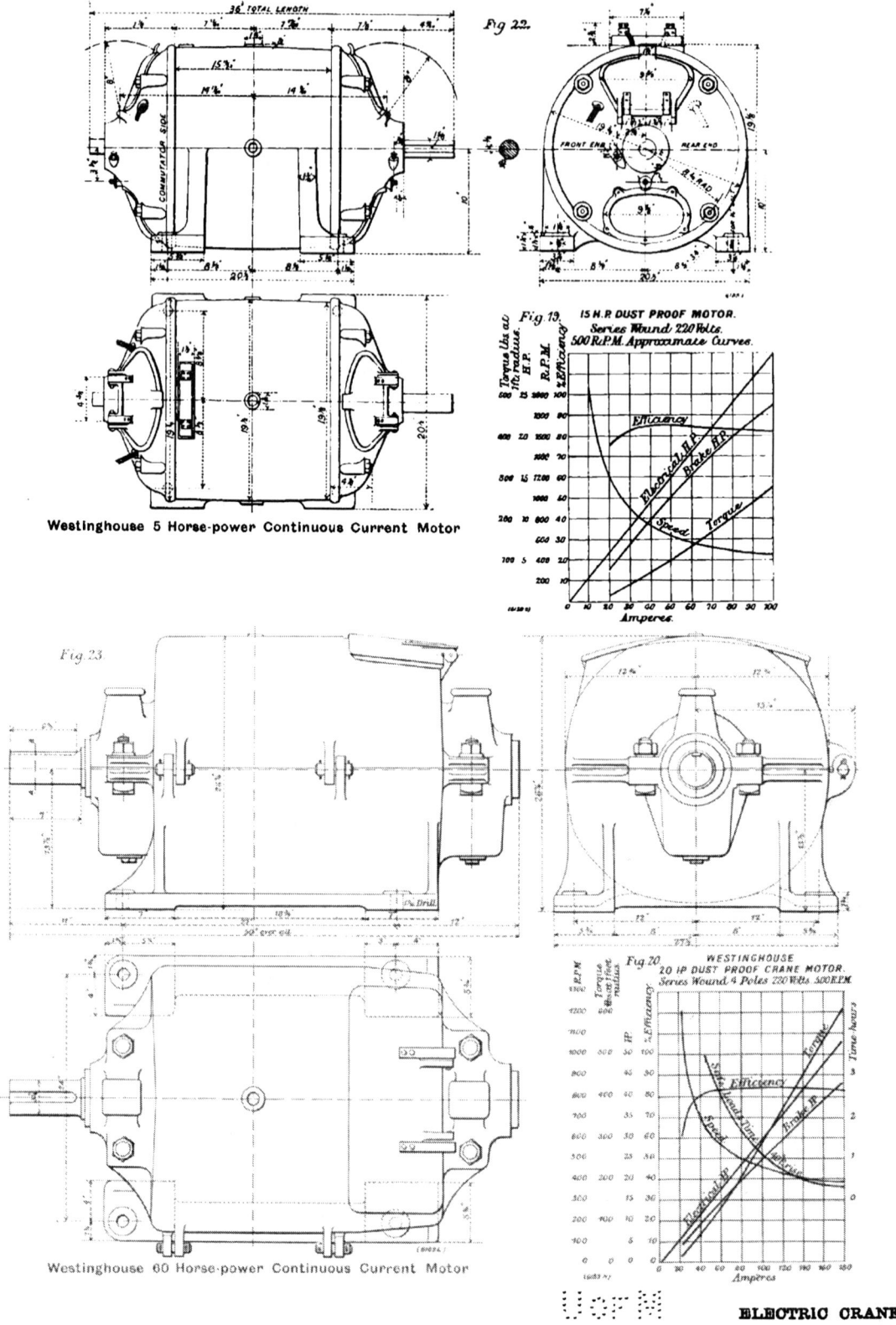

Fig 22.

Westinghouse 5 Horse-power Continuous Current Motor

Fig. 13. 15 H.P. DUST PROOF MOTOR.
Series Wound 220 Volts.
500 R.P.M. Approximate Curves.

Fig 23

Westinghouse 60 Horse-power Continuous Current Motor

Fig 20. WESTINGHOUSE
20 HP DUST PROOF CRANE MOTOR.
Series Wound 4 Poles 250 Volts 500 R.P.M.

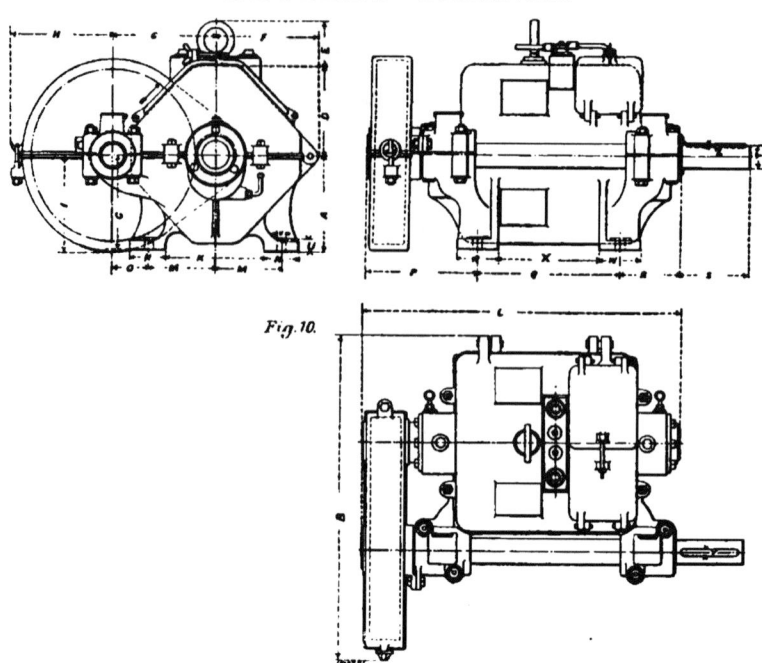

Fig. 10.

Geared Crane Motor by Lahmeyer & Co. (see Table IV)

TABLE IV.—TYPES OF GEARED CRANE MOTORS BY LAHMEYER & CO., FRANKFORT (see Fig. 10)
(Dimensions in Millimetres)

Type.	A	B	C	D	E	F	G	H	I	K	L	M	N	O	P	Q	R	S	T	U	V	W	X	Y	Z
Tr. 2/900	165	570	160	145	80	175	180	215	180	175	580	120	60	60	214	220	124	110	40	20	16	60	150	15	3.5
Tr. 4/800	195	713	190	185	82	218	230	265	225	225	612	152	70	78	202	305	102	150	50	25	16	80	215	18	4
Tr. 7/700	245	865	240	230	100	275	280	310	270	200	775	145	90	135	250	390	130	190	60	25	20	90	300	20	4.5
Tr. 10/600	280	971	275	260	112	306	320	345	302	260	903	182	105	138	335	380	195	220	70	30	23	105	275	22	5
Tr. 15/525	300	1066	295	280	140	336	360	370	325	325	1023	220	115	140	360	460	205	250	80	40	27	130	330	25	5.5
Tr. 20/450	335	1139	330	310	172	372	372	395	340	350	1108	240	130	132	355	570	190	275	90	45	30	130	440	28	6
Tr. 25/400	370	1231	365	345	172	415	410	406	362	380	1226	260	140	150	448	620	195	290	95	45	35	140	480	30	6.5
Tr. 35/320	410	1365	405	402	172	468	465	432	402	430	1395	290	150	175	448	740	195	310	100	55	40	150	590	30	6.5

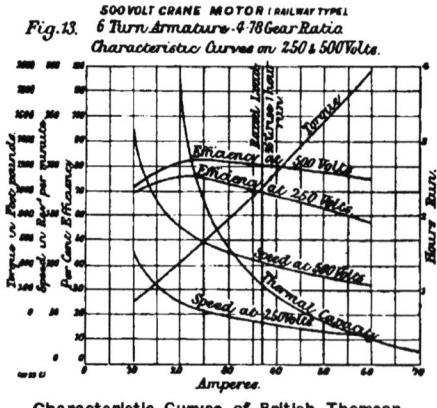

Fig. 13.

500 VOLT CRANE MOTOR (RAILWAY TYPE)
6 Turn Armature - 4.78 Gear Ratio
Characteristic Curves on 250 & 500 Volts.

Characteristic Curves of British Thomson-Houston Motor

the vertical face of a girder or suspended from supports placed above it. The bearings are ring lubricated. The poles are rectangular in section, and are cast solid to the frame. They are fitted with laminated pole shoes of thin sheet steel riveted together. These pole shoes distribute the magnetic flux, and also serve to retain the field coils in position. They are secured to the frame by means of bolts passing through the latter; all field coils are form wound, and can easily be removed. The armature is of the iron-clad type and slotted. The ends of the coils are supported on cast - iron flanges. The motor is so designed that, after an ordinary day's work on cranes or capstans, none of its parts will attain a temperature of more than 70degs. Fahr. above the surrounding atmosphere.

Table V, and Table VI, page 196, give the output, speed, torque, weight, etc., of Messrs. Siemens & Halske's continuous current crane

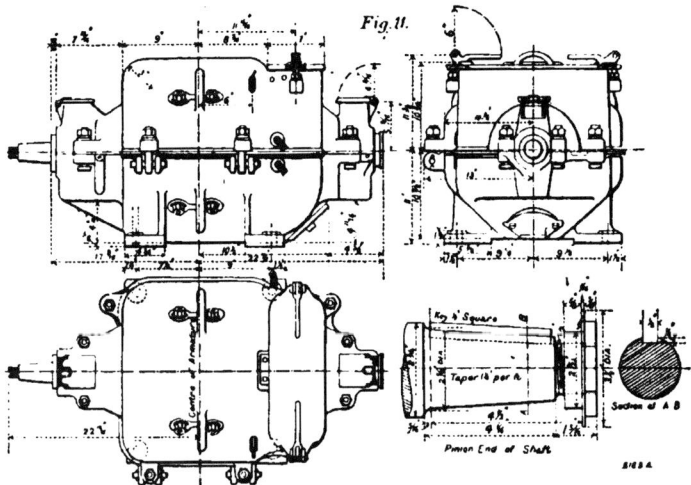

Crane Motor by the British Thomson-Houston Company

The properties of series continuous current motors have already been referred to. These properties are well illustrated by the following figures, which apply to the series wound crane motors manufactured by Lahmeyer,

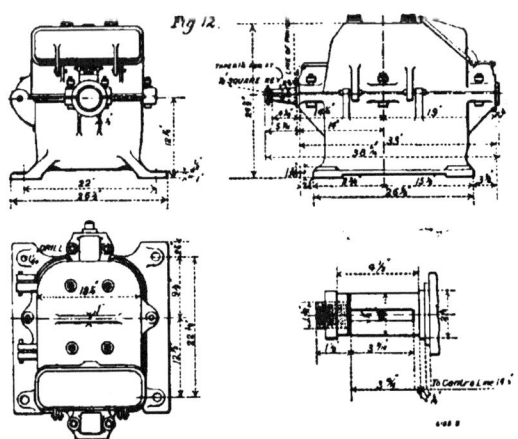

Crane Motor by the British Thomson-Houston Company

motors. Table VI, in conjunction with the outline drawing, Fig. 27, page 196, gives the dimensions of these motors.

Tables VII and VIII, pages 197 and 198, and Figs. 28 to 32 give some particulars and characteristic curves of some of Messrs. Siemens Bros.' standard crane motors.

Table IX, page 195, gives a few particulars of Messrs. Schuckert's continuous current motors.

TABLE V.—SIEMENS & HALSKE CONTINUOUS CURRENT CRANE MOTORS.—100 TO 500 VOLTS
(see Fig. 27, page 196)

Type.	Torque in Metre-kilogrammes.	Low Speed.		High Speed.		Weight in Kilogrammes.
		Brake Horse-power.	Revolutions per Minute.	Brake Horse-power.	Revolutions per Minute.	
K 9	3.2 2.8	2.5	560 635	4	840 950	150
K 11	6.4 5.6	5	560 635	7.5	840 950	260
K 13	10.2 9.0	8	560 635	12	840 950	370
K 15	15.3 13.5	12	560 635	18	840 950	500
K 17	28.6 25.3	18	450 510	27	675 770	710
K 19	55.3 48.5	27	350 400	40	525 600	1100
K 22	82.0 71.6	40	350 400	60	525 600	1540
K 26	143 126	60	300 340	90	450 510	2200

of Frankfort. All the figures are in per cent. of the rated output, speed, and torque.

Output ...	25	40	50	70	90	100	120	140	150	170	190	200
Revs. per minute	240	170	150	122	107	100	89	83	82	80	77	73
Torque ...	6.5	20	31	59	88	100	130	161	180	210	244	260

The rated capacity of Messrs. Lahmeyer's motors is that at which the motor can run

TABLE IX.—ENCLOSED SERIES WOUND DIRECT CURRENT SHUCKERT CRANE MOTORS

Rated Brake Horse-power.	Input in Kilowatts.	Kilogramme-Metres, Torque.	Normal Speed (revs. per min.)	Minimum Speed (revs. per min.)		Weight of Motor (kilogrammes)
				220 Volts.	550 Volts.	
1.3	1.6	.52	1800	500	...	85
2.2	2.3	.92	1700	450	...	125
2.2	2.3	.92	1700	...	700	125
3.4	3.3	1.48	1650	400	...	150
3.4	3.3	1.48	1650	...	600	150
4.5	4.2	2.03	1600	...	500	200
8.0	7.2	3.7	1550	...	480	240
12.0	10.6	5.7	1500	...	470	300
16.0	14.0	8.2	1400	...	435	360
20.5	17.8	10.9	1350	...	420	460

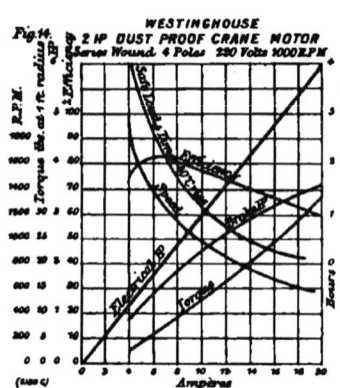

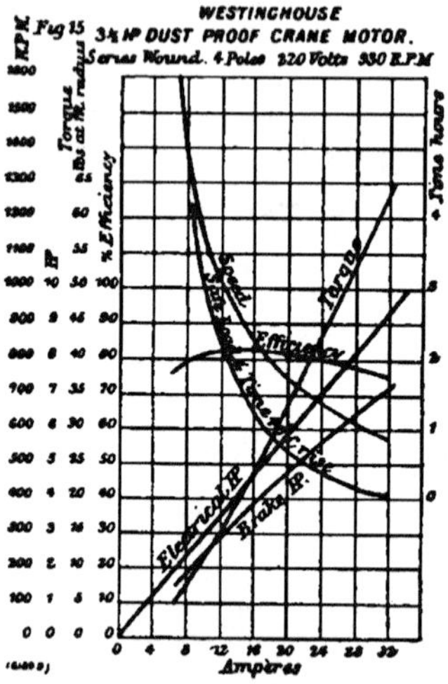

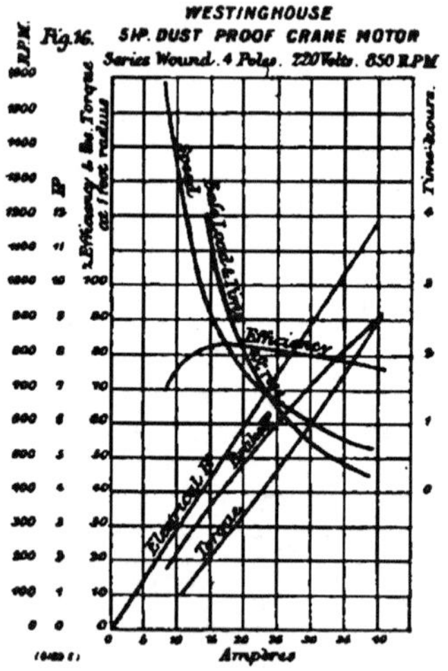

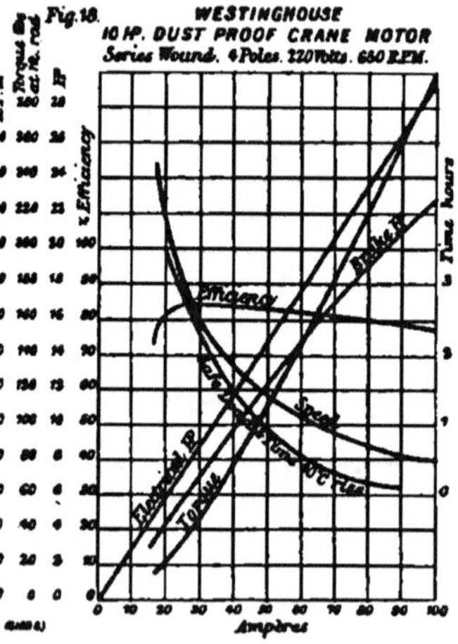

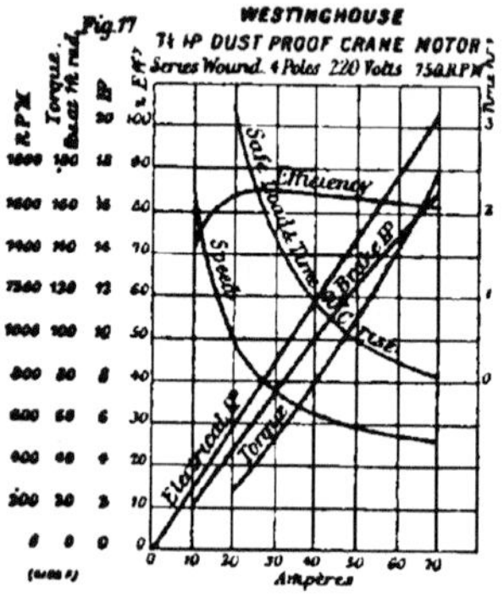

Fig. 14.
WESTINGHOUSE
2 HP DUST PROOF CRANE MOTOR
Series Wound. 4 Poles. 220 Volts 1000 R.P.M.

Fig. 15.
WESTINGHOUSE
3½ HP DUST PROOF CRANE MOTOR.
Series Wound. 4 Poles 220 Volts 830 R.P.M

Fig. 16.
WESTINGHOUSE
5 HP. DUST PROOF CRANE MOTOR
Series Wound. 4 Poles. 220 Volts. 650 R.P.M.

Fig. 18.
WESTINGHOUSE
10 HP. DUST PROOF CRANE MOTOR
Series Wound. 4 Poles. 220 Volts. 650 R.P.M.

Fig. 17.
WESTINGHOUSE
7½ HP DUST PROOF CRANE MOTOR
Series Wound. 4 Poles 220 Volts 750 R.P.M.

Fig 21.

Figs. 14 to 18.—Characteristic Curves of Westinghouse Motors

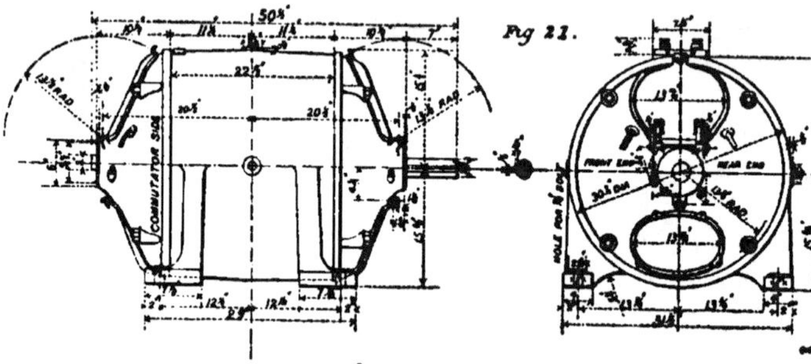

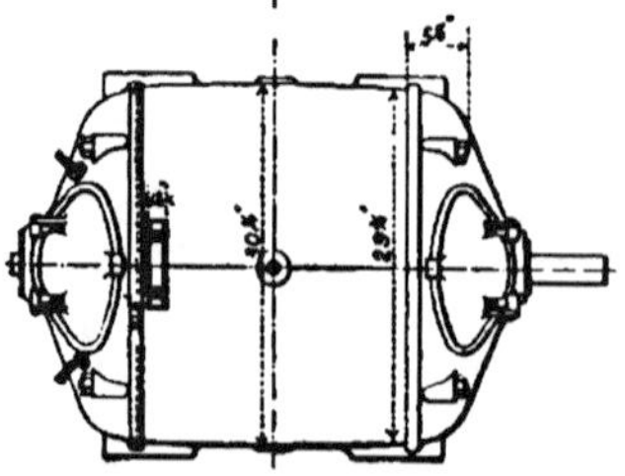

Fig. 21.—20 Horse-power Crane Motor by the Westinghouse Company

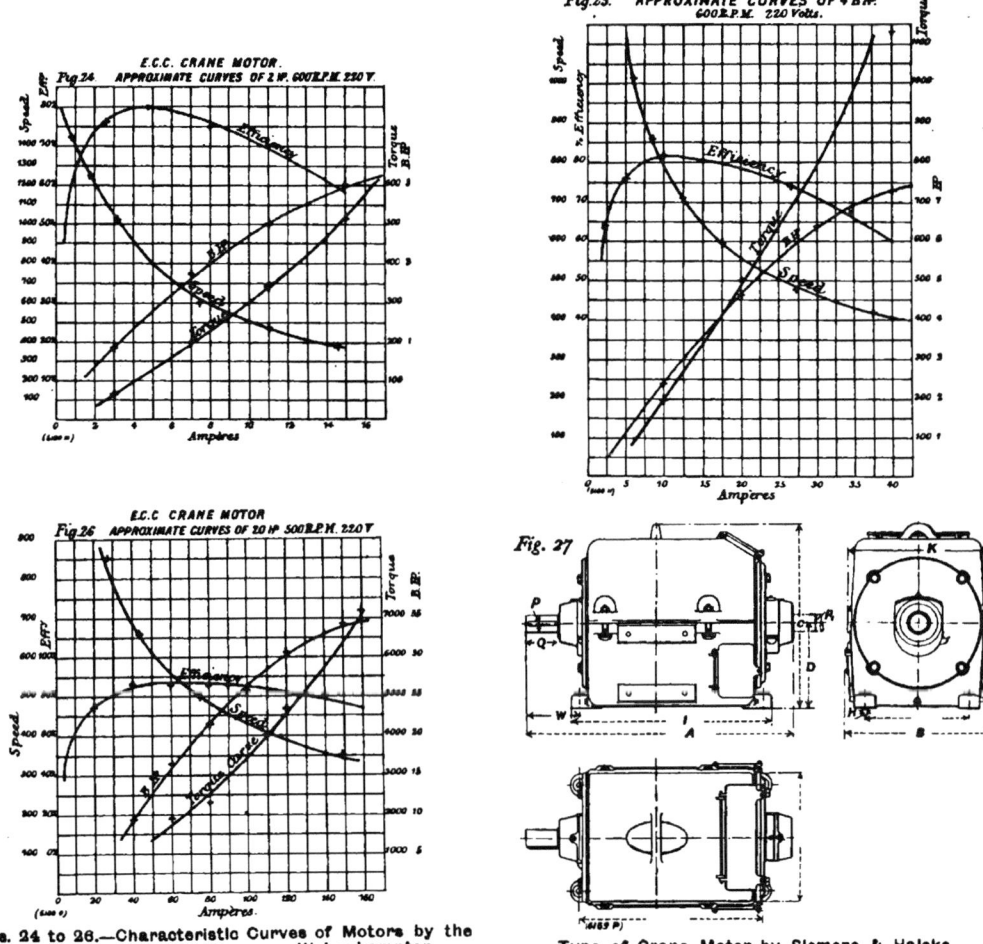

Figs. 24 to 26.—Characteristic Curves of Motors by the Electric Construction Company, Wolverhampton

Type of Crane Motor by Siemens & Halske

TABLE VI.—SIEMENS & HALSKE CRANE MOTORS (see Fig. 27)
(Dimensions in Millimetres)

Type.	A	B	C	D	H	I	K	P	Q	P₁	Key.		W
											Width.	Thick-ness.	
K 9	635	320	427	195	20	529	310	35	75	30	9	5	120
K 11	746	360	525	245	20	558	340	40	85	40	11	6	145
K 13	800	412	570	270	23	605	396	45	100	45	11	6	152
K 15	858	478	612	292	23	672	453	50	115	50	12	7	180
K 17	935	525	680	325	23	754	502	55	130	55	15	8	180
K 19	1,158	600	759	355	23	905	580	65	145	60	18	9	224
K 22	1,288	695	851	400	26	972	650	75	160	70	20	11	258
K 26	1,395	775	961	450	26	1,082	752	85	180	80	22	12	270

for one hour without heating more than 60degs. Cent. above the surrounding temperature. This will be noticed to be a much higher temperature than is usually admitted, and indicates the care that must be exercised when comparing motors of different makes, and the great want that exists for standardisation.

Size of Motor for Cranes.—The motors adopted, although they may be economically operated, owing to the short continuous runs to which they are subjected, must be of ample mechanical strength; in fact, as already said, they are very similar to traction motors, with the exception that they may suitably be mechanically stronger in proportion to their rating.

To calculate the size of lifting motor required for any particular weight and speed of lifting, is very simple. The combined efficiency of the gearing, etc., may be put at 80 per cent., which is sufficiently accurate for most cases.

Let W = weight to be lifted in tons.

S = lifting speed in feet per minute.

Then work done in lifting the load = W × S foot-tons per minute $= \frac{W \times S \times 2{,}240}{33{,}000}$ horse-power.

Hence rated brake horse-power of motor required $= \frac{W \times S \times 2{,}240}{33{,}000 \times .8}$

Thus, if W = 3 tons, and S = 200ft. per minute, the motor would be $\frac{3 \times 200 \times 2{,}240}{33{,}000 \times .8}$ brake horse-power, or 51 brake horse-power (approximate).

Assuming that the diameter of the winding drum is 2½ft., then to obtain a lifting speed of 200ft. per minute, the speed of the drum must be $\frac{200}{\pi \times 2.5}$ revolutions per minute, or 25½ revolutions per minute. Thus, when the speed of the motor is known, the ratio of the gearing required can be settled.

Three-phase Motors.—In cases where the cranes form a very small portion of the load, and where this is distributed over large areas necessitating polyphase transmission, it may

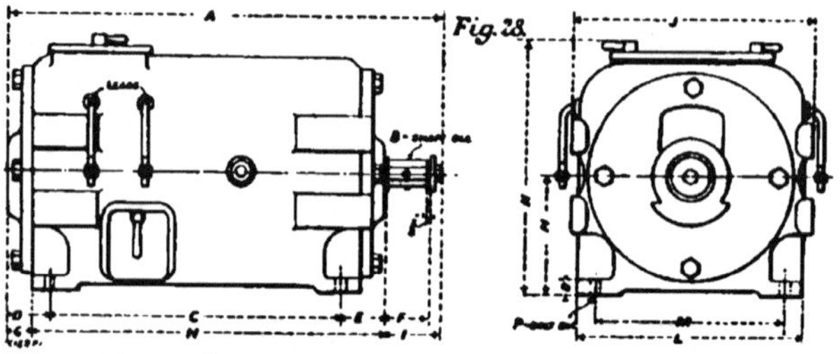

Type of Crane Motor by Messrs. Siemens Bros. (see Table VII)

TABLE VII.—SIEMENS' GEARLESS CRANE MOTORS. TYPE "C," CONTINUOUS CURRENT (see Fig. 28)

(Dimensions in Inches)

Type.	A	B	C	D	E	F	G	H	I	J	K	L	M	N	O	P	Keyway.
C 8	25⅝	1½	17¼	2½	2⅝	2¼	1½	19¼	4⅞	14½	14¾	13¼	11¼	7	13/16	¾	½ by ⅛
C 9¾	31 1/16	1¾	21½	2 13/16	2 15/16	3	1 13/16	23½	5¾	16¾	16¾	15½	13½	8	⅞	¾	9/16 by 9/64
C 11	34 15/16	1⅞	24⅛	2 15/16	3 11/16	4	1 15/16	26⅛	6⅞	18½	18½	17¼	15¼	8⅞	1	¾	9/16 by 9/64
C 13	38 1/16	2⅜	26⅜	3⅛	3¼	4½	1⅞	28⅞	7 5/16	21	21 9/16	19¾	17¼	10¼	1	1	⅝ by 5/32
C 15.1	42⅜	2⅜	27⅞	4	4¼	5	2½	30⅞	8¾	24¼	25	23	20	12	1⅛	1	¾ by 3/16
C 15.2	49⅜	3	35⅛	4	4¼	5	2½	38⅛	8¾	24¾	25⅛	23¼	20¼	12	1⅛	1	⅞ by 7/32

TABLE X.—UNION ELEKTRICITÄTS-GESELLSCHAFT THREE-PHASE CRANE MOTORS (see Figs. 33 and 34)

Type of Motor.	Brake Horse-power.	Speed in Revolutions per Minute.	Torque in Metre-kilogrammes.	Cos φ.	Weight in Kilogrammes.
JNK 4— 1·1500	1.6	1300	0.9	0.87	60
JNK 4— 2·1500	3.2	1350	1.7	0.87	85
JNK 4— 3·1500	4.8	1365	2.6	0.87	120
JNK 4— 5·1500	8	1400	4.2	0.87	140
JNK 6— 5·1000	8	900	6.2	0.83	240
JNK 4—7.5·1500	12	1420	6.5	0.88	240
JNK 6—7.5·1000	12	900	7.5	0.83	300
JNK 4— 10·1500	16	1420	8.7	0.88	300
JNK 6— 10·1000	16	900	12.8	0.88	350
JNK 4— 15·1500	24	1420	13.0	0.88	400
JNK 6— 15·1000	24	930	18.0	0.88	450
JNK 8— 15· 750	24	700	26.0	0.84	520
JNK 6— 20·1000	32	940	24.0	0.88	600
JNK 8— 20· 750	32	705	34.0	0.85	660
JNK 8— 30· 750	48	710	50.0	0.86	850
JNK 8— 40· 750	64	715	65.0	0.86	1000
JNK 10— 50· 600	80	570	103.0	0.85	1250
JNK 10— 60· 600	96	570	124.0	0.85	1400
JNK 10— 75· 600	120	575	160.0	0.85	1900

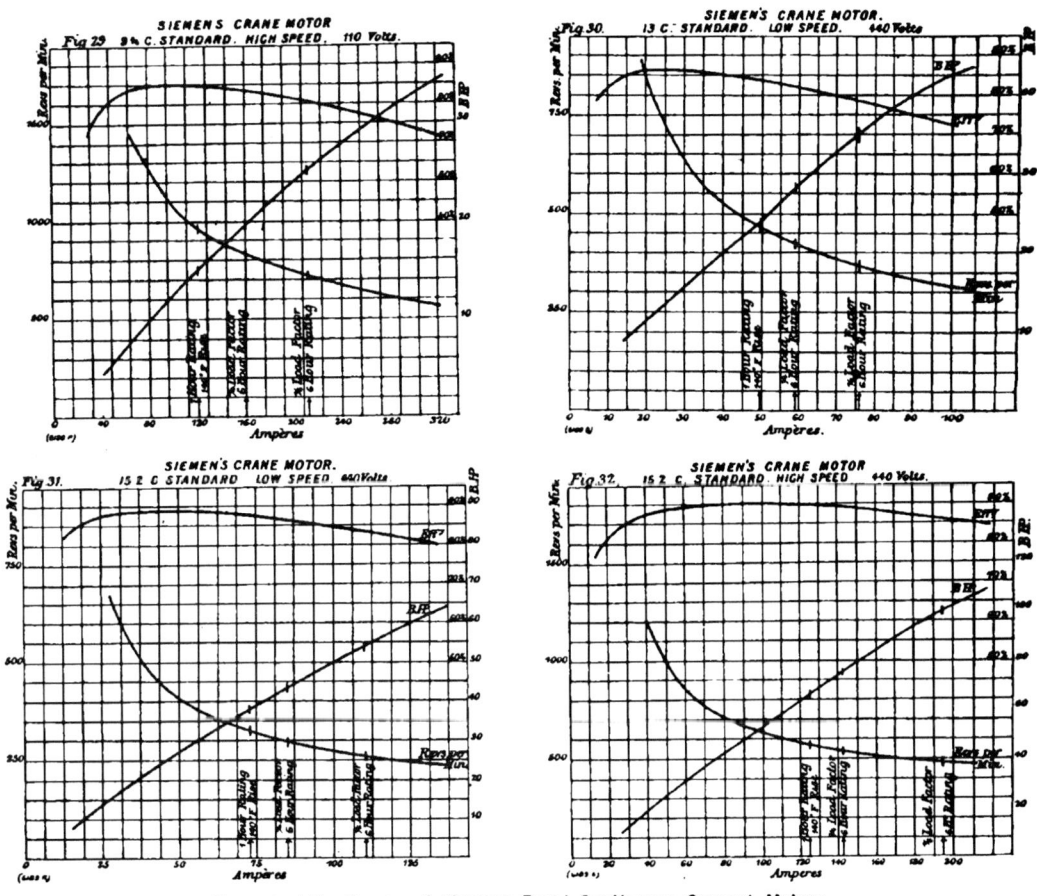

Characteristic Curves of Siemens Bros.' Continuous Current Motors

TABLE VIII.—SIEMENS' GEARLESS CRANE MOTORS. TYPE "C," CONTINUOUS CURRENT
(see Figs. 29 to 32)

Type.	Low Speed Outputs.						Medium Speed Outputs.					
	¼ Load Factor.		½ Load Factor.		¾ Load Factor.		¼ Load Factor.		½ Load Factor.		¾ Load Factor.	
	B.H.P.	Speed.	B.H.P.	Speed.	B.H.P.	Speed.	B.H.P.	Speed.	B.H.P.	Speed.	B.H.P.	Speed.
C 8 }	10	500	8	580	6	700	18	900	14	1020	10	1130
	15	675	10	780	8	900	25	720	19	800	15	1000
C 9¾	15	475	12	540	10	650	35	560	28	670	24	820
C 11	25	420	19	500	15	580	50	525	40	600	33	680
C 13	35	365	28	400	24	480	80	480	62	520	50	570
C 15.1	50	300	40	350	33	370	100	480	75	520	65	550
C 15.2	56	270	45	300	37	320						

The above speeds are for 110, 220, and 440 volts.   For 500 volts, speed will be approximately 10 per cent. higher in each case.

be more economical to use three-phase motors. This is particularly the case in workshops where travelling cranes are used which have continually to move at practically constant speed with occasional stops, from one end of the shop to the other. It need hardly be pointed out that in such cases, even if continuous current motors were used, they

TABLE XI.—UNION ELEKTRICITÄTS - GESELLSCHAFT OPEN TYPE THREE-PHASE CRANE MOTOR WITH SLIP RINGS (see Fig. 33)

(Dimensions in Millimetres)

Type.	A	B	C	D	E	F	G	H	J	K	L	M	N	O	P	Q	R
JNK 4—1-1500	373	198	175	125	50	18	145	175	270	305	140	232	282	10	20	50	25
JNK 4—2-1500	437	240	197	147	50	23	173	209	320	365	165	265	325	13	27	60	30
JNK 4—3-1500	488	265	223	163	60	28	184	224	360	405	185	295	365	13	30	70	35

TABLE XII.—UNION ELEKTRICITÄTS - GESELLSCHAFT OPEN TYPE THREE-PHASE CRANE MOTORS (see Fig. 34)

(Dimensions in Millimetres)

Type.	A	B	C	D	E	F	G	H	J	K	L	M	N	O	P	Q	R
JNK 4- 5-1500	614	324	290	70	173	233	293	30	16	33	430	440	215	225	260	340	420
JNK 6— 5-1000	645	345	300	70	185	245	305	30	16	33	470	480	235	245	270	360	450
JNK 4-7.5-1500	646	345	301	70	185	245	305	30	16	33	470	480	235	245	270	360	450
JNK 6—7.5-1000	690	365	325	70	225	285	345	30	16	33	470	480	235	245	270	360	450
JNK 4—10-1500	695	365	330	70	225	285	345	30	16	33	470	480	235	245	270	360	450
JNK 6—10-1000	667	335	332	80	195	270	345	30	16	33	620	630	310	320	340	460	580
JNK 4—15-1500	792	402	390	70	300	360	420	30	16	33	470	480	235	245	270	360	450
JNK 6—15-1000	715	354	361	90	206	286	366	40	20	43	680	690	340	350	390	520	650
JNK 8—15-750	742	367	375	90	230	310	390	40	20	43	680	690	340	350	390	520	650
JNK 6—20-1000	781	372	409	100	221	301	381	40	23	48	730	740	365	375	420	560	700
JNK 8—20- 750	895	480	415	100	235	315	395	40	23	48	730	740	365	375	420	560	700
JNK 6—30-1000	829	392	437	100	260	341	420	40	23	48	730	740	365	375	420	560	700
JNK 8—30- 750	785	308	477	120	245	345	445	50	23	58	890	900	445	455	510	675	840
JNK 6—40-1000	930	422	508	120	320	401	480	40	23	58	730	740	365	375	420	560	700
JNK 8—40- 750	869	333	536	140	275	375	475	50	26	68	968	979	484	495	560	740	920
JNK 8—50- 750	898	338	560	140	285	385	485	50	26	68	968	979	484	495	560	740	920
JNK 10—50- 600	928	354	574	160	275	375	475	55	26	78	1096	1108	548	560	650	850	1050
JNK 10—60- 600	960	364	596	160	295	395	495	55	26	78	1096	1108	548	560	650	850	1050
JNK 8—75- 750	1101	401	700	200	385	485	585	50	26	78	968	979	484	495	560	740	920
JNK 10—75- 600	1052	402	650	180	305	425	545	65	33	88	1220	1235	610	625	690	920	1150

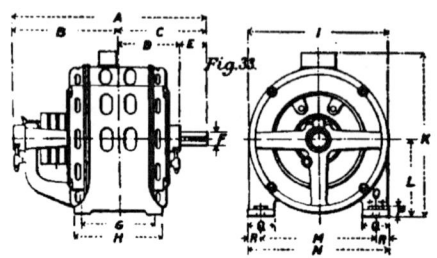 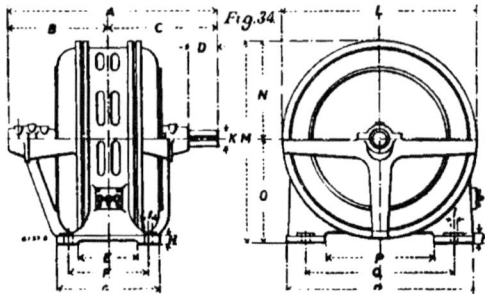

Three-phase Crane Motors, by the Union Elektricitäts-Gesellschaft (see Tables XI and XII)

need not be of the enclosed type, except where they are liable to be damaged by smoke and steam, coal-dust, etc.

The size of the motor is determined by two considerations — the power at which the motor can continuously run, and the maximum torque which it may have to give off. The first case is that where cranes have to be working practically all the time, and where they are heavily forced, having to work at high speeds. This case is met with in steel works, and also in ship-building yards where Goliath cranes have to lift heavy loads through great heights at slow speeds. The second case is generally met with in warehouses and docks, where the motor, after having worked a short time and lifted the load, has time to rest whilst slewing and during lowering. In this case the point to decide in the motor is the maximum torque

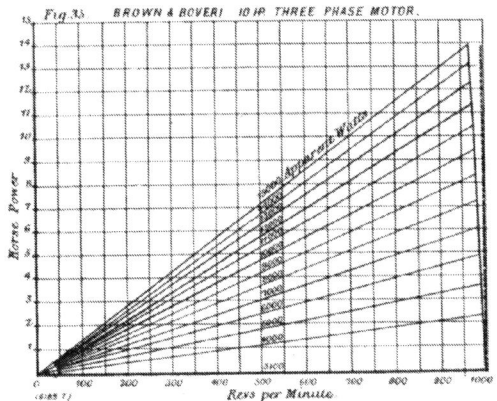

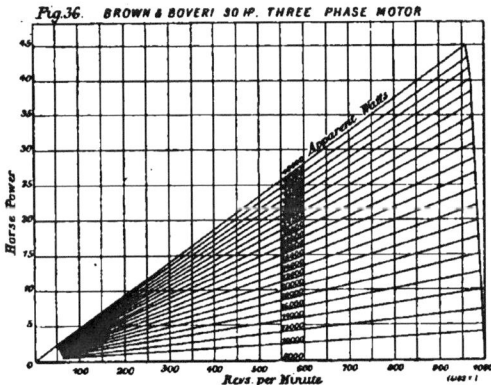

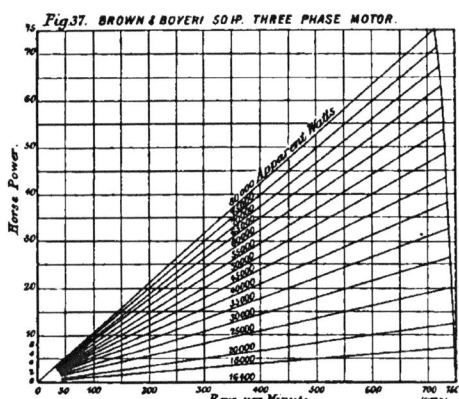

Figs. 35 to 37.—Efficiency Diagrams of Brown & Boveri's Three-phase Crane Motors

TABLE XIII.—SCHUCKERT & Co.'s THREE - PHASE ASYNCHRONOUS OPEN CRANE MOTORS FOR INTERMITTENT WORK—50 PERIODS

Rated Capacity in Brake Horse-power.	Revolutions per Minute.	Normal Torque in Metre-kilogrammes.	Normal Torque in Foot-pounds.	Maximum Torque in Metre-kilogrammes.	Maximum Torque in Foot-pounds.	Approx. Current Consumption at 500 Volts.	Net Weight of Motor in Kilogrammes.	Net Weight of Motor in Pounds.
4	1410	2.0	14.5	6.0	43.39	5.3	75	165.3
5	925	3.75	27.12	11.25	81.37	8.0	135	297.6
8	1430	4.0	28.9	12	86.8	10.5	125	275.6
10	940	7.5	54.2	22.5	162.7	13.5	235	518.1
14	1435	7.0	50.6	21	151.8	17.5	200	440.9
18	950	13.5	97.6	40.5	292.9	24.0	270	595.2
24	960	18.0	130.1	54	390.6	29.5	290	639.3
30	715	30	216.9	90	650.9	42.0	380	837.7
34	960	25.5	184.4	76.5	553.3	44.5	360	793.6
40	570	50	361.6	150	1084.9	58	470	1036.1
50	720	50	361.6	150	1084.9	67	470	1036.1
56	575	70	506.3	210	1518.9	80	710	1565.2
70	720	70	506.3	210	1518.9	92	710	1565.2
86	575	107	773.9	321	2321.8	120	900	1984.1
100	720	100	723.3	300	2169.9	125	900	1984.1

required. The motors must, of course, be constructed so as to occupy the smallest possible space, and also to require practically no supervision. As in the case of continuous current motors, the speed must lend itself to current regulation, and this is done by inserting resistances in the rotor circuit. The motors are generally supplied with slip rings on the rotor. This is comparable to regulating the speed of a shunt-wound continuous current motor by putting a resistance in the armature circuit. The resistances, switchboards, and controllers inserting resistances are determined by the current which circulates through the rotor. We give in Table X, page 197, a list of the standard polyphase crane motors manufactured by the U.E.G. of Berlin. Tables XI and XII, which refer to the Figs. 33 and 34, page 199, give the overall dimensions of such standard motors.

Figs. 35, 36, and 37 show the performances of Messrs. Brown & Boveri's three-phase crane motors at various speeds.

Table XIII gives the sizes of Messrs. Schuckert & Co.'s standard three - phase crane motors. The rated capacity of these machines is that load at which the motor can run for one hour continuously without the temperature of any part exceeding the temperature of the atmosphere by more than 45degs. Cent.

Messrs. Schuckert & Co. give rather an interesting curve, Fig 88, referring to their standard three-phase open crane motors, which enables the requisite size to be ascertained. In this curve the ordinates represent the overload capacity, whilst the abscissæ represent values of a, where $a = \frac{w + r}{r}$, w being the number of seconds in each cycle of the crane during which the motor is working, and r being the time during the cycle in which the crane is not working.

The value of a having been obtained for any particular cycle of operations, the motor to be used will be that which has an overload capacity corresponding to the value of a on the curve.

The conditions which a good polyphase motor generally fulfils are the following :—

The speed from full to no load for a 5 horse-power motor does not vary more than 6 per cent., and for a 100 horse-power motor not more than 3 per cent.

The Maschinenfabrik Oerlikon builds three-phase crane motors without sliding rings and without regulating devices of any kind—the starting torque of which is from two to three times the normal one. The slip under these conditions is about 12 per cent. The following Table XIV is fairly accurate, for general purposes, as regards three-phase induction motors :—

It must be remarked that, as already pointed out, if the power factor can be brought up from .75 to unity, the generators, transformers, and transmitting cables can be reduced 25 per cent.

The important point about three-phase motors is that the current at no load should be as small as possible.

The speed of the motors should be low, so as to reduce the amount of gearing necessary between the armature shaft and the winding drum. The rate generally adopted varies between 200 and 800 revolutions per minute. Table XV, giving approximate comparisons between continuous current and three-phase motors, may be interesting. The horse-power given is brake horse-power for continuous running.

TABLE XV.—COMPARISON OF CONTINUOUS CURRENT AND THREE-PHASE MOTORS

Output.	Continuous Current.		Output.	Three Phase.	
	Revs.	Weight in Kilogrs.		Revs.	Weight in Kilogrs.
2	1000	160	2	1500	120
2	400	400	—	—	—
5	900	300	5	1500	160
5	400	700	—	—	—
10	800	700	10	1000	420
10	320	1600	—	—	—
20	650	900	20	1000	650
20	300	1900	—	—	—
50	550	2000	50	750	1800
50	200	5500	—	—	—
100	400	3300	100	500	4000
100	170	8000	—	—	—

The following Table XVI gives an idea of the capacity and speeds of motor generally to be recommended for crane work :—

TABLE XIV.—OERLIKON THREE-PHASE MOTORS

B.H.P.	Efficiency.		Power Factor.		Slip at Full load.
	Full Load.	Half Load.	Full Load.	Half Load.	
	Per Cent.	Per Cent.			Per Cent.
2	70	65	.75	.68	8—20
5	80	70	.80	.70	6—15
10	84	75	.85	.75	5—12
15	86	78	.85	.75	4—12
25	88	80	.88	.78	3—10
40	90	83	.90	.80	2— 8
100	91	85	.90	.80	1— 6

TABLE XVI.—CAPACITY AND SPEEDS OF MOTORS FOR CRANE WORK

Rated Capacity.	Lifting Motor.		Slewing Motor.	
	Rated Capacity.	Speed in Revs. per Minute.	Rated Capacity.	Speed in Revs. per Minute.
Tons.	B.H.P.		B.H.P.	
1½	25	400—630	4½	900—1,000
2	25	400—630	4½	900—1,000
2½	32	330—550	5	900—1,100
5	50	250—300	6	800—1,000

AN AERIAL ROPEWAY IN SOUTHERN INDIA

By L. Davidson

THE native State of Travancore pays an annual tribute to Britain of £80,000, and has a population of about 2,500,000. It occupies a strip of land of 6,780 square miles on the extreme south-west of India, and Cape Comorin is situated at its southern extremity. From the sea coast, which forms the western limit of this native state, the land rises eastward to the summit of the range of hills which, running almost parallel to the coast, separate Travancore from British territory. On the eastern, or British, side these hills are too steep for railway— and in many places for road—construction, but on them are large areas of rich land, which are to some extent cultivated with very profitable results. The greatest difficulty attending their development lies in easy and cheap means of communication, for the transport of labour and food to the estates, and of the produce to the lower land, where it finds a market.

An example of how this difficulty has been overcome on one large estate is of considerable interest. It is located at a point where the rise from the plains to the cliffs at the top of the "ghaut" is unusually steep and rugged, in some parts there being an almost perpendicular face of rock from 1,000ft. to 1,500ft. in height; below this are several thousand feet of steep, rugged grass land, sparsely dotted with trees and broken up with innumerable ravines. The crest of this ridge is 6,000ft. or more in elevation, and the plains at the foot are about 1,200ft. above sea level, so that there is the extraordinary rise of nearly 5,000ft. in an average horizontal distance of about five or six miles. The eastern side is British territory, and very dry, much cultivation being done with the aid of wells, though the recent completion of the Periya-aar irrigation works, which comprise a dam in one of the valleys on the Travancore side of the range, with a "bund" 150ft. deep, and a tunnel through the hills to the dry British side of the country, enables a large tract of land to be irrigated which would otherwise be subject to the vicissitudes of irregular rainfall, and it is hoped, from this source alone, that 100,000 acres of rice land will be kept under permanent cultivation.

The rainfall on the Travancore side of the range is very heavy, amounting to 250ins. per annum, and even more in some parts; while it is not over 80ins. on the British side, only a few miles distant. An agricultural company secured a concession from the Travancore Government of some 100,000 acres of land, and has of recent years been developing the suitable portions for the cultivation of tea and coffee, cardamoms and cinchona; about 20,000 acres are now under these varied crops. The labourers required in connection with the gardens, together with their families, number about twenty thousand, and in order to feed them some three thousand transport ponies, donkeys, and cattle were employed, besides a large force of probably not less than eight hundred coolies for carrying head loads.

The principal base of operations, Munaar, was thirty-two miles from the end of the cart road on the plains, which ran from that point to a station on the South Indian Railway; along this road it is hoped that a narrow gauge railway will be laid by a company which has secured a concession from the Government. The road has been extended recently by the Agricultural Company ten miles up a valley to the base of the steep ghaut, and from the top of the range about forty miles of cart road have been constructed in various directions to serve the estates. It was to connect those two points that it was decided to erect an aerial ropeway capable of filling the company's requirements, as well as those of the general public, for many years to come. A cart road up this ghaut would have been impossible to make or to work except at a prohibitive cost. The question of cutting a cart road in a westerly direction was also duly considered, but the heavy cost of construction through virgin forest in an unhealthy country, with a rainfall of upwards of 250ins., and the fact that fifty miles of

Plate XLV

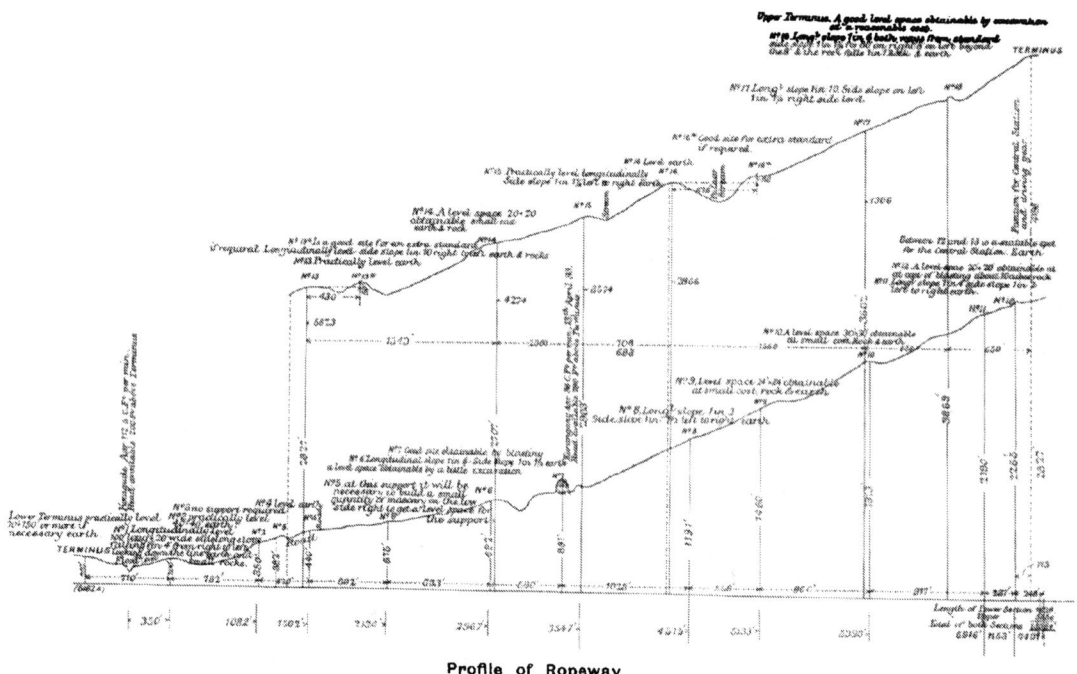

Profile of Ropeway

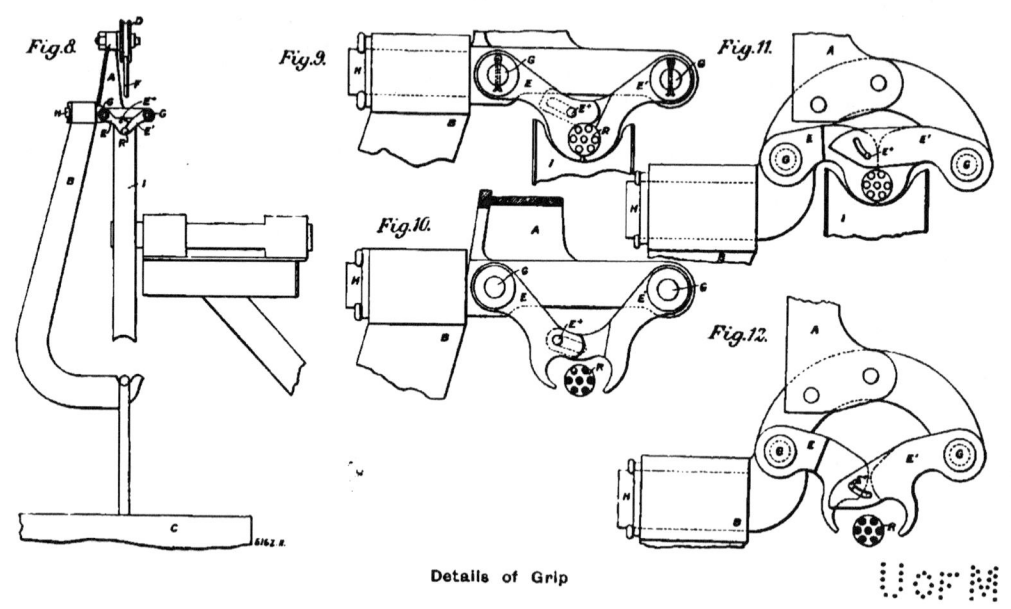

Fig.8.   Fig.9.   Fig.11.

Fig.10.   Fig.12.

Details of Grip

U or M

AN AERIAL ROPEWAY IN SOUTHERN INDIA

UofM

Fig. 2.—Standard Erected on High Cliff

Fig. 4.—Central Station

Fig. 3.—General View of Line

Fig. 5.—View of Upper Zigzag Cart Road

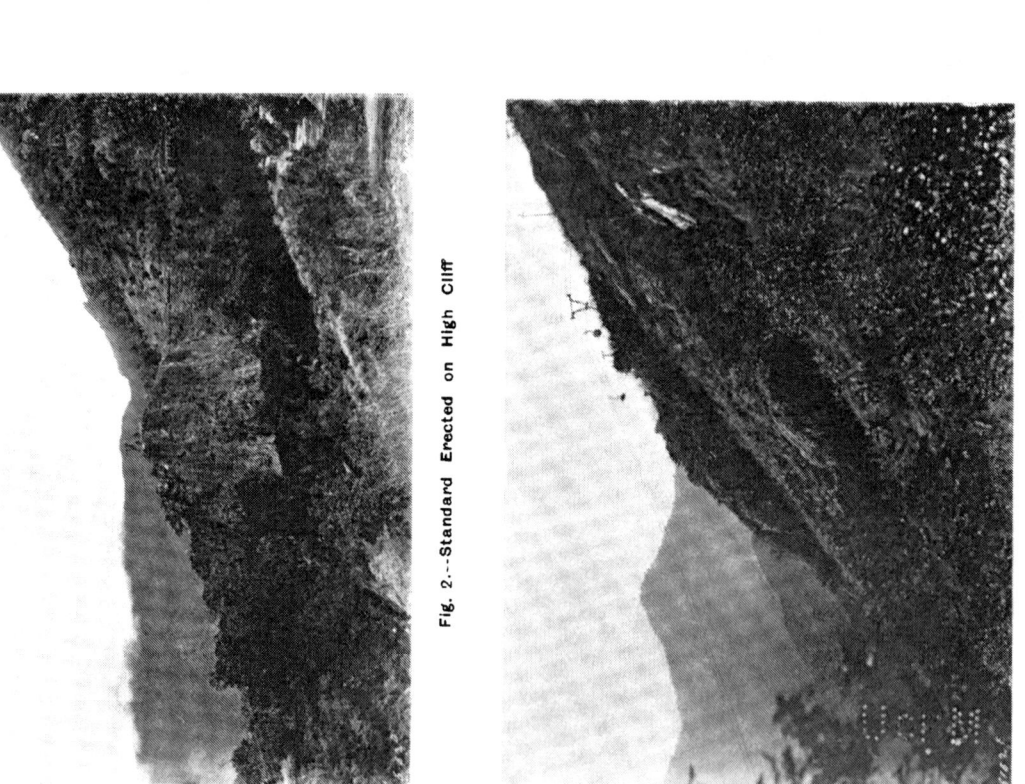

Fig. 2.-Standard Erected on High Cliff

Fig. 3.—General View of Line

Fig. 4.—Central Station

Fig. 5.—View of Upper Zigzag Cart Road

Uor M

Plate XLVII

Fig. 6.—Tension Gear at Top Station

Fig. 7.—Tension Gear at Bottom Station

AN AERIAL ROPEWAY IN SOUTHERN INDIA

Fig. 2.--Standard Erected on High Cliff

Fig. 4.--Central Station

Fig. 3.--General View of Line

Fig. 5.--View of Upper Zigzag Cart Road

U of M

Plate XLVII

Fig. 6.—Tension Gear at Top Station

Fig. 7.—Tension Gear at Bottom Station

AN AERIAL ROPEWAY IN SOUTHERN INDIA

such road would have had to be made and maintained under difficult conditions, resulted in the abandonment of the idea. It was finally decided to join up the steep section between the ends of the two roadways by an aerial rope line, and the type to be adopted received careful consideration. The local engineer of the company, Mr. Kemlo, finally designed the installation with a view to erect an efficient ropeway with materials of as light a section as was compatible with strength, as the cost of transporting material in the very unhealthy ghaut was excessively heavy. His design took the form of a moving rope carrying its own loads, and although the trouble in connection with its installation was great, the results have more than fulfilled expectations. This is probably the steepest ropeway of its class in existence, and its success is in a large measure due to the grip carriers which will be described presently. The total length of the ropeway is 2.6 miles, measured along the slope of the ground, and the rise is about 4,000ft. It is divided into two sections, the lower one being 7,400ft. in horizontal length, with a rise of 2,150ft.; the upper section has a horizontal length of 5,800ft., and a rise of 1,850ft. In the lower section there are thirteen spans, the longest being 1,028ft. horizontal, and in the upper section there are nine spans, the longest 1,560ft. horizontal. The slope is fairly uniform throughout, except that the lowest four spans are less steep than the rest of the line.

Fig. 1, Plate XLV, is a profile of the line. The positions of the standards are numbered consecutively from 1 to 18, and the information on the section is so complete as to render any further reference unnecessary.

The reasons for working the rope in two sections are (1) in the event of a breakdown only half of the installation would be out of work; (2) that part of the stress at the top, which is due to the weight of the rope, is diminished, and thus its load-carrying capacity is increased; and (3) the climate at the foot of the Ghaut is so unhealthy that no European could stand it, while by the present arrangements the ropeway is worked from the central station, which, being at an elevation of nearly 4,000ft., is comparatively healthy. The rope is of good quality plough steel, $\frac{3}{4}$in. in diameter, and about 1lb. weight per foot. It was sent out on eight drums with an interchangeable axle

and wheels, and each drum was rolled into the line of ropeway and unwound on the axle, the hauling being done by $\frac{3}{8}$in. steel ropes on hand winches, a tedious process. Four drums of rope were required for each section; the splices were 60ft. long, and have stood well. The rope is supported on 18in. pulleys, with a groove of 1in. radius, and the pulleys are carried on light angle steel standards of various heights to suit the nature and slope of the ground, varying from 10ft. for the lowest, to 40ft. for the highest standard. The feet are in most cases embedded in concrete blocks, though in some instances they are bolted on to rocks that happened to be in the line of ropeway. One rock shown in the engraving, Fig. 2, Plate XLVI, was 120ft. high, and an iron ladder was fixed to its almost vertical side to enable the work to be done at all.

The engraving, Fig. 8, Plate XLVI, shows the standards very clearly, and indeed gives a good idea of the ropeway generally. The other illustrations on this plate are characteristic of the work. Fig. 4 shows one of the terminal stations, and Fig. 5 shows the zigzag cart road approach to the upper terminus. The tension gears are at the top and bottom stations (see Figs. 6 and 7, Plate XLVII). The tension wheels are 8ft. in diameter, carried on a sliding arrangement 85ft. long. The requisite power is got by a worm wheel winch and three block sheaves with a $\frac{1}{2}$in. specially flexible wire; the anchors are heavy masonry and concrete blocks over 80 tons in weight.

The driving arrangements are at the central station, and consist of two electric motors, either of which can be used geared on to a counter-shaft, which, in its turn, operates, through a rope drive, a vertical shaft and pinion geared on to two 8ft. spur wheels. These spur wheels have bolted on to them hard wood pulleys, by which the ropes are driven. The upper and lower sections of the ropeway are connected by shunt rails, along which the loads pass from one rope to another, and at the termini loads automatically run off the rope on to shunt rails, or off the rails on to the rope, without any loss of time.

The current for supplying the electric motors is generated about a mile further down, at a point where a head of 750ft. of water is available. This operates two Pelton wheels; they in their turn drive two dynamos, each supplying 40 amperes at 500 volts. One of these is sufficient to work the ropeway at two miles an hour, while the other is always ready in case of accidents. No water power was available nearer the central station than at this point, so that electric transmission was indispensable.

The general form of carriers is shown in Figs. 8 to 12, Plate XLV. It consists of a frame or hanger, B, which carries the load clear of the standard head pulleys. To the upper end of this frame the rope-gripping arrangement is attached. It is made up of the frame, A, carrying two pendant jaws, E E, which are so arranged that when the load is run along the shunt rail, and the jaws come in contact with the rope, they automatically close on and grip it with a force proportional to the weight of the load. The other letters on this figure refer to the following parts : I is the carrying pulley ; F is the shunt rail ; and O is the supplementary pulley running on the shunt rail and taking the load off the rope.

Enlarged details of the jaws are given in Figs. 9 and 10. In Fig. 9 the jaws are shown closed over the rope, a result due to, and varying with, the amount of load suspended. In Fig. 10 the jaws are open and the rope released, the weight on it being removed. It will be noticed that the proportions of the jaws do not interfere with the free running over the pulleys.

Figs. 11 and 12 show a somewhat modified form of the grip arrangement.

The large groove in the standard head pulleys has the advantage of altogether preventing the rope from being jerked off, which is a common fault with the ordinary rope-carrying pulleys having a groove only half the diameter of the rope.

The top bracket, A, of the grip frame shown in Fig. 8 carries a rail pulley, D, already referred to. This comes in contact with the shunt rail, F, when the load reaches the end of its journey, and as the shunt rail is laid at a flatter down grade than the rope at this point, the weight of the load is taken up by the rail, and the pendant jaws open and release the rope automatically. This process is reversed at the loading side, the shunt rail being almost level, while the rope has an upward slope at this point, so that as the load travels along the shunt rail, the open pendant jaws close on the rope, and the load is automatically taken up by the rope from the shunt rail.

The loads carried are limited to 5cwt. each, but necessarily most of them are less, as it is easier to handle lighter loads, though the ropeway is capable of taking far more than the existing traffic.

Assuming forty loads as about the average number on the rope at one time, a delivery is ensured of fifteen loads at both ends per hour, when the rope is running at the rate of two miles an hour, and working ten hours with 4cwt. loads. This gives an average of 80 tons a day each way, or more than double the ropeway has actually to carry. The speeds arranged for are one, two, three, and four miles per hour, but at two miles the line handles more than has been required of it hitherto. The economy in working, as compared with the old methods of transportation, is close on £1 per ton. The advantages of being able to erect an aerial rope of this class on steep grades are obvious, as not only does it effect a considerable saving in regard to the original cost of the installation, but by the use of the grip carriers described, the life of the rope is greatly prolonged, owing to the fact that they probably never grip exactly the same part of the rope twice, and the wear and tear is thus equalised throughout its length.

The prospects of success when the work was commenced were small, but the results obtained have been very satisfactory.

THE PATHS OF PROGRESS

A MONTHLY REVIEW

CRIMINAL ASPECTS OF A STRIKE

Touching the uneconomic prejudices of the democracy, there is, in most contemporary public commentaries, a deplorable lack of plain speech. Even in journals which necessarily appeal to but a narrow circle, and even in the utterances of men removed from the exigencies of political opportunism, we have become accustomed to read, concerning many vital problems, nothing more illuminating than polite platitudes varied by smug applications of the principles of suburban humanitarianism. Few politicians, journalists, or ministers of religion, will undertake the painful duty of telling disagreeable truths to the multitude, and their usual attitude in the presence of an imperfectly educated audience suggests that they are much more anxious to please than to instruct. It is as though a schoolmaster should invite his pupils, not merely to dictate the selection of subjects, but also to play what pranks they choose with the elementary rules of the arts and sciences.

Viewed from the standpoint of any sane system of ethics, the instigators or fomentors of a labour struggle which occasions the stoppage of a supply of cheap fuel, are the enemies of the people and a danger to the State. The necessities of civilised humanity being what they are, a great coal strike cannot be otherwise regarded than as an outrage upon society. The withholders of corn who grind the faces of the poor are no more to be execrated than the withholders of coal who do likewise, whether they be colliery owners or unions of working miners. Indeed, if the degree of infamy be proportionate to the public and private hardships inflicted, it would seem almost that the balance of iniquity is on the side of coal, for cereal foods are not essential to life, whereas coal is the indispensable agent in modern industrial productivity, upon the maintenance of which so many millions are dependent, not merely for their comfort, but for their very existence.

Moreover, the excuse may be advanced for the speculator who engineers a corner in wheat that he is in some sort at once a treasurer of stored food and a medium of increased production automatically stimulated by the artificial demand. Minerals, however, are not a product of cultivation, and any interruption of the coal supply, though no doubt it may direct our attention more forcibly to the possible provision of substitutes and the economical husbanding of our limited stocks of fuel, must have an incalculably harmful immediate and prospective effect, in that it brings so much of the world's work to a standstill, and for the rest raises the cost of production of so many articles of common consumption.

Obviously, it is not the rich few, but the poor many, who are afflicted by any cessation of labour such as the recent strike of American coal miners, and the effects of this and other strikes are not by any means merely concurrent with its duration. The disturbance of the manufacturing industries in America and other countries must continue for some time, and it will be long before the last perceptible ripples disappear. Trade unionists are too apt to overlook the universality of the evils they may bring about when they intend no more than a war against their supposed capitalist enemies. The unfortunate helpless non-combatants suffer most, and the responsibility for their troubles must rest upon the parties concerned in the dispute. Proprietors who attempt to swell their profits by unjustly reducing wages, and thus drive their employés into rebellion, are rightly to be denounced; but the very people who are most vehement in their condemnations will hasten to proffer their "sympathy" to workmen who, actuated by the same motive of greed, produce the same result, that is to say, the throwing out of gear a part of our industrial machinery.

Whichever party is the cause of strife is, in ethics, morally liable to a criminal indictment for inflicting damage upon his fellowmen, and when the world becomes a little more civilised, it is practically certain that this view will take legal shape. As population increases and becomes more and more exacting in its demands upon the natural wealth of nations, the sense of common interest in the land and mineral deposits of the country becomes stronger. The absolute right of land owners and coal owners to hoard their property will not be admitted, neither will the absolute right of labourers to prevent the development of such property by "picketing," and other methods of violence.

LABOUR FALLACIES

The English Utilitarians, despised as they seem to be by certain superficial critics, did not live in vain, and the political truths which they enunciated will govern the politics of the future, although not precisely in the manner which they may have conceived. Meanwhile we are living in a period of confusion, out of which, no doubt, a clear line of policy will sooner or later be discerned, and will serve its turn through a generation or two. Thus the present tendency of the several groups professing jointly and singly to represent the interests of labour, is to make a limited, and therefore false, application of the Benthamite principle of "the greatest good for the greatest number." The coal miners are more numerous than the proprietors and shareholders; therefore, in the working and profitable development of mineral deposits, the interests of the miners should have prior consideration, and in so far as they get their wages before the capitalist gets his interest, they are already in enjoyment of a preferential partnership. But there is, of course, a third party to consider, namely, the consumer. His is by far "the greatest number"; his is also the ruling power, able to express his opinions and requirements in legislative form; and, finally, his is "the greatest good" which that legislation will endeavour to procure.

When we consider, for example, how many millions are, directly or indirectly, consumers of coal, either as domestic users or as manufacturers, engineers, carriers, artisans, and labourers; or, again, as travellers, consumers of manufactured articles, and so forth; it becomes brilliantly obvious that the interests which are most injuriously affected by any interruption in the output are the interests of the democracy. Yet, in the higgledy-piggledy confusion of their theories there are labour "leaders" who actually believe that a strike is, on the contrary, beneficial to the proletariat, and is a victory gained at the sole expense of the moneyed classes. Even if it is pointed out to them that, on their own showing, the interests of the many consumers must come before those of the few producers, they will, like Goldsmith's schoolmaster, argue still, and will claim that, inasmuch as the vast majority of the population are wage-earners, the strikers of one trade are fighting the battle of all, and, while inflicting some temporary inconvenience, are by their action raising the social status and improving the prosperity of all workmen.

This is surely confusion worse confounded. A strike of textile operatives raises the price of clothing. If the strike results in higher wages being paid the price remains raised— that is to say, the consumer must pay, if not all, certainly the greater part of the increased wages. Now, if we suppose that this "success" of the textile workers encourages the bricklayers and bootmakers, who are now paying more for their shirts, also to strike for higher wages and to gain their object, the consequence must be that the bootmaker's rent is raised, and the bricklayer finds that more money is needed when he goes to buy boots. A general increase of wages is not an increase of purchasing power.

Unquestionably any sincere and conscientious labour representative should give his diligent attention to the cheapening of production in the interests of the masses. It is decidedly unfortunate that most of the men who claim to represent labour are the nominees of sections only; they are, in fact, merely the servants of a trade union, and they are unable to devote their political efforts to the amelioration of the general condition of the people. It is required of them as their primary duty that they shall resist, not merely reductions in wages, but also other measures having an effect on the cost of production, such as the introduction of labour-saving machinery and even the raising of the wages of the more capable and industrious workers, for even an advance in wages, when it stimulates more efficient specialisation, is sometimes a step in the direction of cheaper manufacture.

The labour leaders under the present system are sectional representatives with sectional interests to serve. It is merely expected of them that they shall protect the pecuniary status of the close corporations who are their clients. They have no authority or justification for posing as friends of democracy at large, whose interests, indeed, frequently clash with the interests of their clients aforesaid. Reluctant as one is to dogmatise, it is difficult to withhold belief from the theory that what benefits the democracy is cheap production of the commodities which are necessary for their existence and comfort, and it is unquestionable, on the other hand, that the several trade unions are actually pulling the other way; they are organised bodies pursuing as an object the increase of the cost of production.

SYMPATHY AND BUSINESS

The process may be a more or less painful one, but there are grounds for the hope that sooner or later this conflict of interests will be more widely recognised. The theory of Liberalism, as applied to the extension of the franchise, is that the power to vote will generate the ability to vote: that, put in another way, responsibility makes men. To a great extent this assumption has been justified by events. Taken in the aggregate, the working men of Great Britain have shown an intelligent appreciation of Imperial policy, and they frequently reject a Parliamentary candidate who endeavours to appeal to their narrower interests.

Is it not fair to assume that their action in relation to industrial policy will also be governed by a quickened sense of responsibility, proportionate to their broader educational horizon, and their growing recognition of the numerous and complicated consequences of rash and unintelligent agitation? The majority of the wage-earners in some of our principal branches of manufacture already discuss the rise and fall of prices and of wages with insight and moderation. They only make claim to such remuneration as the industry will fairly yield, and they accept reductions in slack times as a necessary evil. They know that the welfare of the industry is their welfare, and the troubles of the industry are their troubles.

It is of national importance that this appreciation of the community of interest between labour and capital, directors and employés, in the success of their business should be encouraged. What is wanted is not sentimental sympathy, but industrial sympathy. Probably, indeed, the numerous well-meaning busybodies who are continually raising their appeal for toiling and suffering humanity are actually retarding the alleviation of the burdens of workaday life. It would scarcely improve the victorious prospects of an army if a band of hysterical sentimentalists were permitted to distribute tracts amongst the rank and file, painting in exaggerated colours the hardships of the forced march and the horrors of the combat; and it may be contended, with some force, that to endeavour to make the labourer discontented with his lot is far more likely to produce fresh grievances than to remove those already in existence. It is surely indicative of strength of mind and general intelligence on the part of the British working man that the "sympathy" of the leisured pro-labourer, and the hoarse inventions and revilings of the salaried demagogue, have not had a more demoralising influence upon the general industrial conditions of the country.

Meanwhile, it is not at all easy to discover the right approach to a common understanding between capital and labour bearing some promise of permanence. Their present relationship is not sufficiently defined, even when conferences are held for the plain purpose of attempting such a definition. Capital may be regarded as either a buyer of labour, a partner of labour, or a servant and instrument of labour. Somewhat inconsistently, many trade unionists demand for themselves all the advantages of these three positions. They wish to establish a labour market, and sell their labour at a price which may rise, but must never fall, so that in this respect their market differs from all others. At the same time they claim that, apart from the price received in this curious and unique "market," their remuneration shall bear some proportion to the profits of the industry, so long as those profits are advancing, but not so long as they are declining; in other words, they require a sort of preferential dividend or royalty. And, lastly, when opportunity arises, as in the case of a labour-controlled Municipality establishing works departments, they go into the capital market and purchase what amount they can at the lowest possible rate of interest.

It may be urged in their defence that the capitalists in their turn are open to the same line of criticism; that they endeavour to buy in the cheapest market, while the unionists naturally wish to sell in the dearest market, the one party being "bears" and the other "bulls" of labour. But the various profit-sharing schemes, sliding scales, and premium systems that have been instituted, with, on the whole, no very marked success, show, at least, that attempts have been made to enlist what we have called "industrial sympathy," and to turn to advantage the sense of community of interests. Taken altogether, manufacturers are prepared to regard labour as something to be purchased in a market, and subject to all the ups and downs of market dealings; or to accept the principle of a low, fixed wage to be supplemented by some form of bonus proportionate to the net profit of the business, and to the degree of productive efficiency attained by the individual worker. Most of them would, no doubt, rather pay a price for work done, than a wage for the time occupied; but the constant dread of over production, and consequent lack of employment, impels the trade unions to denounce "piece work" as a device of the enemy.

THE IDEAL PARTNERSHIP

The experiment of Sir Christopher Furness in encouraging his workmen to show an interest in the business by lending them money at 3 per cent. to be invested in the company's shares returning 10 per cent., is not business in the strict sense of the term. The multiplication of small shareholders who are working partners should be a gain to industry and to society at large, but it is questionable whether Sir Christopher Furness is advancing towards this desirable end. So long as the company enjoys its present prosperity, partnership acquired on such terms is purely a free gift, and the only prospect of return to the lender of the money, who is, of course, a very large shareholder, lies in the probability that his new fellow-proprietors, whose partnership he has bought at this high price, will by their personal exertions contribute towards the maintenance or increase of the 10 per cent. dividend. To take an extreme case, let us suppose that the chairman of a company holds £100,000 out of £300,000 capital, on which, at 10 per cent., he receives £10,000 in dividend.

He lends one thousand workmen £100 each at 3 per cent., which they invest in the company. The capital is now £400,000, and if the dividend is maintained the chairman's income will be the same from the company, while he will be drawing £3,000 a year from his advance of £100,000. If, however, the company's profit is not thus increased, the dividend on the higher capital will only yield 7½ per cent., in which case the chairman will receive £7,500, besides the £3,000 interest. Lastly, he might have taken up the additional £100,000 capital himself, and received dividends of £20,000 or £15,000 in all. These figures have, of course, no relation to the actual case, except as representing the sort of calculation that must be made by any capitalist who thinks of following the example of Sir Christopher Furness. Perhaps, however, it is only by results that such an experiment can be judged, costly as it is.

Sir George Livesey, of the South Metropolitan Gas Company, and other eminent industrial chiefs, have adopted profit-sharing schemes, but, on the whole, the theory has not made much headway. Thrifty workmen will invest their money for themselves; the unthrifty will not invest, and will not benefit by any plan that has yet been devised, for in whatever form the bonus or premium is conferred upon them, it is only squandered, and it encourages them to live on a scale which cannot be supported in hard times. The essential difference between the thrifty and the unthrifty workman is that the former endeavours to make his prosperous days carry him over prospective periods of adversity, either by some method of insurance, or by investing his savings, while his improvident companion will lead alternately a merry and miserable life. Unfortunately, the great majority of people live up to their incomes, whatever those incomes may be. The remaining minority accumulate capital by their self-sacrifice, and are roundly abused for their pains, although their savings are used, not exclusively for their own benefit, but for that of the whole community.

It would be of incalculable advantage in settling certain general principles and defining their possible applications if we could have a Capital Congress as well as a Labour Congress. The success or failure of various profit-sharing and other systems could there and then be fully discussed, and in all probability the public mind would be enlightened on many points concerning the relationship between profit-earners and wage-earners, who are popularly supposed to be determined enemies.

THE CONSUMER AS ARBITRATOR

Expression of public opinion is sometimes resented by one side or the other in a labour dispute, and the curious view is taken that the affair is of purely internal and private controversy. It is, however, precisely the general public whose interests are most affected by industrial disturbance. The necessities of the consumer are paramount, and, especially in a democratic state, the consumer will sooner or later take means to make his demands effective. It is little short of ludicrous, for example, that the labours of a large proportion of the population should be interrupted, and that they should shiver in idleness for an indefinite period, merely because coal owners and coal miners have disagreed over a detail of remuneration or regulations. While granting personal liberty to indulge in self-inflicted hardships, it cannot be permitted in any sensibly ordered community that a discontented minority shall revenge themselves upon the whole population.

Economists of a certain school may demur to such propositions, but no intelligent observer can deny that the tendency is in the direction of a growing consciousness of common interests, and that, at present, in a more or less clumsy way, efforts are being made, and will continue to be made, to express this newly acquired consciousness in legislation. The Labour Party are not knowingly working towards that end. Their immediate object is to secure higher remuneration for their members, which, as has been shown, is not *primâ facie* in the interests of the consumer. The South Wales miners who allow themselves "playtime" in order to restrict the output of coal, and thus keep up prices, can scarcely be recognised as public benefactors, and it is astonishing to find their action defended and even applauded by labour representatives, when it is, of course, detrimental to the prosperity of so many other labourers whose work is assisted directly or indirectly by an abundant supply of cheap coal.

Most surprising of all is the enthusiasm with which the advanced section is clamouring for the forging of fetters for Labour by means of Socialist legislation. This aspect of the subject is too large for discussion on the present occasion, and it is sufficient merely to indicate the certain ultimate result of what is called "practical Socialism"; namely, that the interests of the consumer will become more and more clearly predominant, while the selfish interests of the producer, as producer, will be more and more sternly repressed. The curious notion of the communists is that only private capital will be abolished, but the same fate will overtake private labour, and the producer, instead of being a free and independent citizen who can go on strike or take a holiday when he chooses, will be nothing better than the slave of society, with an allotted task to perform before he becomes entitled to his board and lodging.

COLONIAL PARTNERSHIP

It is a curious coincidence that the publication of the results of the conference of Colonial Premiers and representatives of the Imperial Government should occupy the public mind simultaneously with the announcement that the orders given by Lord George Hamilton to German firms for Indian railway locomotives had not been executed according to the contract. The facts are briefly that, while the superiority of British engines is universally acknowledged, and must be known even to the Secretary of State for India, the orders were given to the Germans on the ground of cheapness and quicker delivery. Lower prices for inferior articles do not constitute cheapness, and a promise of rapid construction is not always to be relied upon, and has been broken on this occasion. The India Office has therefore gained no advantage whatever by depriving British manufacturers of business in respect of which they might fairly expect more friendly treatment.

Meanwhile, we have Mr. Chamberlain and the Colonial Conference making a strong point of preferential Imperial trade, which Lord George Hamilton, as Secretary of State for India, is evidently wholly in disagreement with. While our own colonies are considering schemes for favouring British manufactures in their markets, the India Office is purchasing German engines without ensuring anything in the shape of reciprocal advantages.

Altogether, the proposals of the Conference

mark a departure from certain economic principles which have governed the policy of this country for many years past. What we in this country would prefer, of course, is universal free trade. What most of us are still in favour of, is free trade for the United Kingdom, even with its apparent minor disadvantages. But in dealing with our colonies a new set of circumstances arise, which demand consideration on their merits, quite apart from our attachment to the doctrine of free trade.

The plain situation is that, whereas hitherto practically every coast in the world has been a fiscal fortification inflicting more or less injury upon British commerce, an opportunity now occurs of lowering certain of these barriers. Are we to discountenance anything of the kind for fear of exhibiting ourselves in an inconsistent attitude? Hitherto the only form which a bargain could take has necessitated the imposition of some countervailing duty of a differential effect. We could not, for instance, under our system, confer any special favour on the produce of any country in exchange for reciprocal concessions without imposing duties upon similar produce entering our ports from other countries. And no occasion has ever arisen which offered any adequate consideration for the completion of a bargain of this kind, which would threaten to dislocate our commerce in many quarters.

Now we have the proposition put before us that our colonies, having already a protective fiscal system over which we have no control, and for which we have no sort of responsibility, will modify that system for our particular commercial advantage, believing that, directly or indirectly, they will receive compensation. Nothing could be more misleading than to imagine that this proposal rests upon a basis of unreasoning, sentimental patriotism. There are several ways in which our colonies may help themselves by helping us. They have, to begin with, something to sell, and the Government and the people of Great Britain will give preference—or, with the case of Lord George Hamilton before us, we will say, should give preference —to colonial produce whenever possible. They are, again, in need of capital, and this they may the more readily obtain from England, if their territory is, by tariff reform, made a more favourable market for English manufactures.

The intention is obviously to bring about a closer partnership between the various sections of the Empire, to ensure to some extent that the prosperity of Great Britain shall be a good thing for the colonies, and that any successful development of Canada and Australia shall be reflected in the commercial condition of the United Kingdom. In the eighteenth century the British Government endeavoured to raise public revenue from the colonies by enforced taxation. The present proposal is voluntary taxation of the colonies for value received. And although it is not possible to set out in figures the advantages on both sides, there is no question that there will be material benefits of considerable magnitude.

THE ELECTRICAL EQUIPMENT OF SUB-STATIONS*

By E. PARRY and W. CASSON

FUNCTION OF SUB-STATIONS.—The necessity for a sub-station arises when the limit of economical distribution from a single centre is exceeded. The number of sub-stations is determined by the same issue, controlled somewhat in towns having an extensive system of traction, by the limit imposed by the Board of Trade upon the voltage in the earth return, in the interest of the community, and by the self-interest of the traction undertakers.

The limit of the voltage of distribution for all purposes — tramways, motors, and lighting — at the present day is about 500 volts. The limit of economical transmission for this voltage is approximately two miles; hence, for distances exceeding this amount, sub-stations become necessary. In towns such as Glasgow, having a heavy service of cars, a further element is introduced into the problem, owing to the necessity of limiting the field of stray currents, and the number and location of sub-stations is controlled by the proportion of current it is advisable or economical to bring back by means of insulated cables and boosters. In such cases, it is found advantageous to place the sub-stations from one and a half to two miles apart.

The function of a sub-station being to convert energy having characteristics suitable for transmission to a form of energy suitable for distribution, it becomes necessary to define the character of the supply to, and output of, the sub-station. First, as regards transmission, we will fix the voltage at a value beyond which the advisability of transforming up for transmission becomes an element to be considered. At the present time the limit is 12,000 volts, for although generators have been built for pressures up to 20,000 volts, advantages become doubtful beyond 12,000. Having selected this voltage, the distance of maximum transmission is decided, and the area which can be economically served may be fixed. This aspect of the question does not come within the limits of the present article, and we start with an incoming voltage of about 12,000 at the sub-station. We assume that the periodicity has been fixed at 40 cycles per second, this being convenient for alternating current lighting and power, and for conversion to direct current.

With respect to the output, we may consider, as a typical instance, the case of a sub-station in connection with a power distribution scheme, the sub-station having to supply the needs of a manufacturing town of, say, fifty thousand inhabitants. Such a town will require supply for traction, lighting, and industrial purposes. The number of cars in operation would probably be about twenty, for which we may assume an average load of 200 kilowatts during full service, and a probable maximum demand of 400 kilowatts. This will, of course, be direct current at 500 to 550 volts.

The public and private lighting installed will probably be equivalent to about twenty-five thousand 8 candle-power lamps, and will have a maximum demand of 400 kilowatts and a load factor of 10 or 12 per cent. This lighting load we may safely assume to be direct current, since this will certainly be best for public and private arc lighting, and it is very probable that a large proportion of the factories will be lighted with arc lamps. The distribution may be conveniently assumed to be on the three-wire system with 440 volts between outers.

With regard to the motor load, this is a department of electricity supply which has not yet been developed sufficiently to supply figures based on experience, but it is well

* The sub-station arrangements described in this article are those followed by Mr. H. F. Parshall, M.Inst. C.E., M.I.E.E., to whom the authors are indebted for permission to publish the various plans and diagrams illustrating typical sub-stations, all of which were designed by him and carried out under his supervision as consulting engineer.

known from repeated canvassing that a town of the character and size we have under consideration, would utilise some 2,500 horse-power for industrial purposes. In many cases, no doubt, this proportion would be exceeded. It is an undoubted fact that the most satisfactory and convenient form of motive power is the electric motor, and by means of a just and equitable tariff it can also be made the most economical. We may, therefore, take it that we may have a maximum demand of 1,000 kilowatts for industrial purposes. The load factor of this supply would not be less than 20 per cent. This load we may assume to be equally divided between direct and three-phase motors.

During the time of maximum load we shall, therefore, have to meet the following demand :—

	Kilowatts.	Volts.
Traction	400 ...	500 to 550
Lighting	400 ...	440 to 480
Direct current motor load ...	500 ...	440 to 480
Alternating current ,, ...	500 ...	330 to 360

This would require four 500 - kilowatt converting units, one running on the traction load, one each on the direct lighting and power, and one spare, and a group of four 175-kilowatt transformers, three on the alternating current motor load and one spare. It remains to be decided whether our converting units are to be motor generators or transformers and rotary converters, and which will best meet the conditions outlined above.

Comparing the several qualities of motor generator plant and rotary converter plant, experience bears out the following statements :—

(1) The rotary converter is cheaper in first cost in regard to both plant and foundations.

(2) The rotary converter plant is cheaper to maintain, there being only half as many rotating machines as in the case of motor generators.

(3) The rotary converter plant is more efficient than the motor generator plant.

(4) In regard to switch gear, the two systems are on an equality.

(5) The rotary converter plant has a wider range of voltage under ordinary working conditions.

(6) The rotary converter plant is simpler and more satisfactory in operation.

(7) The absence of high - tension machinery enables all the high-tension apparatus to be effectually isolated from the switchboards and running plant, thus minimising risk of fire and shock.

The small size, and therefore small cost, of a converter as compared with a motor generator, is due in the first place to the well-known fact that, owing to the interaction of the alternating and commutated currents, a three-phase rotary will give for the same thermal conditions about 33 per cent. more output, and a six-phase converter about 95 per cent. more than a D.C. generator of the same size and speed, assuming a 0.95 power factor for the A.C. side. The gain from this cause is well brought out in the experience at Dublin, where, on the opening of the new generating station, one of the outlying generating stations of the old system was converted into a sub-station. The old belt-driven generators were provided with collector rings, and are now run as rotary converters, giving just double their former output, at about 25 per cent. greater speed, with the same temperature rise, and an even greater elasticity as regards sparking. Evidently, therefore, the rotary converter will cost considerably less than the generator of a motor generator set of the same rating. But there is even a further gain if the sub-station is to run on a rapidly varying load, for, as there is practically no armature reaction, the load on the machine can be varied enormously without shifting the brushes. A good rotary will carry 150 per cent. overload (two and a half times the load as rated for thermal considerations) without serious sparking. Hence, with a rapidly varying load, it is quite within the limits of good practice to have the rated capacity of the plant running equal to the average load only, letting the overload capacity take care of the peaks. On the Central London Railway the usual practice is to run one 900-kilowatt converter in each sub-station, the average load per sub-station during the heavy load (about two and a half hours in the morning and two and a half in the evening) being about 900 kilowatts, with frequent sudden rises to 1,800 kilowatts. Of course, where the load is of the lighting type as opposed to the traction type, this fact cannot be made so much use of, as thermal considerations would come in in the case of a peak lasting a considerable time; but even here it would be quite within good practice to have the rotaries overloaded for an hour, or even two, the allowable amount of overload depending, of course, on how long the peak lasts. It is necessary to bear in mind, however, that to take full advantage of the great elasticity of the rotary converter, the transformer plant must be liberally designed. As, however, even allowing for this, the transformers cost little more than one-half as much as the rotary converters, this is not a very serious consideration. As regards efficiency, with units of about 500 kilowatts rated output, the efficiency of the motor generator combination may be taken at 87 per cent. at full, and 77 per cent. at half load, the corresponding combined efficiencies of the rotary converter and transformers being 92 per cent. and 87 per cent. In addition to this, as stated above, the rotary converters can safely run at a high average load, owing to their elasticity in respect of overload, so that in the case of a variable load they can be operated on a more favourable part of the efficiency curve than the motor generator.

(4) It is generally assumed that the rotary converter plant requires a complicated system of switches. The switching arrangements of the early plants give some colour to this idea, but as the properties of the rotary converter came to be better understood, a great many switches were dispensed with, and a comparison of the switching apparatus required by the two systems will show an equality in this respect.

As regards the fifth point, the voltage on the direct current side of the rotary converter can be varied by varying the voltage on the alternating current side by means of adjustable reactances, by changing the ratio of transformation in the transformers, by the use of a regulating transformer, and by adjusting the field. In the case of a motor generator, the only available means of varying the voltage is by the last method; consequently the rotary converter is superior in this respect, since such a wide range of voltage as is required in general service would necessitate a very liberal, and therefore expensive, design of generator. In a word, the rotary converter system is more flexible and better suited for the multitudinous requirements of a sub-station for general supply such as we are discussing.

With regard to the relative convenience in operation of the two plants, troubles from surging and similar difficulties of operation, which occurred in early days, are frequently

urged as an objection to rotary converters, but with sub-station plant of good modern design, and with generating plant having a fairly even turning moment, which is obtained without any difficulty, these defects have been practically overcome, and it may be fairly said that none of the installations of rotary converters operating in this country have given serious trouble from any cause peculiar to rotary converters as against motor generators. Rotary converters, in fact, are more easily synchronised than synchronous motors, and will carry far heavier overloads without falling out of step.

In discussing the sub-station arrangements, we may deal first with the rotary converters, since they exercise the greatest influence on the general arrangements of the sub-stations. The relative advantages and disadvantages

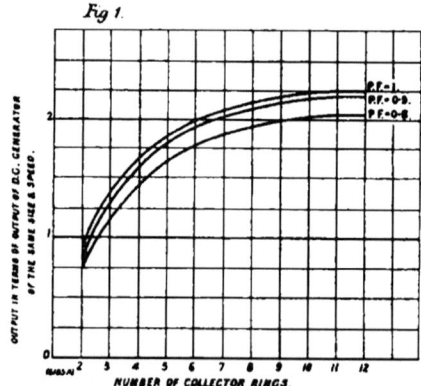

Relative Output of Generator and Rotary Converter

of rotary converters have already been discussed at some length. As regards the type, we have decided above that the transmission is to be three-phase. We may, however, without increasing the number of transformers, employ either three or six-phase converters. The six-phase converter has the advantage that, for the same limits as to heating and sparking, its output is about 40 per cent. greater than that of a three-phase rotary of the same size and speed. Of course, by increasing the number of phases we could still further increase the output, but a reference to the curve on Fig. 1 will show that the gain in having more than six phases will not compensate for the additional complication. The six-phase converter involves six leads on the low-tension alternating side, but with converters of any considerable size this does not make much difference, since in any case it is then desirable to sub-divide these leads, as otherwise they are apt to be of inconvenient dimensions ; for instance, the low-tension alternating connecting cables to an 800-kilowatt rotary converter would be about 1½ square inches per phase in cross section. Troubles are also likely to arise if such heavy alternating currents are carried by single cables. Having fixed on the six-phase rotary converter as the most economical for general purposes, we have the choice of two systems of connection, which have been termed the "double delta" and "diametrical

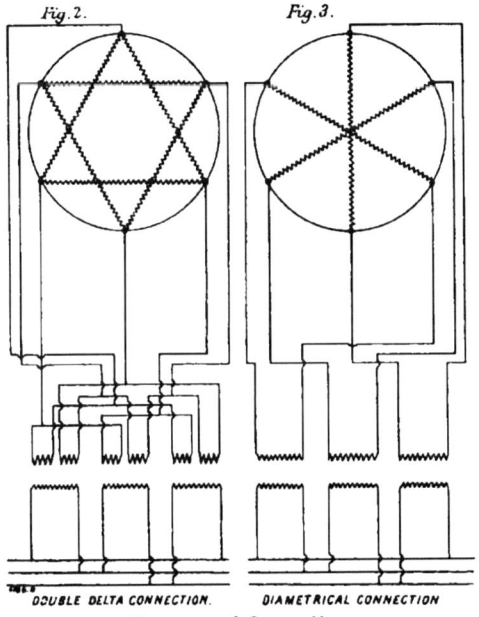

Fig. 2.   Fig. 3.

DOUBLE DELTA CONNECTION.   DIAMETRICAL CONNECTION
Diagrams of Connections

connection." Diagrams of these are given in Figs. 2 and 3. It will be seen that the first involves transformers with double secondaries, whilst the latter does not. With the "diametrical connection," the ratio of collector ring voltage to commutator voltage is 0.707, as against 0.612 for the "double delta," so that with 500 volts on the commutator the low-tension alternating voltage will be about 360. This will be just the right pressure for supplying the three-phase motors which we have assumed to be part of our load, and for which 330 volts is a standard pressure. The adoption of the diametrical connection will, therefore, have the further advantage

of enabling the transformers for the rotary converters to be interchangeable with those for the three-phase motor load. It is therefore evident that in most cases—particularly for a general service sub-station such as we are considering — the diametrical connection will be simple and cheaper, and tend to standardisation of the sub-station plant.

Rotary converters are compounded to compensate for voltage drop, on load, by means of a series winding, in the same way as generators. The ratio between collector and brush voltage, however, being practically fixed, the compounding depends on the action of the leading current set up by the compounding on a reactance inserted in the alternating side. This lowering of the power factor, of course, lowers the permissible output of the machine as regards thermal conditions. There being practically no armature reaction, the compounding required for a "flat" E.M.F. curve is so little that the effect on the power factor is inconsiderable, but with over-compounding it becomes more serious. Generally, however, for traction work the convenience of over-compounding and its practically instantaneous response to rapid changes of load more than compensate for this drawback, especially as the effect on the power factor is greatest at light loads. The rotary converters on the Central London Railway are compounded so as to give 520 volts on no load and 550 on full load. The compounding being only required for the traction load, the switch gear should be arranged to short circuit or cut out the series coil when running on the lighting load, as shown in Fig. 12, Plate L. The series coil will also require to be cut out while starting up on the alternating current side, otherwise a transformer action is set up between the armature and field coils.

As regards transformers, the use of a single transformer for three phases, which is the usual Continental practice, does not hitherto appear to have found favour in this country or in America. It has the drawback that a breakdown involves a complete unit of plant instead of only one-third. On the Central London Railway, for example, seven single-phase transformers, six of which run on load, are found to be ample. With three-phase transformers, three would be the minimum number allowable. On the other hand, three-phase transformers will be so much cheaper for a given output, and will occupy so much less floor space, that the additional spares will hardly be objectionable on either ground. In certain cases, where artificial cooling is not convenient, the smaller size of the single-phase transformers, by enabling artificial cooling to be dispensed with, will be a point in its favour. There is not, however, very much to choose between the two arrangements. Transformers of large size, to be economical, demand some means of artificial cooling. The methods most in use are :—

(1) *Air.*—Air being either blown or drawn through the transformer, usually by means of a fan.

(2) *Oil.*—The transformer case being of large size relatively to the transformer itself, and filled with oil, the circulation of which keeps the transformer cool.

(3) *Water.*—This is usually applied to oil-insulated transformers, water being forced through pipes surrounding the transformers.

The first method is the most economical in first cost and space, but a breakdown is more likely to result in a fire than with either oil or water cooling, and it is difficult to isolate the transformer banks so completely as can be done with oil transformers. If air or water cooling be adopted it will usually be most convenient to drive the fan or pump by means of a three-phase induction motor off the low-tension alternating circuit. On the whole, the oil-cooled transformer will usually be the most satisfactory in working for plants of such size as we are considering. With very large units, however, the transformer cases would have to be enormous to give the required radiating surface, and water cooling then becomes necessary.

As the sub-station under consideration has to be employed for a considerable range of voltage, the transformer will require to have the ratio adjustable. This is usually done by cutting out a certain number of turns. Whether this is best done on the primary or secondary depends on various circumstances. If the unit of plant is small, so that the moving parts of the switches are small and the secondary cables are light, it will be best to have the ratio-changing switches in the secondary, and place them on the transformer panels of the switchboard. This is especially convenient if the sub-station is to supply both traction and lighting, in which case the ratio may want adjusting comparatively often. At the Margate sub-station of the Isle of Thanet Light Railways, the ratio-changing device consists of two triple-pole double-throw switches for each transformer bank, located on the transformer panel. Each blade corresponds to one terminal of a transformer, and three voltages are available according as the switches are closed, both up, one up and one down, or both down. The ratios of all three transformers are changed simultaneously, and the operation can be effected without shutting down the transformer bank, both of which points are important in operating the sub-station. It would obviously be impracticable to carry out this arrangement on the primary, as the switch-gear would be prohibitive. With large transformers requiring heavy secondary leads and switches, it becomes equally impracticable to carry out this arrangement on the secondary, and the ratio-changing device must be on, or close to, the transformer itself. In this case the transformer must be shut down to change over, and it is therefore simpler to have the change in the primary, since the moving parts are smaller. A simple plug connection for the transformer leads, with two or three corresponding sockets for various voltage ratios, forms the simplest method of adjustment. This is the method adopted in the Glasgow tramway installation.

BATTERIES.—Whether a battery should or should not be included in the equipment of any particular sub-station must depend largely on local conditions, especially as regards the character of the motor load. The use of a battery in a general service sub-station may come under one or all of the following three heads :—

(1) It may be charged during the day and used to take the motor and lighting load during the night, and for early morning car service, enabling the running plant to be shut down at those times.

(2) It may be charged during the day and used during the lighting load peak.

(3) It may be employed, in conjunction with a reversible booster, to take the sudden peaks in the traction load, so that the traction supply can be maintained by a smaller unit of plant.

The first of these methods of employment is probably the one that will be found most useful. From the point of view of staff organisation, as will be shown later, it will be most desirable to be able to shut down the running plant at night, unless the night load is sufficiently large to load one converter unit fairly. In the normal case the night load between 12.30 a.m. and 5 a.m. would probably average about 100 kilowatts, with a maximum of perhaps 150 kilowatts. To meet this we should require a battery of 1,000 ampere hours capacity with a three-hour discharge rate. Should the motor load consist to any large extent of colliery or other pumping plant, it is probable that the load will largely exceed the figures given above. In such cases it will prove more economical to dispense with the battery and arrange for a night shift at the sub-station.

As regards the second method of employment, it will be evident that where the motor load forms such a large proportion of the whole, the lighting peak will not be such a serious consideration as to warrant the increased capital and maintenance cost incurred by putting in a battery.

As regards the third method of employment, the real advantage of a battery for meeting the traction peak is that it enables the plant capacity to be reduced to that of the average instead of the maximum load, thereby saving in capital cost by enabling smaller units to be used, and in running cost, due to these units being run on a favourable part of the efficiency curve. In the case of our sub-station, however, we are practically obliged, for the sake of uniformity, to use the same size of unit all through, so that to take any advantage of the reduction in size of the traction unit by using a battery would entail the use of numerous 250-kilowatt units, and this multiplication of running plant, and its lower efficiency, due to the reduction in size of units, would more than compensate for the slight advantage to be gained.

Of course all the above only refers to the case of a general service sub-station, and it is obvious that any very great change in the sub-division of the load, as between traction, lighting, and power, will necessitate separate consideration for each case. For instance, if the demand is very largely for lighting, the use of a battery for meeting the peak may be economical. If, on the other hand, traction forms the greater part, it is simpler to put in a fairly liberal transformer plant, and rely on the overload capacity of the rotary converters to meet the sudden peaks, this being one of the inherent advantages of a rotary converter to which attention

was drawn above, and the use of a battery in this connection being superfluous. Another advantage of employing a battery for carrying the night load only, is that the charging and discharging arrangements are much simplified, the battery being charged from the lighting bus bars by means of a booster, and when the plant is shut down, connected direct to the lighting bus bars. The conclusion is that for a sub-station of the character under consideration a secondary battery would be found a useful adjunct for use under condition No. 1.

Should the circumstances be favourable to the use of a secondary battery it will be found convenient to have two booster sets, one of the semi-automatic type, and suitable for charging off the lighting bus bars, and the other of the automatic type for charging off the traction bus bars at will. In order to attain the desideratum of a constant speed, the boosters should preferably be run by synchronous motors, thus eliminating any difficulty which may arise from the change of speed inherent in a direct current motor.

STARTING DEVICES.—The necessity, or otherwise, for elaborate starting devices, depends largely on the general arrangement of the system. In this connection systems may be divided into three classes:—

(1) Those which run continuously, and in which the sub-stations feed into the same direct current network, or where there is a battery at the sub-station. In this case, as there will always be direct current available, the converters can be started up as direct current motors, and the alternating current switches closed on synchronising.

(2) Where the plant is shut down at night, and the sub-stations feed the same direct current network. Here all that is needed is for one rotary to be switched straight in on the alternating current side, and run up to synchronism—the disturbing effect on the alternating current system being unimportant as the load is off—the remaining sub-stations can then start off the direct current side as in case (1). This is the method used on the Central London Railway, a rotary converter in the power house being usually started up first.

(3) When the sub-stations are not interconnected by feeding the same direct current network. In this case we cannot start up the sub-station on the direct current side, as no current is available. It is not advisable to start up by switching on the rotaries on the alternating current side, owing to the disturbing effect on the other sub-stations; consequently some other means must be found, and this usually takes the form of an induction motor driving the rotary. The rotary is run up to speed by means of this motor,

and synchronised before closing the alternating current switches. This is the method employed in the Glasgow and London United systems.

An arrangement has recently been put forward to enable the rotary converters to be started up from the alternating current side without starting motors, by means of leads connected to intermediate points on the transformer secondaries, a gradually increasing voltage being applied to the collector rings by means of suitable th row-over switches.

A sub-station for general service comes under the first heading, since if it is not provided with a battery there must be arrangements for interconnecting the low-tension networks, so as to keep up the supply in case of a sub-station being shut down. We may therefore conclude that no starting motors will be required in the sub-station under consideration, starting switches on the rotary converter panels being all that is necessary. This arrangement has a minor advantage also in saving the additional switch gear that would be required for cutting out the series coil when exciting on the alternating side.

REGULATING DEVICES.—From the range of voltage to be supplied, and the ratio of commutator to collector voltage, we are now in a position to decide on the regulation required, which is best shown in the following table :

Nature of Supply.	Voltage delivered.	Sub-station Voltage.			
		Direct Current Bus Bar.		Low-tension Alternating Current	
		No Load.	Full Load.	No Load.	Full Load.
Traction	500	500	550	350	390
Lighting and direct current power ...	440	440	480	310	340
Alternating current power	330	...	...	330	360

The sub-station will therefore require regulating devices to give :—

(1) Wide regulation to meet the varied nature of the load, the transformers having to give 310, 330, or 350 volts, as required for the three classes of supply.

(2) Rapid, and therefore of necessity automatic, but not necessarily very accurate, regulation for the rapid variations of the traction load, the low-tension alternating voltage having a range of 40 volts.

(3) Accurate, but probably not very rapid, and

therefore not necessarily automatic, regulation for the lighting and power load, the low-tension alternating voltage having a range of 30 volts.

The first condition is most simply met by having transformers with a ratio-changing arrangement, so as to give 310, 330, or 350 secondary volts, fine adjustment not being required. For the second condition, compounding the rotaries is by far the most convenient and simple arrangement, although it is subject to the drawback which has already been referred to. For the third condition, it would be possible to employ hand regulation of the shunt field, the change of voltage being carried out on the same principle as in the compounding. This could also be done for the first condition, but in neither case would there be any advantage to compensate for the lowering of the power factor. For the fine adjustment some other device is therefore needed. A very simple and efficient regulator consists essentially of a small induction motor, the number of phases of which will depend on that of the general system; in our case it will be three. The stator windings are each in series, and the rotor windings in parallel with a pair of collector rings of the rotary converter, and by altering the relative position of the rotor and stator, their mutual induction can be varied so that the collector ring voltage can be increased or diminished as desired. It would be possible to employ this regulator for condition No. 1, but the size and cost of such a regulator would render it much less advantageous than changing the transformer ratios. The regulator has, from the nature of things, to be operated from the lighting board, but it has to be connected between the transformers and the rotary, and locating it near the lighting board would, in most cases, involve a considerable length of heavy cable; the difficulty is got over by moving the regulator by means of a small induction motor with a double-throw triple-pole switch on the lighting board; this is the method adopted at the Margate sub-station.

Another regulating device consists of an auxiliary boosting rotary converter and group of transformers, the primary coils of the latter supplied from the secondary of the main transformers, and the commutator of the boosting rotary converter being in series with that of the main rotary converter; the maximum voltage of the auxiliary rotary converter should be equal to the maximum boosting required, and can be lowered as desired by field regulation. The auxiliary transformers should be constructed to have considerable inductance, so as to allow of the large variation of voltage by field regulation. The arrangement will, of course, affect the power factor of the system slightly, but this can be readily corrected by adjusting the field of the main rotary converter so as to compensate for the lag, or lead, produced by the booster regulation. The drawbacks of this system are the slightly increased complication and the addition to the rotating machinery of the sub-station. The booster has to be of considerable size, since its commutator must be almost equal in size to that of the rotary.

A somewhat simpler arrangement is to have a booster consisting of a direct current generator on the shaft of the rotary converter. If, however, the rotary converter has a starting motor, and also—as would frequently be the case in a traction sub-station—drives a rail booster, this additional booster would form a somewhat unwieldy arrangement. It has the same drawbacks as regards the size of the commutator as the methods treated above.

Another method which has been proposed consists of placing a synchronous motor on the same shaft as the rotary converter between the armature and collector of the rotary converter. By varying the field of the synchronous motor the voltage drop in its armature, and consequently the voltage on the rotary converter armature, can be varied as required. This method avoids the commutator difficulty, but not the other difficulty alluded to in connection with the direct current booster.

On the whole, it is evident that the first form of regulator presents the greatest advantages in the way of economy and convenience in operation. It is also more rapid in its effect on the voltage than is the case where the adjustment depends on varying the field of a generator.

ARRANGEMENT AND CONNECTIONS OF PLANT.—Sub-stations for traction being so often erected in disused stables, car-sheds, etc., they unfortunately have to be laid out as one can, not as one would, and they seldom approach the ideal as closely as a generating station. A sub-station for general purposes, however, would be less subject to this limitation, which is fortunate, as the general lay-out of such a sub-station demands much more careful attention in order to give convenient and economical working than is required for the comparatively simple conditions of traction. The conditions to be fulfilled in a satisfactory sub-station arrangement are: economy in first cost; convenience in operation; safety from shock; safety from fire.

The first condition necessitates keeping all connections as short and simple as possible. This can best be done by locating each bank of transformers as near as possible to its own rotary converter. The heaviest cables being from the alternating current plant to the rotary converter, and thence to the direct current switchboard, the most economical plan will usually be to have the rotary converters between the alternating current plant and the direct current switchboard. This arrangement also satisfies the second condition. As a protection from fire, it is desirable to have the transformer room entirely separate from the switchboard and the converter room where space will permit, and also to still further sub-divide the transformer room, so that each bank of transformers stands in a separate fire-proof cell, preferably with an arched brick roof.

As regards safety from shock, this is chiefly a matter of switchboard design, which has been dealt with at some length recently in several contemporaries. Briefly, it may be said that a switchboard should either have no back to it, or it should have a back giving ample room for working. On the same principle, it is advisable that all the switchboard connections should be either absolutely insulated and expose no bare metal, or absolutely bare, carried at such a height as to be above the reach of anyone from the floor, and so arranged that, in case of any of the structure falling, it will be effectually earthed.

This latter arrangement generally lends itself best to a convenient arrangement of the buildings, and is adopted on the Glasgow Corporation Tramways, Figs. 4, 5, and 6, Plate XLVIII, and the London United Tramways, Figs. 7, 8, and 9, Plate XLIX. The arrangements here are as follows:—

The sub-station consists of two main divisions, the converter room and transformer room. The transformer room is sub-divided into brick cells, each containing a

Plate XLVIII

Fig. 4.

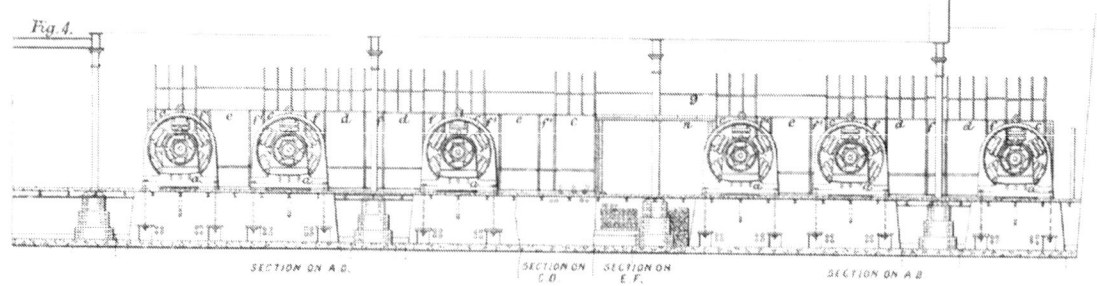

SECTION ON A.B.   SECTION ON C.D.   SECTION ON E.F.   SECTION ON A.B.

Fig. 5.

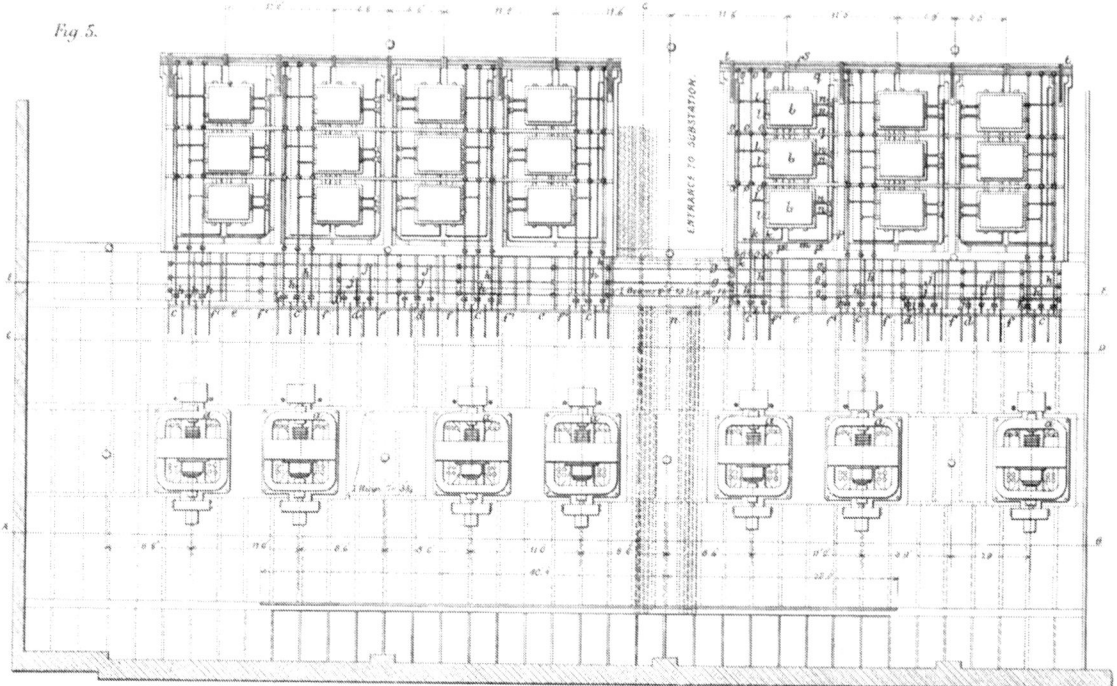

Fig. 6.   SECTION ON G.H.

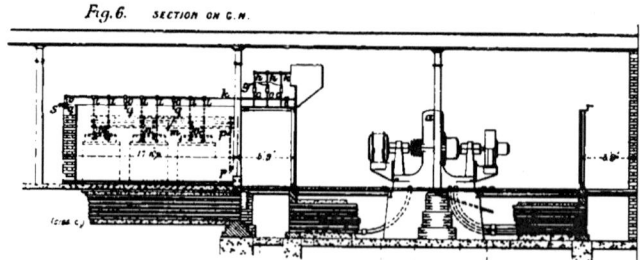

Arrangement of Dalhousie Sub-station, Glasgow Corporation Tramways

U of M

a. 500-kilowatt rotary converter	*g.* High-tension bus bars	*o.* Insulating supports for high-tension bars
b. 200-kilowatt transformer	*h.* Connections to transformer switch	*p.* Insulating supports for low-tension bars
c. Panel for transformer and converter	*j.* Connections to feeder switch	*q.* I Beam, 4ins. by 3ins., 9lbs. per foot
d. Panel for high-tension feeder	*k.* High-tension transformer bars	*r.* Low-tension switchboard
e. Blank panel, 4ft. wide	*l.* Flexible connections to high-tension side	*s.* Tee, 3ins. by 3ins., 7lbs. per foot
f. Blank panel, 2ft. wide	*m.* Low-tension transformer bars	*t.* Rail, 24lbs. per yard
f¹. Blank panel, 1ft. 6ins. wide	*n.* Flexible connections to low-tension side	*u.* Angle, 4ins. by 4ins., supporting slate slabs

THE ELECTRICAL EQUIPMENT OF SUB-STATIONS

MʇoU

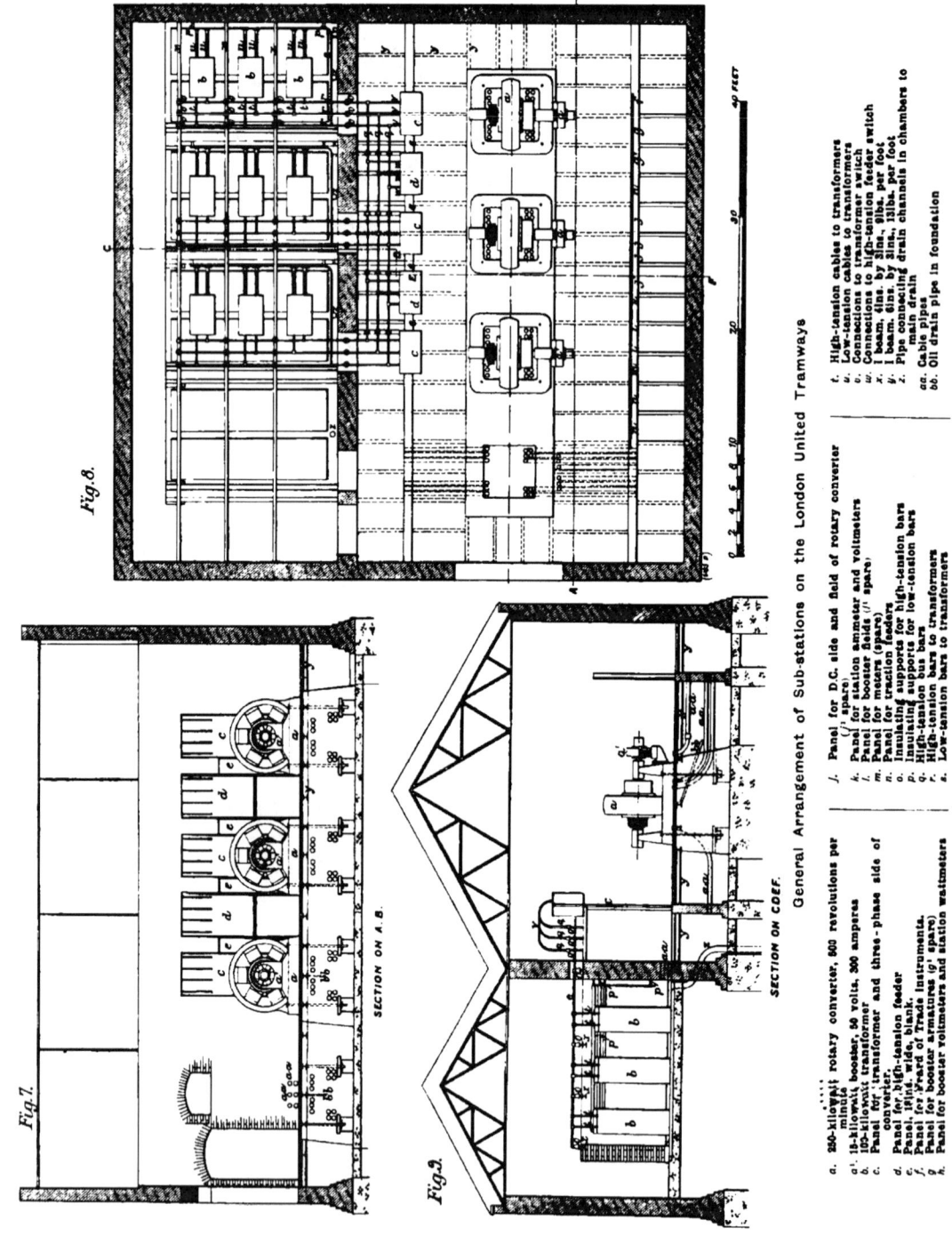

Fig.8.

Fig.7.

SECTION ON A.B.

Fig.9.

SECTION ON CDEF.

General Arrangement of Sub-stations on the London United Tramways

a. 250-kilowatt rotary converter, 600 revolutions per minute.
a¹. 15-kilowatt booster, 50 volts, 300 ampères.
b. 160-kilowatt transformer.
c. Panel for transformer and three-phase side of converter.
d. Panel for high-tension feeder.
e. Panel, 1ft. wide, blank.
f, g. Panel for booster armatures (g¹ spare).
h. Panel for booster voltmeters and station wattmeters.

j. Panel for D.C. side and field of rotary converter (j¹ spare).
k. Panel for station ammeter and voltmeters.
l. Panel for booster fields (l¹ spare).
m. Panel for return (spare).
n. Panel for traction feeders.
o. Insulating supports for high-tension bars.
p. Insulating supports for low-tension bars.
q. High-tension bus bars.
r. High-tension bars to transformers.
s. Low-tension bars to transformers.

t. High-tension cables to transformers.
u. Low-tension cables to transformers.
v. Connections to transformer switch.
w. Connections to high-tension feeder switch.
x. I beam, 4ins. by 3ins., 13lbs. per foot.
y. I beam, 6ins. by 3ins., 18lbs. per foot.
z. Pipe connecting drain channels in chambers to main drain.
aa. Cable pipes.
bb. Oil drain pipe in foundation.

M 10 U

bank of three transformers. The alternating current switchboard is on the side of the converter room next the transformers, and consists essentially of a panel for each high-tension feeder, and one for each bank of transformers. Each transformer panel is

transformers is supplied by a set of three similar bars carried through the party wall and along the cell, and connected to the bus bars by means of a high-tension switch on the transformer panel. The transformers are connected to these bars by short lengths of

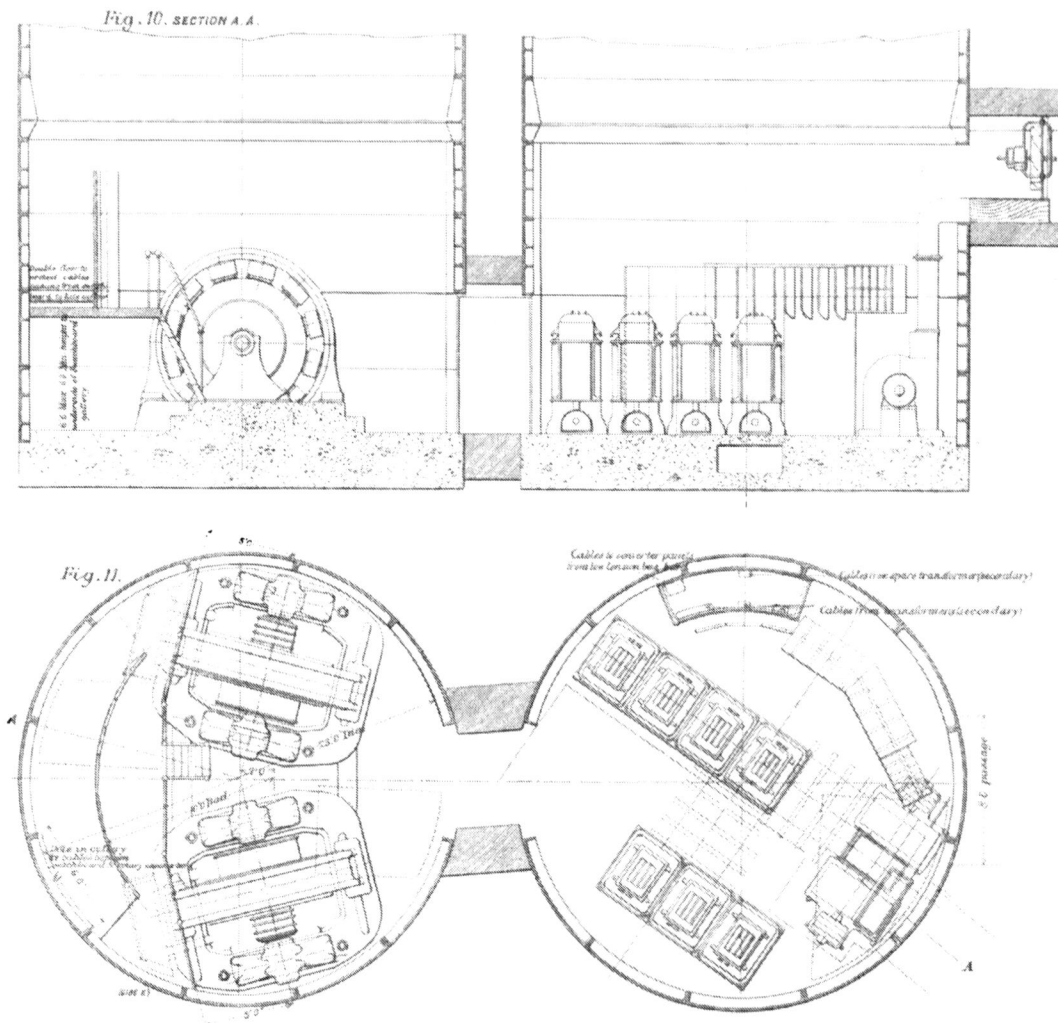

Fig. 10. SECTION A.A.

Fig. 11.

General Arrangement of Sub-station, Central London Railway (see page 220)

located in front of the cell containing the bank it controls and opposite to the corresponding rotary converter. The high-tension bus bars are of bare copper tube on porcelain insulators, supported on iron stems from the framing of the board. Each bank of

flexible cable, having plug connections into the transformers, each having three plug-holes to enable the ratio to be varied. The low-tension connections are similar, the transformers being connected by cables to a set of three copper bars, which are in turn connected

to the three single-pole low-tension switches
on the transformer panel. The connections
from these switches to the collector rings are
carried in the usual way by pipes through
the foundations. The transformer panel also
carries the starting switch for the induction
motor used for running the rotary up to

practically never opened, each rotary with
its transformers being treated as one complete
unit of plant.

A plan is given (Figs. 10 and 11, page 219)
of a sub-station on the Central London Railway; it is, however, more interesting as an
example of how much plant can be got

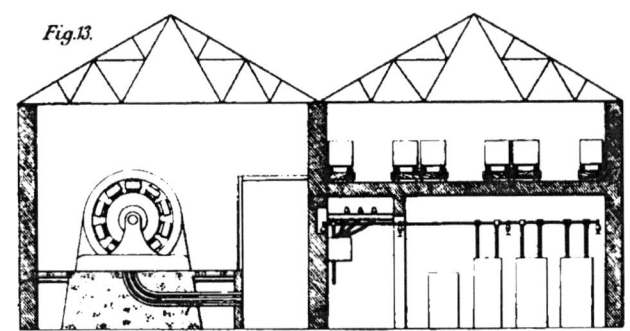

Fig. 13.

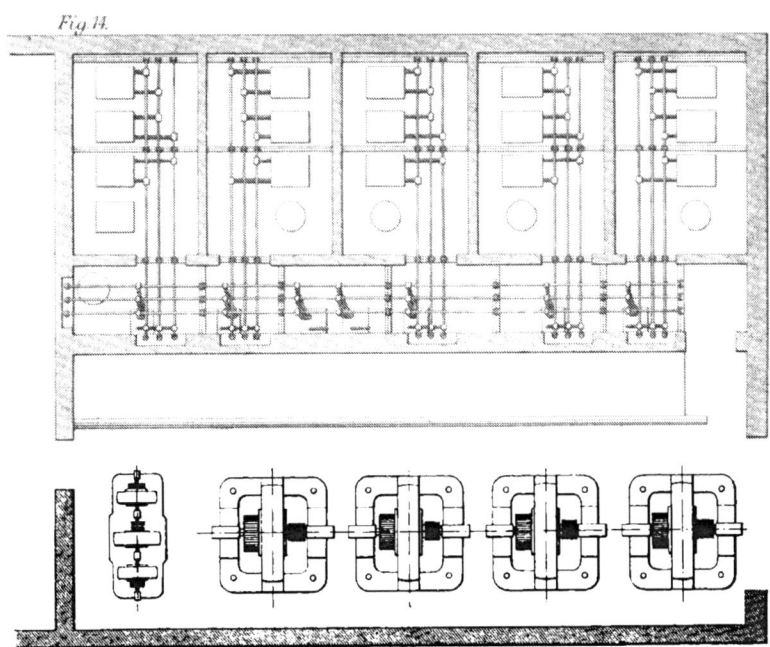

Fig. 14.

Arrangement of Typical Sub-station (see page 221)

synchronism. The direct current switchboard
is situated on the other side of the converter
room, and in its connections and arrangements is practically an ordinary traction
switchboard. Synchronising is carried out
on the high-tension side of the transformers,
and the low-tension transformer switches are

into a limited space under pressure of circumstances, than as a model of sub-station
arrangement. In these sub-stations, synchronising being carried out on the low-
tension side, a triple-pole switch is necessary
on both the secondary and primary of each
bank of transformers, and in addition each

Plate L

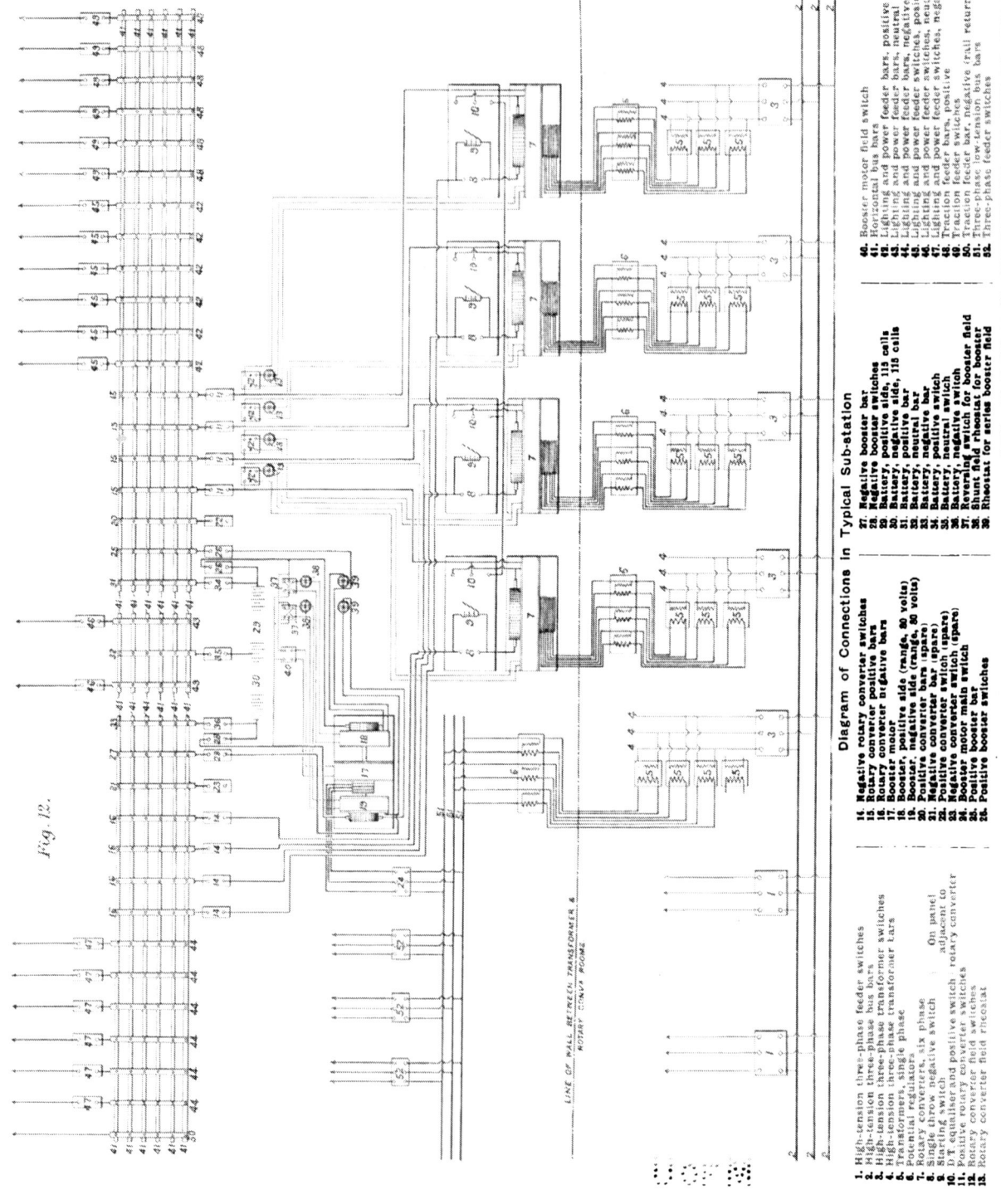

Fig. 12.

Diagram of Connections in Typical Sub-station

1. High-tension three-phase feeder switches
2. High-tension three-phase bus bars
3. High-tension three-phase transformer switches
4. High-tension three-phase transformer bars
5. Transformers, single phase
6. Potential regulators
7. Rotary converters, six phase
8. Single throw negative switch
9. Starting switch
10. D.T. equaliser and positive switch
11. Positive rotary converter switches
12. Rotary converter field switches
13. Rotary converter field rheostat

14. Negative rotary converter switches
15. Negative booster positive bars
16. Rotary converter negative bars
17. Booster motor
18. Booster, positive side (range, 80 volts)
19. Booster, negative side (range, 80 volts)
20. Positive converter bar (spare)
21. Negative converter bar (spare)
22. Positive converter switch (spare)
23. Negative converter switch (spare)
24. Booster motor main switch
25. Positive booster bar
26. Positive booster switches

27. Negative booster bar
28. Negative booster switches
29. Battery, positive side, 115 cells
30. Battery, negative side, 115 cells
31. Battery, positive bar
32. Battery, neutral bar
33. Battery, negative bar
34. Battery, positive switch
35. Battery, neutral switch
36. Battery, negative switch
37. Reversing switch for booster field
38. Shunt field rheostat for booster
39. Rheostat for series booster field

40. Booster motor field switch
41. Horizontal bus bars
42. Lighting and power feeder bars, positive
43. Lighting and power feeder bars, neutral
44. Lighting and power feeder bars, negative
45. Lighting and power feeder switches, positive
46. Lighting and power feeder switches, neutral
47. Lighting and power feeder switches, negative
48. Traction feeder bar, positive
49. Traction feeder switches
50. Traction feeder bar, negative (rail return)
51. Three-phase low-tension bus bars
52. Three-phase feeder switches

LINE OF WALL BETWEEN TRANSFORMER & ROTARY CONVR. ROOMS

individual transformer is provided with a double-pole switch on both primary and secondary. The object of this latter arrangement is to permit of a transformer being cut out in case of a breakdown, and a spare transformer substituted, seven transformers being provided for the two rotary converters, all grouped together so as to be entirely interchangeable. It being impossible in these sub-stations to isolate the transformer banks, this arrangement was adopted as the best one available. Where, however, each bank of three transformers is in a separate cell, there would be no compensating advantage for the increased elaboration of switch gear.

It will be evident from the examples given that synchronising on the high-tension side simplifies the switch gear considerably, even for three-phase rotary converters, and with six phases this is still more the case, as to synchronise on the low-tension side we should require a six-pole switch for heavy currents at 300 to 400 volts. The conditions to be fulfilled as regards switch gear in order to obtain an economical and satisfactory operation are :—

(1) All switch gear required in the ordinary routine operation of the sub-station should be operated from the switch panel corresponding to the apparatus controlled.

(2) Switch gear only occasionally required for tests, etc., should be located so as to necessitate the least possible deviation in the straight cable runs between the various apparatus.

(3) The alternating current transformer switches and direct current converter switches should be located so as to be within reach of one man without necessitating his moving about, so that one man can run up, synchronise, and switch in a rotary single handed.

Fig. 12, Plate L, shows the diagram of connections, and Figs. 13 and 14, page 220, are a plan and elevation of a sub-station designed to fulfil all the conditions that have been given above as to general arrangement and switching arrangements. The transformer room is divided into cells, each containing one bank of transformers and the regulator. The transformer cells have openings, closed by sheet-iron doors, leading into a passage along which the high-tension bus bars are carried on a structure similar to that described in connection with the Glasgow sub-stations. The connection from the incoming high-tension feeders to the bus bars is made through triple-pole switches operated from the converter room.

Each bank of transformers is supplied through a similar switch, each of these switches being operated by a lever on, or adjacent to, the corresponding rotary converter positive panel. There will thus be absolutely no high-tension connections in the converter room, and the switches can be located so as to enable the cable connections to be as short as possible. Each rotary converter is located opposite its own transformer bank ; the transformers are connected direct to the regulator, and the regulators to the collector rings of the rotary converters. Synchronising is carried out on the high-tension side, and consequently the only use of switches between the transformers and rotary converters would be for temporary disconnection for testing purposes. To be of any use, there would have to be twelve such switches or disconnecting links for each unit of plant — six on each side of the regulator—and it is obviously much simpler to arrange so that the cable terminals are easily detachable, and to disconnect in this way.

The switchboard for the alternating current supply may be most conveniently located on the side of the converter room nearer the transformer room, or across the end of the converter room, and would be provided with a transformer panel with ammeter, voltmeter, and switch lever, and with a panel for each feeder, carrying an ammeter and triple-pole switch and fuses.

In order to completely carry out the arrangement of having no high-tension connections in the converter room, the instruments reading on high-tension circuits will be of the transformer type, and all synchronising connections supplied through similar transformers. For the sake of simplicity, these connections are not shown in the diagram, Fig. 12, Plate L.

The high-tension switches should be of the oil-break type. For any class of high-tension work these switches are very desirable on account of their compactness and reliability in action. For the sub-station under consideration, however, they possess still further advantages, as they can be readily located where most convenient for the general arrangement of connections, and are well adapted for operation from a distance by means of relays or by rods carried under the floor.

The direct current switchboard may be

located on either side of the converter room as found most convenient. In its general arrangements it is simply an adaptation of a switchboard for direct current traction, lighting, and power stations. Both terminals of the rotary converters and battery, and the outer booster terminals, are each provided with a vertical bar, and horizontal bus bars are furnished with plugs, so that the feeders can be grouped as desired. The centre of the board is occupied by the neutral battery connection, and taking them in order outwards from this are: the battery positive and negative bars; positive booster bar; negative booster bar; rotary converter positive and negative bars; power and lighting feeder bars; and, at one end of the board, the traction feeder bars; at the other the rail returns and Board of Trade panel. In addition, there will be a switch panel, mounted on a pillar adjacent to each rotary converter, containing a double - throw positive and equaliser switch, starting switch, and negative switch. An alternating current ammeter and voltmeter and synchronising plug connection are located adjacent to each rotary converter panel. It will be evident from the diagram that the double booster and battery can be employed to balance the three-wire distributing system when the main plant is running, in addition to running the night load when the main plant is shut down. For the sake of simplicity only the more important features of the board are shown in Plate L, and are explained by the references annexed to the diagram; the instruments and instrument transformers, the synchronising connections, the relays for operating high - tension switches, all D.C. automatic circuit breakers and fuses, and the Board of Trade panel are omitted.

In starting up a rotary, the *modus operandi* is as follows: Close positive switch on rotary converter switch pillar, so as to short circuit series winding; see that both negative and starting switches are open; insert plug to connect rotary converter to the bus bars on which it is desired to start; close positive and negative rotary converter switches on switchboard; close field switch; close starting switch, and, when up to speed, close the negative switch and open starting switch; regulate speed by field rheostat, and, when synchronised, close transformer switch; regulate direct current volts as required.

If the machine is run on a different set of bars from those on which it has started up, the additional operations required are: Open positive and negative switches on switchboard; adjust direct current volts to the voltage required for the circuit on which the machine is to run; arrange plugs as desired; close positive and negative switches.

It will be evident, from the description and plans, that the alleged complication of the switch gear necessary for operating rotary converters has very little ground in fact. Indeed, there is not a single detail of switch gear essential for a rotary converter that is not equally essential for a motor generator.

SAFETY DEVICES.—The usual safeguards will be required against lightning and against short circuits or heavy overloads. These may be summed up as follows:—

Lightning arresters on traction feeders and on overhead power and lighting feeders, if any are employed.

Reactance coils on traction feeders.

Automatic overload circuit breakers on all feeders.

Automatic overload circuit breakers between the direct current bus bars and the rotary converters, battery, and boosters, to protect these against short circuits on the direct current switchboard or connections.

Automatic overload circuit breakers between the high-tension bus bars and the transformer banks, to protect the high-tension feeders against any short circuits between the high-tension bus bars and the rotary converter direct current circuit breakers.

Automatic return current circuit breakers on the high-tension feeders, to prevent the sub-station returning energy from the direct current network into the high-tension feeders, in the event of a short circuit or breakdown on the latter.

There are numerous types of circuit breakers which will be suitable for the low-tension side. For the high-tension transformer and feeder circuit breaker the most satisfactory arrangement is to have an automatic relay device to open the high-tension oil-break switches. Delayed action circuit breakers have now passed the experimental stage, and are a great convenience in working. By their use the annoyance of having a machine circuit breaker open on a heavy short circuit on a single feeder is avoided, as the machine circuit breaker can be set to have a slightly longer delayed action than the feeder circuit breakers. Similarly the high-tension circuit breakers should be set with a still longer delayed action, since in the case of a short circuit on the low-tension side it is obviously better to ensure that it shall be opened at 500 volts than 10,000 volts.

Cost.—The following schedules as to cost are based on recent quotations from leading British makers, and may be taken as fairly representative. It will be seen that the actual cost of the converting units is only £4 10s. per kilowatt with rotary converters, as against £5 15s. with motor generators.

SCHEDULE OF PLANT AND COST
CONVERTER UNITS

	Rate. £	Amount. £
Twelve transformers, oil type, 175 kilo-watts, with ratio-changing switches	257	3,084
Four rotary converters, 500 kilowatts ...	1,145	4,580
Four reactances (for compounding) ...	119	476
Four potential regulators with operating motors for distant control	213	852
Total cost of four converter units ...		£8,992
Alternative :—		
Four motor generators, induction or synchronous motors, 500 kilowatts	2,875	11,500
Remaining Plant :—		
One battery, 230 cells, 1,000 ampere hours, maximum discharge 300 amperes ...	—	3,000
One charging booster for same, two 30-kilowatt generators, and 70-kilowatt motor	—	800
Four transformers, as above	257	1,028
One potential regulator	—	213
One main switchboard, as shown on diagram	—	2,500
One alternating current switchboard, as shown on diagram		750
Connecting cables		500
Total		£8,791

	£
Total cost of plant with rotary converters...	17,783
Total cost of plant with motor generators...	20,291
Total cost of rotary converter sub-station, with buildings and foundations ...	20,000

With the load factors assumed at the beginning of this article, the units sold for the various classes of load will be approximately as follows :—

	Units.
Traction	1,040,000
Power, alternating current and direct current	1,730,000
Lighting	350,000
Total	3,120,000

The cost of transformation may, therefore, be summarised as follows :—

	£
To depreciation of plant at 5 per cent. ...	1,000
Maintenance	500
Wages, including proportion of superintendent's salary	460
Stores and oil	100
Total	£2,060

Total cost of transformation per unit metered at the sub-station low-tension bus bars ... ...   0.1585d.

RAILWAY ECONOMICS

By the Hon. Robert P. Porter

V.—LONDON LOCOMOTION (continued from page 154)

XL.—A New Situation

THE unexpected and somewhat sensational withdrawal of part of the London Suburban Railway project by the London United Electric Railway interests, and the subsequent rejection of the entire Bill by Parliament, make it impossible to conclude this series of articles, as I had hoped, in this issue of TRACTION AND TRANSMISSION. The motives which led to this action on the part of the United Tramway interests form no part of a discussion in these pages. Both sides of the question have been pretty thoroughly thrashed out by the debates in Parliament or by the daily press, and the public are apparently in possession of all facts relating to the unfortunate incident. I say unfortunate because it may mean still further delay in the solution of the question of London locomotion, and it leaves the situation at the close of the present session of Parliament substantially where it was at the opening. Out of over eighty-two miles of proposed tube railways, only four miles have been sanctioned. Meantime it is fortunate for the public that the side tracking of this important through communication will have the effect of hastening rather than retarding the electrification of the Metropolitan and District undergrounds, and that it will not impede the progress of the tubular railways now in course of completion by the Yerkes group and the Great Northern and City. All these important enterprises are practically out of the wood, so far as legislation is concerned, and in various stages of construction. The London Suburban scheme, as I have explained in a previous article, covered important territory, and in conjunction with the other proposals of the session would have produced something akin to a harmonious system of underground locomotion for London. That part of the battle for the "nether county of London"

will have to be fought over again is to be regretted nearly everyone will admit, but it will be a serious mistake if the incident is made the pretext for unnecessary delay. There never will be any necessity for the construction of two lines under Piccadilly until it has been demonstrated that one will not do the work. As to which particular group of capitalists shall be allotted this important route is not a matter which so deeply concerns the public as the character of the service given. The London Suburban Railway proposal appealed to the Committee of the House of Lords because of its sweeping through route, the lowness of the fares, and the fact that the construction was underwritten by a firm capable and likely, to carry out the undertaking. For the present that scheme has been wiped off the slate. This, however, does not stop progress on the network of tubes now being pushed in various directions by what is known as the Yerkes group, and which, when completed as shown (Plate XVII, "Railway Economics," page 72), connect important north and south districts of London. Unless the present Parliament appoints a Committee with statutory power to act in the matter, there will be proposals and counter proposals from rival interests next session for Parliament to select from. The London Central will undoubtedly again put forward its claims for recognition. There is no reason to suppose that the Morgan interests have abandoned the field, while the Yerkes group, encouraged by the good start they have made, may come forward with both west and north-east proposals that, for scope and economy in operation, may appear attractive to Parliament.

XLI.—THE COUNTY COUNCIL PROPOSALS

The important part which the steam railways play in London locomotion was pointed out in the preceding article, and, though we are not likely to have a concrete proposal from the five or six companies most deeply concerned in London traffic, there is a community of interest here that will exert an influence on the several projects which it will be wise not to ignore. The proposals that carefully consider the interests of these companies will have decided advantages over those which seek to build up traffic districts of their own. The rejection of the London Suburban Railway, and the sudden termination of tubular projects for 1902, was followed, as might be expected, by considerable commotion in Spring Gardens. After a spirited debate the London County Council adopted, by an overwhelming vote, a proposal which seemed to indicate the intention on the part of that body to promote an extensive tube railway scheme itself. After more mature consideration, and a reference to the report of the Joint Select Committee of the two Houses of Parliament held in 1901, the idea of promoting a Bill was abandoned and the following important resolutions adopted :—

(a) That in the opinion of the Council it will be detrimental to the interests of London if any Bill for the construction of a tube railway is proceeded with in Parliament until a full inquiry shall have been held and a report presented upon the following questions :—

(1) How far it is possible to adapt the provisions of the Light Railways Act, 1896, to underground railways in London as recommended by the Joint Select Committee of 1901.

(2) Whether it is possible and desirable to formulate some general scheme of underground railway accommodation capable of serving the requirements of London as a whole, and if so, what should be the main features of such general scheme.

(3) Whether a system of deep level tube railways will afford the best results, or whether it will not be preferable to adopt either wholly or partially the system of underground locomotion in operation in Continental and American cities.

(4) How and by whom such general scheme can best be carried out having regard to :—

The general traffic within London.
The special need of supplying means of access to the suburbs.
The housing problem.
The need for cheap fares.
The raising of necessary capital.
Existing means of locomotion.

(b) That with a view to obtaining such inquiry as above mentioned, a deputation do wait upon the President of the Board of Trade and ask him to assist in obtaining the appointment of a Commission to hold such inquiry, with power to consider all proposals that may be brought before them for the construction and supervision of underground railways in London, and to report as to the desirability of establishing some authority to prepare and issue Provisional Orders for confirmation by Parliament authorising the construction of such underground railways as such authority may be satisfied will be for the public benefit, and in the meantime to use his influence to obtain the suspension of any Bills that may be introduced into Parliament for the construction of tube railways in London.

(c) That it be referred to the Parliamentary, Highways, Housing of the Working Classes, and Finance Committees, to jointly arrange for the proposed deputation, and to report again to the Council as to any further steps they may deem it advisable that the Council should take.

These proposals may involve considerable delay, and the immense money loss due to traffic congestion will soon overtake any possible advantage that may be gained by further reflection on "some general scheme of underground railway accommodation." The Prime Minister, in his remarks on the subject, seems alive to this, and hence hesitates to appoint a Royal Commission. The history of London locomotion is not a particularly attractive one to financiers. The railway companies, underground and surface, within the boundaries of Greater London, the tramway, omnibus, and other companies, have not made immense fortunes for their promoters. Some few have earned respectable dividends, while others, for one cause and another, have lost money. Again, the steam railways centring in London cannot make such great profits out of their suburban business, for three out of the six most important only pay reasonable dividends, while the two south-eastern railways are in far from a flourishing condition. It is well sometimes to face facts as they really exist. No newly constituted authority—and this is said with the greatest respect to the ability and integrity of both Board of Trade and London County Council—is likely to drive a better bargain in the public interest than did the House of Lords Committee when it sanctioned the London Suburban Railway. Expert railway men in all directions shook their heads, and declared the low fares scheduled in that Bill could never be made to pay. It has been repeatedly stated in this series of articles that the advisory work of both Board of Trade and County Council in these matters is excellent, and the fact that the County Council announces that it has instructed its officers to prepare a complete scheme of locomotion for London, is a move in the right direction. Much of the valuable information in existence on this subject has been dug out piecemeal by the permanent officials of the County Council, and by members of that body who have given the subject special attention. Last April the London County Council submitted a report setting forth with considerable detail their views of the situation. It has in its various reports touched upon every one of the questions suggested in the above resolutions.

The powers of the Board of Trade have also been extended in technical matters to a degree that gives that body absolute control as to construction. Under these rules the company is obliged from time to time to submit for the approval of the Board of Trade plans, sections, and other details of their proposals with respect to (a) permanent way, tunnels, platforms, lifts, and other communications; (b) rolling stock; (c) lighting; and (d) ventilation. The railway rolling stock and the other works shall be constructed, reconstructed, and maintained only in accordance with the plans, sections, and other details as approved by the Board of Trade. These clauses are inserted in all the new Bills, and the schemes already authorised have likewise to subscribe to them when they come to Parliament for extension of time, and small extensions, sites for stations, and so forth, for linking up purposes. So much for the general structural side of the question, which the County Council has always been willing to leave to the Board of Trade.

The County Council has taken up in good faith the practical side of this question, and has from time to time advised Parliament at considerable length as to the merits and demerits of the several schemes submitted by promoters. Its minor and unreserved recommendations for the present session were all sanctioned, except the Islington and Euston Railway. These were all in the direction of linking and coupling up tubular railways already sanctioned and partly constructed. The majority of them formed links in the important Yerkes system, which, so far as it goes, and taking into consideration existing conditions when Mr. Yerkes came into the field, could not well be improved by a Royal Com-

mission nor by any public body especially constituted for the purpose. On the most important recommendation of the County Council, namely, that the Brompton and Piccadilly Circus line (Mr. Yerkes's Piccadilly route), and the Piccadilly and City (the Morgan Piccadilly route) be opposed *in toto*, and the Central London Piccadilly route be sanctioned, Parliament disagreed with the County Council. It was really a difficult matter to decide which of these three or four schemes would best serve the public, and there is little doubt that the two features of the London Suburban Piccadilly route which weighed heaviest with the Committee of the House of Lords, were the proposal for a through route from west to north-east, and the advantage to the public in the exceedingly low fares scheduled in the Bill, and which would have been binding on the promoters.

XLII.—Existing Conditions Must be Considered

These points have been ably brought out by Mr. Philip Dawson (pages 89 to 103, TRACTION AND TRANSMISSION for October), and even one so well qualified as Mr. Dawson, seems to realise the impossibility of formulating some general scheme of underground railway which does not take into consideration existing railways—constructed, in course of construction, and authorised—and which does not recognise the several important groups of capitalists who are prepared to find the capital. At least Mr. Dawson makes no proposal for a clean sheet and harmonious system. In his opinion the further extension of the Central London system would have been the wiser plan. Now the Morgan lines have been thrown out, others may agree with Mr. Dawson, and yet others may see the advantage of pushing work as rapidly as possible on the District Railway and its tubular connections, and the Metropolitan with its important steam railway suburban connections. Whatever may be the plan for London locomotion that shall finally be adopted, it would seem to an impartial observer that it must conform with the existing conditions and interests; that, in addition to the ultimate electrification and harmonious operation of all railways at present operating entirely within the area of Greater London, it must include the friendly co-operation of the five or six railway systems centring in London, which, together control such a large proportion of the suburban passenger traffic. The gradual conversion of the suburban lines of these railways, without blocking traffic, from steam to electricity, with a friendly understanding as to fares and territories, would more rapidly bring order out of the present chaos of London locomotion, than further delays and a Royal Commission. The tubes have been so far, and must continue to be, constructed with a view to the surrounding railways and tramways, for otherwise they would merely churn the population up in the centre. It must be remembered that the steam railways at the present time and for all time—unless the British Government or the County Council is prepared to take them over—command every available approach to London. Glance at Plate XXXII, and read page 139 of November TRACTION AND TRANSMISSION, and this fact will become more apparent. To duplicate these lines, even if it were possible, would be expensive folly, when, under modern methods, their carrying capacity can be doubled—possibly trebled. That these modern methods are at the present time under expert consideration by each and every one of these railway companies a reference to the public utterances (see November TRACTION AND TRANSMISSION) of the responsible officers clearly shows. More than this, it is a well-known fact that the general managers and engineering staffs of several of these important railways are preparing plans for the practical application of these principles to suburban traffic. In the large industrial centres of the north these movements in two or three cases have reached the stage where railway companies have publicly asked for tenders to inaugurate electric traction on portions of their lines. In London, where physical conditions are so much more complex, and a greater conflict of interests exists, they have only reached the paper stage; but the most accomplished engineers of nearly all these railways are, nevertheless, seriously at work on the problem. The "branch," and "urban and suburban" lines are being closely examined with a view to electrification, and of making them more than mere feeders for the main lines. By reducing the unit of cost and increasing the efficiency of service, it has been demonstrated that traffic on local lines can be stimulated, and such lines become paying investments. Heavy trains of coaches

running at long intervals, sometimes terribly crowded and at other times empty, cannot be made to pay. It has been demonstrated that increased facilities create traffic, yet the railways have found that with steam, increase may be obtained at too great a cost. In short, steam is handicapped as compared with electrical power, by its inability to provide high acceleration of speed after starting, and by the necessity of either drawing its maximum load or wasting power. The results of these studies, and of the experience of other countries, especially America, in electrical traction, have demonstrated to the British railway manager that electricity can give them the means of improving their suburban service.

XLIII.—ELECTRIFICATION OF EXISTING RAILWAYS

In this connection let me give one concrete example which has recently come under my notice. Last May Mr. J. W. Jacomb Hood, chief engineer of the London and South-Western Railway, read a paper on electric traction before the debating society of that company. This paper was printed for private circulation only, and Mr. Hood had no intention of publishing it. It was so replete with valuable suggestions that, some months afterwards, parts of it found their way into the daily newspapers. On writing Mr. Hood for a copy of the paper he informed me it was written without any intention of publication, but as parts of it had been published, he would not object to my referring to it with this explanation. The courtesy of Mr. Hood will thus enable me to give a practical illustration to the point I am trying to elucidate, and to show how the traffic capacity of the London and South-Western Railway could be increased by the electrification of certain parts of its lines. Mr. Jacomb Hood says :—

Before I close my notes it will be amusing, if it is neither instructive nor profitable, to turn for a few moments from the abstract to the concrete, and with the eye of prophecy to speculate upon the future outlook with regard to our own London suburban services.

We have four lines of way from Waterloo on the main line to Hampton Court Junction, and further, and at comparatively small expense, we can have four lines on the Windsor side, as far as Twickenham. Two of these lines might be devoted exclusively, say, from Nine Elms Junction downwards, to suburban quick services. This would give the means, at practically no capital outlay beyond the cost of a new equipment, of running a series of loop and quick return services as follows :—

WINDSOR LINE.—Waterloo, Barnes, Hounslow, Twickenham, Richmond, and Waterloo, and *vice versa*.

Waterloo, Barnes, Richmond, Twickenham, Kingston, Wimbledon, Wandsworth, Waterloo, and *vice versa*.

MAIN LINE.—Waterloo, Hampton Court, and *vice versa*.

Waterloo, Surbiton, Cobham, Guildford, and *vice versa*.

Waterloo, Wimbledon, Epsom, Cookham, Guildford, and *vice versa*.

Such services could be arranged to give accommodation at normal hours between the points named, as below :—

Between Waterloo and Barnes, and *vice versa*, thirteen trains per hour.

Between Barnes, Hounslow, Twickenham, and Richmond, and *vice versa*, ten trains per hour.

Between Twickenham, Kingston, and Malden, and *vice versa*, three trains per hour.

Between Wimbledon and Wandsworth, and *vice versa*, three trains per hour.

Between Waterloo and Wimbledon, and *vice versa*, ten trains per hour.

Between Wimbledon and Hampton Court, and *vice versa*, eight trains per hour.

Between Surbiton and Guildford, and *vice versa*, three trains per hour.

Between Raynes Park, Leatherhead, and Effingham Junction, and *vice versa*, three trains per hour.

All trains, of course, having the Waterloo terminus as their point of origin and ultimate destination.

Between Nine Elms Junction and Waterloo terminus it might be necessary to provide lines for this traffic at a higher level than the existing roads, ending in loops at the terminus, that would allow of continuous running into and out of the station.

Such services would involve the use of about forty trains.

As power would have to be provided to meet the utmost demand when all the forty trains might be starting together, and when they might all be composed of a maximum of three motor cars, each seating sixty persons, and weighing say 30 tons, the maximum output of power required would probably reach 7,000 horse-power, or say about 5,000 kilowatts.

This could be arranged for in perhaps three power stations of 2,000 kilowatts capacity, each situated conveniently for water, one by the riverside at Wandsworth, another in the fork at Fullwell, and a third, perhaps, by the Mole River at Cobham.

The train mileage per annum by such a service would amount to about 5,000,000, and the ton mileage to about 250,000,000 ; against a present train mileage, on the same routes, of about 1,500,000 per annum.

The capital outlay involved in such a scheme, taking figures quoted by Mr. Langdon, and representing some £9,000 per mile of railway to be equipped, would amount, over the seventy miles that might be so electrified, to £630,000.

The annual interest on this sum, at 3¼ per cent., would amount to, say, £20,500, and this is the annual sum, after deduction for possible economies, and addition of the extra cost of train running, that would have to be earned beyond present takings before a financial improvement could accrue to the stockholders.

Economies in reduction of expenses at stations should average at least £100 per station per annum. Fifty stations are affected, and therefore the saving under this head would be £5,000.

Some form of automatic or simplified signalling would reduce expense of working, that might be put at a moderate estimate at £50 per mile per annum. From this source the saving will therefore amount to £3,500 per annum.

Expenses of running at present cannot be put at less than 10d. per train mile. For the 1,500,000 train miles per annum now run the expenditure is therefore £62,500 per annum.

Under the scheme I have outlined, the cost per train mile for running alone should not exceed 5d. Five million train miles per annum that are contemplated will therefore cost £104,200 — £41,700 more than at present.

This would leave an annual sum of £53,700 that would have to be met by additional traffic. What are the prospects of this ?

Assuming our present trains in suburban services to carry thirty passengers per train mile—no large assumption—the total number now carried one mile is forty-five millions.

Shorter and more frequent trains will not, perhaps, carry more than half the number of passengers per train mile, or say fifteen. If so, our new services per annum would carry seventy-five million passengers one mile, or thirty millions more than at present.

Dividing the increased charges to be met by our increase in number of passengers, we see that each extra passenger must contribute only .43 of a penny per mile to the coffers of the company before a return on outlay is secured, and every fraction of a penny above that means additional profit, so little as one-twelfth of a penny per mile per passenger being all that is necessary to secure 1 per cent. on capital outlay.

It will naturally be asked, what is to become of the goods service on the suburban lines I have spoken of. If any such rapid transit scheme as I foreshadow were to come into operation, goods services would have to be performed, as they are very largely now, at night, the tractive power being electric locomotives. The power specified will provide amply for this.

Mr. Hood, in the above interesting statement, gives us an idea of what could be done in the case of one of the important

London suburban systems. The engineers of other railways could undoubtedly show similar schemes for electrification of the parts of their lines which are engaged in Metropolitan locomotion. It is only just to Mr. Hood to say that the above suggestion was put forward as an indication to speculate on, but coming from a man who has given the question such intelligent consideration, and relating to a railway company that has for its manager Sir Charles J. Owens, one of the most enterprising and capable managers in England, it is well worth consideration in this connection. The conclusions, therefore, we must reach in relation to London locomotion are, that no radical change of principle is necessary. Parliament has at its command all the data necessary for dealing with this problem, and the Committees of that body have the necessary ability and experience to guide these great enterprises in the right direction. For the State or Municipality to interfere at this juncture of affairs would be worse than hopeless. It may be possible for the London County Council to gather up the tramways—with the Act of 1870 hanging over their heads—but it cannot deal successfully with the railway locomotion of London. If that body should promote a scheme of its own it would only add still more to the general confusion. In its advisory capacity it has in the past, and will in the future, greatly aid Parliament. Its officers have been instructed to prepare a complete scheme of locomotion for London, and in particular to report as to what proposals would be most likely to relieve congested and insanitary districts, provide the best means of opening up new areas, and afford the greatest convenience to the travelling public. All this will be as useful and as valuable to a Parliamentary Committee as it would be to a Royal Commission. The advantage to the public of a Parliamentary Committee over a Royal Commission is that it can take up the work where it was left at the present session, and speedily carry it on to completion. An Expert Commission with power to decide routes and make contracts would have an advantage over both Royal Commission and Parliamentary Committee.

XLIV.—Commission of Experts Proposed

In a concise review of the London locomotion question, the *Times* of November 11th

takes the ground that a Royal Commission would be of very little value at this stage of affairs. Such a Commission, the *Times* very rightly contends, in matters of this nature, is traditionally a body to report and advise, not to act, and positive action is required. The question undoubtedly is, how can the present definite foundation which I have depicted in this series of articles, be built upon for the future so that an orderly and homogeneous development of these facilities for transportation may be brought about? A Commission of experts, or persons familiar with the problem, some of whom might be drawn both from the Board of Trade and the London County Council, might be of great help in preparing the ground for the Parliamentary Committees which must finally deal with the matter. The *Times* thinks something far wider than the ordinary machinery is wanted in order to utilise the present situation to the fullest extent for the benefit of the public. It says:—

Certain underground lines are secured. The inquiry we need must be addressed to ascertaining what lines are required to supplement and complete them—grouped, of course, in degrees of urgency—who is to make them, and under what legal, administrative, and financial, conditions. It is surely no reflection on the admirable work done by private Bill Committees, to say that for such a task as this a Parliamentary Committee is quite unsuited. To carry out such an inquiry properly will demand months of the time of the men who, to begin with, can bring to their work a general familiarity with the problems of London locomotion, and who, in addition to that general familiarity, can from within their own body provide special expert knowledge of the legal, administrative, traffic, engineering, and financial, problems involved. In fact, there is required such a body as the Rapid Transit Commission, to which New York entrusted the exhaustive investigation which has resulted in the building of its new four-track railway, right through the heart of the city a few feet below the street level of Broadway, by a contractor, who tendered for the work both of construction and operation, according to the schedule of requirements laid down by the Commission itself.

The New York Rapid Transit Commission has not only dealt with the transportation problem on Manhattan Island, but since the New York Subway was authorised, has been dealing with additional underground facilities between New York and Brooklyn, and New York and Long Island—the latter being an extensive enterprise to be carried out by the

Pennsylvania Railway Company, and, I think, involving as much capital as the twenty-two miles of New York Subway. The Boston Transit Commission is another body that has accomplished useful work of this kind. It has completed one important subway through the very heart of Boston, and has now in progress of completion the East Boston Tunnel, which extends under the Boston Harbour, connecting East Boston. Still another important work has been entrusted to this Commission, and on June 27th, 1902, an Act was passed by the Massachusetts Assembly to provide for the construction of additional tunnels and subways in the city of Boston. These Acts are of a general nature, and only decide the locations of the subways within 1,000ft. or so, all details being left to the Commission, some of the members of which are experts and engineers of great repute. The Commission also executes the contract for leasing the tunnels to the private companies who operate the railways. On the execution of this contract the Commission at once proceeds with the work of construction. It may be possible for Parliament to construct, out of the various authorities now dealing with these matters—including the Light Railway Commissioners — some combination capable of doing what the Rapid Transit Commissioners of New York or Boston do—decide on the general lines of communication required; the exact route such lines shall take ; make the contracts with the companies proposing to operate the lines; supervise the construction; and see that the public interests are protected. In short, what is needed is a competent and active executive. A Commission of this sort would naturally take the initiative in the matter of routes, and lay down such routes as the public needs required, and offer them, as it were, to the best bidder—that is, to the company which offers the best service and the lowest fares. In some cases it might be necessary to pay subsidies for lines intended to relieve congested districts, and to be operated in aid of workmen's housing schemes. A policy of this sort would seem more practical, and more likely to bring order out of chaos, than the curious method now in vogue of letting each promoter fight desperately for the choice routes, and throwing the whole business into confusion if he fails to obtain what he wants. A definite practical statement from some authoritative source as to future routes would, in my opinion, greatly clear up the London locomotion situation, and bring satisfactory responses from responsible persons.

ELECTRIC MOTORS: THEIR THEORY AND CONSTRUCTION*

By H. M. Hobart

SIXTH ARTICLE

THE 35 horse-power, 950 revolutions per minute motor, described in Table XXI differs from that shown in Fig. 130, Plate XXXIV, only in the commutator and windings, which are for 220 volts. The same bearing brackets were used, the bar winding for the 220-volt armature taking up less space than the 440-volt coil winding, and hence permitting the extra room required for the longer commutator.

TABLE XXI.—SPECIFICATION AND CALCULATION FOR FOUR-POLE, 35 HORSE-POWER, 950 REVO-LUTIONS PER MINUTE, 220 - VOLT DIRECT CURRENT SHUNT - WOUND MOTOR

Armature :—

Core diameter (outer)	...	343 millimetres
Core diameter (inner) ...	...	155 ,,
Number of slots	...	71
Conductors per slot ...	...	8
Style winding	...	Multiple circuit single
Turns in series	...	71
Flux (210 internal volts) ...	...	2.35 megalines
Full load current input ...	...	129 amperes

Armature ampere turns per pole $\dfrac{71 \times 129}{4} = 2280$

Size of conductor, bare... ...	...	1.3×9 millimetres
Density in conductor ...	...	275 amperes per sq. cm.*
Resistance of armature winding at 20degs. Cent (measured) ...		.0255 ohm
Size of slot	...	8.5×23 millimetres
Ratio width slot to depth of slot		.37
Width tooth at face ...	...	6.6 millimetres
Width tooth at root ...	...	4.7 ,,
Mean width tooth ...	...	5.65 ,,
Ratio tooth width to slot width		.66
Average length pole arc ...		187 millimetres
Effective length of armature laminations	...	150 ,,

Density in teeth ... ... $\dfrac{2.35}{14\,(5.65 \times 150)} = 19.8$ kilolines

Length of armature between flanges ... ... $150 \times 1.09 + 1$ duct, 6 millimetres wide = 170 mm.

Density at pole face ... ... $\dfrac{2.35}{187 \times 170} = 7.4$ kilolines

Density at magnet core... ... $\dfrac{2.35 \times 1.11}{152^2 \times 785} = 14.4$,,

* The 440 and 500-volt motors of this size have two-circuit wire-wound armatures with current densities of about 450 amperes per square centimetre, the extra loss thereby entailed being offset by the much lower losses at the commutator.

---

* See TRACTION AND TRANSMISSION, Vol. IV, pages 76, 135, 206; Vol. V, 104, 155.

Armature (continued) :—

Density at magnet yoke	...	$\dfrac{2.35 \times 1.11}{2 \times 110} = 11.9$ kilolines
Density at armature core	...	$\dfrac{2.35}{2 \times (150 \times 72)} = 10.8$,,

Magnetic Calculation :—

	Length.	Density in Kilolines per Sq. Cm.	Ampere Turns.
Armature core	9.0 cm.	10.8	60
Armature teeth	2.3 cm.	19.0 (corrected)	600
Air-gap in centre ...	3.5 mm.		
Air-gap at pole tip ...	7.0 mm.	7.4	2220
Average air-gap ...	3.8 mm.		
Magnet core	17.0 cm.	14.4	420
Magnet yoke ...	28.0 cm.	11.9	320
			3620
Further allowance... ...	...	...	380
Calculated total ampere turns	...	...	4000

Field Spool :—

Number of turns	...	4100
Size of conductor { bare diameter		1.10 millimetres
{ single cotton covered diameter		1.23 ,,

Commutator :—

Diameter	...	200 millimetres
Number of segments ...	...	142
Reactance volts ...	...	2.7
I^2R loss	...	200 }
Friction	...	160 } = 400 watts total loss
Stray losses	...	40 }
Effective length of commutator ...		152 millimetres
Watts per square decimetre of cylindrical surface of commutator		$\dfrac{400}{\pi \times 2.0 \times 1.5} = 43$

Brushes :—

Number of spindles ...	...	4
Brushes per spindle ...	...	4
Dimensions of brushes ...	...	16×25 millimetres

Efficiency :—

Measured core loss, brush and bearing friction, and windage (average of several machines) ...	...	1260
Armature I^2R, $129^2 \times 0.0295 =$	...	490
Field losses from saturation curve...		220
Commutator I^2R and stray losses (calculated)... ...	...	240
Total losses (watts) ...	...	2210
Watts output (35 × 736) =	...	25,750
Watts input	...	27,960
Commercial efficiency	=	92.2 per cent.

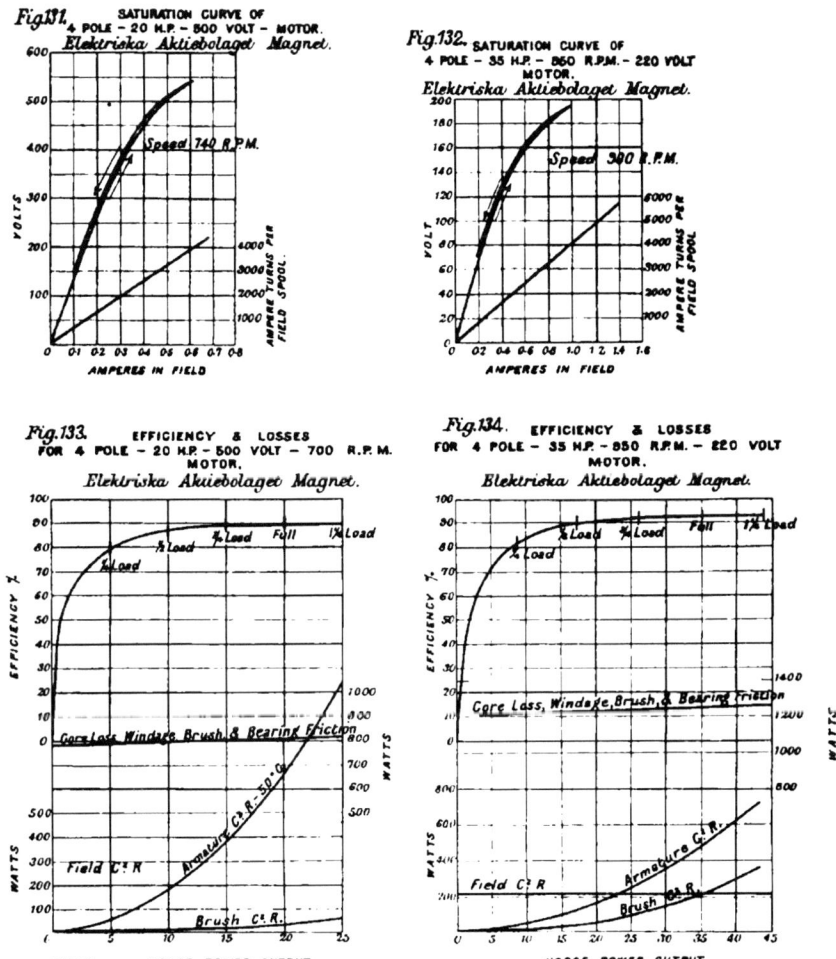

Saturation and Efficiency Curves of 20 and 35 Horse-power Motors

TESTS.— Machine runs from no load to 25 per cent. overload with fixed brushes at two segments backward lead, sparklessly. No complete heating tests were carried out, the only observed temperatures at end of two and a half hours being: Pole-shoe, 30degs. Cent. rise; commutator, 35degs. Cent. rise; armature, 82degs. Cent. rise.

Weight of machine complete = 764 kilogrammes.

TESTS RESULTS OF LUDVIKA 20 HORSE-POWER AND 85 HORSE-POWER MOTORS.— In Figs. 131 and 132 are given saturation curves, and in Figs. 133 and 134 curves of efficiencies and losses for the two motors.

ENCLOSED MOTORS. — As examples of enclosed motors, two designs by Mr. Henry A. Mavor (of the firm of Mavor & Coulson, Glasgow) will be described. They are shunt-wound motors of 5 brake horse-power and 30 brake horse-power normal rated capacity respectively, and have cast-steel frames. Drawings of the 5 brake horse-power motor are given in Figs. 135 and 186, Plate LI, and of the 30 brake horse-power in Figs. 137 to 142, Plate LII. Fig. 148, Plate LIII, is from a photograph of the 80 brake horse-power motor.

Plate LI

Fig. 136.

Fig. 135.

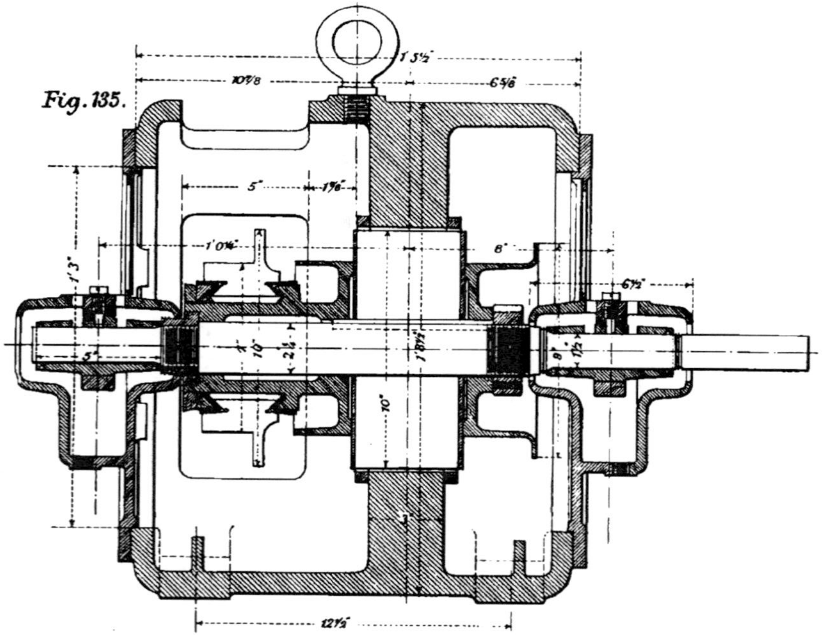

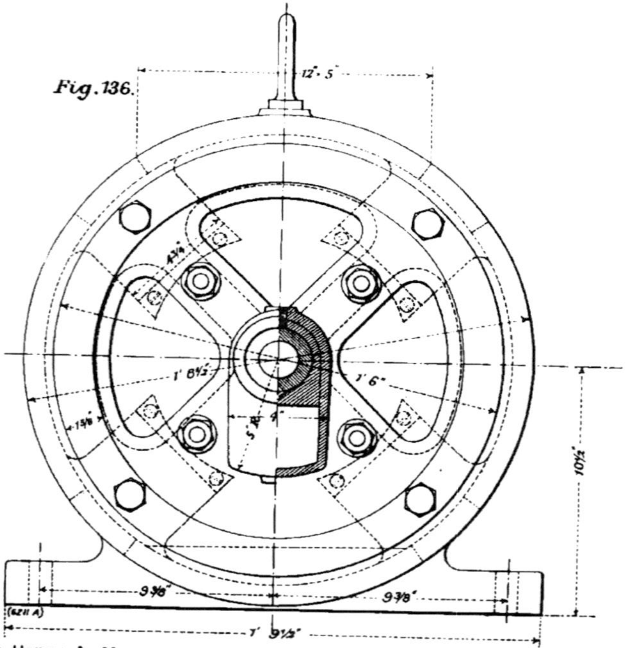

5 Brake Horse-power Enclosed Motor, by Henry A. Mavor

Fig. 147.—Mavor & Coulson Enclosed Motor Geared to Horizontal Mining Pumps

U of M

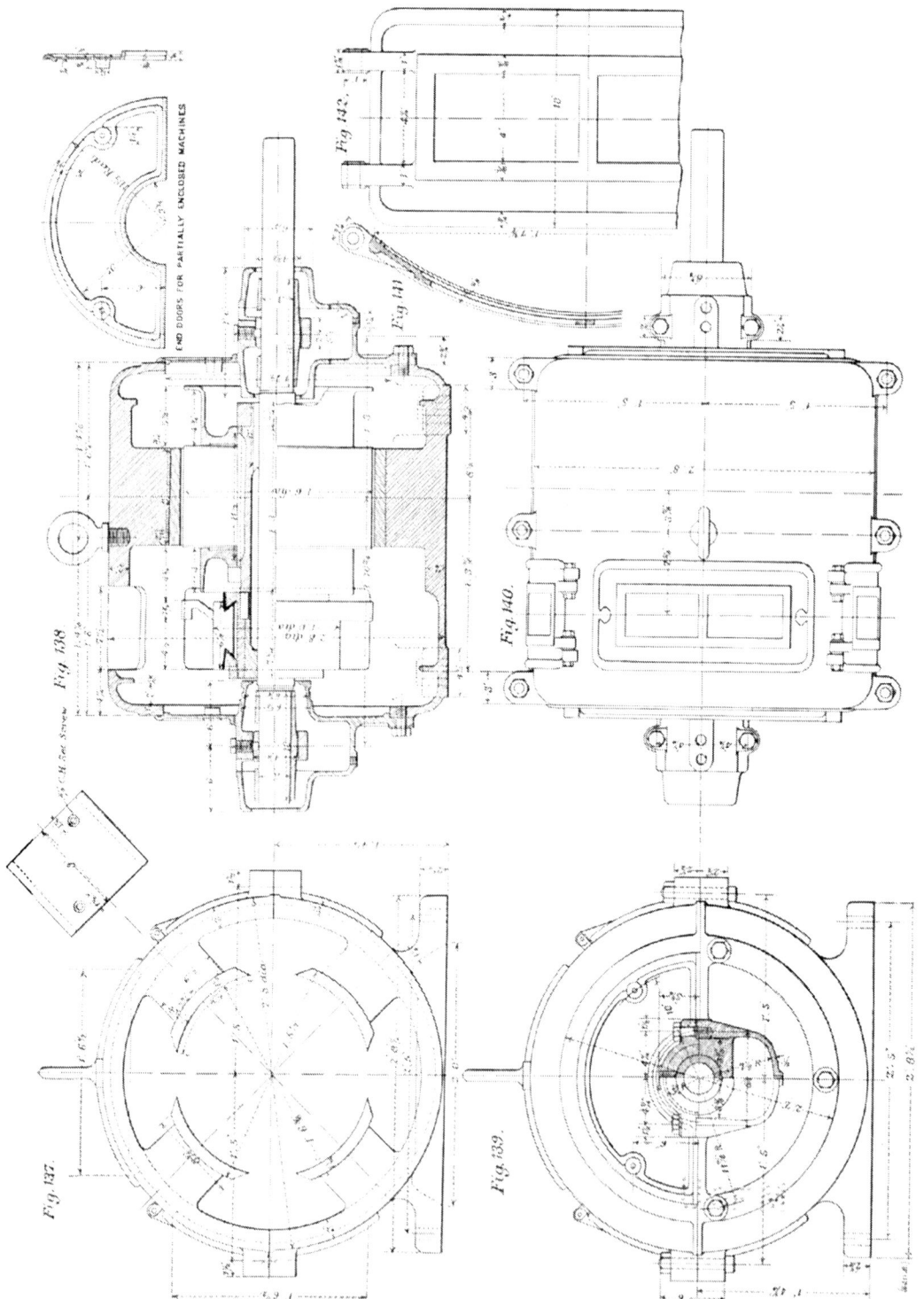

30 Brake Horse-power Enclosed Motor, by Henry A. Mavor

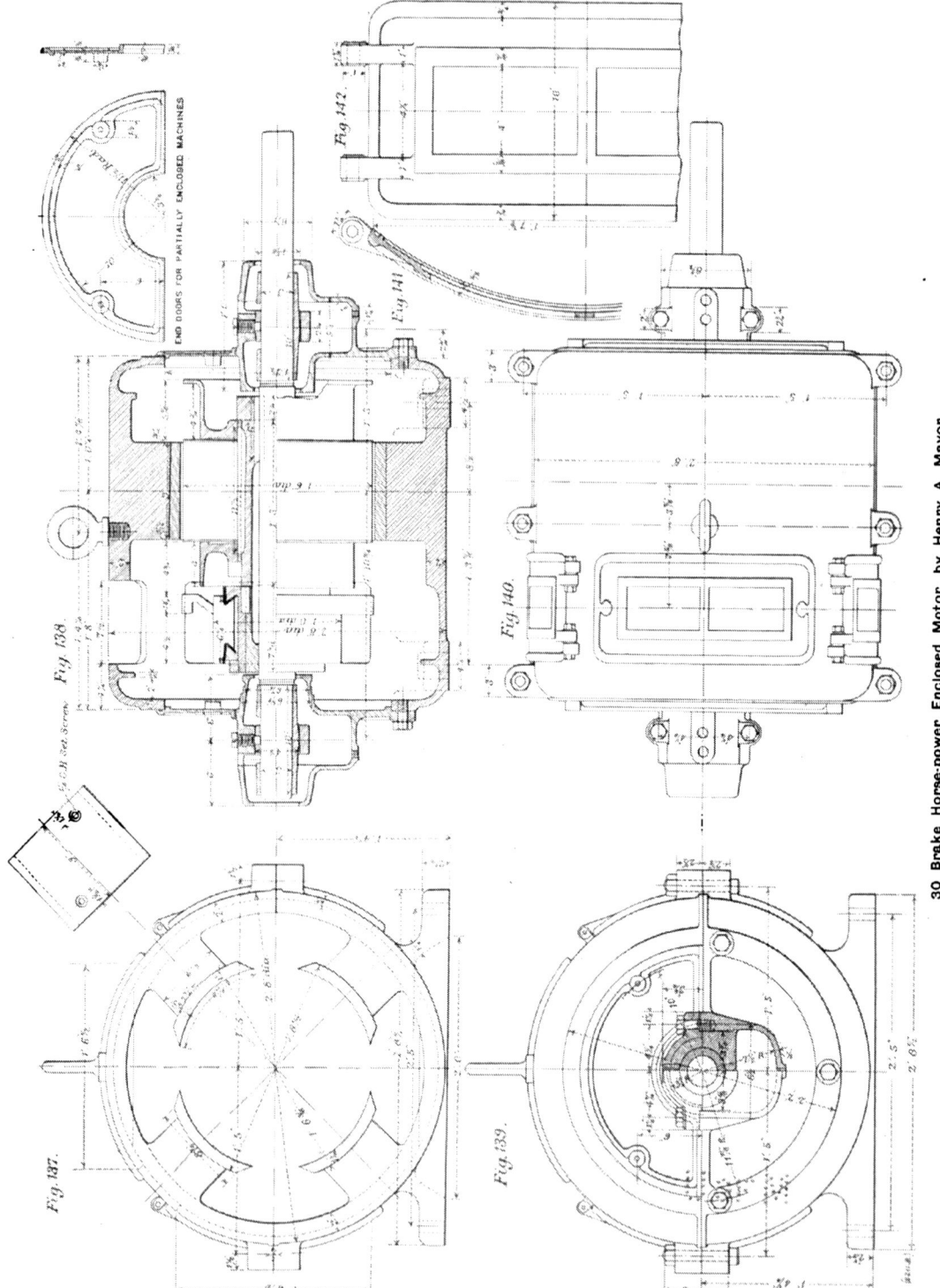

30 Brake Horse-power Enclosed Motor, by Henry A. Mavor

Fig. 142.

Fig. 141.

Fig. 140.

Fig. 138.

END DOORS FOR PARTIALLY ENCLOSED MACHINES

Fig. 137.

Fig. 139.

TABLE XXII.—SPECIFICATION OF ENCLOSED MOTORS

	Rated Output 5 Brake Horse-power.	Rated Output 30 Brake Horse-power.
Speed in revolutions per minute	1000	600
Periodicity in cycles per second	33.3	20
Voltage	250	220
Amperes input at full load	18.8	113
Amperes input at no load	3	9.5
Watts input at no load	750	2090

(Dimensions in millimetres)

Armature :—

External diameter	254	456
Axial length of the winding	241	456
Internal diameter of the laminations	57	191
Axial length of core between flanges	102	228
Effective length of core (magnetic iron)	91	205
Depth of the slot	15.9	31.7
Width of the slot	6.35	11.5
Number of slots	64	70
Width of tooth at periphery, as stamped	6.12	9.1
Minimum width of tooth, as stamped	4.57	6.2

Magnet Core :—

Length of the pole face parallel to the shaft	102	228
Diameter of the bore of the pole face	262	465.5
Pitch at the bore of the pole face	206	367
Length of the pole arc	127	267
Ratio of pole arc to pitch	.61	.73
Thickness of the pole shoe at the centre of the arc	9.5	30
Radial length of the magnet core	89	95
Width of the magnet core parallel to the shaft	76	228
Width of the magnet core at right angles to the shaft	121	165
Radial depth of the air gap	3.81	4.75

Yoke :—

External diameter	520	811
Internal diameter	476	709
Thickness of yoke for magnetic purposes	22	51
Axial width (effective magnetic portion)	222	470

Commutator :—

Diameter	178	305
Number of segments	127	139
Thickness of segment + insulation at periphery	4.4	6.9
Thickness of segment at the periphery	3.6	6.1
Length from external end to commutator connection	51	114

Armature :—

Terminal voltage	250	220
Number of face conductors	762*	278*
Number of conductors per slot	12	4
Arrangement of the conductors in the slot	2×6	2×2
Style of winding	2-circuit	2-circuit
Total amperes to commutator	17.6	110
Amperes per conductor	8.8	55
Mean length of a single turn, centimetres	72	136
Number of turns in series between brushes	191	69.5
Total length of conducting path between brushes, centimetres	13,700	9450

* One "dummy" coil in armature not counted.

	Rated Output 5 Brake Horse-power.	Rated Output 30 Brake Horse-power.
Dimensions of Bare Armature Conductors	1.63 (diameter)	12.7×3.8
Dimensions of Insulated Armature Conductor	1.93 (diameter)	13.5×4.56
Cross section of one conductor, square centimetre	.0209	.482
Cross section of all parallel conductors	.0418	.964
Specific resistance at 60degs. Cent., ohm	.00000200	
Resistance of winding from + to − at 60degs. Cent., ohm	0.65	0.0196
C R loss in armature at 60degs. Cent., volts	12.2	2.25
C R loss in brush contact surfaces, volts	1.5	1.4
Total internal C R loss, volts	13.7	3.65
Total induced voltage, full load	236.3	216.7
Total copper cross section per slot, square centimetres	.250	1.93
Width × depth of slot, square centimetres	1.01	3.64
"Space factor" of slot	.248	.53
Amperes per square centimetre in armature conductor	420	115

Calculation of Reactance Voltage :—

Periphery of the commutator, metres	.560	.959
Revolutions per second	16.7	10
Peripheral speed in metres per second (= A)	9.35	9.59
Length of the arc of contact (= B), millimetres	13.5	20
Frequency of commutation, cycles per second $\left(= \dfrac{1000\,A}{2\,B} = n \right)$	347	240
Width of a segment at the periphery, including insulation	4.4	6.9
Maximum number of coils short circuited under a brush	4	3
Turns per coil (q)	3	1
Maximum number of simultaneously commutated conductors per group (r)	24	6
Mean length of one turn, centimetres	72	136
Effective length of core, centimetres	9.2	20.5
"Free length" per turn (s)	54	95
"Embedded length" per turn (t)	18	41
Lines per ampere turn per centimetre of "free length" (u)	0.8	0.8
Lines per ampere turn per centimetre of "embedded length" (v)	4.0	4.0
Lines per ampere turn for "free length" (u × s)	43	76
Lines per ampere turn for "embedded length" (v × t)	72	164
Lines per ampere for "free length" $\left(\dfrac{r}{2} \times u \times s \right) = o$	515	228
Lines per ampere for "embedded length" (r × v × t) = p	1730	982
Total lines linked with short-circuited coil per ampere (o + p)	2245	1210
Inductance per segment $\dfrac{q \times (o+p)}{10^8} = l$ (henrys)	.0000672	.0000121
Reactance per segment, ohm (2 π n l)	.147	.018
Number of sets of brushes employed	2	4
Minimum series reactance of short-circuit conductors	.294	.018
Amperes per conductor	8.8	55
Reactance voltage	2.58	0.99

TABLE XXII (*continued*)—

	Rated Output 5 Brake Horse-power.	Rated Output 30 Brake Horse-power.
Magnetic Circuit Calculations :—		
Flux entering armature per pole, full load, megalines	0.94	3.90
Corresponding internal voltage	217	236
Corresponding terminal voltage	220	250
Leakage factor	1.2	1.2
Flux generated per pole, full load, megalines	1.12	4.68
Armature :—		
Cross section of the core, square centimetre	151	415
Density, full load, c.g.s. lines	6200	9300
Ampere turns per centimetre, full load	1.0	1.2
Magnetic length per pole, centimetres	7	13
Ampere turns, full load	7	16
Teeth :—		
Number of teeth per pole	16	17.5
Number of teeth directly below a mean pole arc	9.8	12.8
Percentage increase allowed for spread	10 per cent.	10 per cent.
Total number of flux carrying teeth per pole	10.8	14.1
Cross section of one tooth at root, square centimetres	4.2	12.8
Total cross section at the bottom of these teeth, square centimetres	45	180
Apparent density, full load, c.g.s. lines	21,000	21,600
Mean width of tooth ÷ width of slot	.85	.67
Corrected density, full load, c.g.s. lines	20,100	19,900
Ampere turns per centimetre, full load	340	320
Length, centimetres	1.59	3.17
Ampere turns, full load	540	1020
Air Gap :—		
Cross section at pole face, square centimetres	129	610
Density at pole face, full load, c.g.s. lines	7300	6400
Length of air gap, iron to iron, centimetres	.381	.475
Ampere turns, full load	2230	2440
Magnet Core :—		
Cross section, square centimetres	92	377
Density, full load, c.g.s. lines	12,200	12,450
Ampere turns per centimetre, full load	12	13
Magnetic length, centimetres	11	12
Ampere turns, full load	130	160
Yoke :—		
Cross section, square centimetres	99	477
Density, full load, c.g.s. lines	11,400	10,000
Ampere turns per centimetre, full load	10	8
Magnetic length, per pole, centimetres	15	25
Ampere turns, full load	160	200
Ampere Turns per Spool :—		
Armature core	10	20
Armature teeth	540	1020
Air gap	2230	2440

	Rated Output 5 Brake Horse-power.	Rated Output 30 Brake Horse-power.
Ampere Turns per Spool (continued) :—		
Magnet core	130	160
Yoke	160	200
Estimate total number of ampere turns per spool	3070	3840
Actually required*	2600	4100
Shunt Spool Winding Calculations :—		
Voltage per shunt spool at 60degs. Cent.	62.5	55.0
Radial depth of winding, centimetres	5.5	9.0
Internal periphery of spool, centimetres	39.4	79
External periphery of spool, centimetres	83.8	153
Mean length of one shunt turn, metres (*a*)	.616	1.16
Ampere turns per shunt spool (*b*)	2610	4100
a b	1610	5000
.000176 × a^2 b^2	455	4400
Axial length of shunt spool, centimetres	7.5	9
Cross section of shunt spool winding, square centimetres (*r*)	41.2	81
" Space factor " of shunt spool (*s*)	.28	.32
Cross section of copper in shunt spool (*t* = *r* × *s*)	11.6	26
Cubic centimetres copper in shunt spool (100 *a t*)	715	3020
Kilogrammes copper per shunt spool (1 cubic centimetre copper = .0089 kilogramme)	6.3	26.8
Watts per shunt spool (watts = .000176 × a^2 b^2)	72	164
Weight in kilogs.		
External cylindrical surface per spool, square decimetres	6.3	13.8
Watts per square decimetre of external cylindrical spool surface	11.5	11.9
Amperes per shunt spool (watts ÷ volts per spool)	1.17	2.97
Turns per shunt spool	2232	1384
Cross section copper per turn, square centimetre	.0052	.0188
Current density in amperes per square centimetre	225	158
Diameter of bare copper conductor	.81	1.55
Insulation employed on conductor	D.C.C.	D.C.C.
Watts in all shunt spools at 60degs. Cent.	290	657
Weight total shunt copper in kilogrammes, all spools	25.2	107
Resistance four shunt spools at 60degs. Cent., ohms	212	74
Observed total temperature increase by thermometer	38degs. C.	28degs. C.
Ditto per watt per square decimetre external cylindrical surface	3.3degs. C.	2.4degs. C.
Observed total temperature increase by resistance	47degs. C.	44degs. C.
Ditto per watt per square decimetre	4.1degs. C.	3.7degs. C.
Corresponding number of hours run at full load	4.5	3.0

(CALCULATION OF ARMATURE LOSSES AND TEMPERATURE INCREASE)

Armature Copper Loss :—

	Rated Output 5 Brake Horse-power.	Rated Output 30 Brake Horse-power.
Resistance of the winding from + to − at 60degs. Cent., ohm	.65	.0196
Total amperes to commutator	17.6	110
Watts lost in armature copper at 60degs. Cent.	200	235

* The value actually required varies according to the brush position chosen

TABLE XXII (*continued*) :—

Core Loss : —

	Rated Output 5 Brake Horse-power.	Rated Output 30 Brake Horse-power.
Weight of the armature teeth, kilogrammes	4	27
Weight of the armature core, kilogrammes	26	146
Total weight of armature laminations	30	173
Flux density in the core, kilolines (D)	6.2	10
Periodicity, cycles per second (C)	33.3	20
$D \times C \div 100$	2.07	2.00
Watts lost in iron per kilogramme *	5.3	5.0
Total core loss (estimated) watts	159	865
Total core loss (observed) watts	136 †	700

Armature Temperature Increase : —

Armature copper loss, watts	200	235
Armature iron loss, watts	136	700
Total armature loss, watts	336	935
Circumference, decimetres	8.0	14.4
Axial length of the winding, decimetres	2.4	4.6
Peripheral surface, square decimetres	19	66
Watts per square decimetre of peripheral surface	18	14
Observed total temperature increase by thermometer	42degs. C. ‡	24degs. C.
Total thermometrically determined temperature increase per watt per square decimetre	2.3degs. C.	1.7degs. C.
Corresponding number of hours run at full load	4.5	3.0

Commutator Losses : —

Length of brush contact arc, millimetres	13.5	20
Width of brush, millimetres	38	50
Contact surface per brush, square centimetres	5.1	10
Number of sets of brushes	2	4
Number of brushes per set	1	2
Total number of positive brushes	1	4
Contact surface of all positive brushes, square centimetres	5.1	40
Amperes to commutator	17.6	110
Amperes per square centimetre of brush contact surface	3.4	2.7
I^2R loss in watts per ampere§	1.5	1.4
Total I^2R loss at brush contacts, watts	26	154
Peripheral speed of commutator in metres per second	9.4	9.6
Brush friction loss in watts per ampere§	1.5	1.9
Brush friction loss in watts	26	208
Total commutator loss, watts	52	362

Commutator Temperature Increase : —

Total commutator loss, watts	52	362
Circumference, decimetres	5.6	9.6
Length of commutator surface, decimetres	.51	1.14
Cylindrical surface of commutator, square decimetres	2.9	10.9
Watts per square decimetre of cylindrical surface	18.0	34.8
Observed total temperature increase at the peripheral surface	36degs. C.	30degs. C.
Total temperature increase per watt per square decimetre	2.0degs. C.	0.86degs. C.
Corresponding number of hours run at full load	4.5	3.0

* Obtained by curve of Fig. 21, TRACTION AND TRANSMISSION, July 22nd, 1902, page 137.
† Average result for two machines.
‡ 37degs. Cent. for winding, and 47degs. for core.
§ Values taken from Table XVIII (see TRACTION AND TRANSMISSION, November 1st, 1902, page 160).

Efficiency at 60degs. Cent. : —

	Rated Output 5 Brake Horse-power.	Rated Output 30 Brake Horse-power.
(a) Iron loss, watts	136	700
(w) Watts lost in armature copper	200	235
(x) Watts lost at the brush contact resistance at the commutator	26	154
(b) Brush friction loss at the commutator, watts	26	208
(b) Friction loss at bearings and air friction, watts	300	500
(c) Watts lost in shunt winding	290	656
Total of all losses	978	2543
Output at full load, watts	3730	22,400
Input at full load, watts	4708	24,853
Commercial efficiency at full load	79.2	90
,, ,, 1¼ load	80.7	91.1
,, ,, ¾ ,,	76.1	87.6
,, ,, ½ ,,	69.8	83.6
,, ,, ¼ ,,	55.0	72.5

Characteristic Losses : —

$(a+b+c)$ = constant losses, watts	752	2064
$(w+x)$ = variable losses, watts	226	389
External radiating surface of case, square decimetres	120	320
Watts per square decimetre external radiating surface of case	8.2	7.7

When totally enclosed, motors have excellent internal circulation of air, so that air has ready access to all parts, and transfers the heat promptly from those parts to the internal surfaces of the walls of the case; 7 watts per square decimetre of external radiating surface will generally ensure a temperature increase not exceeding 8degs. Cent. per watt per square decimetre of external surface.

When perforated covers, or other departures from absolutely total enclosure are employed, a considerably lower temperature rise is secured.

Weights of the Effective Materials in Kilogrammes : —

Armature laminations, net	30	173
Armature copper	5	82
Commutator segments	9	50
Magnet cores	30	110
Pole shoes	—	50
Yoke	65	450
Shunt copper on magnet spools	25	107
Total effective material	164	1022
Effective material per horse-power	32.8	34
Weight of complete motor	310	1530
Ditto per horse-power	62	51

Total Cost of Effective Materials, in Shillings : —

Armature copper at 24 pence per kilogramme	10	164
Commutator copper at 24 pence per kilogramme	18	100
Spool copper at 24 pence per kilogramme	50	214
Armature laminations at 3.5 pence per kilogramme	9	52
Cast steel at 5 pence per kilogramme	40	255
Total effective material, shillings	127	785
Effective material per horse-power, shillings	25.4	26.2

Fig. 144, Plate LIII, illustrates a 10 horse-power, 110 volts, 700 revolutions per minute, series wound totally enclosed winch motor, derived from the 5 horse-power motor already described by lengthening the core between flanges from 102 millimetres to 152 millimetres, the other parts of the motor being, of course, also lengthened. The above rating is for intermittent working, and is about double the rating which would be given to the motor for a continuous run of six hours with the specified rise of 70degs. Cent.

Fig. 145, Plate LIII, is an engraving of Messrs. Mavor & Coulson's next larger diameter of armature, in an open frame. In all open type motors these makers employ longer and shallower magnet coils.

The 30 horse-power motor described in the preceding specification is, as an open type motor, rated at 42 horse-power (220 volts and 160 amperes) at 600 revolutions per minute for a temperature rise of 39degs. Cent. Including two bearings and bed-plate, its weight is then 2,200 kilogrammes, or 52 kilogrammes per rated horse-power.

Mr. Mavor has also kindly furnished the writer with the results of an interesting series of tests which he has made to compare the 5 horse-power motor described, with a motor constructionally identical in all respects except the following :—

49 armature slots instead of 64.
Slots 23.8 millimetres deep instead of 15.9 millimetres.
Slots 7.6 millimetres wide instead of 6.4 millimetres.
Tooth 8.7 millimetres wide at top instead of 6.1 millimetres.
Tooth 5.6 millimetres wide at bottom instead of 4.6 millimetres.
776 armature conductors instead of 762.
16 conductors per slot instead of 12.
2.03 millimetres diameter for armature conductor instead of 1.63 millimetres diameter.
270 amperes per square centimetre in armature conductor instead of 420.
97 commutator segments instead of 127.
4 turns per segment instead of 3 turns.

The three-turn per coil armature (described in column 1) is, of course, preferable from the commutation standpoint, as its reactance voltage is but 2.6 volts as against 3.5 volts for the four-turn design.

The following results are the average for at least two machines of each design :—

	Three-turn Armature. Watts	Four-turn Armature. Watts
Armature I²R loss at full load	190	121
Armature I²R loss at half load	42	28
Armature iron loss	130	164
Friction loss (estimated)	300	300
Commutator loss, full load	61	61
Commutator loss, half load	41	41
Spool I²R loss	293	293
Total loss, full load	974	938
Total loss, half load	806	826
Efficiency, full load	79.2	79.7
Efficiency, half load	70.0	69·5

The thermometrically determined temperature rise after full load runs for four and a half hours :—

	Degrees Centigrade.	Degrees Centigrade
Temperature of air	18	18
Commutator, above air	36	27
Armature core, above air	47	35
Armature coils, above air... ...	38	30
Field spools, above air ... ' ...	38	36

Full load speed at 220 volts = 1000 revolutions per minute in both cases when hot.

Figs. 146 and 147, Plates LI, LIII, show two applications of small enclosed motors of these types to driving pumps.

FORM WOUND COILS

In the descriptions of these various motors, considerable differences will have been noticed in the shapes of the form wound coils, and in the details of their

Fig. 149.

Alioth's Form Winding

arrangement. The design and construction of these coils is an exceedingly important detail of small motors, especially of those for such speeds and voltages as have more than one turn per commutator segment. One of the earliest methods of form winding is described in the Alioth Company's D.R.P. 34,783, of March 17th, 1885. The illustration in the patent is reproduced in Fig. 149. A different and more clear idea of the winding is, however, obtained

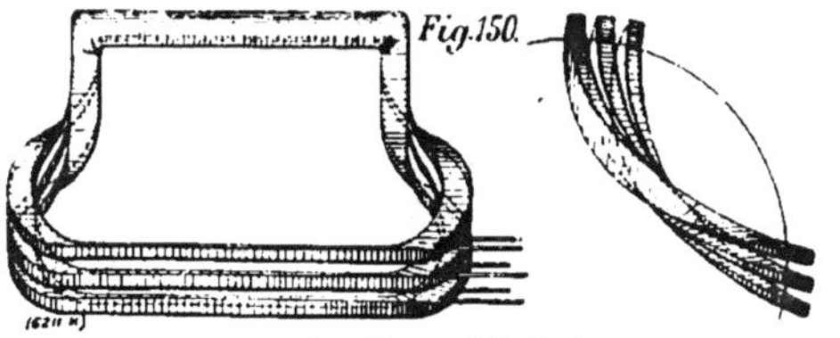

Fig. 150.

Alioth's Form Winding

from Fig. 150, which is reproduced from Arnold's "Ankerwicklungen und Ankerkonstruktionen," page 328 of the third edition. Arnold states that it is winding requiring

Fig. 145.—Small Open Type Mavor & Coulson Motor

Fig. 146.—Enclosed Motor Geared to Vertical Mining Pump

Fig. 143.—30 Brake Horse-power Enclosed Motor, by Henry A. Mavor

Fig. 144.—10 Brake Horse-power 110-volt Enclosed Series Wound Motor

the least length of wire. This, of course, is an important point, since it contributes to increased efficiency, decreased inductance, decreased weight of copper, and more compact construction. It will be noticed that this Alioth winding is more free from sharp bends than many of the other form windings.

The Eickemeyer winding (D.R.P. 45,413, of February 14th, 1888) is the best known, and for many years most widely used form winding. Figs. 151 and 152 are reproduced from the patent, and represent perspective views of coils for two and four-pole motors. The Eickemeyer patent describes winding forms for use in winding such coils. One

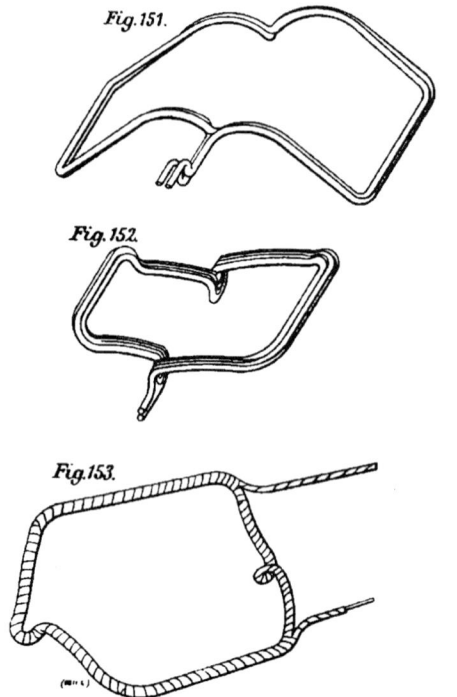

Fig. 151.

Fig. 152.

Fig. 153.

The Eickemeyer and Webber Windings

of the many, more modern methods, is described in Webber's U.S.A. patent, No. 561,636 of 1896. A perspective view of a coil, as wound by this method, is shown in Fig. 153. Other methods of constructing form wound coils are described in Langdon-Davies & Soames' British patent 7,873 of 1900, and in Rothert's U.S.A. patent No. 660,659.

The end connections of windings of the

Eickemeyer type, as well as of bar windings, were at first generally arranged in planes, approximately normal to the armature surface as shown in Fig. 154. By that arrangement one often encountered limitations with reference to the space available for the end connections, these becoming crowded at their lower ends, especially on armatures of small diameter. In a modified type which has been frequently employed, this difficulty is partly overcome by arranging the end connections on a conical surface, as shown in Fig. 155. thus giving more room for the lower ends. Nowadays the most frequently used construction is that shown in Fig. 156, where the end connections are arranged on the same cylindrical surface as the face conductors. This leads to a better mechanical and thermal design. Moreover, it has not been found

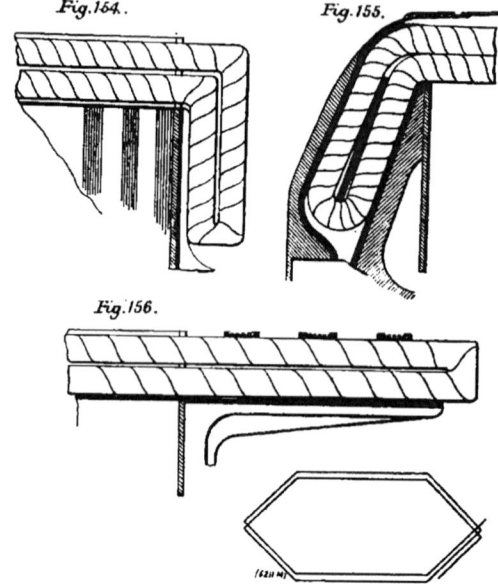

Fig. 154.   *Fig. 155.*

Fig. 156.

Eickemeyer Type of Winding, End Connections

necessary to devote much more space, lengthwise, to the armature winding, although the tendency is to that result. An objection is that it is unsuitable for one layer windings. Figs. 157, 158, and 159 (page 238) show a coil as wound by the method described in Persson & Thomson's U.S.A. patent No. 589,881. A Swiss patent, No. 21,731, of 1900, of Mallett's, illustrates such a coil as wound with flat strip. Fig. 160 is a perspective view of a four-turn coil by this method.

Fig. 161, taken from the same patent, is also a perspective view of a coil wound from flat strip. Fig. 162 is an end view of this coil, which is, at the commutator end, wound in an extension of the armature surface and at the other end has the end connections in planes normal to the armature surface. A

In the windings of Figs. 154 to 164 the outgoing and returning sides of the end connections lie close together; no considerable internal space is enclosed by them; all are, moreover, distinguished by the presence of a quirk at the extreme end where they bend back.

If, as in Fig. 165, a short diagonal ligament

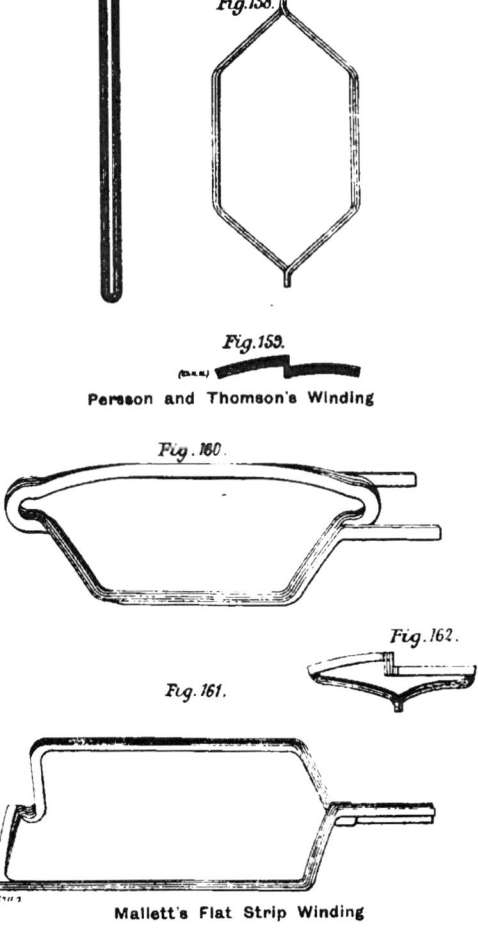

Person and Thomson's Winding

Mallett's Flat Strip Winding

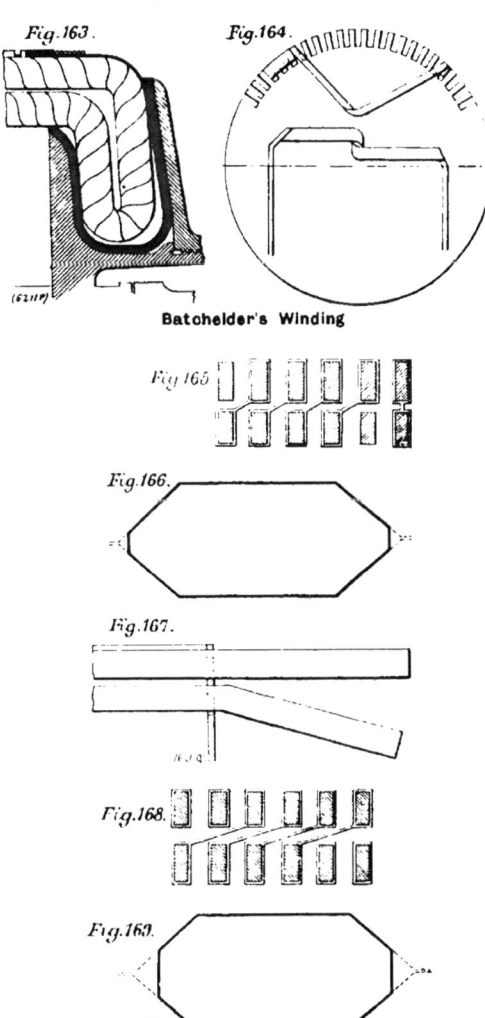

Batchelder's Winding

Diagonal Ligament Connections

modern type intermediate between Figs. 154 and 156 was devised by Batchelder, U.S.A. patent No. 596,136, of 1897. This is shown in Figs. 163 and 164. The end connections start off similarly to the winding of Fig. 156, bend round, and ultimately return to the lower conductors similarly to the winding of Fig. 154.

is used to connect the top to the bottom conductor in windings of the type shown in Fig. 156, the length which the winding occupies in a direction parallel to the shaft is decreased. This is shown diagrammatically in Fig. 166. But to make the winding very much shorter by increasing the length of these ligaments, it is necessary in order to provide the requisite room for them, to bend down the lower conductor as shown in Fig. 167. This permits of making the ligament considerably longer, as shown in Fig. 168, and the length of the winding parallel to the shaft is still shorter, as shown in Fig. 169.

Windings employing these principles to a greater or less extent, have been proposed from time to time (compare also the Alioth winding, Fig. 150), and one of their characteristics is that an annular space is formed by the inner contour of the end connections when the coils are all in place. They are also generally characterised by a smooth gradual bend or twist at the end, as distinguished from the abrupt quirk of the other types. They may also be adapted to use as "one-layer" windings when required.

It has occurred to the writer* that the

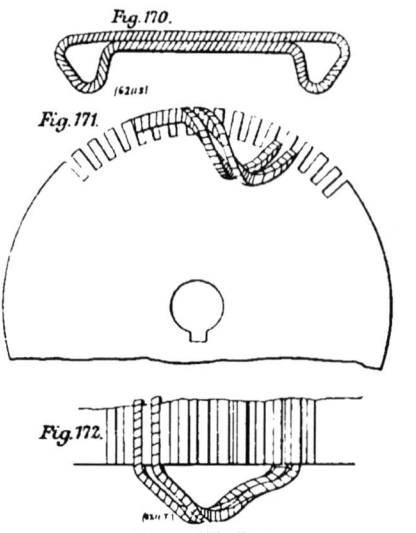

Fig. 170.

Fig. 171.

Fig. 172.

Hobart Winding

shortest coil would have its connections formed on the principle of an equilateral triangle bent out of its original plane, and with the corners rounded off and otherwise modified to adapt it to joining the two corresponding face conductors by an essentially three-sided equilateral end connection.

---

* British Patent No. 17,489 of 1901.

For the case of a two-layer winding it might sometimes be convenient to first wind the coils in one plane, and of the shape shown in Fig. 170. After opening out the coils, and assembling them on the armature core, they will, in end and plan views, have the appearance shown in Figs. 171 and 172.

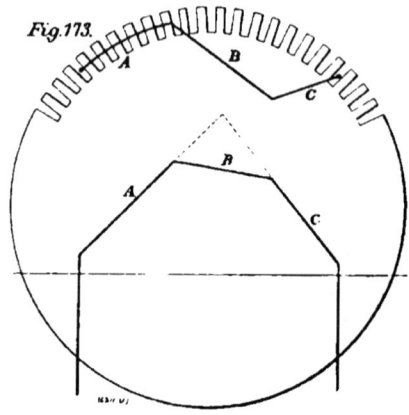

Fig. 173.

Two-layer Winding

From the diagrammatical representation in Fig. 173, it will be seen that the intermediate member, B, of the three equal components of the end connection, lies in principle on a conical surface, as does also the member C. This and the inclination of line B, as seen in vertical projection, together with the general tendency to conform to the proportions of an equilateral triangle, serve to differentiate this winding from others, amongst which one sometimes finds instances where the intermediate link is generally shorter than the others, and lies in a plane perpendicular to the shaft, the intermediate link itself being sometimes radial and sometimes inclined. In other windings sometimes occurring, the component B lies in a conical surface, but the component C lies in a plane perpendicular to the plane of the shaft, and in still another the component A constitutes a straight prolongation of the face conductor. The dotted lines in Fig. 173 show the length which would have been occupied by the winding had it been of the type shown in Fig. 156.

In windings of the type illustrated in Figs. 170 to 172, the annular space may be utilised to contain a solid or hollow annular ring of good conducting material, as indicated in Fig. 174; and windings of the type shown in Fig. 156 may have secondary circuits arranged as shown in Figs. 175 * and 176. Whether internal or external to the end connections, as in Figs. 174 and 175, or interleaved with them as in Fig. 176, these secondary circuits serve the purpose of decreasing the inductance of the armature coils when undergoing short circuit at the commutator brushes, and thus improve the commutation of the motor. It may at first occasion surprise that it should be maintained that a decrease in the inductance of the end connections alone will materially decrease the total induction per coil. This is, however,

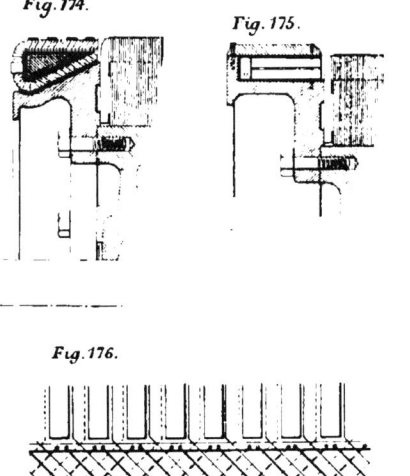

Fig. 174.

Fig. 175.

Fig. 176.

Form Winding Secondary Circuits

in many modern motors, the case. As already explained, rough average values for the magnetic flux set up per ampere turn per centimetre of length of coil are 4.0 and 0.8 c.g.s. lines for "embedded" and "free" length respectively, the former being, therefore, only about five times the latter. For reasons relating solely to the most economical attainment of a given result, one frequently finds cases where the "free" length per turn is from four to eight times the "embedded" length. If, therefore, by such methods as those illustrated in Figs. 174 to 176 one can,

---

* In Fig. 175, the secondary circuits are completed at the inner end by rivets between the end connections. One of these is shown dotted in the figure.

say, halve the inductance of the end connections, one has, in the case of such motors, decreased the reactance voltage per segment by from 14 per cent. to 22 per cent. This arbitrarily chosen illustration is merely cited to illustrate that the proposition should lead to no inconsiderable gain. By the choice of proportions suited to employing the method to best advantage, 20 per cent. to 30 per cent. decrease in the inductance may be regarded as a conservative estimate of the advantage to be gained. It is not the writer's opinion that the extra expense of such constructions would make it desirable to adopt them in any cases except the extremes where commutating considerations impose a limit. With increase in rated output, speed, and voltage, limits are reached where sparkless commutation presents difficulties.

Thus, a satisfactory single commutator shunt motor for operation in either direction with fixed brush position, that is, for operation with the brushes in the neutral point, is, for a rated output of 600 horse-power at 600 volts and 600 revolutions per minute, a relatively expensive machine. If, however, any one of these three values is halved, a satisfactory design is at once possible without excessive cost. Thus, ratings of 600 horse-power at 600 volts and 300 revolutions per minute; 600 horse-power at 300 volts and 600 revolutions per minute; 300 horse-power at 600 volts and 600 revolutions per minute; present no especial difficulties as regards cost and quality, and good motors for 600 horse-power at 300 volts and 300 revolutions per minute; 300 horse-power at 300 volts and 600 revolutions per minute; 300 horse-power at 600 volts and 300 revolutions per minute; are relatively still cheaper. And the same holds true in still greater measure when all three quantities are halved, giving a rating of 300 horse-power at 300 volts and 300 revolutions per minute.

For all the above comparisons, the extra cost of the commutator copper for transmitting the larger currents corresponding to the lower voltages is not taken into consideration, and the conclusions arrived at as to relative cost have to be modified to the extent that the cost of the commutator copper affects the total cost of the machine.

Considerations relating to commutation thus still lead to restrictions in motor design to the extent that, for large capacities and high voltages, the choice of such moderately high speeds as would from other standpoints often be desirable, presents difficulties, and even for smaller motors of lower voltages there exist speeds at which these difficult conditions are encountered whenever it becomes desirable to employ them.

Hence it will be understood that the cost of a motor for a given output and voltage, will at first decrease with increased rated speed, reach a minimum, and then increase. The higher the motor's rated output and voltage the lower is this most economical speed. While the great majority of motors are required for speeds much below this maximum economical speed, and hence, when properly designed, are rated at their thermal limit, modern requirements are tending rapidly in the direction of higher speeds, and motors for speeds at or near these economical limits are becoming more frequently required. In these cases, good commutation is the controlling consideration in the design, and methods of decreasing the inductance are of value in decreasing the cost of machines or of raising the limiting economical speed. When at speeds well below these limits, the commutating properties of a machine are poor, it is an indication of incorrect design, which may be remedied in more economical ways than by resorting to methods such as those described.

TRACTION AND TRANSMISSION IN SOUTH STAFFORDSHIRE

By R. N. TWEEDY and P. J. PRINGLE

SECOND ARTICLE

Canal Systems.—By the courtesy of Mr. Jebb, chief engineer to the Birmingham Canals Navigation Company, we are enabled to include a plan (see Fig. 18, page 243), showing the network of canals in the district about which we write. There are signs that the owners of these canals are not content with the slow and expensive horse haulage now exclusively used, and are investigating electrical methods employed to some extent on the Continent. Not only would electricity be required to propel or to haul the barges; it might also displace the large number of powerful pumping engines which are employed to return the water to higher levels, and it might operate the numerous series of locks on the various systems.

Until the second half of the eighteenth century all local traffic passed of necessity along the roads, which were always in a deplorable condition. There is no navigable river in the Staffordshire coal area, and, of course, there were no railways. In 1767 a public meeting was held in Birmingham to discuss the question of a canal to connect that city with Wolverhampton; the practical result of this meeting was the construction of the canal now running (with modifications) through Smethwick, Oldbury, Tipton, and Bilston. The first barge of coal passed through in 1769, and it is interesting to note that the price of coal in Birmingham immediately fell from 18s. to 7s. 6d. a ton. In 1782 a canal was projected to run from Wednesbury to Birmingham; in 1791 another was commenced to connect Birmingham with the Severn at Worcester. Since then the district has been intersected with canals, so that now every ironworks, and many collieries, are either situated on the banks or have their own branch and quays. Since 1873 the South Stafford-shire iron trade has encountered fierce and ever-increasing competition from newer iron districts located near the sea, and if the building of a ship canal, and the electrical equipment of existing canals, would accelerate delivery and cheapen transit, to a point at which competition was more equalised, the future of the Black Country would be bright indeed. In this era of railroads it may seem out of date to think of canals as a means of salvation, but there appears to be no present hope that the railway companies will change their destructive policy of excessive rates.

The present mileage owned by the Birmingham Canal Navigations is 160. This includes several long tunnels, shown on the map, in which electrical working would be welcomed. Through all these tunnels, barges, whether full or empty, are "footed" by men who make a speciality of the work. Lying on their backs, they press and push on the tunnel roof with their feet, and, practically walking upside down with the barge on their backs, they, with infinite labour, move through the gloom. It is difficult to imagine that such crude, and relatively expensive, methods of "traction" can be practised in the twentieth century.

The table on page 244, kindly furnished by Mr. G. Robinson, is worth examination. It gives the number, capacity, horse-power, and date, of the pumping engines working on the Birmingham Canal Navigations system. Out of twenty-four engines only eleven are less than fifty years old. This fact speaks for the sterling qualities of the engines, and the care with which they have been maintained, but it speaks also of extravagant coal bills, and the company would find itself amply repaid by the substitution of electric motors for the ancient steam plants. The pumps work under conditions which are ideal from the point of view both of the consumer and the electric supply company, as they are pumping practically at full load through the twenty-four hours.

With a total horse-power of 2,600, these

The old company was first incorporated in 1768. The Birmingham and Fazeley Canal Navigations were incorporated in 1788, and amalgamated in 1784; the Company of Proprietors of the Wyrley and Ossington

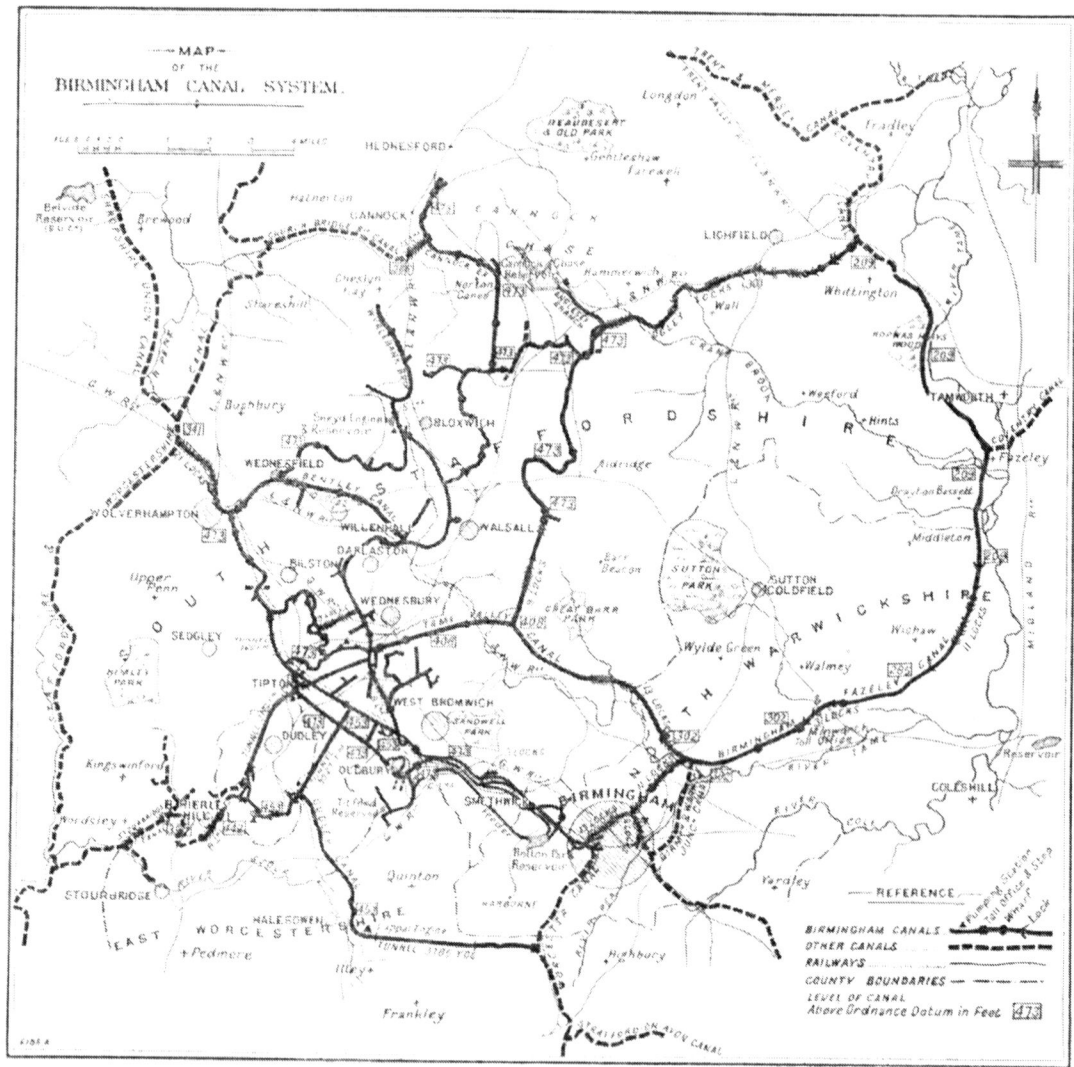

Fig. 18.—Plan of Canal System around Birmingham

engines have a daily pumping capacity of nearly one hundred million gallons.

The present system of the Birmingham Canal Navigations is the result of amalgamations with other companies.

Canal Navigations was incorporated in 1792, and amalgamated in 1840; and the Dudley Canal Navigations were incorporated in 1776, and amalgamated in 1846.

Mines Drainage.—The coal mines in the

TABLE I.—PUMPING ENGINES ON THE
BIRMINGHAM CANAL NAVIGATIONS

Location of Engines.	Numbers.	Gallons per 24 Hours.	Horse-power.	Date of Erection.
Ocker Hill ...	1	4,375,000	120	1883
,, ...	2	5,375,000	226	1800
,, ...	3	2,575,000	63	1867
,, ...	4	4,375,000	120	1883
,, ...	5	3,850,000	150	1851
,, ...	6	6,000,000	227	1857
Walsall ...	1	6,750,000	270	1898
,, ...	2	6,750,000	270	1898
,, ...	3	2,775,000	103 {	Removed from Dudley 1870
Berry Barr ...	1	3,200,000	110	1895
,, ...	2	3,200,000	110	1896
Rotton Park ...	1	3,982,000	100	1818
,, ...	2	3,982,000	100	1818
Ashted ...	1	2,770,000	80	1840 (about)
Smethwick ...	1	5,900,000	50	1892
,, ...	2	5,900,000	50	1892
Titford ...	1	3,125,000	83	1850 (about)
,, ...	2	2,700,000	95	1850 (about)
Park Head ...	1	3,675,000	112	1890
Cannock ...	1	7,125,000	250	1848
Sneyd ...	1	3,875,000	95	1850
Lodge Farm ...	1	2,325,000	70	1839

South Staffordshire district have had always an unenviable reputation for water. When the British Association visited Birmingham in 1865, investigations made by that body showed that about fifty million gallons of water were raised from the mines daily. It was evident that such an enormous quantity could not be supplied by rainfall, and careful examination proved that a vast amount of water was being simply circulated by the pumps, raised to the surface only to find its way back again through broken ground and "swags" caused by subsidences below the natural outfall. Often it was found that one mine unloaded itself of water at the expense of a neighbouring colliery. The canals, streams, and rivers were so disturbed by mining operations that there was a constant and heavy leakage from them, and in time of flood large areas were absolutely inundated.

It was apparent that isolated individual efforts could not cope with this evil in a satisfactory manner, and it was just as evident that a continuation of the evil would result finally in the partial or total extinction of the coal mining industry, so in 1873 the first Mines Drainage Act was passed. This Act granted a universal and compulsory rate for surface works, with a separate tonnage rating for mines drainage.

The surface works include the purchase and removal of water mills, thus reducing the level of the main streams, deepening, straightening, embanking, and clearing all the streams, so as to have a uniform gradient and sufficient sectional area, and a water-tight channel to convey water from the higher grounds where the streams rise right through the broken ground, where mining has most affected them, to the outfall at the boundaries of the district. All the main streams are kept clear of mud and road silt, and frequently have to be cleared of sewage also before a free flow of water can be secured.

Within the thirty-two square miles of the Tipton district, 120 engines used to raise thirty-six millions of gallons of water per diem, but since 1878 the improvements in surface works and pumping engines effected by the Mines Drainage Commissioners have decreased the quantity of water raised daily to nine million gallons.

Notwithstanding this fourfold improvement there are still large areas in which water remains "pounded up" and untouched by the pumps, thereby drowning rich seams of coal.

In 1895 a combined scheme for draining the mines and the surface was brought out. It proposed the establishment of two main pumping and hydraulic power producing plants, underground levels, and a hydraulic power distribution main, which power was not only to be used for working semi-portable deep pumps, but also to be made available for actuating surface pumps situated in the low-lying areas.

Much of the underground level part of this scheme has been carried out with very partial success, owing to the consolidation of the old workings during the time they have been "drowned," rendering the lower measures so close that water will not percolate through them even under a pressure of 45lbs. per square inch.

In order to show the vital importance of clearing the mines of water it may be said that for every ton of coal raised in the Tipton district, $28\frac{1}{2}$ tons of water have to be pumped.

The failure of the costly experiment left no alternative but to deal with the water from an increased number of places, though "the only way to bring down the cost of working" under these conditions, is "to diminish the quantity of water that daily finds its way to the surface."

The advent of the Midland Electric Corporation brought a gleam of sunshine to

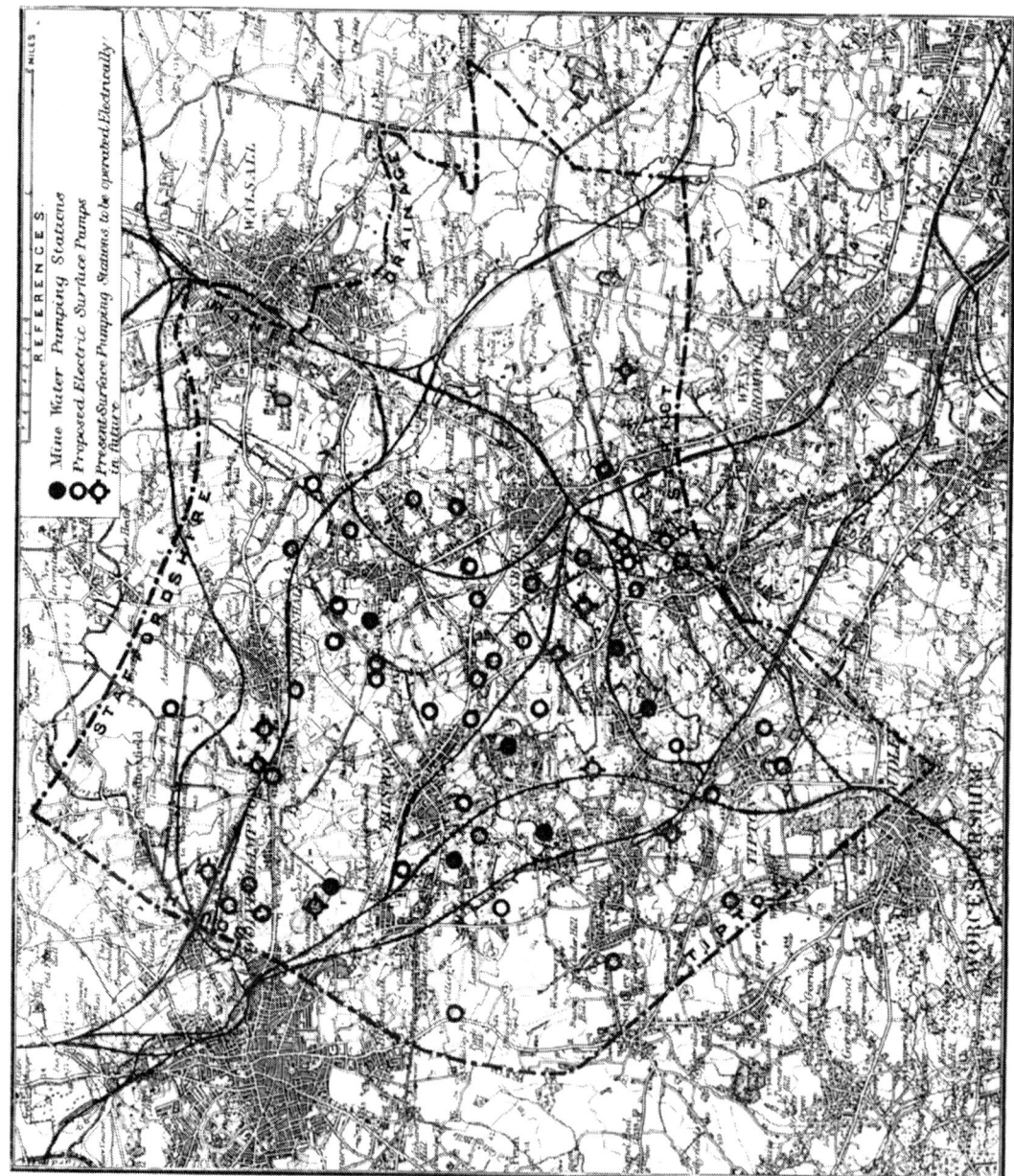

Reproduced from the Ordnance Survey Map with the sanction of the Controller of H.M. Stationery Office.

Fig. 19.—Map of Tipton Mining District, showing Sites for Pumping Stations

the hearts of the commissioners. This company has powers over the whole Tipton drainage area, on which fifty sites have been selected for surface pumps, to be driven by electricity. These sites are shown by rings on the map (Fig. 19, Plate LIV), which has been reproduced from the valuable paper read by Messrs. E. B. Marten and Edmund Howl in 1898 before the Institute of Mining Engineers. The details added have been taken from the same paper.

The leading idea of the scheme is to prevent surface water finding its way into the workings, only to be pumped back, and about three million gallons per diem have to be removed. The pumps proposed will lift as much as twenty-five million gallons per diem, so that they will be able to deal with emergencies in storm - time. It is probable that centrifugal pumps will be used, coupled to motors, which can be started, stopped, and regulated automatically by the level of the water, thereby reducing to a minimum the expense of superintendence and operation. Of course, with steam pumps it is necessary to have a man in constant attendance at every plant, unless the wasteful and time - losing expedient of sending one man in turn to several pumps is adopted.

Ten good and sufficient reasons for electric pumping are given in Messrs. Marten and Howl's paper, which ends as follows :—

Any water that can be dealt with at the surface is so clear and great a gain to the mines, by saving pumping from so great a depth, that it is well worth a further attempt to accomplish it, and the near approach of electric power available for surface pumping seems to offer a reasonable, safe, and ready help.

Mr. Howl, who is the engineer to the Commissioners, and is responsible for the electric power scheme, stated in his reply to the discussion that their best engine cost at that time 3d. per twenty-five thousand gallons per 100ft., and that if the cost of electric pumping were four or five times as much as the present system, they would still save a great deal by pumping on the surface. As the cost of electric pumping would be less than one penny per unit over the twenty - four hours, we believe that it will compare favourably with the actual cost of the best engine in service, so that the advantages to be gained by the change should be very great.

There is no doubt that while the work of the Commissioners has saved many collieries from utter ruin, yet the present charges press hardly on the remainder, so that the introduction of improvements which will not only reduce the drainage rates, but will render the "getting" less expensive, and at the same time clear ground of water, will, in the end, benefit the district considerably.

General Features of Distribution by the Midland Electric Corporation.—What has been said above will give a fair idea of the possibilities which surround the Midland Electric Power Corporation. We shall proceed to describe its methods of transmission and distribution.

From the central station at Ocker Hill two-phase currents at 7,000 volts and 50 periods are sent out.

Under the existing conditions it was thought best to generate two-phase rather than three-phase currents. The Board of Trade insist on an earth shield for extra high-tension (E.H.T.) cables, and, if three-phase had been used, either a fourth wire or cast-iron piping would have been necessary. Owing to the nature of the soil over large portions of the area, it was considered inadvisable to draw cables into cast-iron pipes, so that it was decided to transmit two-phase currents through three-core cable with a common earthed return, laid solid in earthenware troughs filled with bitumen.

The possibilities of overhead transmission were not considered, owing to the apparent inflexibility of the Board of Trade at the time of the inception of the scheme. There are signs now that consideration will be given to proposals of this nature, and it is to be hoped sincerely that we shall be allowed to come into line with America and some Continental countries.

The E.H.T. current is taken over the area by means of trunk mains ranging from eighteen miles to four miles in circumference. Within the largest ring, which serves the least densely populated area, there are two sub-stations; the three remaining sub-stations being served by three other rings. The latter sub - stations and ring mains are so interconnected that, if desired, any sub-station can be supplied by any one ring. Under ordinary conditions all sub-stations are in parallel not only with the main station but with themselves, the various rings, therefore, forming an undivided network. In the event of the direct trunk to Bilston breaking down, it would be isolated primarily by means of the feeder switches at the central station and at the Bilston sub-station, the sub-station then being supplied by the trunk main between Wednesbury and Bilston, or by the trunk between Tipton and Bilston, or by both. Similarly with the other sub-stations.

For the supply of very large consumers it is permitted to carry E.H.T. mains to transformers on their premises, the pressure

Wherever the demand warrants it the 2,700-volt mains are duplicated, one being used to supply large consumers only, the other feeding the lighting and small power demand. This precaution is taken to ensure to the latter class of consumer a supply which shall not be affected by the inevitable variation of pressure caused by the more or less heavy fluctuations due to the large power consumers.

The low-tension distribution is effected at 200 volts. In addition to the purely

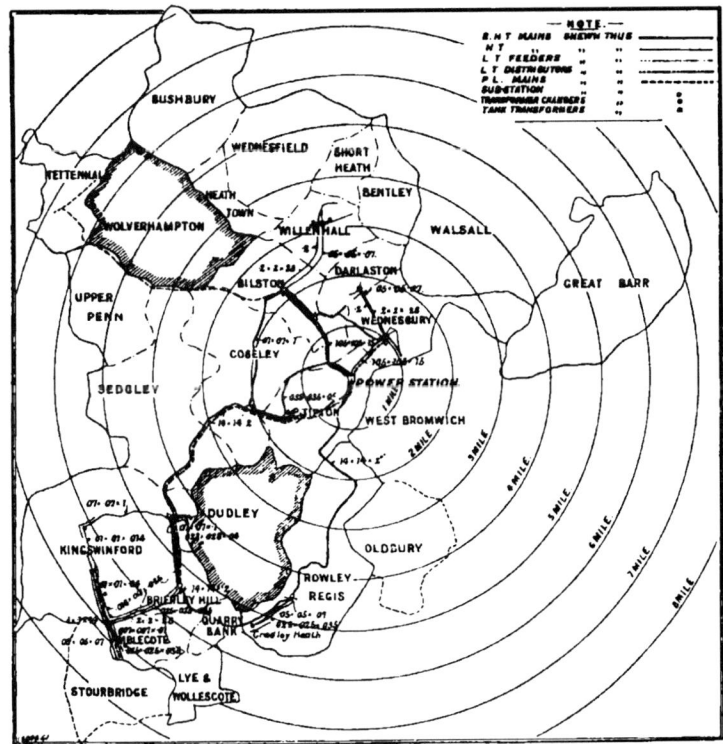

Fig. 20.—Map of Mains

being reduced to any desired amount at the point of supply. In many cases it happens that a large works occupies a position which is so far from the area supplied by the sub-main (H.T.), that this course is both the simplest and most economical to pursue.

From transformers in the sub-stations, current at 2,700 volts is sent into mains radiating to economical distances to supply in their turn the local low-tension distributors from tank transformers.

alternating devices installed in the sub-stations it has been recognised that there will be a demand for continuous current, and to that end each sub-station is provided with, or has space for, rotary converters supplemented by batteries of accumulators.

The map of mains (Fig. 20) is not shown in its entirety, as some of the districts have been acquired so recently that the scheme of mains has not yet been settled finally. For instance, to the north of Bilston there is a large area entirely unfed by an E.H.T.

main, but undoubtedly, in the near future, this will be required to feed one or more new sub-stations.

Great facilities are offered for public lighting, the merest villages within the area being put on equal terms with the largest towns. Such lighting will be effected in various ways to suit local conditions. In the vicinity of a sub-station, which always occurs in a well-populated district, the matter is simple, being provided for by a H.T. main feeding buried transformers supplying twin cables at 200 volts, the lamps being split between the two phases. But where public lighting is required in isolated or rural districts, which are encircled or bordered by an E.H.T. or H.T. main, it would be possible to tap those mains by transformers, or, indeed, to supply direct off the 2,700-volt mains.

The price at which the company supply public lighting, compares favourably with the present charges for gas lighting, and distance is no objection.

The Kingswinford Urban District Council have entered into a twenty-one years' agreement with the Midland Electric Corporation for the lighting, by incandescent lamps, of the main and by-streets and roads, the length of public lighting mains in this district alone being about twenty-two miles.

As showing the difficulty of estimating the probable demand of such a large area, it may be stated that, while the work of cable laying was in progress, further canvassing increased the prospects of the company to such an extent that a large number of mains had to be duplicated immediately; and, in some cases mains were laid about ten times heavier than called for in the original scheme.

Effects of Mining Subsidences. — Cable laying in the Black Country is attended by many difficulties, which assume a still more serious aspect when such high pressures as 7,000 volts are carried. When the whole industrial life of a district may depend upon the safety of one of these E.H.T. mains, every precaution has to be taken against its failure. The country about which we write has been famous for its 10yds. seam of coal, found sometimes almost on the surface. When this coal was first worked, columns and walls of solid coal were left to hold up the roof, as ordinary propping with timbers in such caverns would have been almost impossible, and very expensive.

Of late years, however, the thick coal has been almost worked out, and colliery proprietors have been obliged to " get " these " ribs and pillars," as they are termed. The result is that the roofs of the seams are left unsupported, and the great weight of ground above, breaks them through. Occasionally what is termed locally a " crowning-in " occurs, and the surface falls in suddenly, leaving a yawning chasm of varying extent, and people living over workings seem to be delightfully uncertain when they go to bed as to whether the back-yard, or, maybe the house itself, will not be fathoms below the surface in the morning. Generally, however, nothing so terrifying happens, as the surface gradually slips and falls, often several inches in a night, but not sufficiently to break up a house unless it has been cracked and weakened previously. The tenacity and temerity with which the inhabitants stick to their shaky domiciles is simply marvellous, and it is no uncommon thing to see a fallen house which has been deserted perhaps the day before.

The tramways in the district have an expensive and worrying time with these subsidences, which last for months, and sometimes for years. The line between Dudley and Stourbridge has never been without its subsidence, and it has had to deal with two at once.

It is very curious to see the rail joints opening wider and wider, the track assuming contours and twists never anticipated by the engineers, and the span-wires becoming more and more like drawn bow-strings as the subsidence under a hill gets worse and worse, gradually drawing the hollow part of the hill away from the sound part. The tramway poles move with it, and the fish-bolts are sheared off in their endeavours to arrest the irresistible progress of the rails. As the rail joints open, the spaces are filled, as a temporary expedient, with specially cut pieces of rail, which are replaced with longer pieces as occasion demands. Finally, the road authority and the tramway company agree to raise the road to its original level. This often means a lift of 4ft. to 6ft., and in the process the poles are buried and the trolley wires brought nearer the rails by that depth, thereby necessitating the erection of new poles and the removal of the old.

The houses on the roadside are treated in various ways. If in a lucky position, they sink steadily and evenly; if badly built, or unluckily placed, they may escape for the time with the front or side leaning 20degs. out of the perpendicular, or a wall or two, or the whole building, may have collapsed. Fig. 21, Plate LV, shows a tramway track after lifting, and just before the road on either side has been filled up.

It is hard enough for the tramway company to be incommoded, and for the inhabitants to be rendered houseless or miserably uncomfortable, but this pales before the injustice of the private Acts which have legalised the destruction of property, and permit the coal owners to pull down a town without paying a farthing towards its reconstruction. Over the coal area the whole face of the country has been changed within the last fifty years, the majority of its contours being artificial. This has arisen from the combination of subsidences with the creation of enormous spoil heaps from the collieries and ironworks.

Canals and railways suffer heavily through mining operations. Levels have to be maintained in both cases, and it is not uncommon to see canals, which were originally cut through the earth, raised like aqueducts above the surrounding country. Not long ago a rapid subsidence practically demolished the Daisy Bank Station, together with overbridges near it, on the Great Western Railway, between Dudley and Wolverhampton.

Along the route the tramway cables are laid in wooden troughing filled with bitumen, which makes a fairly flexible job; but the other lines affected by subsidences are fed by lead-sheathed cables drawn into cast-iron pipes, with manholes at frequent intervals, and it is surprising how well a stretch of well-caulked 9ft. pipes will adapt itself to variations in level without injuring the contained cables or breaking joint. In fact, we believe that this system is superior to the solid system under such peculiar conditions.

Until the pipes have sunk about 4ft. it is necessary only to inspect the manholes occasionally in order to pull slack cable from one box into another where the strain is greater. Beyond that depth it becomes essential to raise the pipes and rebuild the manholes, which suffer more than anything else.

When low-tension cables are laid solid, a good method to avoid trouble over subsidences is to cut the troughing for a few yards at either end of the affected length, and to splice in a kind of expansion piece of armoured cable, protected by brick walls covered with sleepers. Any pull on the cable should then be taken up by the coiled slack.

Such a method cannot be relied on when high-tension cables are in question, and Messrs. Kincaid, Waller, Manville & Dawson have taken more elaborate precautions on behalf of the Midland Electric Corporation. The type of "subsidence pit" designed by them is shown in Fig. 22, Plate LV. These pits are spaced 200yds., or less, apart, over subsidences, or, where these are very local, there is a pit at each end. The pits are 8ft. long by 8ft. 6ins. deep, and vary in width, according to the number of cables, from 18ins. upwards. Six feet of slack cable is allowed.

The cable runs from solid troughing into the pit, whence it is drawn through 3in. or 4in. cast-iron pipes, with butt joints, covered by a 2ft. sleeve allowing $\frac{1}{4}$in. clearance. This space is packed with yarn sufficiently tight to prevent pitch fouling the pipe. The pipes are then laid in wood troughs with butted joints, surrounded by 2ft. lengths of loose troughing. These troughs are filled with pitch, and covered with boarding. It is believed that this arrangement will provide sufficient extensibility to protect the cables from undue strain (see Figs. 22 to 24, Plate LV).

Site of Generating Station.—It is obvious that the cost of producing current depends to a very large extent on the position of the power station, and it is difficult to conceive a more favourable location, from every point of view, than that selected by the Midland Electric Power Corporation.

Situated almost in the centre of the area of distribution, and certainly in its most densely populated part, the power station at Ocker Hill is closely adjacent to facilities for cheap transport and for condensing water. On the north side of the triangular site occupied by the station, runs the London and North-Western Railway; the two other sides are bounded by the Birmingham Canal. Fig. 25, page 249, is a general plan of the ground, and from this the great advantage of the location will be at once appreciated.

The subsoil is of stiff virgin clay, excellent for foundations, and as an indication of the wonderful richness of the district it may be

Plate LV

Fig. 21—Track Reconstructed after Subsidence

Fig. 22.—Subsidence Pit

Fig. 23.

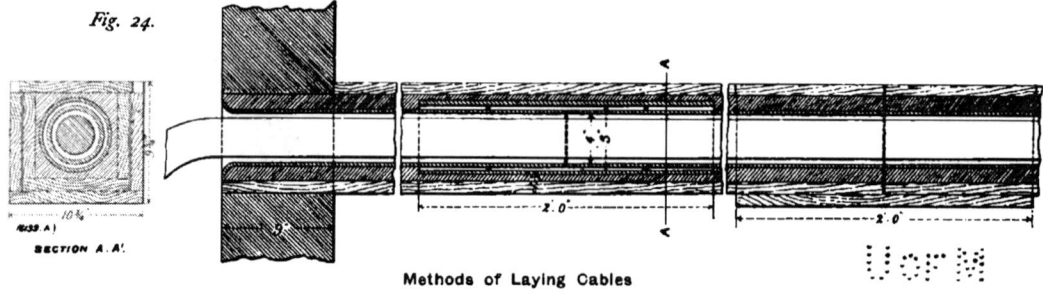

Fig. 24.

SECTION A.A'.

Methods of Laying Cables

TRACTION AND TRANSMISSION IN SOUTH STAFFORDSHIRE

mentioned that the land has been occupied previously by a colliery, a brickworks, and an ironworks, all the raw material having been mined on the spot. It was, indeed, possible to carry the preparation of building material to a pitch which all contractors might envy. The clay excavated for the buildings was used to puddle the sides and bottom of the canal basin; the ruins of the old brick structures were broken up for the concrete of the foundations; and the mortar used in the work was made of slag found

rates. Nevertheless, the rough slack coal used at present is delivered in the basin at 6s. per ton; when the employment of induced draught makes it possible to burn a finer slack this price will be still further reduced. There are collieries working only three-quarters of a mile from the station, so that, at a pinch, "land carriage," as the transport of coal by carts is called locally, could be resorted to. The method of unloading the coal from the barges will be described later.

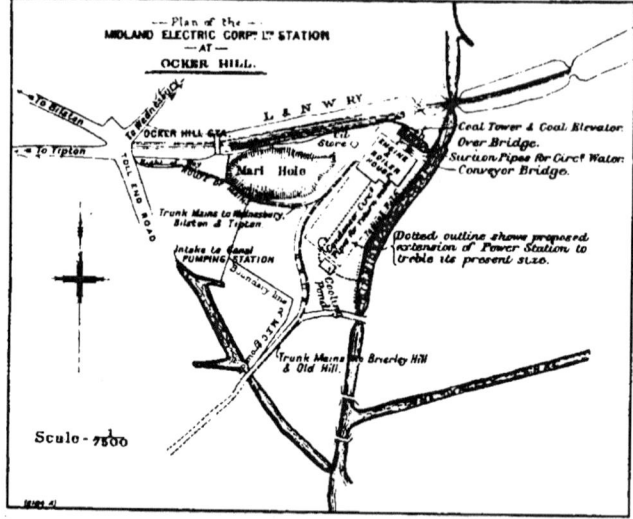

Fig. 25.—Plan of Ocker Hill Power Station (see page 248)

on the site and ground up. All roads and fillings were made with the same *débris*. There are several pit shafts near the station, but any danger from subsidence has ceased.

At right angles to the main canal, and at the northern end of the station, a basin was excavated to serve the double purpose of a receptacle for barges and an inlet for the circulating water. This basin is 180ft. long by 32ft. wide, and can hold eight 30-ton barges at one time. On account of surface leakage into the mines it was imperative that this basin should be quite water-tight, and it was therefore puddled throughout with clay from 3ft. to 4ft. thick.

It is unfortunate that both the canal and railway are owned by the same company, so that it was not possible to initiate any competition with a view to cut down transport

The existence of a canal pumping station in close proximity to the Midland Corporation's works has been the cause of much trouble and delay with respect to the delivery of the circulating water. This pumping station is the largest in the district, and the second largest in the kingdom. It lifts against a head of 66ft. from the low level to the high level canals, the maximum quantity pumped being twenty-five million gallons a day. It was proposed in the first place to discharge the circulating water by pipes running in a direct line from the south of the electricity works into the area of the canal which feeds the pumping station, and the canal company made no objection to this proposal. Later, however, they withdrew their consent on the ground that the large body of ejected water would raise the temperature of the canal branch to such a degree as to interfere with their pumping operations. The Midland Company has therefore been obliged to adopt the scheme indicated on the map, Fig. 25. After the 30in. delivery pipes have been taken out of the existing station in a straight line sufficiently far to allow for the largest extensions contemplated, they turn at right angles into a cooling pond, which is built of concrete, and contains baffling walls, also of concrete, and brought out alternately from either side. This arrangement forces the water to take a circuitous route, which assists the cooling. From the cooling pond the water runs into an open conduit, and discharges into the canal through six pipes, which are splayed out over a weir, so that the water is practically cold by the time the canal is reached. It would seem as if the canal authorities have forced the Power Company to incur considerable extra expense and loss of time without adequate reason. The suction sump and pipe in the basin are duplicated to allow for extensions. The usual straining grids are fitted in the sumps.

Buildings.—The whole of the buildings and foundations were constructed by Messrs. Hughes & Stirling, of Liverpool, to the designs of Mr. Huon A. Matear, of the same city. Mr. W. A. Turner, who has since taken an appointment with the Midland Electric Power Corporation, acted as clerk of the works for the architect during construction. There being no architectural susceptibilities to study, surrounded as the station is by iron works and collieries, it was designed solely for utility, and not for ornament; nevertheless, to the engineering eye, the buildings are sufficiently capacious and satisfactory, as the illustrations show (see Figs. 26 to 30, Plates LVI and LVII). The plans, Figs. 27 and 30, show the area available for extensions.

The whole building is constructed of red bricks of local make, the walls being panelled out to lighten construction, and all interiors are lofty and well lighted. The engine room is wainscoted with brown glazed bricks, the floor of this room being laid in mosaic. The floor of the boiler house is of local blue bricks, but it, as well as that of the engine room, is covered to a large extent by chequer plates supplied by Messrs. Babcock & Wilcox. Engine and boiler rooms were excavated to a depth of 14ft. below floor level, the floors being supported by buckled

plates on girders, and filled in with cement. The boiler room basement is occupied by the ash conveyor and main flue, and in the engine room the space is utilised for air and circulating pumps, exhaust and auxiliary piping, and all cables connecting the machines and switchboards. The ironwork of the roof was supplied and erected by Messrs. Hughes & Stirling. The boilers have been built on arches, a form of construction rendered desirable by the occurrence of an outcrop of coal.

Coal Handling Plant. — It has become the general practice in all large central stations to reduce the handling of coal to a minimum, and many firms make a speciality of dealing with this problem. Where mechanical stokers are used the coal is generally elevated from trucks or barges, and conveyed to overhead bunkers, whence it is delivered by the firemen to the mechanical stokers. This arrangement is adopted at Ocker Hill.

Fig. 31, Plate LVIII, taken from a photograph, shows the canal basin, coal tower, and coal-conveying bridge. Figs. 32 to 35, page 251, show a plan and sections of the coal tower and conveying bridge. This is entirely constructed of girders, angle iron, and plates, with each of the latticed girder stanchions resting on a massive York stone bedded on a good foundation. The whole of the ironwork, excepting the boom for elevating the coal buckets, was made and erected by the Clayton Engineering Company, who were sub-contractors to Messrs. Babcock & Wilcox, Ltd.

The total height of the tower is 50ft., with the top line of the conveyor 40ft. 6ins. from the ground. The tower was placed on the north side of the basin, instead of the south, as would have seemed preferable, principally because the north bank was more convenient for the railway siding. The present method of elevating the coal and feeding it into the conveyor is as follows: The boom, which is of latticed girder construction, has a small trolley working on the upper face of the inclined girders; its whole extent of movement is regulated by two curved wooden blocks. The lower block can be moved to any position best suited for unloading a barge lying close alongside, or if desired to unload from two barges at once it can be moved midway between the two. The boom is long enough to deal with a third barge if necessary.

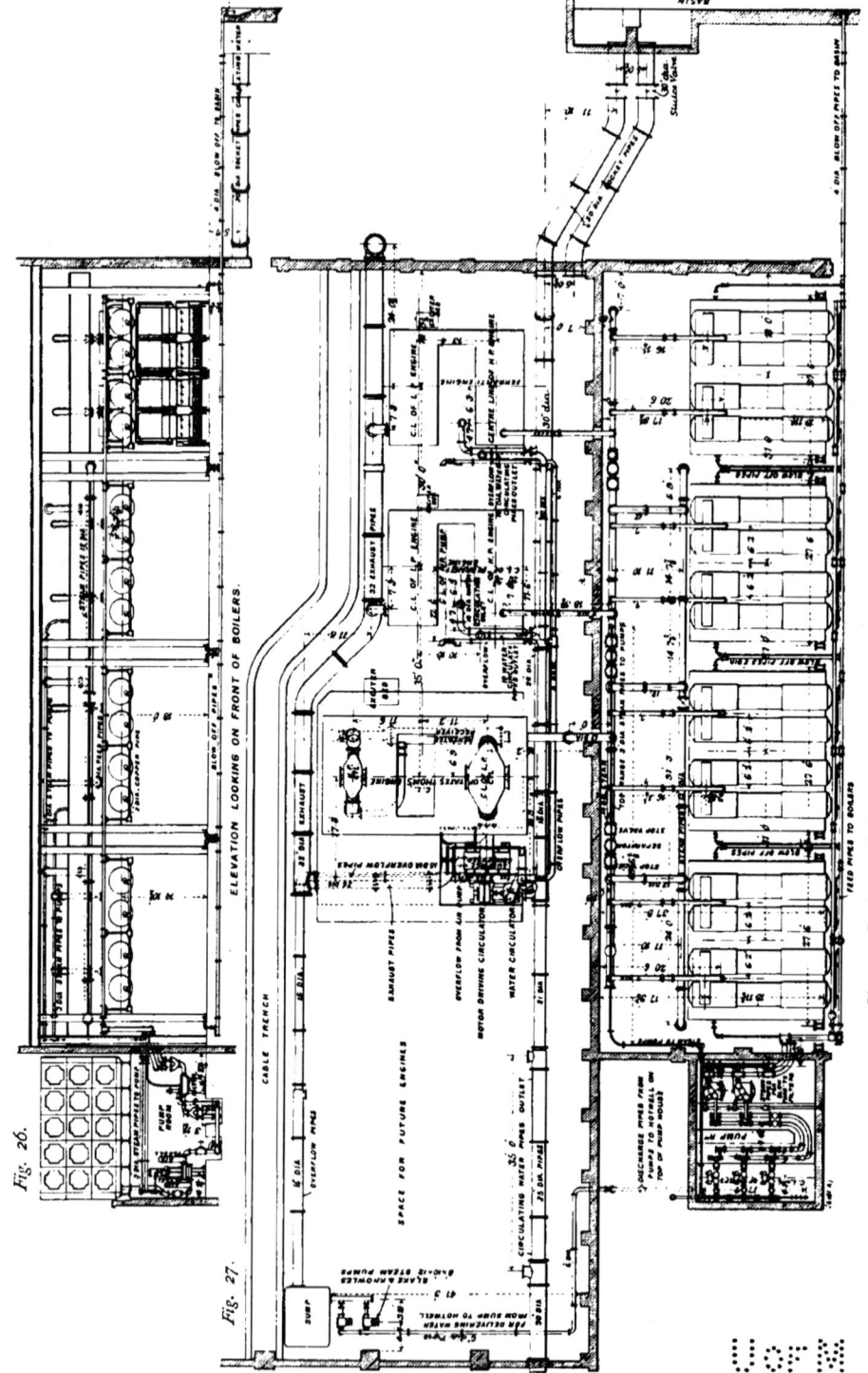

Fig. 26.

ELEVATION LOOKING ON FRONT OF BOILERS.

Fig. 27.

Plan of Engine and Boiler Houses, Midland Electric Power Corporation

M.U

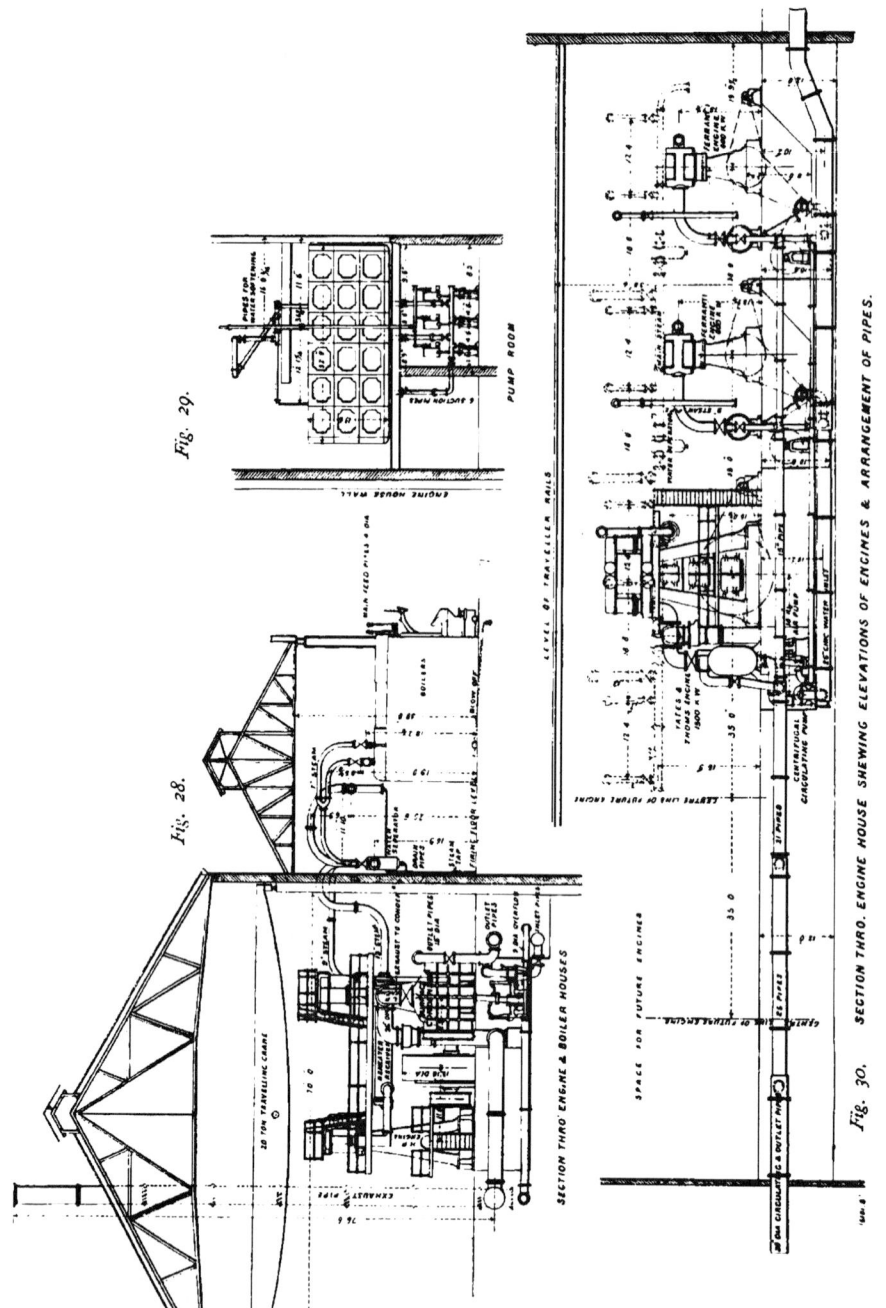

Fig. 29.

Fig. 28.

Fig. 30.   SECTION THRO' ENGINE HOUSE SHEWING ELEVATIONS OF ENGINES & ARRANGEMENT OF PIPES.

Sections through Engine and Boiler Houses, Midland. Electric Power Corporation

MmoU

Plate LVIII

Fig. 31.—View of Coal Tower, Conveying Bridge, and Canal Basin

Fig. 40.—Driving Mechanism of Conveyor Chain

TRACTION AND TRANSMISSION IN SOUTH STAFFORDSHIRE

The cabin on the top floor of the coal tower contains the elevating winch, driven by a 20 horse-power two-phase Westinghouse motor. The man in charge has the the pulley attached to the trolley; it then passes down to the hook, rises again, and is fixed to the trolley. On elevating a bucket, it rises vertically until the hook pulley strikes

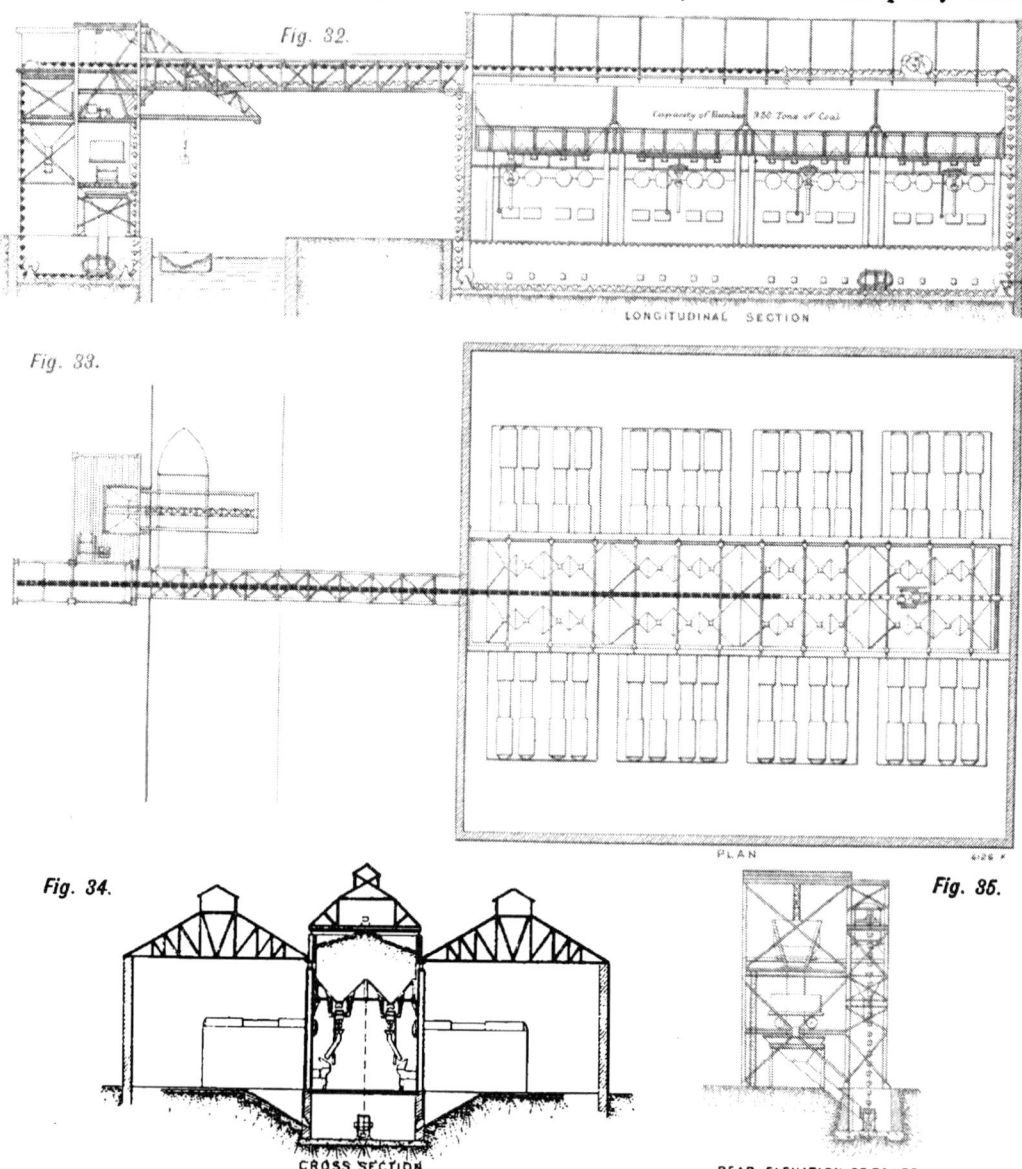

Fig. 32.

Fig. 33.

LONGITUDINAL SECTION

PLAN

Fig. 34.

Fig. 35.

CROSS SECTION

REAR ELEVATION OF TOWER

Plan and Sections of Coal Tower, Conveying Bridge, and Boiler House (see page 250)

motor controller, a handle for working a clutch between winch gear and drum, and a foot-brake on the latter, all within easy reach. The rope from the drum passes round the trolley, when it travels along the inclined beam, and meets the striking rollers over the coal shoot; it then releases a catch on the buckets and automatically tips the coal.

This passes from the top shoot to the bottom one, whence it is fed into the conveyor-filler situated in the basement of the tower.

The buckets are of half a ton capacity,

The buckets are filled by hand, as the type of barge which can be used in the narrow Black Country canals precludes the use of a grab.

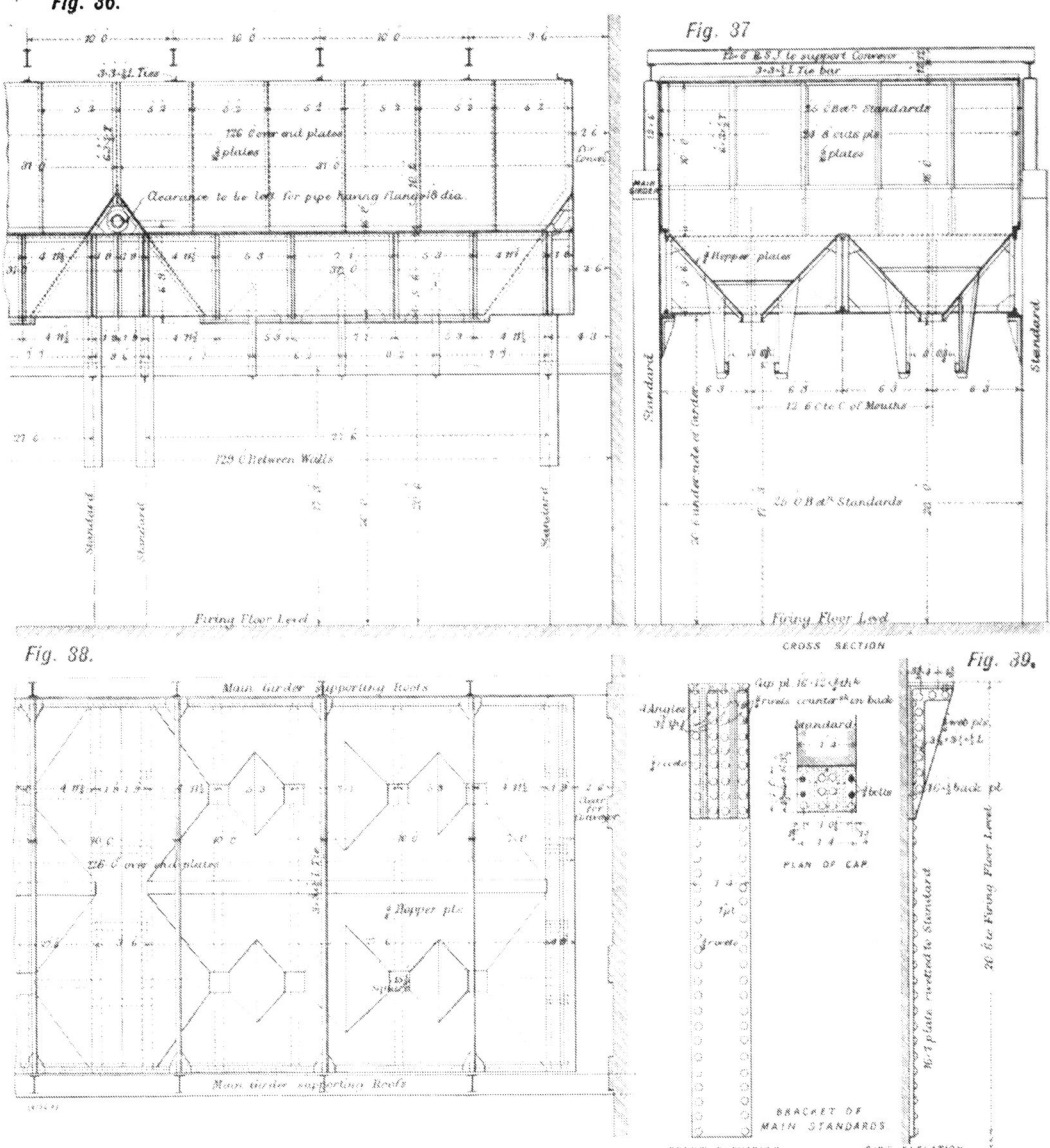

Figs. 36 to 39.—Sections and Plan of Coal Pockets (see page 253)

and three are supplied, so that two can be filled while one is being elevated. The elevating plant and boom are made by the C. W. Hunt Company, of New York.

It should be explained that the above method of elevating, which is at present in use, will have to be reconsidered, as the contractors find that the moving and filling of the buckets demands more time than was estimated, so that the specified elevating output cannot quite be reached.

There are two coal pockets per boiler, or one pocket opposite each grate (see Figs. 36 to 39, page 252); these are closed by a balanced duplex coal valve, actuated from the floor level. Under the line of the two rows of pockets run a pair of rails the whole length of the boiler house. On these run four trolleys, each having a small hopper and an automatic weighing scale contained in a circular box. After the coal has been weighed, a valve in the bottom of the bunker is opened, and the coal gravitates down the long chutes into any stoker hopper. Four of the trolleys are provided for each battery of eight boilers—that is, one trolley to two boilers; but it is obvious that, if necessary, the trolleys can be run under any pocket, and feed any boiler of the series.

Each weighing machine is provided with a registering arrangement, which shows the number of times the hopper has been filled and emptied. This arrangement does not absolutely prevent a stoker taking a small amount more coal than is registered if he is so minded, but with fair treatment the coal consumption can be carefully checked. An apparatus which would prevent any cheating whatever could but introduce many complications on the above arrangement.

The coal hopper, situated on the first floor of the tower, which receives the coal tipped from the buckets, is provided with a valve which, when opened, permits the coal to fall into the travelling conveyor buckets through a filler, that prevents overloading and spilling. Once in the conveyor, the coal travels to the top of the tower, thence in a horizontal direction through the bridge crossing the basin, and so over the bunkers, where the buckets are tipped automatically into any desired bunker. The empty buckets then run to the end of the boiler house, dropping vertically to the boiler room basement, whence they can remove the ashes. Ashes and clinkers are raked direct from the furnaces by the firemen into ashpits with inclined floors, which shoot the ashes into the basement. Here they are slaked and shovelled by hand into a filler, which travels astride the conveyor buckets, on rails fixed to the floor, opposite any ashpit. During this operation the filler is clamped to its rails.

From the basement the conveyor buckets,

either empty or filled with ashes, take another turn of 90degs. up the side of the boiler house on to the bridge; here they assume a horizontal direction along the bridge, then down the elevator tower, under the coal filler from which we started, up the tower again, and over the ash hopper. Beneath this hopper is a cart road, and ashes are loaded into carts direct from the hopper by means of a valve.

If it is found to be desirable to obtain coal by rail, the elevator tower is sufficiently wide to pass a full-gauge truck, which dumps immediately over the coal hopper mentioned above.

The coal hopper has been made large enough to deal with 500 tons per twelve hours. The maximum quantity to be dealt with by the conveyor at present is 250 tons per twelve hours, but it has been made large enough for double the quantity. On the other hand the motors driving the elevating and conveying gears are large enough to deal only with present requirements, but provision has been made for the future installation of larger motors. This was done so that the motors should work always at an economical load.

The coal pockets, or bunkers, which were made by Sir William Arrol & Co., Glasgow, as sub-contractors to Messrs. Babcock & Wilcox, are placed between the boiler fronts, and have a capacity of 920 tons.

These coal receivers have their sides and bottom set at such an angle that coal will gravitate to the chutes without raking or trimming.

At the Glasgow Convention in 1901, Mr. R. A. Chattock read a comprehensive paper on this subject of coal handling, and his opinion of the various types of conveyors in more or less common use is of some interest, especially as it confirms the selection made by the consulting engineers to the Midland Electric Power Corporation.

With the worm type of conveyor the coal is fed in at one end of a semi-circular trough, and is pushed along by the revolution of a spiral of large pitch. This conveyor cannot be used for lengths much greater than 150ft.; it can deal only with small coal, which it makes smaller still in the process of conveying; it is liable to become jammed by lump coal getting fixed between the worm and the trough; the power taken, owing to friction, is very large; and the wear of parts is excessive.

The chain conveyor consists of lines of

bar-iron riveted together, and dragged along a flat-bottomed trough. It is driven by a sprocket wheel, and drags the coal with it. Here, too, the driving power, friction, and wear, are large; and the life of a chain is seldom much more than three years.

The push-plate conveyor was devised in order to keep the chain out of the coal, the chain running on rollers above the trough, with plates depending from the chain into the trough. This is an improvement on the last type, but the friction between coal and trough, and coal and push-plates, involves much loss of energy.

The belt conveyor generally takes the form of a broad, endless rubber belt, running over a pulley at either end of the drive, and supported by rollers throughout its length. Coal is dumped where required by tipping the belt, or by scraping it off with an oblique scraper. This arrangement is cheap to instal, and the belt sometimes lasts from ten to fifteen years, but it is not a very clean method, and shares the objection which applies equally to those mentioned previously, that it can be used only for approximately horizontal work.

The bucket conveyor seems to be the preferable arrangement. It is clean, comparatively noiseless, very flexible, devoid of friction so far as possible, simple in action, long-lived, and requires little driving power. The conveyor installed at Ocker Hill was supplied by Messrs. Babcock & Wilcox, and was made by the C. W. Hunt Company, of New York. We understand that Messrs. Babcock & Wilcox have now a sole manufacturing arrangement with the Hunt Company, and are enlarging their works at Renfrew, in order to undertake this new work.

The conveyor which is illustrated by Fig. 40, Plate LVIII, Figs. 41 to 43, Plate LIX, and Fig. 44, page 255, consists of a double-link chain, carrying a series of pivoted buckets, suspended in such a manner that they maintain their vertical positions, and are free to revolve on their axles at all points of their path, excepting at those points where it is necessary to "dump," or empty them; this dumping is performed automatically in a simple and efficient manner, by means of a cam action, whilst the buckets, on being released from the dumpers, right themselves, and are ready to be refilled. The bucket system passes

through its cycle of action, continuously filling and emptying, the dumping being performed by moving a small lever. The buckets are tipped in such a thorough fashion that nothing remains in them when righted again.

A considerable advantage of this conveyor is the symmetrical and well-balanced arrangement of its parts.

The chain is supported centrally, and is centrally driven, the wheels being placed between the links of the chain, each alternate pair of wheels having an axle passing across the space between the two chains, and correctly maintaining the distance between them, thus preventing distortion of the conveyor system or track gauge. The buckets are suspended on pivots projecting from the inner sides of the chains, and are so arranged that, by withdrawing two pins, any bucket can be removed without disturbing other parts of the mechanism. The wheels are made so that each will carry enough lubricant to provide for a long period of running without attention.

The track consists of a special section of headed rail, connected by double fish-plates, and resting on cast-iron standards, to which the rails are bolted by special hook bolts, thus obviating drilling.

The curves which change the direction of the buckets are, as far as possible, formed as free wheels, and are made each of two wheels accurately bored, turned, and keyed on a steel shaft running in bushed and lubricated bearings. The wheels of the conveyor are thus resting on, and are free to move round, the curved rims, or carry round with them the curve wheels, or have a combined motion of the two, thus minimising friction and wear. By this improvement a great reduction has been effected in the necessary motive power, with a corresponding saving in wear and tear of parts. A "take-up" curve is provided so that any slack of the chain can be adjusted by means of slides and tension screws. The total length of the conveyor at Ocker Hill is 660ft.

The automatic continuous filler consists of a short endless chain carrying seven hoods, and supported in a frame, the hoods covering successively the buckets of the conveyor, and, as the filler chain is driven by projecting lugs engaging with the conveyor chain, the spacing and filling is accurate and uniform. These hoods and chains move around a track formed in the filler frame, and are

Fig. 42.—Automatic Continuous Filler

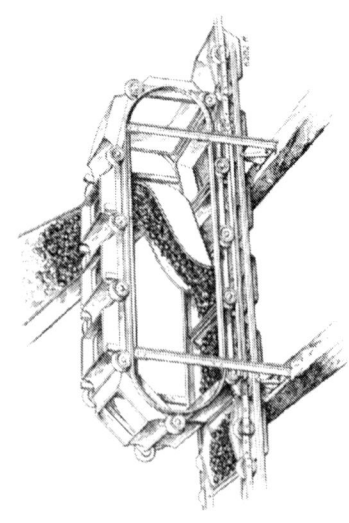

Fig 43.—Charging Conveying Buckets

Fig. 41.—Train of Conveying Buckets

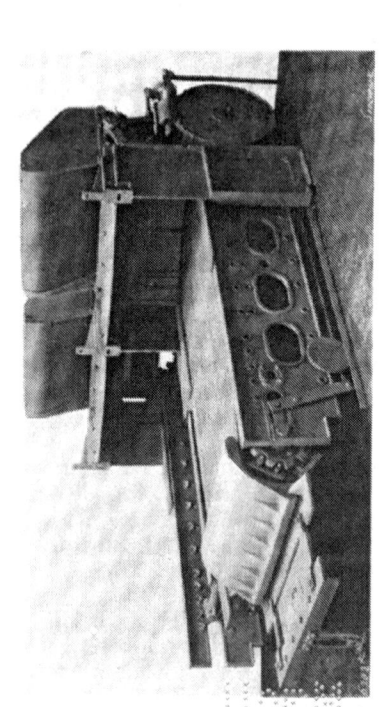

Fig. 45.—Chain Grate Mechanical Stoker

Mroll

supported on wheels similar to those of the conveyor chain.

The driving mechanism is so designed as to propel the chain by means of pawls, which successively engage with the cross studs of the chain, and give a central thrusting action, saving the great wear due to the frictional drives of other systems (see Fig. 44). The

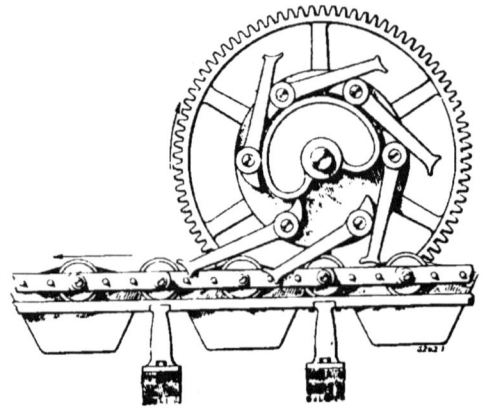

Fig. 44.—Chain Driving Mechanism

motive power is derived from a 12 horse-power, two-phase, 200-volt Westinghouse motor, and even this small power has proved much in excess of actual requirements. It is found that less than 4 horse-power is sufficient to drive the conveyor running light, and about 5 horse-power when loaded —certainly a remarkably good performance.

With a conveyor system such as this, installed in properly arranged stations, it has been possible to reduce the cost of handling coal to about one penny per ton.

Boilers. — The well-known Babcock & Wilcox boiler was selected for steam generation, and at present eight are installed, completely filling one bay of the boiler house (see Figs. 26 and 27, Plate LVI). They are of the double drum type, the drums being 23ft. 7ins. long and 48ins. diameter. These are interconnected with a cross steam drum 8ft. 6ins. long and 20ins. diameter, the total heating surface being 4,650 square feet, each having an evaporative capacity of 12,000lbs. of water from and at 212degs. Fahr.

Each boiler (see Fig. 47, Plate LX), is composed of eighteen sections having twelve tubes 4ins. diameter and 18ft. long, connected

at each end to staggered headers, or up-takes, and down-takes, all provided with hand-holes opposite each tube for cleaning. The mud drum at the bottom of the sections is 10ft. 10ins. long by 10ins. diameter. It is connected through a blow-off cock with a safety cap to a cast-iron discharge, which blows down into the canal basin. Only one spanner for turning the blow-off cock is provided, and the safety cap prevents the spanner being withdrawn unless the valve is closed, so any accident such as a blow-off cock being left open is avoided. Each pair of boilers is slung from cross girders in the usual manner, and these are supported by the box girder stanchions which carry the coal bunkers and roof (see Fig. 26). The boilers are arranged in batteries of two, allowing of easy inspection of back chamber and firing grates, the latter being readily inspected through the two small sliding doors in the side walls.

Each boiler is provided with a Babcock & Wilcox superheater with 454 square feet of heating surface, and consisting of sixty-four U-shaped tubes 1½ins. diameter, expanded at the ends into boxes or manifolds, one of which receives the steam from the boiler, the other collecting the superheated steam after it has traversed the pipes, and delivering it to the superheater stop valve. There is also a second stop valve on each boiler for delivering steam direct, but usually the super-heated steam alone will be used. The super-heater is fitted with cocks for flooding while either the steam is being raised—thus using the superheater as part of the boiler heating surface—or when using saturated steam. The superheater is capable of giving 100degs. to 120degs. Fahr. of superheat.

It is, of course, possible to carry the temperature considerably above this point, still retaining the use of oil as a cylinder and valve lubricant, but it is questionable whether, in every-day working, it will be desirable to go higher than 100degs. to 150degs. Fahr. The main economies are obtained at about this temperature, and although cylinder oil can be used up to a temperature of 800degs. Fahr., additional risks have to be run, and extra allowances must be made for expansion of the working parts, for increased wear and tear, for the sake of a slight extra economy. So long as the steam issues from the exhaust in a just dry condition, practically the most economical conditions are fulfilled, but should it be wet, obviously cylinder condensation must be going on. Undoubted economies are obtained with, say, a superheat of 100degs. to 150degs., which should represent a saving of 10 to 20 per cent. in steam consumption.

Each boiler is fitted with Babcock &

rear, the front drum being revolved by a worm and worm-wheel (see Fig. 45, Plate LIX). The coal is fed over the whole width of the grate, the depth of the fire being regulated by an adjustment of the vertical lifting fire doors. The feed of the coal is so

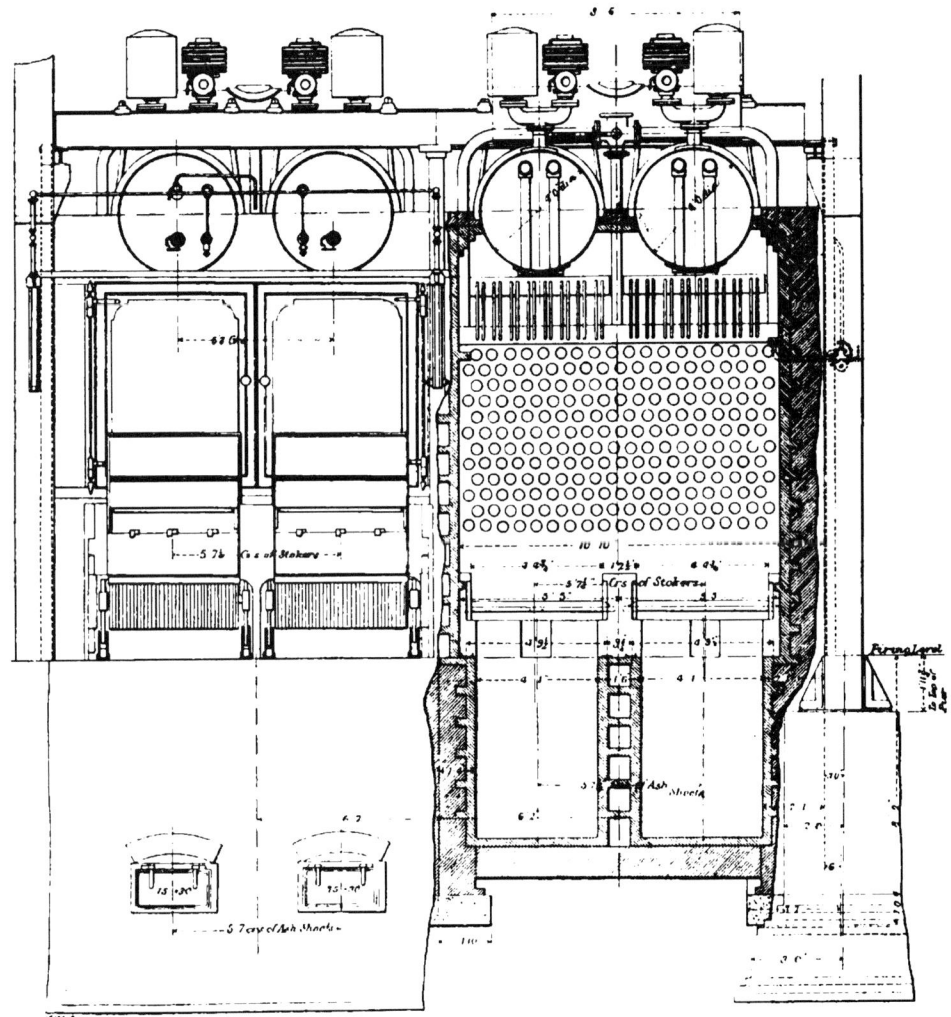

Fig. 46.—Front View and Transverse Section of Babcock & Wilcox Boilers

Wilcox's patent mechanical chain grate stokers. These stokers are suitable for burning a low grade South Staffordshire or other coal.

The stoker consists of an endless chain of grate bars linked together, and connected by passing over drums at the front and

slow that the gas evolved from the fresh fuel, as it drops on to the grate, is efficiently burnt by passing over the incandescent fuel before coming into contact with the boiler heating surface. Thus the fuel is coked and gradually consumed as it travels the length of the grate, falling on to the dumping

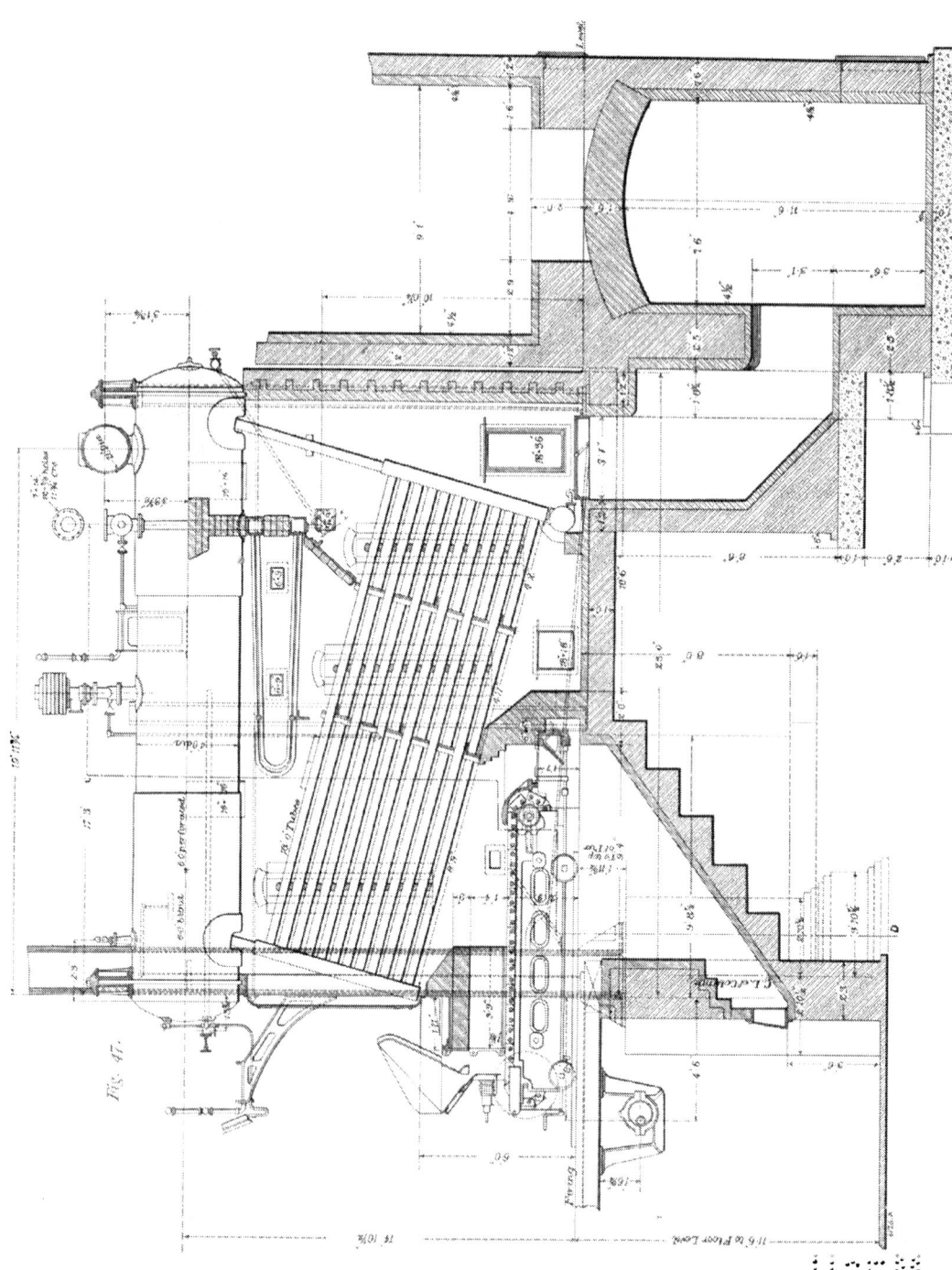

Fig. 47.

Longitudinal Section of Babcock & Wilcox Boiler

UofM

doors at the rear, which are opened to allow the ash and clinkers to fall into the clinkering pit at such intervals as may be required. The

The lifting fire-doors are adjusted to suit the class of fuel to be consumed, and the charge and the speed of the grates can also

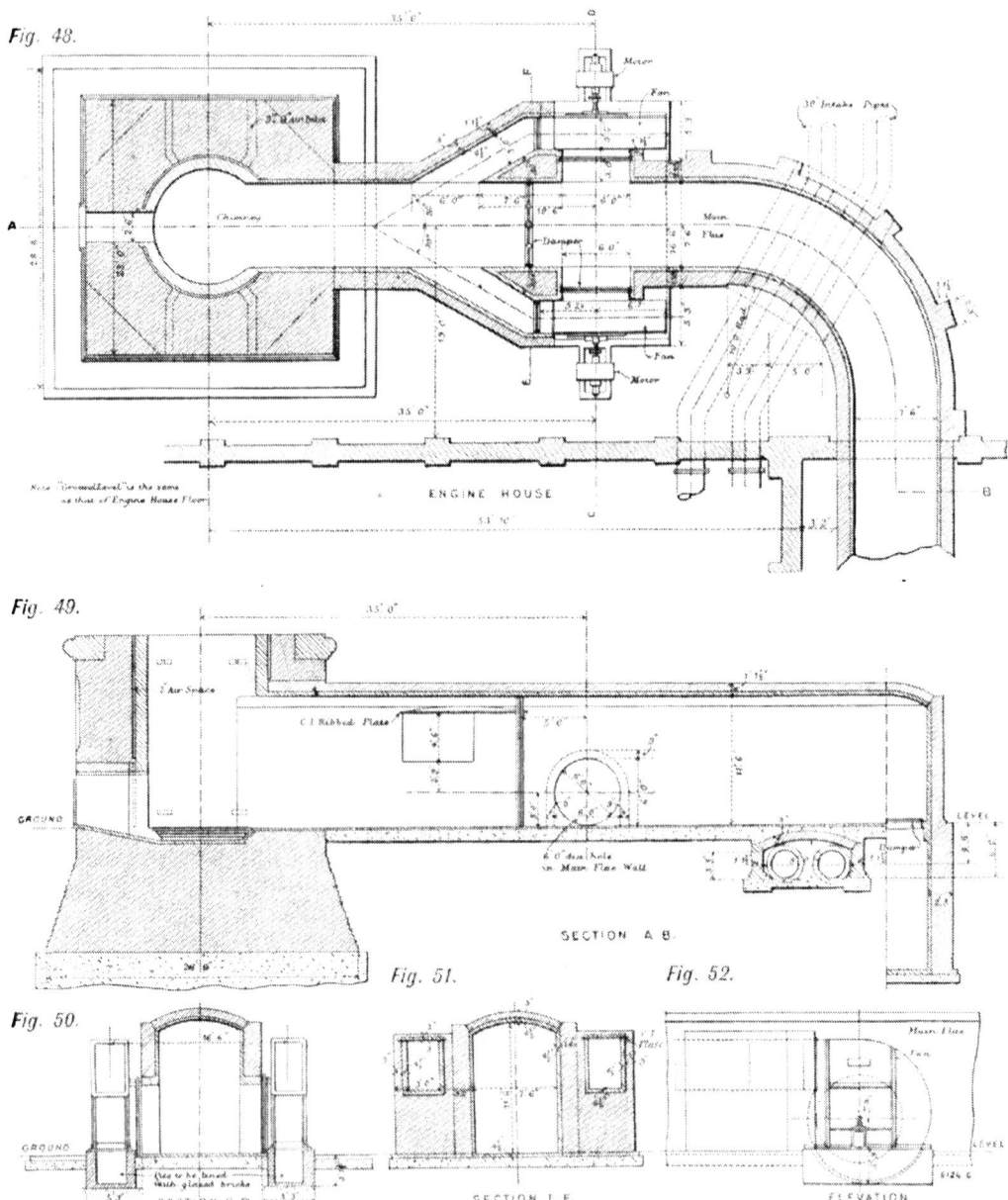

Fig. 48.

Fig. 49.

Fig. 50.

Fig. 51.

Fig. 52.

SECTION C.D.

SECTION E.F.

ELEVATION

Figs. 48 to 52.—Details of Flues (see page 259)

opening and closing of these dumping doors is operated from the front of the stoker by hand gearing.

be regulated. The stoker is self-clinkering, as any clinker that may be found is cleared away when the grate links turn round the back

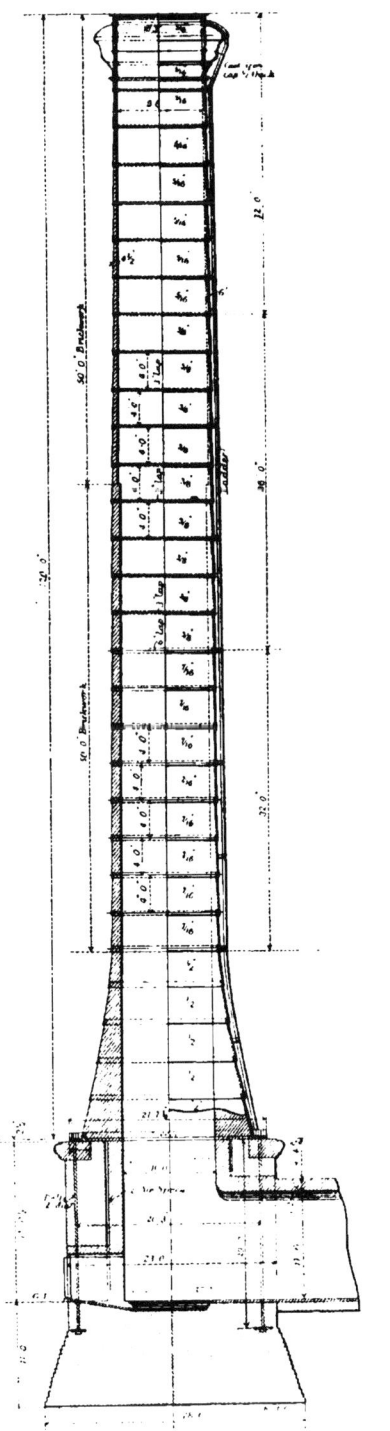

Fig. 53.—Section of Chimney Shaft (see page 259)

drum. The grate links cannot get unduly hot, as by the time they have revolved to re-enter the furnace, they are quite cool. The stoker can be run out clear of the boiler for examination.

The fire doors are hinged to open in the usual way when hand firing is required, and should a mechanical stoker break down, firing can still go on, the grates being occasionally moved by hand gear. In the early stages the station firing was done by hand, but later on, when the stoker could be put in action, its advantages were fully demonstrated. The stokers are driven from a horizontal shaft by

Fig. 54.

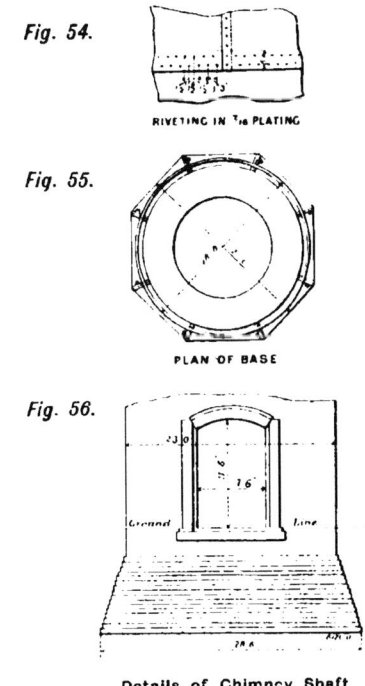

RIVETING IN THE PLATING

Fig. 55.

PLAN OF BASE

Fig. 56.

Details of Chimney Shaft

eccentrics keyed on it, and this is placed in the ashpit basement and driven by a 5 horse-power two-phase Westinghouse motor through worm gearing. Two motors are provided, one as a reserve, and either can be thrown into gear with the shaft. Fig. 46, page 256, and Fig. 47, Plate LX, are respectively a front and side elevation of the boilers. The drawings do not show the tunnel construction, which had to be built to support the boilers on account of the subsoil containing a quantity of coal.

A gangway runs the whole length of the

boiler house opposite the fronts of the steam and water drums, giving access to the boilers and the coal-weighing trolleys. This platform is connected at each passage between the boilers, with an upper platform placed by the side of the stop valves, and another passage by the steam main against the wall, both running the whole length of the boilers, so there is ample provision for readily getting at any part of the entire battery, and the steam ring, a detail which is sometimes overlooked, but which, nevertheless, is important, especially when an emergency occurs.

The boilers are covered with Haacke's composition, canvassed, and black varnished. The boiler house is designed to eventually contain sixteen boilers, the other eight to be placed in the extension bay opposite the present row.

Flues.—Each boiler flue is carried down and enters a main underground flue 11ft. 6ins. high by 7ft. 6ins. wide (see Figs. 48 to 52, page 257), which at each end of the boiler house is closed by three horizontal dampers, and these connect with the economiser flue placed above ground and over the main flue. The economiser is not yet installed, but all provisions are made for its erection.

The main flue is then continued from the north end of the economiser flue into the open, and curves above ground to the chimney stack, as shown in Fig. 48. Provision is made in the main flue, just before entering the chimney stack, for two induced draught fans (Fig. 48), driven electrically, and placed in by-pass flues. The fans are not yet installed, but when they are in operation considerable economy in fuel is expected. Some three or four years ago it was possible to buy a very cheap grade of local slack at 1s. 6d. per ton at the pit mouth, which was burnt extensively in some of the old type of boilers. Coal has increased in price since then, and although it may not be possible to reduce the cost of fuel with induced draught to about the above figure, still, a large reduction on 6s. a ton, the present price of slack, should be made.

The steel chimney shaft (Figs. 53 to 56, page 258) is 120ft. high, with a diameter inside fire-brick lining of 10ft. at the bottom and 9ft. 6ins. at the top. The shaft stands on a massive York stone plinth, built into a brick base about 20ft. high. This base makes the total height from ground level 140ft. The engravings show the construction of the base and shaft. The latter is built entirely of steel plates, three segments completing a ring. The plates vary in thickness from $\frac{1}{2}$in. at the base to $\frac{5}{16}$in. at the top.

The segments are hand riveted, with a double row of rivets to a height of 52ft., above which a single row is used. The splayed part is riveted to a massive cast-iron base, and the top of the chimney is completed by a cast-iron cap. This shaft is designed to be entirely self-supporting, that is to say, its weight and centre of gravity are so proportioned that, with a maximum wind pressure of 60lbs. per square foot, no strain is thrown on the holding-down bolts.

It is possible to erect a shaft of this description at the rate of a ring and a half a day, and with three weeks to a month additional to line the shell with fire-bricks; a complete shaft of the type illustrated can be built in about ten weeks. The engineers adopted this form partly for economical reasons, the cost being less than two-thirds that of a brick chimney. The shaft was erected by Sir William Arrol & Co., as sub-contractors to Messrs. Babcock & Wilcox.

ESCAPING ELECTRICITY AND THE LAW

By W. Valentine Ball

Although a number of Acts relating, directly or indirectly, to electricity may be found in the Statute Books, points arise from time to time upon which those enactments afford no assistance. The advance of electricity in its many practical applications requires modification in the law; hence it is pleasing to find that important changes may be effected in other ways. Thus, by some slight alteration in the common law, resulting from the application of old principles to new methods of using property, it is found that an equitable law of electricity may be produced.

The study of one branch of the law relating to electricity affords a striking example of this species of evolution. Consider the form of a clause which is frequently inserted in private Bills authorising the establishment of a system of electric tramways.

Thus, Sect. 46 of the City of Birmingham Tramways Act, 1901, provides that: "If it be proved that any injury or damage to any gas or water pipes, or other metallic pipes belonging to the Corporation, shall have resulted from fusion or electrolytic action caused by any currents generated or used by the company for the purpose of electric traction under this Act, *nothing in this Act shall relieve the company from any liability to make compensation for any such injury or damage which would not have existed but for the passing of this Act.*"

What, then, is the liability referred to in the passage which we have printed in italics? The statute vaguely hints at the existence of a liability, without stating its scope or extent. The same reluctance to define this liability is to be found in the Electric Lighting Acts. Thus, by Sect. 81 of the Schedule to the Electric Lighting Clauses Act, 1899, which is incorporated with every Provisional Order, it is provided that "Nothing in this order shall exonerate the undertakers from any indictment, action, or proceedings for nuisance, in the event of

any nuisance being caused by them"; but no section states that "nuisance" shall include the electrolytic action of escaping currents.

Setting aside the consideration of such liabilities as the owners of an electrical generating station so frequently incur by reason of their interference with land which they are bound to acquire for the purpose of their undertaking, and the ordinary liabilities for nuisance to which they are exposed, it will be our purpose to consider the liability which the law imposes upon them in respect of the remoter and more subtle consequences which may result from escaping electricity. It is in the course of this inquiry that we encounter a most interesting development of the common law of England, which shows itself peculiarly adaptable to requirements of electrical enterprise.

It is an elementary principle of law that if a man brings into his property any matter, substance, or thing which, in escaping, does damage to a neighbour's property, he shall be held responsible. Thus, if a man keep a lion in his yard, and it escaped and killed cattle in the neighbourhood, the owner of the cattle can bring suit and obtain redress. This principle has been well exemplified in relation to water in the case of *Rylands* v. *Fletcher*.[*] There the defendant had made an artificial lake on his estate. Owing to the occurrence of a violent gale, the water broke from the lake and flooded the plaintiff's property, and it was held that the plaintiff could recover. Mr. Justice Blackburn stated the principle to be that anyone who brings on to his property something which is not naturally there, harmless to others so long as it is confined to his own property, but which he knows to be mischievous if it gets on his neighbour's, "must keep it in at his peril," and ought to be obliged to make good the damage which ensues if he does not succeed in confining it to his own property.

---

[*] L.R., 3 H.L.C., 330.

In the light of this very clearly stated principle, let us examine the position of those who own an electric tramway or other system which involves the use of uninsulated returns. In the first place, they must be regarded as owners of property upon which they generate and keep electricity, "a substance" which is innocuous so long as it is kept within proper bounds, but which, in escaping, may cause damage to property, whether by electrolysis or otherwise. The question whether electric supply companies are liable for the electrolysis of gas and water pipes has already been discussed by the writer in this journal,* but at that time no English cases could be cited to throw light upon the point.

We have now to deal with the question whether liability attaches for the subtler and more remote effects of escaping electricity. Owners of ordinary freehold property could raise no objection to their land being used as part of a return circuit for electricity, but when we consider persons who own delicate instruments which may be affected by electricity, or telephone and telegraphic wires, the use of which may be affected, the nature of the problem becomes altered, for in such circumstances it may be possible to show that property is affected and damage occasioned by the fact that telephonic or telegraphic communication is interfered with. The problem under discussion may be thus formulated: Assuming the escape of electricity from mains carrying a high current is satisfactorily proved, can the owner of those mains be held responsible, or can he say to the owner of the telegraph or telephone, "You are making an extraordinary use of your property, which renders it liable to influences of this kind, and I cannot therefore be held liable. Moreover, you have not taken all possible precautions to prevent the access of stray currents to your delicate apparatus, and since I have as much right to use the earth for return currents as you have, I cannot be held responsible."

The important question whether the doctrine of *Rylands* v. *Fletcher* is applicable to a case where electricity escapes and does injury to the working of a telephone system arose, and was decided, in the *National*

Telephone Company v. *Baker*.* There a tramway company, acting under a Provisional Order, and using the best known system of electrical traction (*i.e.*, overhead wires and return through uninsulated rails), caused electrical disturbance in the wires of a telephone company acting under license from the Postmaster - General. These disturbances prevented the telephone being used. It came to light in the course of the case—and, indeed, the fact was sufficiently obvious—that if the plaintiffs had used a second wire, unconnected with earth, to carry the current back, this would have been a complete cure for the disturbance complained of, but it was also proved that nearly the whole of the plaintiff company's telephone business throughout the country was carried on by means of the single wire system. An action having been brought by the telephone company to obtain redress, the defendants set up three defences, of which the first was that the plaintiffs might by altering their system have minimised the nuisance. With regard to this, Mr. Justice Kekewich said: "They (the plaintiffs) are carrying on their own business lawfully, and in the mode which they deem best, and I cannot oblige them to change their system because they might thereby, possibly, enable the defendants to conduct their business without the mischievous consequences now ensuing." The second defence set up by the defendants was that they were acting under the terms of a Provisional Order granted by the Board of Trade. With regard to this his lordship said: "The defendants are expressly authorised to use electrical power, and the Legislature must be taken to have contemplated this, and to have condoned, by anticipation, any mischief arising from the reasonable use of such power." Judgment was entered for the defendants upon this ground, it having been established that the injury to the telephone system was due to nothing but the natural and ordinary working of their tramway system by the defendants.

In so far as this case is authoritative—for the decision that the defendants would have been liable had they not been protected by statute is partly an *obiter dictum*—it will be seen that the court held that the use of a telephone, even upon a principle which left it exposed to injury from external currents,

---

* See article entitled "The Law of Electrolysis," TRACTION AND TRANSMISSION, September, 1901, Vol. II, page 1.

* [1893] 2 Ch. 186.

was entitled to protection. In other words, Mr. Justice Kekewich held that no distinction could be drawn between escaping electricity and any other commodity, though it is right to say that he said such a distinction would have to be made by a higher tribunal, and not by a judge of first instance.

Fortunately for those who are interested in the progress of electricity, a much higher tribunal has recently had an opportunity of considering the question. The Judicial Committee of the Privy Council have recently considered and have delivered judgment in a case which came before them on appeal from the Supreme Court of the Cape Colony, and which has an important bearing upon the subject now under discussion. We refer to the *Eastern and South African Telegraph Company, Limited,* v. the *Cape Town Tramways Companies, Limited,** which recently came before the Judicial Committee of the Privy Council, on appeal from the Supreme Court at the Cape.

In order to understand this case, it will be necessary to refer to the facts which led up to it.† It seems that the defendant company are the proprietors of an electric tramway system in Cape Town and its suburbs. They obtained statutory authority to lay and maintain all their lines with the exception of one section about a mile and a half in length.

The company adopted the system of overhead wires, and having obtained leave in that behalf from the Municipal authorities, they allowed the current to return through uninsulated rails. The plaintiff company are the proprietors of, *inter alia*, the West Coast Cable, which runs out to sea through Table Bay. When the electric tramway system commenced working in 1896, difficulty was experienced in reading cable messages at Cape Town. This eventually became so severe, that messages could only be received when the cars stopped running. Both companies then took steps to find out and to remedy the cause of the disturbance. It was discovered that at some point in Table Bay, electricity, having escaped and being at large, was attracted by the telegraphic cable. Entering the sheathing it found its way back

to the tramway central station, and so completed the circuit. While travelling along the sheathing the current varied frequently and at irregular intervals, according to the starting or stopping of the cars, with the result that irregular currents were induced in the conducting wire of the cable. These induced currents rendered messages unintelligible, though no physical damage was done to the telegraph company's apparatus. As a result of experiments it was found that the difficulty could be completely obviated by laying a "twin-core" cable for several miles out—the two wires rectifying each other's action. Such a cable was laid in 1897, and a second was laid in 1898, ten miles in length, with the result that at the date when the action was brought, the difficulty was almost entirely obviated. In April, 1899, the present action was commenced, £50,000 being claimed as damages in respect of loss of business, and the estimated cost of remedial measures. The defendants contended (1) that they were protected by the following section in the statute under which the tramway company worked :—

> The company specially undertakes that, in the event of any electric leak taking place, and damage being thereby caused at any time, by electrolysis or otherwise, it will reimburse and make good to the council or other body or person all costs to which the council or other body or person may be put by reason thereof, etc., and provided further that nothing in this Act contained shall entitle the company to use the rails of any of the said lines of tramway as part of its system of conductors for the return electrical current without the consent of the council first had and obtained.

(2) That as regards the section of the line for which statutory authority had not been obtained, the defendants were liable at common law upon the principle of *Fletcher* v. *Rylands*, defendants answered (1) that the escape of electricity from uninsulated rails was not an electric leak within the meaning of the section; (2) that the words " or otherwise " referred only to things *ejusdem generis* with electrolysis; (3) that the doctrine of *Fletcher* v. *Rylands* was not recognised by the common law in use at the Cape. The Supreme Court at the Cape found for the defendants on all points, laying it down with regard to their third contention " *that as regards the unauthorised section of the line, the construction and working of it in a*

---

* (1902) A.C., 381.

† An admirable statement of these facts appeared in the *Electrical Review* for March 28th, 1902, page 502.

proper manner and without negligence was not an infringement of any legal right of the plaintiffs." On appeal to the Privy Council the judgment of the Supreme Court at the Cape was upheld upon all points. With regard to the question of leakage, their lordships said that, while giving to the word "leak" whatever expansion might be appropriate to its application to electricity, they could not hold that what had occurred fell within the undertaking and condition mentioned in the protecting section. The escape was, on the contrary, a natural incident of the operations legalised under the statutes.

The Privy Council also affirmed the opinion of the Colonial Court that no legal right of the plaintiffs had been infringed. Lord Robertson said :—

The question of common law is raised directly, because the defendants are unprotected in respect of one portion of their line. If regard be had solely to the action of the respondents in storing electricity on their lands, it must be allowed that the analogy is very close to the illustrations given in *Fletcher* v. *Rylands* of the kind of things which a proprietor can only do at his own peril. Electricity (in the quantity which we are now dealing with) is capable, when uncontrolled, of producing injury to life and limb and to property, and in the present instance it was artificially generated in such quantity, and it escaped from the respondent's premises and control. So far as they are concerned, it appears to us that, given resulting injury such as was postulated in *Fletcher* v. *Rylands*, the principle will apply.

It will be seen from the above extract that, in the opinion of the Privy Council, the doctrine of *Fletcher* v. *Rylands* only applies to electricity where very substantial damage is caused by escaping currents. Lord Robertson continued :—

But that is only one half of the question, and it remains to be seen whether the injury postulated was present. Was there any injury upon which a claim could be founded? In the present case, neither person nor property were injured—unless the ingenious suggestion of Mr. Bousfield can be entertained that physical injury was done to the paper, which was smudged by the eccentric action of the recording apparatus. Certainly there was here no injury of the same genus with the tangible and sensible injuries which have hitherto founded liability on the principle in question, and which have always constituted some interference with the ordinary use of property. Now, the kind and degree of interference with the respondent's property is well illustrated by the fact that it could only take place if the cable was constructed without certain precautions, for, given the cable as it now is, there is no injury. That is referred to

because it shows that it cannot be predicated of the electric escape in question that it was destructive of telegraphic communication generally, but only because it affected instruments made in a certain way. If the instrument be taken as it was when the injury occurred, its nature was such that to ensure its immunity from disturbance was a somewhat serious liability to cast on neighbours. . . . The true comparison is with things used in the ordinary enjoyment of property, and that instrument differed from such things in its peculiar liability to be affected by even minute currents of electricity. Now having regard to the assumptions of the appellants' argument, it seems necessary to point out that the appellants, as licensees to lay their cable in the sea, and as owners of the premises in Cape Town, where the signals are received, cannot claim higher privileges than other owners of land, and cannot create for themselves, by reason of the peculiarity of their trade apparatus, a higher right to limit the operations of their neighbours than belongs to ordinary owners of land who do not trade with telegraphic cables. If the apparatus of such concerns requires special protection against the operations of their neighbours, that must be found in legislation. The remedy at present invoked is an appeal to a common law principle which applies to much more usual, and less special conditions. A man cannot increase the liabilities of his neighbours by applying his own property to special uses, whether for business or pleasure. The principle of *Fletcher* v. *Rylands*, which subjects to a high liability the owner who uses his property for purposes other than those which are natural, would become doubly penal if it implies a liability created and measured by the non-natural uses of his neighbour's property. Nor need the law be regarded as showing any want of adaptability to modern circumstances, if that be the true view, for the liability thus limited is of insurance and not for negligence, and all the remedies for negligence remain.

The following conclusions may be drawn from this judgment: (1) Leaking electricity may in certain cases subject to liability the person who allows it to escape ; (2) in deciding the question of liability regard must be had to the nature of the damage done, and to the steps which the complainant has taken to guard against injury from stray currents in the earth.

It might appear at first sight that this judgment presses hardly upon the telegraph companies, but this is not so. *Ubi jus, ibi remedium* is an ancient maxim of law, with which the Privy Council have been careful to comply. They have merely laid it down that the right of a telegraph company to claim damages for the consequences of escaping currents does not accrue until every precautionary measure has been taken.

ELECTRIC CRANES*

By Philip Dawson

FIFTH ARTICLE

Motor Heating.—In the last article the design of crane motors was discussed, and the characteristic curves of several types were reproduced. The question of temperature rise is one of great importance, and in this connection the curves on this and the next page, showing temperature rise in the field magnets, coils, and armatures of some typical series wound motors, will be found of interest. The curves have been plotted from actual tests, and the motors to which they refer are of standard types, constructed by the Union Elektricitäts-Gesellschaft, which have given first-rate results in practice.

Motor Speed and Power.—As is well known, the speed of the series wound motor varies according to the load. This is clearly shown by the various diagrams given in the preceding article. In order to ascertain the variations in speed, it is necessary to know the various loads at which the motor will have to work, and from this information the torque can be ascertained.

Let Q_m be the maximum load which the crane has to lift.

Then, if the efficiency of the lifting gear is "E," the actual load, W_m, lifted by the motor is $\frac{Q_m}{E}$.

When lifting the empty hook, the actual load, W_o, will be due to the friction, etc., in the gearing. Hence $W_o = W_m - Q_m = \frac{Q_m}{E} - Q_m$.

It may be assumed that this amount is constant for all loads. Then when lifting a given load, Q, the actual load on the motor will be $W = W_o + Q = \frac{Q_m}{E} - Q_m + Q$.

The torque exerted by the motor is proportional to the load on the motor. Hence, if T_m is the torque for maximum load, and T the torque for load Q, then—

$$\frac{T}{T_m} = \frac{W}{W_m} = \frac{\frac{Q_m}{E} - Q_m + Q}{\frac{Q_m}{E}} = 1 - E + \frac{Q\,E}{Q_m}$$

---

* See Traction and Transmission, Vol. IV, pages 145 and 247; Vol. V, pages 47 and 188.

The following table gives values of T for various values of Q, assuming E equals 80 per cent. :—

Q	0.0 × Qm	0.5 × Qm	1.0 × Qm	2.0 × Qm
T	0.2 × Tm	0.6 × Tm	1.0 × Tm	1.8 × Tm

Figs. 1 to 3 give characteristic curves of a motor constructed by the Union Elektricitäts-Gesellschaft (Thomson - Houston system) of

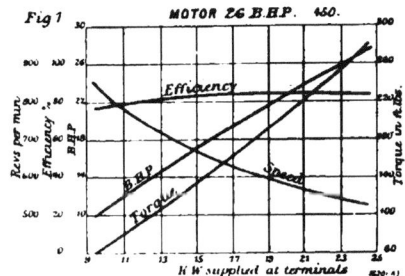

Fig 1. MOTOR 26 B.H.P. 450.

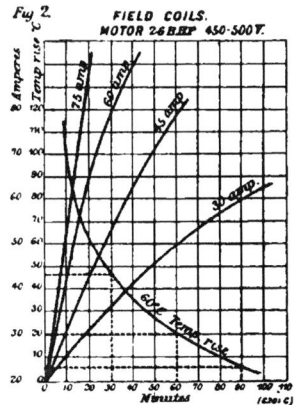

Fig 2. FIELD COILS. MOTOR 26 B.H.P. 450-500 V.

Berlin, which has been extensively used for crane work. The motor is rated at 26 brake horse-power at 540 revolutions and 500 volts, which corresponds to the minimum power the motor will have to give out in lifting the maximum load for which the crane is designed, at the maximum speed specified.

Thus, supposing a load of 3 tons has to be lifted at a rate of 100ft. per minute, and if the efficiency of the crane gearing (not including the motor) is 80 per cent., the rated brake horse-power of the motor will have to be $\frac{3 \times 2240 \times 100}{0.8 \times 33,000} = 25.5$ brake horse-power.

For this purpose the above-mentioned

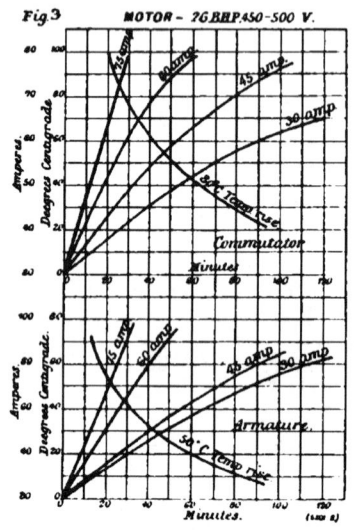

Fig 3. MOTOR - 26 B.H.P. 450-500 V.

Assuming (see Fig. 3) a pressure of 500 volts, which corresponds to a little over 46 amperes input, we see that the motor can work for one hour at 26 brake horse-power without a rise of more than 45degs. Cent. in the armature, and slightly over 65degs. Cent. at the commutator; the field coils would nearly reach 115degs. Cent., as seen from Fig. 2. Figs. 4 and 5 give data of a 12 brake horse-power motor at 700 revolutions, and Figs. 6 and 7, of a 5 brake horse-power motor at 400 revolutions, both designed for 500 volts.

The Table on page 266 giving particulars

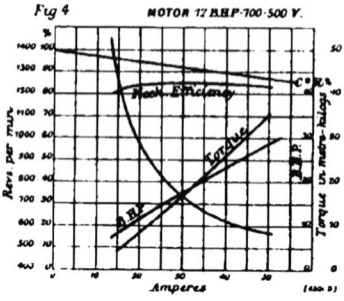

Fig 4. MOTOR 12 B.H.P. 700-500 V.

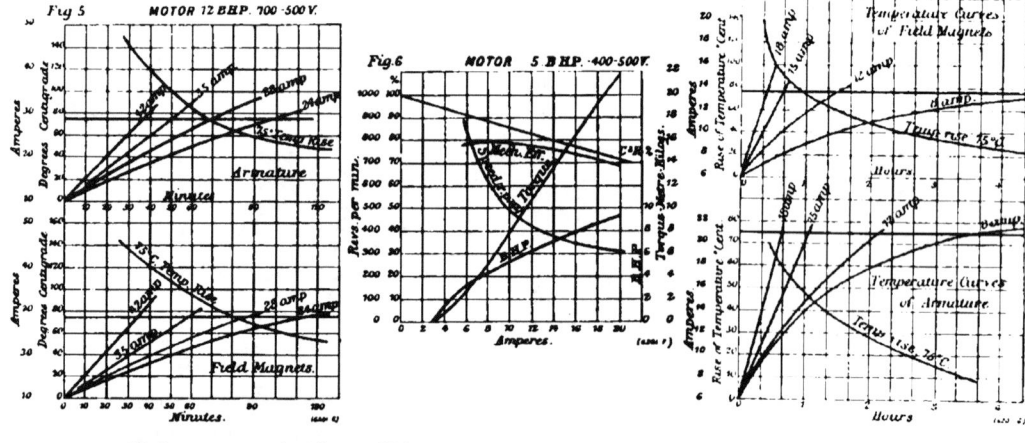

Fig 5. MOTOR 12 B.H.P. 700-500 V.

Fig 6. MOTOR 5 B.H.P. 400-500 V.

Fig 7. MOTOR 5 B.H.P. 400-500 V.

motor would be very suitable. This motor gives a torque of 255 foot-pounds at 540 revolutions, and a mechanical efficiency of 84 per cent. Assuming that the diameter of the winding drum is 27ins. (2.25ft.), the gear ratio will have to be $\frac{540 \times 2.25 \times \pi}{100} = 38$ (approximate); that is to say, the revolutions of the armature of the motor will be thirty-eight times greater than those of the winding drum.

ot Messrs. Schuckert's crane motors will be found of interest; it gives the complete series from 1.3 to 209 brake horse-power, and method on which the rating is based.

Brakes.—One of the most necessary details in a well-designed crane is a powerful, reliable, and instantaneous acting brake. In hydraulic cranes the command which the driver has over the loads is practically perfect, and although additional band brakes are generally

TABLE I. — ENCLOSED SERIES WOUND DIRECT CURRENT SCHUCKERT CRANE MOTORS

Two-pole Type—

Rated Brake Horse Power.	Input in Kilowatts.	Torque.		Normal Speed. R.P.M.	Minimum Speed. R.P.M.		Weight of Motor.	
		Kilog-metres	Foot-pounds.		220 Volts.	550 Volts.	Kgs.	Lbs.
1.3	1.6	0.52	3.76	1800	500	..	85	187
2.2	2.3	0.92	6.65	1700	450	..	125	275
2.2	2.3	0.92	6.65	1700	..	700	125	275
3.4	3.3	1.48	10.7	1650	400	..	150	330
3.4	3.3	1.48	10.7	1650	..	600	150	330
4.5	4.2	2.03	14.7	1600	..	500	200	440
6.0	7.2	3.7	26.8	1550	..	480	240	528
12.0	10.6	5.7	41.2	1500	..	470	300	660
16.0	14.0	8.2	59.25	1400	..	435	390	792
20.5	17.8	10.9	78.8	1350	..	420	400	1012

Four-pole Type—

Rated Brake Horse Power.	Input in Kilowatts.	Torque.		Normal Speed. Revolutions per Minute.	Minimum Speed. Revolutions per Minute.	Weight of Motor.	
		Kilog-metres.	Foot-pounds.			Kgs.	Lbs.
26	22.3	14.3	103.3	1300	400	510	1122
34	29	20.3	146.8	1200	370	700	1540
43.5	37	29.6	214.0	1050	325	940	2068
46.5	39.4	31.7	229	1050	700	1000	2200
46.5	39.4	31.7	229	1050	320	1200	2640
65	54.5	49	354	950	300	1550	3410
93	78	75.5	546	880	280	1750	3850
122	100	105	760	830	280	3000	6600
165	138	153	1106	770	240	3400	748
209	172	226	1634	660	220	4200	9240

N.B.—The rating of these motors is made on the assumption that they run for three minutes and rest for six minutes. The rated speed is attained at one quarter the rated torque. Should the motor have to be run continuously, the rated capacity would be one-third that given in the table.

furnished, they are not absolutely necessary. It is otherwise with the ordinary steam, and electrically driven, cranes, in which a powerful and reliable band, or other, brake is essential. Where electricity is used as a motive power, the band brake is frequently made dependent on the current in such a way that, unless it is specially held off by the hand of the operator, it is always put on hard except when current is going through the motor during the operation of lifting. The brakes must be of sufficient power to compensate instantly for the inertia due to the revolving parts, and to stop all movement the moment the current is cut off. It is sometimes desirable, as in the case of lifts, that an automatic safety device should be provided to prevent the load being lifted so high as to damage the crane, or do other mischief, should the crane operator fail from any cause to cut off the current when the load has attained its maximum height. This automatic device must cut off the current from the lifting motor and apply the brake so as to hold the load in the position at which it has arrived, and prevent

it coming down with a run. In many cases the motors are so connected to the controller that they can be short circuited, and used (as in traction work) as emergency brakes should anything go wrong with the band brakes. These brakes must be capable of instant application, either for stopping or for regulating the movement of the load. On the ease with which this operation can be performed, the efficiency of cranes greatly depends. Brakes can also be applied to control the travelling and revolving movements; and in some cases centrifugal governors have been used to cut off the energy and throw on the brakes, should the speed, either in lifting or lowering, exceed a safe limit.

Both the type of brake used, and the method of applying it, vary in different types of cranes. Where the motor is permanently connected by means of gearing to the winding drum, i.e., where no friction clutch is used, it is generally the practice to apply a band brake to the motor shaft. The brake is normally held on by a counterweight, but is lifted by a solenoid, and frees the shaft as soon as the current is put on to the motors. This arrangement is very useful, because, as soon as the current is cut off the motors, the band brake is applied; otherwise it would be quite possible for the inertia of the motor to continue lifting after the current has ceased. To prevent a too sudden application of the brake, and an undesirable jarring motion, a dashpot is generally employed to modify the action. Such brakes are so arranged that they cannot be on when the current is going through the motors; without this precaution the motors might burn out. A hand or foot lever is also supplied, with which the brake can be worked by the driver, so that he can either take it off entirely when necessary, or regulate it so as to let the load run down by gravity. The mechanical details of these brakes are comparatively simple, and there are several different types, all of which have been well worked out by a large number of crane makers in the past; they do not differ materially from those which have been used on steam cranes for many years.

There are, however, important electrical details, as well as mechanical arrangements, by which the brake and controller commanding the current can be so interlocked as to prevent any possible accident due to carelessness on the part of the driver.

Where the winding drum is operated by means of a friction clutch for lifting, and is disconnected from the hoisting motor when lowering, the band brake is applied direct to the drum, and is generally controlled mechanically.

In other forms the brake is applied by springs or counter-weights, and taken off by an electro-magnet (Figs. 8 and 9); the following diagrams illustrate a few of the many varieties of this type.

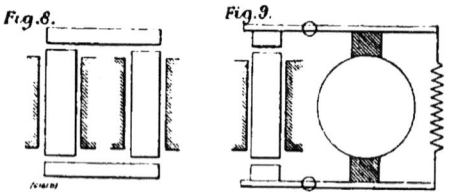

Fig. 8. Fig. 9.

Diagram of Brake Magnet

Fig. 10 shows the method employed by Sprague. In this a magnet attracts two armatures, thereby causing the two levers which hold the band brake to oscillate and

circuit, thus decreasing the current used in its operation. It is also possible to employ a fixed core with a movable coil. The general design of such an arrangement has been very successfully adopted by the Union Elektricitäts-Gesellschaft in crane installations. In their device, the solenoid attracts a core attached to the lever, and lifts the weight which holds on the band brake. To prevent the action being too sudden and rapid, the top of the core is connected to a piston working in a cylinder, and by means of a small valve, the rapidity with which the air is sucked in can be regulated in such a way as to allow a perfect working of the brake. The general size and design of the solenoid is shown in Figs. 17, 18, page 268, and Table III gives the standard sizes in which it is constructed. Figs. 11 and 12 illustrate diagrammatically such a solenoid, in one case acting by attraction, in the other by repulsion. In order to prevent the brake acting too suddenly, it has been found necessary to fit a dashpot on to it, as shown in Fig. 11. With motors up to 12 horse-power the smallest size is generally sufficient.

Tables II and IV, page 268, give particulars,

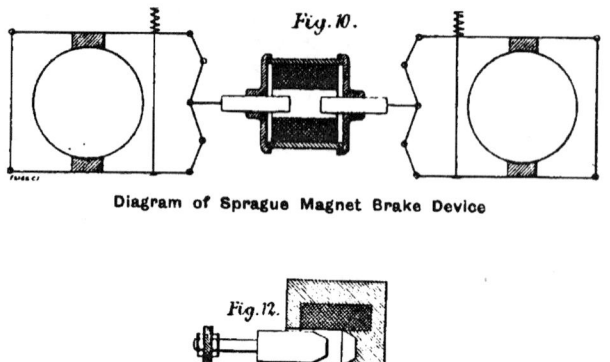

Fig. 10.

Diagram of Sprague Magnet Brake Device

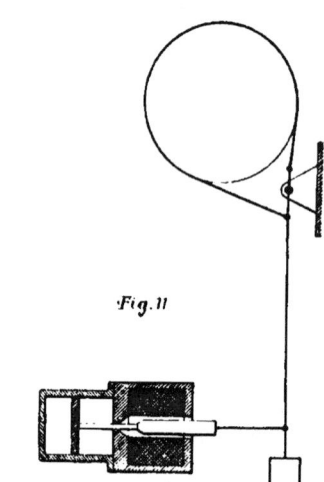

Fig. 11

Fig. 12.

Diagrams of Solenoid Brakes

counteract the effect of the spring, thus releasing the brake-blocks and setting the drum free to revolve. Instead of using an electro-magnet to attract the armature, a solenoid may be advantageously adopted; in this case it should be designed in such a way as to have an economical magnetic

ticulars, and Figs. 13 to 18 are diagrams, of cut-outs and magnet brakes of the Union and Lahmeyer Companies.

The solenoids which are now generally used by the Union Elektricitäts-Gesellschaft, and which are the standard adopted by the Benrather Maschinenfabrik, are generally

TABLE II.—SAFETY CUT-OUT FOR CRANES—UNION ELEKTRICITÄTS-GESELLSCHAFT TYPE (Figs. 15 and 16)
(Dimensions in Millimetres)

Amperes.	A	B	C	D	E	F	G	H	I	K	L	M	N	O	P	Q	R	S	T	U	V	W	β
50	218	196	11	102	98	10	115	152	45	110	2	50	18	26	24	74	41	2	10	95	8	30	45°
150	292	260	16	139	135	14	146	185	55	130	0	50	20	30	25	87	55	6	12	119	9	35	45°

TABLE III.—DIMENSIONS OF UNION ELEKTRICITÄTS-GESELLSCHAFT BRAKE MAGNET (Figs. 17 and 18)

Pull in Kilogrammes.	Pull in Lbs.	Lift in Millimetres.	Lift in Inches.	A	B	C	D	E	F	G	H	I	K	L	M	N	O	P	Q	R	S	T	U
10	22	40	1.575	186	108	33	144	100	42	30	250	16	15	15	287	190	77	20	7	18	15	112	50
20	44	30	1.181	186	108	33	144	100	42	30	250	16	15	15	287	190	77	20	7	18	15	112	50
20	44	60	2.362	242	110	58	174	130	54	42	320	20	20	20	375	244	111	20	24	21	21	141	60
30	66	50	1.969	242	110	58	174	130	54	42	320	20	20	20	345	244	81	20	24	21	21	141	60
25	55	100	3.94	242	110	58	174	130	54	42	320	20	20	20	475	344	111	20	24	21	21	141	60
40	88	80	3.15	242	110	58	174	130	54	42	320	20	20	20	445	344	81	20	24	21	21	141	60

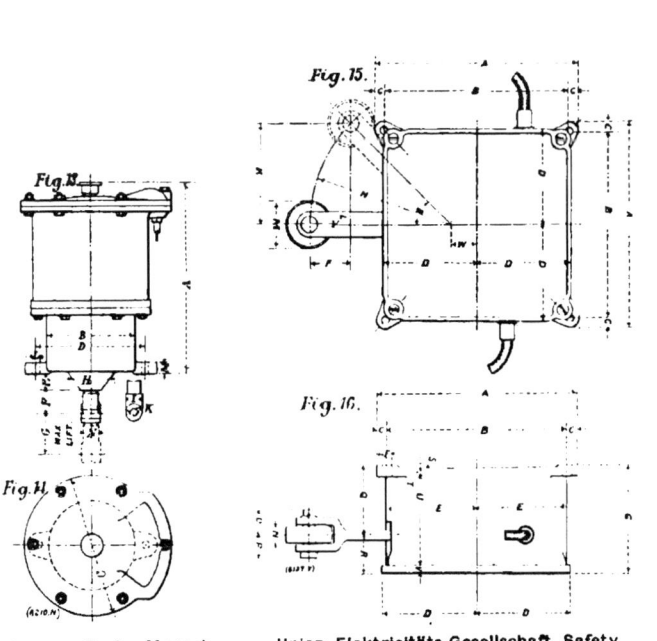

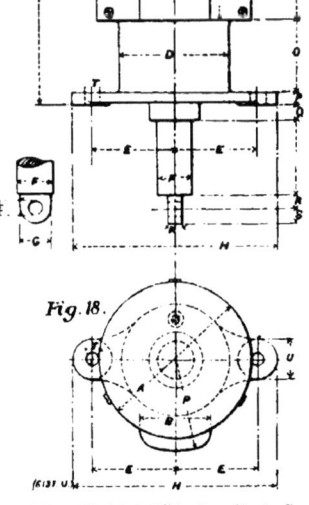

Lahmeyer Brake Magnet

Union Elektricitäts-Gesellschaft Safety
Cut-out (Table II)

Union Elektricitäts-Gesellschaft
Brake Magnet (Table III)

TABLE IV.—DIMENSIONS IN MILLIMETRES OF LAHMEYER
BRAKE MAGNET (Figs. 13 and 14)

Size.	A	B	C	D	E	F	G	H	I	K	L	M	N
3 × 1½	430	210	320	260	40	55	105	105	40	20	20	26	41
3 × 2	330	160	250	200	30	40	80	80	30	15	15	20	32
3 × 3	230	110	175	140	21	30	60	60	21	13	13	20	24

provided with two windings, one a series
and one a shunt winding. Both of these
are in circuit when the current first goes
through the motor, and they give the pull
required to suck in the core. When the
latter has once been attracted, the current

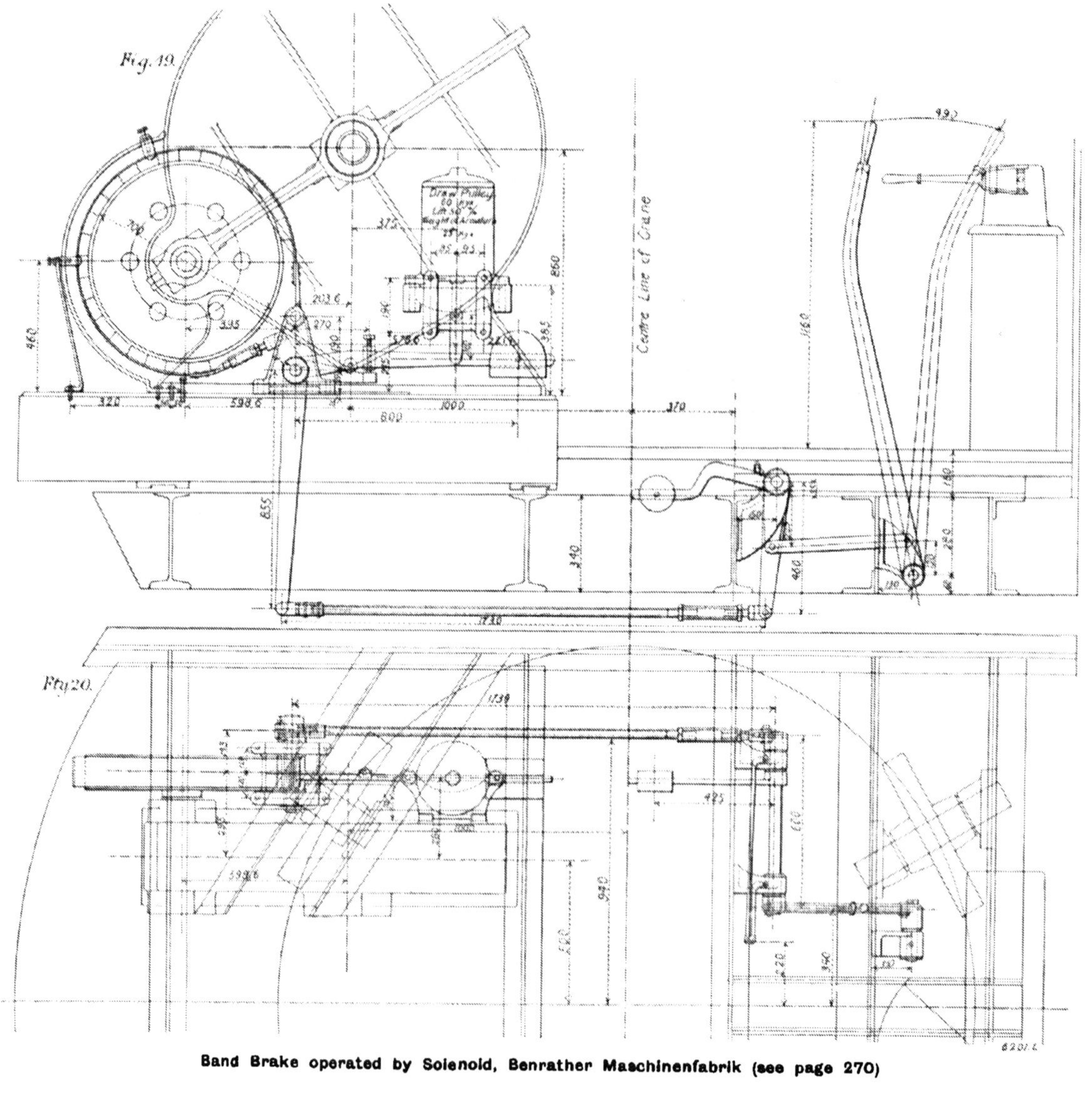

Fig. 19

Fig 20.

Band Brake operated by Solenoid, Benrather Maschinenfabrik (see page 270)

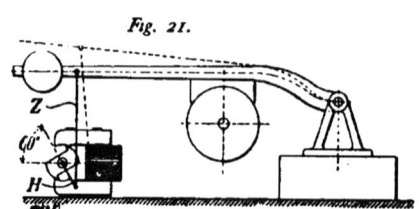

Fig. 21.

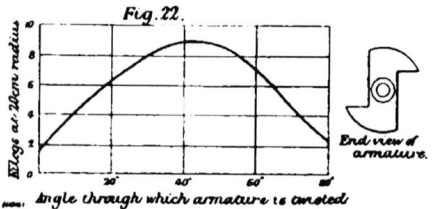

Fig. 22.

Siemens' Revolving Magnet Governor (see page 270)

through the shunt coil is cut off, and the core is held in place by the series coil alone. This considerably reduces the amount of current required to work the solenoid. The cutting out of the windings is generally effected by contacts in the controller.

Figs. 19 and 20 (page 269), show details of a band brake, and a method of its application by means of the solenoid, and how the brake can be taken off by the use of a hand lever. The dimensions given on these drawings are in millimetres. The pull of the solenoid is 60 kilogrammes through a lift of 50 millimetres, and the weight which it has to attract is 25 kilogrammes. The sketch shows the contrivance as actually installed on the cranes.

Solenoids have the disadvantage of not being able to give a very long stroke or lift, and to overcome this difficulty Messrs. Siemens & Halske, in Berlin, and Messrs. Siemens Bros., in London, have brought out a type of revolving magnet governor, the general arrangement of which is shown in Fig. 21, page 269.

Messrs. Siemens & Halske build their electric governor in the following three sizes :—

Approximate Torque in Kilogramme-centimetres.	Approximate Energy Consumption in Watts.	Approximate Weight in Kilogrammes.
125	180	30
250	280	60
500	540	130

The arrangement practically resembles a small motor with a solid iron armature of the shape shown in the figure, and which is caused to rotate through a certain angle by the two poles of the magnet frame. The action of this is shown diagrammatically in Fig. 21. The levers are arranged in such a way that at the beginning, when the amount of work to be performed is small, the attraction produced on the armature is also small, and the strongest pull occurs when most power is required. The curve, Fig. 22, shows the results obtained with this type of apparatus.

All the solenoids which have been described have a very large air gap, and could not be used in connection with three-phase machinery, as the power factor would be

exceedingly small, probably not exceeding .2. In consequence of this, instead of using solenoids or magnets, the governing arrangement, with three-phase machines, is composed of an induction motor which has to revolve a few times to operate the brake gear to which it is connected. It would be quite possible to use a similar method with continuous current machinery, but this need

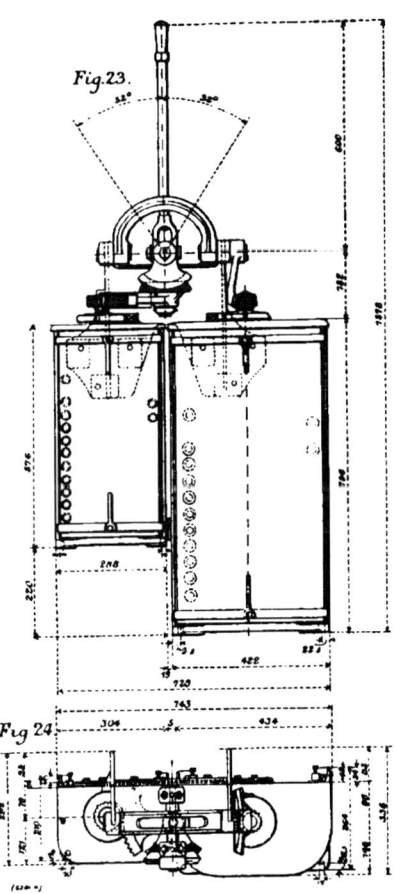

Fig. 23.

Fig 24.

Union Elektricitäts-Gesellschaft Controller

never be taken into consideration except when dealing with the largest cranes.

Electrical Speed Control. — With continuous current series motors, controllers which are practically the same as those used for traction purposes give the best results, and should always be employed. In order to simplify the handling of these as much as possible, the controllers operating the lifting and the slewing motors respectively may,

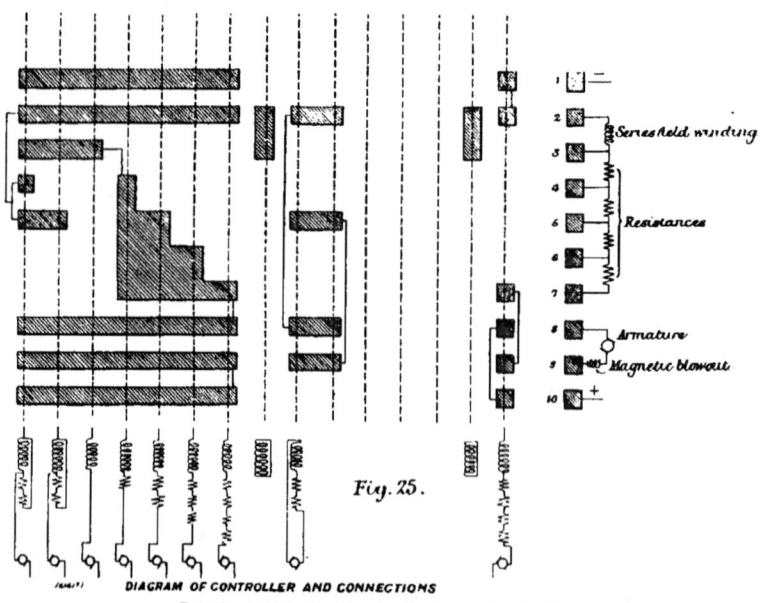

Fig. 25.

DIAGRAM OF CONTROLLER AND CONNECTIONS
Development of Schuckert Crane Controller

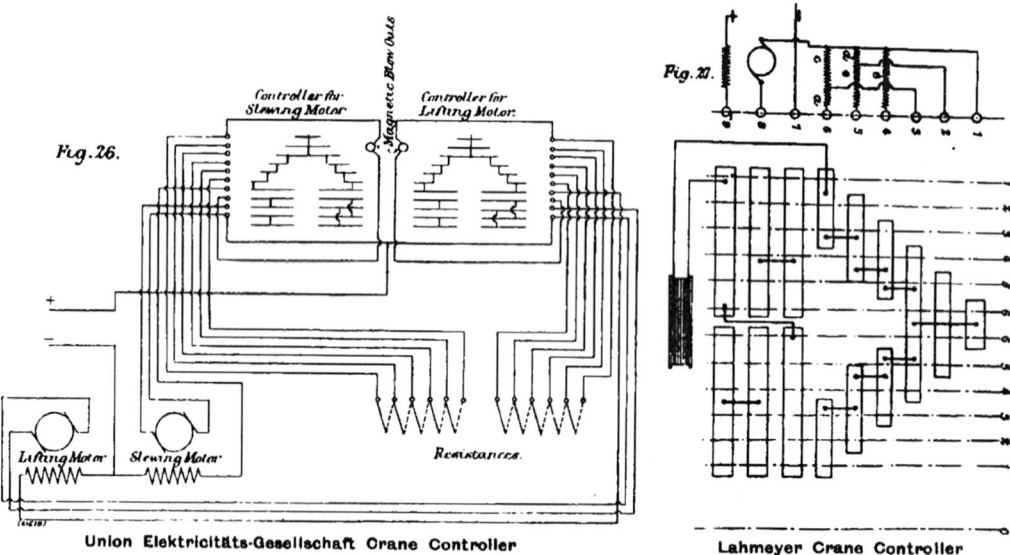

Fig. 26.

Union Elektricitäts-Gesellschaft Crane Controller

Fig. 27.

Lahmeyer Crane Controller

with advantage, be connected in such a way that one handle will command both motions. The Union Elektricitäts - Gesellschaft, of Berlin, and Messrs. Lahmeyer, of Frankfort, have a very neat arrangement of this kind (see Figs. 23 and 24, page 270). By a universal joint one handle operates two ratchet wheels, each of which works a pinion connected to the controller spindle. The handle in its normal "off" position is vertical; when pressed downwards and forwards it means *lowering ;* when pressed backwards, *lifting ;* when pressed to the left, *slewing to the left ;* and to the right, *slewing to the right.* In this way it is practically impossible for the driver to make any mistake in the direction of the load. Lifting and slewing can proceed simultaneously, and the operator can combine the motions so as to lift at maximum, while slewing at minimum, speed ; or he can make any other desirable combination. The Union Elektricitäts-Gesellschaft manufacture their controllers in several different sizes to suit various requirements.

Variations of speed in smaller cranes where only one motor is used is effected by placing resistances in series, and the controllers are built with six, seven, eight, or nine notches of resistance. If the crane be a traveller, and a third motor is used for this purpose, a special controller is supplied for travelling purposes only. In such a case the driver would have two controller handles, one in each hand, and would command the release of the brake by means of his foot. When necessary, the controllers can be arranged with a brake device, so as to supplement the band brake, or for use in case of emergency. By means of this braking arrangement the motors are practically short circuited through various grades of resistance, according to the amount of retardation required.

The diagram, Fig. 25, page 271, shows the connections of the crane controllers adopted by the Schuckert Company. It will be seen that for the lifting motor, resistances are slowly taken out till the maximum speed is reached, and that, when passing from lifting to lowering, the motor goes through the braking position in which the motor is short circuited through the resistance, and acts as generator. The connections of a slewing and lifting controller, as arranged by the Union Elektricitäts - Gesellschaft, are shown in Fig. 26. Fig. 27 shows the development of the controller as used for lifting motors by Messrs. Lahmeyer & Co.

Resistances.—The resistances used in connection with the controllers are similar to those employed in traction work. They generally consist of flat spirals of iron strip, with the turns insulated from each other with asbestos. Each spiral is well insulated

Fig.28.

Steel punching for rheostats.

from earth, and the whole construction is substantial. For the larger currents cast-iron grids are employed. The resistances

should be liberally designed, so that they can be left in circuit for considerable intervals without damage, thus enabling the crane to run at reduced speeds when desired. Resistances are also formed of steel punchings of the shape shown in Fig. 28. The ideal resistance would be one which could take maximum current for an indefinitely long time, and which possessed a large coefficient of resistance and of radiation; or, in other words, one that could get rid of a large amount of heat quickly without great variation of the resistance.

The resistance, R, of a conductor $= 6\frac{l}{S}$, where :—

R = resistance in ohms.
l = length of conductor in millimetres.
S = cross section in square millimetres.

The resistance at a temperature, t, which is designated by R_t is : $R_t = R_0 (1 + a t)$, where R_0 is the resistance for $t = O$, the temperature being given in degrees Centigrade. The following table gives the value of "6" and "a" for various metals :—

				a	6
Iron	...	...	...	0.004	0.10
Copper	...	...	...	0.004	0.018
Brass	...	...	...	0.0015	0.07
Nickelin	...	...	...	0.0002	0.45
Carbon	...	...	...	0.0005	0.50

Some manufacturers prefer to use liquid resistances. These are easy to make, but in the writer's opinion they are to be avoided in practice, as being neither mechanical nor absolutely reliable, although for testing purposes nothing could be better. German engineers are particularly addicted to the use of liquid resistances both for cranes and for central station work. Amongst the advantages claimed for them may be mentioned a gradual variation of the resistance in circuit, compactness, low first cost, and absence of destructive sparking when the current is broken. The resistances are short circuited metallically when they are cut out; this operation, however, can rarely be done without causing considerable variation in current, and in constant use they are liable to heat rapidly, and sometimes boil over. When they are used with continuous currents the contact plates are rapidly eaten away by electrolysis. The liquid employed is usually a solution of washing soda, the proportion varying from about ½lb. to 1½lbs. of soda to a pint of water.

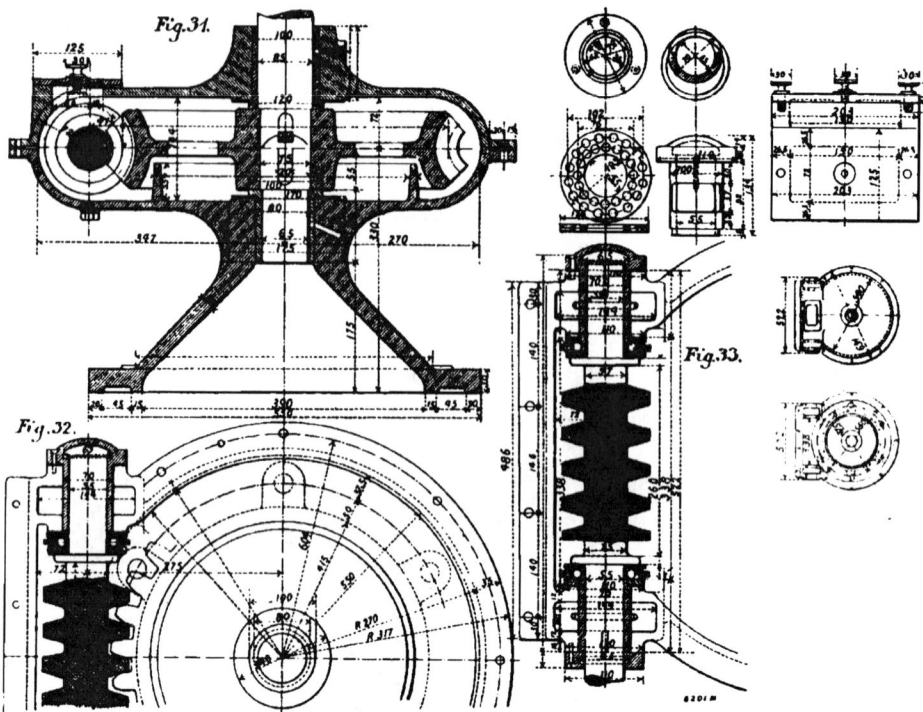

Fig. 31.

Fig. 32.

Fig. 33.

Benrath Worm Gear for 26 Horse-power Motor (see page 274)

Care must be taken to replenish the water as it evaporates. Creeping of the soda solution must be avoided, one means of doing this being to paint the rims of the resistance boxes containing the liquid with a mineral oil or grease. Attempts have been made to substitute a powdered carbon resistance

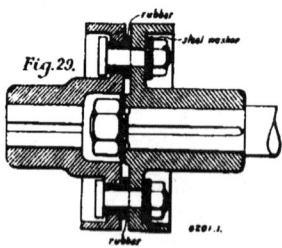

Fig. 29.

Benrath Elastic Coupling

for the liquid, but so far without any very satisfactory result.

Some Constructional Details.—The design of gearing connecting the winding drum and the motor varies considerably with different makers. The method which has found great

favour in Germany, and has given good results, is that adopted by the Benrath Factory, in which, as far as possible, a single reduction, effected by a worm and worm-wheel running in oil, is used. The worms are cut out of a solid steel forging, and the worm-wheels are of phosphor bronze. To reduce vibration there is an elastic coupling between the motor shaft and the worm-wheel. The shaft of the motor has a half-coupling, and that on the worm-wheel has another half-coupling, these being connected by bolts; the holes of the coupling on the motor shaft are lined with rubber tube, through which the bolts pass (see Fig. 29). The efficiency obtained with this gearing is very high, and it has the advantage of being practically silent. The Benrather Maschinen-fabrik state that the combined efficiency of the worm and worm-wheel exceeds 83 per cent. This figure is not at all improbable, and the experience which the writer himself has had with worm gearing has always been satisfactory. The Maschinen-fabrik Oerlikon has made extensive use of worm and worm-wheels fitted with ball bearings. These have also been used by the Benrath Factory with excellent results.

The curve (Fig. 80) is a result of several tests which were recently made on worm and worm-wheels by the Oerlikon Factory. The worm in question had five threads, with a diameter of 95 millimetres at the pitch

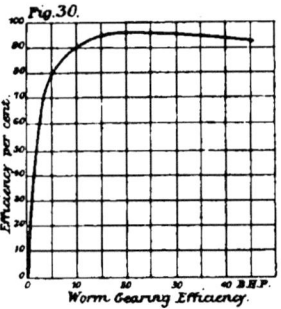

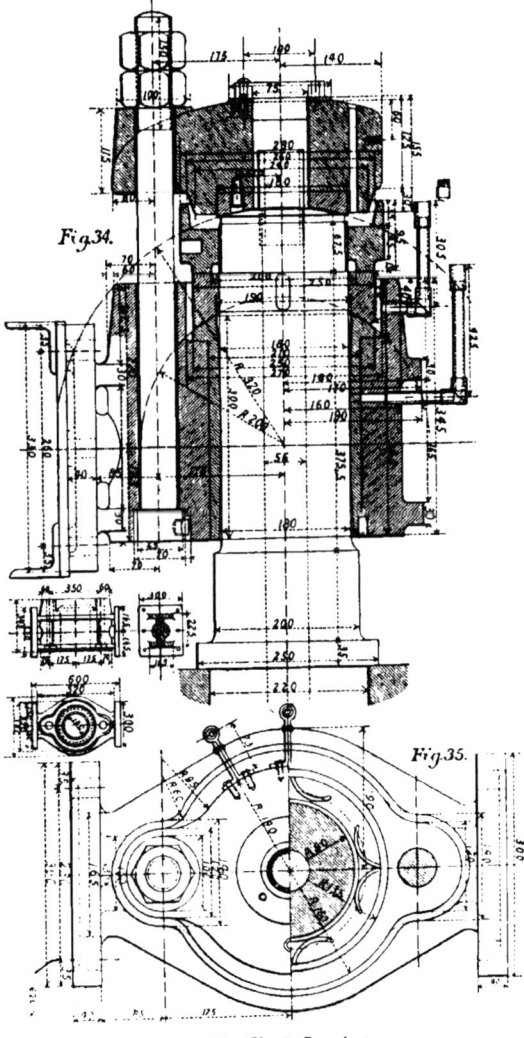

Fig.34.

Fig.35.

Adjustable Pivot Bearing

illustrations on page 273 of a worm designed to transmit 26 brake horse-power at rated load, and running at 560 revolutions, is of interest. It is the standard type of construction used by the Benrath Company in their 3-ton cranes (see Figs. 31 to 33).

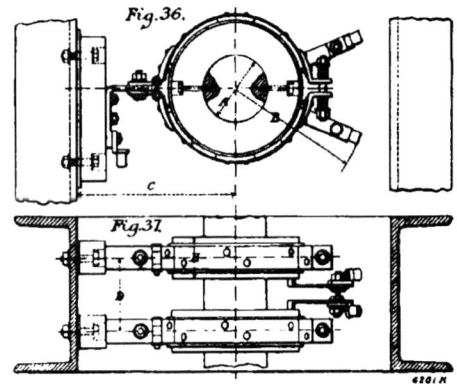

Union Elektricitäts-Gesellschaft Collecting Rings
(see page 275)

It will be seen that a simple form of ball bearing is used on the thrusts, the ball being held in place by spherical bearings with two brass plates riveted together, as shown in Fig. 33. The illustrations give the dimensions in millimetres.

Pivots.—Another interesting detail in the construction of cranes is the method for adjustment, so that when slewing without the load, the crane revolves on a pivot, without any weight being carried by the wheels. The ingenious method of doing this is shown in Figs. 34 and 35, which represent the operating gear of a 3-ton crane such as has already been described. This new construction has been patented both in Germany and in England, and has been adopted for the cranes now being built for the harbour

line, and a pitch of 185 millimetres; the worm-wheel had sixty-eight teeth, and the diameter at the pitch was 801 millimetres. The motor connected to the worm ran at 780 revolutions, and the ratio was 5—68.

In connection with this class of gear, the

at Hamburg. The pivot is of steel, the bottom part being firmly fixed. The cap is of cast iron, having gun-metal bearings grooved to secure proper circulation of oil, and by means of the bolts shown in the drawing, it is possible to adjust the balance so as to secure the minimum friction when revolving. These pivots have a hole drilled through them for the electric conductors to pass to the collecting ring, from which the current is taken to operate the crane. The collecting rings as constructed by the Union Elektricitäts - Gesellschaft are shown in Figs. 36 and 37, page 274. In some cases a separate motor is supplied for moving the crane laterally, and where this motor is controlled from the revolving part of the crane, five contact rings are necessary.

The following table gives the dimensions of the collecting rings in general use for various types of cranes. The minimum

TABLE V.—DIMENSIONS OF CURRENT COLLECTOR FOR JIB CRANES MADE BY THE UNION ELEKTRICITÄTS-GESELLSCHAFT (Figs 36 and 37)

A	B	C
100—140	220	250
141—190	250	270
191—225	270	290
226—250	290	315
251—300	300	340
301—350	320	365
351—400	340	390
401—450	365	420
451—500	390	445

distance between two rings must not be less than 75 millimetres for 110 volts, 85 millimetres for 220 volts, and 100 millimetres for 500 volts. The maximum current for each ring as shown is 300 amperes. Between the metal contact ring and the steel pivot of the crane insulating rings made of stabilite are screwed on.

Safety Devices.—Cranes should be supplied with circuit breakers devised to open automatically without doing damage, if the current supplied, exceed the proper limit. Preferably the arrangement should be such that the circuit breaker can be operated by hand, but if this is not possible an auxiliary switch should be added so that the crane can be completely isolated from the main should occasion arise. It is possible to arrange the controller handle in such a way that it is actuated

by a spring, and returns to the "off" position the moment the driver releases the handle; there is also a mechanical arrangement to pull the handle into the "off" position when the load has reached a certain height. A very simple form of safety device for controlling lifting or revolving limits has been used by the Union Elektricitäts-Gesellschaft. This is now standardised in two sizes. It is simply

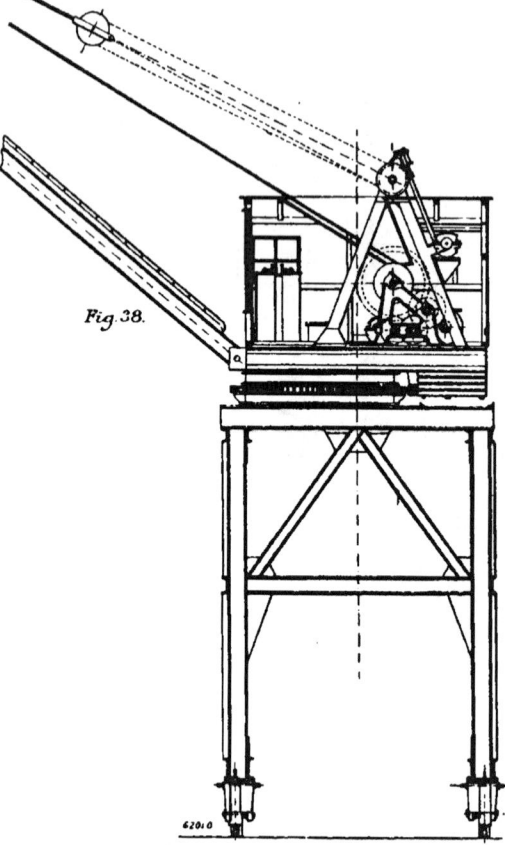

Fig. 38.

3-ton Crane, Stothert & Pitt (see page 276)

a switch operated by a conveniently arranged trigger.

German and English Crane Practice.—It is a feature of German crane practice that derricking cranes are very little used, and that even where the motion is provided, it is generally only operated by hand, the crane being set at a fixed radius as may be required, and not constantly altered, as is the general practice in this country. In this connection it may be of interest to give

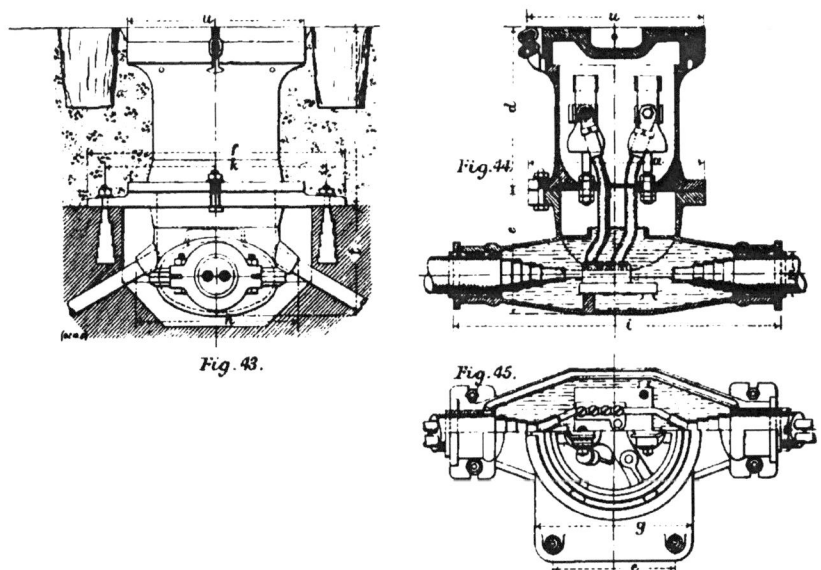

Fig. 43.

Fig. 44.

Fig. 45.

Allgemeine Elektricitäts-Gesellschaft Two-pole Connectors and Sockets up to 200 Amperes and 500 Volts
(see page 278 and Table VI)

TABLE VI.—ALLGEMEINE ELEKTRICITÄTS-GESELLSCHAFT SOCKETS AND JUNCTION BOXES
(see Figs. 43 to 45)

Connecting Cables.		Dimensions in Millimetres.			Weight in Kilogrammes.	Feeder Cables.		Dimensions in Millimetres.									Weight in Kilogrammes.
Square Millimetres.	Amperes.	A	D	U		Square Millimetres.	Amperes.	A	E	F	G	H	I	K	L	M	
2 × 25	60	230	195	225	17	2 × 50	100	230	142	360	200	215	420	300	140	60	22
2 × 120	200	300	276	300	36	2 × 150	300	300	207	440	270	260	560	380	210	80	40

some illustrations (Figs. 38, and 39 to 42, Plate LXI), of a type of derricking crane, in which the motion is controlled by means of an electric motor. These cranes were constructed by Messrs. Stothert & Pitt, of Bath, for the Table Bay Harbour, Cape Town, and another for Buenos Ayres. As in nearly all the jib cranes which have been constructed by the same firm, a detachable winding drum is employed, which is connected to the motor gearing by means of a friction clutch of the Lindsay patent coil type. The clutch is an exceedingly simple one, and this may account for the great success which this type of crane, manufactured by Messrs. Stothert & Pitt for the past seven years, has had. The lifting barrel is not keyed directly to the shaft, but runs loose on it, and is connected or disconnected by the clutch. The barrel shaft carries the main spur-wheel, which is

keyed on it, and this is driven by a pinion keyed on the shaft of the armature of the lifting motor; as in tramway practice, the spur-wheel is of cast iron, and the pinion of forged steel, both having machine-cut teeth, running in an oil bath. The hand lever actuating the electric controller operates an electric solenoid which controls the lifting friction coil clutch, the arrangement being such that, on moving the lifting handle forward from the "off" position, current is switched on to the solenoid, the clutch is put in the gear, and the lifting motor is started simultaneously. If the clutch is in gear, the movement of the lever cuts out the resistance and accelerates the motor. Provision can also be made to mechanically connect the lifting controller handle with the friction coil clutch, or this can be done electrically.

The large friction brake drum is carried

Plate LXI

Fig. 39.—3-ton Electric Crane, Stothert & Pitt

Fig. 40.—Buenos Ayres 3-ton Derricking Crane

Figs. 41 and 42.—Buenos Ayres 3-ton Crane, showing Slewing Motor and Derricking Gear

Plate LXII

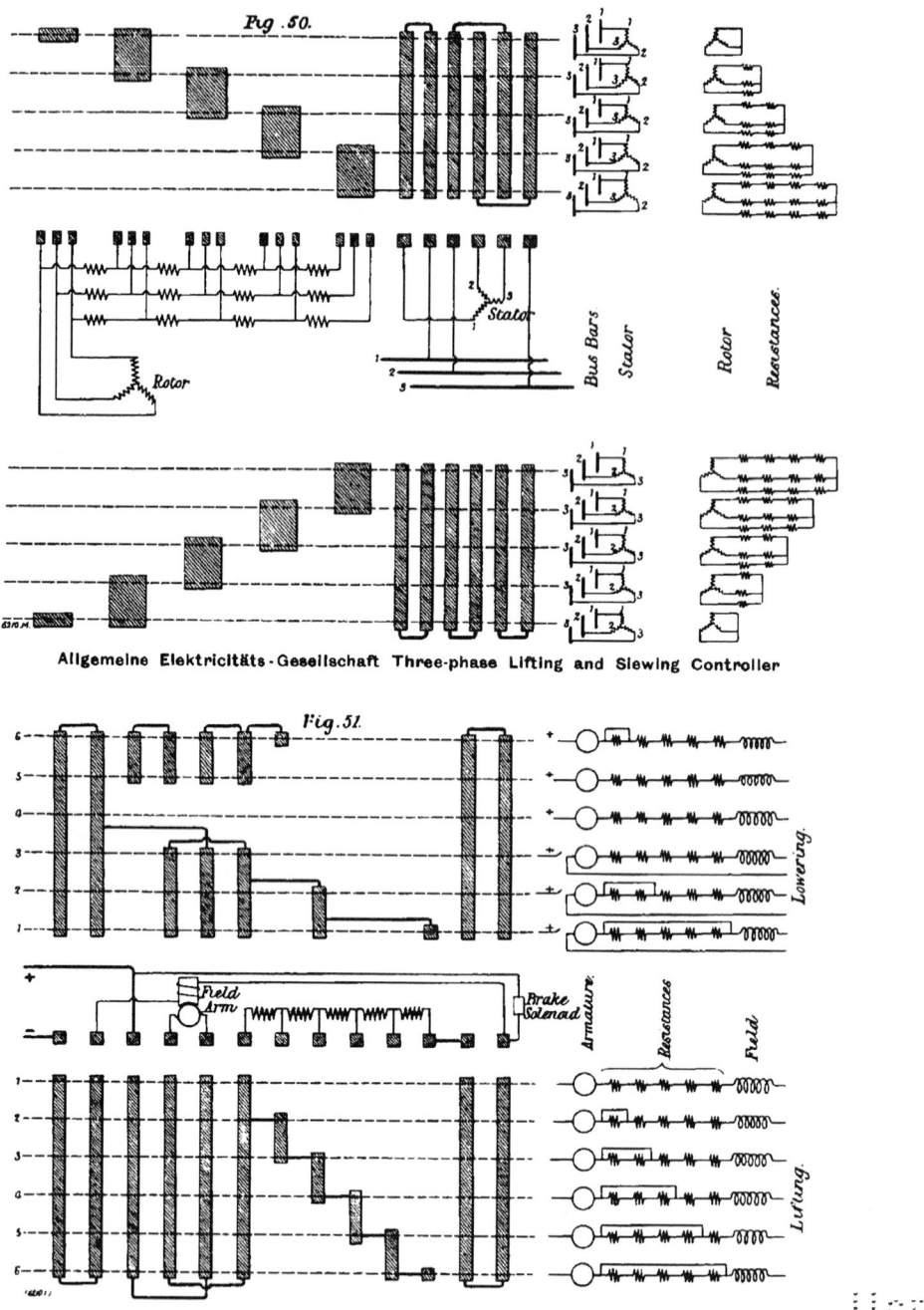

Fig. 50.

Rotor

Stator

Bus Bars

Stator

Rotor

Resistance.

Allgemeine Elektricitäts-Gesellschaft Three-phase Lifting and Slewing Controller

Fig. 51.

Lowering.

Field
Arm

Brake
Solenoid

Armature

Resistances

Field.

Lifting.

Allgemeine Elektricitäts-Gesellschaft Continuous Current Lifting Controller

U of M

ELECTRIC CRANES

Plate LXIII

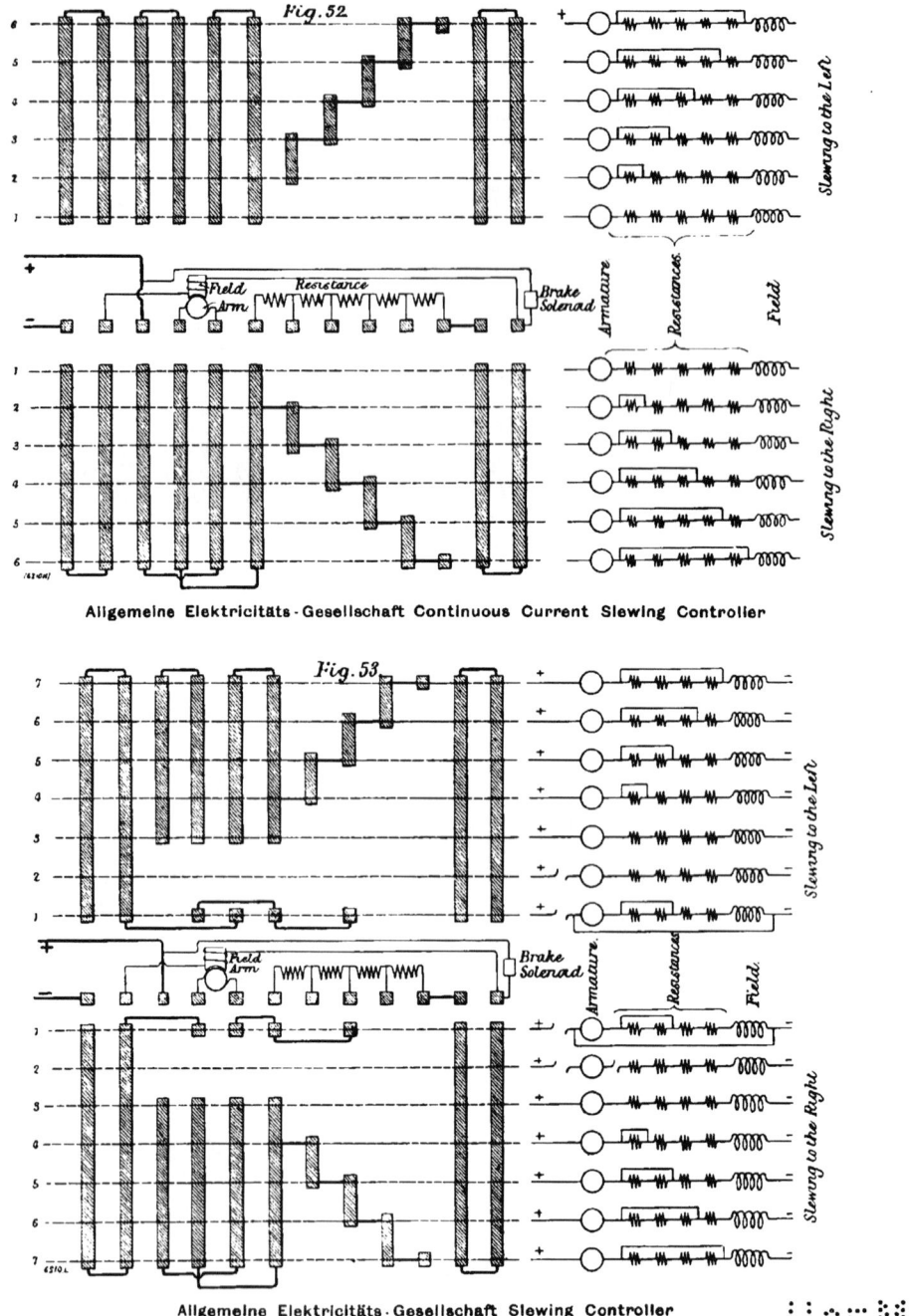

Fig. 52

Allgemeine Elektricitäts-Gesellschaft Continuous Current Slewing Controller

Fig. 53

Allgemeine Elektricitäts-Gesellschaft Slewing Controller

Plate LXIV

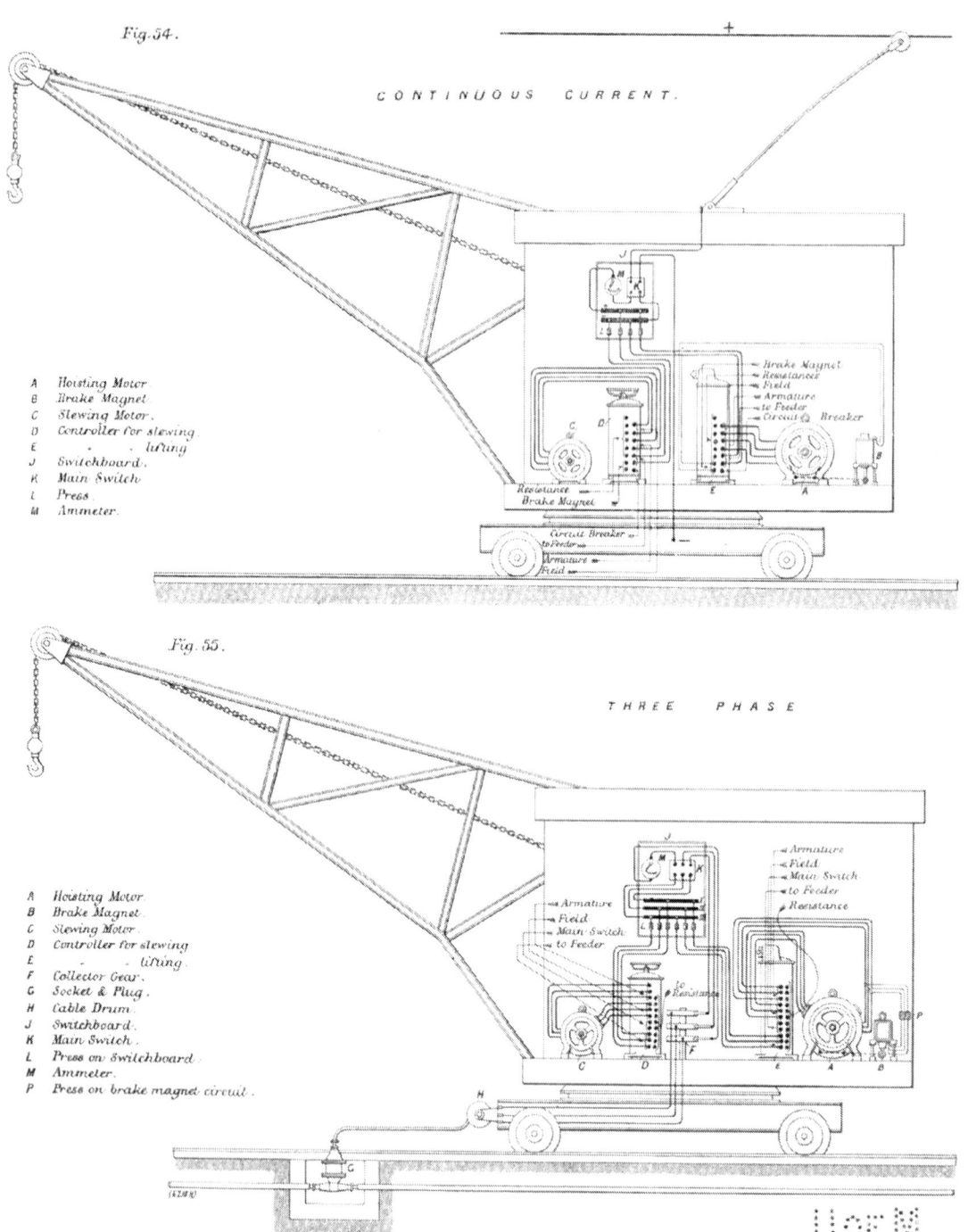

Fig. 54.

CONTINUOUS CURRENT.

A   Hoisting Motor.
B   Brake Magnet.
C   Slewing Motor.
D   Controller for slewing.
E   "   "   lifting.
J   Switchboard.
K   Main Switch.
L   Press.
M   Ammeter.

Brake Magnet.
Resistance.
Field.
Armature.
to Feeder.
Circuit Breaker.

Resistance
Brake Magnet.

Circuit Breaker
to Feeder
Armature
Field

Fig. 55.

THREE PHASE

A   Hoisting Motor.
B   Brake Magnet.
C   Slewing Motor.
D   Controller for slewing.
E   "   "   lifting.
F   Collector Gear.
G   Socket & Plug.
H   Cable Drum.
J   Switchboard.
K   Main Switch.
L   Press on Switchboard.
M   Ammeter.
P   Press on brake magnet circuit.

Armature
Field
Main Switch
to Feeder
Resistance

Armature
Field
Main Switch
to Feeder

Resistance

Diagram of Crane Connections, Continuous and Three-phase Current

ELECTRIC CRANES

TABLE VII.—ALLGEMEINE ELEKTRICITÄTS - GESELLSCHAFT TWO - POLE PLUGS AND SOCKETS, CONTINUOUS CURRENT UP TO 200 AMPERES AND 500 VOLTS (see Figs. 46 and 47)

PLUG WITHOUT FUSE							PLUG WITH FUSE						
Connecting Cables.		Dimensions in Millimetres.				Weight in Kilogrammes.	Connecting Cables.		Dimensions in Millimetres.				Weight in Kilogrammes.
Square Millimetres.	Amperes.	B	C	C₁	U		Square Millimetres.	Amperes.	B	C	C₁	U	
2 × 25	60	170	37	24	225	6.5	2 × 25	60	228	37	24	225	10
2 × 50	100	225	45	28	300	} 16	2 × 50	100	275	45	28	300	28
2 × 120	200	225	63	37	300		2 × 120	200	275	63	37	300	28

TABLE VIII.—TERMINAL SOCKETS (see Figs. 48 and 49)

Feeder Cables.		Dimensions in Millimetres.										Weight in Kilogrammes.
Square Millimetres.	Amperes.	A	F	G	K	L	N	O	P	Q	R	
2 × 50	100	230	360	200	300	140	130	150	50	155	62	14
2 × 150	300	300	440	270	380	210	175	240	80	200	85	27

TABLE IX.—COMMON DIMENSIONS IN MILLIMETRES

Connecting Cables. (Square Millimetres.)	Feeder Cables. (Square Millimetres.)	S	T
25	50	215	124
25	150	215	185
120	150	300	185

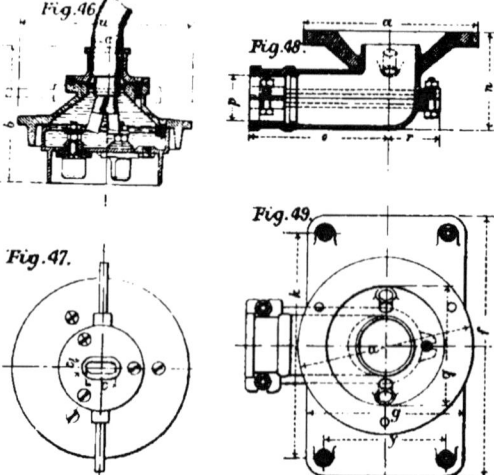

Fig. 46.
Fig. 48.
Fig. 47.
Fig. 49.

Allgemeine Elektricitäts-Gesellschaft Plugs and Sockets (see page 278)

on the lifting barrel, the encircling brake strap being made of steel and lined with wooden blocks; this brake is mechanical, but it is interlocked with the controller, so that when the brake is holding the barrel, the motor cannot be started. The lifting controller does not reverse the motor, the lowering being carried out independently by the loose drum.

The makers claim for this arrangement a large increase in the speed of working, both in lifting and lowering. It has been found

in practice that the load can be lowered 60ft. before the lifting armature has ceased to revolve in the direction of hoisting.

The gearing and clutch arrangement used for this purpose by Messrs. Stothert & Pitt is clearly shown in the illustrations, Figs. 41 and 42, Plate LXI. These figures show the front and back view of a crane with the housing removed, as well as the derricking motor, which, by a combination of spur and mitre gearing, drives the worm and worm wheel that lifts or lowers the derrick. Fig. 40, Plate LXI, shows this crane erected.

With one of these cranes which has been installed for the Clyde Navigation Trustees by Messrs. Stothert & Pitt, it has been found possible to make 84 cycles in the hour. The efficiency obtained was very high; even when the crane was quite new, that is to say, while the gears and other parts were working stiff, the absolute efficiency between load lifted and current supplied (which therefore includes all losses) was 73 per cent.

In comparing the various gantry cranes which have been described, it will be noted that the tendency exists to reduce and simplify the gear as much as possible, and that there are two different schools of crane makers, the one believing in permanent connection of the motor to the hoisting drum, and the other in working the drum by means of friction clutches. It would seem clear that an economy in energy consumption, as well as an increase of speed in operating, should be obtained by the use of friction clutches. It is undoubtedly true that good results have been obtained by both methods, and time alone can demonstrate which really is the better of the two.

Sockets and Connections.—The connections or sockets are manufactured both for continuous and three-phase motors, and are of two types, according as they are branched on a circuit, or at the end of the same. The sockets are fixed in cast-iron boxes, and after the necessary connections have been made, they are run in with a bitumen compound. A vent is allowed in the bottom of the socket, which must be connected to the drains or sewers to dispose of any water which may find its way into the cast-iron box. The boxes are generally fixed in place by means of Lewis bolts on a concrete foundation (see Figs. 43 to 45, page 276).

Plugs and sockets form very important details in a crane installation, and the annexed data of the practice of the Allgemeine Elektricitäts-Gesellschaft in this connection is of value (see Figs. 46 to 49, page 277, and Tables VII to IX).

The diagrams, Figs. 50 and 51, Plate LXII, show the general arrangement adopted by the Allgemeine Elektricitäts-Gesellschaft for hoisting motors, and Figs. 52 and 53, Plate LXIII, for slewing motions, and they clearly show the electric braking arrangements which the Allgemeine Elektricitäts-Gesellschaft employ.

The connections of the motors and resistances where three-phase motors are used, are shown in the diagram (Fig. 50).

If electric braking is required, it is simply done by connecting on to the line, and sending current into the motor as if it were lifting. According to the amount of resistance inertia, the weight can be lowered slowly or stopped entirely. Many claim that it is possible by the use of three-phase motors, to return power into the line when lowering, but the amount returned in reality is so small a portion of the total energy used as to practically become a negligible quantity. Solenoids to act on the band brake are built by the Allgemeine Elektricitäts-Gesellschaft for their three-phase work.

Figs. 54 and 55, Plate LXIV, show diagrammatically the wiring of jib cranes worked by means of continuous and three-phase current motors.

UNIVERSITY
MAR 30 1911
OF MICHIGAN